T0297718

Blockchain Applications for Healthcare Informatics

Blockchain Applications for Healthcare Informatics

Beyond 5G

Edited by

Sudeep Tanwar

Computer Science and Engineering Department, Institute of Technology, Nirma University, Ahmedabad, Gujarat, India

ACADEMIC PRESS

An imprint of Elsevier

ELSEVIER

Academic Press is an imprint of Elsevier
125 London Wall, London EC2Y 5AS, United Kingdom
525 B Street, Suite 1650, San Diego, CA 92101, United States
50 Hampshire Street, 5th Floor, Cambridge, MA 02139, United States
The Boulevard, Langford Lane, Kidlington, Oxford OX5 1GB, United Kingdom

Copyright © 2022 Elsevier Inc. All rights reserved.

No part of this publication may be reproduced or transmitted in any form or by any means, electronic
or mechanical, including photocopying, recording, or any information storage and retrieval system,
without permission in writing from the publisher. Details on how to seek permission, further
information about the Publisher's permissions policies and our arrangements with organizations such
as the Copyright Clearance Center and the Copyright Licensing Agency, can be found at our website:
www.elsevier.com/permissions.

This book and the individual contributions contained in it are protected under copyright by the Publisher
(other than as may be noted herein).

Notices
Knowledge and best practice in this field are constantly changing. As new research and experience
broaden our understanding, changes in research methods, professional practices, or medical treatment
may become necessary.

Practitioners and researchers must always rely on their own experience and knowledge in evaluating
and using any information, methods, compounds, or experiments described herein. In using such
information or methods they should be mindful of their own safety and the safety of others, including
parties for whom they have a professional responsibility.

To the fullest extent of the law, neither the Publisher nor the authors, contributors, or editors, assume
any liability for any injury and/or damage to persons or property as a matter of products liability,
negligence or otherwise, or from any use or operation of any methods, products, instructions, or ideas
contained in the material herein.

ISBN 978-0-323-90615-9

For information on all Academic Press publications
visit our website at https://www.elsevier.com/books-and-journals

Publisher: Mara Conner
Editorial Project Manager: Rafael Guilherme Trombaco
Production Project Manager: Swapna Srinivasan
Cover Designer: Miles Hitchen

Typeset by STRAIVE, India

Working together
to grow libraries in
developing countries

www.elsevier.com • www.bookaid.org

Contents

viii

Contributors

K. Aditya Information Science and Engineering, Ramaiah Institute of Technology (Affiliated to VTU), Bangalore, Karnataka, India

Harsha Aggarwal Dream Technology, Delhi, India

Puneet Kumar Aggarwal ABES Engineering College, Ghaziabad, India

Nurshod Akhmedov Data Communication Networks and Systems Department, Tashkent University of Information Technologies, Tashkent, Uzbekistan

Arun Arora SWINGER (Security, Wireless IoT Network Group of Engineering and Research) Lab, USIC&T, GGSIP University, New Delhi, India

P. Aruna Department of Computer Science and Engineering, Annamalai University, Chidambaram, Tamil Nadu, India

Jitendra Bhatia Computer Engineering Department, Vishwakarma Government Engineering College, Gujarat Technological University, Ahmedabad, India

Neeraj Bisht Birla Institute of Applied Sciences, Bhimtal, India

Shilpi Bisht Birla Institute of Applied Sciences, Bhimtal, India

Uttam Chauhan Computer Engineering Department, Vishwakarma Government Engineering College, Gujarat Technological University, Ahmedabad, India

Jais Dargan Department of Computer Science and Engineering, Amity University, Noida, Uttar Pradesh, India

Shray Dasila Birla Institute of Applied Sciences, Bhimtal, India

Mrittika Dey Department of Web and Data Science, The University of Koblenz and Landau, Mainz, Germany

Aditya Garg Amity School of Engineering & Technology, Amity University, Noida, Uttar Pradesh, India

Vansh Gaur ABES Engineering College, Ghaziabad, Uttar Pradesh, India

Ahona Ghosh Department of Computer Science and Engineering, Maulana Abul Kalam Azad University of Technology, West Bengal, Kolkata, West Bengal, India

Ananya Ghosh Department of Computer Science and Engineering, University of Calcutta, Kolkata, India

R. Gopal Information and Communication Engineering, College of Engineering, University of Buraimi, Al Buraimi, Sultanate of Oman

Kalpana Gupta Centre for Development of Advanced Computing (C-DAC), Noida, India

Megha Gupta IMS Engineering College, Ghaziabad, India

Muskan Gupta ABES Engineering College, Ghaziabad, Uttar Pradesh, India

Neha Gupta ABES Engineering College, Ghaziabad, Uttar Pradesh, India

Rabab Jafri Department of Computer Science and Engineering, Amity School of Engineering and Technology, Amity University, Lucknow, Uttar Pradesh, India

Ankush Jain School of Computer Science Engineering and Technology, Bennett University, Greater Noida, India

Garima Jain Department of Computer Science and Engineering, Noida Institute of Engineering and Technology, Greater Noida, India

Rahul Johari SWINGER (Security, Wireless IoT Network Group of Engineering and Research) Lab, USIC&T, GGSIP University, New Delhi, India

Deepti Kakkar Department of ECE, Dr. B.R Ambedkar National Institute of Technology, Jalandhar, India

Pooja Khanna Amity School of Engineering and Technology, Amity University, Lucknow, India

Doston Khasanov Data Communication Networks and Systems Department, Tashkent University of Information Technologies, Tashkent, Uzbekistan

Khalimjon Khujamatov Data Communication Networks and Systems Department, Tashkent University of Information Technologies, Tashkent, Uzbekistan

Vrinda Kohli ABES Engineering College, Ghaziabad, Uttar Pradesh, India

Komal ABES Engineering College, Ghaziabad, Uttar Pradesh, India

Anil Kumar Amity School of Engineering and Technology, Amity University, Lucknow, India

Ashwani Kumar Amity Institute of Information Technology, Amity University, Noida, Uttar Pradesh, India

Sachin Kumar Amity School of Engineering and Technology, Amity University, Lucknow, India

Sunil Kumar Department of Computer Science, Central University of Rajasthan, Ajmer, India

M. Kumaresan Department of Computer Science and Engineering, Jain Deemed-to-be University, Jakkasantra Post, Kanakapur Taluk, Ramanagar, India

Roshan Lal Amity School of Engineering & Technology; Department of Computer Science and Engineering, Amity University, Noida, Uttar Pradesh, India

Amir Lazarev Data Communication Networks and Systems Department, Tashkent University of Information Technologies, Tashkent, Uzbekistan

Ratnesh Litoriya Medi-Caps University, Indore, Madhya Pradesh, India

M. Mahasree Department of Computer Science and Engineering, SRM Institute of Science and Technology (Ramapuram), Chennai, Tamil Nadu, India

S.R. Mani Sekhar Information Science and Engineering, Ramaiah Institute of Technology (Affiliated to VTU), Bangalore, Karnataka, India

M. Mathivanan Department of Electronics & Communication Engineering, ACS College of Engineering, Bangalore, India

Neetu Mittal Amity Institute of Information Technology, Amity University, Noida, Uttar Pradesh, India

Megha Modi Yashodha Super Speciality Hospital, Ghaziabad, Uttar Pradesh, India

Krishna Kumar Mohbey Department of Computer Science, Central University of Rajasthan, Ajmer, India

Poorvika Singh Negi Amity School of Engineering & Technology, Amity University, Noida, Uttar Pradesh, India

K.S. Nisar Prince Sattam bin Abdulaziz University, Al-Kharj, Saudi Arabia

Naitik Panchal Computer Engineering Department, Vishwakarma Government Engineering College, Gujarat Technological University, Ahmedabad, India

Prateek Pandey Jaypee University of Engineering & Technology, Guna, Madhya Pradesh, India

Rahil Parmar Computer Engineering Department, Vishwakarma Government Engineering College, Gujarat Technological University, Ahmedabad, India

Dhruval Patel Computer Engineering Department, Vishwakarma Government Engineering College, Gujarat Technological University, Ahmedabad, India

T. Poongodi School of Computing Science and Engineering, Galgotias University, Greater Noida, Delhi, NCR, India

Aakash Puri Department of Computer Science and Engineering, Amity University, Noida, Uttar Pradesh, India

N. Puviarasan Department of Computer and Information Science, Annamalai University, Chidambaram, Tamil Nadu, India

K. Raghavendra Department of ECE, Dr. B.R Ambedkar National Institute of Technology, Jalandhar, India

Aarushi Rai ABES Engineering College, Ghaziabad, Uttar Pradesh, India

Vibhavari B. Rao Information Science and Engineering, Ramaiah Institute of Technology (Affiliated to VTU), Bangalore, Karnataka, India

Rohit Rastogi Department of CSE, ABES Engineering College, Ghaziabad, Uttar Pradesh, India

Ernazar Reypnazarov Data Communication Networks and Systems Department, Tashkent University of Information Technologies, Tashkent, Uzbekistan

B.L. Sandeep Information Science and Engineering, Ramaiah Institute of Technology (Affiliated to VTU), Bangalore, Karnataka, India

Indranil Sarkar Department of Computational Science, Brainware University, Kolkata, India

Sudhriti Sengupta Amity Institute of Information Technology, Amity University, Noida, Uttar Pradesh, India

Ankur Sharma ABES Engineering College, Ghaziabad, Uttar Pradesh, India

Anupam Sharma HMR Institute of Technology and Management, Delhi, India

Bhuvneshwar Prasad Sharma Department of CSE and MBA, ABES Engineering College, Ghaziabad, Uttar Pradesh, India

Meenu Sharma Department of Computer Science, Central University of Rajasthan, Ajmer, India

Savita Sharma Department of Computer Science, Central University of Rajasthan, Ajmer, India

Bela Shrimali LDRP Institute of Technology and Research, Kadi Sarva Vishwavidyalaya, Gandhinagar, India

G.M. Siddesh Information Science and Engineering, Ramaiah Institute of Technology (Affiliated to VTU), Bangalore, Karnataka, India

Mandeep Singh HMR Institute of Technology and Management, Delhi, India

Pankaj Singh Birla Institute of Applied Sciences, Bhimtal, India

Robin Singh Amity Institute of Information Technology, Amity University, Noida, Uttar Pradesh, India

Shikha Singh Department of Computer Science and Engineering, Amity School of Engineering and Technology, Amity University, Lucknow, Uttar Pradesh, India

Swapnil Soner Jaypee University of Engineering & Technology, Guna, Madhya Pradesh, India

Prajwal Srivastava ABES Engineering College, Ghaziabad, Uttar Pradesh, India

Namrata Sukhija HMR Institute of Technology and Management, Delhi, India

Shivangi Surati LDRP Institute of Technology and Research, Kadi Sarva Vishwavidyalaya, Gandhinagar, India

Kumud Tiwari Amity School of Engineering and Technology, Amity University, Lucknow, India

Deo Prakash Vidyarthi Parallel and Distributed System Lab, School of Computer and Systems Sciences, JNU, New Delhi, India

Blockchain-based transaction validation for patient interoperability in Healthcare 4.0

1

Kumud Tiwari, Sachin Kumar, Pooja Khanna, and Anil Kumar
Amity School of Engineering and Technology, Amity University, Lucknow, India

1 Introduction

Healthcare is one of the largest and fastest-growing industries, accounting for the majority of the economy. The medical business, often known as the healthcare industry, is a sector of the economy that offers health goods and services to individuals or patients, regardless of their socioeconomic level, for curative and rehabilitative purposes. Health professions include doctors, nurses, and administrators [1]. In the previous 20 years, hospital services as well as their structure, growth, operation, and administration have experienced significant changes. The implementation of issues such as changing the quality of life and cost-effectiveness, extensive media coverage of system flaws, increasing demands and awareness of patient rights, and limited resources in the age of expensive high-tech medical support systems and trajectories have all contributed to public dissatisfaction with the traditional role of the healthcare provider[2]. Patients and experts see a lack of access to medical records as a hindrance to transparency and effective medical care. While electronic clinical records frameworks assist adapt to this issue a bit, a considerable lot of these frameworks are heterogeneous, they end up being variable effective reconciliation into clinical work processes and show insignificant interoperability between stages. As a result, many EHR frameworks are now fighting to provide vital advantages of computerized innovation, including as improved customer experience, information trade advanced skills, and examination. This lack of interoperability is becoming more of a test of how complicated individuals present themselves to a variety of care providers in various medical care wards using multiple EHR systems [3]. The blockchain-based framework is a potential arrangement that presents a few advantages that could be used for information organization. However, blockchain is a fledgling innovation and there are key specialized, administrative, and institutional obstructions that limit its maximum use in the clinical field [4].

Blockchain innovation is a peer-to-peer (P2P) network digital data distributed ledger system that can be distributed privately or publicly to all users, allowing any type of data to be stored reliably and verifiably [5]. Fig. 1 describes the application of blockchain in the healthcare industry. Another vital aspect of blockchain is the contract, which is a set of protocols. This is known as a smart contract, which is a legally

Blockchain Applications for Healthcare Informatics. https://doi.org/10.1016/B978-0-323-90615-9.00017-7
Copyright © 2022 Elsevier Inc. All rights reserved.

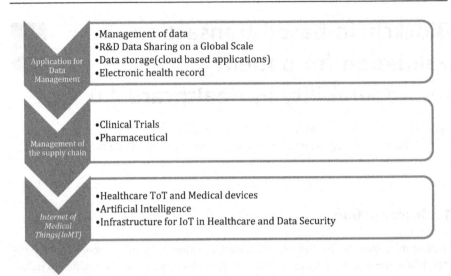

Fig. 1 Blockchain-based healthcare applications.

binding strategy that contains a bunch of customizable guidelines/rules under which different parties agree to cooperate with each other in the form of decentralized automation. Several smart contract applications have emerged as a result of blockchain in different areas, including energy resources, financial services, voting, and healthcare. Blockchain innovation offers transparency while also eliminating the need for intermediaries. In an untrusted and untrustworthy environment, it uses consensus and encryption mechanisms to validate the legality of a transaction. In a P2P transaction network, the receiving node verifies the message and saves it in a block if it is correct. The data in each block are then confirmed using a consensus process known as "proof of work (PoW)." After the consensus method is completed, a block will be added to the chain and every node in the network will accept it, spreading the chain indefinitely [6].

Taking the healthcare sector as a target, blockchain as a support technology can address challenges such as data sharing, privacy issues, data security, and storage. Interoperability is a requirement in the healthcare industry. Interoperability refers to the capacity of two parties, whether machine or human. Interoperability as a feature targets the information flow of healthcare personnel and patients in an efficient and secured manner, such as EHR, so that data can be shared and dispersed across multiple hospital systems. Regardless of provider location or trust connections, interoperability allows providers to securely share patient health records (with patient permission) [7]. It is particularly vital considering that health data sources are different. Blockchain technology solves this element of interoperability, and has demonstrated the potential to securely manage, store, and share electronic medical records between healthcare communities. In addition, the rising costs of healthcare infrastructure and software have put a terrific strain on global economies. Blockchain technology is influencing healthcare results in a beneficial way for businesses and stakeholders by streamlining business processes, managing patient data, improving patient outcomes, reducing costs, improving compliance, and enabling better use of health data [8].

1.1 Motivations

The motivation of conducting this study is to dissect the blockchain as a central innovation. It is as of now a piece of Bitcoin, but it is considered part of the "new internet." The goal of this study is to track down the current situation of blockchain on the worldwide technological scene, to talk about potential outcomes of innovation execution, and track down various techniques for the secured transaction and validation methods of healthcare data that are evolving rapidly. We are studying the role of blockchain technology in securely sharing medical data among healthcare practitioners while also looking at how we might make blockchain adoption easier from a technological standpoint. Researchers want to learn about the application issues that blockchain presents and debate the technology's future potential. The aim of this study is to determine the factors that can enhance the patient interoperability structure with blockchain technology while focusing on state-of-the-art security and privacy aspects as well as showcase the potential of blockchain technology. Further, researchers get to know about open issues, and challenges that blockchain technology is facing at the time of implementation.

1.2 Contributions

Patient-driven interoperability is a recent trend that has the capacity to set a new base for information sharing between medical service associations. However, patient-driven interoperability brings with it new challenges and requirements, such as security and protection, innovation that can deal with a variety of issues related to patient-driven interoperability, and the majority of these challenges for traditional interoperability have yet to be resolved. Blockchain is a novel innovation that can be used to further develop interoperability. Blockchain can possibly give sharing, security, protection, stability, information liquidity, information sharing, and encryption of health information. In this chapter, we propose improved blockchain-based patient-driven interoperability for medical care information.

1.3 Organization

This how the rest of the chapter is organized. The basic ideas for comprehending blockchain technology are presented in Section 2. In Section 3, healthcare 4.0 as the next step in innovation is presented. Functional blocks of blockchain integration with EHR systems are discussed in Section 4. In Section 5, blockchain-assisted secured transaction-validation for patient interoperability is explained. In Section 6, we suggest a model for flexible smart contracts for enhanced interoperability. The investigation's problems and prospects are described in Section 7. Finally, Section 8 brings the paper to a close and makes recommendations for future development.

2   Intricacies of blockchain

Blockchain has evolved as one of the most promising technologies of the last decade, garnering the interest of academics as well as industry specialists. Satoshi Nakamoto first proposed this concept in a white paper published in 2008 [9]. It is a distributed, decentralized, and immutable ledger that's used to securely record transactions over a network of computers on a P2P basis without the need for third parties. Bitcoin [9], the first blockchain implementation based on cryptocurrency applications, is supported by the first version of blockchain, Blockchain 1.0. The new Blockchain 2.0 generation introduces the concept of a smart contract, which is a piece of code specified by a set of rules that is performed, and recorded in the distributed ledger. The third version of blockchain technology, Blockchain 3.0, is mostly utilized in nonfinancial applications, including government, energy, and healthcare. Some healthcare institutions have accepted this technology and put it to use in a variety of ways. Decentralization, privacy, and security are the most exciting properties of blockchain that are helpful for healthcare applications. This is because blockchain technology can provide patients and other stakeholders with safe access to medical data, so it has great potential (hospitals, insurance companies, doctors, etc.). Bitcoin is based on blockchain technology, which stores an encrypted ledger in a public database. Blockchain is a technology used in a worldwide database that can be accessed by anybody, anywhere with an Internet connection. Unlike traditional databases that are held by central parties such as banks and governments, a blockchain is not owned by anybody. With an entire network dealing with it, cheating the system by forging papers, transactions, and other information becomes exceedingly difficult. Blockchain is a network of nodes that preserves information indefinitely. It's not only about decentralizing data; it's also about disseminating it. Each network node can store a local copy of the blockchain system that is updated on a regular basis to ensure consistency across all nodes. A blockchain is a distributed computing and information-sharing network that enables several nodes to make decisions, even if they do not trust one another. The only point of failure in the centralized system is the problem. There are several coordinate points in a decentralized system that exceed the single point of failure. In a distributed system, each node collaborates to complete the task [10,11]. Fig. 2 depicts blockchain's basic architecture. Each user is represented as a linked node in a dispersed network. Each node maintains a copy of the blockchain list, which is updated on a regular basis. A node can perform a variety of functions, including initiating transactions, validating transactions, and mining.

The structure of the blockchain technology includes:

1. Block: A collection of valid transactions; the transaction may be started by any node in a blockchain system and broadcast to the remaining network. The network's nodes confirm the transaction by comparing it to previous transactions, and then the next step is added to the existing blockchain. During that period, the number of transactions that occurred is gathered into a block and then put in the blockchain block. "A block can include on average more than 500 transactions," according to Bitcoin, and "a block's average size is around 1 MB (an upper limit suggested by Satoshi Nakamoto in 2010)." It can grow to be as large as 8 MB in size, and occasionally much larger. Larger blocks can help with the simultaneous processing of many transactions.

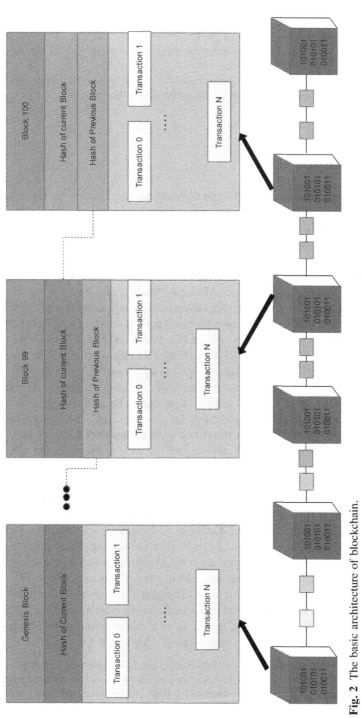

Fig. 2 The basic architecture of blockchain.

2. Previous Block Hash: Every block inherits from the previous block. As the blockchain algorithm employs a hash of previous blocks to produce the next block's hash, the sequence of generation makes the series tamper-proof.
3. Block header and list of transactions form the third and fourth components. The block header contains the metadata about a block.
4. The block was built using the following mining statistics. The mechanism needs to be complicated enough, to make the Blockchain tamper-proof Bitcoin Mining:

$$H_k = Hash(H_{k1}|T|nonce|)$$

3 Healthcare 4.0

Healthcare 4.0 refers to the final stage of healthcare digitization, in which advanced analytics tools and artificial intelligence (AI) assist clinicians and hospital administrators in making more precise diagnoses and better therapy choices [12–14]. Large volumes of data flow into the archiving cloud, not just from medical offices and imaging centers but also from distant gadgets and sensors operated by patients. At the same time, data assist in the formation of better-informed health management decisions, with the prospect of considerable efficiency benefits and cost control in the near future. Healthcare 1.0 was at the beginning of digitization in the early 1990s, when doctors changed hands written notes to record patient data on computers which were then archived and managed with systems like PACS and RIS. Although the shift has improved and accelerated access to patient data, the doctor-patient process has remained the same. Then came Healthcare 2.0, which saw hospitals develop systems to incorporate and handle digital data that employees were collecting via computers and tools. Workflow in hospitals and physician clinics began to change with the adaptation of managers to patient trends; this became apparent to all aggregated data in clinical settings. Healthcare 3.0 flourished with the primary focus of collecting all patient data in EHRs to which everyone had full access. People could upload extra information to their accounts, such as portable device self-test data or genomic information, in addition to the data obtained by doctors. With the growing avalanche of data processed with AI, the momentum has come in the last iteration, Healthcare 4.0. These huge volumes of information come from a variety of sources related to the IoMT's expansion. Healthcare 4.0 suggests digitization is much more than a mere technological solution, but rather is an innovative technique that impacts sanitary practices and industry frameworks, allowing healthcare practitioners to boost precision medicine, alter care delivery, and improve the patient experience. Fig. 3 shows the revolution from Healthcare 1.0 to 4.0. The goal of Healthcare 4.0 is to collect vast amounts of data and put that to use in applications. Remote aid and telemedicine are becoming more common, indicating that these applications are becoming a reality.

The following are the major components of Healthcare 4.0:

1. Intelligence: The application of artificial intelligence (AI) algorithms to enhance the accurate identification of diseases, diagnosis, and interaction between doctors, patients, and stakeholders to achieve individualized and patient-centric smart health management systems, includes the following points of view:

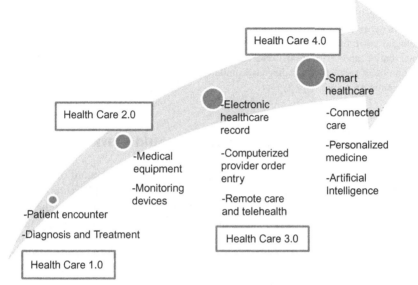

Fig. 3 Revolution from Healthcare 1.0 to 4.0.

a. Stratification and classification: Patient requirements and characteristics must be better recognized for patients to be classified into distinct classes (for example, risk assessment platforms for cancer and stroke [15,16]). It is possible to uncover key variables associated with a given illness using stratification and classification methods. We can go beyond examining this correlation to determine the causative link between patient variables and a specific condition, which will aid physicians in developing patient-specific intervention strategies that address these factors. This may be used as a starting point for improving diagnosis support and therapy to match the needs of patients.

2. Preventive-prognostic care: Prognostic detection can be employed to develop proactive and preventative treatment strategies [17]. This can help to effectively address how to provide minimized relevant medication with fewer mistakes and enhance patient safety in addition to preventing or delaying disease progression [18,19]. An investigation of key factors influencing patient outcomes and therapy responsiveness might lead to recommendations for creating treatment regimens.

3. Prediction analysis: For each patient, accurate predictions of disease development and results based on stratification and classification can be made to aid diagnosis and prognosis (e.g., prediction of hospital readmission, cardiovascular disease, and diagnosis of infection by COVID-19) [20]. Not only must such models predict risk levels, but they must also identify and understand the factors that influence those levels. The importance of prioritizing related components as well as the potential influence of causative elements might be investigated further to give recommendations and assistance for medical decision-making [21].

4. Closed loop: In a closed loop, all components of Healthcare 4.0 are dynamically interconnected. To put it another way, the outcomes of medicine and treatment decisions must be submitted to the prognostic analysis model so that prognoses, significant factors, and treatment and intervention plans may be dynamically updated in real time.

Deep learning, NLP, statistical analysis, augmented reality and virtual reality modeling, and optimization approaches all play key roles in the development of a smart healthcare system. In cyber-physical systems, robots, IoT, wearable devices, RFID, and blockchain technologies, as in Industry 4.0, provide a framework for data gathering, analysis, monitoring, intervention, and verification. Connecting them to customized medicine can aid in the implementation of genetics-based diagnostic and treatment techniques as well as increase patient therapeutic efficacy.

4   How a blockchain EHR system would work

Blockchain is a decentralized ledger technique that generates a record of immutable transactions. Distributed ledger technology produces an immutable record of transactions and an immutable exchange. Transactions in the healthcare industry are defined by parts of patient health information. Before reaching blockchain permanence, each occurrence of entering patient data into file registration was double-checked to keep a universal patient data record. There are numerous ways to verify a blockchain. With various governance and accessibility levels, there is no research procedure for participants in a public blockchain system, thus anybody may participate; this characteristic is employed in Bitcoin. Instead, a trustworthy consortium governs the blockchain and evaluates possible participants in a file with permission or a private blockchain. While both private and public blockchains might be useful in healthcare, a private blockchain mode potentially allows for additional monitoring because only authorized parties with a private digital key will have access to the blockchain. Both patients and clinicians would have access to relevant health information because of this. In this approach, the blockchain might expand access to documents while maintaining enough supervision, therefore impacting care quality. Transactions in the healthcare industry are defined by parts of the patient's health information. Each transaction or occurrence of putting patient data into the file registration is evaluated before reaching blockchain permanence in order to preserve a universal patient data record.

Even if they are not ready for time being, blockchain offers an incredible opportunity to address the above problems. As a result of this strategy, the blockchain may be able to increase document access while still retaining enough oversight, therefore affecting care quality. MedRec, for example, allows patients and physicians to share HER files across doctors. In the same way, the European Union established MyHealthMyData, a blockchain network that permits healthcare providers, government entities, vendors, and patients to exchange data. Despite these advancements, its usage is hampered by regulatory and institutional obstacles. Blockchain has several distinguishing characteristics. This makes it particularly well-suited to dealing with problems in EHR systems (Table 1).

Because data are immutable, they offer a trustworthy event record and make it nearly difficult for bad actors to modify it. Furthermore, cryptography initiatives built into the blockchain make any erroneous data harder to comprehend. From the standpoint of accessibility, health data might be accessed by anybody, anywhere, with a

Table 1 Features of a desirable health information sharing system as well as blockchain properties.

Features for healthcare model	Blockchain properties
Accessibility, transparency	Decentralization, clear visibility, and auditing
Accuracy	Immutable and deterministic data
Efficiency	Reduced transaction costs between agents
Security, privacy	Cryptography and dual private/public key
Interoperability	Harmonized between healthcare datasets
Utility	Availability of digitized, structured data

wireless connection and authenticated credentials. This technique might result in a significant reduction in information exchange transaction costs. Data tampering and unauthorized access are concerns with any digital system, and these concerns reach the bare minimum with the blockchain technique. Innovation and research are minor factors that may benefit from the vast amount of data that blockchain would make available. EHRs are made accessible to patients, clinicians, and research organizations by utilizing blockchain technology. There are numerous advantages to working for the government. Consumerization of healthcare is a well-known trend among patients, and it has led to a significant volume of patient data being produced via mobile devices, apps, and other tools. It is expected that patients might take a proactive and involved part in their care if health information was made more available to them. Furthermore, at each appointment, physicians would be supplied with all essential health data, allowing for accurate and targeted care as well as avoiding diagnosis mistakes. Enhanced access to patient data on a wide scale might aid researchers in creating a large number of datasets, resulting in improved evidence-based decision-making. Likewise, easily accessible data and the capacity to handle consent through a patient-centric platform might result in cheaper research and development expenses for developers and pharmaceutical firms, allowing for a faster time to market and lower prices for both patients and providers.

5 Blockchain-assisted secured transaction validation for patient interoperability

Blockchain technology has the potential to improve interoperability across a global medical tourism sector by removing both system and geographical barriers. Access to patients' accumulated clinical data– their medical history–to assist better care delivery "in country" is, however, a big problem. Blockchain technology may be used to create a decentralized, uniform worldwide EHR system. Members/patients can have global mobility thanks to blockchain, which ensures that their medical history data can be securely accessible by any provider, anywhere in the world, over the Internet. Clinics may share healthcare information without limits in an interoperable healthcare system, and they can also optimize their healthcare procedures [22–24]. Interoperability can be divided into three categories:

1. Structural interoperability: structured data formats facilitate data sharing. The use of these standardized data formats ensures data interpretation.
2. Data sharing across various healthcare facilities (fundamental interoperability). The responder is not needed to understand the data.
3. Semantic interoperability: information interpretation is facilitated at the semantic layer, allowing data meaning to be interpreted.

The three types of interoperability enable various information technology (IT) systems and data collection devices, such as mobile handsets for recording blood sugar or health monitoring devices for blood pressure, pulse, and other indicators. This can help ensure the quality, security, and cost-effectiveness of structured data [25,26]. In addition, seniors in the medical domain must exchange clinical domain information to scientists from the data domain. Advanced standards for data are needed for the preparation of unstructured data, which is acquired from mobile handsets and health data devices that monitor patients constantly for diagnostic data. The integration of clinical knowledge and data standards that exchange this knowledge from various case studies will be critical in the future [27,28] because a substantial number of health information sources are difficult for information systems to comprehend.

Advancements in EHR, cloud-based health data storage, and patient data as well as new privacy protection rules have opened new prospects for health data management, allowing patients to reach and forward their health data more easily [29–31]. Data security, transactions, and storage as well as the administration of continuous integration are the backbone to any data-assisted organization, especially for healthcare services, where blockchain has the ability to take care of these open issues securely and efficiently [32–34]. Fig. 4A depicts seven phases in the blockchain system's health data management, which are explained further below. Blockchain-based applications include data sharing, data management, data storage, e.g., cloud-based applications and EHR.

When a patient interacts with a physician or specialist, primary data are created. This information includes the patient's present issue, medical history, and other physiological facts. The primary data collected before are used to construct each patient's EHR. Other medical information is also provided, such as that gained from nursing care, medication history, and medical imaging. The owner of this property is the sole patient who has access to confidential EHRs and individualized access control. Those who want access to this sensitive data must first submit an authorization request, which is then submitted to the EHR's owner who decides who has access. The database, blockchain, and cloud storage are the three steps that make up the complete activity. Logs are kept in databases and cloud storage in a scattered manner, ensuring exceptional privacy as well as legal and customized user access. The end user is a health professional, such as ad hoc clinics, social care centers, or hospitals, who wishes to get access to a safe care service that is approved by the owner. For example, medical records will be available on the handset and authenticated employing a blockchain decentralized platform.

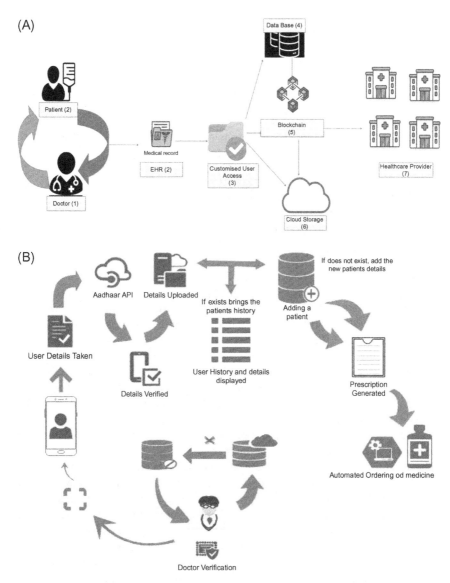

Fig. 4 (A) Health data management in blockchain. (B) Features available for the doctor's domain.

5.1 Data flow and operation

(a) After collaborating and registering on the app, doctors would be given authorization after confirming their authenticity through the medical board. Their data would then be stored permanently in cloud storage.

(b) The customer details along with their location would be saved on the cloud service after their biometric and key confirmation.
(c) The above step would take place depending on the chosen plan or as prescribed by the doctor himself.
(d) A doctor's prescription along with a diet plan and necessary reminders would be sent for execution as entered.
(e) The names of the medicines would be searched and their prices fetched through registered sites, based on the minimal cost shown on the app. The doctor, with the patient's approval, can place the order.
(f) Similarly, fruits, vegetables, and other items suggested by the doctor would all reach the patient's registered location.
(g) Upon receiving the order, the patient would be required to confirm their received order.
(h) Reminders would be generated as scheduled.
(i) Throughout the registered period, both patients as well as doctors would be able to communicate with each other through the video/voice call facility provided.

5.2   Model design

Modeling of data flow for functional operation at the doctor domain:

In doctor-end functionalities: Healthcare experts will be authorized to access the application only upon verification as a licensed expert. The task will be achieved by establishing his/her entries (registration identification and region) in the licensed expert database, and concurrently in the blacklisted database. After access, the expert may go through a list of his former clients and scan their history, or simply see a new patient's unique ID or Aadhaar card during the appointment. On scanning the patient's unique identity, his/her complete medical record will be available to the expert if it exists; if the need arises, a new entry will be created. Depending on the medical record, the expert can add a new prescription, diet plan/precautions, or reminders for food, medications, and other items, as shown in Fig. 4B. The costs of prescription and medicine can be worked on by a price comparison tool.

The data of a chronic care patient can be upgraded to make medical history records available on a worldwide network, as shown in Fig. 5. This would allow any hospital in the world to obtain this information, regardless of where it is situated (once authorized by the patient). As a result, when a patient travels to another city or country to obtain treatment as outlined by the medical tourism policy, they no longer need to bring their medical documents with them. Smart contracts can be set up in an interoperable blockchain to act as a gateway for storing standardized data that are instantly accessible to any parties that have been granted access to the blockchain. To drive the smart contract, an application program interface (API)-oriented architecture might be created. The APIs will be made public and available to all collaborating organizations. All participating organizations connected to the blockchain will have access to the APIs, which will allow for seamless integration with each organization's existing systems. The content of the patient interaction is sent to a blockchain-based smart contract when the API is called. Querying data from the blockchain is also possible via a set of API calls that may be used by any linked organization. These APIs allow organizations to query specific blocks in the chain or submit preset query criteria (patients

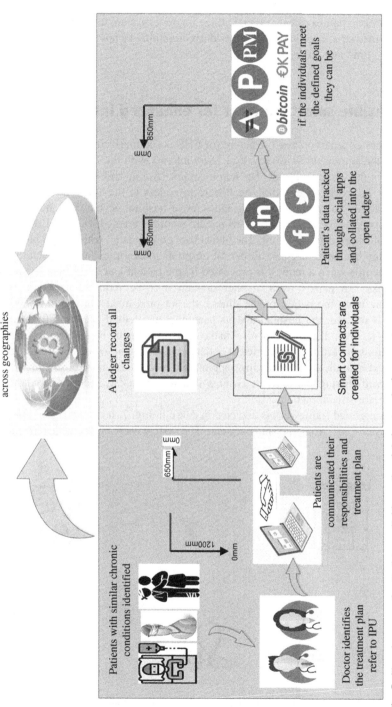

Fig. 5 Chronic care patient's data available on the global network via a smart contract.

Interoperability of data at multiple locations across geographies

Patients with similar chronic conditions identified

Doctor identifies the treatment plan refer to IPU

Patients are communicated their responsibilities and treatment plan

A ledger record all changes

Smart contracts are created for individuals

Patient's data tracked through social apps and collated into the open ledger

if the individuals meet the defined goals they can be

older than 25, for example). APIs can be used to create a common portal that all linked healthcare companies can access and utilize for direct system integration. Because the API-oriented structure only necessitates the redirection of a few data fields, businesses may save time and money.

6 Flexible smart contract for enhanced interoperability

The suggested smart contract structure for EHR is summarized in Fig. 6. The parameters of the agreement as well as how users interact with the Ethereum network are defined in this smart contract. The administrator (Admin in Fig. 6) is the governing authority in charge of enrolling healthcare providers in the app. The administrator has the ability to create, edit, add, and remove hospital accounts. A new block is produced on the backend when a new patient record is created, validated, and broadcast to all nodes in the network. The blockchain gets updated with a fresh block. The technology has been designed to permit hospitals to examine and formulate patient health records when a request is processed by the patient and the patient has permitted access. An expert from another domain may be required to aid a patient depending upon the nature of the illness; the hospital makes this request. When a request is refused, the hospital and its personnel are denied access to the patient's medical records. Patients can also make an appointment by calling the facility. Two actions govern the boundaries of patient contact: (1) allowing or refusing access to medical records, and (2) viewing appointment records. Because blockchain is used as a record-sharing platform, it ensures that data transfer, security, privacy, and integrity are streamlined.

The suggested framework is depicted in detail in Fig. 7. It is made up of three primary layers: User, front end, and back end. The system user classes, which include the

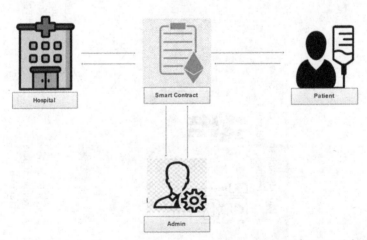

Fig. 6 For an electronic healthcare record system, a basic smart contract framework is required.

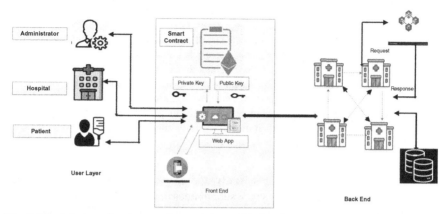

Fig. 7 Blockchain-assisted secured transaction validation for patient interoperability in electronic health records.

administrator, hospital personnel, and patient modules, make up the user layer. The following modules are discussed in detail:

1. The administrative module

This module creates user interfaces for applications that are straightforward and simple to use. It is divided into six submodules that allow the administrator to manage hospital accounts. All administrator submodules are listed below:

(a) The Create-Hospital-Record Module allows administrators to create or update hospital records. It's a completely verified online form that contains the programming logic for registering patients and creating hospital records.
(b) The Dashboard Module generates and provides all hospitals in the suggested blockchain network. Using the explore tag offered by the targeted hospital available on the dashboard, the administrator may investigate these hospital data and run the hospital.
(c) The Hospital Record Details Module permits the administrator to see facility data as well as do other administrative tasks related to the hospital's present needs. Add personnel to the hospital, modify hospital records, suspend hospital accounts, and so on are examples of administrative tasks.
(d) Using the Create Hospital Staff Record Module, the administrator appends health center staff data to the present health center records.
(e) Edit Hospital Record Module allows administrators to make changes to hospital records.
(f) The Administrator Menu Module is integrated with all other modules of the administrator module. There are two possibilities. Administrator Dashboard and Create Hospital Record modules utilize one variation, whereas the Hospital Record Details and Create Hospital Staff-Record modules use the other.

2. Patient module

This module incorporates user-friendly and easy-to-use app interfaces that permit logged-in patients to communicate with the mode. There are six submodules in total:

(a) The Grant Access to Request Module permits a logged-in person to view and accept or reject all hospital requests for access to their medical information. After a patient

authorizes a request, it is active for that day, and upon completion of patient consultation, access is revoked.
(b) The Patient-Menu Module is interconnected to all other modules. The module consists of a set of links that allows logged-in users to access additional content.
(c) The Dashboard Module displays logged patient alerts, such as notifying users of a new request from a hospital to reach their data or displaying the patient's daily appointment. This module also shows the logged-in user's profile information.
(d) The Medical History of Patients Module permits the logged user to access their own medical records. The information in their medical history cannot be modified or tampered with by the registered user; they can only see the data.
3. Hospital module

The hospital module presents user-friendly and easy-to-use user interfaces in the administration module. It contains seven submodules that allow logged-in individuals to complete activities that assist the hospital in managing their patients. Hospital submodules are:

(a) Medical Records for Patients Module: The logged hospital person has reached the patient's records and they may then see the patient's data and medical records. This module also gives hospital personnel the ability to update patient records following a thorough conversation with the patient as well as plan a follow-up meeting with the patient. The doctor's access authorization is revoked when the expert exits the patient record page after successfully finishing the consultation. If the doctor needs access to the record again, he or she must make a new request.
(b) Dashboard Module: This module displays statistics on the number of patients the hospital has seen for the day, the total number of scheduled appointments, and scheduled appointments the hospital intends to keep for that day to log hospital personnel. This module also includes a list of all medical record access requests that have been granted as well as several appointments that the hospital has kept for the patient.
(c) Seek Access to Patient Medical Records Module: Logged hospital professionals (doctors) can use this module to request access to a patient's medical record. A search function in the module allows the doctor to get a patient's record by providing the public key or account token. The program searches the patient's records in the back end using the provided token, and if the record is present, the doctor asks for access and waits for approval. If the user account cannot be discovered, the doctor must register the patient, prepare a patient report, and request access to the patient's previous record. On approval of the request, the expert can access and analyze patient records.
(d) Hospital Appointment Module: This module displays the logged user's hospital appointment logs. Appointments for the present day are first on the list, followed by all other appointments, which are displayed underneath the current day's appointments.
(e) Add Medical Report Module: The module allows logged hospital staff to update the patient's history and create a record depending on the doctor's consultation and diagnosis.
(f) The Hospital Menu Module is integrated with all other modules of the hospital module. The module is a list of links that permits the logged user to access additional resources.
(g) Module for Scheduling Appointments: The module enables logged hospital person to plan a patient's next hospital visit. This module is a completely verified procedure that creates an appointment record when filled out with the correct information.

The smart contract that is distributed on the Ethereum network serves as the back end, and the smart contract is created by the dapp application. To deploy the smart contract, it must first be completed and the binary application interface, a json representative of a smart contract in terms of the user agreement, must be produced. The created smart contract gets interfaced using migration tools. The front end will have access to the smart contract, which will allow MetaMask to communicate with the distributed file. The program may be accessed via a web browser and MetaMask, a web3 protocol for accessing a decentralized network from your browser (dapp). To use the application, the user's private key will be needed to import the user account into the browser using MetaMask and connect to the Ethereum network (administrator, hospital personnel, or patient).

With the Ethereum network, a public key is employed to identify and address an account. A request (login request) from the dapp application initiates the delivery backend transaction (smart contract). A processing charge known as gas is required for the submitted transaction. On the Ethereum network, gas is the needed cost for successfully completing a transaction or contract on the platform. The transaction is then transmitted to the backend, where it will be processed, after the commencement of the access request and the request confirmation opens in the MetaMask dialog. The miner employs mining algorithms to create new blocks on the blockchain to execute a transaction. The mined block may include several transactions, each of which is checked and validated by the network. After completion of block extraction and transaction, the back end sends its response to the front end, which changes the user interface based on the contents of the file server response.

The flowcharts above outline the functions aimed at delivering efficient and precise healthcare support for its users as well as simplicity of use and data management for doctors. The initial app activity allows a user as well as a doctor to log in. In the instance of a user, the following Flowchart, Fig. 8, explains the subsequent activities. In the case of a doctor, he may input his registration identification and region (which as one unit will constitute a unique identification key), and the OTP delivered to the doctor's registered contact number guarantees that no nondoctor may get access. If any of these credentials are discovered in a database of authenticated doctors (and it should not possess any banned doctors), the doctor is granted access. The doctor can then check or see if any fresh pathology reports have been updated, analyze any existing records or contacts (mostly for persons he or she is presently taking care of), or simply scan the QR code on the patient's unique ID card. If the patient's current information and medical records are present, the Aadhaar card scanning procedure will bring them all, and if they are not, the new patient's personal credentials will be added to the database. Any prescriptions, reminders, or other details added by the doctor will be saved with the patient's records. A charge for the prescriptions, drugs, and vaccines available online would be created immediately after a prescription was filed. Whether to place an order is up to you, but in any case, all your information will be saved in the patient database. Fig. 9 depicts a snapshot of the electronic healthcare app.

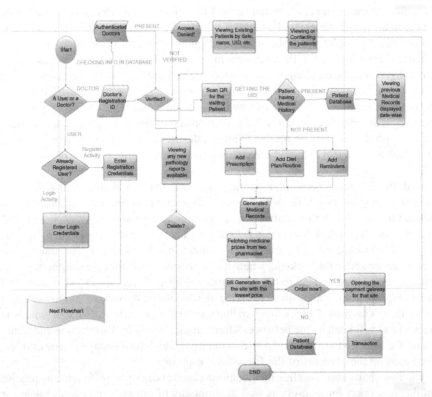

Fig. 8 Flowchart illustrating how the electronic healthcare app works (mostly from the doctor's perspective).

Fig. 9 Snapshot of the electronic healthcare app.

The app's operation is depicted in the diagram below.

Step 1: Begin.

Step 2: If you are an existing user, enter your credentials; if you are a new user, select the registration option and proceed. If you are a doctor, go to Step 4 and pick DoctorLogin from the option, as shown in Fig. 9.

Step 3: After logging into the app, the user can choose from one of the following seven options:

(a) Doctor search by any field.

(b) Doctors near me option.

(c) Viewing the Gantt chart based on the previous sickness investigated.

(d) Finding a list of medical tests/check-ups needed and nearby pathologies depending on the disease/symptom input (These details are collected through the fog layer reduction system).

(e) Uploading a date-stamped test report (added to the patient's record).

(f) Examining the patient's prior medical records and visits (If needed, the patient can even contact the doctor in any of three ways: messaging, telephone calling, or video chat).

(g) Submitting a feedback form for each doctor seen.

Step 4: For doctors, the initial step in gaining access to the app is to get verified. He must give his registration number as well as the state in which he was registered, as shown in Fig. 10.

Step 5: Upon successful verification, access is granted.

Step 6: The doctor can then review or make an addition to the list of those who have already seen him.

Step 7: The following action contains the basic personal information (such as name, age, gender, and so on) as well as any medical history that may be discovered. Fig. 11 depicts the snapshot of the working of the app for personal details (name, age, gender, and address).

Step 8: There's also the option to add a medication, diet plan, or reminder, which is shown in Fig. 12.

Fig. 10 Snapshot of doctor's side.

Fig. 11 Snapshot of working of the app for personal details (name, age, gender, and address).

Fig. 12 Snapshot of the app working for medicine prescription by a doctor.

Step 9: Submission of the prescription generates a bill comprising the lowest price medications.

Step 10: Upon selection of a payment gateway for the online pharmacy, the transaction is initiated; otherwise, the prescription is saved for a later stage.

Step 11: Diet charts are emailed to the patient's login account, and medication reminders are created.

Step 12: Come to an end (Exit)

Digitized medicare is the need of today's world and providing what is needed is the best possible thing we can do to help mankind. The system has various benefits, and some characteristics may include the following:

1. Electronic prescription and report generation: The usual method of manually writing a prescription might be easy at first for the doctor, but in the long run these data are hard to maintain, search for, and reread by someone else. They are also prone to wear and tear, leading to data loss. The electronic generation of prescriptions, bills, and pathology reports makes the management of data far easier. The patient's personal information is automatically read and retrieved from the QR code, and no human entry is required. AutoComplete recommendations and checkbox inputs of often-used names make entering symptoms, medicines, and tests a breeze.
2. Locating directions via app: One of the biggest issues that elderly individuals or patients in general experience is the difficulty in locating a nearby doctor's clinic or pathologist for visits. Other problems include searching for doctors through their specialization or by the symptoms or the patient's disease. This problem is overcome because the app makes use of Google Maps API; it can also give step-by-step directions to reach there too.
3. Automated procurement of medicines with an online transaction: as previously said, patients generally do not have the patience, time, and energy to rush for their medicines. As a result, they frequently skip doses, which can result in health issues and a patient's delayed recovery. Automation and the ease of getting the medicines delivered at home reduce the chances of carelessness.
4. Storing a massive quantity of patient data in one place: Earlier, the prescriptions and patients' records were maintained manually through registers or Excel files, which were often hard to manage and maintain. Tracking these huge sets of records seemed far beyond imagination, even searching for any of them was quite difficult. However, because a patient's history, from symptoms to prescriptions and required tests, is kept in one place through this app, any reference to previous data may be made at a click and additional treatment can be carried out.

7 Open issues and challenges

Blockchain technology has to find a number of applications in the healthcare industry; the potential is not yet completely explored and is not a panacea for instant use. Techniques, organizational structure, and behavior are all different. Before businesses can implement a healthcare blockchain across the country, they must overcome economic hurdles.

1. *Scalability constraints: trade-offs between available computing power and transaction volumes*:
    Organizations can use blockchain technology in permissionless or permissioned ways, according to the blockchain. Unauthorized blockchains are appealing because they allow for more access, unauthorized open innovation, and the utilization of additional network processing power. Existing permissionless blockchains like Ethereum and Bitcoin, on the other hand, have transaction volume limits. The Bitcoin network now processes about seven transactions per second, even though there are more than 10 million users and 200,000 transactions each day. Many in the business are asking for advancements in technology to allow for faster processing times. Authorized blockchains, on the other hand, can reduce transaction processing times while also limiting computational power owing to reduced network

engagement. The US Department of Health and Human Services (HHS) could theoretically provide the computing power required to process all blockchain transactions through an authorized network for selected participants; however, this would make HHS the relative owner of the blockchain, limiting the value of a truly decentralized system. With so many people involved in healthcare, a nationwide blockchain would not only make the system more interoperable but also safer.

2. *Data standardization and scope*:

Organizations should examine what information the blockchain stores in addition to permissionless and approved blockchains. The most urgent worry for healthcare data stored on the blockchain is the scale of the data. Free data submission to the blockchain, such as doctor's notes, could result in needlessly huge transaction sizes, which could harm the blockchain's speed. However, given a restricted range of data, such as medical history, demographic information, and service codes, the blockchain may still be used effectively. Organizations must align with a framework to determine what data, size, and format may be provided to standardize the data stored on the blockchain and control performance. Technical APIs can concatenate and deconcatenate stored and transmitted data to shrink data size in particular circumstances. Finally, users can make the blockchain private, limiting access to only registered and confirmed users.

3. *Operating costs*:

While blockchain technology allows for near-instant transactions, the costs of running such a system remain unclear. Traditional data interchange and information systems are time- and money-intensive to create and maintain, and they necessitate a significant amount of manpower to troubleshoot, update field settings, perform backup and recovery processes, and extract data for reporting. The open-source technology, functionality, and distributed nature of blockchain can assist in lowering the cost of these operations. The parameters of a blockchain and its smart contracts become absolute once they are put up, reducing the need for frequent upgrades and troubleshooting. Rollback contingencies are unneeded because blockchain records are immutable and shared among all participants. Furthermore, the transparent information structure of the blockchain could eliminate many integration points for time-consuming data exchange and reporting activities.

A blockchain, on the other hand, uses a lot of computational power to process transactions. The quantity and volume of transactions sent across the network affect the cost of processing power, which varies even more even more depending on the type of transactions in the chain (for example, data warehousing versus value exchange).

4. *Adoption and participation incentives*:

Two sorts of incentives are required for blockchain to be effective. A network of networked computers (nodes) is necessary on a technical level to provide the computing capacity required to create blocks when a transaction is submitted. People are attracted to donate their processing power to the network on a permissionless blockchain by monetary incentives in the form of cryptocurrencies. Monetary benefits or reach to blockchain data in return for processing exchanges might be used to promote involvement in the blockchain. In addition to the technological incentives, further help may be required for the blockchain to flourish. While some businesses are presently experimenting with blockchain technology to verify and manage medical information and complaints internally, the blockchain will increase in strength as the number of individuals who use the shared network rises. Programs that are comparable to those offered by the Center. Programs similar to the ones provided by the Center The Medicare and Medicaid Significant Use of Services (CMS) Program, which promotes clinicians to migrate to electronic health records, could lead to an increase in the number of people using electronic health records.

5. *Regulatory considerations*:

To comprehend and stimulate ecosystem expansion within the constraints of the present regulatory framework and new administrative policy goals, health officials should consider a deep partnership with the industry. The ramifications of the blockchain's distributed storage, who owns the data (and when ownership changes), and how access is provided through the blockchain may all be considered. HHS establishes national guidelines to preserve the privacy of people's medical records through the HIPAA privacy act. The rule outlines the conditions under which personal health information is kept confidential as well as the limits and situations under which it can be used and disclosed without the patient's agreement. Due to these circumstances, a blockchain system might be able to comply with the HIPAA privacy guideline by segregating and encrypting IDs, PHI, and PII into different entities that can be retrieved. At the same time, it demands a comprehensive analysis of the types of high-level demographic data kept on the blockchain; a combination of this demographic data and location data may possibly allow triangulation of exact individuals. A rural locale, for example, may have a higher likelihood of recognizing someone with a rare health condition than a densely populated urban center. Some of these concerns can be alleviated with the use of a licensed blockchain. As blockchain tests develop, however, the questions will need to be carefully explored.

8 Conclusion

Blockchain technology offers one-of-a-kind possibilities for reducing complexity, enabling trustless cooperation, and generating safe and immutable data. The electronic health record is ideally positioned to keep track of this rapidly evolving sector, highlighting patterns and areas where government help may be necessary for the technology to realize its full potential in healthcare. Blockchain technology has the potential to enhance health information sharing while also enabling better data openness, more secure treatment, increased health efficiency, and more robust medical research. Over the previous laborious and inefficient manual operations method, this technology offers the following advantages:

1. Paperwork reduction: No need for large files.
2. Redundancy: Data input redundancy can be eliminated.
3. Speed: The computer is far faster than a person in retrieving and modifying data.
4. Storage is simple and long-lasting.
5. Cost-cutting: Paper and file costs can be reduced.
6. Authorization and security are both important.
7. Ease in the process of handling accounts such as bill payments and receipts.
8. If a user encounters any security issues, they can use the hospital's online software and reset their password. Administrators, CMOs, doctors, operators, and patients will all have the proper authority to view the database.

Despite the positive qualities, several basic issues must be addressed before mass adoption can be successful and safe. Healthcare companies must examine blockchain in the context of their requirements, just as they do with any other technology adoption, and strengthen providers with techniques to employ these algorithms successfully. Although blockchain can provide a stronger platform for information exchange, it would be naïve to expect the benefits to appear immediately. Blockchain platforms must have a certain amount of flexibility in implementation to allow widespread usage and acceptance to adapt to local practical variations to attain their full potential. In addition, the primary focus cannot be just on technology solutions; human concerns and issues must also be considered, as any digital platform would pose. To optimize the exchange of information while preserving patient safety, solutions should be decentralized and must involve a broad multidisciplinary expert group, including healthcare vendors, legal professionals, technology developers, and patients, just as the blockchain is fundamentally opposed to siloed approaches through decentralization principles.

References

[1] K. Tiwari, S. Kumar, R.K. Tiwari, Real time mobile-phone aided melanoma skin lesion detection using triangulation technique, Int. J. E Health Med. Commun. 11 (3) (2020) 9–31. article 2.

[2] K. Tiwari, S. Kumar, R.K. Tiwari, FOG assisted healthcare architecture for pre-operative support to reduce latency, in: 1st International Conference on Computational INTELLIGENCE and Data Science (ICCIDS-2019), Procedia Computer Science Journal, vol. 167, Elsevier, 2020, pp. 1312–1324.

[3] S. Mehta, K. Grant, A. Ackery, Future of blockchain in healthcare: potential to improve the accessibility, security and interoperability of electronic health records, BMJ Health Care Inform. 27 (3) (2020) 1–6.

[4] S. Tanwar, K. Parekh, R. Evans, Blockchain-based electronic healthcare record system for healthcare 4.0 applications, J. Inf. Secur. Appl. 50 (2019) 1–14.

[5] J. Hathaliya, P. Sharma, S. Tanwar, R. Gupta, Blockchain-based remote patient monitoring in healthcare 4.0, in: 9th IEEE International Conference on Advanced Computing (IACC), Tiruchirappalli, India, 13-148th December, 2019, pp. 87–91.

[6] S. Khezr, M. Moniruzzaman, A. Yassine, R. Benlamri, Blockchain technology in healthcare: a comprehensive review and directions for future research, Appl. Sci. 9 (9) (2019) 1736.

[7] G.G. Dagher, J. Mohler, M. Milojkovic, P.B. Marella, Ancile: privacy-preserving framework for access control and interoperability of electronic health records using blockchain technology, Sustain. Cities Soc. 39 (2018) 283–297.

[8] D. Mehta, S. Tanwar, U. Bodkhe, A. Shukla, N. Kumar, Blockchain-based royalty contract transactions scheme for Industry 4.0 supply-chain management, Inf. Process. Manag. 58 (4) (2021) 102586. ISSN 0306-4573 *https://doi.org/10.1016/j.ipm.2021.102586.*

[9] S. Nakamoto, Bitcoin: A peer-to-peer electronic cash system, Decentralized Business Review, Bitcoin.org, 2008, p. 21260. URL: *https://bitcoin.org/bitcoin.pdf.* (Accessed 24 February 2021).

[10] I. Haq, O.M. Esuka, Blockchain technology in pharmaceutical industry to prevent counterfeit drugs, Int. J. Comput. Appl. 180 (25) (2018) 8–12.

[11] J. Zhang, C. Thomas, P. FragaLamas, T.M. Fernández-Caramés, Deploying blockchain technology in the supply chain, in: Computer Security Threats, IntechOpen, 2019.

[12] R. Gupta, S. Tanwar, S. Tyagi, N. Kumar, Tactile-internet-based telesurgery system for healthcare 4.0: an architecture, research challenges, and future directions, IEEE Netw. 33 (6) (2019) 22–29, https://doi.org/10.1109/MNET.001.1900063.

[13] R. Gupta, A. Shukla, S. Tanwar, AaYusH: a smart contract-based telesurgery system for healthcare 4.0, in: IEEE Conference on Communications (IEEE ICC-2020), Dublin, Ireland, 2020, pp. 1–6. 07-11th June.

[14] V. Gatteschi, F. Lamberti, C. Demartini, C. Pranteda, V. Santamaría, Blockchain and smart contracts for insurance: Is the technology mature enough? Future Internet 10 (2) (2018) 20.

[15] J. Alzubi, B. Bharathikannan, S. Tanwar, R. Manikandan, A. Khanna, C. Thaventhiran, Boosted neural network ensemble classification for lung cancer disease diagnosis, Appl. Soft Comput. 80 (2019) 579–591, https://doi.org/10.1016/j.asoc.2019.04.031.

[16] M.W. Newman, L.C. O'Dwyer, L. Rosenthal, Predicting delirium: a review of risk-stratification models, Gen. Hosp. Psychiatry 37 (5) (2015) 408–413.

[17] J.A. Damen, L. Hooft, E. Schuit, T.P. Debray, G.S. Collins, I. Tzoulaki, K.G. Moons, Prediction models for cardiovascular disease risk in the general population: systematic review, BMJ 353 (2016) 1–17.

[18] L. Wynants, B. Van Calster, G.S. Collins, R.D. Riley, G. Heinze, E. Schuit, M. van Smeden, Prediction models for diagnosis and prognosis of covid-19: systematic review and critical appraisal, BMJ 369 (2020) 1–19.

[19] V. Struckmann, F.R. Leijten, E. van Ginneken, M. Kraus, M. Reiss, A. Spranger, M. -Rutten-van Mölken, Relevant models and elements of integrated care for multi-morbidity: results of a scoping review, Health Policy 122 (1) (2018) 23–35.

[20] C. Mistry, U. Thakker, R. Gupta, S. Tanwar, N. Kumar, J.J.P.C. Rodrigues, M.S. Obaidat, MedBlock: an AI-enabled and blockchain-driven medical healthcare system for COVID-19, in: IEEE International Conference on Communications (IEEE ICC 2021), Montreal, Canada, 14–18 June, 2021.

[21] S. Tanwar, Q. Bhatia, P. Patel, A. Kumari, P.K. Singh, W. Hong, Machine learning adoption in blockchain-based smart applications: the challenges, and a way forward, IEEE Access 8 (2020) 474–488, https://doi.org/10.1109/ACCESS.2019.2961372.

[22] A. Kumari, R. Gupta, S. Tanwar, N. Kumar, Blockchain and AI amalgamation for energy cloud management: challenges, solutions, and future directions, J. Parallel Distrib. Comput. 143 (2020) 148–166, https://doi.org/10.1016/j.jpdc.2020.05.004.

[23] A. Hendry, E. Vanhecke, A.M. Carriazo, L. López-Samaniego, J.M. Espinosa, D. Sezgin, R. O'Caoimh, Integrated care models for managing and preventing frailty: a systematic review for the European joint action on frailty prevention (ADVANTAGE JA), Transl. Med. UniSa 19 (5) (2019) 5.

[24] J. Li, P. Carayon, Health Care 4.0: a vision for smart and connected health care, IISE Trans. Healthc. Syst. Eng. 11 (3) (2021) 171–180.

[25] C.U. Correll, B. Galling, A. Pawar, A. Krivko, C. Bonetto, M. Ruggeri, J.M. Kane, Comparison of early intervention services vs treatment as usual for early-phase psychosis: a systematic review, meta-analysis, and meta-regression, JAMA Psychiat. 75 (6) (2018) 555–565.

[26] P. Bhattacharya, P. Mehta, S. Tanwar, M.S. Obaidat, K.F. Hsiao, HeaL: a blockchain-envisioned signcryption scheme for healthcare IoT ecosystems, in: International Conference on Communications, Computing, Cybersecurity, and Informatics 2020 ((CCCI 2020)), Sharjah, United Arab Emirates, 2020, pp. 1–6. 3–5 November.

[27] C. Gulden, R. Blasini, A. Nassirian, A. Stein, F.B. Altun, M. Kirchner, M. Boeker, Prototypical clinical trial registry based on fast healthcare interoperability resources (FHIR): design and implementation study, JMIR Med. Inform. 9 (1) (2021) e20470.

[28] R. Gupta, A. Kumari, S. Tanwar, N. Kumar, Blockchain-envisioned softwarized multi-swarming UAVs to tackle COVID-19 situations, IEEE Netw. 35 (2) (2020) 160–167, https://doi.org/10.1109/MNET.011.2000439.

[29] R. Gupta, A. Shukla, S. Tanwar, BATS: a blockchain and AI-empowered drone-assisted telesurgery system toward 6G, IEEE Trans. Netw. Sci. Eng. 8 (4) (2020) 2958–2967, https://doi.org/10.1109/TNSE.2020.3043262.

[30] J. Vora, S. Tanwar, S. Tyagi, N. Kumar, J.J.P.C. Rodrigues, Home-based exercise system for patients using IoT enabled smart speaker, in: 2017 IEEE 19th International Conference on e-Health Networking, Applications and Services (Healthcom), 2017, pp. 1–6, https://doi.org/10.1109/HealthCom.2017.821082.

[31] U. Bodkhe, D. Mehta, S. Tanwar, P. Bhattacharya, P.K. Singh, W. Hong, A survey on decentralized consensus mechanisms for cyber physical systems, IEEE Access 8 (2020) 54371–54401, https://doi.org/10.1109/ACCESS.2020.2981415.

[32] R. Gupta, S. Tanwar, F. Al-Turjman, P. Italiya, A. Nauman, S.W. Kim, Smart contract privacy protection using AI in cyber-physical systems: tools, techniques and challenges, IEEE Access 8 (2020) 24746–24772, https://doi.org/10.1109/ACCESS.2020.2970576.

[33] U. Bodkhe, S. Tanwar, A. Ladha, P. Bhattacharya, A. Verma, A survey on revolutionizing Healthcare 4.0 applications using blockchain, in: International Conference on Computing, Communications, and Cyber-Security (IC4S 2020), Lecture Notes in Networks and Systems, Springer, Chandigarh, India, 2019, pp. 1–16. 12-13th October.

[34] R. Gupta, S. Tanwar, N. Kumar, S. Tyagi, Blockchain-based security attack resilience schemes for autonomous vehicles in industry 4.0: a systematic review, Comput. Electr. Eng. 86 (2019) 106717, https://doi.org/10.1016/j.compeleceng.2020.106717.

NFC-enabled packaging to detect tampering and prevent counterfeiting: Enabling a complete supply chain using blockchain and CPS

2

Rohit Rastogi[a], Bhuvneshwar Prasad Sharma[b], Neha Gupta[c], Vansh Gaur[c], Muskan Gupta[c], Vrinda Kohli[c], Ankur Sharma[c], Komal[c], Prajwal Srivastava[c], and Aarushi Rai[c]

[a]Department of CSE, ABES Engineering College, Ghaziabad, Uttar Pradesh, India, [b]Department of CSE and MBA, ABES Engineering College, Ghaziabad, Uttar Pradesh, India, [c]ABES Engineering College, Ghaziabad, Uttar Pradesh, India

1 Introduction

1.1 Scope and motivation

As technology is improving day by day, every new technology solves problems in human lives. Near field communication (NFC) is one such technology that will help us stop illegally tampered with and counterfeit medicines that are affecting human beings. A project like AKSHAT provides us the opportunity to analyze how these things are working because all the data and information about the authenticity of the product will be stored and cannot be changed.

Such projects motivate us to do something good and beneficial. If this technology is used on a large scale, then a huge percentage of fake drugs and medicines can be detected and the lives of people can be saved. People and the public will have no trust issues with healthcare and doctors because they will be so sure that the medicines they are using are 100% pure. Also, greedy and inhuman people behind all these activities will be exposed [1,2].

Amid the global threat of COVID-19, the governments of many countries as well as healthcare industries, hospitals, doctors, and patients are also facing a crucial threat of tampering and counterfeiting of vaccines and drugs. This is not an issue that can be ignored easily, as it troubles all of society in a significant way. The current trend of technology such as blockchain, the Internet of Things (IoT), and artificial intelligence (AI) is a boon now as they encourage fast and easy access, transparency, and authentication. Using the NFC technique, many applications are being developed and the aforesaid issues can also be addressed efficiently. The Hyperledger blockchain combined with IoT and web servers applied with NFC seem to provide an efficient

Blockchain Applications for Healthcare Informatics. https://doi.org/10.1016/B978-0-323-90615-9.00002-5
Copyright © 2022 Elsevier Inc. All rights reserved.

solution and proof of concept (PoC) for a prototype. A product perspective has been presented.

1.2 Contributions of authors

Rohit Rastogi was the team lead to apply the manuscript and finalize the documentation. He acted as the corresponding author with handling all reviews, etc. Dr. B. P. Sharma originated the project and provided the seed idea. Team member Neha did the data collection and reference management while Vansh, Muskan, and Vrinda worked on blockchain execution. Komal and Aarushi designed the prototype, and App and Prajwal enabled the IoT part.

1.3 Chapter organizations

This chapter contains the abstract, followed by an introduction and background that presents the global analysis of NFC and drug interrogation. The introduction presents all the basic concepts in detail, followed by a literature survey covering four related papers and their gist. The next section shows the market analysis and product perspective. The Android app in the front end and blockchain-based execution in the back end, the output, and snapshots of the functioning are also demonstrated.

In the next phase, the manuscript covers the recommendations, novelties, future research work, and concluding remarks, followed by acknowledgments and references.

1.4 Technological shift from Healthcare 1.0 to Healthcare 4.0

With the IoMT, improved analytics, and an overlay of invisible users, a quiet revolution is afoot in the healthcare industry globally. Public Healthcare 4.0 is going to be a reality within the next few years (Swartz et al., 2014) [1].

Medicines play a vital role in human lives and the market size of medicines is quite large. Some greedy people are selling tampered and counterfeited medicines at the same rate, which is adversely affecting humans.

With this illegal activity, doctors, patients, healthcare, and governments are all suffering in one or another. The public is losing trust in them. Because of all this, medical tourism gets affected. Many doctors may end up losing their jobs, and much more is happening because of this activity [3].

1.5 Significance of blockchain and its advanced features

1.5.1 Blockchain in AWS and blockchain in IBM

The popularly known blockchain is said to be the peer-to-peer network that improves the efficiency, immutability, transparency, and security of transactions for business processes such as international payments, supply chain management, land registration, crowdfunding, governance, financial transactions, and more. This helps people and organizations who are unknown to one another to trust and independently verify their transaction records.

Many organizations provide and include blockchain as a service, due to its credibility and exceeding significance on account of its advanced features. The modular blockchain framework at IBM and Amazon's AWS cloud service's managed blockchain are two popular instances of the same [4–6].

1. **Increased financial and time efficiency**: The decentralized blockchain allows individual-to-individual transactions without the involvement of a third party. It also helps save a lot of money and time while making transactions secure and reliable when compared to traditional bank transactions.
2. **Transparency**: As blockchain is an open-source ledger, so to decrease the discrepancies and frauds, every transaction is recorded and everything is displayed on the network.

1.6 Security threats to blockchain and its possible solutions

The main security threat to blockchain infrastructure is identity theft. Several attacks and vulnerabilities can be done on the infrastructure such as majority attacks where an attacker may have all the processing power and mining capabilities across the network. He is able to verify or validate things that didn't happen in real time such as double payments, smart contracts, and endless things. Government interventions can also be a reason.

Access has been the major issue for blockchain infrastructure. Due to the lack of access, fake participants can take advantage of this. Once the money is lost, there is no option to recover it.

Then comes the question of how can we protect access?

For example, an employee is fired from the organization, but he has access to the key and has the right capabilities to get access to those frauds [7].

Measures can be taken to prevent these attacks and fraud activities.

First, we need to monitor who is accessing the infrastructure and what that person is doing on the infrastructure. Right now, we can digitally monitor any person's information such as GPS tracking, credit card information, etc. Elimination of third-party approvals is required.

Antimoney laundering (AML) and know your customer (KYC) are the two systems that help to monitor and watch the activities of users, so they can help in tracing data [6].

The above process involves all stakeholder contributions, from the manufacturer to global quality control organizations (QCO), then partners of logistics and end consumers.

1.7 Applications of blockchain and DL in NFC and IoT applications of pharmaceuticals

NFC is an enabling technology for IoT platforms and solutions in pharmaceutical companies in the digitalization and connection of vital functions, elevating efficiencies, and assuring product quality and compliance. The Internet of Things (IoT) lets one perform an incredible array of fascinating tasks, using NFC [8].

Drugs and medicine such as injection vaccines and various relevant drug packing are too basic to guarantee item quality. Organizations must follow exacting rules for deciding the manner in which a medication is moved, controlled, and burned through. Smart pharma packing can help guarantee that shipments and meds are precisely followed and that the chain stays proficient and practical.

(a) This is an unorthodox system constructed on the IoT for drug identification and a remote information-based interconnected system.
(b) Medicines can be actualized with the help of an interchangeable mobile device and considering NFC technology and a legacy overidentification solution such as a barcode.
(c) Once the medicines have been recognized, these data are shipped to the pharmaceutical intelligent information system [9].

One can see the above for different diseases contributing to the global health crisis and NFC labels can provide an efficient mechanism for tamper-proof product design.

For tamper-proof product sealing with NFC labels, when the consumer receives the product and finds that the NFC seal is broken, or if it looks intact but the NFC data cannot be read, then apparently the product has been tampered with.

1.8 How NFC works and its advantages

NFC is a communication convention for electronic gadgets. It is most ordinarily used to help portable installment frameworks such as Apple Pay, Google Pay, and Samsung Pay. It is additionally used to share media between nearby gadgets, make access tokens and keycards, and bootstrap remote associations.

Organizations depend now on the cloud to play out a wide range of significant undertakings, and NFC can give admittance to the physical to digital world in the pharma industry. For instance, through NFC, you can connect IoT sensors [10]. See Fig. 1 for authentication using blockchain.

Practically speaking, all NFC-based innovations share proximity ID technologies. When converged with cloud-based applications, proximity ID technology innovations empower total cooperation between the physical and advanced universes.

The intensity of NFC is consistent, secure way through as basic tap. Many individuals associate a cell phone with objects to start a wide range of collaborations. By extraordinarily associating the physical to the advanced universes, NFC can empower totally new encounters and discover its way into new business applications, for example, temperature and other physical information (for detailed advantages, see Fig. 2).

NFC sensors are about gathering information from the physical world. This means NFC sensors gather data for a small bunch of properties and spotlight use cases that require activity when those characteristics change. By and large, these sensors are explicitly recognized.

Convenient: Easy to integrate payment system in the medical field, verification of drugs, and ability to connect the unconnected [7,11].
Versatile: Works with more than just payment systems such as drug authentication. Seamless communication between interconnected devices.

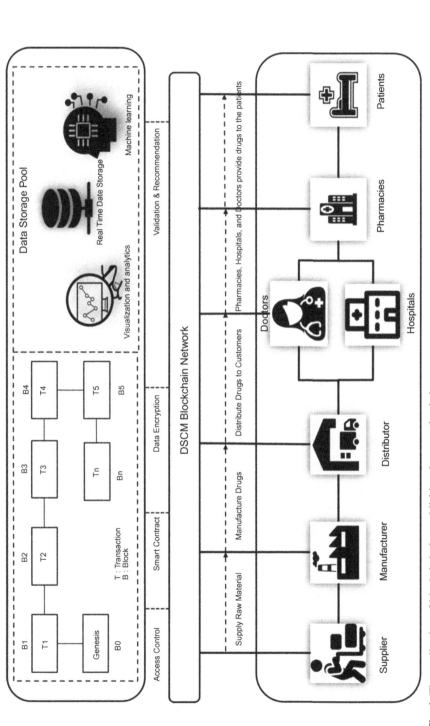

Fig. 1 The application of blockchain in establishing drug supply chain management.
Courtesy: https://www.mdpi.com/2079-9292/9/5/852/html.

Fig. 2 Competitive advantage of proposed Akshat research project in India and South Asia.

NFC payments are generally more secure than credit cards, as many encryption algorithms are implemented on it [12].

1.9 Technical threats to current drug discovery

The following are challenges or threats to drug discovery.

1. **There should be proper system security**: Suppose one country discovered drugs for any disease, but if the cybersecurity of that country is not good enough, then any country can hack the systems and copy the drug discovery.
2. **All labs and instruments should be well developed and up to date**: Suppose one country is willing to develop drugs, but they don't have the proper availability of labs and other instruments. It will become a technical challenge.
3. **Testing of drugs is very crucial**: The country must have a proper technique and technical equipment to test drugs with as many people as possible to collect their responses and analyze whether anything is wrong with the drugs. If they don't have good technology, then it will have a harmful impact on people (Fig. 2).

2 Literature survey

In their paper, Aniello, L and his team proposed a method to demonstrate that there has been a growth in international free trade that has led to the expansion of drug distribution. This expansion in trade leads to drug counterfeiting, which means that some unwanted materials are mixed in the drugs. To prevent this, many technological means were used. For example, in countries such as the United States, the radio frequency identification (RFID) method is used whereas in European countries, the two-dimensional (2D) barcode method is being used. Now, even pharmaceutical companies are employing such technologies to monitor their supply chains. India produces 22–25% of pharmaceutics, hence such technological methods will be of great benefit to Indian industries [13].

The team has applied a methodology that uses track and trace technology that remains with the product throughout the supply chain. The types are:

1. **Pedigree**: It tracks and traces the drugs in a location. It is generally a document or an electronic file that has records of the prescribed drugs until received by the physician. It ensures authentication and that the drugs cannot be replaced and counterfeited.
2. **Mass Serialization**: It is the process of verifying the identity of an individual physical item. It is an important part of the pedigree system. It helps in tracing the product after adding a track.
3. **Global Trade Number**: GSI has been denoted and Prefix in its manufacturing. It has an item reference number and a check digit.
4. **Data Carriers**: For product identification, a graphical system is used to convey the product identifier through computers. It is represented by a mark or tag on the label.

Generally, a multileveled approach is used to ensure the safety and purity of a pharmaceutical product, but the disadvantage is that this approach is very costly.

The author team applied the dataset and algorithm efficiently. In developing countries such as India, a mobile-based authentication company has designed a system called Epothecary. It is cost-effective and requires minimum network infrastructure. Some brand companies have developed devices such as Rocephin, which is a handheld device like an infrared spectrometer developed by Hoffmann-La Roche.

Researchers have proposed that in the future, counterfeiting is expected to decrease. This can only happen when strict rules and regulations are brought into order. Apart from that, the technologies used should be highly authenticated and secure. Drug packaging should be done in a way that the purity of its components is not compromised [13].

They also revealed the limitation that the counterfeited process should be rotated or changed every 12–16 months, because a duplicate of the same process can be made very easily. The physician or the patient is not expected to be aware of it. Also, repackaging a drug will make it useless [14].

In their concluding remarks, the authors stated that drug counterfeiting is a huge problem in the world. It has been taken very seriously and the supply chain is monitored by pharmaceutical companies through track and trace systems. Also, in India, it has become necessary that each product should have a barcode on the label [15].

In their interesting manuscript, Arner, D.W. and his team determined that drug counterfeiting has become an issue worldwide. Initially, it was a problem associated only with developing nations, but with technology advancing and greed increasing daily, the concern has widened to all nations. It has become an immediate patient safety issue. Because these drugs aren't made by legitimate manufacturers, they tend to affect our bodies differently, contributing to early mortality and drug resistance. These drugs may be smuggled in or made in poorly equipped industries [16]. The team applied the following methodology in their execution:

1. **Improving legislation**: Legislation should ensure timely scrutiny and regulate the importation, distribution, and sale of drugs. Counterfeit drugs should be banned. All manufacturers should be licensed.
2. **Assign drug inspectors to perform timely examinations of documents**: There should be a random sampling of drugs being produced. Preliminary tests should be done. When required, there should be a proper method for seizing counterfeit drugs.
3. **Verification methods using blockchain**: Blockchain technology is being used to maintain data integrity. It can be used to track down the manufacturer and give an idea of the product quality. Authentication of drugs includes using holograms, color-changing inks, chemical marks, etc.
4. **Spreading awareness**: People should be aware of the risks of these drugs. Mostly, these drugs are sold at a cheaper price and are widely bought without paying heed to the quality or the manufacturer. Spreading awareness will allow people to make proper judgments.
5. **Electronic tracking**: This can be done using RFID technology. Countries are adopting medicine tracking. RFID adoption will include purchasing tags and integrating the information with the internal system.
6. **Mass serialization**: This uniquely identifies the object to which it is attached. It uses unique alphanumeric identifiers adhered to the particular drug [17].

In their manuscript, the authors applied the dataset and algorithm efficiently and a few new technologies have been resolved to stop drug counterfeiting. These include using Epedigree. The system is used to give the history of the product along complex chains. The two-way SMS system is another system which will appear ahead. It allows pharma companies and customers to interact with each other through a free two-way SMS system. This system is useful in places with no or little Internet access [16].

The team stated that the technology is evolving and new ways to stop drug counterfeiting are emerging. This gives a clear picture that drug counterfeiting will be stopped in the future. Also, with World Health Organization (WHO) guidelines being implemented, the production of these medicines has been lowered. The main aim will be poor or developing countries where cheaper medicines are still bought.

Researchers have propounded the limitations that problems arise when people within the system cause the mess-up due to greed and send the wrong information. Many people are still not aware of these fake drugs. There is confusion in the definition of standard and counterfeit medicines. Many consumers are shifting from actual medicines because they are unable to distinguish the difference [18].

They concluded their manuscript with the fact that according to the WHO, counterfeit drugs make up 10% of the global medicine market. The production of counterfeit drugs in India has not only affected patient health, but also the country's reputation globally. With these problems increasing everyday, it is important for the pharmaceutical industry to come up with the most effective and cost-efficient solutions [16].

In their paper, "Lightweight Authentication Protocol for NFC Based Anti-Counterfeiting System in IoT Infrastructure," the authors put a new approach for the validation of drug doses online using mobile devices. In their protocol, NFC is enabled in the mobile device, which forms an interface with the NFC server and checks for mutual authentication between the server and NFC tag. This process is more secure. The drug dosage form is then authenticated and the review is sent to the user's smart phone. The whole paper is divided into eight sections that deal with the introduction, the flow of control of the underlying system, the common notations used in the paper and the preliminaries, the schemes in related works, explanation of the whole devised process, security, the performance of the system, and it's comparison followed by the conclusion that their system is able to resist known attacks and provide better security. The protocol is evaluated using PyCharm and shows better computational cost [19].

In their paper, "Toward Blockchain-Enabled Supply Chain Anti-Counterfeiting and Traceability" Neo C.K. Yiu and team introduced Blockchain 2.0, which is a new approach to decentralize the existing product anticounterfeiting system. The manuscript talks about the existing technologies and methods used and their issues to stop counterfeiting of medicines. The current architecture is a centralized architecture that has a dedicated server for everything. However, their proposed solution has a decentralized architecture of a blockchain.

It concluded with the authors stating that there are two types of attacks that can take place on the existing anticounterfeiting system. These are system threats and physical NFC tag threats. The decentralized system also presents a few threats such as limited scalability, security vulnerabilities, and privacy concerns such as distributed denial-of-service (DDoS) attack [20].

3 Methodologies and structural design

3.1 Methodology

The methodology used in this research project called AKSHAT is that an NFC chip will be installed in the caps of medicines. When a consumer scans a label on a product with their phone or any NFC-enabled device, they authenticate the product and are informed as to whether it is genuine.

When a consumer receives the product and finds that the NFC seal is broken, or if it looks intact but NFC data cannot be read, then apparently the product has been tampered with.

3.2 Structural design

1. Checking for tampering and counterfeiting

The above diagram (see Fig. 3) explains how NFC will play a vital role in reducing tampering and counterfeiting of medicines. Basically, the NFC role has been defined. One NFC chip will be installed in the medicine bottle that will be scanned by an NFC-enabled device. In this, a smart phone or any other NFC-enabled device is the receiver and the NFC chip is the transmitter. The transmitter produces a short-range radio

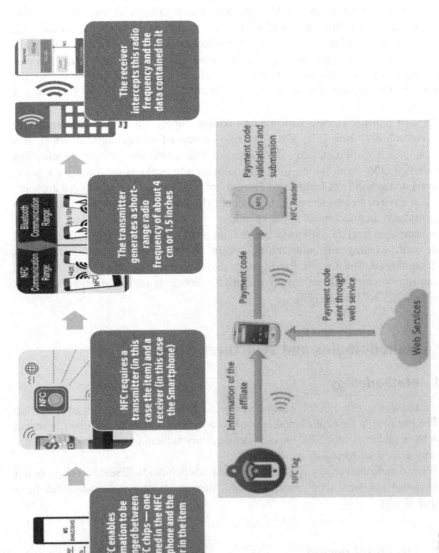

Fig. 3 Functioning of NFC.

frequency of 4 cm and the receiver intercepts this radio frequency to store or contain the data [21].

2. Complete track of product lifecycle using blockchain

Akshat maps digital assets with the physical product through NFC tags that are made with their revolutionary anticounterfeiting technology. Information on the authenticity of the product will be provided as soon as the doctors/patients scan the label (see Fig. 4). Akshat's blockchain will store all the information with a high-security process. This data will be secured and everlasting because the data are read-only, as written on the blockchain. This process tracks the product's lifecycle from the origin to the destination where it is consumed [14,22].

3.3 Tools and techniques applied

The tools and techniques used in these proposed products are as follows:

(a) **NFC chips**: These chips are to be inserted in the caps of medicine bottles.
(b) **NFC-enabled device**: This would act as a receiver and will receive all the information about the medicine so that the person will know whether the medicine has been tampered with. Examples include smart phones.
(c) Medicine bottles.
(d) **Medicine Caps**: The NFC chips will be installed in medicine caps [23,24].

3.4 Market analysis of proposed product

As the market size of medicines is very large across the world, then the chances of drug tampering and counterfeiting are also very high because people want to make more profit by selling inferior products. If this type of behavior is shown in the medical field, then all four main groups—patients, doctors, the government, and healthcare–will have problems. It is estimated that the Indian pharmaceutical sector will increase to $100 billion by 2025 while the medical device market is expected to expand to $25 billion. Pharmaceutical exports from India stood at $20.70 billion in fiscal year 2020 [25].

In the future, it is expected that NFC will grow to include more opportunities in healthcare sectors [26].

Various other companies are working toward the same cause:

a. Schreiner Protech
b. Sta Twig
c. CCL
d. TechRock

All these companies are working for the same thing and using technologies like blockchain [27].

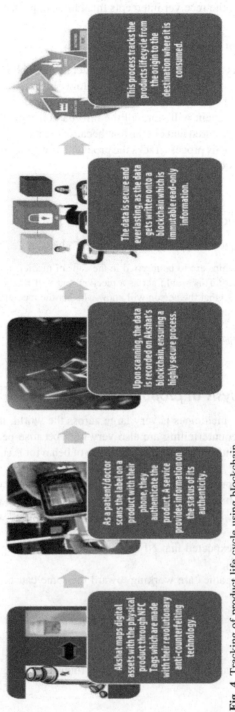

Fig. 4 Tracking of product life cycle using blockchain.

4 Application development

Application development in blockchain technology totally depends upon the need of the traditional database technologies or blockchain.
Blockchain technology can add more value to the platform:

1. More transparency–history of transactions becomes more transparent.
2. Enhanced traceability–when the supply goes from one place to another, it can be tracked easily.
3. Increased speed–execution of fast and secure transactions can be automated.
4. Reduced costs–there is no need to pay third parties or intermediaries.

Security challenges in blockchain application development include:

- Initial cost.
- Energy consumption.
- Security.
- Privacy.

5. Visual and technical designs–creation of user interface for software components.
6. Development–development should be done in stages such as prealpha, alpha, and beta.

Technologies used in blockchain application development are Geth, Remix IDE, Mist, Ganache, Solium, Ether Scripter, Truffle, and Embark.
See Fig. 5 to understand in detail the flowchart of product searching and interconnectedness among each component.

4.1 Timeline analysis

Due to the growth of advanced technology, a rapid change has been observed in the analysis of NFC-enabled Packaging to Detect Tampering and Prevent Counterfeiting: Enabling Complete Supply Chain Using BlockChain. Over time, many analyses have been done including the analysis of visual identifiers, the analysis of images and audio, the analysis of induced emission, sensor analysis, etc. See Fig. 6 for a timeline analysis.

The applications of visual identifiers are easily applied to various goods in different domains [28–30].

In the analysis of image recognition against counterfeiting, the advantage we have is the simplicity and cost-effectiveness. We only require cameras and a connection with proper bandwidth whereas in the analysis of induced emission, the biggest problem is cost; it is expensive but it has a higher level of accuracy for testing counterfeits. We do not need to damage the product to identify and distinguish proper goods from counterfeit ones [31].

The validation of the products is also done based on digital samples. Many analyses have been done on this as data are taken from the device itself. For example, a law enforcer can take a picture from a suspect phone using a test SIM and compare it

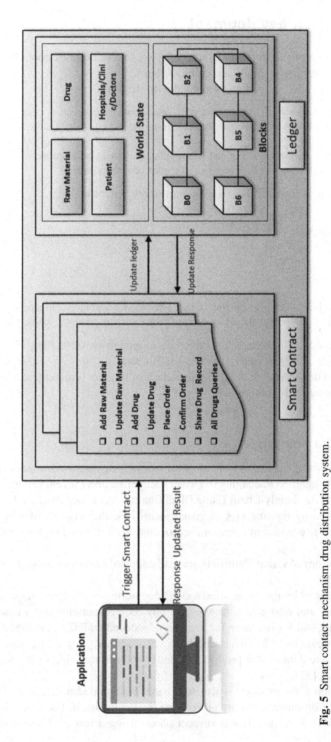

Fig. 5 Smart contact mechanism drug distribution system.

Courtesy: https://www.mdpi.com/electronics/electronics-09-00852/article_deploy/html/images/electronics-09-00852-g003.png.

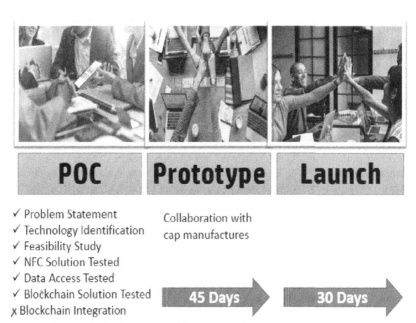

Fig. 6 Timeline analysis of proposed Akshat research project.

to a reference library of phones of the same model to check that the suspect phone is counterfeit [32,33].

Identification of counterfeit devices with image acquisition capability can be achieved by distinguishing image artifacts, whereas the detection of counterfeit devices with audio addition capability can be achieved by analyzing the response of the audio circuit to a standard stimulus [34,35].

There are statistical analyses of sensors that cannot fulfill the authentication process. In other words, the data collected by the sensors are used for device identification, which has enough granularities to perform identification [36–38].

4.2 S/W and H/W requirement

4.2.1 Software requirements

1. **Origin**
   - It is an open platform for accessing NFC technology, and it provides opportunity for all product manufacturers and brand owners.
   - This software as a service (SaaS) platform anticipates a perfect solution to protect a product from counterfeiting.

- Due to cost-effectiveness of anticounterfeiting, the solution allows use of exclusive standard NTAG 213-based tags.
- The NFC tag embedded in our system cannot be cloned as it is protected by our trademarked algorithms that are enhanced by blockchain technology.
- This software is also used to protect any item, from standard retail products to high-value luxury items [39].

2. iL00 S50
- It is a user-friendly platform.
- It is the smartest investment for advanced industry because of its simplified daily operation, enhanced security, and lifecycle savings [19].

3. IMAporter
- Homeowners can easily govern their homes from their mobile devices because of IMAporter.
- It is the basic solution to send fully secured. credentials
- It comes in the form of a universal NFC and Bluetooth reader.
- While maintaining a high level of security, the identification process is done by itself.
- There is no need for a mobile application to be opened and also no screen lock needs to be unlocked.
- We only require them to light up the display of their phone and tap the NFC reader.
- IMAporter comes in many forms [40].

4. Ward London
- The NFC has a tiny NFC disk in the back of the wallet.
- By using an app such as NFC tools, we can then add information to the NFC tag.

5. PoolMate Sport
- It is a keen swim tracking watch that tracks all our swims.
- It has an accelerometer and patented algorithm that helps when we swim and gives many metrics such as speed, distance, calories, and laps.
- There are mainly two watches that currently use NFC technology to send swim data rapidly and productively to iPhone and Android apps: PoolMatePlus and PoolMateSport.
- NFC technology is consolidated so we can sync the watch to all our smartphones to transfer data, which further enables the use of a simple coin cell battery and improves battery life using NFC [41].

6. NTAG 424 DNA tags

The NTAG 424 DNA and 424 DNA TagTransfer support real-time validation [42].

7. APPSWED Genuine check NFC

It enables pharmaceutical companies to ensure that their items or products are genuine and trustable.

With the help of smartphones, users can tap the Genuine Check NFC on the package and identify the product, its details, and location tracking. The benefits of Genuine Check NFC are as follows:

(a) It is inexpensive.
(b) It does not need an Internet connection.

(c) there are options for SMS line information and GPS tracking.
(d) It prevents counterfeiting medicines and other products [43].

8. TimeTac

It is a time tracking solution for organizations and their employees, projects, and leave management [44].

4.2.2   Hardware requirements

1. Toppan and Amcor
- It recommends Intact.
- It acts as a high-security solution to minimize damage due to counterfeiting in the market.
- The Intact is a capsule for wine and spirits with an integrated NFC tag that detects opening or tampering [43,45–48].
- The NFC acts as a high-security solution to prevent fraudulent refilling.
- Amcor has both metallic and nonmetallic films.
- Amcor developed a capsule construction that can incorporate an NFC tag with flawless communication [49–51].

2. Smart E-labels
- Digital authentication makes Smart E-labels easy.
- It enhances patient safety.
- These labels have integrated NFC chips and can be easily applied to primary containers during production because of their thin and bendable structures.
- They include online and offline verification, password protection, and signatures to encryption techniques [52,53].

3. Evermee necklace
- It symbolizes a revolutionized locket and invisibly carries one single photo memory of your choice. The photo is stored on an NFC tag inside a gemstone and can be collected by hovering your smart phone over the pendant.
- Each pendant allows us to wear different photo memories on different days.
- It is an essential single photo memory [54,55].

4. NFC Wristband
- It provides an easy way for a cashless payment option that reduces the risk of fraud as organizers spend less time behind the scenes.
- The wristband is easily identified by any NFC-enabled smartphone.
- It helps users experience short wait times.
- It also enables faster payment transactions.
- This wristband is a huge option for an RFID access control and cashless payment system.
- This is fully secured and tested.
- The DO RFID tag manufacturer produces a large range of RFID wristbands and NFC wristbands that can be used in accessing control with security, proximity range, involuntary access control, and events and festivals [56].

5. Leveraging the pharma IoT
- Nowadays, the number of pharmacy companies with the advanced features, i.e., power of putting smart NFC tags on their product, are in the market, which serves with many advantages.
- NFC tags provide a direct link to the cloud for joining pharmaceuticals through IoT to connect with several products.

Examples include Vivacy France, Stylage, Biolog-id, and Schreimer-Mediphorm [57].

4.3 Coding snap shots with captions and output analysis

See Figs. 7–13 for detailed script-written Hyperledger (main components) and Android app snippets to understand the flow and execution (Table 1).

4.4 Analysis of the results

In the above histogram, the x-axis represents the latency time in milliseconds, the time required to process the submitted query by the client on the web interface, and the Y-axis represents the number of users accessing the server to get the information about the field. The server has a minimum time to serve the particular user denoted by the

Fig. 7 Execution of smart contract through the script to update drug information.

Table 1 Execution of query transactions with latency time in milliseconds.

Users	55 Users	110 Users	330 Users	660 Users
Min	45	110	107	137
Average	57	150	172	465
Max	135	225	417	1210

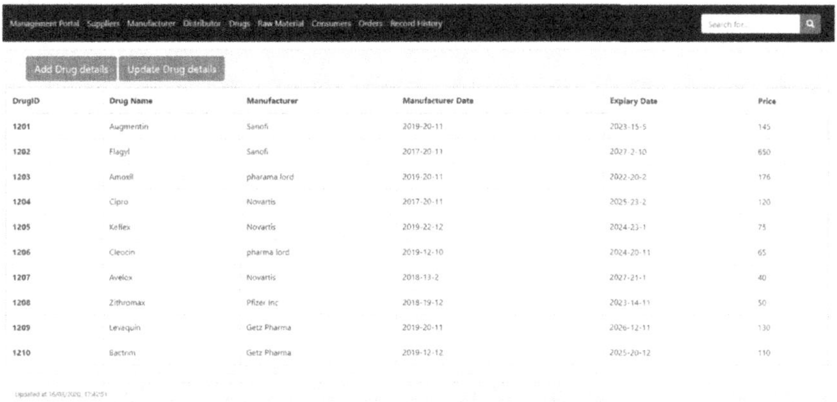

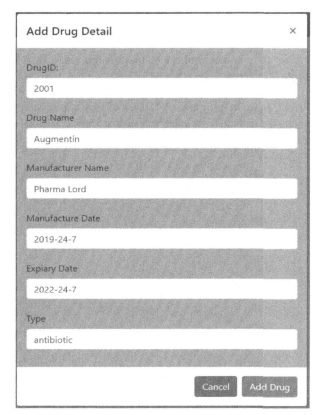

Fig. 8 E-portal design for tracking, editing, and checking drugs.

Fig. 9 An end-user graphical user interface to update the drug info on the web page.

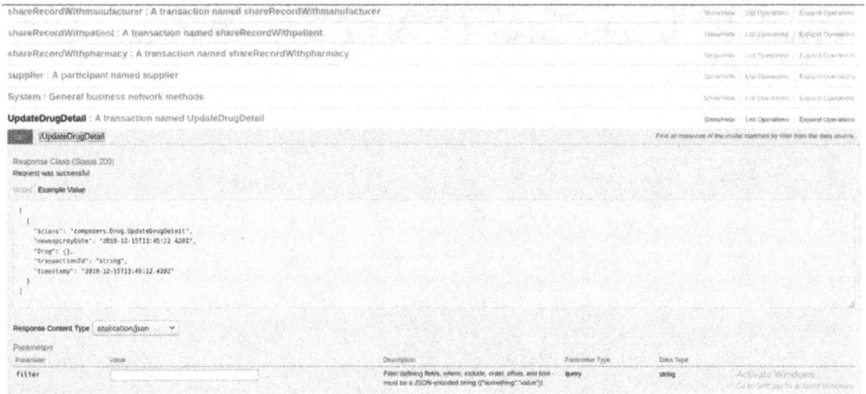

Fig. 10 Rest server user interface and communication using API.

blue bar. The red bar denotes the average time required for the server to fetch the information and display in the client side, and the green bar represents the maximum time for the server to respond to the client or user.

In the above graph, we can see that if the user is 55 then the minimum latency time required by the server to serve the user is 45 while 57 ms is the average latency time required to complete the execution of query transactions and 135 is the maximum latency time for the 55 clients.

One can also observe that when the user is 660, then the minimum latency time required by the server to serve the user is 137 while 465 ms is the average latency time required to complete the execution of query transactions and 1210 ms is the maximum latency time for the 660 clients. The web server on the client-side displays the details of executed transactions (Table 2).

Date Time	Entry Type	Participant	Actions
2019-12-10, 01:36:35	UpdateDrugDetail	admin (NetworkAdmin)	View Transaction
2019-12-10, 01:32:25	AddAsset	admin (NetworkAdmin)	View Transaction
2019-12-10, 01:30:30	ActivateCurrentIdentity	none	View Transaction
2019-12-10, 01:30:24	StartBusinessNetwork	none	View Transaction
2019-12-10, 01:30:24	IssueIdentity	none	View Transaction
2019-12-10, 01:30:24	AddParticipant	admin (NetworkAdmin)	View Transaction
2019-12-10, 01:36:35	AddParticipant	admin (NetworkAdmin)	View Transaction
2019-12-10, 01:36:35	AddParticipant	admin (NetworkAdmin)	View Transaction
2019-12-10, 01:36:35	updateRawmaterial	admin (NetworkAdmin)	View Transaction

Fig. 11 Displaying the transaction history on the portal.

Fig. 12 The web page on the client side to display the executed transactions (view-only mode).

4.4.1 Comparative analysis of results

Counterfeit medicines have become a global issue, leading many to try to find solutions to this problem. However, the greed of people is pushing us to come up with new approaches all the time. All the approaches are equally effective. Our approach presents a more convenient method to detect counterfeit medicines. Here, the user just has to use a smart phone to get medicines validated. We are taking full advantage of the NFC and blockchain technology to develop a more secure and convenient system. This way we save both time and money for the user (see Table 1).

5 Recommendations

Some of the problems faced in NFC packaging to detect tampering and prevent counterfeiting include:

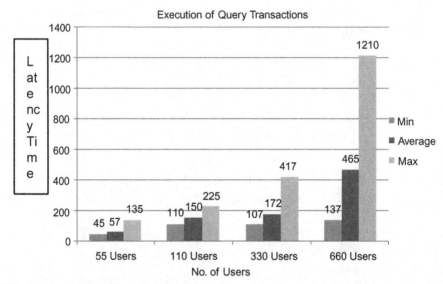

Fig. 13 The bar chart shows the latency of different users in the submitted query transaction.

(i) Risk of adverse effects.
(ii) Loss of confidence and trust.
(iii) Potential loss of life.
(iv) Create unrest in the masses.
(v) Medical tourism gets impacted [58].

The team recommends solutions to the above problems such as:

(a) Enable NFC packaging to detect tampering and prevent counterfeiting along with the ability to track a complete lifecycle using blockchain, as it is a simple, cost-effective, reliable, and secured method.
(b) Track and trace authenticity using contactless NFC. When consumers scan the label on a product with their phone or any NFC-enabled device, they authenticate the product and are informed of its counterfeit status.
(c) Tamper-proof product sealing with NFC labels.
  When a consumer receives the product and finds that the NFC seal is broken, or if it looks intact but NFC data cannot be read, then apparently the product has been tampered with [59].

As the demand for medicines is rising, it must be assured that customers are getting quality products and not fake products.

NFC technology will play a very vital role in stopping tampering with medicines, which will affect society in one way or another.

6   Novelties in the work

NFC has been trending lately and is going to be the future of the pharmaceutical industry. Selling counterfeit drugs is not something new. According to the WHO, these drugs account for around 15% of all pharmacy products sold worldwide. NFC uses

Table 2 Tabular comparisons among available applications and our approach.

Method name	Blockchain design	Limitation	Novelty	Efficiency	Technology-used
Method 1	Multilevel blockchain system	Multilevel approach, though safe is not cost-effective	Devices such as Rocephin, which is a handheld device like an infrared spectrometer	In India, they made a mobile-based application called epothecary that is cost-effective	Track and trace technology, Pedigree, mass serialization, data carriers
Method 2	Blockchain is used for verification purposes	People may mess up the system due to greed	Use of Epedigree and two-way SMS system	Effective for places with no or little internet access	Using blockchain for verification and RFID for tracking
Method 3	Authentication protocol where the NFC is updated after every verification	IoT systems have security issues sometimes and can be slightly expensive	Uses IoT, cloud, and hashing to maintain security	Effective in most all cases	Cloud and IoT system for anticounterfeiting
Method 4	Decentralized blockchain design	Takes more computational time	Choosing a decentralized architecture over a centralized one	Improves data integrity and strengthens security More effective than a centralized system	Peer-to-peer blockchain network and decentralized NFC-enabled anticounterfeiting system
NFC with blockchain (proposed approach)	Blockchain for validation	Blockchain's initial cost is high	New approach using NFC, blockchain, and IOT to prevent integrity attacks	Effective and easy system for common people	Blockchain and CPS

blockchain to provide the means to check the information of the drug manufacturer while authenticating the product and its transportation route. NFC tags made using IoT can be used for everyday business purposes as well. This technology gives us the following benefits, which were not available until now:

a. Building customer engagement.
b. Ensuring safety and integrity.
c. Informing pharmacies as well as patients about illegal companies and expiration dates.

7 Future research directions and limitations

The future direction is very simple. Anticounterfeit solutions are established on NFC technology and available to high brands that have enough income to invest in the research and development as well as implementation of the technology. Because of this, there has not been widespread use of this technology among general people. This is mainly due to the absence of standardization and methods that consumers can easily adapt to.

Our project provides the option for all product manufacturers and brand owners to integrate NFC technology at a fraction of the money.

This blockchain project offers a readily available end-to-end solution to protect a product against counterfeiting.

Our anticounterfeiting solution applies standard NTAG 213-based tags, which are cost-effective as well as have mutual understanding with all NFC-enabled smart phones.

NFCs could work in short ranges such as 10–20 cm. Also, it provides very low data transfer rates of almost 106 or 212 or 424 Kbps, which makes it costly for businesses to embrace NFC-enabled devices. However, it is safer when compared to credit/debit card-based systems [60,61].

8 Case studies

Here, two case studies are presented to give a better idea to readers. It informs about the roles for emerging communication technologies which play in improving healthcare by preventing diseases. These diseases are caused by improper waste disposal. Using deep learning also, the latest characteristics and challenges of this integration has been demonstrated.

8.1 Medical waste disposal using NFC

Medical waste collection is a very important aspect of healthcare because this waste material if not disposed of properly can lead to foul smells, infections, and environmental hazards. In the article, author Claire Swedberg talks about a Dutch company Less2Care, which is using the Vacusan system to provide vacuum sealing and safe disposal of medical waste. This Vacusan uses NFC technology. Jop van Hareen, the founder of Less2Care, sells vacuum packaging machines that help in the easy and safe disposal of waste. Also, the bags they are using are made of recycled material that is 110 µm thick. NFC tags are attached in these bags. When workers collect the waste in the bag, the bag is positioned in the Vacusan machine and then the NFC tags are authenticated, which captures the unique ID number. The vacuuming process then begins. In case of any error while scanning the NFC tag, Vacusan will not work [62].

8.2   AI waste sorting system

Artificial intelligence (AI) is nowadays used in many applications, including waste sorting. In the article, the authors Kah Chun Tan and Chiqin Tan wrote that the AI waste sorting system predicts the waste category by capturing images and the weight of the waste. When the waste is put in the bin, the cameras take photos to help the system determine the volume and weight of the waste in a deep learning AI technique. This helps in sorting the trash to the correct category. If the waste is biodegradable, it will form compost. Without contamination, the waste can be recycled. Similar processes are followed for different types of waste materials [63].

9   Concluding remarks

In this manuscript, the authors proposed NFC-enabled packaging to detect tampering and prevent counterfeiting using blockchain and CPS. A new anticounterfeiting supply chain using NFC and blockchain was used that was programmed as a new decentralized supply chain that uses blockchain and NFC technologies.

With the rapidly growing challenges in product counterfeiting, the benefit of this research is to find out whether anticounterfeiting and traceability solutions of blockchain are useful. The solutions defined are based on blockchain and IoT to provide high availability and strong tolerance against integrity attacks.

Physical goods are associated with a blockchain, which helps transactions of the items to be stored safely with the help of IoT. Manufacturers use this system to store applicable information on product sales in blockchain that is provided to everyone. As the demand for medicines is rising, it must be assured that customers are getting quality products. NFC technology will play a very vital role in stopping tampering with medicines, which will affect society in one way or another. So, mainly the problem of product counterfeiting attacks using blockchain was the focus.

Tag reapplication detection is also used, which helps detect reapplication attacks using low-cost NFC tags and public-key cryptography that are very essential. The key idea in our solution is to exploit the read-only NFC tag counter to track the number of times the tag has been read in the supply chain. Blockchain detects tag modification, cloning, and reapplication attacks without the need for a centralized authentication authority.

Acknowledgments

The authors wish to pay gratitude to the ABES Engineering College, Ghaziabad, senior offi-cials, Sh. Sachin Goel, Dr. Gaurav Kansal, Dr. Pradeep Kr. Singh, and officers of Data Ritz Technologies, CARE, CBSE Verticals, and Department of CSE for arranging the necessary facilities for this innovative research work. We would also like to extend our thanks to COE of blockchain and IoT for their support and guidance in accomplishing our research paper. We thank the authorities and management department of IIT (Delhi and Roorkee) for arranging all the facilities, their direct and indirect support are the reasons for bringing this research work to this stage, which is much appreciated.
We are very much thankful to Almighty God for showering His blessings upon each one of us throughout this project. The authors felt extremely energetic and happy and had life-long cher-ished experiences. This research work would not have been possible without their tireless ded-ication. We acknowledge all of them with respect.

References

[1] N.D. Swartz, Bursting the bitcoin bubble: the case to regulate digital currency as a security or commodity, Tul. J. Technol. Intell. Prop. 17 (2014) 319–335.

[2] A. Teja, Indonesian fintech business: new innovations or foster and collaborate in business ecosystems? Asian J. Technol. Manag. 10 (1) (2017) 10–18, https://doi.org/10.12695/ajtm.2017.10.1.2.

[3] M. Swan, Anticipating the economic benefits of blockchain, Technol. Innov. Manag. Rev. 7 (10) (2017) 6–13, https://doi.org/10.22215/timreview/1109.

[4] S. Abboushi, Global virtual currency. Brief overview, J. Appl. Bus. Econ. 19 (6) (2017) 10–18.

[5] L.J. Trautman, A.C. Harrell, Bitcoin versus regulated payment systems: what gives? Cardozo Law Rev. 38 (3) (2017) 1041–1097.

[6] M. Abramowicz, Cryptocurrency-based law, Ariz. Law Rev. 58 (2) (2016) 359–420.

[7] S. Vassiliadis, P. Papadopoulos, M. Rangoussi, T. Konieczny, J. Gralewski, Bitcoin value analysis based on cross-correlations, J. Internet Bank. Commer. 22 (S7) (2017) 1–12.

[8] E. Al Kawasmi, E. Arnautovic, D. Svetinovic, Bitcoin-based decentralized carbon emis-sions trading infrastructure model, Syst. Eng. 18 (2) (2015) 115–130, https://doi.org/10.1002/sys.21291.

[9] V. Alcazar, Data you can trust: blockchain technology, Air Space Power J. 31 (2) (2017) 91–101.

[10] H.J. Allen, $=€=bitcoin? MD. L. Rev. 76 (4) (2017) 877–939.

[11] S. Wang, J.-P. Vergne, Buzz factor or innovation potential: what explains cryptocurrencies' returns? PLoS One 12 (1) (2017) 1–17, https://doi.org/10.1371/jour-nal.pone.0169556.

[12] S.H. Ammous, Blockchain Technology: What Is It Good For?, SSRN, 2016. August 8.

[13] L. Aniello, R. Baldoni, E. Gaetani, F. Lombardi, A. Margheri, V. Sassone, A prototype evaluation of a tamper-resistant high performance blockchain-based transaction log for a distributed database, in: Paper Presented at 13th European Dependable Computing Con-ference (EDCC), Geneva, Switzerland, September 4–8, 2017.

[14] S.B. Wesley, A.M. Ray, Practice or lip service: exploring collaboration perspectives in purchasing, IMP J. 11 (3) (2017) 452–467, https://doi.org/10.1108/IMP-05-2016-0009.

[15] R. Gupta, S. Tanwar, F. Al-Turjman, P. Italiya, A. Nauman, S.W. Kim, Smart contract privacy protection using AI in cyber-physical systems: tools, techniques and challenges, IEEE Access 8 (2020) 24746–24772, https://doi.org/10.1109/ACCESS.2020.2970576.

[16] D.W. Arner, J. Barberis, R.P. Buckley, FinTech, RegTech, and the reconceptualization of financial regulation, Northwest. J. Int. Law Bus. 37 (3) (2017) 371–413.

[17] R. Gupta, A. Shukla, P. Mehta, P. Bhattacharya, S. Tanwar, S. Tyagi, N. Kumar, VAHAK: a blockchain-based outdoor delivery scheme using UAV for healthcare 4.0 services, in: IEEE International Conference on Computer Communications (IEEE INFOCOM 2020), Beijing, China, 27-30th April, 2020, pp. 1–8.

[18] G. Wolfond, A blockchain ecosystem for digital identity: improving service delivery in Canada's public and private sectors, Technol. Innov. Manag. Rev. 7 (10) (2017) 35–40, https://doi.org/10.22215/timreview/1112.

[19] Y.B. Kim, J. Lee, N. Park, J. Choo, J.-H. Kim, C.H. Kim, When bitcoin encounters information in an online forum: using text mining to analyse user opinions and predict value fluctuation, PLoS One 12 (5) (2017) 1–14, https://doi.org/10.1371/journal.pone.0177630.

[20] M. Marshall, IBM and Shipping Giant Maersk Launch Blockchain Company for Global Logisics, VentureBeat, 2018. January 16 (Accessed 20 January 2018) *https://venturebeat-com.cdn.ampproject.org/c/s/venturebeat.com/2018/01/16/ibm-and-shipping-giant-maersk-launch-blockchain-company-for-global-logisics/amp/*.

[21] R. Gupta, A. Shukla, S. Tanwar, AaYusH. A smart contract-based telesurgery system for healthcare 4.0, in: IEEE Conference on Communications (IEEE ICC-2020), Dublin, Ireland, 07-11th June, 2020, pp. 1–6.

[22] U. Bodkhe, D. Mehta, S. Tanwar, P. Bhattacharya, P.K. Singh, W. Hong, A survey on decentralized consensus mechanisms for cyber physical systems, IEEE Access 8 (2020) 54371–54401, https://doi.org/10.1109/ACCESS.2020.2981415.

[23] V. Babkin Alexander, D.D. Burkaltseva, W.W. Pshenichnikov, A.S. Tyulin, Cryptocurrency and blockchain-technology in digital economy: development genesis, St. Petersburg State Polytech. Univ. J. Econ. 621 (2017) 319–334, https://doi.org/10.18721/JE.10501.

[24] P. Bailis, A. Narayanan, A. Miller, S. Han, Research for practice: cryptocurrencies, blockchains, and smart contracts; hardware for deep learning, Commun. ACM 60 (5) (2017) 48–51, https://doi.org/10.1145/3024928.

[25] J. Basden, M. Cottrell, How utilities are using blockchain to modernize the grid, Harv. Bus. Rev. (2017). *https://hbr.org/2017/03/how-utilities-are-using-blockchain-to-modernize-the-grid*.

[26] E. Bouri, G. Azzi, A.H. Dyhrberg, On the return-volatility relationship in the bitcoin market around the price crash of 2013, Economics 11 (2) (2017) 1–17, https://doi.org/10.5018/economics-ejournal.ja.2017-2.

[27] R.-Y. Chen, A traceability chain algorithm for artificial neural networks using T–S fuzzy cognitive maps in blockchain, Futur. Gener. Comput. Syst. 80 (2018) 198–210, https://doi.org/10.1016/j.future.2017.09.077.

[28] I.H.Y. Chiu, A new era in fintech payment innovations? A perspective from the institutions and regulation of payment systems, Law Innov. Technol. 9 (2) (2017) 190–234, https://doi.org/10.1080/17579961.2017.1377912.

[29] L. Cocco, A. Pinna, M. Marchesi, Banking on blockchain: costs savings thanks to blockchain technology, Future Internet 9 (3) (2017) 25, https://doi.org/10.3390/fi9030025.

[30] J. Cunliffe, J. Martin, D. Décary-Hétu, J. Aldridge, An island apart? Risks and prices in the Australian cryptomarket drug trade, Int. J. Drug Policy 50 (2017) 64–73, https://doi.org/10.1016/j.drugpo.2017.09.005.

[31] J. Hathaliya, S. Tanwar, S. Tyagi, N. Kumar, Securing electronics healthcare records in healthcare 4.0: a biometric-based approach, Comput. Electr. Eng. 76 (2019) 398–410.
[32] K. Dandapani, Electronic finance—recent developments, Manag. Financ. 43 (5) (2017) 614–626, https://doi.org/10.1108/MF-02-2017-0028.
[33] P. Davy, J. Wouter, I.-Z. Elisabeth, Trustworthy data-driven networked production for customer-centric plants, Ind. Manag. Data Syst. 117 (10) (2017) 2305–2324, https://doi.org/10.1108/IMDS-10-2016-0419.
[34] D. Mehta, S. Tanwar, U. Bodkhe, A. Shukla, N. Kumar, Blockchain-based royalty contract transactions scheme for Industry 4.0 supply-chain management, Inf. Process. Manag. 58 (4) (2021) 102586. ISSN 0306-4573 *https://doi.org/10.1016/j.ipm.2021.102586.*
[35] F. Dotsika, A. Watkins, Identifying potentially disruptive trends by means of keyword network analysis, Technol. Forecast. Soc. Chang. 119 (2017) 114–127, https://doi.org/10.1016/j.techfore.2017.03.020.
[36] G.L. Evans, Disruptive technology and the board: the tip of the iceberg 1, Econ. Bus. Rev. 3 (17) (2017) 205–223, https://doi.org/10.18559/ebr.2017.1.11.
[37] S. Isaacson, The bamboozling bite of bitcoin: bitcoin doesn't make white collar crime possible, but it does make it easier! Utah Bar J. 30 (4) (2017) 32–36.
[38] R.J. Kauffman, K. Kim, S.-Y.T. Lee, A.-P. Hoang, J. Ren, Combining machine-based and econometrics methods for policy analytics insights, Electron. Commer. Res. Appl. 25 (2017) 115–140, https://doi.org/10.1016/j.elerap.2017.04.004.
[39] M.A. Khan, K. Salah, IoT security: review, blockchain solutions, and open challenges, Futur. Gener. Comput. Syst. 82 (2017) 395–411, https://doi.org/10.1016/j.future.2017.11.022.
[40] I. Klaus, Don Tapscott and Alex Tapscott: blockchain revolution, New Glob. Stud. 11 (1) (2017) 47–53, https://doi.org/10.1515/ngs-2017-0002.
[41] N. Kshetri, Blockchain's roles in strengthening cybersecurity and protecting privacy, Telecommun. Policy 27 (10) (2017) 1027–1038, https://doi.org/10.1016/j.telpol.2017.09.003.
[42] Y. Kurihara, A. Fukushima, The market efficiency of bitcoin: a weekly anomaly perspective, J. Appl. Financ. Bank. 7 (3) (2017) 57–64.
[43] K.B. Letourneau, S.T. Whelan, Blockchain: staying ahead of tomorrow, J. Equip. Leas. Financ. 35 (2) (2017) 1–6.
[44] K.F.K. Low, E.G.S. Teo, Bitcoins and other cryptocurrencies as property? Law Innov. Technol. 9 (2) (2017) 235–268, https://doi.org/10.1080/17579961.2017.1377915.
[45] S. Mansfield-Devine, Beyond bitcoin: using blockchain technology to provide assurance in the commercial world, Comput. Fraud Secur. 5 (2017) 14–18, https://doi.org/10.1016/S1361-3723(17)30042-8.
[46] E. Mik, Smart contracts: terminology, technical limitations and real world complexity, Law Innov. Technol. 9 (2) (2017) 269–300, https://doi.org/10.1080/17579961.2017.1378468.
[47] A. Mikolajewicz-Wozniak, A. Scheibe, Virtual currency schemes—the future of financial services, Foresight 17 (4) (2015) 365–377, https://doi.org/10.1108/FS-04-2014-0021.
[48] A. Milne, Competition policy and the financial technology revolution in banking, Commun. Strateg. 213 (103) (2016) 145–161.
[49] J.H. Mosakheil, Security threats classification in blockchains, in: Culminating Projects in Information Assurance, 2017, p. 48. *https://repository.stcloudstate.edu/msia_etds/48.*
[50] M. Morisse, C. Ingram, A mixed blessing: resilience in the entrepreneurial socio-technical system of bitcoin, J. Inf. Syst. Technol. Manag. 13 (1) (2016) 3–26, https://doi.org/10.4301/S1807-17752016000100001.

[51] S. Nakamoto, Bitcoin: a peer-to-peer electronic cash system, Bitcoin (2020). *https:// bitcoin.org/bitcoin.pdf.*

[52] W. Nowiński, M. Kozma, How can blockchain technology disrupt the existing business models? Entrep. Bus. Econ. Rev. 5 (3) (2017) 173–188, https://doi.org/10.15678/ EBER.2017.050309.

[53] J.H. Park, J.H. Park, Blockchain security in cloud computing: use cases, challenges, and solutions, Symmetry 9 (8) (2017) 1–13, https://doi.org/10.3390/sym9080164 (20738994).

[54] F. Piazza, Bitcoin in the dark web: a shadow over banking secrecy and a call for global respoonse, South. Calif. Interdiscip. Law J. 26 (3) (2017) 521–546.

[55] C. Prybila, S. Schulte, C. Hochreiner, I. Weber, Runtime verification for business processes utilizing the bitcoin blockchain, Futur. Gener. Comput. Syst. (2017), https://doi. org/10.1016/j.future.2017.08.024. Advance online publication.

[56] H. Rooney, B. Aiken, M. Rooney, Q&A. Is internal audit ready for blockchain? Technol. Innov. Manag. Rev. 7 (10) (2017) 41–44, https://doi.org/10.22215/timreview/1113.

[57] P. Ryan, Smart contract relations in e-commerce: legal implications of exchanges conducted on the blockchain, Technol. Innov. Manag. Rev. 7 (10) (2017) 14–21, https:// doi.org/10.22215/timreview/1110.

[58] Y. Shiyong, B. Jinsong, Z. Yiming, H. Xiaodi, M2M security technology of CPS based on blockchains, Symmetry 9 (9) (2017) 1–16, https://doi.org/10.3390/sym9090193.

[59] F.W. Samuel, J. Robert, K. Kamdjoug, R.E. Bawack, J.G. Keogh, Bitcoin, blockchain and fintech: a systematic review and case studies in the supply chain, Prod. Plan. Control 31 (2–3) (2020) 115–142, https://doi.org/10.1080/09537287.2019.1631460.

[60] J.J. Sikorski, J. Haughton, M. Kraft, Blockchain technology in the chemical industry: machine-to-machine electricity market, Appl. Energy 195 (2017) 234–246, https://doi. org/10.1016/j.apenergy.2017.03.039.

[61] J.M. Sklaroff, Smart contracts and the cost of inflexibility, Univ. Pa. Law Rev. 166 (1) (2017) 263–303.

[62] C. Swedberg, J.V. Harren, Catthoor, NFC Ensures Quality of Bags Used in Medical Waste Disposal System, 2021, Case Study Blog *https://www.rfidjournal.com/nfc-ensures-qual ity-of-bags-used-in-medical-waste-disposal-system.*

[63] K.C. Tan, Z. Tan, Smart Land, AI Waste Sorting System, Univ. of Malaya, 2019, Blog *https://www.iotchallengekeysight.com/2019/entries/smart-land/201-0515-002718- a-i-waste-sorting-system.*

Optimized segmentation of white patches in skin lesion images

Sudhriti Sengupta[a], Neetu Mittal[a], and Megha Modi[b]
[a]Amity Institute of Information Technology, Amity University, Noida, Uttar Pradesh, India,
[b]Yashodha Super Speciality Hospital, Ghaziabad, Uttar Pradesh, India

1 Introduction

Medical images are used by doctors and healthcare personnel around the world to understand the nature of a disease and to treat it accordingly. There are many varieties of medical images for different organs and body parts. Some common examples of medical images are computerized tomography (CT) images, magnetic resonance imaging (MRI) images, X-rays, dermascopic images, etc. Image analysis and processing collaborates with a blockchain-based healthcare system to enable remote patient monitoring for viewing patients by using wearable devices [1–3]. These technologies can be extended to medical image analysis. Skin images are used by doctors to understand the nature and condition of the skin tissue. This leads to more efficient and effective diagnoses and treatments for patients. Doctors use various types of techniques to check skin lesions such as biopsies, dermascopic images, etc. Doctors use skin lesion images to perceive the skin conditions or occurrence of lesions. The analysis of the skin images is a noninvasive procedure and is less painful to patients compared to operations. Image processing and analysis can lead to the creation of an automatized disease diagnosis system, which will lead to a quicker and accurate diagnosis of diseases. Another use of the automatic disease diagnostic system is to help people living in far-flung areas access an efficient disease prediction system easily [4]. With the integration of blockchain technology, healthcare applications have shifted to a decentralized system of storing and analysis of images. Segmentation of patches in skin images is one of the most important steps toward the creation of automatic skin disease detection and analysis systems. Skin is one of the essential organs of the human body and often is subjected to different types of lesions. These lesions are indicative of diseases pertaining to the skin [5]. Patches are a kind of lesion that occurs due to distorting or discoloration of skin pigments. Psoriasis, tinea vesicular, tinea corpuses, eczema, etc., are some examples of white patches. One of the significant challenges in the detection of these patches is the different sizes and shapes of these patches [6]. Segmentation of white patches in a skin image is an important step in developing a computer-aided diagnostics system for skin lesion analysis. These systems will help detect skin diseases by using a noninvasive technique.

Sengupta et al. proposed a split and merge threshold method for the segmentation of skin lesion images [7]. Jayade et al. used images taken by dermascopy to extract the

Blockchain Applications for Healthcare Informatics. https://doi.org/10.1016/B978-0-323-90615-9.00009-8
Copyright © 2022 Elsevier Inc. All rights reserved.

important features using the gray-level cooccurrence matrix technique [8]. Jahanifer et al. used the saliency-based segmentation technique for skin lesions [9]. Global threshold was used for skin lesion identification by Kharazmi et al. Threshold integrated with mimicking expert dermatologist segmentation (MEDS) was used for melanocytic lesion segmentation [10]. Nezambadi-Pour utilized ant colony optimization (ACO) for edge derivation of images [11]. Dalia et al. proposed an ant colony-based segmentation technique for skin lesion images [12]. The adaptive threshold technique combined with ACO was applied to extract the borders of skin lesion images [13]. Sengupta et al. proposed an ACO-based improved lesion border detection technique for skin images [14].

In this paper, we have introduced segmentation optimization of white patches by the well-known genetic algorithm (GA) and ACO techniques for improving the segmentation quality by a threshold method. We have done a comparative analysis of these techniques by using three parameters, that is, entropy, dice similarity index, and structural similarity content. Also, before applying the optimization method, we preprocessed the image to obtain better quality input by using the L*a*b color space-based histogram equalization technique. Medical images such as skin lesion images are often susceptible to different types of noise and distortions due to the contrast in the image, which leads to the poor nature of the image. The aim of preprocessing is to enhance the nature of the image, as better image quality led to better segmentation. In this chapter, a luminosity-based preprocessing technique has been introduced. As per this technique, the image is first acquired and then transformed into L*a*b color space. This color space perceives colors as three values: L for lightness and a* and b* to represent four principle colors—red, yellow, green, and blue. Then, the popular histogram equalization is applied to the luminosity channel of the test image. The motivation for applying equalization on the luminosity channel is to preserve the detailed colors of the lesion image while adjusting the contrast factor to properly view the details in the image [15]. The next part of the proposed methodology is applying segmentation for detecting white patches from skin lesion images. Segmentation partitions the image into multiple parts, enabling focusing on the area of interest. We have applied two segmentation techniques and quantitatively compared the results of these techniques to determine the better technique. The first technique of segmentation is an ACO-based segmentation technique. In this technique, the image is segmented by using the edge detection method. This segmented output is enhanced by using ACO [16]. The second technique is the GA-based clustering technique. In this approach, clusters are created on the basis of red, blue, and green color space, and then GA is applied to reach the optimized cluster to obtain the segmented image [17]. To test the efficiency of these methods and to determine the best approach, we have used three quantitative parameters to measure the image quality: entropy, dice similarity index, and structural similarity content. As per all three parameters, the GA-based segmentation technique proved to be better than the ACO-based segmentation technique. The details of the proposed techniques and their implementation along with test results are shown in the following subsection. An efficient and effective segmentation can be integrated into a blockchain-based electronic health system (EHS) for controlling and sharing medical records or changes in medical images [18,19].

This chapter is categorized into the following sections: Section 2 describes the proposed method. Results and analysis are discussed in Section 3. Section 4 presents the conclusion.

2 Proposed methodology

Computerized diagnostics tools for disease detection help doctors and healthcare providers in the earlier and more efficient diagnosis and treatment of patients. Segmentation plays a very important role in developing an automatic system and a blockchain-enabled healthcare system. The main challenge in the segmentation of skin images is the skin lesion irregularity in terms of color, pattern, size, etc. To get a better-quality segmented image, two approaches have been proposed in this chapter. First, an ACO-based edge detection technique has been proposed. The second technique is a GA-based clustering approach. Prior to the application of the segmentation process, a preprocessing step is used. This proposed preprocessing step involves the application of histogram equalization on the luminosity channel of the image. This method of preprocessing tends to increase the perception in the image by affecting lightness while preserving the details of colors. Preprocessing steps are applied to improve the image quality by removing noise, adjusting contrast, etc. The better quality image affects the performance of the segmentation.

The work flow of the discussed technique is given in Fig. 1.

In the discussed technique, we first applied a preprocessing step to enhance the intricacies of the lesion in the skin image. After that we used two strategies to optimize the image segmentation. One of the strategies is the ACO-optimized enhanced edge detection method. Another technique is the GA-based segmentation technique. The resultant images obtained by both these techniques are analyzed by using Entropy, Dice Similarity Index, and Structural Content to determine the best technique of skin lesion image segmentation.

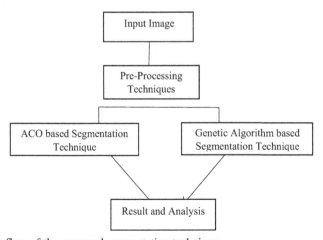

Fig. 1 Work flow of the proposed segmentation technique.

2.1 Preprocessing

In this chapter, we apply preprocessing techniques based upon the luminosity histogram equalization technique, which is shown in Fig. 2.

This technique preserves the color details of the image while increasing the luminance. The details of the preprocessing step are given below:

2.1.1 L*a*b color space

In L*a*b color space, a three-axis color system is used to define the color dimension, where L is for luminosity and a and b are for color dimension. This color space can imitate human vision approximately and is device-independent. This is widely used in different industries such as printing and designing. In the proposed image processing technique, the test images are first converted into L*a*b color space.

2.1.2 Histogram equalization

The method of adjusting the image contrast by changing the intensity distribution using a histogram is called histogram equalization. In this technique, the cumulative probability function plays a prominent role. The steps in histogram equalization are as follows:

1. Calculate the image histogram.
2. Compute the normalized sum of the histogram.
3. Convert the input image to the output image.

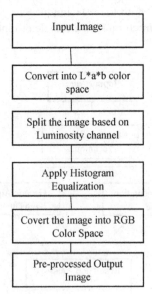

Fig. 2 Flowchart of preprocessing steps.

The above techniques result in better-quality skin lesion images, which improves the chance of better segmentation and feature extraction.

In the proposed preprocessing technique, the skin lesion image is separated based on the luminosity channel. Then we apply the histogram equalization technique on the luminosity component. After that, the image is converted back into RGB space. This image is further taken for the application of GA-based segmentation and ACO-based segmentation to compare and comprehend the best results of segmentation.

2.2 Image segmentation

The method of portioning a digital image into subparts for better understanding and analysis of the region of interest is called image segmentation. Image segmentation depends on image attributes such as points, edge, region, etc. It is an important step in digital processing as it is an essential stage in the creation of the computerized analysis procedure of an image. There are several methods of image segmentation, such as threshold, edge detection, clustering, region based, watershed, artificial neural network based, etc. However, the issue in the segmentation of skin lesion images is the wide variety of skin lesions that occur due to various diseases and the physiology of the human body [20]. In this chapter, ACO-based edge detection and GA-based clustering for histogram equalization segmentation of white patches in the skin is discussed.

2.2.1 Thresholding

The threshold is a very popular segmentation process in which each pixel is exchanged with a black pixel or white pixel determined by some fixed value T. This is given by the following equation

$$I_{x,y} < T \tag{1}$$

$$I_{x,y} \geq T \tag{2}$$

In the above equation, $I_{x,\,y}$ represents the image (I) intensity at the pixel (x,y).

The threshold can be single-level thresholding or multilevel thresholding. In single-level thresholding, we separate the information of an image based on the single threshold value. In multilevel thresholding, more than one threshold value is considered for the separation of image formation.

For ACO-based segmentation, we first obtain the image map by applying edge detection on the skin images to obtain a basic segmented image to enhance the quality of the output image.

2.2.2 Ant colony optimization (ACO)

ACO was inspired by the natural behavior of ants. ACO was introduced by Dorigo and Gambard in 1970. It mimics the basic instincts of ants in collecting and gathering food for their habitat. It has been observed that a chemical substance called a pheromone is deposited on the optimal path to be followed by all ants in the colony. Pheromone deposition in the optimal path and its updating, leading to the use of the optimal path, are the main inspirations behind ACO. ACO is very popular in the research community to solve a variety of problems such as image processing, vehicle routing, packet routing, etc. Edge detection and segmentation are often optimized by applying ACO.

The initialization of ants for each pixel position in the test image is done by using an eight-pixel clique. The pheromone matrix is initialized by using the equation below:

$$
n^{mn} = \frac{\begin{pmatrix} |tI((m-1, n-1) - tI(m+1, n+1)|, \\ |tI((m-1, n+1) - tI(m+1, n-1)|, \\ |tI((m, n-1) - tI(m, n+1)|, \\ |tI((m-1, n) - tI(m+1, n)| \end{pmatrix}}{n_{max}}
\tag{3}
$$

Here, n^{ij} is the heuristic information of pixel (m,n) and n_{max} is the maximum heuristic value. tI is the pixel value. The creation of a probabilistic transition matrix and updating the pheromone matrix are the main stages in the ACO algorithm. Developing the transition matrix implies that ant k has moved from node i to node j, as given by the equation:

$$
P_{i,j}^{(n)} = \frac{\left(\Upsilon_{i,j}^{(n-1)} \right)^{\propto} \left(n_{i,j} \right)^{\beta}}{\sum_{j \in \omega_i} \left(\Upsilon_{i,j}^{(n-1)} \right)^{\propto} n_{i,j} \Big)^{\beta}} \quad \text{if} \quad j \in \omega_i
\tag{4}
$$

In the above equation, the information value of the pheromone arc that joins node i with node j is denoted by $\Upsilon_{i,j}^{(n-1)}$. ω_i represents the neighboring node of ant k. α and β denote the matrix influence and heuristic information, respectively. The traversing rule from node i to node j is given by the constant denoted by $n_{i,j}$.

Updating the pheromone is done in two stages: a local update and a global update. The local update is completed if an ant has completed its solution. When all the ants in the colony have completed their solution, it is called a global update.

The stop criteria of ACO is when the ants have covered all paths or when each ant has covered its respective neighboring pixel. The overall edge trace for segmentation is obtained from the pheromone matrix, which is merged with the edge map to obtain the resultant segmented image.

We applied ACO on the binary image obtained by applying the edge detection method. Some artificial agent "ants" are placed on the end points of the edge map. The pixel intensity variations led to the ant's movement. Undetected neighbors are considered to be the next target for ant movement. In this way, all pixels are covered by the ants to determine the strongest edge in the edge map. These edges are cumulated to form the segmented image.

2.3 Clustering

The second method of segmentation of white patches from skin lesion images is the GA-based clustering method. Clustering is the process of partitioning data points into several parts so that each data point is grouped with similar data points. These groups are called clusters. In this process, clusters are formed based on red, green, and blue color space. Then, the minimum distance of each pixel point in the cluster with the central pixel is found out and selected as the best solution by applying a GA.

2.4 Genetic algorithm

GA is a popular search technique inspired by Darwin's theory of evolution. GA is a soft computing and metaheuristics of machine learning (ML) that takes inspiration from evolution in nature. According to this algorithm, the fittest entity is chosen to generate new offspring. Once the new generation is created, small tweaks are introduced for employing random variations in the offspring. This process will continue until some stop criteria are met. To select the best entity to engage in reproduction, the fitness function is used.

We have applied a clustering-based image segmentation technique with a GA where the RGB components are used to create clusters. A fitness function is used to set the iteration, which results in creating a structure leading to the final segmented image.

This chapter aims to explore two segmentation techniques to compare and comprehend the most efficient and effective method of segmentation of white patches in skin lesions. The first segmentation process is an ACO-based edge detection technique. In this technique, the first edge detection method is used to obtain a binary image from the experimental image. After this, ACO is applied to optimize the segmentation. In the second segmentation technique, a GA-based clustering method based upon red, green, and blue color space is applied. Both methods are used on the same experimental images and the outputs for each image obtained by these techniques are compared by three image measuring parameters, entropy, dice similarity index, and structural similarity index. The details are mentioned in the next sections.

3 Results and discussion

For evaluation of the proposed method, we used four skin lesion images for testing the proposed system. These images were taken from a public access website. For evaluating the results quantitatively, we used three parameters, such as entropy, dice similarity index, and structural similarity index. We used Octave 4.0 on Windows 10 with a 64-bit operating system with Intel to conduct the experiments. Table 1 shows the original image taken for conducting experiments, the preprocessed enhanced image, the segmented image obtained by applying GA, and the edge map obtained by applying ACO.

Table 1 (a) Test image, (b) preprocessed image, (c) segmentation by genetic algorithm, (d) edge detection by ACO.

Serial no.	Original image	Enhanced image	Genetic algorithm-based segmentation	Optimized edge detection with ACO
1				
2				
3				
4				
	(a)	(b)	(c)	(d)

Table 1 depicts the images obtained by performing different segmentation techniques along with the preprocessing image. We compared the output images by using three performance measuring parameters:

3.1 Entropy

Entropy is a widely used parameter to determine the quality of an image [21,22]. It is a statistical attribute for determining the texture characteristics of an image. The volume of data in an image is quantified by entropy. It shows the information quantity in an image. The mathematical definition of entropy is given as:

$$E_n = - \sum_{x=0}^{g} p_i \log_2 p_i \tag{5}$$

Here, E_n signifies the image entropy, g denotes the gray level of the test image, and p_i denotes the probability occurrence. A higher value of information present in an image indicates better image quality. If the value of entropy is high, then the quality of the image is also high. In 2018, Sengupta et al. used entropy to measure the quality of edge detection in skin lesion images [23].

3.2   Dice similarity index

The dice similarity index is a popular technique used to measure segmentation results. This method determines the similarity between the area of interest in the original image and the output segmented image, giving maximum value where two segmented images overlap. The dice similarity index is widely used to measure the effectiveness of the segmentation technique used in medical images, In 2017, Nilesh et al. used this technique to calculate the effectiveness of detection of a brain MRI image [24]. This method was applied to measure the performance of the border detection of renal contours by Gomalavali et al. in 2018 [25].

The mathematical equation of dice similarity is as follows:

$$Dice = \frac{2*PT}{2*PT + PF + NP}$$

In this, dice is the dice similarity index value, PT is the quantity of true positive, and PF is the quantity of false negative. NP denotes a false positive. A higher value of the dice similarity index denotes a better quality of image.

3.3   Structural similarity content

This helps to understand image quality and calculate the similarity between two images. The spatial orientation of the image is considered in this parameter. If the segmentation quality is poor, then the value of the structural content between the original and segmented image will be high. In 2015, Menon et al. used this measure to assess the quality of image segmentation [26]. In 2019, Supriya et al. used structural similarity content to compare the change between the original and recreated ECG signal [27].

The mathematical equation of this parameter is as follows:

$$\text{Structural content}: SC = \frac{\sum_{i=1}^{m}\sum_{j=1}^{n}[f(i,j)]^2}{\sum_{i=1}^{m}\sum_{j=1}^{n}\left[f^{s}(i,j)^2\right]} \tag{6}$$

Here, SC indicates the structural content. The size of the image is denoted by m and n. f and f^{s} denote the original and segmented images, respectively. The better-quality images will have a lower value of structural content.

The values of entropy, dice similarity index, and structural similarity content of the segmented image obtained by GA-based segmentation and ACO-based edge detection are shown in Table 2. From Table 2, we can see that the entropies of an image obtained by GA segmentation are larger than the entropies of ACO edge detection images. Further, the dice similarity indices of the first method are larger than the images obtained

Table 2 A relative comparison of state-of-the-art approaches.

Serial no.	Methodology	Entropy	Dice similarity index	Structural similarity content
1	Genetic algorithm-based segmentation	**6.9197**	**0.95683**	**1.1650**
	Optimized edge detection with ACO	4.9838	0.75581	2.6365
2	Genetic algorithm-based segmentation	**7.4199**	**0.95987**	**1.1772**
	Optimized edge detection with ACO	6.2376	0.85755	1.8113
3	Genetic algorithm-based segmentation	**7.1569**	**0.95520**	**1.1876**
	Optimized edge detection with ACO	5.2651	0.78331	2.4647
4	Genetic algorithm-based segmentation	**7.4508**	**0.98083**	**1.0776**
	Optimized edge detection with ACO	6.7329	0.89775	1.5806

by the second method. Also, the structural similarity content of the output images obtained by the GA technique shows better results than the ACO edge detection technique.

From the table, we can see that the images obtained by the GA technique are better than the images obtained by the ACO edge detection method. The result is the same for all four test images used to perform the result analysis. The quality of the output segmented image can be further seen in Fig. 3, which demonstrate the value of entropy.

In Fig. 3, the entropies of the segmented output images are plotted to perceive the quality of segmentation. For this, we have considered four test images: Image 1, Image 2, Image 3, and Image 4. From the above graph, we can see that the entropy of the images obtained by applying GA segmentation is higher than the entropies of the images obtained by applying ACO edge detection.

Similarly, Figs. 4 and 5 depict a comparison graph on the basis of the dice similarity index and structural similarity content of the segmented output image obtained by the proposed method, respectively. The comparison of the proposed techniques on the basis of the dice similarity index is shown below.

From Fig. 4, we can understand that the dice similarity index of the images obtained by applying GA segmentation is higher than that of the images obtained by applying the ACO edge detection technique. Thus, as per the dice similarity index, the GA segmentation technique is proved to be more efficient than the ACO edge detection technique.

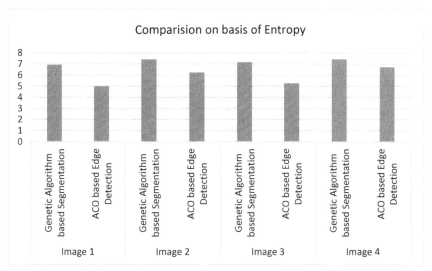

Fig. 3 Comparison of the proposed techniques on the basis of entropy.

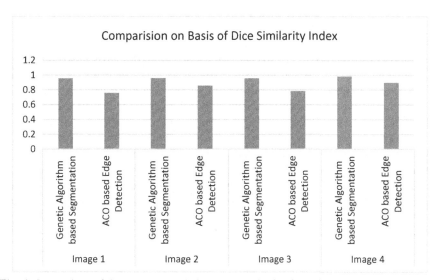

Fig. 4 Comparison of the proposed techniques on the basis of the dice similarity index.

The comparison chart proposed techniques on the basis of the structural similarity index of the output images is shown in Fig. 5. In this index, a lower value denotes better segmentation.

As per Fig. 5, the value of structural similarity content for the segmented output image obtained by applying the GA segmentation technique in all the four test images is less that the values obtained by applying the ACO edge detection technique.

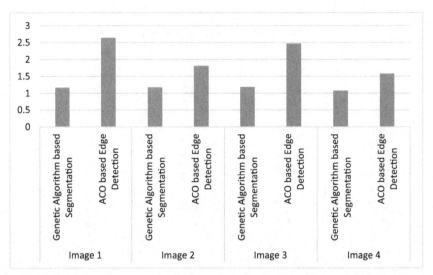

Fig. 5 Comparison of the proposed techniques on the basis of the structural similarity content.

Therefore, we can state that as per the structural similarity content, the proposed GA technique is superior to the ACO technique.

Three well-known image quality parameters are used in this study to demonstrate the validity of the proposed method such as entropy, dice similarity index, and structural content. For entropy and dice similarity index, a higher value denotes better image quality, whereas for structural similarity content, a lower value denotes better quality. For testing, we have taken four images of skin lesions with white patches, then applied preprocessing to the test images. On these test images, the two discussed methodologies were applied separately. In this way, two output images were obtained from one input image. The different quality measuring parameters are applied to the output images for all test images. As per all these measures, the GA segmentation technique proved to be more efficient than the ACO edge detection the for all the test images. Edge detection of a medical image is an important tool in the creation and development of computer-aided diagnostics [28]. In this chapter, we have introduced an optimal procedure for skin lesion identification.

4 Conclusion

In this paper, optimized segmented methods for the detection of white patches in skin images was done. At first, a histogram equalization-based image preprocessing step was introduced that will enhance the quality of the image. Then, we applied two segmentation techniques by using the popular ACO and GA techniques. Performance analysis was done quantitatively by using three parameters: entropy, dice similarity index, and structural similarity content. In all three cases, GA segmentation was found to be better than ACO segmentation. Further, the proposed work can be done to introduce a more efficient GA segmentation technique as a precursor step in the classification stage to develop automatic computer-aided diagnostics for skin disease detection.

References

[1] J. Hathaliya, P. Sharma, S. Tanwar, R. Gupta, Blockchain-based remote patient monitoring in healthcare 4.0, in: 9th IEEE International Conference on Advanced Computing (IACC), Tiruchirappalli, India, 13–14th December 2019, 2019, pp. 87–91.

[2] S. Tanwar, K. Parekh, R. Evans, Blockchain-based electronic healthcare record system for healthcare 4.0 applications, J. Inf. Secur. Appl. 50 (2019) 1–14.

[3] P. Bhattacharya, S. Tanwar, S. Tyagi, N. Kumar, BINDaaS: Blockchain integrated deep-learning as a service in healthcare 4.0 applications, IEEE Trans. Netw. Sci. Eng. (8, 2019) 1–14.

[4] S. Sengupta, N. Mittal, Analysis of various techniques of feature extraction on skin lesion images, in: S.K. Khatri (Ed.), Proceedings of 6th International Conference on Reliability, Infocom Technologies and Optimization (Trends and Future Directions), ICRITO, Noida, India, September 20–22, vol. 6, 2017, pp. 651–656.

[5] Q. Abbas, I. Fondón, Unsupervised skin lesions border detection via two dimensional image analysis, Comput. Methods Programs Biomed. 104 (2011) 1–15.

[6] Healthline, What is Skin Lesions? 2020. https://www.healthline.com/health/skin-lesions. (Accessed 6 April 2021).

[7] S. Sengupta, N. Mittal, M. Modi, Color space based thresholding for segmentation of skin lesion images, Int. J. Biomed. Eng. Technol., n.d. (Inderscience Publication (Forthcoming Article)).

[8] S. Jayade, D.T. Ingole, M.D. Ingole, MRI brain tumor classification using hybrid classifier, in: Proceedings of International Conference on Innovative Trends and Advances in Engineering and Technology, ICITAE, Shegoaon, India, 2019, pp. 201–205.

[9] M. Jahanifar, N. Zamani Tajeddin, B. Mohammadzadeh, A. Gooya, Supervised saliency map driven segmentation of lesions in dermoscopic images, IEEE J. Biomed. Health Inform. 23 (2) (2019) 509–518.

[10] M. Kharazmi, H. AlJasser, Z. Lui, Z.J. Wang, T.K. Lee, Automated detection and segmentation of vascular structures of skin lesions seen in dermoscopy, with an application to basal cell carcinoma classification, IEEE J. Biomed. Health Inform. 21 (6) (2017) 1675–1684.

[11] S. Kashef, H. Nezamabadi-pour, An advanced ACO algorithm for feature subset selection, Neurocomputing 147 (2015) 271–279.

[12] F. Dalila, A. Zohra, K. Reda, Segmentation and classification of melanoma and benign skin lesions, Optik 140 (2017) 749–761.

[13] A. Mahmood, H. Mahmood, Automatic triple-A segmentation of skin cancer images based on histogram classification, Al-Rafdain Eng. J. 23 (2015) 31–42.

[14] S. Sen Gupta, N. Mittal, M. Modi, Improved skin lesion edge detection method using Ant Colony Optimization, Skin Res. Technol. 25 (2019) 46–856.

[15] S. Sengupta, N. Mittal, M. Modi, Contrast enhancement for color dermascopy images using equalization based on luminosity, in: A. Rana (Ed.), International Conference on Reliability, Infocom Technologies and Optimization (Trends and Future Directions) ICRITO, Noida, India, June 4–5, 2020, pp. 845–848, https://doi.org/10.1109/ICRITO48877.2020.9197874.

[16] O. Verma, P. Signal, S. Garg, et al., Edge detection using adaptive thresholding and Ant Colony Optimization, in: World Congress on Information and Communication Technologies, 1, 2011, pp. 313–318.

[17] Color Image Segmentation Using Genetic Algorithm (Clustering), MATLAB Central File Exchange, 2020. https://www.mathworks.com/matlabcentral/fileexchange/64223-color-image-segmentation-using-genetic-algorithm-clustering. (Accessed 22 April 2020).

[18] C. Mistry, U. Thakker, R. Gupta, S. Tanwar, N. Kumar, J.J.P.C. Rodrigues, M.S. Obaidat, MedBlock: an AI-enabled and blockchain-driven medical healthcare system for COVID-19, in: IEEE International Conference on Communications (IEEE ICC 2021), Montreal, Canada, 14–18 June 2021, 2021.

[19] A. Shukla, N. Patel, S. Tanwar, B. Sadoun, M.S. Obaidat, BDoTs: Blockchain-based evaluation scheme for online teaching under COVID-19 environment, in: International Conference on Computer, Information and Telecommunication Systems (IEEE CITS-2020), Beijing, China, 5–7 October, 2020, pp. 1–5.

[20] R. Gonzalez, R. Woods, Digital Image Processing, Pearson, United Kingdom, 2009.

[21] N. Mittal, S. Tanwar, S.K. Khatri, Identification and enhancement of different skin lesion images by segmentation techniques, in: S.K. Khatri (Ed.), Proceedings of IEEE International Conference on Reliability, Infocom Technologies and Optimization, Noida, India, September 20–22, 2017, pp. 609–614.

[22] N. Mittal, H.P. Singh, R. Gupta, Decomposition & reconstruction of medical Images in MATLAB using different wavelet parameters, in: International Conference on Futuristic Trends on Computational Analysis and Knowledge Management (ABLAZE), Greater Noida, India, 2015, pp. 647–653.

[23] S. Sengupta, N. Mittal, M. Modi, Edge detection in dermascopic images by linear structuring element, in: S.K. Khatri (Ed.), Proceedings of International Conference on Reliability, Infocom Technologies and Optimization (Trends and Future Directions) (ICRITO), Noida, India, August 29–31, 2018, pp. 419–424.

[24] N. Bahadure, A. Ray, T. HarPal, Image analysis for MRI based brain tumor detection and feature extraction using biologically inspired BWT and SVM, Int. J. Biomed. Imaging 1 (2017) 8–120.

[25] R. Gomalavalli, S. Muttan, S. Venkata, Boundary detection of renal using contour segmentation, Int. J. Biomed. Eng. Technol. 28 (2018) 53–66.

[26] H. Menon, K. Narayanakutty, Comparative performance of different perceptual contrast fusion techniques using MLS, Int. J. Biomed. Eng. Technol. 18 (2015) 52–71.

[27] O. Supriya, S. Talbar, Adaptive thresholding of wavelet coefficients using generalised false discovery rate to compress ECG signal, Int. J. Biomed. Eng. Technol. 29 (2019) 155–173.

[28] B. Dhruv, N. Mittal, M. Modi, Comparative analysis of edge detection techniques for medical images of different body parts, in: Data Science and Analytics. Communications in Computer and Information Science, Springer, 2017, pp. 164–176.

Blockchain applications for the healthcare sector: Uses beyond Bitcoin

Rabab Jafri and Shikha Singh
Department of Computer Science and Engineering, Amity School of Engineering and
Technology, Amity University, Lucknow, Uttar Pradesh, India

1 Introduction

Medicine is an inevitable part of our lives, making medical data such as prescriptions, patient medical history, etc., an essential part of treatment. Traditionally, medical data was written on paper, which was vulnerable to damage or human modifications. Therefore, to mitigate this impairment, it became necessary to safely store this data in an electronic format. Even after this, the medical database is still prone to tampering or even permanent deletion. Information blocking is another issue that occurs when someone from the outside wants to access data without the permission of the patient or hospital. Sharing medical data securely without any modification is necessary, as one disease could be the result of a prior one. This data may be needed when monitoring a patient or when the practitioners need to know the medical history of the patient for treatment. Furthermore, there are numerous issues with time, speed, storage, and protection when data are transmitted on paper or via email. Relying on a centralized database for keeping sensitive data is also not an option. Also, it is believed that cyberattackers are prone to medical data as it has huge revenue potential. So, access to a distributed instead of a centralized ledger for sharing medical data can ensure data security. There should be a patient-centric model to give priority to patients. The patient should be aware of data provided to an insurance company, data provided to a blood bank, etc., to provide flexibility. Therefore, researchers began using blockchain in medical healthcare. Frost and Sullivan highlighted tagging medical equipment with useful identification, and integrating confidence in device identification and tracking as a critical problem. When a gadget fails, tracking it can disclose the source of the problem and save wasteful repurchasing in the case of lost devices. These dangers are expected to be reduced by a strong trust infrastructure based on the identification of medical equipment. Due to security and privacy concerns, just 20%–30% of medical equipment is connected within hospitals, according to the survey. As a result, blockchain can assist the pharmaceutical business in overcoming the rising risks of counterfeit and unapproved pharmaceuticals. There are numerous areas of healthcare and well-being where blockchain technology could be beneficial, including device tracking, clinical trials, pharmaceutical tracing, and

Blockchain Applications for Healthcare Informatics. https://doi.org/10.1016/B978-0-323-90615-9.00022-0
Copyright © 2022 Elsevier Inc. All rights reserved.

health insurance. Hospitals can use a blockchain infrastructure to track the entire life-cycle of their assets through device tracking. Following that, the data gathered can be used to improve patient safety and give an aftermarket analysis to save money. In today's digital age, academics are concerned about another issue: how to deal with data of a specific size. Applications such as big data, data analysis, image processing, and data mining help in processing an enormous amount of data in gigabytes and terabytes today. Digitalizing systems in the healthcare sector is evidenced by increasing interest and various initiatives taking place in different sectors worldwide. The aim of doing so is to benefit patients and society through the adoption of electronic health records (EHR). The ability of EHR systems includes public healthcare management and online patient access, which has become of interest to various research communities. This can also be seen in the novel coronavirus (COVID-19) pandemic, where remote patient monitoring and other remote healthcare deliverables are used to tackle the situation in the most secure way possible. The medical sector is looking for newer technology to detect and control the COVID-19 pandemic in this global health disaster. As a result, accurate and trustworthy data are required to track and manage the spread of any virus. However, contemporary technology lacks reliable data that could provide correct information regarding the transmission of a novel coronavirus in the current setting. Although public hospitals and clinical laboratories can provide information on COVID-19 patients, the information may not be valid because it is not properly managed, preserved, or collected according to approved processes. Blockchain technology (BT) can assist in tracking the spread of the coronavirus, identifying high-risk individuals, and controlling the infection in real time to address these challenges. BT is a digital database that holds information that can be utilized and shared in a huge decentralized and publicly accessible network at the same time. Blockchain's properties of immutability, transparency, and decentralization can be leveraged to provide security and trust in the healthcare domain.

1.1 Motivation and contribution

Compared to the previously published articles, this work provides a comprehensive assessment and analysis of BT's application in healthcare. The goal of this study is also to demonstrate the obstacles of blockchain research as well as the potential applications of blockchain in healthcare. Only research that presents a novel solution, algorithm, method, methodology, or architecture for the topic of healthcare is included in this systematic review. Research of the review type, discussions of possible blockchain uses and applications, and other irrelevant publications are not included. The remainder of this chapter is organized as follows. In Section 1 we present background information on blockchain technology and EHR systems and its concepts and the current implementation of blockchain in healthcare. A deeper insight into the importance of mobile health, remote monitoring, and the motivations for using blockchain-based EHR systems is listed in Section 2. Section 3 covers the details of a patient-centered blockchain model along with its promising features. Furthermore, a discussion on the present pandemic and how blockchain is striving to help in this ongoing situation is in Section 4. The chapter is summed up in Section 5 where conclusions are drawn to support the entire contents of the chapter.

1.2   Fundamentals of blockchain

A software system is said to have typically two main architectural approaches: the centralized approach and the distributed approach [1]. Currently, trading and exchanging goods over the Internet depends on financial institutions that monitor any electronic payments and act as a trusted third party to process these payments. There is a cost to these intermediary parties, which increases the transaction cost, thus limiting small casual transactions. This system may work well but still suffer from various hindrances such as the inherited trust-based model drawbacks. The possibility of nonreversible transactions is almost negligible because the intermediary disputes cannot be overlooked and cannot be neglected. This is the basic working of a "centralized system." In a centralized approach, the nodes are distributed and connected with one central node acting as a coordinator. The distributed approach, in contrast, has several nodes connected to each other directly but not centrally. Fig. 1 illustrates the comparison of these two approaches.

Blockchain is a distributed ledger technology with the potential to drastically transform many industries globally. The term "blockchain" was first introduced by Satoshi Nakamoto in his published white paper, which was a technical manifesto released in October 2008 under an MIT public license. He introduced this peer-to-peer, no intermediary system that helped in the electronic cash system by introducing the first digital currency, named Bitcoin. Security in this system is ensured as the nonmalicious nodes collectively control more than 50% of CPU power, which is more than any other group of hoax nodes [2]. This distributed ledger technology is a time-stamped chain of blocks containing the transactions and encoded with a cryptographic hash function and a digital signature, which helps in enabling a trustless protocol. Fig. 2 depicts how each block is associated with the one prior via the previous hash, thus forming

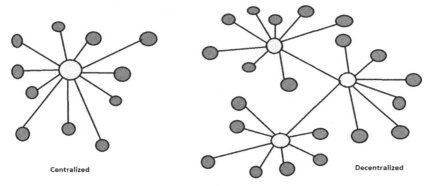

Fig. 1 Centralized vs. decentralized network architecture.

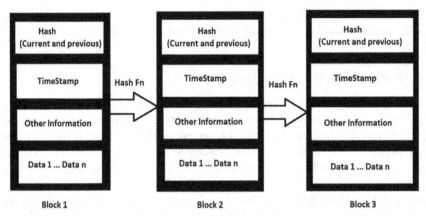

Fig. 2 A blockchain structure.

a chain. The block prior to the present one is called its *parent block* and the first-ever mined block is known as the *genesis block* or *the 0th block*. Data are stored and verified across the entire network of computers. Blockchain verifies, secures, confirms, and records each transaction. Data are stored in a decentralized way across a wide network, saving it from a single point of failure and hence ensuring less fraud and tampering with greater security. There is an effective limit on the speed of new transactions being added. Right now, each new block in the chain must be 1 MB or smaller. A typical Bitcoin transaction is about 250 bytes, so that means 1 MB/250 bytes equal to 4000 transactions that can fit in each new block. Once a block is added to the chain, then anyone who tries to alter it would need to recompute the altered block as well as all the other subsequent blocks, thus making blockchain permanent. This in return demands an enormous amount of computation power. The trust among nodes is obtained by solving mathematical puzzles and cryptography instead of a central bank. As data are stored in an encrypted form, this ensures the preservation of data privacy. Smart contracts were introduced to support different functions for different application scenarios to work toward robustness, as the terms of this smart contract can be preset by users and will only be executed if the conditions are fulfilled. Hence, this hands over control to the owner of the data. The blockchain is a decentralized network that has no central authority and thus all nodes should agree on the validity of the transactions occurring. This is achieved with consensus. A special peer node known as a "miner" validates the transaction and facilitates the consensus process. These are the powerful computers executing software defined by blockchain protocols. The miners are in competition with each other to add their block to the chain first. This is done by a consensus algorithm that makes sure all the nodes agree on the same state of the blockchain. They use proof of work (POW), which is a consensus protocol that confirms transactions and produces new blocks. Miners compete with each other to validate the transaction and whichever node adds a new block to the chain by solving a mathematical puzzle wins a reward. In addition encryption and decryption, one more concept is associated with it, called hashing. Hashing along with encryption provides security. Hashing basically refers to the process that takes an input of varied length and gives an output of a fixed length. This fixed-length output is called a "hash." Tracing a hash makes it easier to track a transaction. The basic function of a hash is to verify the integrity of the block and form a chain link by including the previous hash block in the current block header. If another node tampers with the block, the hash value changes, causing a hash value mismatch and rendering the local chain invalid. Bitcoin's secure hashing algorithm 256, also known as SHA-256, is a good example. It also ensures the anonymity, immutability, and compactness of the block. This gives a fixed output of a length of 256 bits. The consensus process determines how the miners are chosen and what data are included in the block. The blocks are then broadcast to the network, where the validation nodes verify that the received block contains valid transactions and that it references the previous block in the chain by using the corresponding hash. If both requirements are fulfilled, the nodes add the block to the blockchain. The block is discarded if the prerequisites are not met. The function of network nodes is defined by this. In the blockchain network, each node has its own copy. The same blockchain is disseminated across the whole network in multiple copies. Even if each copy is identical, the fact that it is dispersed throughout the network makes it harder for the wicked node to change it. Thus, a hacker would need to manipulate each and every copy on the entire network, making it a distributed ledger [3].

These properties make blockchain seem ideal for healthcare data management. Although blockchain in healthcare is relatively new, more research is becoming available each day. There are many real-world blockchain healthcare systems such as Gem, Guardtime, and Healthbank, to name a few. The application of blockchain in healthcare transforms the ecosystem in a variety of ways that benefit patients and improve treatments, outcomes, security, and prices. Blockchain has the potential to revolutionize healthcare delivery by putting patients at the center of healthcare ecosystems and increasing healthcare data security, privacy, and interoperability. By making electronic medical records more efficient and secure, this technology can establish a new model for health information exchanges. Its immutable, time-stamped, tamper-proof ledger, accessible by all or preapproved participants, is one of blockchain technology's key offerings, making it a no-brainer for supply chains across industries [4]. Because of its numerous qualities, blockchain can handle many real-world health science goals and criteria, which is a compelling justification for its adoption. Decentralized administration, for example, is extremely valuable for organizing digital assets created by diverse entities. There is no one point of permission, ownership, or control as a result of this. When users don't want to rely on a single central authority, or when patients (users) wish to double-check their data and records, this is advantageous. In clinical and surveillance systems, for example, data provenance is vital. This is ensured because blockchain generates an immutable trail that records transactions in perpetuity, ensuring that crucial records are always available in the network to be inspected if necessary. A block could be used to record transactions in healthcare or research. The actual patient data as well as access records such as requests for and receipts of records are recorded as transactions in blocks on a chain. An example of a health informatics exchange would be: Patient P1 requests that clinician C use data, institution I1 grants access, and the transaction is visible to the patient P1 or primary care clinician C2. Again, consider a human subject research scenario: researcher R1 requests trial data, institution I2 grants access, and participant P2 and/or principal investigator R2 can view the transaction [5]. Researchers and businesses are growing increasingly interested in the Internet of Things (IoT) cybersecurity and blockchain technology due to its ability to bring answers to a variety of difficulties, most notably those relating to traditional centralized design. Blockchain technology provides a single source of truth that is permanent, verifiable, and immutable. About $1.4 billion was invested in blockchain-related start-ups back in 2016 and the hype cycle shows no sign of slowing anytime soon. Much of the focus on blockchain has been on cryptocurrency, particularly Bitcoin, and the impact that blockchain is expected to have on the financial sector. Despite the focus on financial services, many other areas, including voting, real estate, supply chain management, and healthcare, are vulnerable to upheaval. Healthcare is ripe for disruption because it faces a slew of issues that blockchain can address with its immutability, fraud prevention, and ability to transfer data between institutions without the requirement for third-party trust. Current issues within the modern healthcare industry are:

1. **Healthcare data interchange:** Data must be shared between healthcare providers, necessary third parties, insurers, and patients while adhering to data privacy regulations.
2. **Nationwide interoperability:** Having a uniform standard for patient data sharing makes it easier to transfer data between healthcare providers, which is something that outdated systems often lack.
3. **Medical device tracking:** From supply chain to decommissioning, medical device tracking provides for quick device retrieval, avoidance of wasteful repurchasing, and fraud analytics.
4. **Drug tracking:** As with medical devices, blockchain allows for frictionless recalls and the prevention of counterfeit medications by tracking the chain of custody from the supplier chain to the patient.

1.3 Types of blockchains

There are basically three types of blockchains depending on the managed data, the availability of such data, and the actions that can be performed by the user, namely:

1. **Public blockchain:** As the name suggests, this blockchain is publicly accessible and there are no restrictions on the participants or the validator. The main advantage is that nobody will have complete overall control of the network. There is no central authority, which assures that the data are secure and that the records are immutable. Bitcoin, Ethereum, and Litecoin are some examples of this type of blockchain.
2. **Private blockchain:** To become a member of this blockchain network, participants must be invited. Only persons who are members of the network may see what's going on here. These are primarily used in private organizations to store the organization's sensitive information.
3. **Consortium/hybrid blockchain:** This blockchain network is divided into two different types where some nodes are private while the other nodes are public. As a result, only some nodes will be allowed to participate in transactions while the others will be in charge of the consensus protocols. This is a type of hybrid blockchain consisting both of private and public blockchain. Table 1 states various examples of each of the three kinds of blockchains.

Table 1 Summary of types of blockchain.

	Public blockchain	Private blockchain	Consortium blockchain
What is it?	Anyone anywhere can read and write on the network. Data are validated by every node in the network, thus making it very secure	There is a highly trusted organization (owner of the blockchain) that provides permission to read and write data onto the blockchain	Permissions to verify, read, and write onto the blockchain are controlled by a few predetermined nodes
Benefits and challenges	It is secure and transparent as all transactions made are public with individual anonymity It can be inefficient as all nodes need to verify the transaction	It is efficient and private as the owner has the power to control who can read/write on the blockchain This also gives controlling power to a single consolidated entity	Efficient as fewer nodes verify transactions. It is also private as read/write access can be controlled by predetermined nodes. There is no consolidation of controlling power
Example	Bitcoin, Ethereum, Litecoin, etc.	Ripple and Hyperledger	Corda and quorum

2 Implementations of blockchain in healthcare

Many medical services and blockchain-oriented organizations have successfully delivered blockchain frameworks to improve these medical services for both doctors and patients. By decentralizing patient wellbeing history, following drugs, and improving choices, blockchain is turning into an important instrument for medical services, changing the business around the world. Nonetheless, there are various exploration and operational difficulties trying to integrate blockchain technology with existing EHR systems. Research about blockchain's applications to medical care is presently restricted, yet more exploration opens up consistently. Blockchain apparently is one of the hottest programming research topics right now. It can change medical services by returning ownership over clinical information to the patient. This is advantageous from a patient-focused perspective. Current medical care frameworks are described as being exceptionally complex and exorbitant. This can be diminished through improved health record management, utilization of insurance agencies, and blockchain technology. Healthcare accounts for a significant portion of the gross domestic product (GDP) in developed countries. Hospital costs, on the other hand, are continuing to climb, as are unnecessary operations and data breaches. This is one area in which blockchain technology has the ability to make a difference. It has the ability to a wide range of tasks, including secure encryption of patient data and the management of epidemics. A new type of blockchain trust model, a consortium trust, is also gaining traction. Microsoft has released the Coco framework, which enables the creation of blockchain-agnostic consortiums. A predefined group of trusted parties is used in these consortium structures. Multiple hospitals, medical device makers, and third parties are examples of this in healthcare. Smart contracts are executed on a trusted partner's hardware to generate consensus without the use of miners. This has resulted in far better performance, with a Coco-optimized blockchain capable of processing 1600 transactions per second, bringing blockchain much closer to the big payment processors. Blockchain can assist the pharmaceutical business in overcoming the rising risks of counterfeit and unapproved pharmaceuticals. With integrated GPS and chain-of-custody logging, it is possible to build smart contracts for pharmaceuticals and then identify pill containers, just as it is for devices. Blockchain can be used in clinical trials to solve concerns such as false results and data deletions that go against the researcher's bias or the funding source's goal. As a result, clinical investigations will be more reliable. It also allows for the creation of an irreversible log of trial subject consent. The pharmaceutical industry may save $200 billion by identifying a chain of custody in the supply chain. Many sectors of health insurance could benefit from a reliable record of events surrounding the patient pathway, such as improved incident reporting and automated underwriting operations. Contracts, such as automated payments for segments of the patient journey, could also be precisely stated and then implemented. The following are some of the current blockchain application cases, primarily in healthcare [6]:

1. **Clinical trials:** Clinical trials are one area where blockchain has the potential to improve medical practitioner and researcher transparency, auditability, and accountability. Regulators may readily monitor clinical trial standards by keeping an immutable ledger of patient consent, ensuring that the experiment complies with informed consent rules. This is especially important because faked informed consent forms, along with tampering with data and faking patient agreements, are among the most common types of clinical fraud. A high level of trial subject authentication would be required to prevent this scam. This system could be enhanced even further by developing a smart contract system that blocks clinicians from accessing patient data until a key is released at the end of an auditable smart contract procedure that requires agreement from the patient at each stage of the trial. Clinical trial subjects gain ownership of their data by using a blockchain clinical trial consent ledger, which also provides an audit trail for clinical staff, researchers, and regulators.
2. **Patient records:** Blockchain has the potential to revolutionize healthcare by putting data in the hands of people. MedRec keeps a permanent record of healthcare data for patients and providers. Its strategy is to reward miners by giving them access to unidentified healthcare data in exchange for helping to keep the network running [7]. MedRec maps patient-provider relationships (PPR) using smart contracts, in which the contract displays a list of references that details the relationships between nodes on the blockchain. It also gives patients control over PPRs, allowing them to accept, reject, or change partnerships with healthcare providers such as hospitals, insurers, and clinics.
3. **Drug tracking:** Drug monitoring on the blockchain is another possibility, as it improves the blockchain's immutability and allows for the development of tracking and chain of custody from the manufacturer to POW patient. An example is a technology start-up producing a solution that generates a chain that shows where a drug was created, where it is now, and when it was distributed to patients, eliminating pharmaceutical fraud and theft. This enables

healthcare providers to comply with current healthcare requirements in terms of pharmaceutical supply security, with an emphasis on interoperability between providers. The Counterfeit Medicines Project was recently started by Hyperledger, the open-source blockchain working group, to address the problem of counterfeit drugs. The sources of counterfeit drugs may be traced and discarded from the supply chain using blockchain. The advantage of blockchain in drug monitoring over traditional methods is the inherent decentralization of confidence and authority in the technology's principles. While central authorities can be bribed or falsified, bribing a consensus of those on the blockchain is considerably more difficult. Counterfeit drugs can be totally eradicated from participating supply chains if they can be updated and tracked utilizing blockchain's intrinsic tamper-proofing capabilities at the moment of manufacture.

4. **Device tracking:** Medical device tracking is another opportunity for blockchain in disrupting healthcare from the manufacturer to decommissioning. The use of blockchain in conjunction with this technology allows for an immutable log that shows not only where the device is, but also where it has been in its lifecycle as well as which manufacturer, reseller, and serial number are associated with it, assisting in regulatory compliance. Deloitte identified this feature as one of the potential game-changers for blockchain in the healthcare sector in a white paper. According to an IBM survey, 60% of government stakeholders in healthcare say medical device integration and asset management are the most disruptive areas in the industry. In comparison to traditional location tracking technologies, a blockchain method has various advantages. The immutability and tamper-proof properties of blockchain are the most obvious. This prohibits a malicious user from altering a device's location history or erasing it from the database. This is especially relevant given that medical equipment theft has become a huge problem in the United States and the United Kingdom. This immutability also prevents gadgets from being misplaced and reordered, which costs a lot of money in terms of both care and equipment expenditures. This method should not add significantly to nurse, porter, or support worker burden because it simply requires a tap on the device with a mobile phone or scanner, followed by the entry of the device's present location.

2.1 Electronic health records systems

Technology's recent advancements are touching many aspects of our lives and altering how we use and view things. Technology is finding new methods to improve the healthcare sector, just as it has in other areas of life. The key advantages of technological innovation include improved security, user experience, and other aspects of the healthcare business. EHR and electronic medical record (EMR) systems provide these advantages [8]. EHR is the collection of the patient's electronic health information serving as a data source fetched from and to healthcare providers for medical purposes. It follows a centralized architecture that has a central authority responsible for managing, coordinating, and controlling activities on the network. On the contrary, in a decentralized architecture such as blockchain, all nodes are managed without any dependence on a central authority, as described previously. Ideally, EHR systems should ensure the confidentiality, integrity, and availability of the data, which should be shared with authorized users only to carry on with diagnosis and other medical help when needed. With the right implementation, this system can reduce the replication of data and the risk of losing the data. However, the challenge of data security in such

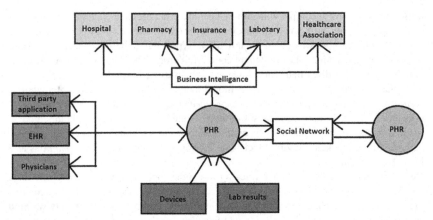

Fig. 3 Personal health record.

systems is threatened by the increasing connections to these systems. They are vulnerable to attack vectors while mobile devices issued by hospitals can be exploited with malware software installed to gain access to sensitive data. EHR systems provide us with enormous data in terms of volume, which can be used to carry out data analysis and machine learning. For example, it can be beneficial to inform others about disease forecasting such as in the case of the 2019 coronavirus. Also, wearable IoT devices can provide relevant information that can help facilitate healthcare monitoring and personalized medical services. But that can be difficult to manage as one healthcare provider's EHR for a patient may differ from the same patient's other information provider. Blockchain offers the ability to create a single system for securely storing and retrieving health records by authorized users in a timely and safe manner. Innumerable mistakes can be avoided by minimizing communication gaps between different healthcare personnel and the patient. Faster diagnosis and interventions are possible, and care can be individualized to each patient, even remotely. The personal health record (PHR) is the personal healthcare information obtained from wearable devices such as smart watches that are owned and controlled by patients themselves, as shown in Fig. 3. This information collected by PHRs can be made available to healthcare providers by patients.

2.2 The essence of mobile health and remote monitoring

Mobile health or mHealth technologies have the potential to significantly impact health research, healthcare, and health outcomes. A **mHealth App** is offered by a healthcare organization to their patients. Patients use these apps to access self-service tools to pay their medical bills, schedule an appointment with the doctor, access lab results, find a suitable physician, and view medical records. The most common applications for mHealth include spreading awareness, diagnostic and treatment support, tracking disease and epidemic outbreaks, healthcare supply chain management, remote data collection, remote monitoring, and healthcare worker telecommunication.

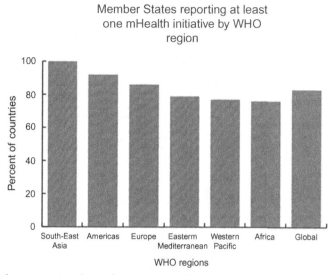

Fig. 4 Member states reporting at least one mHealth app [9].

Top mHealth apps on the market are Fitbit, Apple Heart Study, GoogleFit, Samsung Health, Practo, Medlife, etc. Fig. 4 shows the outcome of a recent study by the World Health Organization of regions where at least one mhealth application is in use [9].

The global mobile health industry is predicted to reach $311.98 billion by 2027, according to a new report from Reports and Data. With the expanding use of smart phones and the advent of innovative technologies in the healthcare sector, the industry has experienced an increase in demand in recent years. Not only for stakeholders in the healthcare industry but also for various companies outside of healthcare, digital health is proving to be a profitable venture. Advanced technologies have revolutionized the healthcare industry. The rate of increase in investment in health startups has accelerated, increasing the market's need. Newcomers are creating innovative ways to make these apps more user-friendly while also attempting to expand the app's potential. To digitalize the US healthcare system, a total of $7.5 billion has been invested in several start-ups. Babylon Health, based in the United Kingdom, received almost $500 million in private funding in 2019, followed by Ginkgo Bio Works, a bioengineering firm that designs microorganisms, which received $300 million. Currently, the COVID-19 pandemic has triggered a wave of fear, prompting lockdowns virtually everywhere to maintain social distancing. As a result, the market has shrunk in the short term, but producers believe that demand for these products will increase in the long run, especially as a result of the pandemic. The use of mobile health will grow, especially in rural areas. Fitness-tracking devices are projected to be in high demand, and home workout sessions are becoming increasingly popular. Fig. 5 represents the percentage of revenue of publishers of mHealth applications.

Blockchain has shown considerable adaptability in recent years, as almost every sector finds a way to incorporate its abilities into its domain. The financial industry

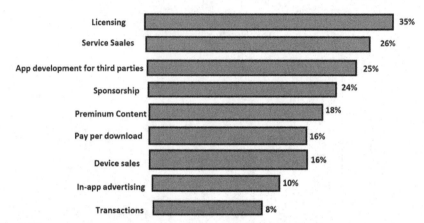

Fig. 5 The percentage of revenue of publishers of mHealth applications.

has received most of the attention thus far, but numerous projects in other sectors, such as healthcare, are beginning to show signs of change in areas such as public healthcare administration, user-oriented medical research, and medication counterfeiting in the pharmaceutical sector [10]. Patient data management is one of the most popular blockchain applications in healthcare. MedBlock is a blockchain-based information management system that enables electronic information access and retrieval through distributed blockchain parameters. The improved consensus mechanism ensures that the network is not overly burdened by activities. It is highly secured due to the features of access control and cryptography. Similarly, a data preservation system (DPS) is also blockchain based for medical data [11]. DPS uses similar cryptographic algorithms to ensure security. One more system called omniPHR places all the PHRs in one accessible place. OmniPHR combines attribute-based encryption (ABE), identity-based encryption, and identity-based signatures to create a new type of cryptographic framework called combined attribute or identity-based encryption and signature. This cryptographic framework maximizes security, as sharing healthcare data in a secure way is also an integral part of healthcare. Diseases in general are becoming more widespread. To treat and monitor these diseases ideally requires going to hospitals, increasing the burden of both hospitals and patients. This process can take a significant amount of time and may often result in mistakes due to human error. Presently, enhancements in wearable devices, sensors, and communication through these devices contribute to modifying the healthcare system in a way that will reshape medical management in no time. Remote patient monitoring (RPM) is the foremost of these advancements visible to us. RPM systems are based on the collection of patient vital signs extracted using presumptuous as well as chronic techniques and then sending them in real time to physicians. These data enable physicians to take the timely, right decision. Developed on the Ethereum blockchain, **MedRec** is a system that prioritizes patient agency and hence gives a transparent and accessible view of medical history. It stores all the patient's information in one place, making it simple for both patients and doctors to view when required. Providers maintain the blockchain through the proof of authority (POA) mechanism to safeguard authenticity and security. **SimplyVital** Health also has two projects running on blockchain technology. **ConnectingCare** uses care coordination and financial forecasting to help providers in bundled payments get insight into what happens to patients when they leave the hospital. It is currently on the market, helping healthcare providers determine how much a patient's care will cost. **Health Nexus** stores a patient's information on a blockchain for all parties to view. It will also allow patients to sell their data to researchers for profit. The Taipei Medical University Hospital and Digital Treasury Corporation (DTCO) have recently released **phrOS**. It seeks to improve medical institution transparency by storing all the patient's medical records on a blockchain, which contains photographs and other information about the patient's condition. This information can be accessed by doctors and patients through a mobile app. This in turn increases the security of medical information through the decentralized ledger technology (DLT). A blockchain-based system would allow for data to be added and tracked through a ledger, therefore providing a live feed of multiple agencies' relief efforts. It has the potential to save lives and money. Hashed Health, a health-focused blockchain development company, intends to make credentials in the health sector more transparent and easily accessible. With professional credentials exchange, members of the chain can verify the credentials and track records of various health professionals. This streamlines the hiring process while also providing an unalterable history of a professional's healthcare career history. Change Healthcare develops a wide variety of products focused on payments and data management in the healthcare sector. According to their website, 92% of top US health plans use their services. One of their most recent developments simplifies claims management and revenue cycle management. It helps hospitals and health systems manage and improve the collection of patient payments, minimize denials and underpayments, and manage daily revenue cycles and business operations more effectively. **MedicalChain** helps in ensuring full access and control over our own personal health data. Users can easily grant doctors immediate access to their health records via their mobile devices while keeping the data secure on the blockchain. Patients can also wear wristbands, which medical professionals can scan to access a person's medical history if they are unconscious in case of emergencies. It also offers telemedicine communication, enabling online video consultations with doctors. Healthcare Data Gateway (HGD) is another such application presented for organizing patient data. The application uses a simple unified indicator-centric schema to organize this data and a secure multiparty computing system. This prevents privacy violations without any ownership over the information. Smart contracts based on blockchain could aid in ensuring that devices are operated safely. To improve remote monitoring, a private blockchain based on Ethereum was developed. Before participating in this blockchain, participants must first be invited. Here, the transactions are visible only to persons who are part of the blockchain ecosystem. Private blockchain usually has a network administrator who can take care of user permissions in case any particular user requires additional authority. These are typically used in private organizations to store sensitive information. Smart devices interact with sensors that record events in this private blockchain. The smart contracts enable patient monitoring in real time. This is possible because notifications are sent to patients and healthcare providers securely. This is essential for care at home for patients while a healthcare provider is always accessible remotely. We can upload our health data easily from various devices such as smart gadgets, mobiles phones, etc., and store them on the cloud platform using blockchain. This makes it easier for people trying to access our data from a distance. **Guardtime** provides a specialized cybersecurity module called **Guardtime Cybersecurity** for several industries, including healthcare. Guardtime Health is a platform for patients, providers, regulators, and others that provides all with a single, immutable copy of health data shared across all the involved parties. This system signs every data asset in the network with a cryptographic stamp, which allows tracing the originality of each piece. Thus, any attempt at corruption is immediately spotted in real time. The start-up creates blockchain networks for chain of custody in drug supplies. Because of this, pharmacies can trace the origins of supplies, detect suspicious activities such as drug trafficking, and forge drugs during the process. In 2017, Chronicled created **MediLedger**, which is a blockchain-based project that allows checking the pharma supply chains with local regulations. The solution keeps a forgery-proof record of transactions on a blockchain, thus helping to authenticate raw materials that drugs are made of and detect counterfeits promptly. Currently, the US Centers for Disease Control explores blockchain-related use cases for disease control. In particular, it's mapping out blockchain usage for time-stamping of records to detect and report disease outbreaks in real time in a quick manner. For the same purpose, CDC teamed up with IBM to create a surveillance system for public agencies that will gather and accumulate data about patients and prescriptions effectively. **Dentacoin** is an ecosystem of applications focused entirely on the dental industry. Those include loyalty programs and dental insurance powered by smart contracts; own-issued tokens for payments among patients, dentists, suppliers, manufacturers, and other involved parties; and a platform for affordable care services that is currently under development. The new project will be a wholly new ecosystem that will reportedly encompass:

1. **Dentacare**—It is an app for oral hygiene notifications and reminders for the same.
2. **DentaVox** surveys—It is an online platform for surveying patients.
3. **Trusted reviews**—It is a platform for collecting patient reviews about dentists.
4. **Dentacoin assurance**—Preventive dental care with lower costs based on patient income.

Blockchain use cases in healthcare are plentiful and have the ability to transform the entire sector. The only issue now is getting healthcare providers to adopt blockchain systems on a wider scale. Once mass adoption occurs, it will foster the improvement of the entire healthcare system. More than ever, we are in charge of our own health and well-being. Many of us have devices that count our steps or tell us how we slept. All this information tells a complete story about what we're going through and who we are. This is a unique opportunity to bring all that together technologically to enable us to take charge of our own health. There are high chances of EGRs being adopted. There is an opportunity now to weave all that information meaningfully. The best health systems are those that provide the patient with the most visibility and access as well as those that enable the most inputs to be added to that core set of data. One of the biggest trends we are seeing in digital health is remote monitoring. Say you are treated for a particular condition at a hospital and then you go home. It has the capacity to deliver continuous monitoring of your vitals. In terms of providers, they are absolutely looking at technologies such as blockchain. Mobile health applications are becoming more important nowadays with the advancements in technology. In this context, EMRs were found to be kept secure in a blockchain network. The data can be sent to medical practitioners rapidly as well as being available for self-monitoring and home care as well. This area is particularly sensitive to malware; however, particularly a root exploit can give the hacker access to the patient's private key. Mobile applications and remote monitoring machines are an integral part of this technological era and blockchain can further enhance this. Blockchain has also been applied to clinical trials and very recently to medical insurance storage as well. A recent study outlines that **MIStore** is a blockchain-based medical insurance storage system that utilizes different servers of hospitals, patients, and insurance companies to verify each other's activity and security concerns. Such systems can encourage a more productive relationship between patients' hospitals and insurance companies.

3 Motivations for using the blockchain-based EHR system

Patients are increasingly empowered to access medical information and services digitally and securely on blockchain by a growing number of organizations. "Blockchain is exploding in clinical trials right now," says Maria Palombini, the IEEE Standards Association's director of emerging communities and projects development. Despite all this promise, just 5% of healthcare chief information officers (CIOs) and 12% of payer CIOs have blockchain in their written business strategies. According to a poll of 3700 physicians, nearly half of them (47%) are unaware of BT. There are a variety of scientific and operational hurdles, as with any maturing consumer technology. Hence, security and privacy become necessary for such data. Some of the challenges include a single point of failure of centralized servers and malicious attacks. Patients' whose data are saved in EHR systems lose control over who has access to it and for what purposes it could be utilized, which is a breach of personal privacy. This information may also be passed from malicious users to another organization such as an insurance company that may deny insurance to a patient based on a leaked medical history. The coronavirus pandemic, in which remote patient monitoring and other healthcare deliveries are being used to limit the situation, demonstrates the potential of EHRs. The following requirements should be met when implementing secure EHR systems:

1. Any unauthorized modification to data is not allowed and can be detected.
2. Security and privacy of data.
3. An efficient data-sharing mechanism.
4. It returns the control of EHRs back to patients so that patients can see their records and be notified of loss or malicious acquisition.

Jarzbek started **TrustedHealth**, a virtual platform that connects patients with life-threatening or rare illnesses with the best physicians for their needs. It's like telemedicine on steroids because it allows for virtual interactions and knowledge sharing while also collecting data for future research. Blockchain is used by Trusted Health to accomplish all of this. By making EHRs more efficient and secure, this technology could create a new model for health information exchange (HIE). It becomes an easier and more efficient information exchange. More security is achieved in terms of confidentiality, meaning only rightful users can access the data. Integrity implies that data must be accurate and should not be altered by any users and availability means that legitimate users' access to data and resources is accepted. The audit logs inside the blockchain have information about who accesses which EHR or PHR. It has information about the aim of accessing this information and also the time stamp of any operation in the entire life cycle. A person or an entire organization will be accountable and responsible for misconduct with any type of information. The above properties can be achieved using blockchain as explained below [12]:

Decentralization: Blockchain-based networks provide fault-tolerance architecture as end-to-end replications remove the reliance on a single point of failure. A significant amount of time has been saved after applying the decentralization in the process, which manage security and privacy.

Consensus mechanism: The winner from the miners releases this block to all other nodes in the network, which confirm and validate this block and add it to their chain; the winner gets a financial incentive for doing the work [13]. There are many consensus algorithms used to ensure data integrity and to validate blocks such as proof of stake, proof of burn, etc.

Immutability: Blockchain is immutable and tamper-free, hence it ultimately provides security. The hash function makes it tamper-resistant to any sort of change. A hash value is calculated by applying some hashing algorithms such as SHA-256, RSA, and RIPEMD-16, to name a few [1].

Traceability: Blockchain is a ledger that keeps on growing as the number of blocks grows. A block is comprised of a list of all done transactions. In this chain of blocks, every block has a parent block. The first block in the chain is the genesis block or the 0th block. The hash code of the 0th block is added to the header of the next block, then the hash code for the second block is computed. The hash of the second block becomes the parent of the third block and so on. This feature of blockchain provides data provenance to keep chronological track of activities and track the chain backward for investigations. The blocks are hence linked with each other, having a time stamp as well. This link can be chased back to the origin, the 0th block.

Smart contract: A smart contract is a computerized logic or terms of a contract written in a programming language, mostly Solidity. It implements transactions between two or more parties only after fulfilling the coded logic or when certain conditions are met. This implementation makes the blockchain flexible as well as programmable [14]. Smart contracts can enforce traceability and transparency.

Open source: Blockchain projects are mostly open source. Developers or any person can make contributions to it freely. Blockchain technology can accommodate evolution in the future. Various transformations from financial blockchains to nonprofit blockchains have been announced, as there is big interest of the community. Ethereum and Counterparty have paramount interest in building more value-added services for the future of blockchain.

4 Proposed patient-centered blockchain model

Fig. 6 is an overview of the model based on this very concept. It is secure and allows patients to claim ownership over their own records while allowing hospitals to have easy access to these records too [12]. This is based on Ethereum, which is a decentralized platform that allows developers to run various applications on a custom blockchain. Because blockchain may not offer sufficient storage many times, the actual medical records are on decentralized cloud storage such as Ethereum Swarm, which is a native base layer service of the Ethereum acting as a distributed storage platform. Each medical record has a unique swarm hash that is then combined with the decryption key. Only those that know the reference to this root can access the content within it. These root chunks are stored in smart contracts securely and are released only under certain conditions when required. Smart contracts are lines of code that are stored on a blockchain and automatically execute when predetermined terms and conditions are met. They are programs that run and have been set up to run by developers. Smart contracts are most useful in cases of business. They are used to implement some agreement so that all participants can be aware and certain of the outcome without any involvement of a third party. Say you have bought a car at a dealership and there are several steps, hence it can be frustrating. If cannot pay for the car, you will have to obtain financing. This will require a credit check and you will have to fill several forms with personal information to verify your identity. We will also have to interact with several different people such as the salesperson, finance broker, lender, and so on. To compensate for their work, various commissions and fees are added to the basic cost of the car. Smart contracts can streamline this complex process involving several intermediaries as there can be a lack of trust among various participants in the entire transaction. With our identity stored on a blockchain, lenders can quickly make a decision about credit, etc. A smart contract will be created among our bank, the dealer, and the lender so that once the funds have been released, the lender will hold the car's title and repayment will be initiated based on the agreed terms. The transfer of ownership would be automatic as the transaction gets recorded to a blockchain, is shared among the participants globally, and can be cross-checked at any time. The problem of data ownership and control can be solved by the concept of multisignature contracts. Multisignature requires multiple users to use their private keys to sign a transaction for

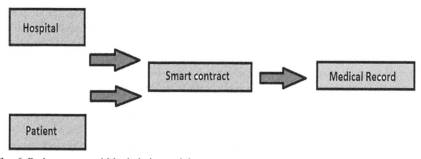

Fig. 6 Patient-centered blockchain model.

authentication. So the patient cannot tamper with the record without the permission of the hospital. But the patient still has control over who can access their record. A new swarm hash must be generated every time the data was accessed so a "last accessed" time stamp was added. Changes in data will automatically change the swarm hash, which is secured again until the required permissions for access are received. This paradigm improves blockchain's security and immutability while also providing a multisignature solution for data ownership and accessibility. Interoperability, secure storage, and dependable access to patient data are also included in this proposed paradigm.

5 Applications of blockchain technology to combat COVID-19

The different areas in which blockchain can play a key role in tackling the COVID-19 pandemic include outbreak tracking, user privacy protection, medical supply chain management, and donation tracking. The key purpose of blockchain is to aid in the control of the pandemic's propagation. Improved solutions, outbreak tracking, user privacy protection, the performance of the medical supply chain, donor tracking, and secure day-to-day operations are all things that technology can aid with during this pandemic crisis. Blockchain should be used in a way that reduces network latency while still providing a secure environment for storing and transmitting essential data. The ultimate combination of blockchain technology and other developing technologies such as artificial intelligence, big data, and cloud computing can effectively handle fatal pandemics such as the coronavirus. The primary areas where blockchain is helping in combating coronavirus are listed below [15]:

1. The first area is controlling the disease [16]. Effective and reliable disease surveillance is required for infectious disease control and pandemic prevention. Diseases that can be tracked and controlled with blockchain include the Ebola virus, yellow fever, cholera in Africa, Nipah in Asia, coronavirus, and others. This is accomplished by putting the blockchain network in people's electronic devices so they can be used globally to track the development of COVID-19 and other diseases among humans. In COVID-19, blockchain technology is critical for assisting virus sufferers by immutably recording patient symptoms of infection. BurstIQ's platform enables healthcare organizations to manage huge amounts of patient data in a safe and secure manner. Its blockchain allows for the secure storage, sale, sharing, and licensing of data while adhering to HIPAA regulations. BurstIQ's platform, which has complete and up-to-date information about an individual's health and healthcare activity, could aid in the detection of opioid and other prescription drug abuse. Factom develops tools to assist the healthcare business in securely storing digital information on the company's blockchain network, which is exclusively accessible to hospitals and healthcare managers. Physical papers can be embedded with Factom security chips that save patient information as private data that are only accessible by authorized individuals. The US Department of Homeland Security awarded Factom a roughly $200,000 grant in June 2018 to beta test a platform aimed at combining secure data from Border Patrol cameras and sensors to better evaluate the benefits of blockchain in "a realistic field scenario."

2. The second area is related to traceability. The term "traceability" refers to the ability to track infected patients. Controlling the spread of coronavirus is critical. With blockchain, infected patient travels can be tracked, real-time data about impacted areas can be provided, and direct fighting actions may be reported. BT can also be used to track people's movements in virus-free zones. The chain blocks are used to record information on safe zones, such as population, location, and the current condition of the coronavirus outbreak. To ensure transparency in the medical supply chain, goods and medical supplies must be tracked constantly. This tracking is possible thanks to the blockchain network's transaction logging and monitoring capabilities. The Centers for Disease Control and Prevention are investigating blockchain as a means of tracking infections in a supply chain-like fashion. The time stamps, peer-to-peer health reporting, and data-processing capabilities of blockchain, according to the US government agency, can assist in recording disease outbreaks in real time. Scientists can discover the origin of a disease and trends that aid in disease suppression by investigating the trail of reported outbreaks. The CDC may use blockchain to track the opioid epidemic. IBM is collaborating with the CDC to create a blockchain-based monitoring system that will allow public health organizations to collect data on patients and prescriptions more efficiently.

3. Maintaining a steady supply of medicines and nutrients has become a significant concern for the healthcare industry during this pandemic crisis. So the third area revolves around the use of blockchain in the commodities supply chain, and the trade supply chain has proven to be extremely beneficial. It can ensure the medical chain's stability by securely linking blocks and transactions. As a result, blockchain encryption is utilized to protect supply chain data privacy. During COVID-19, IBM announced the launch of a blockchain network to support the medical supply chain, named Rapid Supplier Connect. Chronicled creates blockchain networks that show proof of ownership. The networks assist pharmaceutical businesses in ensuring that their drugs arrive on time, and also allow law enforcement to investigate any suspect activities such as drug trafficking. In 2017, Chronicled launched the Mediledger Project, a blockchain-based ledger focused on medical supply chain security, privacy, and efficiency. Results from this project, according to the business, show that their blockchain-based system "is capable of operating as an interoperable system for the pharmaceutical supply chain" and "can meet the data privacy standards of the pharmaceutical industry."

4. One of the most important characteristics of blockchain is its transparency. It is critical to protect the personal data and information of patients undergoing treatment. Due to unconfirmed data, the spread of fake news on social media causes anxiety and panic. Because of its ability to check information and deliver real-time data updates, blockchain could be a promising solution to ensure data accuracy. It can help with the move from interoperability driven by institutions to interoperability driven by patients. Robomed blends AI and blockchain to provide a single point of care for patients. To collect patient data and share it with the patient's medical team, the company uses chatbots, wearable diagnostic gadgets, and telemedicine sessions. The Panacea platform from Robomeds involves patients in smart contracts that encourage and guide them toward improved health. Robomed collects patient data securely and shares it with the patient's healthcare providers using blockchain. To more securely store and distribute medical records, the Taipei Medical University Hospital recently integrated blockchain, including Robomed's network.

5. During the COVID-19 epidemic, BT could be critical in tracking healthcare tools, medications, and other items. It guarantees that healthcare instruments are transported safely and securely from one location to another. Alipay, in collaboration with the Zhejiang Provincial Health Commission and the Chinese Ministry of Economy and Information Technology, recently established a blockchain-based platform. Blockpharma provides an

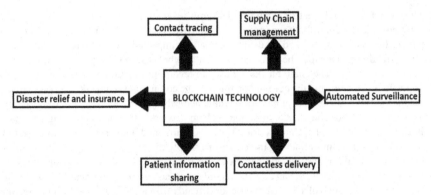

Fig. 7 Various domains in healthcare leveraging blockchain technology.

anticounterfeiting and medicine tracking solution. The company's software scans the supply chain and verifies all points of shipment, alerting patients if they are receiving counterfeit medications. Blockpharma picks out the bogus 15% of all pharmaceuticals in the world with the use of a blockchain-based SCM system. The company's blockchain-based solution can help people avoid counterfeit drugs through its app. Fig. 7 showcases various domains in the healthcare sector leveraging blockchain globally.

6 Conclusion

Blockchain is the buzzword of the year, and as this new technology evolves, it appears that it is ready to disrupt everything from banking to supply chain operations. Particularly in healthcare, there is a massive opportunity for a blockchain revolution to disrupt and lead a digital transformation. From medical records to pharmaceutical supply chains to smart contracts for payment distribution, there are plenty of opportunities to leverage this technology. Every modern healthcare system is built on the foundation of EHR. Each visit to our doctor tends to get longer and more complicated. Every hospital as well as every doctor's office has a different way of keeping these records. As a result, obtaining them is not always simple for healthcare providers. Some companies such as Patientory, Medibloc, or Medicalchain aim to solve this very problem. The goal is to give patients authority over their entire medical history and one-stop access to it for patients and physicians as well. Blockchain would not only simplify and make access more efficient but inherently bring data security to the field as well. The pharmaceutical industry has one of the highest standards for product safety, security, and stability; it is ripe for disruption. For example, supply chain management with blockchain can be monitored securely and transparently. This can greatly reduce time delays and human mistakes. It may also be used to track coats, labor, and even waste emissions throughout the supply chain. It may be used to check the validity of items by following them back to their source, battling the counterfeit medication business, which loses $200 billion each year. Companies such as Chronicled, Blockpharma, and Modum are already working toward more efficient blockchain logistic solutions. Modumin particular works in compliance with EU laws that require proof that medicinal products have not been exposed to particular conditions, especially certain temperatures that may compromise their quality. Companies such as EncrypGen and Nebula Genomics are building blockchain platforms to enable people to share genomic data safely and securely on a new emerging market. They bet in the future that opportunities around personnel genome sequencing will create a data market worth billions of dollars, and what is the best technology to solve data security issues and to ensure that data gets from the source to its end users without any middleman? It is the blockchain. Along with the pros, there are definite cons to this technology. Because each transaction necessitates the utilization of strong hardware resources, it consumes a lot of energy. The technology's main drawback is its scalability. Because the majority of nodes must approve transactions before they can be validated, this takes time. Another disadvantage of blockchain is its complexity, which necessitates the creation of a large user network. Another significant problem that this technology faces is maintaining privacy.

References

[1] B.A. Tama, B. Kweka, Y. Park, K.H. Rhee, A critical review of blockchain and its current applicat ions, 2017, pp. 109–113, https://doi.org/10.1109/ICECOS.2017.8167115.

[2] S. Nakamoto, Bitcoin: A peer-to-peer electronic cash system, 2008, p. 9. www.bitcoin.org.

[3] https://www.investopedia.com/terms/b/blockchain.asp.

[4] K. Rabah, Challenges & opportunities for blockchain powered healthcare systems: a review, in: ISSN 2523-5680, no-1, 2017, pp. 45–52.

[5] T.-T. Kuo, H.Z. Rojas, L. Ohno-Machado, Comparison of blockchain platforms: a systematic review and healthcare examples, J. Am. Med. Inform. Assoc. 26 (5) (2019) 462–478, https://doi.org/10.1093/jamia/ocy185.

[6] L. Bell, W.J. Buchanan, J. Cameron, O. Lo, Applications of blockchain within healthcare, in: 2020 Blockchain in Healthcare Today™, 2020, https://doi.org/10.30953/bhty.v1.8. ISSN 2573-8240 online.

[7] A. Azaria, A. Ekblaw, T. Vieira, A. Lippman, MedRec: Using Blockchain for Medical Data Access and Permission Management, in: 2nd International Conference on Open and Big Data, 2016, pp. 25–30.

[8] A. Shahnaz, U. Qamar, A. Khalid, Using Blockchain for electronic health records, IEEE Access 7 (2019) 147782–147795, https://doi.org/10.1109/ACCESS.2019.2946373.

[9] S. Salam, B. Faith, P.P. Martín, B. Ramalingam, The contribution of digital technologies to service delivery: an evidence review, 2017, https://doi.org/10.13140/RG.2.2.28618.16329.

[10] M. Mettler, Blockchain technology in healthcare: The revolution starts here, in: 2016 IEEE 18th International Conference on e-Health Networking, Applications and Services (Healthcom), 2016, pp. 1–3, https://doi.org/10.1109/HealthCom.2016.7749510.

[11] H.S. Chen, J.T. Jarrell, K.A. Carpenter, D.S. Cohen, X. Huang, Blockchain in healthcare: a patient-centered model, Biomed. J. Scient. Tech. Res. 20 (3) (2019) 15017–15022.

[12] T. Ahram, A. Sargolzaei, S. Sargolzaei, J. Daniels, B.A. Amaba, Blockchain technology innovations, in: 2017 IEEE Technology & Engineering Management Conference (TEMSCON), 2017, pp. 137–141.

[13] T. Nugent, D. Upton, M. Cimpoesu, Improving data transparency in clinical trials using blockchain smart contracts, F1000 Research 5 (2016) 2541, https://doi.org/10.12688/f1000research.9756.1.

[14] P. Mamoshina, L. Ojomoko, Y. Yanovich, A. Ostrovski, A. Botezatu, P. Prikhodko, E. Izumchenko, A. Aliper, K. Romantsov, A. Zhebrak, I. Ogu, A. Zhavoronkov, Converging blockchain and next-generation artificial intelligence technologies to decentralize and accelerate biomedical research and healthcare, Oncotarget 9 (2018) 5665–5690, https://doi.org/10.18632/oncotarget.22345.

[15] A. Sharma, S. Bahl, A.K. Bagha, M. Javaid, D.K. Shukla, A. Haleem, Blockchain technology and its applications to combat COVID-19 pandemic (published online ahead of print 2020 Oct 22), Res. Biomed. Eng. (2020) 1–8, https://doi.org/10.1007/s42600-020-00106-3.

[16] ZIGURAT, Innovation and technology business school. Blockchain in healthcare: the case of coronavirus, 2020, Available from: https://www.e-zigurat.com/innovation-school/blog/blockchain-in-healthcare/.

Artificial intelligence and blockchain: Implementation perspectives for healthcare beyond 5G

Ananya Ghosh[a], Indranil Sarkar[b], Mrittika Dey[c], and Ahona Ghosh[d]
[a]Department of Computer Science and Engineering, University of Calcutta, Kolkata, India, [b]Department of Computational Science, Brainware University, Kolkata, India, [c]Department of Web and Data Science, The University of Koblenz and Landau, Mainz, Germany, [d]Department of Computer Science and Engineering, Maulana Abul Kalam Azad University of Technology, West Bengal, Kolkata, West Bengal, India

1 Introduction

In today's world, among some trending technologies, arguably blockchain has the widest spread. The Internet has affected all big industries the same way blockchain is affecting the industrial field. Due to its complex yet distributive nature, this innovative technology has been broadly adopted in a variety of fields. From its creation, blockchain has revolutionized communication, safe transaction, transparency, trust between strangers and organizations, and privacy. Now when we talk about blockchain we automatically talk about Bitcoin. Bitcoin is nothing but digital currency and the technology behind creating this cryptocurrency is blockchain. Blockchain can be highly cost-effective as it does not need any centralized authority to govern and it also provides high security with the help of asymmetric cryptography. Another driving force in the world of innovation is artificial intelligence (AI). AI permits an instrument to simulate cognitive skills to learn, reason, amend self-correction, etc. Similar to blockchain, AI can also be applied to different sectors and industries. AI technologies are quickly evolving because AI processes the massive generation and production of data much faster. To perform analytics, such data can be utilized by AI applications that use various deep learning and machine learning techniques to quickly produce usable information. However, AI relies on a centralized form of training that risks the possibility of a data modification to some extent, that is, data can be manipulated and hacked. This raises a big question mark on the authenticity of the sources generating the data as these can be highly risky and erroneous. To solve these issues, decentralized AI can steal the spotlight by combining blockchain and AI. Data are stored on the blockchain in a decentralized and distributed way, which provides security without trusting any third parties. Across a huge number of self-reliant agents that can vote, coordinate, participate in later stages of decision making, the decentralized

Blockchain Applications for Healthcare Informatics. https://doi.org/10.1016/B978-0-323-90615-9.00003-7
Copyright © 2022 Elsevier Inc. All rights reserved.

learning-based AI techniques may provide less vulnerability among the results of certain decisions and information sharing. But one of the biggest disadvantages of blockchain is the operating cost. Also, mining nodes in blockchain need an exorbitant amount of energy to be completed. In that case, AI can be helpful as it is already established that AI can be very competent in optimizing energy utilization.

1.1 Motivation

In this subsection, we discuss the motivations behind blockchain and 5G convergence.

(1) To integrate these two, we first have to remember the most important features of both mechanisms. Via its secure distributed ledger, blockchain will provide secure 5G data services. Immutability, decentralization, openness, and privacy are some of the features that make this possible. As a result, the most important features of blockchain in this context are its ability to support encryption and network management, and applications for 5G networks. 5G, on the other hand, applies to the next-generation wireless networks that are designed to offer higher bandwidth, higher data rates, lower latency, vast device connectivity, improved end-user quality of experience (QoE), lower operating costs, and reliable service provisioning. As a result, the benefits of 5G here are its ability to provide quick and high-quality data with the security requirement and networking performance enhancement. The impetus for combining blockchain and 5G stems primarily from blockchain's potential benefits in addressing problems in 5G networks in terms of protection, safety, networking, and service management. 5G is expected to address emerging barriers and open new markets for blockchain 5G-based applications with the aid of creative blockchain designs. Following that, we'll go over the impetus for the integration, which stems from existing 5G problems, and then we'll go over the benefits of blockchain-5G integrations.
(2) Security and privacy challenges in the 5G paradigm: One of the main considerations for 5G and beyond networks has been the protection associated with 5G technologies. Due to its centralized architecture, the current 5G technology infrastructure has not yet solved problems in terms of computing performance, networking, and security [1]. Edge/cloud computing models, for example, currently depend on centralized service systems, such as Amazon Web Services, that expose several security flaws. Indeed, single-point failures are a risk in this configuration, posing a threat to the accessibility of cloud/edge services on demand. However, in 5G networks, network feature virtualization and service function chaining present new security problems. As the end-to-end service purpose chains can use network function virtualizations in a multicloud architecture, data broadcasts may be intercepted by interested cloud units, leading to data leakage scenarios. In addition, in a virtualized environment, tenants frequently share the same cloud organization. In this regard, the attack risk within the cloud could upsurge, jeopardizing service provider transparency and accountability. Virtualization servers execute at virtual machines (VMs) network function virtualizations for providing particular functions for different operating systems such as resource assignment via orchestration rules or virtual machine migration. Communication protection, on the other hand, between the physical machine and orchestrator is a real challenge.

The rapid growth of mobile data traffic as well as rising consumer demands on 5G networks present new security and efficiency challenges. For example, demand for bandwidth-hungry 5G services such as mobile video streaming and big data processing necessitates a proper spectrum resource management plan to escape resource constraints to ensure uninterrupted service. As a result, spectrum sharing is needed between mobile users and mobile network operatives. Spectrum sharing, on the other hand, poses security issues and offers a central point of attack for malicious users in such scenarios [2]. Using certification authorities to deliver certificates for cognitive radios within each cell is one choice. Furthermore, it necessitates a higher level of computing sophistication, which raises spectrum sharing overheads and, as a result, lowers the quality of services (QoS) of the concerned system. Importantly, using such centralized frameworks introduces single-point-of-failure issues if the system fails, which in turn disrupts the complete spectrum sharing framework.

1.2 Contribution

The chapter can be summarized as follows:

(i) A detailed implementation-based analysis of blockchain consensus algorithms applied in the healthcare domain.
(ii) Probable future direction for further research in the area of AI technique-induced blockchain beyond 5G.

The next section describes and analyzes the state of the art in the concerned domain. Existing benchmarks have been compared by their performance evaluation and the drawbacks or limitations have been attempted to find out for getting a direction for future research in this topic. The application areas along with their prospects will be described in Section 3. Implementation perspectives such as the sensors used in the existing literature and the machine learning methods applied are explained in detail in Section 4. Finally, the concluding statements and future scope in this area are presented in Section 5.

2 Literature survey

Blockchain along with the Internet of Things (IoT) and AI have acquired a fair amount of attention from researchers as well as industry persons over the last decade as they are being widely adopted by numerous applications in a smart city. Salah et al. in [3] taxonomically discussed the implementation, types, infrastructure, and consensus of blockchain in decentralized applications of AI. Different research challenges such as security, privacy, trust, consensus protocol, interoperability, and scalability exist here that should be addressed in the near future for a better understanding of the problems in the existing literature. Machine learning as well as deep learning methods integrated with big data acquired by smart contracts was the area of focus by Sgantzos et al. [4] for analyzing the use cases of AI implementations in blockchain. Various possibilities of intersecting AI with blockchain were discussed by Corea et al. [5]. In the case of blocking malware on an interconnected blockchain platform, an AI-based decision-making algorithm has been introduced to overcome the issues of existing systems and to acquire learning, perception, optimization, reasoning, and so on. Xing et al.

in [6] discussed the infancy of blockchain despite its efficiency and effectiveness in various areas. A bug-free smart contract has been attempted to deliver with the use of AI techniques by Xing et al., using which, not only the start ups, but also older companies can benefit. In this way, in addition to start-ups, older companies also utilize the benefits of blockchain [7].

The roles of blockchain and AI in the evolution of cloud computing, an emerging paradigm allowing metered and on-demand access to resources for worldwide applications, were discussed in [8]. Future systems in smart cities such as automated vehicles, microgrids, etc., can benefit from this paradigm when it is integrated with blockchain [9,10]. Security in robotic systems, the organization and regulation of these systems, and pledges that machines will act inside some specific moral and ethical restrictions [11] are mainly the issues that robotics have to deal with where the proper use of blockchain may solve these problems. Blockchain was initially introduced for cryptographic currency transactions, but being powerful, it allows data decentralization and homogeneous registries among every peer [12]. Blockchain is also useful in the data-sharing system where separation among different mobile networks becomes a barrier in communication. Zhang et al. proposed a system combining fine-grained data access regulation [13]. However, the system has been analyzed only from a technical perspective, so economic analysis should be done to make it adoptable by companies, which is more challenging [14]. Transfer learning is a deep learning tool that achieves successful outcomes in healthcare data transforming, biomarker development, and drug discovery [15]. A structured and systematic review [16] of security issues in existing blockchain and AI-empowered energy-efficient systems was presented in [17], and a solution taxonomy was developed. The challenges of AI and blockchain-induced energy cloud management systems include the lack of a proper selection of suitable consensus techniques, professional experience and expertise, and proper methods for creating consensus, scalability, and sustainability [18]. The probable techniques applied to design smart contracts for achieving Blockchain 2.0 involving decentralized autonomous organizations and smart asset goals were discussed in [19]. These can be assisted by various AI techniques for a better range of possibilities [20] in the fourth industrial development [21]. The role of blockchain for healthcare using the beyond 5G network is summarized in Table 1, where the shortcomings found in the existing literature have been highlighted and are to be explored in near future.

3 Application domains

The different areas where integrated AI and blockchain have been used are described below.

3.1 Personalization and privacy in healthcare

In a blockchain-based system, security is incorporated by installing applications such as data encryption and/or a smart contract system. Potential threat monitoring is done by two mechanisms, an intrusion detection system and an intrusion protection system,

Table 1 Comparative analysis of blockchain-embedded healthcare applications using beyond 5G.

References	Objective	Method used	Outcome	Shortcomings found (if any)
[22]	Study of a joint radio resource allocation algorithm according to LDD	Dual-band mmWave network created on CDSA, providing a new dimension to spectrum heterogeneity	– Comparison with maxRx, DSA, and JPRA algorithms – Analysis of interaction among use of unlicensed and licensed mmWave properties – Analysis of achieving efficient utilization of licensed and unlicensed mmWave resources by dynamic spectrum	– No employment of DBS switching mechanism for analyzing the network performance according to the traffic patterns
[23]	To address resource allocation challenges such as dispersion, heterogeneity, and uncertainty of resources	Identification and analysis of cloud workloads and design patterns using K-Means clustering	Resource scheduling based on different scheduling parameters	– No extraction and storage of context information such as node position for smooth coordination
[24]	Energy efficiency-based case study of blockchain framework for AI-enabled 5G	Complete intelligence and protected data analytics architecture for 5G systems converging AI and blockchain	20% less energy consumption at the radio access network level	– No assurance of integrity and security of permanent and nonmodifiable smart contracts used in AI applications – User privacy issue in public blockchain and restriction in data generation in private blockchain

Continued

Table 1 Continued

References	Objective	Method used	Outcome	Shortcomings found (if any)
[25]	Analysis of blockchain slice leasing ledger concept for future factory	– Network slice trading in blockchain – Slice orchestration by smart contract from slice broker	– Reduced service creation time – Enabled industrial apparatus autonomously – Acquired the slice required dynamically for more effective processes	– No comparative study with other multitenant, multiservice, context-aware use cases – No consideration of applicability checking for real-life collaborative regulations and business models
[1]	– To enable flexible and secure resource sharing – To increase system utility	Blockchain-empowered content caching problem using deep reinforcement learning	Four blockchain-induced resource management schemes, that is, computation offloading, V2V energy trading, D2D caching, and spectrum sharing have been presented	Selection of learning rate based on the optimization mode and circumstances state
[26]	Network slicing for 5G with blockchain and user equipment state-based assignment approach	Blockchain-based latency aware functionalities for security, transparency, and efficiency in resource management	Network resource efficiency is achieved using performance parameters, that is, handover ratio in the concerned area and user equipment blocking	No machine learning architecture-based modeling of user equipment density aware intelligent network slice handling system

in several applicative domains. To make the intrusion detection system even better, an approach is taken called swarm intelligence. In cryptography, AI applications are vast and as in a blockchain-based system, data encryption plays a big part in ensuring a stakeholder's privacy by hiding or encrypting sensitive or private data. The role of AI is to make a system with blockchain more flexible by creating tougher ciphers to crack. Hash function optimization has played its role to preserve personalized data. On the other hand, several other self-reliant intelligent algorithms have been used to search for solutions to the problems at hand such as secret keys, depending on the environment. A real-world example is a popular blockchain-based system, that is, Bitcoin currency's use of an elliptic curve depending on the creation of a public or private code or key (Fig. 1).

3.2 Autonomic computing

There are so many popular applications of AI that are capturing the interest of the world. Eventually, one of them will perform autonomous operations, where some small computer programs called intelligent agents recognize their part of the environment, save the internal states, and consequently carry out specific actions [27]. Modern computing machines require immense heterogeneity handling across all verticals, such as certain devices, data sources, storage systems, data processors, and application interfaces for autonomous operations. Along with heterogeneity handling, the large use of multiagent systems also facilitates intralayer and interlayer functionality across the systems [28]. On the other hand, the contribution of blockchain architecture is the incorporation of operational decentralization and keeping track of communications between data, devices, users, applications, and systems, resulting in the full decentralization of systems and autonomy.

3.3 Strategizing

AI systems and applications execute planning strategies to solve complex problems in new environments by teaming up with other systems and applications. Different strategies turn out to be pretty valuable, keeping in mind the efficiency of an operation plus the flexibility of AI systems and applications to reach predefined goals, by considering present input state and implementing diverse logic or protocol-based algorithms [29]. At present, centralized planning is a complex and lengthy task; hence, the requirement of comparatively more robust strategies that preserve permanent footprints and original history is fulfilled by blockchain-based AI strategies. Moreover, to devise unchangeable yet critical plans in some occasions and mission-critical systems, blockchain proves to be very useful.

3.4 Optimization

A major characteristic of AI-based systems and applications is selecting the optimal solutions among all potential solutions, that is, a set of bests among all [30]. Modern AI systems and applications venture to a wide range of domains, including pervasive

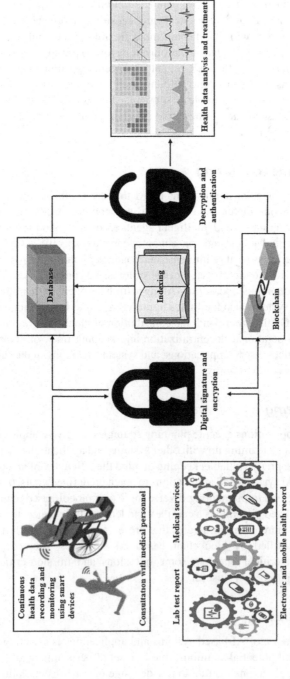

Fig. 1 Application of blockchain in privacy and personalization in healthcare.

environments (e.g., IoT systems for smart homes) [31]; geographically clustered systems (e.g., LAN, WAN, etc.); limited resource settings (e.g., mobile systems/devices); and massively parallel distributed yet centralized systems (e.g., cloud computing systems) [32]. Depending on the goals at the system and application layers, the optimal set of plans works out in unconstrained or constrained environments [33]. These plans smooth the progress of finding optimal solutions, such as choosing the most appropriate dataset in pervasive and ubiquitous environments, picking the best cloud or edge servers for processing data and applications, and facilitating data management that is resource-efficient in distributed environments on a large scale. Present optimal strategies are done using centralized management to accomplish application-wide/system-wide optimization targets that produce off the point and irrelevant data, that is, unclean data processing and poorer application/system performance [34]. In contrast, decentralized strategies, based on blockchain, give new openings to research works and provide development prospects. For this kind of optimization, systems perform better by processing relevant and clean data, especially across those systems and applications, where several strategies with diverse optimization goals are run in parallel.

3.5   Knowledge discovery and handling

Nowadays, huge amounts of data are handled by AI applications, which need to hold up such centralized systems that process big data. The discovery of centralized knowledge along with proper information handling profits the scope of machine intelligence. On the other hand, for some particular groups of users, machines, and systems, the applications facilitate personalized knowledge patterns [35]. Now, the process of knowledge discovery has been made decentralized; this decentralized managing of information is for the visualization of personalized knowledge patterns, judging by the demands of every stakeholder in this arrangement. Moreover, safe and secure tracking of information transmission is what blockchain can exploit between all stakeholders in intelligent environments.

3.6   Perception

Using artificial machine intelligence, multiple bots and agents constantly gather data, interpret them, choose the selective ones, and eventually arrange them using ambient intelligence; this ends up as a collection of monolithic data [36]. This collection of data can be analyzed differently by some decentralized perception tactics. One of these can be implemented using blockchain, which can map out perception routes and securely transport data without any unintended modification during storage, making all these works a lot easier in the process. As an AI system or application does not require collecting data streams to achieve highly qualified and successful perceptions repetitively, the concept of decentralized perception yields a positive response. Finally, blockchain should not store anything more than the successful perception footprints to maintain consistency and its characteristic of permanency.

3.7 Learning

The core idea to create AI is to make machines learn from datasets, so the learning algorithms are the reason behind intelligent automation and improvisation of knowledge with time. These algorithms can be classified based on several parameters. Supervised learning, unsupervised learning, regression, classification, deep learning, ensemble, reinforcement, frequent pattern mining, and transfer are all kinds of learning algorithms. Traditionally, the global intelligence is accomplished by training a system to predict accurately and launched centrally. But to achieve high distribution and autonomy during the training process, decentralized learning models come into the play which stands totally in a synchronized way but applies intelligence across every dimension of AI environment [37,38]. Apart from all these things, through maintenance of some input dataset's original features, a high level of security and immutability of learning models is protected by blockchain. But again, considering the permanency of smart contracts and data encryption, proper training and testing of learning models should be done before deploying on top of the blockchain.

3.8 Reasoning

When it comes to developing inductive or deductive reasoning policies to arrive at some conclusion, logic programming plays a vital role in the AI domain. Now, the main concern becomes when blockchain-based decentralized AI is our main implementing factor, but centralized reasoning is the traditional guide to generalize global behavior among all components of the AI-based systems [39]. Resolving this problem can be done by accelerating the progress of custom-made reasoning strategies that may execute better throughout perception, learning, and model employment by the prediction of blockchain-based distributed reasoning. Moreover, the availability of the reasoning processes, which cannot be forgotten, is guaranteed by smart contract-based distributed decentralized reasoning; this might result in the potential implementation of the same type of strategies later on.

4 Implementation perspectives

Blockchain offers immutability (no change is admissible) and disintermediation (no requirement of third-party verification due to the assurance of trust). These features make it disruptive, which is why the prospects are very high for this technology [40,41]. Different implementation aspects of blockchain technologies are described below.

4.1 Types of blockchain applied in AI applications for a smart city

Mainly, there are two categories of blockchain technology for implementation in AI applications: permission-less blockchain that is open to all users via the Internet and permission-required blockchain, where only allowed users can contact the blockchain platform in cloud-based, private, or consortium settings.

4.1.1   Public blockchain

A no-restriction environment where a customer can download and update the blockchain code on his/her device and use it just the way he/she wants to is called a public blockchain [8,42]. Additionally, public blockchains can be accessed with no difficulty, whereas even reading and writing access are given to every participant on that network. Because of this openness, user identity and information on his/her transactions on public blockchains are handled through anonymous and pseudonymous data to ensure privacy. In addition, some complex protocols along with some consensus methods are used by public blockchains for security purposes. Here, for each public blockchain, asset and data transfer are completed using value pointers or cryptocurrencies, which are nothing but a form of local tokens. These blockchains are widely accepted because of their mass honest openness and decentralization. However, the customers/or validators of the system remain undisclosed, making this platform vulnerable to malicious security attacks that can lead to important data theft or missing values. Agreement of at least 51% of validators is needed and complicated math is used to crack the security codes; this end up consuming large amounts of energy for public blockchaining. Moreover, if the attackers manage to get control of 51% of validators on the network, they are likely to exploit this loophole. Another pitfall of the public blockchain is that the transactional procedure response time is comparatively longer than private and consortium blockchains.

In a real-world scenario, 10 minutes or more is the approval time taken on a public blockchain for a transaction, but that mainly matters on some factors such as the time complexity of the deployed consensus algorithms or how many participants a network has. An overview of a public blockchain is depicted in Fig. 2.

4.1.2   Private blockchain

Usually, a single organization manages a private blockchain. Compared to public ones, a private blockchain is intended to be a system where all participants are preapproved for read/write operations, that is, the system is permissioned, and the participants over a network are always known to each other within their circle [43]. For the preapproval of members on a particular network and this recognized identification of them, the mathematical computations performed in private blockchains are less complicated compared to their public counterparts; hence, they also run faster when it comes to transaction validation in the permissioned system. Plus, all types of native values, data, and assets within the network can be transferred by private blockchains. So, transferring assets and transaction approvals are carried out by either voting or multiple-party consensus algorithms, which cause lower energy consumption than public blockchains and make faster transactions. In a real-world scenario, in the case of private blockchains, transaction approval time generally is less than a second. An overview is shown in Fig. 3.

4.1.3   Federated blockchain

A federated blockchain, also known as a consortium blockchain, is managed by a group of associations. Grouping is usually done by considering the common interests of the contributing associations [44]. Different types of federated blockchains are

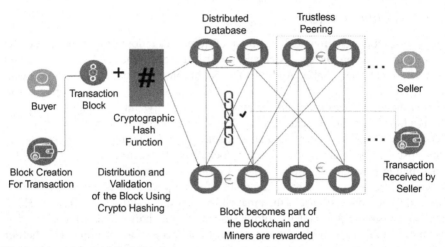

Fig. 2 Overview of public blockchain.

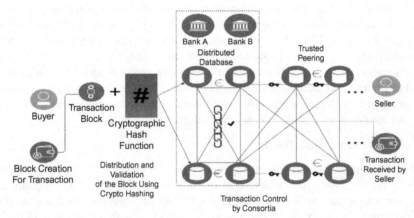

Fig. 3 Overview of private blockchain.

offered by different clusters such as governmental organizations, banks, or private blockchain corporations. Similar to a private blockchain, a federated blockchain functions like a permissioned system, although access is restricted to a few participants of a network who can do both read/write operations. This is unlike the private counterpart, where all participants of a network have read/write access. In this case, data can be read by every member of a particular network of the blockchain, but only some trusted and sanctioned participants on the blockchain have access to writing data. Also, for preapproval of members on a particular network and this recognized identification of them, a federated or consortium blockchain is relatively faster than a public blockchain. Again, a consortium blockchain consumes less energy than a public one, as multiparty approval or voting-dependent consensus algorithms are executed. In an ideal test case scenario, the approval time of a transaction on a consortium blockchain is 1 second.

4.1.4   Blockchain as a service

Due to wide acceptance by large enterprises and governments, cloud service providers are looking forward to blockchain technologies. For the development and testing of blockchain-based systems, IBM, Amazon, Microsoft and so many other popular cloud vendors are activating their environments for their customers [45,46]. Both private and consortium blockchain companies are expected to benefit by the increasing acceptance of blockchain as a service (BaaS) at a rapid rate. Adding values by developing applications, testing, and eventually deploying computational infrastructure, consideration of underlying network, and storage continue to be their main goal. Apart from the modern cross-industry private-public consortia, the enabling of BaaS also takes part in influencing new industry openings and customer-business interactive models. For writing smart contracts, single-click stipulations of BaaS services are also given to developers. As an excess amount of cloud services are already offered to the main cloud vendors for AI applications, a new window of opportunity is opening in support of developers along with BaaS incorporation with AI.

4.2   The infrastructure required in AI implementation

Conventional blockchain implementation was decentralized using two types of data structures: hashing and linked list. Queuing information models and graph theory-based nonlinear infrastructures are promising to handle big data and accommodate real-time application needs.

4.2.1   Linear infrastructure

The linear infrastructure of blockchain architecture means a single chained blockchain expanding on a linear path where at the chain's end, appending of new blocks is done. At the beginning, decentralized organizations used to do operations on a single chain, but this kind of system had several drawbacks. These single chains used to mature to a slower extent; as a result, decentralized application real-time performance was hampered [8,42]. Moreover, for every industrial state of affairs, different singular chains are necessary, so information value plus asset exchange on several chains is highly unlikely. For single job AI applications doing operations such as searching, learning, optimizing, or autonomous working, single chained blockchains might prove to be useful in homogeneous environments. Blockchains based on a single chain can have more use when some log of system performance needs to be stocked up enduringly, instead of AI application execution for only smart contracts. The successful exploration tracks of isolated industrial robots are another good example in this context. Since the AI applications operate in unrestrained settings, hence the entire AI application components are not a reasonable option on the blockchain.

4.2.2   Nonlinear infrastructure

Traditionally, in the multiple chain architectures, where blockchain topology is used as main-side chains, parallel chains, and parent-child chains, there nonlinear blockchains are put into practice [47]. From miscellaneous business settings, cross-chain value transfers, and being scalable in real-time performance, multichain architectures maintain all these things properly. Here, one or a few chains, serving as the main or parent chain, maintain information about other chains. A similar type of operation is observed in side and child chains, although the operations of side chains can be completely independent of the main chain. In child chains, the business settings are strongly coupled with parent chains. In parallel chains, even from the name, it is evident that the operations are independent of other chains. An approach called pegging is a two-way peg process to execute bidirectional value transportation at a constant swapping rate in the chains involved. Between different chains, transferring of value is executed using pegging. By local tokens or coins within a blockchain system, each exchange value is characterized. In AI, several interlinked or independent AI assignment executions in decentralized applications are made easy by nonlinear blockchains. Additionally, the flexible characteristics permit the execution of AI applications in both developing and deploying states simultaneously. In production settings, components based on AI are employed on the parent chain. Mostly on side chains or test nets, training and testing are implemented. Moreover, nonlinear blockchains benefit up-and-coming applications such as those using adaptive learning strategies and reinforcement where continuous updating of the performance of learning models by retraining them with every iteration is a must for the main applications. For this scenario, learning models are deployed on main chains but developed on side chains.

4.3 Consensus protocols in AI implementation

Some widely used protocols for consensus in implementing AI at the blockchain are described in Fig. 4. Some other protocols that are relatively new or not that widely accepted can be studied by interested readers, including proof of retrievability (PoR), proof of ownership (PoO), proof of exercise (PoE), proof of luck (PoL), etc.

4.3.1 Proof of activity

This is a mixture of proof of work and proof of stake as at the beginning, it works on empty blockchain as proof of work. After solving 51% attack issues, it solves complex mathematical problems for which the validators receive different awards, resulting in increasing the stake as well. Proof of stake then gets activated and applied to validators who have an acceptable stake in the blockchain; this makes the process more effective, secured, and efficient. The algorithm for proof of activity works as shown in Fig. 5.

4.3.2 Proof of burn

Validators get accepted by proof of burn only when they employ coins to public, invalid, and verifiable addresses. After burning the coins, users get permission to create blocks while also getting rewarded. Coin burning results in a decrease in the number of coins in the system, which gradually increases the coin value, helps balance the number of coins, and utilizes the unsold coins. Proof of burn can be useful in giving incentives to users for maintaining the underlying decisions. The workflow diagram is shown in Fig. 6.

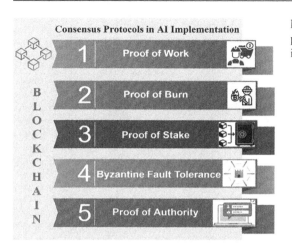

Fig. 4 Blockchain consensus protocols used in artificial intelligence applications.

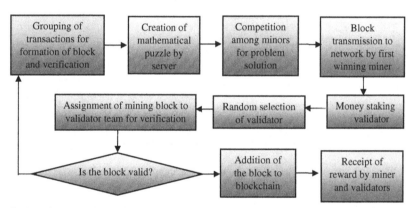

Fig. 5 Workflow diagram of proof of activity consensus.

4.3.3 Proof of work

It's the most fundamental and popular consensus protocol used by Ethereum and Bitcoin for validating transactions initiated by 51% of the total participating nodes after joining the network. As the validating nodes are mostly anonymous and huge in quantity, the blocks get mined and the hash code gets broken for reading the transaction. The successful one conveys the solution on the network to get added to the system. Proof of work (PoW) is appropriate mostly in a situation when energy consumption is high and when there is a chance of delay in approving transactions. But it results in a less secured system, as 51% of attack is compromised by PoW. The algorithm for PoW works as shown in Fig. 7.

4.3.4 Proof of stake

The big stakeholders following the proof of stake (PoS) protocol get declared as the authority to create new blocks in the system. The categories of validator include delegate validator, random validator, validators keeping coins for a long duration, and

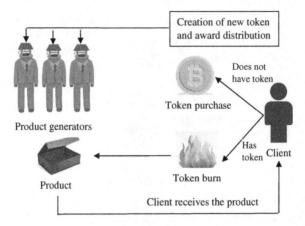

Fig. 6 Workflow diagram of proof of burn consensus.

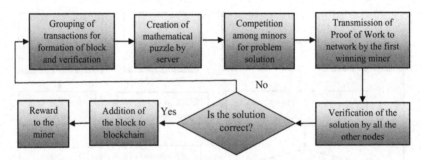

Fig. 7 The working mechanism of the proof of work consensus algorithm.

validators performing frequent transactions. Based on these categories, stakeholders get selected by PoS, which in turn gets energy-efficient and secured when compared to PoW. The working mechanism of PoS is shown in Fig. 8.

4.3.5 Byzantine fault tolerance

This is a process based on majority voting that rules the suspicious nodes in the network out of validations as they misguide other nodes and corrupt data directly/indirectly. The implementation of the different protocols of Byzantine fault tolerance is a little tough as it enforces digital signatures and limits communication between nodes. But once it is implemented successfully on time, it becomes very useful and handy for AI applications from a smart city perspective [48]. The algorithm for Byzantine fault tolerance works as shown in Fig. 9.

4.3.6 Proof of importance

The rank of a node depends on the number of validations it has been approved in. Nodes are ranked according to their validator's frequencies. Proof of importance (PoI) decides a threshold empirically that should be satisfied by the nodes to get

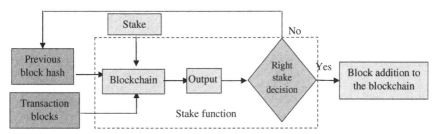

Fig. 8 The working mechanism of the proof of stake consensus algorithm.

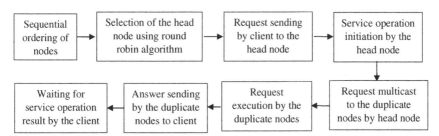

Fig. 9 Workflow diagram of Byzantine fault tolerance.

validated and maximum trust between them is assured by the PoI protocol as they are selected by their past successful validations. In consortium and private networks, some conflicts may arise between the stakeholders as important stakeholders get a chance to monopolize the market. The workflow of the PoI consensus algorithm is shown in Fig. 10.

4.3.7 Proof of authority

The energy consumption issue faced by proof of work gets resolved by proof of authority as it declares some specific nodes as the authority to create a consensus depending on the majority of votes. Proof of authority is energy-efficient and causes minimum delay; it is more appropriate for private networks. The security threats to the nodes are always high as the security attack can be performed on validator nodes, resulting in gradually becoming the source of attack in the network.

5 Blockchain beyond 5G for healthcare

Not only can next-generation networks offer exceptionally high data speeds and low latency, but they also promise ubiquity and a huge IoT. Today, compressed network positioning is a very important technique for meeting 5G cellular system's capability and accessibility demands [22]. The previous generations of wireless mobile communications are 2G, 3G, and 4G. Faster data, less latency, less energy consumption, efficient cost, increased system volume, and large concurrent node connectivity are all anticipated with 5G [23]. The primary goal of 5G networks is to serve applications with a high device density. Enhanced mobile broadband communications,

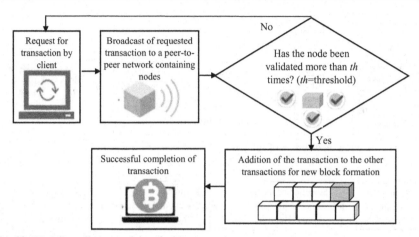

Fig. 10 Workflow diagram of proof of importance consensus.

ultrareliable low-latency communications (URLLC), and massive machine-type communications (mMTC) are the terms that come to mind in this regard [24]. 5G would revolutionize network and networking infrastructure by enabling ultrahigh-speed data transfer up to 100 times faster than current 4G networks [25].

Edge computing, as a branch of cloud computing, moves application hosting from centralized data centers to the network edge, bringing users and data produced by applications closer together [25]. Edge computing is seen as one of the most important enablers of 5G's challenging key performance indicators (KPIs), such as improved mobile broadband, low latency, and massive convergence. The growing number of mission-critical tasks in emerging networks, combined with the number of computation-intensive applications in the IoT era [1,26], is a major bottleneck in the architecture of the network. Mobile edge computing (MEC) is a capable approach to improve mobile user computation capabilities and comprehend low-latency infrastructures to address massive computing demands and shortage of available resources [49] at the mobile device. At the network's edge, there's a cloud-like MEC server as well as an access point (AP) [2]. The probable system architecture of integrated beyond 5G and blockchain-based smart telemedicine is shown in Fig. 11.

The benefit of MEC is that it allows resource-constrained mobile handlers to offload tasks for distant implementation at a more efficient MEC server in their vicinity, resulting in increased computing ability and lower latency [50]. The introduction of 5G and cloud storage would increase network operator capability, functionality, and flexibility, allowing them to provide a wider variety of services. Thanks to fast data speed and low latency promises, 5G and AI-based data analytics can handle vast amounts of data from a large number of sensors in industrial IoT use cases cost-effectively. To deliver encrypted communication, 5G networks would need to use blockchain technology.

Trends and Open Challenges: Readers interested in learning more can further explore 5G and beyond by conducting an extensive literature survey. The open challenges can be summarized as follows:

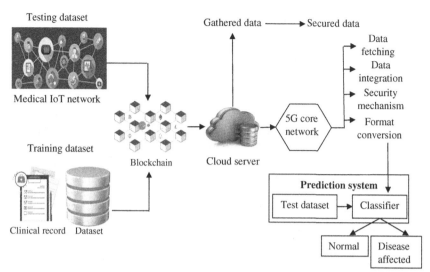

Fig. 11 Integrated beyond 5G and blockchain-based smart telemedicine framework.

- The rising area of mission-critical applications in emergent 5G networks, combined with the number of computation-intensive requests of the IoT age, is a major holdup in implementing real-time frameworks.
- Data analytics on vast amounts of data obtained from a high number of sensors in the industrial IoT use cases may be handled cost-effectively by using 5G-powered AI-based approaches.

6 Benefits and challenges of AI and blockchain convergence

Blockchain is becoming more popular as a safe way to transmit data among organizations. The technology is being utilized to conduct medical license audit reports, identify and track medications, and understand patient health outcomes. Bhattacharya et al. projected a deep learning framework integrated with blockchain [51] to collect and monitor electronic health records. This has been assessed with performance metrics including security, throughput, and latency to obtain an improved outcome. Blockchain-based healthcare solutions for Industry 4.0 can result in automatic data collection and verification techniques as well as correct and aggregated data from a variety of safe, tamper-resistant, and immutable sources with a lesser chance of cybercrime [52,53]. However, challenges in integrating blockchain with AI tools in healthcare applications may include:

- Ethical issues in placing sensitive clinical data to the immutable blockchain may arise, given that no completely secure system exists in the world.
- A so-called 51% attack, in which a fraudulent person gains majority control, might also make blockchain vulnerable.

7 Case study based on a recent scenario

Studies have suggested that almost 55% of all healthcare sectors will integrate blockchain by 2025. Global expenditure in healthcare in 2040 is expected to reach $18 trillion [54]. In COVID-19-safe clinical practice, blockchain plays a critical role. The integration of blockchain and AI capabilities helps to quickly detect and arrange treatment toward COVID-19 sufferers as well as contribute to the formulation of clinical guidelines for similar epidemics in the future. Data collected by pediatricians, primary care physicians, hospitals, clinical laboratories, and additional foundations are shared via blockchain technology while preserving security and privacy. AI solutions are used to analyze data. This paradigm is useful for risk management as well as for promoting research into appropriate therapies and the creation of novel pharmaceuticals. According to worldwide surveys conducted from 2009 to 2017, 176 million enduring archives have been exposed to data breaches. Table 2 summarizes some of the industries applying blockchain in their healthcare frameworks from where it is obvious that blockchain is a trustworthy solution to AI-based systems employed in the recent pandemic. Fig. 12 gives an insight into blockchain-based healthcare models being used in recent industries. Our case study highlights some of them as follows:

- Verida, a blockchain-based industry collaborated with CareProtocol, an AI-based company, to create a decentralized health statistics market powered by AI and blockchain [55]. To give hyperpersonalized healthcare references and apply datasets in a clinical study, AI will be combined with blockchain.
- The Atlanta-based Centers for Disease Control and Prevention (CDC) use a real-time blockchain framework to track different epidemics [56].
- To fight the opioid problem, BurstIQ's health wallet mixes big data, blockchain, and AI to store patient data and share the same with healthcare experts [57].
- For neurology, heart and kidney illnesses, and hormone replacement remedies, Vytalyx is developing AI-powered blockchains [58].

8 Conclusion

The role of blockchain in different domains such as healthcare, business, and finance is growing every day, and integration with different aspects of AI makes it more effective in smart city implementation. Though blockchain has been able to find solutions to some security challenges faced by IoT, an analytical study of various recent works in this domain has helped us to find different challenges and limitations of the existing methods. These are to be addressed shortly and can help researchers explore some new research directions. This chapter summarized the existing efforts and discussed the promising future of their integration. AI and blockchain beyond 5G are definitely promising tools in the healthcare domain and future researchers may explore more real-life testbed-oriented implementation perspectives in this domain.

Table 2 Healthcare industries employing blockchain and artificial intelligence tools [59].

Company name	Industry	Location	Benefits
Factom	IT, Enterprise Software	Austin, Texas	Produces tools that contribute to healthcare by the safe storage of digital records on the business's blockchain platform, only accessible by healthcare administrators
Medicalchain	Electronic Health Record and Clinical	London, England	Use of blockchain in maintaining the accuracy of medical records while creating a single source of truth that every healthcare operator can request patient records with a detectable source that preserves the patient's identity and keeps a safe distance from malicious entities
GUARDTIME	Cybersecurity, Blockchain	Irvine, California	Guardtime and Verizon Enterprise Solutions recently partnered to launch a number of platform services based on Guardtime's keyless signature infrastructure (KSI) blockchain

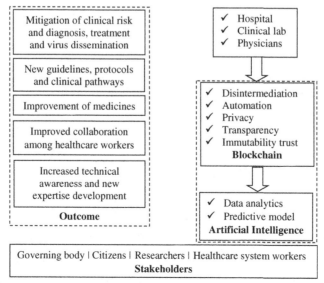

Fig. 12 Insight into the blockchain-based healthcare model inducing artificial intelligence.

References

[1] Y. Dai, D. Xu, S. Maharjan, Z. Chen, Q. He, Y. Zhang, Blockchain and deep reinforcement learning empowered intelligent 5G beyond, IEEE Network 33 (3) (2019) 10–17.
[2] C.-X. Wang, F. Haider, X. Gao, X.-H. You, Y. Yang, D. Yuan, H.M. Aggoune, H. Haas, S. Fletcher, E. Hepsaydir, Cellular architecture and key technologies for 5G wireless communication networks, IEEE Commun. Mag. 52 (2) (2014) 122–130.
[3] K. Salah, M.H.U. Rehman, N. Nizamuddin, A. Al-Fuqaha, Blockchain for AI: review and open research challenges, IEEE Access 7 (2019) 10127–10149.
[4] K. Sgantzos, I. Grigg, Artificial intelligence implementations on the blockchain. Use cases and future applications, Future Internet 11 (8) (2019) 170.
[5] F. Corea, The convergence of AI and blockchain, in: Applied Artificial Intelligence: Where AI Can Be Used in Business, Springer, Cham, 2019, pp. 19–26.
[6] Y.V. Vertakova, T.A. Golovina, A.V. Polyanin, Synergy of blockchain technologies and "big data" in business process management of economic systems, Institute of Scientific Communications Conference, Springer, Cham, 2019, pp. 856–865.
[7] S. Makridakis, A. Polemitis, G. Giaglis, S. Louca, Blockchain: the next breakthrough in the rapid progress of AI, in: Artificial Intelligence-Emerging Trends and Applications, IntechOpen, 2018, pp. 197–219.
[8] G. Wood, Ethereum: a secure decentralised generalised transaction ledger, Ethereum Proj. Yellow Pap. 151 (2014) (2014) 1–32.
[9] M. Swan, Blockchain for business: next-generation enterprise artificial intelligence systems, in: Advances in Computers, vol. 111, Elsevier, 2018, pp. 121–162.
[10] V. Lopes, L.A. Alexandre, An overview of blockchain integration with robotics and artificial intelligence. arXiv preprint arXiv: 1810.00329, 2018.
[11] V. Lopes, L.A. Alexandre, N. Pereira, Controlling robots using artificial intelligence and a consortium blockchain. arXiv preprint arXiv:1903.00660, 2019.
[12] T.N. Dinh, M.T. Thai, AI and blockchain: a disruptive integration, Computer 51 (9) (2018) 48–53.
[13] G. Zhang, T. Li, Y. Li, P. Hui, D. Jin, Blockchain-based data sharing system for ai-powered network operations, J. Commun. Inform. Netw. 3 (3) (2018) 1–8.
[14] J. Chen, K. Duan, R. Zhang, L. Zeng, W. Wang, An AI based super nodes selection algorithm in blockchain networks. arXiv preprint arXiv:1808.00216, 2018.
[15] P. Mamoshina, L. Ojomoko, Y. Yanovich, A. Ostrovski, A. Botezatu, P. Prikhodko, E. Izumchenko, A. Aliper, K. Romantsov, A. Zhebrak, I.O. Ogu, Converging blockchain and next-generation artificial intelligence technologies to decentralize and accelerate biomedical research and healthcare, Oncotarget 9 (5) (2018) 5665.
[16] S.S. Gill, S. Tuli, M. Xu, I. Singh, K.V. Singh, D. Lindsay, S. Tuli, D. Smirnova, M. Singh, U. Jain, H. Pervaiz, Transformative effects of IoT, blockchain and Artificial Intelligence on cloud computing: evolution, vision, trends and open challenges, Internet Things 8 (2019) 100118.
[17] A. Kumari, R. Gupta, S. Tanwar, N. Kumar, Blockchain and AI amalgamation for energy cloud management: challenges, solutions, and future directions, J. Parallel Distrib. Comput. 143 (2020) 148–166.
[18] M. Mylrea, AI enabled blockchain smart contracts: cyber resilient energy infrastructure and IoT, in: 2018 AAAI Spring Symposium Series, 2018.
[19] J.D. Harris, B. Waggoner, Decentralized and collaborative ai on blockchain, in: 2019 IEEE International Conference on Blockchain (Blockchain), IEEE, 2019, pp. 368–375.
[20] T. Marwala, B. Xing, Blockchain and artificial intelligence. arXiv preprint arXiv:1802.04451, 2018.

[21] A. Ekblaw, A. Azaria, J.D. Halamka, A. Lippman, A case study for Blockchain in Healthcare: "Med Rec" prototype for electronic health records and medical research data, in: Proceedings of IEEE Open & Big Data Conference, vol. 13, 2016, p. 13.
[22] R.I. Ansari, H. Pervaiz, S.A. Hassan, C. Chrysostomou, M.A. Imran, S. Mumtaz, R. Tafazolli, A new dimension to spectrum management in IoT empowered 5G networks, IEEE Network 33 (4) (2019) 186–193.
[23] S. Singh, I. Chana, Efficient Cloud Workload Management Framework (Master's Thesis), Thapar University, Patiala, Punjab, India, 2013.
[24] A. El Azzaoui, S.K. Singh, Y. Pan, J.H. Park, Block5gintell: blockchain for ai-enabled 5G networks, IEEE Access 8 (2020) 145918–145935.
[25] J. Backman, S. Yrjölä, K. Valtanen, O. Mämmelä, Blockchain network slice broker in 5G: slice leasing in factory of the future use case, in: 2017 Internet of Things Business Models, Users, and Networks, IEEE, 2017, pp. 1–8.
[26] P. Gorla, V. Chamola, V. Hassija, D. Niyato, Network slicing for 5G with UE state based allocation and blockchain approach, IEEE Network 35 (3) (2020) 184–190.
[27] D. Ye, M. Zhang, A.V. Vasilakos, A survey of self-organization mechanisms in multiagent systems, IEEE Trans. Syst. Man Cybern. Syst. Hum. 47 (3) (2016) 441–461.
[28] Y. Rizk, M. Awad, E.W. Tunstel, Decision making in multiagent systems: a survey, IEEE Trans. Cognit. Dev. Syst. 10 (3) (2018) 514–529.
[29] M.A. Contreras-Cruz, J.J. Lopez-Perez, V. Ayala-Ramirez, Distributed path planning for multi-robot teams based on artificial bee colony, in: 2017 IEEE Congress on Evolutionary Computation (CEC), IEEE, 2017, pp. 541–548.
[30] F. Fioretto, E. Pontelli, W. Yeoh, Distributed constraint optimization problems and applications: a survey, J. Artif. Intell. Res. 61 (2018) 623–698.
[31] J.C. Augusto, Ambient intelligence: the confluence of ubiquitous/pervasive computing and artificial intelligence, in: Intelligent Computing Everywhere, Springer, London, 2007, pp. 213–234.
[32] M.H. ur Rehman, C.S. Liew, T.Y. Wah, M.K. Khan, Towards next-generation heterogeneous mobile data stream mining applications: opportunities, challenges, and future research directions, J. Netw. Comput. Appl. 79 (2017) 1–24.
[33] M.H. ur Rehman, A. Batool, C.S. Liew, Y.W. Teh, Execution models for mobile data analytics, IT Professional 19 (3) (2017) 24–30.
[34] L. Bottou, F.E. Curtis, J. Nocedal, Optimization methods for large-scale machine learning, SIAM Rev. 60 (2) (2018) 223–311.
[35] S.J. van Zelst, B.F. van Dongen, W.M. van der Aalst, Event stream-based process discovery using abstract representations, Knowl. Inf. Syst. 54 (2) (2018) 407–435.
[36] H. Lu, Y. Li, M. Chen, H. Kim, S. Serikawa, Brain intelligence: go beyond artificial intelligence, Mob. Netw. Appl. 23 (2) (2018) 368–375.
[37] A.B. Kurtulmus, K. Daniel, Trustless machine learning contracts; evaluating and exchanging machine learning models on the ethereum blockchain. arXiv preprint arXiv:1802.10185, 2018.
[38] H. Kim, J. Park, M. Bennis, S.L. Kim, On-device federated learning via blockchain and its latency analysis. arXiv preprint arXiv:1808.03949, 2018.
[39] S. Banerjee, P.K. Singh, J. Bajpai, A comparative study on decision-making capability between human and artificial intelligence, in: Nature Inspired Computing, Springer, Singapore, 2018, pp. 203–210.
[40] J. Mattila, The Blockchain phenomenon – the disruptive potential of distributed consensus architectures (No. 38), 2016. ETLA working papers.
[41] R. Adams, G. Parry, P. Godsiff, P. Ward, The future of money and further applications of the blockchain, Strateg. Change 26 (5) (2017) 417–422.

[42] S. Nakamoto, Bitcoin: A Peer-to-Peer Electronic Cash System, Manubot, 2019.

[43] T.T.A. Dinh, J. Wang, G. Chen, R. Liu, B.C. Ooi, K.L. Tan, Blockbench: a framework for analyzing private blockchains, in: Proceedings of the 2017 ACM International Conference on Management of Data, 2017, pp. 1085–1100.

[44] Z. Li, J. Kang, R. Yu, D. Ye, Q. Deng, Y. Zhang, Consortium blockchain for secure energy trading in industrial internet of things, IEEE Trans. Ind. Inform. 14 (8) (2017) 3690–3700.

[45] D. Joshi, IBM, Amazon & Microsoft Are Offering Their Blockchain Technology as a Service, Business Insider, 2017, p. 24.

[46] C. Xu, K. Wang, M. Guo, Intelligent resource management in blockchain-based cloud datacenters, IEEE Cloud Comput. 4 (6) (2017) 50–59.

[47] G.H. Hwang, P.H. Chen, C.H. Lu, C. Chiu, H.C. Lin, A.J. Jheng, Infinite chain: a multi-chain architecture with distributed auditing of sidechains for public blockchains, in: International Conference on Blockchain, Springer, Cham, 2018, pp. 47–60.

[48] A. Ghosh, C.C. Ho, R. Bestak, Secured energy-efficient routing in wireless sensor networks using machine learning algorithm: fundamentals and applications, in: Deep Learning Strategies for Security Enhancement in Wireless Sensor Networks, IGI Global, 2020, pp. 23–41.

[49] S. Kekki, et al., MEC in 5G Networks, ETSI White Paper No. 28, first ed., 2018. ISBN No. 979-10-92620-22-1.

[50] S. Li, et al., Energy-efficient resource allocation for industrial cyber physical IoT systems in 5G era, IEEE Trans. Ind. Inform. 14 (6) (2018) 2618–2628.

[51] S. Tanwar, K. Parekh, R. Evans, Blockchain-based electronic healthcare record system for healthcare 4.0 applications, J. Inform. Secur. Appl. 50 (2019) 1–14.

[52] P. Bhattacharya, S. Tanwar, S. Tyagi, N. Kumar, BINDaaS: blockchain integrated deep-learning as a service in healthcare 4.0 applications, IEEE Trans. Netw. Sci. Eng. 8 (2) (2019) 1–14.

[53] S. Tanwar, Q. Bhatia, P. Patel, A. Kumari, P.K. Singh, W. Hong, Machine learning adoption in blockchain-based smart applications: the challenges, and a way forward, IEEE Access 8 (2020) 474–488, https://doi.org/10.1109/ACCESS.2019.2961372.

[54] E. Gurgu, M. Andronie, M. Andronie, I. Dijmarescu, Does the convergence of the blockchain, the Internet of Things and artificial intelligence changing our lives, education and the known world of the internet?! Some changes and perspectives for the international economy, in: International Conference on Economic Sciences and Business Administration, vol. 5, Spiru Haret University, 2019, pp. 69–88. No. 1.

[55] M. Hanke, F. Hauser, On the effects of stock spam e-mails, J. Financ. Mark. 11 (1) (2008) 57–83.

[56] S.B. Thacker, A.L. Dannenberg, D.H. Hamilton, Epidemic intelligence service of the centers for disease control and prevention: 50 years of training and service in applied epidemiology, Am. J. Epidemiol. 154 (11) (2001) 985–992.

[57] D. Senthilkumar, Cross-industry use of blockchain technology and opportunities for the future: Blockchain technology and aritificial intelligence, in: Cross-Industry Use of Blockchain Technology and Opportunities for the Future, IGI Global, 2020, pp. 64–79.

[58] S. Phansalkar, P. Kamat, S. Ahirrao, A. Pawar, Decentralizing AI applications with block chain, Int. J. Sci. Technol. Res. 8 (9) (2019) 9.

[59] S. Makridakis, K. Christodoulou, Blockchain: current challenges and future prospects/applications, Future Internet 11 (12) (2019) 258.

Combining blockchain and machine learning in healthcare and health informatics: An exploratory study

Swapnil Soner[a], Ratnesh Litoriya[b], and Prateek Pandey[a]
[a]Jaypee University of Engineering & Technology, Guna, Madhya Pradesh, India,
[b]Medi-Caps University, Indore, Madhya Pradesh, India

1 Introduction

1.1 Motivations

A blockchain is a public ledger of transactions associated with a distributed database of systems where different parties are participating. Here, public ledger transactions are verified by consensus algorithms such as proof of work, proof of stake, proof of burn, etc. [1–3]. Due to the distributed database data stored at a local machine, the blockchain helps secure data because of the cryptographic algorithm, that is, sha256. Bitcoin is the digital currency based on blockchain technology, which is a distributed peer-to-peer network. Bitcoin is the most popular cryptocurrency example that uses blockchain technology. Bitcoin is a controversial cryptocurrency because of some government and legal aspects. Government has many disputes over Bitcoin in the financial and nonfinancial sectors. The white paper [4] first explains the Bitcoin peer-to-peer network in the market from where blockchain technology comes under the financial market. Bitcoin is now used in many kinds of financial and nonfinancial sectors such as banks, healthcare, cryptocurrency exchanges, etc.

In 2008, Satoshi [1] published a paper titled "Bitcoin: A Peer-To-Peer Electronic Cash System." This paper suggested a peer-to-peer network of electronic cash that allows electronic payments directly from one party to another party without third-party access. This introduced the Bitcoin concept, which is based on blockchain technology. The advantage of Bitcoin over the previous system is that transactions are speedy, no third party such as a bank is involved in transactions, and low cost. Each transaction is broadcast to every node in the Bitcoin network and recorded in a public ledger after verification. Every single transaction needs to be verified for validity before it is recorded in the general ledger [5] (Fig. 1).

There are four primary categories of blockchain, which do not include traditional databases or distributed ledger technology (DLT) that are often confused with blockchain. Public blockchains are open source that allow anyone to participate as users, miners, developers, or community members. Public blockchains are also

Blockchain Applications for Healthcare Informatics. https://doi.org/10.1016/B978-0-323-90615-9.00014-1
Copyright © 2022 Elsevier Inc. All rights reserved.

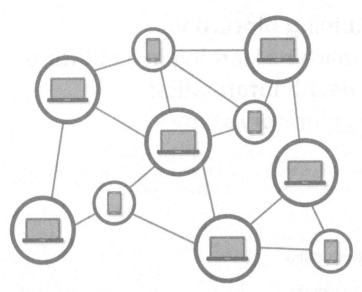

Fig. 1 Blockchain architecture.

designed to be fully decentralized and highly resistant to censorship [6]. In the public blockchain, we are getting incentivized and rewarding participants in the network. Bitcoin and Ethereum are two examples of a public blockchain. A private blockchain is known as a permissioned blockchain, where no participant could be added without permission. A private blockchain is also centralized, but it is more centralized than a public blockchain. Examples of a private blockchain are Hyperledger and Corda. The next type of blockchain is a combination of public and private blockchains known as a hybrid blockchain, which combines the privacy benefits of a permissioned and private blockchain with the security and transparency benefits of a public blockchain [7]. An example of a hybrid blockchain is Dragonchain. When multiple groups are associated with a private blockchain, a new type is introduced, known as a consortium blockchain, which has all the benefits of a private blockchain and could be considered a subcategory of private blockchains. A consortium blockchain is more efficient. An example of a consortium blockchain is a quorum [5].

In Fig. 2, blockchain working will be explained between two parties based on this healthcare system. Suppose node 1 and node 2 exist. The very first process shows that node 1 wants to share information with node 2. The next process represents the transaction block. The block will be broadcast to every node. All other nodes have to approve the transaction. After that, the block will be added in the blockchain and money will be transferred successfully. While approving the different transaction, different types of consensus algorithm is used in other cryptocurrencies. Some basic consensus algorithms are proof of work, proof of burn, proof of stack, proof of authority, etc.

A Merkle tree is used as a blockchain data structure, allowing efficient and secure content verification in a large body of data stored in that blockchain database [8–10].

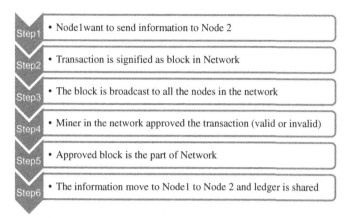

Fig. 2 How blockchain works in the healthcare system.

It is used to verify the consistency and scope of the data. Merkle trees combine hashing pairs until there is only one hash left, which is considered the root hash. It follows the bottom-up approach from hashes of individual transactions (known as transaction IDs) to the root hash (known as the Merkle root). Bitcoin is a cryptocurrency that uses the Merkle tree as a data structure. Here, the SHA-2 cryptographic hash function is used to prove the validity and integrity of the data. Merkle tree in which every node has a hash value, each node's hash is decided by the SHA 3 hash value of its contents. This hash is also used as the key that refers to the node. Ethereum is an example that uses a Merkle tree [11].

The blockchain ensures the data integrity and validity of transaction data using SHA 256 hash algorithm. SHA256 is a simple algorithm where a 256-bit hash is generated. Cryptography plays a vital role in blockchain technology, where a hash function is generated using some cryptographic algorithm. Some basic features of blockchains are given below:

- Scaling capacity
- Better security
- Immutability
- Minting
- Faster settlement
- Decentralized system

A fork is a process where a blockchain diverges into two potential paths forward or a change in protocol, that is, a place where two or more blockchains diverge. Here, different users have to use a standard protocol to maintain the history of the blockchain. Forks are responsible for adding new features to a blockchain. So, some of the forking techniques are used for adding a new element into the blockchain. Soft fork and hard fork are two types of fork techniques. A soft fork is that which changes the protocol by changing software rules. Changes in hardware technology do the hard fork [12] (Fig. 3).

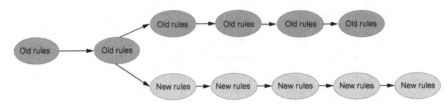

Fig. 3 Fork process of blockchain.

A smart contract is a computer program or computer protocol that is automatically executed and controls the event and action of agreement. Blockchain technology is used to register, verify, and execute smart contracts. Ethereum is a technology that has smart contracts. The purpose of smart contracts is reducing the need for trusted intermediates. For the business perceptive, a smart contact is used. Some early applications that will use the smart contract of Ethereum are e-governance, independent banks, keyless access, crowdfunding, financial derivatives trading, and settlements [13].

Some latest technology is also coming which is associated with blockchain that is Hashgraph and tangle. A hash graph is a data structure that will work for a distributed blockchain. Here is a community of users agreeing on a consensus algorithm to verify the transaction. The two consensus algorithms used for the hash graph are gossip about gossip and virtual voting. Tangle is a system of transactions not gathered in a block, but a directed acyclic graph is used here. DAG is architecture and a mathematical model used to organize, record, store, and verify information. IOTA tangle is a novel cryptocurrency based on the tangle technology for the Internet of Things for industry [14].

1.2 Contributions

The most important thing is the implementation of a systematic blockchain with a smart contract. The system is more flexible with a smart contract and applies so much logic to implement the system smoothly. The healthcare domain is one of those potential research areas where we can improve various healthcare activities. When a blockchain healthcare system with IoT and sensors gives a real-time environment of patients to the doctor, and vice versa, hospital management and patient caretakers also know the entire system's status [15]. Especially for doctors, the machine learning concept will be easy to evaluate and predict details of their patients. So finally, a combination of these three emerging technologies will bring a revolution to the healthcare system with 5G technology. Blockchain's use of 5G technology will give many benefits that are sometimes lacking in implementing various use cases.

1.3 Organization

Section 1 introduces blockchain and its structure. Section 1.2 explains the contribution of blockchain in emerging technologies. Section 1.3 is the organization of sections. Section 2 explains the survey of different research papers with their comparisons. Section 3 presents blockchain, how another technology is helpful, and their details. Section 4 explains the proposed methods of this healthcare system. Section 5 concludes the chapter.

2 Literature survey

Blockchain has made a considerable mark in various domains since its inception. It has proved to be a trust-less technology to execute a number of daily transactions, not only in healthcare but also in diversified domains [16–19].

Casino [20] explains how the blockchain-based application uses multiple domains. The paper explores the current state of blockchain technology and applications based on this technology. With the help of these specific characteristics, we can revolutionize "business as usual" in the practices.

A payment channel is a technique designed for off-chain payments. An off-chain payment means only starting and ending the payment channel of the transaction will be executed by the decentralized note. The transaction will be limited among participants. In this technique, a smart contract will allow a user to have the minimum number of invocations for multiple token transactions. Once the payer and payee initiate the transaction with a specific token amount, the payer sends the continuous micropayments to the payee, deprived of alerting the smart contract. Off-chain will help us to maintain the system in a suitable model.

With Hasselgrena [21], the purpose of the study of this paper is to understand blockchain and areas within the health domain that are potentially highly impacted by blockchain technology. The author explores health information system domains of different publications on knowledge infrastructures, picture archiving and communications systems, automated diagnostic services for patients, administrative systems, population health management systems, and pharma supply chains. The final research plan of this paper is to address the concrete result in the healthcare industry and how the blockchain provides secure and immutable data sharing to data management in a diverse medical workflow.

With Hussien [22], the purpose of the study of this paper is to understand blockchain usability in the healthcare system. The researcher here studies and surveys different blockchain and healthcare-related articles. The initial solution is to increase the transparency and operating efficiency of health. After the initial implementation of this system, we need to improve the security, privacy, and scalability of a blockchain-based application. An electronical health system is now feasible and convenient to its users by providing safety and confidentiality. Still, clinical care systems need to enhance the blockchain healthcare system. All the applications use the blockchain to eliminate the intermediate, and this system is most useful for all the users to improve the system.

McGhin et al. [23] presented applications based on blockchain technology that have a significant challenge in their scalability. When the application, especially Internet of Medical Things devices using this application and no users are increasing, scaling is biggest. When we grow applications, especially healthcare-based systems, a challenge could lead to a computational requirement for the blockchain-based application. If the system faces less computational power, it will increase the data delays and capabilities of any application due to less processing and response time. So, the healthcare-based system also requires a high computational power for their big data and multimedia data. Mobile app development is a popular process by which a mobile application is developed for mobile small handheld devices, such as personal digital assistants, enterprise digital assistants, or mobile phones [24–28]. As part of the development process, mobile user interface (UI) design is also essential in the creation of mobile apps.

The healthcare system still uses Chukwu [29] and the electronic health record (EHR) system, but there are many loopholes. The biggest issue in the current system is that data sharing is not trustworthy. In this system, data storage at the central place may cause hacking, failure, etc. The alternate solution is using blockchain technology; we will achieve a trusty, secure, and decentralized environment. Blockchain nowadays is used fully in nonfinancial applications also. As per the research, 120 medical specialties and subspecialties in the health sector are either online or physically. To maintain this massive data, blockchain is the best option with its available features. As per the author, the central authority concept will use blockchain to provide a more secure system, which is a minor amendment in the architecture in the blockchain. In the end, research is still lacking in blockchain, communication overhead, and scalability, especially in the healthcare system. Blockchain future work also concentrates on cost and performance issues in the nonfinancial sector and where to maintain the heavy data or multimedia data required to transfer or share. Decision-making through data mining and other techniques such as fuzzy logic and various other tools have made it easy to make good and efficient decisions in many fields [30–37].

Jiang et al. [38] advocated for the application of block chaining in the healthcare system; blockchain will benefit from building facilities. Healthcare systems have EHRs and personal health data, which are required to store bulk space and need high bandwidth for computation. The paper also explains the off-chain storage to maintain the distributed database of the EMR chain of hospitals and on-chain verification for both computation and storage capacity. When the healthcare system uses blockchain, it also needs to keep extra security and authority agency authorized certificates to maintain a more secure environment. A node will hold the data backup. The teaching-learning pedagogy is also impacting a lot in studying and applying new technologies [39].

Randall [40], in his paper, illustrates the practices of blockchain used by the US Medicaid program. There are so many difficulties or challenges to adopting such a system. But when the DARPA government agency involves using blockchain to remove the numerous challenges and achieve the goal of the blockchain concept to be use in an interoperable, and flexible, environment. The system that uses blockchain in healthcare will involve lots of innovative approaches and improve the future scope to use blockchain applications (Table 1).

Table 1 Relative comparison tables.

Sr. no.	Author name	Key contribution	Limitation
1	Fran Casinoa and Thomas K. Dasaklis	Classification of different blockchain applications	Scalability and durability are the problems to implementing blockchain for a new application
2	Anton Hasselgrena	Blockchain is helpful in the healthcare system to manage the flow of information	Secure and immutable data for large applications is a problem in the blockchain in the healthcare system
3	H.M. Hussien, S.M. Yasin	To increase the transparency and operating efficiency of health	After the initial implementation of this system, there is a need to improve the security, privacy, and scalability of blockchain-based applications
4	McGhin, T., Choo, K. R., Liu	Mainly focus on authentication of patient's information and integrity, interoperability of records, IoT security	The healthcare-based system requires high computational power for their big data and multimedia data
5	Emeka Chukwu and Lalit Garg	PRISMA framework is used for the systematic work of blockchain in the healthcare system. Also, including the other health-related domains for the betterment of the system	Concentrate on cost and performance issues in the nonfinancial sector and maintain the heavy or multimedia data required to transfer or share
6	S. Jiang, J. Cao, H. Wu, Y. Yang	BlocHIE system gives privacy and authenticity. The help of this system also improves the system throughput	System needs to maintain extra security, so the authority agency authorized certificate to maintain a more secure environment also works on system interoperability
7	David Randall	Blockchain-based applications remove the difficulties and achieve the goal of the blockchain concept in a nonfinancial system such as interoperability, flexibility, and privacy	Deploying the new system will cause the problem of costs and maintenance. Also, we need to work on efficiency and efficacy
8	Prateek Pandey, Ratnesh Litoriya	BFT gives better performance than POW	The blockchain-based system needs to work on scalability and throughput

3   Overview of blockchain technology

3.1   Blockchain

Blockchain is based on a distributed database system for the transaction of crypto-currency. Blockchain uses a public ledger of the transaction, which is based on a distributed environment. When the system is based on a distributed database for the transaction, it is essential to achieve security. Cryptographic algorithms such as SHA 256 and 512 are the most usable concepts in the blockchain system and add new nodes through miners with the help of a consensus algorithm (proof of work, proof of stake). Blockchain is so popular because it solves the problematic and time-consuming process of a centralized system. Blockchain technology with a financial system is also usable in nonfinancial systems to improve the work environment with security. Blockchain uses the hash function and Merkle tree concept to provide the authenticated system (Fig. 4).

3.1.1   Different types of blockchain

Blockchain uses the distributed ledger technology network, a different case that varies by the nature of use by the user. There are three types of blockchains: public blockchain, private blockchains, and consortium blockchains (Table 2).

(a) **Public blockchain**—As per the name, a public blockchain is available publically. Anyone can join and perform a transaction through the mining technique. In this chain, every user or node has a copy of the ledger. In case of any tempering will not be acceptable by the system

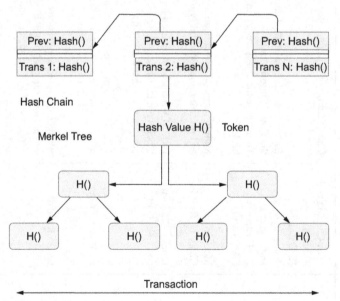

Fig. 4 Blockchain structure.

Table 2 Comparison of different types of blockchains.

Property	Public blockchain	Private blockchain	Consortium blockchain
Participants	Free, anonymous could be malicious	Permissioned Identified and trusted	Permissioned Identified and trusted
Consensus determination	All miners	One organization	Selected set of nodes
Read permission	Public	Public or restricted	Public or restricted
Immutability	Yes	Partial	Partial
Efficiency	Low	High	High
Consensus process	Permissionless	Permissioned	Permissioned

because this public blockchain is more secure and follows all the security rules. Bitcoin and Litecoin cryptocurrency use the public blockchain concept.

(b) **Private blockchain**—The private blockchain is a permissioned blockchain, usually used within any organization. The organization selects members for participation in the network. Compared with a public blockchain, a private blockchain provides less security because it is controlled by enterprises, and permissioned nodes are allowed. Most of this is used in voting and supply chain management systems. Multichain and Hyperledger use the private blockchain concept.

(c) **Consortium blockchain**—A federated blockchain or consortium blockchain is a semi-decentralized type of blockchain. Usually, more than one organization manages the system, and the node exchanges information through mining. The preset nodes control the consensus procedures in a consortium blockchain. Banks and government organizations mostly use the consortium blockchain concept. R3 and Web Foundation use this concept.

3.1.2 Consensus mechanism

Blockchain is a distributed decentralized network with built-in facilities such as immutability, privacy, security, and transparency. It has no central authority, so we have to consider that no need for validation and verification of transactions will provide a secure and verified system. All these facilities are possible only because of a consensus algorithm that has proper verification of nodes before joining the network. Consensus means agreement between all the peer nodes available or wanting to join the distributed environment for a transaction or other work. Use the consensus protocol to achieve reliability in this distributed blockchain network and automatic trust between all the peer nodes. This process continues whenever a system is required for further execution. Many consensus algorithms are available to enter the blockchain such as proof of work, proof of stake, practical Byzantine fault tolerance, proof of capacity, proof of activity, delegated proof of stake, etc. Still, a few are mentioned in Table 3 with a comparison chart that are highly used and give more relevant results [41].

Table 3 Comparison chart of consensus algorithms.

	Proof of work (PoW)	Proof of stake (PoS)	Byzantine fault tolerance (PBFT)
Energy consumption	High	Low	Very low
Transaction per sec	7–30	30–173	100–2500
Transaction fee	High	Low	Very low
Structure	Decentralized	Decentralized	Decentralized
Example	Bitcoin	Neo	Stellar

3.2   Smart contract

Smart contracts work as logic in a blockchain-based system to automatically implement the transactions in the system. A smart contract system will work very efficiently
with the systematic execution of the concept. A smart contract is a self-executing contract with the agreement terms among patients, hospitals, and Mediclaim (medical
claim). The arrangement helps to execute the patient's and hospital terms and conditions with the Mediclaim department as well as the future use of the patient's disease
history through doctors. Hospital management and patient caretakers also know the
status of the entire system. Especially for doctors, the machine learning concept will
be easy to evaluate and predict patient details. So finally, a combination of these three
emerging technologies will bring a revolution in the healthcare system [42].

3.3   Distributed ledger

A distributed ledger means a shared database in the network for all participants. All
nodes maintain the data through which the system will adequately synchronize data
copies [43]. This ledger allows all members to keep data secure, verified, and immutable. This concept highly supports the safe functioning of decentralized digital databases with the help of the cryptography concept. In Fig. 5 (smart contract), all the
nodes or participants have the patient's data, records, hospital bills, prescriptions,
etc. Nobody can tamper with this data, making it secure and immutable. In case of
tampering, the system will acknowledge all the nodes.

3.4   IOT

The Internet of Things (IoT) is used in the healthcare system to support the entire system in a very effective way. IoT sensors are used to monitor patient health-related
issues and report to the system [44–46]. Sensors are used for a wide range of observations or calculations such as pulse rates, oxygen level, sugar level, blood pressure,
body temperature, electrocardiograms, calories, etc. [47]. The hospital staff maintains
the record to show doctors. With the help of this record, doctors provide treatment. But
if the sensors are joined with blockchain, they send all the records to all the stakeholders, which will provide quick monitoring and treatment to hospitalized patients

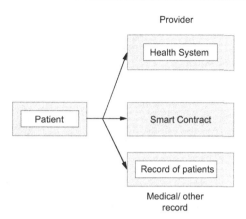

Fig. 5 Smart contracts in the healthcare system.

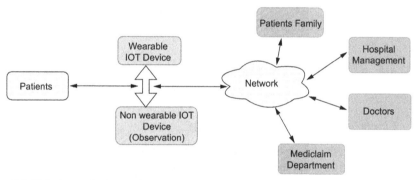

Fig. 6 IoT device and other nodes.

or others. All the prescriptions are also in the form of a ledger with their bill. The combination of all these technologies gives an impressive improvement to the healthcare system. Applying smart contracts in this communication supports the better applicability of the entire architecture. In Fig. 6, a patient's support is hospitalized; observations from wearable and nonwearable devices will be reported to doctors, family members, hospital staff, and in case of medical-claim facilities too.

3.5 Machine learning

Machine learning (ML) with the blockchain, especially in a nonfinancial section such as healthcare, helps reduce the effort and provide efficiency in the system. In a healthcare system, machines with the dataset learn many things and circulate that to all the nodes, which are part of the system. This will allow the doctors and hospital staff to understand the patient's disease predictions. The system collects all data from IoT devices. When blockchain with the smart contract and ML is used, it definitely helps the whole system and give better results and have a significant impact on their

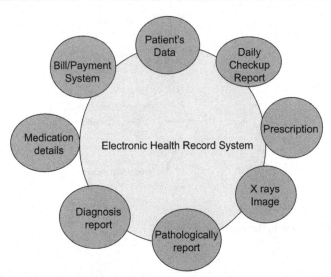

Fig. 7 Electronic health record system.

users. Also, with ML, we can work on energy and resource management with the security of blockchain [48].

3.6 Electronic health record system

An electronic health record (EHR) is a soft-copy record of a patient's medical history, prescriptions, and all the billing records and sanctioned amount by the Mediclaim. It is maintained and updated over time by the administrator of the system. In this, the system has all the records of a patient's disease, treatment, geographical location, tests, reports, etc. With the help of this kind of system, clinical work is very supportive to all the related persons and their observations in an effortless way. When such a system is available to the medical system, it will produce accurate results while providing patient clarity and transparent information that will quickly help doctors (Fig. 7).

4 Proposed work

The proposed model of a healthcare system is based on blockchain technology and using IoT-based sensors to collect patient data for continuous monitoring. These collected data are stored for some analytics purpose and to apply ML algorithms to predict patient treatment. Other stakeholders are also part of the blockchain network node to help maintain and support the EHR system in the blockchain technology. The use of smart contracts in this system will ease the application of all the legal logic or agreements among all active participants of the system (Fig. 8).

The figure explains the entire concept of a healthcare system-based blockchain and applies IoT and ML. The system is understood in the following process.

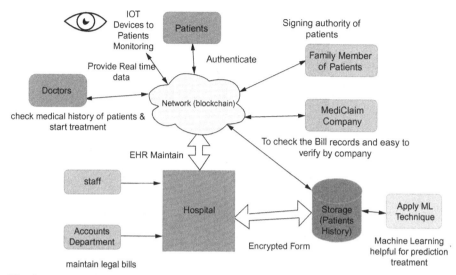

Fig. 8 Integrated frameworks of the proposed healthcare system.

Suppose a patient is hospitalized due to some disease and is under the supervision of a doctor. Hospital staff have been allocated to arrange the facilities. If patients have some medical history, doctors and staff check records and predict a cure or medication through ML techniques. Simultaneously, in the hospital, patients are monitored by staff, and a sensor is attached with IoT devices. Regular patient updates are sent to a repository to maintain the records. A doctor's treatment is based on both their predictions and the current problem. But maybe the data available have been tampered with. Blockchain plays a vital role in maintaining and producing the entire record through a secure channel. The doctors, medical staff, and family members check the patient's status. All patient treatments were recorded in the storage place. Any time when doctor checks the patients he may apply machine learning methods to diagnose the futuristic problem of patients. Hospitals and their account departments never face issues regarding bills and other issues. The medicine department of the hospital never cheats on the patients. All the bills and other records in the network are easily checked by the Mediclaim department to release the amount.

All the current technology will give an easy life; EHR is the only software that has limitations. But we have to include the blockchain with IoT sensors and artificial intelligence through ML to give a better result in our system and ease the patient's treatments.

Surveillance through IoT devices and medicine tracking is also essential through the blockchain with advanced sensors. Nowadays, fraud is done by their staff by not providing the costly medicines to the patients, but sold it in the market. This patient may cause a bigger problem and one more aspect of blockchain to properly trace medicine toward the system to avoid the forgery and black marketing of medication, injection of other medical equipment.

4.1 Algorithm implementation

(i) Registration of a User (PatientAdd())

```
Input: Enter registration details.
Output: Registration process Successful completed
If (doctor. Approved= true) {
    Print "patient recommend for hospitalization";
    If (Enter. Record=true) {
    {enter -> Uid, doctor name, address, hospital name}
    Generate Hash value for the patients.
    Patient.Hashvalue();}
else (Doctor. Approved= false)
    Print "patient not recommend for hospitalization"
End}
```

(ii) Registration of Mediclaim company (MediclaimComAdd())

```
Input: Enter Mediclaim company details.
Output: Registration process Successful completed
    If (AuthorizedAdd= true) {
Print "Company is authorized approve by government";
Generate Hash value for the Company persona to particular case.
Agent.Hashvalue(); }
    else (AuthorizedAdd = false)
Print "Company is authorized to approve by the government"
    end
```

(iii) Registration of Doctor (Doctor. Add())

```
Input: Enter Doctor's details.
Output: Registration process Successful completed
    If (AuthorizedAdd= true) {
Print "Eligible for prescription Process in the system";
Generate Hash value for the doctor.
Doctor.Hashvalue(); }
    else (AuthorizedAdd = false)
Print "Not Approved"
    end
```

(iv) Registration of a Hospital (HospitalAdd())

```
Input: Enter Hospital complete details.
Output: Registration process Successful completed
If (Hospital. Approved= true) {
    Print "Hospital recommended for patient's admission";
    If (Enter. Record=true) {
    {enter -> Uid, doctor list, address, hospital name, location}
    Generate Hash value for the hospital.
    Hospital.Hashvalue();}}
else (Hospital. Approved= false)
    Print "Hospital not recommended for patient's admission."
end
```

4.2   Smart contract implementation

A smart contract is a logical program among all the implemented classes for the trans-action. For the implementation of smart contracts, apply the protocol for the terms and conditions among nodes. It increases the trust on all sides and protects them from any accidental or illegal concept of the program. In this system, smart contracts work every node and application program, that is, the registration of all (hospital, patients, doctors). With the help of this, we can improve the authentication and integrity of different functions. Use of smart contract or contract between parties having various features to recognize the genuineness of customers with efficiency, effectiveness and secure environment. The smart contract in the blockchain works as a safe and effective programmable asset that runs as scheduled [49].

Smart contracts in this healthcare system have various functions: (i) register uses, (ii) verify all the users, (iii) send reports for diagnosis, (iv) analyze the report, and (v) continue monitoring patients and tracking medicine availability. Fig. 9 shows the major classes with their attributes and methods for the implemented smart contract in the system.

4.3   Results and discussion

The proposed healthcare system will give many benefits when we merge all the new technology with 5G.

1. The mode has better interoperability with all connected nodes.
2. This model is secure and efficient as it's based on blockchain and smart contracts as an agreement between all the parties.
3. The use of machine learning to predict patients' data will be helpful to the entire system.
4. IoT devices will help to remove the forgery and give proper results.
5. Lab report of patients and bill of the hospital to open for Mediclaim department.

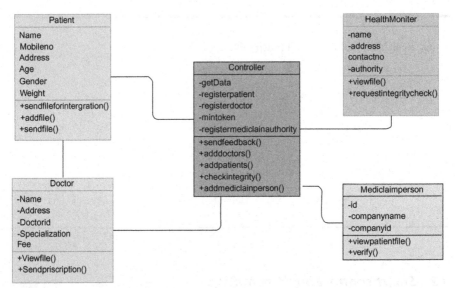

Fig. 9 Smart contract in blockchain.

5 Conclusion

The healthcare system is the digital platform for the whole medical procedure that will help to improve the working of all stakeholders. Especially for the patient's perspective with hospital facilities, it will provide ease of work. There are so many issues with this current healthcare system, but we have to merge this healthcare system with new and vital blockchain technology. When blockchain is in the healthcare system with its features, it is secure, transparent, and authorized. The distributed network includes all the nodes such as doctor, hospital, Mediclaim, and patient care in peer-to-peer communication that will be helpful to society. In this proposed model architecture, we have included IoT devices for monitoring and controlling patient activities. The medical transaction field is equally compliant with social, ethical, and regulatory issues, which is why every country must consider different issues as per the law [50]. We have also used machine learning for the analysis of the actual data to predict the report. We have also used smart contracts to achieve ease of work in the blockchain because code will automatically execute and perform the assigned task. This proposed architecture will be helpful for the medical sector to achieve potential growth toward use and performance with a secure channel to satisfy their users. As we know, there is a lot of fraud in the medical sector. This kind of system will protect the records of medicines, injections, and other equipment. Further, we have to add this system to pathology labs, medical suppliers, and pharma companies to track and, as per the demand, provide the required thing. Also, we will try to convert the mobile applications and software for less consumption of power.

References

[1] N. Satoshi, Bitcoin: A Peer-to-Peer Electronic Cash System, 2008.

[2] R. Gupta, S. Tanwar, S. Tyagi, N. Kumar, M.S. Obaidat, B. Sadoun, HaBiTs: blockchain-based telesurgery framework for healthcare 4.0, in: 2019 International Conference on Computer, Information and Telecommunication Systems (CITS), 2019, pp. 1–5.

[3] P. Pandey, R. Litoriya, Promoting trustless computation through blockchain technology, Natl. Acad. Sci. Lett. 44 (2020) 225–231.

[4] V. Buterin, Ethereum white paper, Etherum White Paper, Etherum no. January, 2014, pp. 1–36.

[5] M. Hölbl, M. Kompara, A. Kamišalić, L. Nemec Zlatolas, A systematic review of the use of blockchain in healthcare, Symmetry 10 (10) (2018) 470.

[6] P. Pandey, R. Litoriya, Securing E-health networks from counterfeit medicine penetration using Blockchain, Wirel. Pers. Commun. 117 (2020) 7–25.

[7] L.G. Jaeger, Public Versus Private: What to Know Before Getting Started With Blockchain, IBM, 2018. Available from: https://www.ibm.com/blogs/blockchain/2018/10/public-versus-private-what-to-know-before-getting-started-with-blockchain/.

[8] P. Pandey, R. Litoriya, Implementing healthcare services on a large scale: challenges and remedies based on blockchain technology, Health Policy Technol. 9 (1) (2020) 69–78.

[9] S. Soner, R. Litoriya, P. Pandey, Exploring blockchain and smart contract technology for reliable and secure land registration and record management, Wirel. Pers. Commun. 121 (2021) 2495–2509.

[10] P. Pandey, R. Litoriya, Securing and authenticating healthcare records through blockchain technology, Cryptologia 44 (4) (2020) 341–356.

[11] P. Zhang, D.C. Schmidt, J. White, G. Lenz, Blockchain technology use cases in healthcare, Adv. Comput. 111 (2018) 1–41.

[12] S. Tanwar, K. Parekh, R. Evans, Blockchain-based electronic healthcare record system for healthcare 4.0 applications, J. Inf. Secur. Appl. 50 (2020) 102407.

[13] A. Bartolomé, J. Adell, L. Castañeda, Block chain in education: introduction and critical review of the state of the art, EDUTEC. Rev. Electron. Tecnol. Educ. 61 (2017) 1–14.

[14] M.A. Ansari, S. Soner, An approach to improve the production using recycling on products, Int. Res. Fellows Assoc. Res. Journey 167 (C) (2019) 185–188.

[15] P. Pandey, R. Litoriya, Ensuring elderly well being during COVID-19 by using IoT, Disaster Med. Public Health Prep. (October) (2020) 1–10.

[16] P. Pandey, R. Litoriya, Technology intervention for preventing COVID-19 outbreak, Inf. Technol. People 34 (2021) 1233–1251.

[17] S. Leible, S. Schlager, M. Schubotz, B. Gipp, A review on blockchain technology and Blockchain projects fostering open science, Front. Blockchain 2 (2019) 1–28.

[18] N. Kabra, P. Bhattacharya, S. Tanwar, S. Tyagi, MudraChain: blockchain-based framework for automated cheque clearance in financial institutions, Futur. Gener. Comput. Syst. 102 (2020) 574–587.

[19] R. Ben Fekih, M. Lahami, Application of blockchain technology in healthcare: a comprehensive study, The Impact of Digital Technologies on Public Health in Developed and Developing Countries, vol. 12157, LNCS, 2020, pp. 268–276. https://doi.org/10.1007/978-3-030-51517-1_23.

[20] F. Casino, T.K. Dasaklis, C. Patsakis, A systematic literature review of blockchain-based applications: current status, classification and open issues, Telematics Inform. 36 (2019) 55–81.

[21] A. Hasselgren, K. Kralevska, D. Gligoroski, S.A. Pedersen, A. Faxvaag, Blockchain in healthcare and health sciences—a scoping review, Int. J. Med. Inform. 134 (2020) 104040.

[22] H.M. Hussien, S.M. Yasin, S.N.I. Udzir, A.A. Zaidan, B.B. Zaidan, A systematic review for enabling of develop a blockchain technology in healthcare application: taxonomy, substantially analysis, motivations, challenges, recommendations and future direction, J. Med. Syst. 43 (10) (2019) 320.

[23] T. McGhin, K.-K.R. Choo, C.Z. Liu, D. He, Blockchain in healthcare applications: research challenges and opportunities, J. Netw. Comput. Appl. 135 (2019) 62–75.

[24] M. Pandey, R. Litoriya, P. Pandey, Applicability of machine learning methods on mobile app effort estimation: validation and performance evaluation, Int. J. Softw. Eng. Knowl. Eng. 30 (1) (2020) 23–41.

[25] M. Pandey, R. Litoriya, P. Pandey, Application of fuzzy dematel approach in analyzing mobile app issues, Program. Comput. Softw. 45 (5) (2019) 268–287.

[26] M. Pandey, R. Litoriya, P. Pandey, Novel approach for mobile based app development incorporating MAAF, Wirel. Pers. Commun. 107 (4) (2019) 1687–1708.

[27] M. Pandey, R. Litoriya, P. Pandey, Identifying causal relationships in mobile app issues: an interval type-2 fuzzy DEMATEL approach, Wirel. Pers. Commun. 108 (2019) 683–710.

[28] M. Pandey, R. Litoriya, P. Pandey, Mobile app development based on agility function, Ingénierie Des Systèmes d'information RSTI Série ISI (IIETA) 23 (6) (2018) 19–44.

[29] E. Chukwu, L. Garg, A systematic review of blockchain in healthcare: frameworks, prototypes, and implementations, IEEE Access 8 (2020) 21196–21214.

[30] P. Pandey, R. Litoriya, Fuzzy cognitive mapping analysis to recommend machine learning based effort estimation technique for web applications, Int. J. Fuzzy Syst. 22 (4) (2020) 1212–1223.

[31] N. Sharma, R. Litoriya, D. Sharma, Forecasting the most predictable municipal solid wastes for improving the quality of waste management system in urban & rural areas of India, Mukt Shabd J. 10 (1) (2021) 403–408.

[32] N. Sharma, R. Litoriya, A. Sharma, Application and analysis of K-means algorithms on a decision support framework for municipal solid waste management, in: A. Hassanien, R. Bhatnagar, A. Darwish (Eds.), Advanced Machine Learning Technologies and Applications. AMLTA 2020. Advances in Intelligent Systems and Computing, Springer, Singapore, 2021, pp. 267–276.

[33] N. Sharma, R. Litoriya, D. Sharma, An analytical study on the importance of data mining for designing a decision support system, J. Harmonized Res. 7 (2) (2019) 44–48.

[34] M. Pandey, R. Litoriya, P. Pandey, Perception-based classification of mobile apps: a critical review, in: A.K. Luhach, K.B.G. Hawari, I.C. Mihai, P.-A. Hsiung, R.B. Mishra (Eds.), Smart Computational Strategies: Theoretical and Practical Aspects, Springer Singapore, Singapore, 2019, pp. 121–133.

[35] P. Pandey, R. Litoriya, A predictive fuzzy expert system for crop disease diagnostic and decision support, in: Fuzzy Expert Systems and Applications in Agricultural Diagnosis, IGI Global, 2019, pp. 175–194.

[36] P. Pandey, R. Litoriya, Software process selection system based on multicriteria decision making, J. Softw. Evol. Process 33 (2) (2021) e2305.

[37] S. Singh Bhadauria, V. Sharma, R. Litoriya, Empirical analysis of ethical issues in the era of future information technology, in: 2010 2nd International Conference on Software Technology and Engineering, vol. 2, 2010, pp. V2-31–V2-35.

[38] S. Jiang, J. Cao, H. Wu, Y. Yang, M. Ma, J. He, BlocHIE: a blockchain-based platform for healthcare information exchange, in: 2018 IEEE International Conference on Smart Computing (SMARTCOMP), IEEE, Taormina, Italy, 2018, pp. 49–56.

[39] R. Prakash, R. Litoriya, Pedagogical transformation of bloom taxonomy's LOTs into HOTs: an investigation in context with IT education, Wirel. Pers. Commun. 122 (2021) 725–736.

[40] D. Randall, P. Goel, R. Abujamra, Blockchain applications and use cases in health information technology, J. Health Med. Inform. 8 (3) (2017) 1–4.

[41] Y. Sun, R. Zhang, X. Wang, K. Gao, L. Liu, A decentralizing attribute-based signature for healthcare blockchain, in: 2018 27th International Conference on Computer Communication and Networks (ICCCN), IEEE, Hangzhou, China, 2018, pp. 1–9.

[42] R. Gupta, A. Shukla, S. Tanwar, AaYusH: a smart contract-based telesurgery system for healthcare 4.0, in: 2020 IEEE International Conference on Communications Workshops (ICC Workshops), IEEE, Dublin, Ireland, 2020.

[43] T.-T. Kuo, H.-E. Kim, L. Ohno-Machado, Blockchain distributed ledger technologies for biomedical and health care applications, J. Am. Med. Inform. Assoc. 24 (6) (2017) 1211–1220.

[44] P. Pandey, R. Litoriya, An activity vigilance system for elderly based on fuzzy probability transformations, J. Intell. Fuzzy Syst. 36 (3) (2019) 2481–2494.

[45] P. Pandey, R. Litoriya, An IoT assisted system for generating emergency alerts using routine analysis, Wirel. Pers. Commun. 112 (1) (2020) 607–630.

[46] P. Pandey, R. Litoriya, Elderly care through unusual behavior detection: a disaster management approach using IoT and intelligence, IBM J. Res. Dev. 64 (1) (2019) 15:1–15:11.

[47] R. Litoriya, S. Soner, M. Lovanshi, Preventing road accidents caused by drunk driving using machine learning & internet of things, Int. J. Adv. Sci. Technol. 29 (3) (2020) 11060–11070.

[48] M. Vahdati, Applications of Blockchain in Healthcare, vol. 83, Springer Singapore, Singapore, 2021.

[49] I. Mistry, S. Tanwar, S. Tyagi, N. Kumar, Blockchain for 5G-enabled IoT for industrial automation: a systematic review, solutions, and challenges, Mech. Syst. Signal Process. 135 (2020) 106382.

[50] R. Litoriya, A. Gulati, M. Yadav, R.S. Ghosh, P. Pandey, Social, ethical, and regulatory issues of fog computing in healthcare 4.0 applications, in: Fog Computing for Healthcare 4.0 Environments, Springer, Cham, 2021, pp. 593–609.

IoT and blockchain technology in 5G smart healthcare

Anupam Sharma[a], Mandeep Singh[a], Megha Gupta[b], Namrata Sukhija[a], and Puneet Kumar Aggarwal[c]

[a]HMR Institute of Technology and Management, Delhi, India, [b]IMS Engineering College, Ghaziabad, India, [c]ABES Engineering College, Ghaziabad, India

1 Introduction

Effective, efficient, and smart healthcare services play a crucial role in the provision of medical services. Smart healthcare accounts for 10% of the gross domestic product (GDP) in Europe, and it is estimated that smart healthcare will save billions of euros in healthcare costs. In health services, the Internet of Things (IoT) promises many benefits for streamlining and improving health care delivery from proactively predicting and diagnosing health issues to treating and monitoring patients, both in and out of the hospital. IoT applications can include telemedicine, mobile health, ambient assisted living, and smart medications, among others [1,2]. The IoT market segment in medical care services is estimated at over $100 billion [3]. Smart healthcare applications are growing and changing how healthcare is being delivered, in innovative ways. Wireless communication technologies, IoT, and 5G-based approaches have been suggested for continuously monitoring a patient's health [4]. For consistent assessment and monitoring of diabetes patients, a portable medical care system based on 5G and IoT has been suggested [5].

Wearables that use IoT will be recommended to support smart medical care applications (for remote assessment and remote clinical assistance) [6]. Wearable devices such as smart watches, sensors, and smart articles of clothing collect data on heart rate, length of rest periods, and activity levels for continuous health monitoring (e.g., pulse, circulatory stress, blood sugar levels). Using the IoT opens the door to many opportunities within the healthcare environment, such as improved outcomes and improved disease management [7]. The IoT is praised for its use in healthcare to enable remote monitoring of chronically ill patients [8]. Wearable devices are proposed for telehealthcare services using cloud servers and, a virtual specialist (rather than an actual server) working in a distributed computing environment that could be obtained remotely using the Internet [9]. The wearable devices assemble data, for instance, activity levels and proportion of resting, and send it to a cloud server via the internet. The use of smart devices can be enhanced by 5G and IoT technologies.

Smart healthcare provides medical services across smart devices (smart phones, smart watches, remote glucometers, remote blood pressure monitors) and networks (body area network, extensive area network, and wireless local area network). Smart

Blockchain Applications for Healthcare Informatics. https://doi.org/10.1016/B978-0-323-90615-9.00004-9
Copyright © 2022 Elsevier Inc. All rights reserved.

devices measure health information by using various sources such as biomedical systems and sensors. The IoT benefits from having a foundation with the capacity of self-arrangement based on set communication protocols and interoperability, using concepts from the IoT European Research Cluster (IECR) project. The IoT is an adaptable, intricate, and dynamic organizational framework that associates anybody and anything, whenever and wherever, for any application [10]. The various applications of the IoT in healthcare services are used for observing smart sensors and clinical device combinations. Now, there is a developing pattern in the combination of detectors and systems of sensor-based device-to-device (D2D) interchanges [11]. The remote systems of 5G are not too far off, and the IoT is becoming the overwhelming focus as devices are required to shape critical portions of this 5G organizational worldview. In any case, the innovations are still advancing. While one difficulty of IoT in healthcare services is to deal with data from many different sources, future IoT healthcare applications will rely upon gaining significant understanding from the assembled data [12]. 5G is a recent advancement over 4G in communication technology that provides various advantages over the previous technology, such as high-speed data transmission. It also improves the connectivity issues in networks. Principles, abilities, and advances in the vision for 5G are as yet being examined, and many limitations still exist in the 5G technologies [13].

Healthcare, like other industries, went through various developmental phases to get to where it is today. Healthcare 1.0 was based on the interaction between the doctor and the patient. The technology use was limited to examining the reasons for disease. Records of patients were kept either by the doctor or the patient. The treatment was based on the efficiency of conditional factors and the knowledge of the doctor. Healthcare 2.0 highlighted the role of technology in enabling health interactions. It outlined the systematic use of social development tools to encourage collaboration among people, physicians, and caregivers. It aimed to improve patient experience, economy, clinical uniformity, and payment plans. Social networking, extensive clinical practice, negotiation, interaction, and public openness were the five primary elements of this breakthrough technology. The technology allowed patients to have a significant say in their own healthcare decisions. Healthcare 3.0 established a patient-centered approach to recover the art of treatment by combining the best aspects of Healthcare 1.0 and 2.0. The goal was to reduce the workload and make better use of physician skills and knowledge by boosting doctor-patient engagement. Healthcare 4.0 is a program that builds a reimagined healthcare system to be empowered by evidence. As a result, medicine is unrestrained by it, as long as patients are recognized as distinct individuals. Industry 4.0 inspired a step-by-step approach to prior healthcare versions. Its goal is to create a caregiver system through the use of an augmenting simulation domain. It is based on healthcare providers sharing patient records through electronic health record (EHR) repositories. Data sharing has improved clinicians' ability to access data from any location.

Blockchain is an inalterable, shared record of peer-to-peer transactions built from linked transaction blocks that are shared in a digital ledger. It makes use of established cryptographic techniques to allow each participant in a network to interact without preexisting trust between them, with no central authority. Blockchain has potentially beneficial application in healthcare. In a variety of healthcare settings, distributed ledger technology (DLT) can be used, but not all activity in healthcare is tied to transactions. Also, because the data in digital currencies, the original primary use of blockchain, are readily available, they cannot be utilized to store private information such as identifiable health data. As a result, providers are required to consider security problems to ensure that protected health information (PHI) is maintained. Even though blockchain data are immutable, they should never be used senselessly in healthcare. Large files, particularly ones that change frequently, may be excluded. All protected information data should be protected as something off the chain. Some benefits of blockchain are traceable data, decentralized management, unchangeable databases, calculated forces, robust data, and the amount of information to any authorized user, and keeping data out of the hands of unauthorized users through encryption, which is dependent on a patient's private key. All of these are advantages of using blockchain over traditional methods of healthcare information systems.

1.1 Motivations

Nowadays, smart health services play an important role in healthcare. Healthcare costs are projected to be cut by nearly a billion dollars because of smart healthcare. The IoT is expected to play a key role in smart health services, enabling a wide range of functions such as e-health, assisting the elderly, smart drugs, remote and on-the-spot resource monitoring in clinics, therapy consistency, and patient social change. According to a recent report from Grand View Research, Inc., the market for IoT in healthcare services will reach USD 534 billion by 2025. Smart healthcare applications are expanding the scope of the diverse relations already offered in the structure. Healthcare services are benefiting from both 5G and IoT technologies, with both as reliable drivers.

1.2 Contributions

For smart healthcare, consider the explicit key focus on technology in the 5G smart healthcare framework. The establishment of a scientific categorization for smart healthcare services in 5G covers interchange innovations, targets, requirements, and execution measures. The research is evaluated at the network layer, which covers routing protocols, addressing, and planning. It is applied to future 5G research prospects and smart healthcare. In 5G and IoT-based smart healthcare, there are some current and future research studies as well as problems.

1.3 Organization

The arrangement of this chapter is described as follows. The solutions for smart healthcare regarding network architecture in 5G are covered in Section 2. The 5G smart healthcare taxonomy, communication technologies, objectives, specific requirements, and specific performance measures are described in Section 3. Network layer solutions of 5G smart healthcare are described in Section 4. Issues and challenges are examined in Section 5. Section 6 covers blockchain potential use in smart healthcare. The conclusion is in Section 7.

2 Architecture of 5G network for smart healthcare solutions

The new 5G wireless mobile network technologies are emerging and are having significant impacts on healthcare connectivity. Fig. 1 depicts 5G architecture.

2.1 Architecture of 5G

Several kinds of small cells play a fundamental role in 5G smart healthcare, which means improved coverage and throughput for IoT applications, such as in healthcare. The high data demand rates of smart healthcare applications (such as the wireless medical procedure required range of data up to 1.6 gbps [14]) are suitable for small cell zones [15]. Ranging from shorter to larger, these cells are of three types—micro, pico, and femto. All three are small cells compared to the macrocell, with a range of

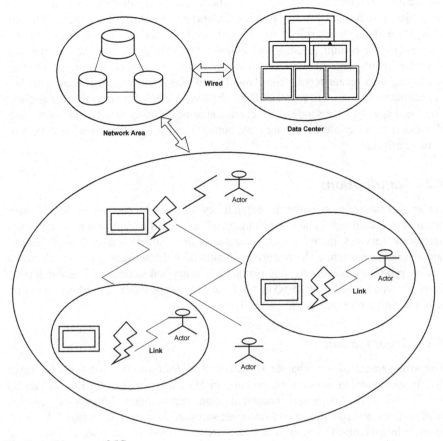

Fig. 1 Architecture of 5G.

20 miles. Femtocells are small cells that are expanded between areas and are limited to a small region such as a home or a hospital. The picocells can hold up to 100 clients over an area of 1 km. In a major contrast, the microcell inclusion zone supports more users, up to 2000 users in the 2 km range. This gives large area coverage with a highly proficient output range [16]. Macrocells are assembled on different stations, which have a highly effective power output with a range of tens of watts. It also supports more than 2000 users in the 30 km range.

Small cells are used in the network to increase the area of spectrum efficiency by higher frequency reuse [17]. The client hardware (CH) makes use of both small cell and macrocell stations all the while. The base station of the macrocell uses minimum frequency bands to give network and portability (control plane), and higher recurrence uses the base station for small cells to give high-throughput transit information [18]. In the 5G cellular network, femto, pico, micro, and macrocell base stations are all found to regularly combine in heterogeneous networks (HetNets).

2.2 Enabling features and technologies of 5G

These are the features/technologies described in this section: device-to-device (D2D), millimeter wave (mmWave) communication, software-defined network, network function virtualization (NFV), and edge computing.

2.2.1 Device-to-device (D2D)

An immediate communication of two devices (i.e., users) in the system is not included in the base station (BS) or central organization. With D2D (device-to-device) communication, difficult network issues can be addressed [19]. In D2D communication, every terminal can connect with another directly or share their automatic access connection to transfer data [20]. There is little use of D2D communication in 4G networks. All interchanges are directed through the passage and base station. This steering is wasteful, particularly when devices are close to one another. When it comes to machine-to-machine communication, a large number of devices are included and more reasonable in between direct correspondence. Devices may link with one another in the range of the cell network by utilizing various technologies such as WLAN in ad-hoc mode or Bluetooth. In any case, these connections have few defenses against interference. Then again, in D2D the quality of service in the authorized range is ensured if the connection is overseen appropriately by the telecom operator [21].

2.2.2 Millimeter wave (mmWave) communication

The 5G mmWave is in the range of 20–300 GHz. Because of the absence of a range beneath 3 GHz, 5G stretches out the mmWave band in general form between 20–90 GHz, on the grounds that there is an immense amount of unused data transfer capacity. By making use of small cells, mmWaves will help meet the capacity needed in 5G [22], which will be useful in smart healthcare technology applications. The best part is that mmWave alleviates the strain of lower frequencies while expanding remote communication to the limits of cognitive radio networks.

2.2.3   Software-defined network (SDN)

The SDN is a dynamic, reasonable, adaptable, and practical means to convey high transmission capacity needed for smart healthcare applications. The network technologies in SDN make the network more agile and adaptable, efficient, and secure. SDN systems represent a way to deal with fabricating, planning, and taking care of networks by isolating organization control planes and sending planes [23]. It can provide the different necessities of 5G smart healthcare. SDN enables both virtualization and cloud technologies, providing easier management of network components.

2.2.4   Network function virtualization (NFV)

NFV is a method for enabling the costly committed equipment devices such as firewalls and switching routes with programming-based network devices that are running as virtual machines on network servers. 5G has empowered D2D communication in smart healthcare, and as a result a huge measure of data is unsurprisingly being produced. It is not possible to expect to send the entirety of the produced data to the concentrated server for processing. Subsequently, some innovations are needed to oversee information on cloud servers and the edge cloud. NFV guarantees in-network adaptability and network scalability.

2.2.5   Edge computing

Edge computing is a distributed paradigm in which client data is processed at the edge of the network, as close as possible to the initial source. Machines will need to be able to make decisions and react appropriately in the future of smart healthcare. In such cases, edge computing plays a significant role, and decision time is crucial in 5G-based organizations [24].

2.3   Performance enhancement of 5G

The characteristics and performance enhancement comparison of 4G and 5G are shown in Table 1 [25].

- Level of data collection under various conditions and scenarios; 20 gigabits per second are predicted with peak data rates hitting 10 gigabits per second.
- Support highly dense network and enable massive machine-type communication.
- Allows for a three-fold increase in spectrum performance and a ten-fold increase in energy efficiency.

Table 1 4G and 5G comparison.

Name of attributes	Performance result	
	4G	5G
Movability	Up to 350 km/h	Up to 500 km/h
Spectral efficiency	1.5	4.5
Energy efficiency	0.1 µJ/100 bits	0.1 µJ/100 bits
Density	100 k/km^2	1000 k/km^2
User plane	10 ms	1 ms
Control plane	100 ms	50 ms
Transfer rate	0.01–1 gbps	0.1–20 gbps

3 Classifications of 5G smart healthcare

The classifications of 5G smart healthcare are shown in Fig. 2. Communication systems, criteria, goals, success metrics, and methods are the foundations of this classification.

3.1 Smart healthcare communication technologies

In smart healthcare, there are various brief and long-term connection enhancements that rely on data transfer between devices and servers [26]. GPRS, GSM, Long-Term Evolution (LTE), and LTE advanced are all technologies used in a base station to send data from a local server in smart healthcare. The 3rd Generation Partnership Project (3GPP) needs to improve battery life, inclusion, and device complexity in Discharge 13 [27]. Unlike other existing protocols, the LoRaWAN protocol is standardized by

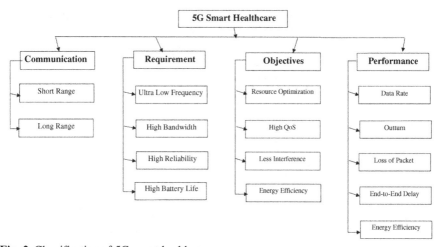

Fig. 2 Classification of 5G smart healthcare.

Table 2 Communication technology comparison for smart healthcare.

	Technology name	Transfer rate	Power	Range
Long-range communication	4G	12 Mbps	Up to 2600 MHz	10 km
	5G	3.6 Gbps	Lower bands	10 km
	5G	10 Gbps	Higher bands	<1 km
	LoRa	50 Kbps	868/915 MHz	25 km
	LoRaWAN	0.3–50 kbps	Various	45 km
	Sigfox	300 kpbs	868/915 MHz	50 km
	WiMAX	11–100 Mbps	10–66 GHz	50 km
	LTE-M (M1)	0.144 Mbps	Up to 5400 MHz	35 km
	NB-IoT (NB1)	250 kbps	900 MHz	35 km
	EC-GSM	140 kbps	900 MHz	100 km
Short-range communication	WiFi	802.11(b)11M	Up to 5 GHz	50 m
	Bluetooth 4	1 Mbps	2.4 GHz4 GHz	0.1 km
	Bluetooth 5	2 Mbps	2.4 GHz	0.25 km
	Z-Wave Alliance	9.6/40/100 kpbs	900 GHz	30 m
	NFC	100–400 kbps	13.56 GHz	10 cm
	ZigBee	250 kbps	2.4 GHz	10–100 m

the LoRa Association to aid smart healthcare applications in ensuring interoperability among multiple operators. As shown in Table 2, a SIGFOX is an ultra-narrowband wireless technology that provides an extremely scalable overall network for smart healthcare applications with extremely minimal use of power [28].

3.2   Prerequisites of smart healthcare

3.2.1   Ultralow latency

Smart healthcare applications can have extremely low latency communication requirements [29]. For instance, telesurgery requires communication latency commensurate with the latency of automated instruments. Start-to-finish latency under 200 ms is required for future telesurgery [30]. Be that as it may, the characteristic latency of an automated system is practically under 100 ms. For future prospects, 5G can meet most of the conceivable requirements in the healthcare environment. Surgeons in hospitals can operate with robots for all intents and purposes from any place in the hospital [31].

3.2.2   High bandwidth

The bandwidth capacity is the maximum capacity of a wireless or a wired network communication link to send an amount of data at a certain time [32]. But in the case of biomedical sensors, only a fixed data amount can be sent because of limited bandwidth capacity in the current network scenario [33]. In a 5G network, a vital need is higher frequencies (more than 10 GHz). By utilizing these frequencies, greater range is accessible, which prompts better strength of transmission (in Gbps). Doctors can remotely view high-resolution pictures and send healthcare services with the ultrahigh-definition 5G network, allowing good transfer speed in a versatile and adaptable manner during communications, which can empower D2D systems for the healthcare field [34].

3.2.3   Ultrareliability

The ability of a network system to complete a certain activity with low error rates is called its reliability. The use of IoT with huge numbers of sensors that surpass the network limit [35]. Therefore, the increased data limit and an enormous number of connections should be provided by the new communication infrastructure. Biomedical devices with various traffic patterns such as traffic signaling and transmission should be handled by new organization infrastructure. The main requirement in smart healthcare is scalability, given that the network should allow for the addition or removal of nodes without compromising network execution [36]. As a result, massive-machine-type communications with a broad scope necessitate a very flexible and adaptable network.

3.2.4   High battery life

The battery's performance and longevity is estimated as the battery's lifetime; improvements in battery life can improve the network lifetime. Low-cost, long-lasting devices are needed to interface with massive amounts of sensors and biomedical equipment [37]. The aim of a continuous monitoring system is to attach self-contained devices to cover the entire spectrum of clinical activities [38]. The low-cost detectors are proposed in 5G to work off the same battery for a very long time [39]. Thus the network lifetime should be improved.

3.3   Main objectives in smart healthcare

3.3.1   Resource optimization

These methods are utilized to extend the network lifetime and use less energy [40]. In a 5G-based smart healthcare network, resource optimization strategies play a big role. The increasing numbers of devices connected produce a lot of data and consume more network bandwidth. Improper resource optimization can prompt some issues in the network [41]. To expand network proficiency without additional software or hardware, network resource optimization must guarantee the optimal use of system resources. Thus one of the most important priorities for smart healthcare is resource optimization.

3.3.2   High QoS

The network's ability to handle high bandwidth and other network performance is related to quality of service, for example, uptime, latency, and error rate. An alternate type of information in the network quality of service (QoS) additionally includes overseeing and controlling network resources. The primary objective is to provide networks with controlled jitter, improved loss characteristics, low latency, and dedicated bandwidth capacity [42]. Because smart healthcare systems have different types of data, one of the primary goals of smart healthcare is to improve QoS.

3.3.3   Decreasing interference

In the smart healthcare system, frequency reuse can be utilized to accomplish better resource utilization. Also, user throughput densification and traffic capacity can be improved. Along these lines, frequency reuse and densification can result in greater improvement regarding effective load sharing among local access networks and macrocells. These advantages can cause various issues, for example, the density of the network and load can cause cochannel interference [43], which is a threat to smart healthcare systems. Consequently, effective interference strategies are required.

3.3.4   Energy efficiency

Because of environmental considerations, the main reason for creating a smart healthcare network focuses on energy efficiency. The energy consumption of the network increases as the density of access points in the network increases [44]. To reduce costs and increase the life of the devices in the network, the minimization of energy consumption is important for network administrators [45].

3.4   Measures of performance

(i) Data rate, the rate at which data are transferred in communications.

(ii) Throughput, the number of packets transmitted per unit of time.

(iii) The average packet loss, or packet loss ratio, during network transmission from source to destination.

(iv) The time it takes for packets to travel through a network from source to destination is referred to as end-to-end delay.

(v) To transmit/receive data, the source/destination must use energy efficient routing protocols.

4   Research on smart healthcare and 5G

Many studies have looked at the ability of networks to support smart healthcare applications. This section examines some of these research works.

4.1   Congestion in the network

Congestion control is proposed at the priority level in the low-asset transmission capability of the network, such as remote multimedia sensor networks, in the priority rate-based routing protocol (PRRP) [46]. Because of the large transfer speed, congestion may easily occur in low-asset transmission capacity networks. Bad sound and visual quality transmitted in multimedia files for application areas will undoubtedly be induced by node energy and application-specific QoS requirements (for example, remote health monitoring, remote medical procedure). The plan's key objective is to boost the QoS by reducing network congestion. PRRP empowers blockage identification and notices, just as rate transformation does. The estimation of congestion at every hub is calculated by the maximum and minimum values of the threshold. As a result, it provides three possible scenarios. First, the estimate of congestion is not exactly the base limit, which shows no blockage, and the source node in the congestion method takes into account the energy levels of the upstream nodes. Consequently, to maintain the data rate, it sends traffic to them. Second, a moderate level of congestion means that the value of the congestion is somewhere between the higher and lower threshold values. Along these lines, to prevent congestion, the data rate at which data are sent to the node is adjusted based on the energy level, buffer size, or whether the data are to be sent to another node. Third, the maximum threshold is less than the congestion value, which means the congestion level is high, thus the data rate is reduced at the next node. In 5G smart healthcare applications, the protocol is suitable. PRRP appears to increase throughput by lowering packet drop rates and end-to-end delays.

To prevent congestion, congestion control based on reliable transmission (CCRT) is designed for continuous streaming-based media services, such as remote surgery [47]. For reliable transmission of genuine information data, CCRT employs a need-based congestion management component. The main target of a congestion detection system is to increase the QoS in the network's line variation rate and line length. Each packet in a queue of these packets has a low, medium, or high priority to prioritize high-priority packets for solid transmission. Congestion can be detected by the receiver node using two standards. First, the response time is divided into three categories: high, medium, and low. The packet type means that the packet has been attached to the tail of the queue. High-priority packets are the first to ensure that information is available and has a low latency. Moderate and high-priority packets will be kept before the top priority queue is full. Second, the queue volatility level looks at both the positive and negative sides of the queue. A positive queue variety ratio indicates that queue length will intensify in the future, implying that congestion levels will increase, while a negative queue variety ratio indicates that queue length will drop, implying that congestion levels will decrease in the future. Along these lines, for queue variation rate, the receiver node has modified the information rate based on the congestion detection strategy. As a result, CCRT has shown that increasing throughput decreases packet loss and end-to-end latency.

A congestion control and energy balance hierarchy (CcEbH) is preferred to maintain a strategic distance from congestion in a profoundly congested network with restricted assets, such as continuous health monitoring [48]. The principal aim is to improve the QoS in the network by lessening congestion. First, a solitary node in a network is arranged in the CcEbH network into progressive form, so every node is able to be an upstream (or upper progressive level node), a downstream (or lower progressive level node), and a comparable various leveled stage endpoint. The size of the queue can be determined by looking at the congestion at a hub, where the approaching output signal is more prevalent than the active output power. Upstream nodes may measure the buffer occupancy (or queue size) of downstream nodes. A downstream node is selected to collect and forward information in the form of bundles, and a downstream node becomes congested (for example, the prominence of buffer inhabitance exceeds the right action in the total scaling factor). CcEbH appears to decrease energy utilization.

Healthcare-aware optimized congestion avoidance (HOCA) is proposed to dodge congestion in healthcare applications, such as monitoring vital signs of patients or health-related crises, as a result of the significance and criticality of the sent information [49]. The basic target is to decrease congestion in a network by improving energy efficiency. Every packet has a priority, requiring a high data rate or a low data rate. There are four major steps for a health center (sink node) to accumulate events or data from nodes embedded in patients. First, a request for data to nodes is broadcast by the sink node. Second, the nodes embedded in patients reply with data and events identifying the importance level. Third, the last node is chosen by the sink node to lessen congestion from the sink node dependent on the level of importance and multiple paths are set up to the destination node to avoid congestion. Fourth, the node detects the event and generates the packet. Low-priority packets select the next jump from the low-priority table to send data, and high-priority packets choose from the high-priority table to send data. HOCA has extended the network's lifetime and reduced end-to-end delay, by lowering energy consumption.

The transmitting rate of a source node and buffer size of a destination node can be modified using a window-based rate control algorithm (W-RCA) to reach a trade-off between peak to mean ratio and standard deviation to optimize the QoS of video transmissions for telesurgery [50]. Machine learning algorithms are used to shape the buffer (temporary storage) for upcoming frames [51]. It results in smoothing the video transmission over a single-hop from a remote site (such as anyplace on the internet) in 5G networks. The peak-to-mean ratio, the delay standard deviation, and the jitter are optimized. Various protocols (i.e., user datagram protocol, transmission control, session description protocol) are utilized in the plan for exchanging video frames on both the client and server side. This proposed approach has appeared to lessen jitter and also minimize end-to-end delay in video transmission.

4.2 Scheduling approaches

Wearable networks based on network slices have been introduced in the 5G network, helping to improve the energy-efficient use and network resource sharing [52]. The main target of a network slice is to use network function virtualization (NFV) and software-defined networking to maximize energy efficiency and resources in the network (SDN). NFV disperses the capacity of the network into different utilitarian zones; virtualization technology and software programming are helpful instead of physical hardware. SDN can handle both planes (data and control) and can provide adaptable control of the network stream subsequently. By distributing communication resources, storage, and processing, network slicing can provide for the low latency requirements and reduce end-to-end delay. Further, a data-driven resource management executive structure is introduced. By getting service knowledge, a machine learning algorithm is used in the cognitive service machine to execute wearable service layers to consumer services. In the cognitive source, acknowledgment for tight coupling is sent to services and resources to improve QoE utilization of clients and resources.

A network service chaining (NSC) was introduced that creates flexible coordination between SDN and NFV; it can create self-operating network devices, as opposed to utilizing manual associations, for healthcare services in 5G [53]. Its primary goal is to improve QoS. In order to provide fast services (less delay) in a 5G environment, a model was incorporated with the assistance of different communication protocols, including low-power and loss-networks routing schemes. In addition, to improve the QoS, cell technologies, small base stations, and WiFi were utilized. Further, an authentication server was introduced for a secure model with Kerberos to protect the cloudlet network from data DoS attacks. TLS protocol is sent inside the server to provide secure communication between both clients. This approach improves QoS by decreasing the high-security end-to-end delay.

A 5G cognitive system (5G-Csys) has been proposed to improve the QoS by accomplishing ultrahigh dependability and ultralow latency for cognitive applications (i.e., remote medical procedures) in a heterogeneous organization [54]. Given the knowledge of network configurations, the resource cognitive engine has cognized the resources in the network to accomplish the required ultralow latency and ultrahigh reliability of the system. The data cognitive engine uses machine learning and deep learning algorithms (i.e., uses computer programs to acquire data that is used to learn independently [51]) to investigate healthcare data. This framework has appeared to improve QoS by decreasing the network end-to-end delay.

A 5G-based Smart Diabetes approach was introduced for resource improvement, to give better QoS for continuous remote monitoring of patients [68]. The plan comprises three layers: the sensing layer gathers information from various resources (sensors) progressively. The customized diagnosis layer measures the gathered data for present-day machine learning algorithms (can acquire data and use it to find out on their own [51]) to investigate the illness. The data exchange layer distributes information from the social media space to medical professionals and patient family members through social networking. The smartphone and medical wearable devices (i.e., smart garments) arising from the 5G network are utilized this approach, which has demonstrated the ability to precisely reduce packet loss and end-to-end delay.

A small cell network in the 5G approach was introduced for upgrading QoS by accomplishing a high data rate [55]. The medical ultrasound videos were transferred from moving emergency vehicles (ambulance) to the hospital or clinic uplink in emergency situations. The macrocell contains a heterogeneous network, with eNodeB coinciding with a mobile small cell. This small cell network will send the mobile small cells to permit clients to move around and interface with the administrator's network nearby. The LTE-Sim test level system was used to obtain the reported results. The outcome showed that the QoS in the network was improved with regard to throughput, end-to-end delay, and packet loss rate (PLR).

4.3 Routing approaches

A handover scheme was introduced to help the cell client for D2D communications at the edge of the cell [56]. The approach was to lessen interference by overseeing mobility to limit delay during movement of cells. To provide a more consistent network with better channel quality during a handover, nodes (or UEs), can move from one cell to another, and can form D2D links with adjoining nodes. eNB controls resource management, the board, D2D meeting foundation, and power control. The handover choice is dependent on the channel quality indicator (CQI) created by eNB. The handover interaction is isolated into three stages. During the preparatory stage, the UEs send information to its serving eNB identified with the channel and it chooses whether to recruit the handover process upon certain conditions. In the execution step, the conduct and data of UEs will be sent to other cells or not, depending on the decision-making scheme. In the completion step, acknowledgment is shared among existing cells and the status of the UEs is refreshed within the new cells. This approach was shown to be an energy-efficient plan.

A device-aware routing and scheduling algorithm (DARA) in a multihop network was introduced for device-to-device communication [57]. The resource optimization is the primary target of the network to increase network lifetime (energy efficiency). In DARA, each node decides the amount of data to handle dependent on its remaining energy and processing power. For decisions on device cap abilities, a network utility maximization (NUM) formula is used. A node concludes whether to advance information (routing choice) or switch on the connection for the following hop node (scheduling choice). In this way, the algorithm is calculated on both routing and scheduling choices. A testbed was utilized for implementing, and, compared with the conventional back-pressure algorithm, DARA showed a major improvement in throughput.

Interference-aware routing (IAR) was introduced for D2D communication [58]. The goal of this approach was to decrease interference. The route is enabled between the source and the destination by utilizing cell edge nodes. First, the data are sent by the router to the current nodes on the edge, and then it travels in the direction of the destination. Finally, data are sent to the destination from the cell edge. Now, IAR exhibits shortest path routing (SPR) at each stage; and IAR is longer when compared with the direct shortest path, but has less interference. This is demonstrated to be energy efficient, with a high data rate.

A trust-based secure relay node selection method was also is introduced in 5G for D2D communication [59]. The plan involved keeping a trusted node for data transmission from interference selection. At each node, the level of trust is determined by experience and is based on the success of the packet conveyance rate and the error. Every node keeps track of its neighbor nodes in a trust table. The four parameters on which trust is based are reliability, energy, buffer capacity, and SNR. This scheme was demonstrated to be energy efficient.

A 5G-based approach and routing protocol was introduced for continuous monitoring of chronic patients. This scheme aims to leverage network capacity to minimize start-to-finish delays and provide high data delivery to clients, while preventing congestion. The creator utilized a PDA, wearable devices, and the 5G network to divide data among advanced mobile phones, sensors, and base stations. The designer used a machine learning algorithm (depends on computer programming to obtain data and learn on its own [51]) having a decision-making algorithm to examine the data to take needed actions. This decision-making algorithm investigates the data information and initiates an alert in unusual situations. It has the capacity of data collection in real time with quick reaction. This present scheme has been utilized in 4G and 5G by the creator and the performance was dissected. The 5G version shows the result of improvement in throughput, network lifetime, and end-to-end delay.

A plan based on the femto cell network and a cloud computing scheme was introduced to enhance network resources to arrive at a high data information rate [60]. A body sensor network gathers client data and sends it to the client's cellular devices, which are registered in the femto cell. A low-power home base station is used by the femto cell station with good coverage in the indoor location. A database is maintained by the femto cell to confirm the information received with the data in the database. If any irregularity is noted, then the information is sent to the cloud through the femto cell for additional analysis by medical specialists. A Markov Chain Model is used in the cloud to find the best solution. As compared to a macrocell network, this strategy restricts the use of network resources to achieve high energy efficiency and high security.

5 Issues and challenges of 5G

There are various difficulties and open research issues other than the previously mentioned problems in adopting 5G for smart healthcare. These issues give research direction talking points for researchers. The future exploration topics and their significance are shown in Table 3.

5.1 How to connect with IoT

Billions of devices are employed in smart healthcare networks. Smart healthcare has the potential to provide access to any computer in the network as well as the ability to detect significant data. IoT devices, such as WiFi, Bluetooth, and cellular networks (5G, LTE), can be used in any available communication network. Nonetheless, ensuring connectivity in smart healthcare has numerous difficulties, including:

- Ensuring that a large number of devices are available in a network with a wide range of coverage.
- Linking devices in the network with high mobility (high-speed ambulances carrying patients).

5.2 Interconnecting networks and devices

Another issue is the ability for exchanging data between at least two unique devices and networks to create interconnection with one another. Distinctive IoT devices from different areas of smart healthcare (remote health monitoring, ECG monitoring, remote surgery) are used for delivering smart healthcare services. Different communication technologies are used depending on availability between various devices, which assumes a significant part of interoperability in smart healthcare. A critical constraint for IoT development is interoperability between different devices in different domains because of the absence of universal norms [61]. Recognition at different

Table 3 Future issues and challenges.

Features	Challenges	Requirements
Connectivity	– How to guarantee connecting with massive IoT devices in a wide range during high mobility? – How to guarantee resource management in a highly dense network? – How to use power/energy for IoT devices?	– Use of spectrum for efficient communication of IoT devices. – Smartly use communication mediums (LTE, LTE ADV, WLAN, WiMAX, etc.). – Design of intelligent algorithms to give connectivity to a high number of devices in the network in the absence of communication networks.
Interoperability	Incorporating devices for retailer locked in services.	Models universal, integrated, and flexible in IoT devices to incorporate and communicate.
Low-cost and low-power communication	How to extend IoT device battery life?	– Advancement in wireless communication domain and microelectronics to deliver low-cost communication and extend battery life. – Design of artificial intelligence-based routing protocols.
Big data	– Lack of useful tools to process huge amount of generated information. – Resourceful centralized data acquisition and information.	– Big data centralized processing center. – Public appreciation of how to use IoT network resources securely.
Security	– Secure integration and deployment of services (cloud-based) at both device and network levels. – Early detection of both outsider and insider threats. – Standardized security solutions without delaying data integrity.	Identification of vulnerabilities at various levels in the network that work as entry points for numerous attacks.

levels (devices, application, network, and communication) should be a test of interoperability. For instance, the FIRARE and oneM2M standards are working on these interoperability issues in collaboration with other standards groups.

5.3 Communication with minimum power and minimum cost

In smart healthcare, IoT devices are restricted in size and associated with an assortment of sensors. To drive these devices, a consistent source of energy is needed, which presents a serious test regarding battery life and cost. These types of issues are addressed in smart healthcare, so devices should have low power consumption with low cost. Hence, to communicate with each other, intelligent algorithms are required with less energy utilization. Another technique is miniature devices and remote communication [62].

5.4 Big data analytics

Billions of devices are associated with smart healthcare, which create a need for information analysis and a huge amount of data. These data consist of private user information (for example, patient data) and information on the surrounding environment (for example, pulse rate checking). Intelligent techniques and intelligent algorithms are needed to analyze this data. For instance, by adopting deep learning algorithms, data created by privately associated devices can be broken down productively. The key issues are as follows:

- User privacy during data analysis should be ensured.
- Sensitive information should be protected and secure.
- Infrastructure for an enormous amount of data should be provided for collecting, storing, and analysis.
- Computational power for extracting actual information from the big data.

5.5 Security in smart healthcare

Smart healthcare necessitates security. Because smart healthcare relies on the Internet to connect various devices, security becomes a significant issue. Complex security protocols and algorithms are difficult to implement due to the restricted existence of IoT devices (limited processing and battery life) [63]. As a result, 70% of IoT devices will be open to attack in the future. There are frequent attacks and risks to security and privacy. The following concerns must be addressed when planning a viable smart healthcare network for the emerging 5G network.

- Simple communication between smart healthcare devices and a cloud-based application center is required for data integrity and authenticity.
- Strong privacy must be provided to ensure user acceptance and confidence.

To detect current and new threats, a thorough risk assessment is needed.

6 Blockchain use in smart healthcare

As defined earlier in this chapter, blockchain is an immutable, shared record of peer-to-peer transactions, built from linked transaction blocks and stored in a digital ledger. With the problems of information and system security intrinsic to smart healthcare, blockchain technology has the potential to alleviate some of the most troublesome points, since it has beneficial characteristics like decentralization, anonymity, tamper-proof capability, and auditability. Information sharing in a blockchain network eliminates the data duplication and inconsistency problem of the traditional system and it also eliminates the need of middlemen for information and contract sharing [2]. With the growing prominence of blockchain, the technology is now shifting towards developing end-to-end solutions for medical stakeholders, with a number of tools and technologies emerging to support blockchain-based smart healthcare applications [6]. A number of technological challenges in smart healthcare can be potentially met by blockchain. Information transmitted between IoT devices devours more energy. Hence, a long battery life (up to 10 years) is necessary for reasonable performance [64]. Different organization layer arrangements such as directing, congestion control, planning, resource improvement, QoS upgrades, energy production systems, and interference moderation are implemented in 5G and IoT to handle difficulties, with solutions to these difficulties projected to improve throughput productivity, dependability, transmission inclusion, and delay. Smart healthcare from various research perspectives is shown in Table 4, which sums up several investigations of work identified on smart healthcare found in the literature [65–69]. As far as we could possibly know, this paper is the sort to introduce a survey on healthcare. Specifically, our commitment is to convey an audit of 5G smart healthcare services with various perspectives as follows:

- Thinking about explicit key empowered technologies in 5G smart healthcare architecture for smart medical care.
- To enhance the security and privacy of patient data, a permissioned blockchain-based healthcare architecture has been presented, which discusses the challenges and their solutions. This work describes the applications of blockchain and the usage of machine learning with blockchain technology, which can impact smart healthcare development [1].

As seen in Table 4, in 2014 Baker et al. gave a model of a future smart healthcare system that can be used in both general and specialized systems. In [67], they found different uses of IoT in smart healthcare from an alternate point of view (such as checking of heartbeat, blood pressure). Mahmoud et al. [68] presented the Cloud of Things (CoT) and used it in smart healthcare service applications. In the same year, Islam et al. focused on IoT-based healthcare technologies and designed a smart healthcare network to support the network as an IoT backbone. In [29], the authors created various IoT-based smart healthcare systems for remote information gathering and transmitting to required destinations.

The blockchain technologies characteristics, including privatization (no need for a central authority), integrity, authenticity, and transparency, have already found some

Table 4 Smart healthcare survey.

Author	Year	Details
Baker et al. [65]	2014	The author gives a model for future smart healthcare systems, which is used for both general and special systems.
Dhanvijay et al. [29]	2020	The authors zeroed in on various IoT-based healthcare systems for remote body area networks that can empower smart healthcare information gathering and information transmission.
Qi et al. [25]	2017	The investigation is different in the use of IoT in smart healthcare from alternate points of view (such as checking of oxygen level, heartbeat monitoring, and blood pressure measurement).
Mahmoud et al. [68]	2018	The review is on Cloud of Things (CoT), stages, and how to carry it out in smart healthcare service applications.
Islam et al. [26]	2018	The main focus is on IoT-based healthcare technologies and the design of healthcare networks and support backing admittance to the IoT backbone.

uses in the healthcare industry. A major advantage of using blockchain technology in smart healthcare is that it can change the interoperability of healthcare databases, providing better access to patient medical records, prescription databases, and hospital resources, including the complete life cycle of a device within the blockchain infrastructure. Access to patients' medical histories is crucial for correctly prescribing medications [3]. Blockchain-based Electronic Health Record (EHR) systems can be beneficial in creating greater trust, security, and privacy among healthcare users. A framework has been proposed called Blockchain-Based Deep Learning as-a-Service (BinDaaS), that integrates blockchain and deep-learning techniques for sharing EHR records among multiple healthcare users [4]. Blockchain technology allows for real-time remote continuous monitoring devices, remote diagnosis, and therapy for patients. A blockchain telesurgery framework was developed in which security along with immutability and interoperability are achieved using Smart Contracts (SCs) to establish trust between all the parties connected via blockchain [2, 5]. A blockchain-based system with Smart Contracts, such as with a sensor to monitor the heart rate, collects and sends data to a smart device such as a smartphone or tablet, which then sends the data to the blockchain framework [70]. The nodes in the network can establish secure connections using sensor and mobile device addresses to record the heart rate on the blockchain in this architecture, which is an upgraded version of the IEEE 802.15.6 standard. Smart devices and body sensors store all the information. The primary advantage of this method is that patients may not need to maintain the blockchain records or take a full node on the blockchain system. Authorized applications can be integrated into the health environment thanks to the smart contract's design. Because only medical experts actively participate in data validation and consensus, the suggested approach's consensus mechanism can be altered from the existing solid evidence method to a clear evidence or verification consensus mechanism. Then it would necessitate available materials other than the blockchain's present actual evidence authentication.

Blockchain and smart contract (SC) appear to offer technological solutions to overcome many security issues in smart healthcare, including supply chain issues. A recent study proposes an Ethereum blockchain-based smart contract for a healthcare supply chain using unmanned aerial vehicles (UAVs) called VAHAK, which ensures transaction reliability and security. It is a peer-to-peer (P2P) distributed scheme where each peer has a copy of the entire BC, with no chance of single-point failure. VAHAK also ensures trust between all stakeholders via the immutability and transparency of records. Finally, the VAHAK performance evaluation demonstrates its effectiveness as compared to traditional systems, outperforming existing approaches with respect to various performance metrics, including scalability, latency, and network bandwidth [7].

However, the application of blockchain in the smart healthcare field is not yet mature. Most of the existing research is on the combination of blockchain and existing information technology to create a new system or platform, such as the construction of an electronic medical system based on blockchain or of a data privacy protection platform based on blockchain. Some studies examine the role of blockchain in smart healthcare sustainable supply chains, such as monitoring substandard or counterfeit drugs or the operating environment of medical products.

7 Conclusion

The long-term improvements offered by blockchain to the smart healthcare system are mainly reflected in ten factors: top-level design, doctor management, medical records management, treatment optimization, community building, cost savings, internal and external regulation, medical insurance, and environmental governance.

The existing applications of blockchain in the field of smart healthcare have mostly been at the private chain level, in which the permissions are controlled by an organization and the general public does not have access, and there is a lack of exploration at the alliance chain level, which would allow at least some decentralization. Because the leading companies control the information, the information is not transparent enough in private blockchain and its application is limited. Although, compared with the private chain, the public chain has a greater improvement in the credibility of information, the public chain must include many participants, and it is difficult to ensure the privacy and security of those participants. In addition, the private chain is "completely decentralized," which negatively affects the design of the healthcare system. In contrast, the alliance blockchain has the characteristic of "partial decentralization," and it is more conducive to the application of blockchain in the field of smart healthcare by adding a limited main body in the application process to reduce the cost decrease risks and increase the degree of trust. Research is ongoing for methods to utilize alliance blockchain level more effectively in smart healthcare applications [71].

We have presented a review of recent works as well as various research opportunities and openings in the areas of IoT blockchain, and 5G for smart healthcare. First, a concept for 5G smart healthcare was presented as well as the required techniques, D2D communication, network function virtualization, and edge computing (mmWaves) to allow 5G smart healthcare services. Second, the scientific classification of 5G smart healthcare was presented, and the new prerequisites (ultrahigh reliability, ultralow latency, high transfer speed, and high battery lifetime) and goals for 5G smart healthcare were investigated. The goals are to increase resources, upgrade QoS, reduce interference, and improve energy efficiency. Third, a point-by-point audit of network layer arrangements, such as routing, scheduling, and congestion management, was applied to the IoT-based 5G smart healthcare system, and it covered research openings in both future and current prospects. Because of the network's versatility and changing nature, it was difficult to present all the methodologies; however, an attempt was made to cover all the fundamental methodologies. Blockchain technology was discussed in the context of applications to better enable IoT in smart healthcare and provide solutions to some of the major issues. Some current applications were presented, and limitations and challenges were examined as well. As we discussed, there are open problems and obstacles to be faced in the future of 5G smart healthcare.

References

[1] J. Hathaliya, P. Sharma, S. Tanwar, R. Gupta, Blockchain-based remote patient monitoring in healthcare 4.0, in: 9th IEEE International Conference on Advanced Computing (IACC), Tiruchirappalli, India, 13-148th December, 2019, pp. 87–91.

[2] R. Gupta, S. Tanwar, S. Tyagi, N. Kumar, M.S. Obaidat, B. Sadoun HaBiTs, Blockchain-based telesurgery framework for healthcare 4.0, in: International Conference on Computer, Information and Telecommunication Systems (IEEE CITS-2019), Beijing, China, August 28–31, 2019, pp. 6–10.

[3] S. Tanwar, K. Parekh, R. Evans, Blockchain-based electronic healthcare record system for healthcare 4.0 applications, J. Inf. Secur. Appl. 50 (2019) 1–14.

[4] P. Bhattacharya, S. Tanwar, S. Tyagi, N. Kumar, BINDaaS: blockchain integrated deep-learning as a service in healthcare 4.0 applications, in: IEEE Transactions on Network Science and Engineering, 2019, pp. 1–14.

[5] R. Gupta, A. Shukla, S. Tanwar, AaYusH: a smart contract-based telesurgery system for healthcare 4.0, in: IEEE Conference on Communications (IEEE ICC-2020), Dublin, Ireland, 07-11th June, 2020, pp. 1–6.

[6] U. Bodkhe, S. Tanwar, A. Ladha, P. Bhattacharya, A. Verma, A survey on revolutionizing Healthcare 4.0 applications using blockchain International Conference on Computing, Communications, and Cyber-Security (IC4S 2020), Lecture Notes in Networks and Systems, Springer, Chandigarh, India, 12-13th October, 2019, pp. 1–16.

[7] R. Gupta, A. Shukla, P. Mehta, P. Bhattacharya, S. Tanwar, S. Tyagi, N. Kumar, VAHAK: a blockchain-based outdoor delivery scheme using UAV for healthcare 4.0 services, in: IEEE International Conference on Computer Communications (IEEE INFOCOM 2020), Beijing, China, 27-30th April, 2020, pp. 1–8.

[8] J. Hathaliya, S. Tanwar, S. Tyagi, N. Kumar, Securing electronics healthcare records in healthcare 4.0: a biometric-based approach, Comput. Electr. Eng. 76 (2019) 398–410.

[9] D. Mehta, S. Tanwar, U. Bodkhe, A. Shukla, N. Kumar, Blockchain-based royalty contract transactions scheme for Industry 4.0 supply-chain management, Inf. Process. Manag. 58 (4) (2021) 102586. ISSN 0306-4573 *https://doi.org/10.1016/j.ipm.2021.102586*.

[10] U. Bodkhe, D. Mehta, S. Tanwar, P. Bhattacharya, P.K. Singh, W. Hong, A survey on decentralized consensus mechanisms for cyber physical systems, IEEE Access 8 (2020) 54371–54401, https://doi.org/10.1109/ACCESS.2020.2981415.

[11] J. Hathaliya, S. Tanwar, An exhaustive survey on security and privacy issues in healthcare 4.0, Comput. Commun. 153 (2020), https://doi.org/10.1016/j.comcom.2020.02.018.

[12] R. Gupta, S. Tanwar, S. Tyagi, N. Kumar, Tactile-internet-based telesurgery system for healthcare 4.0: an architecture, research challenges, and future directions, IEEE Netw. 33 (6) (2019) 22–29, https://doi.org/10.1109/MNET.001.1900063.

[13] P. Bhattacharya, P. Mehta, S. Tanwar, M.S. Obaidat, K.F. Hsiao, HeaL: a blockchain-envisioned signcryption scheme for healthcare IoT ecosystems, in: International Conference on Communications, Computing, Cybersecurity, and Informatics 2020 ((CCCI 2020)), Sharjah, United Arab Emirates, 3–5 November, 2020, pp. 1–6.

[14] J. Santos, J.J.P.C. Rodrigues, B.M.C. Silva, J. Casal, K. Saleem, V. Denisov, An IoT-based mobile gateway for intelligent personal assistants on mobile health environments, J. Netw. Comput. Appl. 71 (2016) 194–204.

[15] I. Chiuchisan, I. Chiuchisan, M. Dimian, Internet of things for ehealth: an approach to medical applications, in: Proceedings of IEEE International Workshop Computational Intelligence Multimedia Understand. (IWCIM), 2015, pp. 1–5.

[16] M. Chen, Y. Ma, Y. Li, D. Wu, Y. Zhang, C.-H. Youn, Wearable 2.0: enabling human-cloud integration in next generation healthcare systems, IEEE Commun. Mag. 55 (1) (2017) 54–61.

[17] W.D. de Mattos, P.R.L. Gondim, M-health solutions using 5G networks and M2M communications, IT Prof. 18 (3) (2016) 24–29.

[18] S. Kraijak, P. Tuwanut, A survey on IoT architectures, protocols, applications, security, privacy, real-world implementation and future trends, in: Proceedings of 11th International Conference on Wireless Communication, Networking Mobile Computation (WiCOM), Sep, 2015, pp. 1–6.

[19] W. Ejaz, A. Anpalagan, M.A. Imran, M. Jo, M. Naeem, S.B. Qaisar, W. Wang, Internet of Things (IoT) in 5G wireless communications, IEEE Access 4 (2016) 10310–10314.

[20] M. Elhoseny, G. Ramírez-González, O.M. Abu-Elnasr, S.A. Shawkat, N. Arunkumar, A. Farouk, Secure medical data transmission model for IoT-based healthcare systems, IEEE Access 6 (2018) 20596–20608.

[21] M.H. Alsharif, R. Nordin, N.F. Abdullah, A.H. Kelechi, How to make key 5G wireless technologies environmental friendly: a review, Trans. Emerg. Telecommun. Technol. 29 (1) (2018), e3254.

[22] M. Agiwal, A. Roy, N. Saxena, Next generation 5G wireless networks: a comprehensive survey, IEEE Commun. Surv. Tutor. 18 (3) (2016) 1617–1655. 3rd Quart.

[23] M. Series, IMT vision-Framework and overall objectives of the future development of IMT for 2020 and beyond, Tech. Rep. Recommendation ITU-R M.2083-0, 2015.

[24] M.R. Palattella, M. Dohler, A. Grieco, G. Rizzo, J. Torsner, T. Engel, L. Ladid, Internet of things in the 5G era: enablers, architecture, and business models, IEEE J. Sel. Areas Commun. 34 (3) (2016) 510–527.

[25] J. Qi, P. Yang, G. Min, O. Amft, F. Dong, L. Xu, Advanced Internet of Things for personalized healthcare systems: a survey, Pervasive Mob. Comput. 41 (2017) 132–149.

[26] S.M.R. Islam, D. Kwak, M.H. Kabir, M. Hossain, K.-S. Kwak, The internet of things for health care: a comprehensive survey, IEEE Access 3 (2015) 678–708.

[27] R. Gupta, S. Tanwar, N. Kumar, S. Tyagi, Blockchain-based security attack resilience schemes for autonomous vehicles in industry 4.0: a systematic review, Comput. Electr. Eng. 86 (2019), https://doi.org/10.1016/j.compeleceng.2020.106717.

[28] I. Budhiraja, S. Tyagi, S. Tanwar, N. Kumar, J.J.P.C. Rodrigues, DIYA: tactile internet driven delay assessment NOMA-based scheme for D2D communication, IEEE Trans. Ind. Inf. 15 (12) (2019) 6354–6366, https://doi.org/10.1109/TII.2019.2910532.

[29] M.M. Dhanvijay, S.C. Patil, Internet of things: a survey of enabling technologies in healthcare and its applications, Comput. Netw. 153 (2019) 113–131.

[30] Q. Zhang, J. Liu, G. Zhao, Towards 5G Enabled Tactile Robotic Telesurgery, 2018, pp. 1–7.

[31] S. Tanwar, J. Vora, S. Tyagi, N. Kumar, M. Obaidat, A systematic review on security issues in vehicular ad hoc network, Secur. Priv. 1 (2018) 1–26, https://doi.org/10.1002/spy2.39.

[32] T.Q. Duong, X. Chu, H.A. Suraweera (Eds.), Ultra-Dense Networks for 5G and Beyond: Modelling, Analysis, and Applications, Wiley, Hoboken, NJ, USA, 2019.

[33] R. Gupta, S. Tanwar, N. Kumar, Secrecy-ensured NOMA-based cooperative D2D-aided fog computing under imperfect CSI, J. Inf. Secur. Appl. 59 (2021) 102812. ISSN 2214-2126 https://doi.org/10.1016/j.jisa.2021.102812.

[34] W.H. Chin, Z. Fan, R. Haines, Emerging technologies and research challenges for 5G wireless networks, IEEE Wirel. Commun. 21 (2) (2014) 106–112.

[35] F. Jameel, Z. Hamid, F. Jabeen, S. Zeadally, M.A. Javed, A survey of device-to-device communications: research issues and challenges, IEEE Commun. Surv. Tutor. 20 (3) (2018) 2133–2168. 3rd Quart.

[36] D. Reebadiya, T. Rathod, R. Gupta, S. Tanwar, N. Kumar, Blockchain-based secure and intelligent sensing for autonomous vehicles activity tracking beyond 5G networks, in: Peer-to-Peer Networking and Applications, 2021, https://doi.org/10.1007/s12083-021-01073-x.

[37] D. Fang, F. Ye, Y. Qian, H. Sharif, Small base station management-improving energy efficiency in heterogeneous networks, in: Proceedings of the 14th International Wireless Communication and Mobile Computing Conference (IWCMC), 2018, pp. 1191–1196.

[38] N. Al-Falahy, O.Y.K. Alani, Millimeter wave frequency band as a candidate spectrum for 5G network architecture: a survey, Phys. Commun. 32 (2019) 120–144.

[39] R. Gupta, S. Tanwar, N. Kumar, Blockchain and 5G integrated softwarized UAV network management: architecture, solutions, and challenges, physical communication, 47 (2021) 101355. ISSN 1874-4907 https://doi.org/10.1016/j.phycom.2021.101355.

[40] N. Hassan, S. Gillani, E. Ahmed, I. Ibrar, M. Imran, The role of edge computing in Internet of Things, IEEE Commun. Mag. 56 (11) (2018) 110–115.

[41] R. Gupta, A. Kumari, S. Tanwar, Fusion of blockchain and AI for secure drone networking underlying 5G communications, Trans. Emerg. Telecommun. Technol. 32 (2020), https://doi.org/10.1002/ett.4176.

[42] S. Madakam, R. Ramaswamy, S. Tripathi, Internet of Things (IoT): a literature review, J. Comput. Commun. 3 (5) (2015) 164–173.

[43] Y. Mehmood, F. Ahmad, I. Yaqoob, A. Adnane, M. Imran, S. Guizani, Internet-of-Things-based smart cities: recent advances and challenges, IEEE Commun. Mag. 55 (9) (2017) 16–24.

[44] M.M. Alam, H. Malik, M.I. Khan, T. Pardy, A. Kuusik, Y.L. Moullec, A survey on the roles of communication technologies in IoT-based personalized healthcare applications, IEEE Access 6 (2018) 36611–36631.

[45] I. Mistry, S. Tanwar, S. Tyagi, N. Kumar, Blockchain for 5G-enabled IoT for industrial automation: a systematic review, solutions, and challenges, Mech. Syst. Signal Process. 135 (2019), https://doi.org/10.1016/j.ymssp.2019.106382.

[46] Q. Han, S. Liang, H. Zhang, Mobile cloud sensing, big data, and 5G networks make an intelligent and smart world, IEEE Netw. 29 (2) (2015) 40–45.

[47] A. Kumari, S. Tanwar, S. Tyagi, N. Kumar, Verification and validation techniques for streaming big data analytics in internet of things environment, IET Netw. 8 (2019) 155–163, https://doi.org/10.1049/iet-net.2018.5187.

[48] J. Alzubi, B. Bharathikannan, S. Tanwar, R. Manikandan, A. Khanna, C. Thaventhiran, Boosted neural network ensemble classification for lung cancer disease diagnosis, Appl. Soft Comput. 80 (2019), https://doi.org/10.1016/j.asoc.2019.04.031.

[49] J. Vora, S. Tanwar, S. Tyagi, N. Kumar, J.J.P.C. Rodrigues, Home-based exercise system for patients using IoT enabled smart speaker, in: 2017 IEEE 19th International Conference on e-Health Networking, Applications and Services (Healthcom), 2017, pp. 1–6, https://doi.org/10.1109/HealthCom.2017.8210826.

[50] A. Kumari, R. Gupta, S. Tanwar, N. Kumar, Blockchain and AI amalgamation for energy cloud management: challenges, solutions, and future directions, J. Parallel Distrib. Comput. 143 (2020), https://doi.org/10.1016/j.jpdc.2020.05.004.

[51] H. Shariatmadari, R. Ratasuk, S. Iraji, A. Laya, T. Taleb, R. Jäntti, A. Ghosh, Machine-type communications: current status and future perspectives toward 5G systems, IEEE Commun. Mag. 53 (9) (2015) 10–17.

[52] Y.-G. Yue, P. He, A comprehensive survey on the reliability of mobile wireless sensor networks: taxonomy, challenges, and future directions, Inf. Fusion 44 (2018) 188–204.

[53] C. Mistry, U. Thakker, R. Gupta, S. Tanwar, N. Kumar, J.J.P.C. Rodrigues, M.S. Obaidat, MedBlock: an AI-enabled and blockchain-driven medical healthcare system for COVID-19, in: IEEE International Conference on Communications (IEEE ICC 2021), Montreal, Canada, 14–18 June, 2021.

[54] A. Shukla, N. Patel, S. Tanwar, B. Sadoun, M.S. Obaidat, BDoTs: blockchain-based evaluation scheme for online teaching under COVID-19 environment, in: International conference on computer, information and telecommunication systems (IEEE CITS-2020), Beijing, China, October 05-07, 2020, pp. 1–5.

[55] A. Ahad, S. Al Faisal, F. Ali, B. Jan, N. Ullah, Design and performance analysis of DSS (dual sink based scheme) protocol for WBASNs, Adv. Remote Sens. 6 (4) (2017) 245–259.

[56] M.A. Jan, S.R.U. Jan, M. Alam, A. Akhunzada, I.U. Rahman, A comprehensive analysis of congestion control protocols in wireless sensor networks, Mob. Netw. Appl. 23 (3) (2018) 456–468.

[57] R. Gupta, A. Kumari, S. Tanwar, N. Kumar, Blockchain-envisioned softwarized multi-swarming UAVs to tackle COVID-19 situations, IEEE Netw. (2020), https://doi.org/10.1109/MNET.011.2000439.

[58] D. Vekaria, A. Kumari, S. Tanwar and N. Kumar, "Boost: an AI-based data analytics scheme for COVID-19 prediction and economy boosting," IEEE Internet Things J., doi: *https://doi.org/10.1109/JIOT.2020.3047539.*

[59] W. Mwashita, M.O. Odhiambo, Interference management techniques for device-to-device communications, in: Predictive Intelligence Using Big Data and the Internet of Things, IGI Global, Hershey, PA, USA, 2019, pp. 219–245.

[60] S. Samarakoon, M. Bennis, W. Saad, M. Debbah, M. Latva-Aho, Ultra dense small cell networks: turning density into energy efficiency, IEEE J. Sel. Areas Commun. 34 (5) (2016) 1267–1280.

[61] L. Tshiningayamwe, G.-A. Lusilao-Zodi, M.E. Dlodlo, A priority rate-based routing protocol for wireless multimedia sensor networks, in: Advances in Nature and Biologically Inspired Computing, Springer, Cham, Switzerland, 2016, pp. 347–358.

[62] A. Shukla, N. Patel, S. Tanwar, B. Sadoun, M.S. Obaidat, BDoTs: blockchain-based evaluation scheme for online teaching under COVID-19 environment, in: International conference on computer, information and telecommunication systems (IEEE CITS-2020), Beijing, China, October 05-07, 2020, pp. 1–5.

[63] A. Ahad, S. Al Faisal, F. Ali, B. Jan, N. Ullah, Design and performance analysis of DSS (dual sink based scheme) protocol for WBASNs, Adv. Remote Sens. 6 (4) (2017) 245–259.

[64] A. Kumari, S. Tanwar, Secure data analytics for smart grid systems in a sustainable smart city: challenges, solutions, and future directions, Sustain. Comput.: Inform. Syst. 28 (2020) 100427. ISSN 2210-5379 *https://doi.org/10.1016/j.suscom.2020.100427.*

[65] 5G-PPP White Paper on E-Health Vertical Sector, document 5G-PPP, Sep. 2015, [Online]. Available *https://5g-ppp.eu/wp-content/uploads/2014/02/5G-PPP-White-Paper-one-Health-Vertical-Sector.pdf.*

[66] T.J. McCue, $117 Billion Market for Internet of Things in Healthcare by 2020, Forbes technology, 2015. [Online]. Available: *http://www.forbes.com/sites/tjmccue/2015/04/22/117-billion-market-forinternet-of-thingsin-healthcare-by-2020/2715e4857a0b2536043d2471.*

[67] J. Lloret, L. Parra, M. Taha, J. Tomás, An architecture and protocol for smart continuous eHealth monitoring using 5G, Comput. Netw. 129 (2017) 340–351.

[68] M. Chen, J. Yang, J. Zhou, Y. Hao, J. Zhang, C.-H. Youn, 5G-smart diabetes: toward personalized diabetes diagnosis with healthcare big data clouds, IEEE Commun. Mag. 56 (4) (2018) 16–23.

[69] F. Xiao, Q. Miao, X. Xie, L. Sun, R. Wang, Indoor anti-collision alarm system based on wearable Internet of Things for smart healthcare, IEEE Commun. Mag. 56 (4) (2018) 53–59.

[70] S. Hua, Congestion control based on reliable transmission in wireless sensor networks, J. Networks 9 (3) (2014) 762–768.

[71] X. Du, B. Chen, M. Ma, Y. Zhang, Research on the application of blockchain in smart healthcare: constructing a hierarchical framework, J. Healthcare Eng. 2021 (2021) 6698122, https://doi.org/10.1155/2021/6698122.

Smart healthcare using blockchain technologies: The importance, applications, and challenges

Shilpi Bisht[a], Neeraj Bisht[a], Pankaj Singh[a], Shray Dasila[a], and K.S. Nisar[b]
[a]Birla Institute of Applied Sciences, Bhimtal, India, [b]Prince Sattam bin Abdulaziz University, Al-Kharj, Saudi Arabia

1 Introduction

The healthcare industry has seen enormous changes with the development of technologies. It is considered to be the substratum of any economy and certainly affects the overall development of a country. In India, the healthcare sector is a significant contributor in terms of employment and revenue generation. The transformation of this industry from traditional healthcare to smart healthcare is definitely a boon to society as well as to the economy.

Smart healthcare is an advanced health service system that is equipped with modern technologies such as a new generation of wireless networks, the Internet of Things (IoT), smart wearable gadgets, blockchain technology, and artificial intelligence (AI) to provide convenient, highly efficient, secure, and personalized services to patients and medical personnel. This multilevel technological advancement in traditional health services is a gradual process that is still in its developmental phase.

Blockchain, a decentralized, distributed, efficient, and secure technology, has emerged as the dominant technology to bring a digital revolution to the healthcare industry. Medical records of any patient are very critical data that demand extreme privacy. However, due to the digitization of health data, they are more prone to breaches and cyberattacks. The decentralized nature of blockchain provides transparency and more control over personal medical records to both patients and health service providers. Also, the feature of immutability reduces the probability of fraud and also protects against liability. Blockchain provides a better solution to the privacy and security concerns of smart healthcare systems.

The fifth-generation wireless network, known as 5G technology, in the healthcare sector is envisioned to bring a paradigm shift in this industry. Telehealth services with IoT have proved to be fruitful in providing healthcare services remotely. These IoT and technical devices demand faster network speed and bandwidth because increased congestion and slower network speeds create challenges for healthcare providers who have to interface with dozens of patients a day. 5G technology appears to be a better solution to these challenges.

According to a report from Bitglass [1], healthcare breaches in the United States increased 55.1% in 2020 in comparison to the previous year. The report states, "This

Blockchain Applications for Healthcare Informatics. https://doi.org/10.1016/B978-0-323-90615-9.00006-2
Copyright © 2022 Elsevier Inc. All rights reserved.

year, hacking and IT incidents led to 67.3% of all healthcare breaches, more than three times that of the next highest category. Additionally, breaches caused by hacking and IT incidents exposed 91.2% of all breached records in healthcare in 2020-24.1 million out of 26.4 million." It is clear that data breaches and cyberattacks in the healthcare industry are currently major challenges for smart healthcare. The implementation of blockchain-enabled 5G technology in health services may provide for better security and privacy of personal records.

1.1 Research contribution

This chapter provides a detailed literature review of the research done in the development of smart healthcare. It introduces basic concepts of blockchain, 5G technology, and healthcare informatics. It discusses the applications and challenges for 5G-enabled blockchain in smart healthcare. A comparative study of existing electronic health record (EHR) models and a case study are done to understand developments in this field.

1.2 Organization

This chapter is divided into six subsections. Section 1 provides the introduction. A detailed literature review that is the motivation behind understanding smart healthcare is provided in Section 2. Precise descriptions of blockchain technology, its working mechanisms, 5G technology, and 5G-enabled blockchain are provided in Section 3. Section 4 deals with healthcare informatics and applications of Blockchain 5.0. Section 5 presents potential challenges for the proposed technique in healthcare. We discuss a case study in Section 6. A comparative study of existing blockchain-based smart healthcare systems is presented in Section 7. The future scope and conclusion are presented in Section 8.

2 Literature review

The healthcare sector is important and needs improvement as far as taking care of patients is concerned. There is a necessity of adopting a "patient-oriented" system. Healthcare is currently transforming to a distributed patient-centered approach from a conventional hospital and specialist-based approach. Azaria et al. [2] stated the various types of challenges faced in integrating the blockchain and healthcare sector. In their work, they proposed MedRec. It will be used for maintaining the electronic medical records (EMR). They also discussed a unique approach to access all EMRs. Ichikawa et al. [3] used the Hyperledger fabric blockchain platform to work on medical records they collected through smart phones. In their work, they shared medical data to the blockchain platform and verified that data is successfully recorded. Vora et al. [4] performed a study to check the efficiency of smart speakers with IoT. Gordon et al. [5] in their work stated that blockchain technology is important for the healthcare sector. They published a review defining how blockchain technology can be used in healthcare. Blockchain can share patient-centric data over institution-centric control. Blockchain technology will allow and identify patients on its own, access rights digitally, and store and manage the data and information of patients. Rouhani et al. [6] also talked about the Hyperledger fabric blockchain platform. They used Hyperledger to manage the healthcare records of patients. Vora et al. [7] stated that the data records of patients such as name, age, sex, and other personal information are either lost or illegally disclosed. In their work, they presented a system and framework needed by doctors and patients for managing and taking care of EHR. Shen et al. [8] discussed in detail the management of medical records and data through blockchain and MedChain, which is a peer-to-peer network. They analyzed the system efficiency with that of a therapist present physically. Hathaliya et al. [9] presented and discussed the problems along with the solutions of a permissioned blockchain based upon healthcare architecture. Gupta et al. [10] discussed in detail how 5G can use the tactile Internet for various applications in the healthcare sector. They also compared IoT and the tactile Internet. Kumari et al. [11] analyzed how data can be securely streamed as well as security issues before IoT. A detailed analysis of various research challenges was done. Budhiraja et al. [12] presented an Internet-driven delay assessment, known as a DIYA (Driven Delay Assessment) scheme. Their study showed that DIYA achieved more accuracy with reduced delay time as compared to OMA and NOMA schemes. Gupta et al. [13] proposed HaBiTs (a framework based on blockchain) and highlighted challenges for the telesurgery system and how the HaBiTs framework overcomes them. Bhattacharya et al. [14] proposed the blockchain-based deep learning as a service (BinDaaS) framework and deep learning as a service (DaaS). DaaS stores EHRs so they can be used for predicting future diseases with the help of machine learning.

Khezr et al. [15] analyzed and described in detail the various types of challenges and problems in the healthcare management system. These problems and issues faced can be erased using blockchain technology. Blockchain technology with distributed ledger technology can be very important and vital for the healthcare sector. In their work, they also discussed the Internet of Medical Things (IoMT) delivery system and the client-centered approach from a conventional hospital and specialist-based approach. The main features of the valuable work by Ahad et al. [16] are the taxonomy, challenges ahead, IoT, and 5G-enabled smart healthcare. Siyal et al. [17] in their work stated that smart contracts are important and advantageous for the healthcare sector. They further explained in detail that it is very important and mandatory to store and properly manage healthcare records. Introducing and combining blockchain technology with the healthcare sector can help in minimizing the data and information of patients. Jamil et al. [18] discussed the issues regarding drug regulations and how to standardize drugs using blockchain. In their work, they highlighted the difficulties in detecting falsified drugs and proposed blockchain as a way to detect counterfeits. Agbo et al. [19] in their valuable work described in detail the various types of applications of blockchain technology. Drug supply chains, storing and maintaining EMRs, and various research fields can be implemented using blockchain technology. There is a need to overcome the various problems and issues in integrating healthcare and blockchain.

Basholli et al. [20] proposed a 5G-enabled sensor-based networks architecture and a data structure stating the transmission of data without the use of any intermediate devices. Bittins et al. [21] reviewed the research results of the blockchain-based healthcare sector. They presented the application of blockchain for data sharing in the healthcare sector. This ensured proper tracking and management of a patient's data. Multiaccess edge computing (MEC) is prevalent in supporting 5G technology. Lin et al. [22] proposed an algorithm that is helpful in reducing the end-to-end delay in data computation. Minimization of the end-to-end delay of the applications in the healthcare sector is a major proposal of their work. Security and privacy concerns are important due to confidential data and information. They shared details on the technologies used in the security models of 5G technology and the PHY (physical) layer. The IoT is estimated to connect more than 33 billion devices by 2021. Khan et al. [23] and Haris et al. [24] defined in detail the security and privacy concerns, including the performance on the integration of blockchain and 5G-enabled IoT. Chen et al. [25] stated that blockchain is a transparent and decentralized system. Thus, it can be used for storing as well as sharing data and information. Moreover, the system is secure and safe, henceforth no third party has excess to the stored data. The data remain only among the allowed individuals or groups. This technology has evolved and has many applications, including the healthcare sector.

Blockchain and 5G-enabled IoT altogether are a complete package for bringing a revolution to various sectors. Blockchain and 5G-enabled IoT industrial automation can be important for sectors such as healthcare, smart city, and supply chain management. Open issues and challenges are in front of this technology. Mistry et al. [26] compared previous proposals with a number of parameters, thus allowing users to select the best proposals on the basis of a comparison. 5G technology is considered the elementary network infrastructure for Healthcare 5.0. Mohanta et al. [27] in their work elaborated that artificial intelligence (AI), high-speed transmission of data, and smart intelligent devices have set high standards as far as the healthcare sector is concerned. A detailed evaluation and summary of the fundamental concepts including AI and 5G technology are also presented. Sectors such as healthcare, defense, lifestyle wearable gadgets, and technologies have played a crucial role. Hence, the role of 5G technology becomes important. Sharma et al. [28] in their work presented the design and structure of wearable smart watches based on 5G technology in the defense sector. Adebusola et al. [29] reviewed the changes and improvements from a new generation of wireless technology over previous generations. Uddin et al. [30] elaborated in detail about how drones can be important for blockchain in terms of privacy and decentralization. They reviewed the background of 5G-IoT ecosystems, unmanned aerial vehicles (UAV), and their capability and research challenges. Also, they proposed an architecture of blockchain and 5G-enabled medical delivery drones and satellites providing communication ease and support. Today's era includes smart technologies in sectors such as transport, smart cities, healthcare, and telecommunication. Tanwar et al. [31] stated that the advent of blockchain in the healthcare sector can be beneficial. Later, they proposed an access control policy algorithm (ACPA) allowing data and information to be accessed successfully. Gupta et al. [32] proposed AaYusH, a telesurgery system based upon the Ethereum smart contract (ESC) and the interplanetary file system (IPFS). Further, they analyzed AaYusH's performance on various parameters such as cost and data storage. Kumari et al. [33] reviewed various approaches to AI, including challenges facing blockchain technology and AI energy cloud management system. Hewa et al. [34] in their work explored the importance of blockchain for sixth-generation technology in terms of future challenges, research opportunities, and applications.

COVID-19 has had a great impact on almost everyone around the world. In some countries, the situation has been quite crucial. Some myths and rumors were spreading all around. Chamola et al. [35] discussed in detail how technologies including 5G-enabled IoT, AI, and blockchain can be integrated to slow the impact of this pandemic. Siriwardhana et al. [36] also presented the technical challenges and requirements in reference to 5G and IoT. 6G-based blockchain-enabled software reducing human intervention with THz frequency bands including the physical protocols required was presented by Gupta et al. [37] in their valuable work. Chen et al. [38] proposed a 5G-based smart security system. The main elements included behavior, object, subject, and environment. Thus, it met the need for a smart medical system based on 5G. Mazurczyk et al. [39] further evaluated that 5G technology has great potential to offer the finest and superior range of five-star services. The main focus was on the research results achieved by scientists and developers who worked on problems and challenges for 5G technology. Hewa et al. [40] proposed an architecture based on blockchain and MEC (multiaccess edge computing). Elliptic Curve Qu-Vanstone (ECQV) provided data privacy and MEC, cloud, and IoT integration. The system also ensured an enormous storage capacity for storing the medical records. Ciampi et al. [41] elaborated with an example about the challenges in integrating health level seven (HL7) fast healthcare interoperability resources (FHIR) with distributed ledger technology (DLT). Blockchain has gained a lot of appreciation in the recent years. Berdik et al. [42] in their survey integrated this technology with the current information systems. Modern languages and the structure of blockchain technology are key elements for the further development and spread of the technology.

3 Blockchain and 5G technology

Blockchain is an ordered chain consisting of blocks. Every individual block contains data and information based on the references of the previous block. A block stores information such as transaction details, digital certificates, papers, encrypted identities of users, and other personal and public information. Each individual block also has a unique hash code or value. The input stored in each block is converted into unique encrypted output. This output has a fixed length and is generated using a mathematical function.

A hash value resembles a student's ID card, which identifies the student and gives certain important information about him/her. Now, here student refers to a block and information refers to the content and data that specific block contains. Also, every single block contains the previous block's hash value for reference. Suppose a group or individual somehow manages to get access to a blockchain. Now, when they change anything in a block, this in turn creates a new hash code for that particular block. Hence, this makes the whole blockchain invalid or not found. This feature protects the other blocks of the blockchain from getting hacked or attacked by third parties or suspicious individuals.

Blockchain is a decentralized and distributed form of technology. It is mostly governed by a network called peer-to-peer. Next comes the proof of work (PoW) mechanism. PoW is basically an algorithm that verifies and then confirms a transaction in a "blockchain. After successfully completing the verification process, a new block is created and added to the blockchain. This process is necessary for security and privacy.

Chatterjee and Chatterjee [43] described that PoW is a process where miners compete to find a random string. Once they find the string, it has to be hashed with hash and the transactions of the previous block, hence, generating a new hash. Hashing is a process of converting a given input string to a certain length output. This newly generated hash contains x leading zeros, where x depends upon the difficulty level. Fig. 1 describes the working mechanism of blockchain.

5G is the fifth generation of wireless networks, and it follows 4G. This wireless network technology was launched in early 2019. It's designed for attaining high and fast multi-Gbps peak data speeds with greater reliability and a low latency rate compared to all previous generations of mobile networks. Continuity as well as uniformity will be greater and more developed in 5G. 5G is supposed to be 10 times faster than 4G. This technology works on orthogonal frequency-division multiplexing (OFDM), which helps to reduce interference and results in smooth connectivity. 5G is designed to provide higher peak data rates and greater bandwidth.

Ericsson, Samsung, Nokia, Qualcomm, and other companies have contributed to developing 5G. It's estimated that 5G is successfully deployed in more than 60 countries. In India, 5G is supposed to be launched around the middle of 2021. 5G technology can also be integrated with the IoT. Hence, IoT devices can share data with higher speeds and great connectivity. Gupta and Jha [44] proposed the architecture of the 5G cellular network. In their work, they stated that IoT is capable of working with 5G. Smart healthcare, smart cities, industry, tourism, and many other sectors can benefit

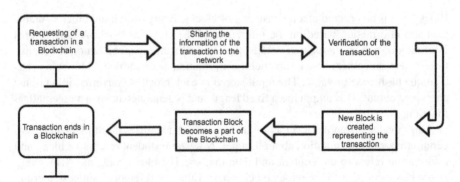

Fig. 1 Working mechanism of blockchain.

with the integration of 5G and IoT. Advancement and development in the mobile network generation are significant to overcome future problems and challenges.

In 5G networks, the data and information are transferred through radio waves. Information and data are transferred through higher frequency bands. These frequency bands have a range of 30–300 GHz, with a latency rate of about 1–3 ms. A faster speed of about 10 gigabytes per second is also a key feature of these advanced 5G networks. This helps in transferring large amounts of data packets without delay and in less time. Hence, 5G is important for the healthcare sector because of these salient features.

We now understand that blockchain is a decentralized group of blocks. The main features of blockchain include transparency and reliability; the fact that it is a trustworthy and decentralized platform; maintaining user privacy; and also providing a safe and secure environment. 5G is designed to provide high bandwidth, faster data and information transfer, great continuity, and uniformity. Now, both these technologies integrated together are referred to as 5G-enabled blockchain.

Sectors such as smart healthcare, smart homes, and tourism will become more developed and advanced with this integration. We should also keep in mind that there will be various challenges and flaws in developing 5G-enabled blockchain. Chaer et al. [45] in their work mentioned the opportunities and challenges in creating a blockchain-enabled 5G environment. They also evaluated the architecture with flow diagrams related to blockchain-enabled-5G. If in the near future blockchain and 5G are integrated, then a lot more applications of these technologies can come into existence.

4 Applications of 5G-enabled blockchain in healthcare informatics

Healthcare is a very old industry that is resistant to changes and defiant to new practices. Sharing of patient's clinical records, medical supply chain management data, and record verification of medical personnel are major challenges due to the concerns of privacy, security, and integrity of information. These issues are being scrutinized, and have been gaining attention in recent years. Demand for the secure exchange of patient clinical data with medical practitioners and other fellow medical researchers has also grown in recent years. To resolve these issues, 5G-enabled blockchain is being identified as a secure technology for the distribution and sharing of clinical data. In recent years, 5G-enabled blockchain has gained a lot of popularity in various fields such as cryptocurrency, smart contracts, IoT, logistic and supply chain control and supervision, and personal identity security, due to its novel approach to authenticate, verify, and control the access mechanism of data. According to a recent report from Market Research Future [46], blockchain technology accounts for more than $42 million in the global healthcare industry and is expected to grow by 71.8% by 2027. This substantial rise of 5G-enabled blockchain in the healthcare industry is steered by the decentralized, transparent, traceable, efficient, secured, privacy-oriented, and cost-effective nature of blockchain.

The healthcare sector is a broad area where there is a huge scope for the utilization of blockchain technology. Moreover, blockchain has been exercised successfully in several biomedical studies and academia. There are many use cases of blockchain in clinical investigations where it has been used to counter the manipulation of a clinical investigation's conclusion. Blockchain can also be used to make patient medical data anonymous so that patients can be motivated to make available their data for various ongoing clinical studies. Moreover, the integrity of patient data can be assured on the immutable substructure of blockchain. It will be much simpler to replicate the research generated from blockchain-based technology. According to Chen et al. [47], blockchain has the potential of revolutionizing the peer review system for healthcare-related research publications because of its transparency as well as decentralized and immutable nature. Disparate ingenious ideas have been suggested to take advantage of blockchain-based applications in healthcare, as shown in Fig. 2. A few of them are discussed below.

4.1   5G-enabled blockchain-based EHR system

According to Burton et al. [48], patient-centric EHR systems are developed for creating, storing, and managing a patient's clinical and other health data. Storing and managing clinical communication between a patient and medical practitioner and data pooled through various biomedical sensors could provide ample sources of intelligence that can be utilized for healthcare-related decisions. There is an increasing demand that a patient's clinical data and other related information should be easily accessible to the patient at any given time. Moreover, medical practitioners also need to access the patient's health record at varying levels. In such scenarios, only a patient

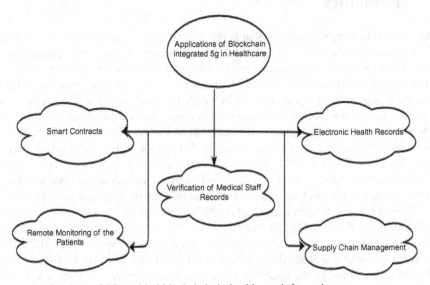

Fig. 2 Applications of 5G-enabled blockchain in healthcare informatics.

should be in control of the conditions and information that they want to share with a medical practitioner. This requires a patient-centric solution that guarantees access to proper data to the right person at the right time and provides privacy and security of the patient's clinical data. Such patient-centric solutions can be developed with the help of 5G-enabled blockchain technology, which provides complete control to the patient of their health data.

5G-enabled blockchain EHR systems provide the following benefits over traditional systems.

• Quick and easy access to the patient's clinical data at any time.
• Privacy and security-centric system that ensures trusted access to data.
• Eliminates redundant and multiple copies of data.
• Enhances patient and caregiver interactions.
• Enables detailed insight into patient clinical data.

4.2 5G-enabled blockchain-based supply chain management systems

Supply chain management poses a major challenge in the healthcare industry where a lot of counterfeit medical goods and medicines make their way to hospitals and consumers, causing thousands of deaths globally [49]. It is necessary to ensure the originality of medical commodities to affirm their authenticity. Manufacturers and customers can utilize a blockchain-based system to track the medical commodities they have ordered from the production plant to each stage of the supply chain to ensure the originality and authenticity of the product.

There are several other benefits of blockchain-based supply chain management. Some of the key benefits are listed below.

1. Customer's trust: blockchain-based supply chain management systems ensure customer trust in the provenance of the product as well as timely information on its whereabouts.
2. Compliance: medical and pharmaceutical manufacturers must bear the responsibility of ensuring the patient's safety. Therefore, compiling all supply chain-related data into a single system helps manufacturers streamline compliance.
3. Supply chain optimization: a blockchain-based system helps in aggregating supply chain data into a single place and in its optimization.

4.3 5G-enabled blockchain-based smart contract

Blockchain-based smart contract systems provide a common platform to all stakeholders of the healthcare sector [19]. Smart contracts in the healthcare sector have huge potential for providing a common platform for trading. They can cater to the needs of all stakeholders of the healthcare sector such as pharmaceutical companies, healthcare providers, medical device manufacturers, and insurers. Such platforms could provide services such as logging details of contracts, managing transactions, and settling payment disputes. With help of a shared 5G-enabled blockchain ledger, pharmaceutical companies, healthcare providers, medical device manufacturers, insurers, and other participating entities can significantly reduce the time taken for settling any dispute they may have. Some of the advantages of 5G-enabled blockchain-based smart contracts are listed below:

- These contracts do not involve any broker or any other third party, thus eliminating the risk of any kind of tampering or manipulation.
- Cost-effective and do not require any paper trail.

4.4 5G-enabled blockchain-based medical staff record verification

Blockchain-based systems could also be used to maintain, track, and validate the experience and other credentials of medical personals [15]. To establish such a system, reputed medical organizations can record the credentials of their employees to smoothen the recruitment process of medical staff. Any changes made in the record of an employee may need to be verified by the previous employer, thus ensuring the authenticity of the records. ProCredEx is a United States-based company that has made such a record verification system. It uses the R3 Corda blockchain protocol for medical staff record verification. Some of the main advantages of such systems are:

- Simple and swift record verification of medical personnel during the hiring process.
- Provides assurance of the quality of the medical staff being hired.
- Preserves reliance on the excellence of medical staff, and keeps costs down.

4.5 5G-enabled blockchain-based security of remote patient monitoring

Remote monitoring of patients by using sensors to assess vital signs helps medical practitioners to have a detailed insight into patient health [50]. With this kind of data, patients could receive preventive and proactive care. However, security is a major challenge in remote monitoring to make sure that a patient's clinical data stays private and secure and is not meddled with to generate imprecise information. It is important that the supporting technology for remote monitoring is strong enough to thwart distributed denial of service (DDoS) or any other attack that may interrupt monitoring. Blockchain-based cryptography makes sure that only the allowed entities can read the patient's medical information, which is stored in a very unique hash function. Once a patient's clinical data are stored in a hash function, then it is difficult to tamper with the data. Some of the benefits of blockchain-based security of remote monitoring are listed below:

- Improved access to quality healthcare.
- Prevent patient's health data leakage.
- Secure tracking of patient's health.

5 Challenges for blockchain in healthcare

The healthcare sector is a major element for the economic growth and gross domestic product of any nation. Integrating the blockchain and healthcare sectors will help boost and upgrade the healthcare sector. But there are some challenges ahead for making this integration fruitful. Onik et al. [51] discussed in detail the challenges in integrating blockchain and healthcare. They also designed an architecture, related issues, and problems for proper management and storage of patient data and information in the present as well as in the future. These challenges and problems, as presented in Fig. 3, include the following:

5.1 Issues in storing patient data

The proper management and security of patient's personal information and data are required to avoid loss or leaking of EMRs. According to a report by Munro [52], more than 12 million data records get deleted, disclosed by illegal means, lost, or stolen. So, issues in storing patient data and information must be resolved while integrating blockchain and healthcare.

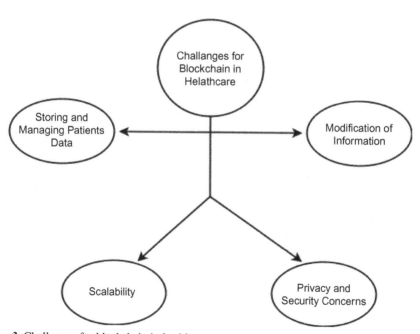

Fig. 3 Challenges for blockchain in healthcare.

5.2   Updating and modifying information

Once data are stored in a blockchain, it's next to impossible (except by creating a new block) to update and modify the data. But it's also a good option from a security point of view. So if the patient data gets leaked or stolen, then the third party can't edit or modify it.

5.3   Higher energy consumption and scaling issues

Blockchain technology is designed in such a way that it uses large amounts of energy. Scalability is also a minor issue but is important in integrating blockchain and healthcare. Scalability and high energy consumption rate issues must be resolved before integrating blockchain and healthcare.

5.4   Privacy and security issues

Blockchain is a transparent, decentralized, independent, and reliable form of technology. Now, if the blockchain containing patient data faces any of these attacks, then all data might be leaked. There exist a number of threats and attacks prevailing all around, as presented in Fig. 4. They include:

1. **DDoS attack:** In DDoS attacks, the attacker doesn't allow the particular attacked block to work normally. The block gets slowed down as the attacker transfers a larger amount of transactions and information. Hence, this makes the block slower.
2. **51% vulnerability attack:** In these types of attacks, the attacker or third party takes control over access to more than 50% of the blockchain mining hash rate. But such attacks don't continue for a long time period as a huge amount of power is required for this.

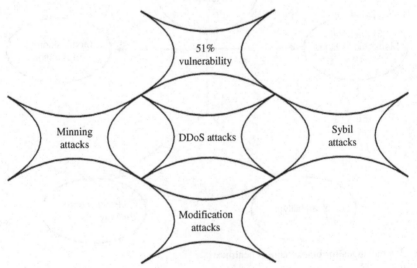

Fig. 4 Showcasing some types of attacks in a blockchain.

3. **Modification attacks:** As the name suggests, modification means change. Hence, the attacker can modify or update any information in the blockchain.
4. **Sybil attacks:** The attacker passes a number of nodes, making the network crowded with these nodes. Once the attacker is successful, he tries to get access to the network of blocks through these multiple nodes.
5. **Mining attacks:** In mining attacks, the malware tries to mine larger amounts of cryptos for the miner or attacker. It's believed that the malware hides inside the system without getting easily spotted.

In these attacks, the data contained in the block are at risk. Suppose a record of around 10,000 patients is stored in block A. Now, block A faces any of the above-mentioned attacks. So, the attacker now has full access to the data stored. Hence, this also affects the privacy of many patients.

Also, permission-seeking blockchain solves the issue to some extent. A stranger or any third party can't access the data present in any block of permission-seeking blockchain until and unless the users grant permission. There is an urgent need for a model that can make blockchain more secure and private. It's important to give the main emphasis on how to protect the blockchain from threats and attackers.

6   Case study

6.1   Problem statement

For smart healthcare, all records of patient histories are required over the network, so that it can be accessed easily whenever it is necessary to maintain the privacy and security of data.

6.2   Proposed solution

Tanwar et al. [31] considered a case where a history of all the test records and previous consultancy and treatment of the patient was required. For this, they proposed a DLT-based blockchain approach for designing an EHR-sharing architecture with an access control policy. Their proposed algorithm is patient-centric and the patient has the authority to share data with other healthcare providers. The four stakeholders in the proposed EHR sharing system are the administrator, doctors, patients, and laboratory. An EHR is distributed securely with other participants of the blockchain network by sharing a symmetric key and a private key. Permission-based symmetric key cryptography ensures the security of private data. The administrator has all the rights to access the system, including read, write, update, and remove participants. The administrator provides a unique ID to each valid participant so that they can access the blockchain network. Any suspicious participant can be removed from the network by the administrator. Patients can add their records through software development kit or client applications. Once a transaction is committed, it is distributed over the blockchain network and cannot be altered or deleted by any unauthorized users. The security is claimed by timestamping. The doctors and laboratory staff can view and update the records of the patient into the EHR ledger network only if the patient grants access to them for the same.

The authors performed a performance evaluation of their proposed system using the caliper and attained optimization for throughput, latency, and network security.

7 Comparative study of existing blockchain-based EHR systems

Table 1 presents a comparative study of the existing blockchain-based EHR systems.

Table 1 Existing blockchain-based EHR systems.

Author	Proposed algorithms	Proposed model	Advantages
Tanwar et al. [31]	Admin working, patients working, clinician working, lab working	Proposed architecture and algorithm related to patient's data and information security	Performance was enhanced by $1.75 \times$ and the latency rate was reduced by $1.5 \times$
Xia et al. [53]	Smart contract and package transaction model	Designed data-sharing model with the help of blockchain between cloud service	Data can be shared between the cloud users without privacy threats
Jiang et al. [54]	APP-KTH-SUM algorithm, FAIR-FIRST and TP&FAIR	BlocHLE system	Proposed algorithms for enhancing BlocHLE system
Uddin et al. [55]	Session key generation algorithm, characteristic-based miner selection algorithm, random selection of miner node, nonce generation algorithm, block verification algorithm	Patient-centric agent-based architecture	Provided better security and privacy
Gupta et al. [56]	–	Telesurgery system	Low latency rate, security, privacy, reliability

Table 1 Continued

Author	Proposed algorithms	Proposed model	Advantages
Vora et al. [4]	–	IoT-based smart speaker for patients	Patients can easily consult doctors from home
Bhattacharya et al. [14]	–	BinDaaS system	Privacy and security are governed through integrating framework
Budhiraja et al. [12]	–	DIYA scheme	Reduces the cochannel interference
Gupta et al. [13]	Transaction tuples of a block, execution of smart contracts	HaBiTs framework	Illustrates how consortium blockchain ensures the security and privacy of patients
Hathaliya et al. [9]	–	Blockchain-based architecture	Provides better security and privacy to blockchain system

8 Conclusion

Future advancements in blockchain-based IoT healthcare devices that are compatible with 5G networks will have prospective to newer healthcare transformation, providing high-quality health services to patients and reducing disparities in healthcare in remote areas. Blockchain-based smart healthcare services would be able to successfully target their aim with faster speed and higher bandwidth. To achieve improved healthcare with easy and fast access to these services, 5G technology plays a pivotal role.

Digitized healthcare data with the help of blockchain can be safely and securely exchanged among patients, doctors, and other concerned healthcare providers. The combination of these techniques will ensure security, privacy, availability, and control of information access in the healthcare sector. This will reduce administrative loads, simplify the tedious process of data collection, reduce transaction costs, and eliminate intermediaries.

These salient features of blockchain technology propose an open scope for researchers to explore applications of IoT and blockchain in the healthcare sector with 6G or future technologies for better results. Also, there are still challenges such as storage problems, high energy consumption, and 51% vulnerability attacks that need attention for a more efficient, smart, and green healthcare system.

References

[1] Bitglass, Healthcare breach report, 2021. https://www.bitglass.com/press-releases/2021-healthcare-breach-report.

[2] A. Azaria, A. Ekblaw, T. Vieira, A. Lippman, Medrec: using blockchain for medical data access and permission management, in: 2016 2nd International Conference on Open and Big Data (OBD), 2016, pp. 25–30.

[3] D. Ichikawa, M. Kashiyama, T. Ueno, Tamper-resistant mobile health using blockchain technology, JMIR Mhealth Uhealth 5 (7) (2017), e7938.

[4] J. Vora, S. Tanwar, S. Tyagi, N. Kumar, J.J. Rodrigues, Home-based exercise system for patients using IoT enabled smart speaker, in: 2017 IEEE 19th International Conference on e-Health Networking, Applications and Services (Healthcom), 2017, pp. 1–6.

[5] W.J. Gordon, C. Catalini, Blockchain technology for healthcare: facilitating the transition to patient-driven interoperability, Comput. Struct. Biotechnol. J. 16 (2018) 224–230.

[6] S. Rouhani, L. Butterworth, A.D. Simmons, D.G. Humphery, R. Deters, MediChain TM: a secure decentralized medical data asset management system, in: 2018 IEEE International Conference on Internet of Things (iThings) and IEEE Green Computing and Communications (GreenCom) and IEEE Cyber, Physical and Social Computing (CPSCom) and IEEE Smart Data (SmartData), 2018, pp. 1533–1538.

[7] J. Vora, A. Nayyar, S. Tanwar, S. Tyagi, N. Kumar, M.S. Obaidat, J.J. Rodrigues, BHEEM: a blockchain-based framework for securing electronic health records, in: 2018 IEEE Globecom Workshops (GC Wkshps), 2018, pp. 1–6.

[8] B. Shen, J. Guo, Y. Yang, MedChain: efficient healthcare data sharing via blockchain, Appl. Sci. 9 (6) (2019) 1207.

[9] J. Hathaliya, P. Sharma, S. Tanwar, R. Gupta, Blockchain-based remote patient monitoring in healthcare 4.0, in: 2019 IEEE 9th International Conference on Advanced Computing (IACC), 2019, pp. 87–91.

[10] R. Gupta, S. Tanwar, S. Tyagi, N. Kumar, Tactile internet and its applications in 5g era: a comprehensive review, Int. J. Commun. Syst. 32 (14) (2019), e3981.

[11] A. Kumari, S. Tanwar, S. Tyagi, N. Kumar, Verification and validation techniques for streaming big data analytics in internet of things environment, IET Netw. 8 (3) (2018) 155–163.

[12] I. Budhiraja, S. Tyagi, S. Tanwar, N. Kumar, J.J. Rodrigues, DIYA: tactile Internet driven delay assessment NOMA-based scheme for D2D communication, IEEE Trans. Ind. Inf. 15 (12) (2019) 6354–6366.

[13] R. Gupta, S. Tanwar, S. Tyagi, N. Kumar, M.S. Obaidat, B. Sadoun, HaBiTs: blockchain-based telesurgery framework for healthcare 4.0, in: 2019 International Conference on Computer, Information and Telecommunication Systems (CITS), 2019, pp. 1–5.

[14] P. Bhattacharya, S. Tanwar, U. Bodke, S. Tyagi, N. Kumar, Bindaas: blockchain-based deep-learning as-a-service in healthcare 4.0 applications, IEEE Trans. Netw. Sci. Eng. 8 (2) (2021) 1242–1255.

[15] S. Khezr, M. Moniruzzaman, A. Yassine, R. Benlamri, Blockchain technology in healthcare: a comprehensive review and directions for future research, Appl. Sci. 9 (9) (2019) 1736.

[16] A. Ahad, M. Tahir, K.L. Yau, 5G-based smart healthcare network: architecture, taxonomy, challenges and future research directions, IEEE Access 7 (2019) 100747–100762.

[17] A.A. Siyal, A.Z. Junejo, M. Zawish, K. Ahmed, A. Khalil, G. Soursou, Applications of blockchain technology in medicine and healthcare: challenges and future perspectives, Cryptography 3 (1) (2019) 3.

[18] F. Jamil, S. Ahmad, N. Iqbal, D.H. Kim, Towards a remote monitoring of patient vital signs based on IoT-based blockchain integrity management platforms in smart hospitals, Sensors 20 (8) (2020) 2195.

[19] C.C. Agbo, Q.H. Mahmoud, J.M. Eklund, Blockchain technology in healthcare: a systematic review, Healthcare 7 (2) (2019) 56.

[20] A. Basholli, H. Cana, A novel sensor-based architecture using 5G and Blockchain for remote and continuous health monitoring, in: Eighteenth International Symposium for Health Information Management Research, 2020, https://doi.org/10.15626/ishimr.2020.xxx.

[21] S. Bittins, G. Kober, A. Margheri, M. Masi, A. Miladi, V. Sassone, Healthcare data management by using blockchain technology, in: Applications of Blockchain in Healthcare, Springer, 2021, pp. 1–27.

[22] D. Lin, S. Hu, Y. Gao, Y. Tang, Optimizing MEC networks for healthcare applications in 5G communications with the authenticity of users' priorities, IEEE Access 7 (2019) 88592–88600.

[23] R. Khan, P. Kumar, D.N. Jayakody, M. Liyanage, A survey on security and privacy of 5G technologies: potential solutions, recent advancements, and future directions, IEEE Commun. Surv. Tutorials 22 (1) (2019) 196–248.

[24] R.M. Haris, S. Al-Maadeed, Integrating blockchain technology in 5g enabled iot: a review, in: 2020 IEEE International Conference on Informatics, IoT, and Enabling Technologies (ICIoT), 2020, pp. 367–371.

[25] H.S. Chen, J.T. Jarrell, K.A. Carpenter, D.S. Cohen, X. Huang, Blockchain in healthcare: a patient-centered model, Biomed. J. Sci. Tech. Res. 20 (3) (2019) 15017.

[26] I. Mistry, S. Tanwar, S. Tyagi, N. Kumar, Blockchain for 5G-enabled IoT for industrial automation: a systematic review, solutions, and challenges, Mech. Syst. Signal Process. 135 (2020), 106382.

[27] B. Mohanta, P. Das, S. Patnaik, Healthcare 5.0: a paradigm shift in digital healthcare system using artificial intelligence, IOT and 5G communication, in: 2019 International Conference on Applied Machine Learning (ICAML), 2019, pp. 191–196.

[28] P.K. Sharma, J. Park, J.H. Park, K. Cho, Wearable computing for defence automation: opportunities and challenges in 5G network, IEEE Access 8 (2020) 65993–66002.

[29] J.A. Adebusola, A.A. Ariyo, O.A. Elisha, A.M. Olubunmi, O.O. Julius, An overview of 5G technology, in: 2020 International Conference in Mathematics, Computer Engineering and Computer Science (ICMCECS), 2020, pp. 1–4.

[30] M.A. Uddin, A. Stranieri, I. Gondal, V. Balasubramanian, Blockchain leveraged decentralized IoT eHealth framework, Internet Things 9 (2020), 100159.

[31] S. Tanwar, K. Parekh, R. Evans, Blockchain-based electronic healthcare record system for healthcare 4.0 applications, J. Inf. Secur. Appl. 50 (2020), 102407.

[32] R. Gupta, A. Shukla, S. Tanwar, Aayush: a smart contract-based telesurgery system for healthcare 4.0, in: 2020 IEEE International Conference on Communications Workshops (ICC Workshops), 2020, pp. 1–6.

[33] A. Kumari, R. Gupta, S. Tanwar, N. Kumar, Blockchain and AI amalgamation for energy cloud management: challenges, solutions, and future directions, J. Parallel Distrib. Comput. 143 (2020) 148–166.

[34] T. Hewa, G. Gür, A. Kalla, M. Ylianttila, A. Bracken, M. Liyanage, The role of blockchain in 6G: challenges, opportunities and research directions, in: 2020 2nd 6G Wireless Summit (6G SUMMIT), 2020, pp. 1–5.

[35] V. Chamola, V. Hassija, V. Gupta, M. Guizani, A comprehensive review of the COVID-19 pandemic and the role of IoT, drones, AI, blockchain, and 5G in managing its impact, IEEE Access 8 (2020) 90225–90265.

[36] Y. Siriwardhana, C. De Alwis, G. Gür, M. Ylianttila, M. Liyanage, The fight against the COVID-19 pandemic with 5G technologies, IEEE Eng. Manage. Rev. 48 (3) (2020) 72–84.

[37] R. Gupta, A. Kumari, S. Tanwar, N. Kumar, Blockchain-envisioned softwarized multi-swarming uavs to tackle covid-i9 situations, IEEE Netw. 35 (2) (2020) 160–167.

[38] B. Chen, S. Qiao, J. Zhao, D. Liu, X. Shi, M. Lyu, H. Chen, H. Lu, Y. Zhai, A security awareness and protection system for 5G smart healthcare based on zero-trust architecture, IEEE Internet Things J. 8 (13) (2021) 10248–10263.

[39] W. Mazurczyk, P. Bisson, R.P. Jover, K. Nakao, K. Cabaj, Special issue on advancements in 5G networks security, Future Gener. Comput. Syst. 110 (2020) 314–316.

[40] T. Hewa, A. Braeken, M. Ylianttila, M. Liyanage, Multi-access edge computing and blockchain-based secure telehealth system connected with 5G and IoT, in: GLOBECOM 2020–2020 IEEE Global Communications Conference, 2020, pp. 1–6.

[41] M. Ciampi, A. Esposito, F. Marangio, M. Sicuranza, G. Schmid, Modernizing healthcare by using blockchain, in: Applications of Blockchain in Healthcare, Springer, 2021, pp. 29–67.

[42] D. Berdik, S. Otoum, N. Schmidt, D. Porter, Y. Jararweh, A survey on blockchain for information systems management and security, Inf. Process. Manage. 58 (1) (2021), 102397.

[43] R. Chatterjee, R. Chatterjee, An overview of the emerging technology: blockchain, in: 2017 3rd International Conference on Computational Intelligence and Networks (CINE), 2017, pp. 126–127.

[44] A. Gupta, R.K. Jha, A survey of 5G network: architecture and emerging technologies, IEEE Access 3 (2015) 1206–1232.

[45] A. Chaer, K. Salah, C. Lima, P.P. Ray, T. Sheltami, Blockchain for 5G: opportunities and challenges, in: 2019 IEEE Globecom Workshops (GC Wkshps), 2019, pp. 1–6.

[46] Blockchain Technology in Healthcare Market Size, Trends, Share by 2027, 2021. https://www.marketresearchfuture.com/reports/blockchain-technology-healthcare-market-6475. (Accessed 1 April 2021).

[47] G. Chen, B. Xu, M. Lu, N.S. Chen, Exploring blockchain technology and its potential applications for education, Smart Learn. Environ. 5 (1) (2018) 1–10.

[48] L.C. Burton, G.F. Anderson, I.W. Kues, Using electronic health records to help coordinate care, Milbank Q. 82 (3) (2004) 457–481.

[49] E.A. Blackstone, J.P. Fuhr Jr., S. Pociask, The health and economic effects of counterfeit drugs, Am. Health Drug Benefits 7 (4) (2014) 216.

[50] F. Jamil, L. Hang, K. Kim, D. Kim, A novel medical blockchain model for drug supply chain integrity management in a smart hospital, Electronics 8 (5) (2019) 505.

[51] M.M. Onik, S. Aich, J. Yang, C.S. Kim, H.C. Kim, Blockchain in healthcare: challenges and solutions, in: Big Data Analytics for Intelligent Healthcare Management, Academic Press, 2019, pp. 197–226.

[52] D. Munro, Data Breaches in Healthcare Totaled over 112 Million Records in 2015, 3, Forbes, New York, NY, 2015.

[53] Q. Xia, E.B. Sifah, K.O. Asamoah, J. Gao, X. Du, M. Guizani, Medshare: trust-less medical data sharing among cloud service providers via blockchain, IEEE Access 5 (2017) 14757–14767.

[54] S. Jiang, J. Cao, H. Wu, Y. Yang, M. Ma, J. He, Blochie: a blockchain-based platform for healthcare information exchange, in: 2018 IEEE International Conference on Smart Computing (SMARTCOMP), 2018, pp. 49–56.

[55] M.A. Uddin, A. Stranieri, I. Gondal, V. Balasubramanian, Continuous patient monitoring with a patient centric agent: a block architecture, IEEE Access 6 (2018) 32700–32726.

[56] R. Gupta, S. Tanwar, S. Tyagi, N. Kumar, Tactile-internet-based telesurgery system for healthcare 4.0: an architecture, research challenges, and future directions, IEEE Netw. 33 (6) (2019) 22–29.

Device-to-device and millimeter waves communication for 5G healthcare informatics

Khalimjon Khujamatov, Nurshod Akhmedov, Ernazar Reypnazarov,
Doston Khasanov, and Amir Lazarev
Data Communication Networks and Systems Department, Tashkent University of
Information Technologies, Tashkent, Uzbekistan

1 Introduction

Information technologies penetrate deeper and deeper into all spheres, including healthcare. Health informatics is the discipline of transferring, processing, storing, distributing, and delivering medical information through information technologies. With the development of the healthcare system, its needs for modern methods of data processing and exchange have also grown. Exobytes of information are generated by medical equipment, personnel, and patients on a daily basis. It is clear that new methods and networking technologies are required for the further development of the system.

The development of medicine makes it possible to think not about the treatment of the disease, but about its early detection and prevention. In recent years, healthcare services have become more personalized, adaptive, and technological. Medicine is based on new priorities. One of these priorities is real-time remote patient monitoring. In recent years, new terms have emerged such as the Internet of Medical Things.

Rapid development is definitely affecting telecommunication networks. Traditional networks simply cannot handle huge healthcare traffic. Technology is required that is competent at fathoming a number of issues such as high data transfer rate, high bandwidth, quality of service (QoS), and much more. As a result, 5G technology has been rapidly developing in recent years in response to growing needs [1]. Small cells are used to achieve spectral efficiency in 5G. Small cell sizes lead to lower power consumption, higher data rates, and decreased delays due to the close proximity of users and evolved node base stations (eNB).

Another promising technology with the potential to provide networked resources for healthcare informatics is device-to-device communications (D2D) [2]. D2D technology is a composite 5G technology providing optimal spectrum allocation. Although D2D was developed for use in the unlicensed spectrum, in this chapter we will show that it is more effective in the licensed spectrum, in particular in integration with 5G. To expand the bandwidth and increase the spectrum, we consider the use of the millimeter wavelength range, which suggests the use of a previously unused high-frequency spectrum.

Blockchain Applications for Healthcare Informatics. https://doi.org/10.1016/B978-0-323-90615-9.00019-0
Copyright © 2022 Elsevier Inc. All rights reserved.

1.1 Motivation

5G technologies are gaining popularity in healthcare for the ability to adapt networks to the requirements of individual users. So in the many medical services offered, device-to-device communications (D2D) technologies are very often used to interconnect wearable devices for monitoring patients. Many works are devoted to the use of D2D technologies in various fields, including healthcare. The authors of [3] gave a comprehensive review of the use of 5G in the healthcare system, where they touched upon the use of D2D and millimeter waves for the provision of medical services. The authors of [4] proposed using D2D as a means of providing cloud computing for use in various fields. In addition, there are many similar works devoted to D2D and millimeter waves (mmWave) used in conjunction with 5G.

Despite all the contributions of the available work, there is an acute lack of systematic work that combines all aspects of D2D and millimeter waves as well as research that takes into account the peculiarities of health informatics when implementing these technologies.

1.2 Contribution—Paper structure

The chapter is divided into five sections. The second section is devoted to the modern requirements of the healthcare system and health informatics. Unlike other similar works, we focused on the accordance of D2D and mmWave with the requirements of health informatics. The third and fourth sections explore D2D communications and millimeter waves and their integration into 5G. We have given a detailed analysis of the application of these technologies in healthcare as well as the integration of features and technologies that make this possible. Another contribution of this chapter is the study of the impact of blockchain on D2D communication. In the fifth section, we studied the issues of introducing D2D and millimeter waves in healthcare.

2 Healthcare informatics requirements

2.1 Security system

The main requirements for the security of healthcare informatics are access control, authentication, and nonrepudiation. Modern securing methods show their ineffectiveness, and the use of complex encryption algorithms leads to problems associated with the diversity of standards in different systems. General requirements for secure healthcare informatics are given in Table 1.

2.2 Data sharing

The exchange of data and access to data in medicine are very important tasks that can be a problem in healthcare. The reason is that patients can visit different hospitals and their records are stored in separate databases in a scattered form without any

Table 1 Security requirements.

Requirements	Description
Integrity	Medical records must be correct, uncensored, and unmodified.
Access control	The system must provide control and authorized access to medical records.
Availability	Medical data have to be accessible. If necessary, in any situation, the physician should have access to the data immediately.
Data freshness	Medical data must be received in real time, delays are unacceptable.
Anonymity	The system must guarantee the confidentiality of the patient's identity.
Auditing	The transaction registration process must be provided to ensure trust in applications.
Authenticity	Only an authentic party should have access to health data.
Nonrepudiation	The data must be encrypted by a digital signature so that no one can deny it.

identifiers that allow them to be combined. That causes a gap in patient data, making it difficult for service providers to obtain up-to-date records.

A healthcare network can share terabytes of data every day. Such a volume of information requires a high data transfer rate, a huge bandwidth, and most importantly, high reliability.

2.3 Interoperability

Usually, in medical centers, patient data are stored in centralized databases. Every day, the records of different patients are recorded in the databases of different hospitals. That means the records of one patient can be scattered across different hospitals, and some of these records are sometimes lost. Such storage restricts obtaining complete data and leads to a reduction of interoperability, fragmentation of medical records, slow access, and a lack of quantity and quality of medical data. Therefore, the system architecture of the network serving healthcare must ensure the interconnection of scattered data and the interoperability of different databases while preventing fragmentation and data loss.

2.4 Mobility

The mobility of healthcare is associated with patient mobility because patients refuse to be tied to one point. In addition, the use of IoMT devices and wireless technologies makes them mobile without interrupting the treatment process. Besides, the rapid development of vital infrastructure requires healthcare to be in touch with patients from different countries. The fact that the healthcare database must be accessed by any device from anywhere in the world complicates the task of protecting and ensuring data security.

3   D2D communications for 5G healthcare informatics

D2D is a direct connection of two devices with or without a core network or base station. This technology was developed as a solution to the problem of high-density networks [5]. The area of application of D2D technologies was considered as a network for devices in close range to each other because, in such scenarios, traditional routing through the gateway and the base station (BS) is ineffective. It makes more sense to use end-to-end forward machine-to-machine transmission, especially on networks where numerous devices are involved. With D2D, each terminal can directly communicate with each other to share its radio access connection or exchange information. To ensure communication between devices, there can be both a licensed spectrum and an unlicensed spectrum outside the cellular network, such as WLAN or Bluetooth in ad hoc mode. The use of an unlicensed spectrum improves the mobility and scalability of this network but decreases its reliability and security. The use of a licensed spectrum guarantees the quality of service and high reliability, but usually requires base stations to ignore intracell interference [6].

D2D is an emerging 5G technology, but it is not typical for earlier generations of the network. D2D provides a number of advantages to fit modern network requirements. D2D provides high bandwidth due to spectrum reuse as well as good mobility. Thus, it is ideal for building networks with a high density of devices that transmit large amounts of data, in particular healthcare networks. Because gadgets based on IOMT technologies are used in healthcare, it really needs technologies that provide proper autonomy with high efficiency. At the same time, there is no better contender than D2D today.

3.1   D2D communications classification

D2D communications can be divided into three classifications: level of control, coverage, and modes of communication. This is shown in Fig. 1. A detailed definition of the classifications is given in the following chapters.

3.1.1   D2D control level

The D2D control level characterizes the degree of controllability of the D2D data transmission from the side of the core network. According to the control level, D2D can be divided into two categories: autonomous and full control networks. In case D2D units (DU) are controlled by an operator or a cellular network that controls cellular units (CU) is participating in the process, the mode is called a fully controlled mode; otherwise, the mode is called autonomous. The autonomous mode implies the databases to be involved in management. To summarize, Table 2 illustrates the significance, advantages, and disadvantages of both modes.

Full control mode is characterized as a network in which devices are controlled by an operator or a cellular network is participating in the process of network management. The process of device authentication, D2D initiation, power control, D2D pair discovery, D2D connection, and resource allocation occurs on the operator's side,

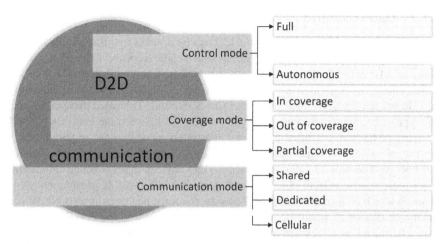

Fig. 1 Classifications of D2D communications.

Table 2 Control levels.

	Full control	Autonomous
Meaning	The network is responsible for D2D pair discovery, D2D authentication procedure, D2D connection, D2D initiation procedure, power control, and allocating radio resources	The devices are totally or partly responsible for D2D pair discovery, D2D authentication procedure, D2D connection, D2D initiation procedure, power control, and allocate radio resources
Advantages	Less interference among CUs and DUs. Better QoS for users and network	Negligible signaling overhead
Disadvantages	High signaling overhead is required	Interference on CU by DU

which has a number of advantages and disadvantages. The controllability of the core network or the operator provides a higher CBS, higher transmission reliability, and less interference between nodes because the interference is controlled at the network core level. However, to provide such control, a high signaling overhead is required, which is a clear disadvantage.

Autonomous D2D networks are independent and the main processes of D2D connection are performed on the devices themselves. This mode requires negligible signal overhead, but at the same time, the network is subject to interference due to the effects of DUs on each other.

3.1.2 D2D coverage

According to the 3GPP classification, D2D can be divided into three categories [7]. The first is called "in coverage" of D2D, in which all devices are in the coverage area of the cellular network and use a licensed network for communications. DUs located in the cellular coverage area have the ability to use an increased spectrum; in addition, they do not require additional interfaces for interaction. The main disadvantages of this type of communication are the high interference between the controllers due to the reuse of the same channel by several controllers as well as the requirements for the use of additional algorithms and mechanisms for the allocation of resources and energy. The second category includes D2D devices that exchange information in the unlicensed spectrum. Such network deployment is possible in emergency situations in which eNB malfunctions and cellular coverage becomes impossible. In such situations, industrial, scientific and medical (ISM) spectra in the 2.4 GHz range are most often used, and they are implemented according to the ZigBee, Bluetooth, or WiFi standards. This coverage allows using a wide range without fear of interference between DUs and control systems. The main disadvantage of such a D2D connection is the requirement for the use of additional interfaces for the interaction of the DU and network node. The third category includes devices with partial coverage of the cellular network, where one of the devices is in the coverage area and the other is out of the area. In this scenario, one of the remote DUs can operate as a repeater and broadcast data to the eNB area or to the coverage area of the unlicensed spectrum, depending on which network is the priority; this is shown in Fig. 2 [8].

3.1.3 D2D communication mode

The D2D communication mode indicates how network end equipment use network resources for data exchange. Thus, the D2D communication mode can be divided into three different types: shared, dedicated, and cellular.

Shared is a communication mode in which both the DU and CU use the same network to exchange data. This mode is also called the underlay mode, in which the

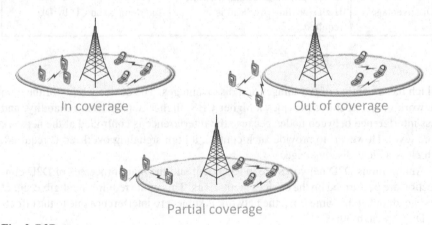

Fig. 2 D2D coverage.

communication between the DU and the CU uses a single spectrum. In other words, the D2D communicating device uses the resources allocated for the CU, which increases the effectiveness of the spectrum. Blocks of resources are appointed to cellular users and DU reuses these blocks for end-to-end data transmission.

Dedicated is a D2D communication mode in which DUs use a separate spectrum allocated to them for transmission. The mode is also referred to as the overlay mode, where part of the spectrum intended for the cellular device is dedicated to D2D communications. This reduces the interference between the DU and CU by several times, increases the efficiency of the network, and improves the power control during end-to-end transmission of D2D [9–11]. Despite this, this mode has a serious drawback—it is very difficult to achieve effective use of the dedicated spectrum because remote DUs do not have load balancing mechanisms, which leads to poor system throughput and resource utilization.

Cellular is a mode in which DUs use the cellular network to exchange data and behave like ordinary control systems. This mode is easy to implement and does not require additional tools, but does not have the proper performance. A comparison of all modes is given in Table 3.

3.2 D2D applications

Many emerging services and medical practices in the healthcare system are associated with the transmission of large amounts of information in real time. Due to the specific characteristics of the devices used in these processes in most cases (energy consumption, bandwidth requirements, the requirements for interference in the transmission environment), the use of D2D technology is considered appropriate. Many areas of the healthcare system are interested in D2D communication, as shown in Fig. 3.

3.2.1 D2D for telemedicine

The concept of telemedicine is defined as the remote provision of medical services, which include teleconsultation of a doctor, remote monitoring of the patient's condition with further manipulations (remote administration of medications, emergency assistance, etc.), doctor's advice on request, control of the patient's daytime activities,

Table 3 Communication modes.

	Shared mode	Dedicated mode	Cellular mode
Advantages	Spectrum efficiency is very high.	Simple interference management.	Easy to deploy. Simple interference management.
Disadvantages	High level of interference between DUs or DUs vs CUs.	Spectrum utilization is low. Capacity is small.	Spectral efficiency is low

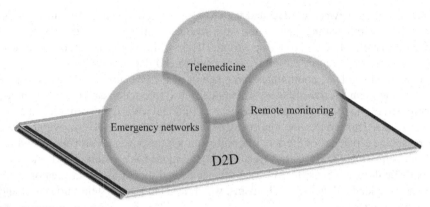

Fig. 3 D2D for healthcare system.

teleoperations, and much more. Key network services that determine the quality and quantity of telemedicine services are video streaming, voice, and data transmission.

Video streaming is based on sending compressed video in real Internet mode via telecommunication networks while the sent compressed files are separate video fragments, which allows you to watch the excerpts as they arrive without waiting for the content to be fully downloaded. Another way to transmit video content is to continuously stream data played back immediately after it arrives. Video streaming is a key traffic volume not only in healthcare but also on the Internet. According to the American company Cisco, more than 90% of the traffic on the Internet is video traffic [9]. Recently, the exchange of video data between users through a direct connection using point-to-point technology (P2P) is gaining more and more popularity, and this can slow down traffic transmitted over wireless networks. P2P technology is on a large scale, gaining more and more users. The daily clients of the technology exceed 32 million [10], including in the healthcare sector. D2D technology can significantly increase network performance when transmitting P2P video streaming. Applications based on D2D will allow creating video chats and video conferencing between devices in one cell, such as cells of private networks of clinics.

In remote monitoring of the patient's daytime activity, the transmission of voice and data is very important. The use of traditional mobile devices operating in the cellular coverage area has a number of inconveniences in healthcare, such as delays, constant signal emission, and high signal power of transmitters. The use of D2D improves network performance and reduces transmission delay, which meets the requirements for providing high-quality remote monitoring services. In addition, D2D networks based on Zigbee or Bluetooth are characterized by low radiation and low energy consumption, which improves mobility and patient autonomy while reducing health risks.

3.2.2 D2D for remote monitoring

Remote patient monitoring is a trend in modern healthcare; all new methods and services for monitoring the patient's condition are being developed and applied in healthcare. When monitoring mobile patients, data exchange technologies are most often used between humanoid machines that process or transmit information collected through built-in sensors to servers. This technology of information exchange between machines is often used as M2M technology, where machines are used to track specific events and changes as well as to instruct actuation [12].

M2M technology is mainly based on wireless networks while the end-to-end transmission among machines is provided by the network. Because very often the machines are scattered a short distance from each other, D2D can be useful to provide end-to-end communication between machines. The use of D2D significantly increases the efficiency of the network because D2D provides a high-quality communication channel in the near range of transmission. In addition, D2D has a number of advantages in the use of M2M, such as greater autonomy of machines due to a decrease in transmission power, lower network delay due to direct routing of D2D traffic, and a decrease in the load on servers in the local network [13].

3.2.3 D2D for emergency networks

Sometimes there are emergencies when it is necessary to deploy emergency medical services in an area without traditional network coverage. As a rule, during natural disasters, data networks can fail, and their reconstruction can take a long time. But unfortunately, in such situations, the healthcare system needs to transmit a huge amount of traffic such as reports on victims, video broadcasts with remote online support of medical personnel, and support for communication between medical teams. Many researchers, having studied such scenarios, concluded that D2D is capable of providing broadband network access services, creating small networks for a large number of devices, and providing highly efficient data interchange in a very short time [14]. The research results have shown the good quality of service, lower power consumption, and long autonomy as well as less delay when using D2D to organize emergency networks. Another group of researchers suggests using D2D in emergencies with intermediate relay nodes serving as intermediate processing points for data exchanged between devices [15]. Also in this scenario, it is proposed to use energy harvesting (EH) algorithms to extend the life of individual devices used in intermediate relay nodes. Such interaction is able to expand the coverage area of the D2D network by ensuring the energy efficiency of the entire network [16].

3.3 D2D integrated features

Modern D2D technologies are multifunctional, as many other technologies are integrated into them. The next chapter discusses the integration of technologies such as millimeter waves (mmWave), vehicle-to-vehicle end-to-end (V2V) technologies, artificial intelligence (AI), and the Internet of Things (IoT). The benefits in conjunction with D2D are given in Fig. 4.

3.3.1 mmWaves for D2D

mmWaves include a band from 30 to 300 GHz and are very rarely used for transmission of communication channels. But recently, the widespread bands above 300 GHz have been very clogged with signals from television, satellite, and mobile

Fig. 4 D2D integrated features.

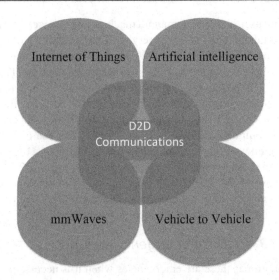

communications, which makes the use of this spectrum ineffective for private corporate networks, including healthcare networks. Thus, millimeter waves are of increasing interest, as they are capable of providing a huge bandwidth due to a large amount of unused spectrum [17]. Millimeter waves provide high data transmission rates and are therefore being increasingly applied to build networks of modern technologies such as 5G. Millimeter waves have a number of distinctive properties that make their use impractical in different network, including large losses during their use. Second, millimeter waves have a low coefficient of penetration through solid materials, which in some cases makes their use impossible without direct line of sight. These differences require the use of antennas with higher power and special design as well as the use of millimeter waves only in small radii or indoors [18].

The small radius of application and high gear speeds make mmWaves ideal for use in D2D communications. A lot of studies carried out on the integration of mmWaves into D2D have revealed a number of problems, such as requirements for special device designs and the use of additional interfaces [19].

3.3.2 *Artificial intelligence for D2D*

Artificial intelligence is widely used in the healthcare system in model forecasting, real-time data processing, and uninterrupted communication. Artificial intelligence mechanisms are able to manage resources for large capacity, reduce nonlinearities of radiofrequency [RF] components, optimize network QoS, manage nonlinear data-driven approximations and allow the appropriate network operator to establish cognitive and comprehensive data storage through signal processing and classification, partitioning, and resource planning [20].

Recent studies show the effectiveness of 5G in building corporate and private networks such as networks of private clinics or healthcare providers. However, D2D, with its peculiarities, makes the tasks of resource allocation and interference mitigation in 5G more difficult. AI allows networks in such cases to perform self-optimization and self-configuration, increasing the efficiency of algorithms and resource allocation mechanisms [21]. Learning algorithms have been applied in various studies to increase the throughput and optimize D2D networks for the requirements of CBS [22].

3.3.3 Internet of Things for D2D

IoT is a promising technology that is able to make our lives easier by developing infrastructure of many areas of modern society through the use of innovative services. For the application of IoT in healthcare, it is necessary to solve a number of basic tasks to meet the stringent requirements of the system, such as analyzing and storing a huge amount of information generated by patient devices, maintaining a reliable data exchange channel between machines and patients, providing complex interfaces for the exchange of big data and their processing, and minimizing power consumption to increase the autonomy of wearable devices. In addition, there are a number of indirect tasks to solve, such as restoring data transmission channels between machines in case of failures and establishing alternative communication paths to maintain uninterrupted communication. Devices with multimedia functions such as monitoring a patient's condition are very sensitive to delays and network failures.

D2D in integration with IoT is able to meet the requirements of healthcare by achieving a higher data-transmitting rate and low latency, providing a wide coverage area, supporting interaction in heterogeneous networks, and consuming minimal power from the DU [23].

Most of the works on the integration of D2D and IoT show that these technologies complement each other, covering a number of disadvantages of each. Therefore, for example, the cross-cell frequency resource multiplexing [CFRM] scheme allows allocating resources for CUs in accordance with the division of the cell area and providing efficient multiplexing of resources for DUs, thereby reducing interference between devices and increasing network bandwidth [24]. Based on the results of the study, this scheme showed an increase in bandwidth and connection stability between devices.

3.3.4 Vehicle-to-vehicle (V2V) communication for D2D

Currently, the growth in the number of vehicles makes it difficult for emergency vehicles such as ambulances to move around. The healthcare system is in dire need of vehicle warning systems for road accidents, the number of cars on specific roads, the speed of movement, the direction and location of cars, and so on. V2V communication technologies can become a solution to this problem. For several years, this technology has been among the leading research subjects in the field of wireless communication.

A V2V communication network is a network of vehicles and roadside devices that serves as communication nodes for transmitting data to each other [25]. Various technologies are used to ensure V2V communication, for example, the IEEE has already released the IEEE 802.11p standard, according to which the exchange of data between machines depends on dedicated short-range communication [DSRC] technology, which in turn is not able to provide sufficient speed and transmission range, thereby reducing reliability and network performance. Other communication technologies previously proposed for V2V such as Bluetooth, WiFi direct, ad hoc communications, and ultrawide band (UWB) were mainly developed for wireless local area networks, which means that they cannot provide the proper mobility of nodes at high speeds and wider coverage area, as shown in Table 4.

According to studies, V2V technology can exist with the condition of providing high reliability of about 99.99% and low latency of about 1 ms [26]. Some of the main challenges faced by V2V technology are interference, resource allocation, and mobility. D2D is a strong candidate to solve the problems of spreading V2V technology, as it can provide a reliable communication channel as well as minimum latency according to IEEE 802.11p.

3.3.5 Blockchain for D2D

The D2D idea is based on a direct connection of gadgets with minimal participation, or even without the participation of intermediaries at all. They are very useful in designing networks with minimal latency, efficient resource allocation algorithms, and minimal energy costs. However, an end-to-end connection of devices can create peculiar barriers in the design of 5G networks because it is necessary to solve a number of problems related to network performance, manageability, and security of network connections.

A very important task in D2D is security and confidentiality, as there is a paradox here. On the one hand, information security can be solved through authentication mechanisms. However, in D2D, authentication takes place with the participation of third parties, which increases network delays. On the other hand, the simplification of authentication mechanisms allows reducing the network load, but at the same time, untrusted devices can gain access to resources, thereby creating a threat of unauthorized access to service servers.

The integration of blockchain mechanisms in the 5G network and, in particular, in D2D allows solving the above problems and providing a highly secure closed system for the exchange, collection, and distribution of information. Blockchain has several leverages to improve quality and security in D2D:

- The mining process carried out by D2D users on the basis of the blockchain, which is supported by a reward policy, increases the security of D2D.
- Participants in the D2D network get the opportunity from tracking the transmitted and received information using the blockchain consensus mechanisms, which reduces cases of fraud.
- Decentralized blockchain mechanisms are able to provide functions for offloading computations, which increases the performance of D2D.

3.4 D2D challenges

Due to its properties, D2D is gaining increasing popularity among consumers and providers of mobile communications. However, this technology has a number of issues of deployment, without the solution of which the use of D2D becomes ineffective. Issues as well as some solutions to these issues are given in the following subsections and in Fig. 5.

Table 4 Comparison among communication technologies.

	Standardization	Distance	Data rate	Frequency	Mobility	V2V
ZigBee	802.1504	100 m	1250 kb/s	868/915 MHz–2.4 GHz	Low	Ad Hoc
Bluetooth	Bluetooth SIG	100 m	24 mb/s	2.4 GHz	Low	Ad Hoc
UWB	802.1503a	10 m	480 mb/s	3.1–10.6 GHz	Low	Ad Hoc
WiFi Direct	802.11a	200 m	250 mb/s	2.4/5 GHz	Low	Ad Hoc
5G	3GPP	1000 m	1 Gb/s	Licensed band	Up to 350 km/h	D2D
DSRC	IEEE 802.11p	200 m	27 mb/s	5.86–5.92 GHz	Up to 60 km/h	Ad Hoc

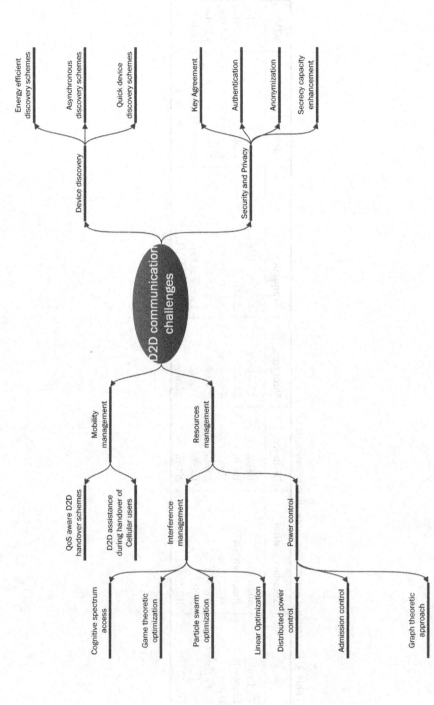

Fig. 5 D2D challenges.

3.4.1   Device discovery

One of the fundamental tasks of the creation and design of D2D networks is to solve the problem of device discovery. Device discovery is the process of detecting and locating potential candidates in a coverage area and then communicating directly with them. The discovery of devices occurs through several stages. To begin with, devices listen to channels to find potential nodes, then exchange basic information such as the device identifier, its location or distance to a given device, and channel status. Subsequently, this information is used to form pairs of nodes during data exchange. Device discovery can be either centralized or distributed.

Centralized device discovery usually occurs through intermediaries. Intermediaries are usually BSs, which in turn provide the transfer of important information such as communication protocols, power control policies, and the state of the communication channel or the level of interference. In this case, the BS can play the role of a control node. Each message sent to detect devices passes through the BS, so the devices do not have the ability to independently search. On the other hand, in another scenario, depending on the settings and protocols used, DUs may be able to independently detect devices. The BS partially participates in the process. It determines the possibility of communication between devices, then sends data on the gain of the path and the level of the signal-to-noise ratio [SNR] of all devices [5].

Distributed discovery occurs without the involvement of third-party resources, in particular BS. Devices at regular intervals send control messages to detect nearby devices. This scenario allows for cost savings and technology independence but has several disadvantages, including high power consumption of the DU, synchronization problems, and possible interference.

Device discovery is supported by a variety of methods and schemes. These include quick device discovery schemes, asynchronous discovery schemes, and energy-efficient discovery schemes. A lot of research was done for the development of algorithms and protocols to work with these schemes. The tic-toc rendezvous protocol [27], the multicarrier transmission method [28], the optimization of scanning sequence architecture [29], and the bouncing strategy protocol [30] are used to provide asynchronous discovery schemes. Connected open platform for smart objects [COAST] [31], the use of common channels and group channels [32], service advertisement, and access mechanisms [33] are capable of providing quick device discovery. A social application-based discovery mechanism [34], a three-dimensional iterative matching algorithm [35], and a social overlapping community-aware [SOCA] neighbor discovery scheme [36] are some of the many ways to provide energy-efficient discovery.

3.4.2   Mobility management

The scope of D2D mainly covers mobile devices, that is, devices that frequently change location or are in constant motion. Including patients with wearable sensors and transmitters, ambulances serving a specific area need mechanisms to ensure the mobility of their devices. Thus, the task of managing the mobility of D2D devices is a frequently discussed issue.

There are two main operations in the mobility management task. The first of these is the operation of location management—determining the connection point of the device among individual connection sessions. The second operation is to track changes in the location of the device, that is, handoff [handover] management—transfer of control to the location of the device. The process of handoff management can occur at a horizontal plane or at a vertical plane, depending on the initiator of the process. So, for example, if the signal level decreases below the normal threshold, or in the event of a deterioration in the quality of the channel, the user initiates a handoff between homogenous networks, which is called horizontal transfer. In another case, the handoff occurs between heterogeneous systems, initiated by the network to distribute the total load between the networks. This type of handoff is called a vertical handoff. A vertical handoff is influenced by many factors, including minimum bandwidth, application type, observed network load, latency preferences, estimated data rates, power requirements, and more. These data are considered very important in optimizing the management of the D2D device network.

Modern network technologies on the basis of which D2D networks are built, such as 5G, mainly have a multilevel topology, meaning they are built as a structure consisting of many small cells [femto cells, pico cells]. In addition, given the fact that most devices support multiple radio access technologies [RATs], D2D is able to provide sufficient network density and spectrum reuse, and, as a result, high bandwidth. However, this advantage has another effect—a more complex handoff process. Constant interference between small nonpermanent cells, which forms and disappears depending on the movement of devices, slows down the handoff, which leads to a deterioration in mobility. Additional solutions are required to provide optimal mobility without a loss of bandwidth. One of the solutions is to separate the user and control plane, as shown in [26]. Division of the control plane and user plane allows flexible handover decision making through a small amount of control information.

Mobility management tasks in D2D mainly depend on handoff management. In this case, it is required to achieve the fulfillment of several conditions that provide an optimal balance of mobility and bandwidth. One of the main conditions is the use of D2D for the handover of cellular users. So, for example, in [37], the possibility of using eNB as a control link is investigated during handover and creating a direct D2D connection between control systems when they move from one cell to another. The eNB is responsible for power control, establishing D2D sessions, and functions for controlling resources. Based on the channel quality indicator [CQI] received from the CUs, the eNB decides to establish the handoff procedure for ensuring continuous downloads and takes advantage of the best channel quality.

Another prerequisite is the use of QoS-aware D2D handover schemes. To ensure the proper level of QoS during the handover, the authors of [38] proposed applying a strategy of using seamless handover schemes, which consider the handover process for a pair of CUs involved in D2D communication jointly. To ensure proper QoS, the handover request from the source eNB is sent to the target eNB. Upon receipt of a request, the target eNB analyzes the state of the channel for compliance with QoS requirements. If these are met, it launches the ProSe function. This function is responsible for the authentication of the UE, the reservation of radio resource control [RRC] resources for the UE, and allocating a cell radio network temporary identifier

[CRNTI] for the UE. Only after the ProSe function has been performed does the hand-off between the source and target eNB occur. This approach allows optimally allocating eNB resources before transferring the DUs to the coverage area.

3.4.3 Security and privacy

D2D communications are based on a hybrid architecture, which means that it combines centralized and distributed architectures. Thus, having a similar structure with wireless ad hoc and cellular networks, it is vulnerable to the vulnerabilities of each of the architectures. These vulnerabilities include security threats that can affect network availability, confidentiality, authentication, and integrity. Thus, to ensure secure exchange between DUs, effective solutions are required that can eliminate threats from the cellular network as well as the direct network between devices.

In cases where D2D communication occurs through base stations of cellular networks, it is necessary to apply protective measures in the form of cryptographic encryption to protect the channel between the DU and the eNB from eavesdropping, message modification, replay attacks, and node impersonation. Modern encryption methods require the use of public key infrastructure [PKI] managed open keys. However, the variety of devices and standards as well as a large number of DUs loading keys into each device is a very difficult task that does not justify itself from the performance side. In decentralized systems such as D2D, it is advisable to use decentralized methods of ensuring security and confidentiality. For example, the authors of [39] proposed a cross-layer security structure where security at the physical layer and at the application level is provided by various mechanisms. The authors proposed a security architecture where the watermarking authentication is provided by the application layer while the physical layer provides wireless security.

In scenarios where DUs are located at a great distance from each other, communication from the source to the destination node can go through many relay points. On the one hand, relay nodes expand the coverage area of the network as well as improve the service quality at the communication boundaries. However, each node in itself is a weak link, which is a risk for transmitted data confidentiality and integrity.

Confidentiality is another difficult task, and if it is not solved, D2D communications are doomed to failure. It is known that D2D is a dynamic environment in which communication between different devices has a different context-dependent level of sensitivity with varying degrees that strongly depend on the user's desire to publish their personal data. It is necessary to develop a policy for the transfer of personal information, to solve the problem of what information to send to whom. Even taking into account the fact that DU systems transmit encrypted data, long term listening to the channel by an intruder can provide an opportunity to identify natural data about the user, such as the user's communication patterns, location, and time of access to the network. Thus, ensuring the anonymity of the user is another task in solving the problem of theft of D2D networks. This problem is especially expressed in group communications.

Modern methods of ensuring security and privacy in D2D are reduced to solving several subtasks. These include reliable user authentication, secrecy capacity enhancement, and creating conditions for a key agreement. Different sources in their research provide different methods for solving these subtasks. Secrecy capacity enhancement can be provided by optimization of wireless networks [40], the method of random array transmission in massive systems [41], the use of stochastic geometry, random matrix theory to optimize cellular networks [42], and much more.

Different researchers solve the problems of user authentication in different ways. For example, the authors of [43] use authentication algorithms based on biometric data, [44] uses a carrier frequency shift that changes over time in mobile networks, and [45] uses wireless channel exploitation as a function for authentication. Opportunistic beamforming and frequency diversity algorithms [46], vector quantization and clustered key mapping [47], lightweight information reconciliation [48] algorithms, and much more are used to secure the key agreement.

3.4.4 Resource management

Resource management is a very important task for D2D because in most cases, large autonomy is required from the DU, which means low energy consumption or a large amount of its supply. Modern technologies are limited for the development of large volume power supplies; therefore, the development and application of energy efficient D2D protocols, the reduction of interference, and the improvement of transmission quality are the only ways to ensure proper autonomy.

The resource management problem has two separate areas of development. Reduction of interference to ensure high performance at low power and the second direction is to reduce energy consumption.

The optimal allocation of network and spectrum resources is a critical issue in maintaining the QoS level required by the network. Wearable devices serving as DUs in healthcare have a variety of architectures and send heterogeneous data streams, which complicates solving the problem of interference in cellular networks. Due to the two-tier architecture, cellular networks with integrated D2D services are susceptible to interference at two layers, at the layer of cells—microcells, and at the layer of D2D devices. Interference at the cell level occurs between the DU and CU levels when the same spectrum is reused. This is because the resource block allocated to the cellular user is reused by one or more DUs. Most often, D2D devices are sources of interference and CUs are their victims. At the level of D2D devices, interference appears between pairs of DUs in the case when the same resource block is allocated to several devices from the same level.

The results of the research carried out provide various solutions to the problem of interference. However, three main subjects of research exist:

- Centralized approach. In this approach, the node in the center [controller, base station] examines the network and determines the interference level and channel state information for each user and cell-wide information regarding SNR. As a result, it issues a decision of resources allocation to D2D users and cellular users. This approach is applicable only to small networks because if the number of devices connected to the network increases, the information processed by the central link also increases, which will certainly lead to its failures.
- The distributed approach does not require the use of central nodes, is highly scalable, devices have constant access to communication channels of cellular devices, and adapts to the network architecture. However, this approach is very energy-intensive because the devices

constantly exchange administrative data and also have to constantly listen to communication channels to detect interference and determine the quality of the channels.
- A semidistributed approach is a hybrid approach where a variety of algorithms are applied to allocate resources with different roles of participation of D2D and eNB devices.

The problems of interference control are solved by different authors with different algorithms. The authors of [49] proposed algorithms for linear optimization, which made it possible to maximize the total rate while maintaining the requirements of QoS for D2D devices. The authors of [50] investigate the use of the particle swarm optimization algorithm. Its use allowed the authors to maximize system throughput and reduce interference. The authors of [51] successfully investigated the application of game theory optimization methods to increase bandwidth. The cognitive spectrum access method is applied to increase spectral efficiency [52].

The power level adjusting process during transmission in the base station is known as power control. Power control algorithms help save energy. The power control processes are based on resource allocation techniques that include strategies for allocating radio resources to different users/devices. Optimizing resource allocation and power management is very important to improve overall system throughput performance.

Power control algorithms also have a two-pronged approach. Power distribution can be performed from the side of the central unit [53], as in D2D based on 5G, or from the side of the devices themselves [54].

4 Millimeter waves for 5G healthcare informatics

mmWaves are a bandwidth of the spectrum above the conventionally used frequencies. Frequencies from 20 GHz to 300 GHz belong to the mmWave band. The spectrum below 3 GHz is already very clogged with a variety of frequencies for television broadcasts or other technologies. For 5G technology to show efficiency, the use of higher frequencies is required, mainly from 20 GHz to 90 GHz, because there is a huge untapped potential bandwidth. Thus, the use of millimeter waves can solve the problem of high transmission path losses [55] and will be useful for a variety of applications, including smart healthcare. Modern developments allow the use of millimeter waves at low cost, which makes this spectrum very popular. Millimeter waves are expanding wireless applications beyond radio technology.

The millimeter wave theory is not a new concept; its history began in the 1890s, as shown in Table 5. However, millimeter waves have been gaining popularity in recent years due to the widespread adoption of 5G technology. Of course, modern wireless networks employ various technologies to increase spectral efficiency, such as orthogonal frequency division multiplexing (OFDM), interference coordination, efficient channel coding techniques, and complex systems. In addition, in 5G to optimize wavelength division multiplexing, heterogeneous infrastructure, distributed antennas, and macro, pico, and femto cells are used. However, to meet the requirements imposed on 5G technology, increasing the spectral efficiency alone is not enough. The solution to this problem is the use of millimeter waves.

Table 5 History of millimeter waves.

Period	mm Waves development
1897 year	Demonstration of mmWaves
1960 year	mmWaves are used in radio astronomy
1970 year	First use of mmWaves in military applications
1980 year	First use of mmWaves in commercial applications
1990 year	First use of mmWaves above 40 GHz by consumers
2003 year	71–76 GHz and 81–86 GHz spectra authorized by FCC were first used for licensed point-to-point communication

Despite the clearly expressed advantages, the use of millimeter waves requires mechanisms for working with channel distortions in high-frequency ranges as well as effective methods of working with propagation attributes. It is necessary to solve many problems, primarily related to reducing the effect of noise as millimeter waves are highly susceptible to noise because they use large bandwidth. In addition, a high carrier frequency leads to high path losses and weak paths outside the line of sight contribute to an increase in the blocking effect.

4.1 Advantages, disadvantages, and parameters affected by mmWaves

4.1.1 Advantages of mmWaves

- A wide spectrum, high transmission rate, and high immunity to interference are provided by a huge bandwidth, some of which are given in Table 6.
- The sizes of the antenna for receiving millimeter waves are minimal, which ensures the minimum size of the equipment.
- The ability to reuse the same frequency multiple times enables communication on the same frequency without interfering with each other.

Table 6 Available spectrum.

Band	Frequency range (GHz)	Available spectrum (GHz)
23 GHz	22.55–23.55	1.0
28 GHz	27.50–28.35, 29.10–29.25, 31.075–31.225	1.3
38 GHz	38.6–40.0	1.4
40 GHz	40.50–42.50	2.0
46 GHz	45.5–46.9	1.4
47 GHz	47.2–48.2	1.0
49 GHz	48.2–50.2	2.0
E-Band	71–76, 81–86, 92–95	12.9

4.1.2 Disadvantages of mmWaves

* Development of devices for this spectrum is more expensive as most of the parts are miniature.
* Millimeter waves have very poor penetration characteristics. Therefore, this range is applicable only at short distances.
* Very high attenuation rates.
* Strong interference occurs when passing through the air or through vegetation.

4.1.3 Parameters affected by mmWaves

Security. The beamwidth of millimeter waves is very narrow. To ensure safety, the receivers must be in line of sight or at close distances from each other because they have poor passability and fade when passing through hard objects.

Bandwidth. Service providers are provided with a wide range of bandwidth. In this case, it is possible to provide full duplex at one high frequency.

Beam width interference resistance. Millimeter waves are interesting because they are ideal for all network topologies. The main reason is the use of a single frequency in a close range for several designs due to narrow-focused beams. Low-frequency signals are not adequately protected against crosstalk in the ring, point-to-point, beam, and hub topologies.

Propagation characteristics of mmWave. Important characteristics of millimeter wave propagation are path loss, blockage, atmospheric and rain absorption, and foliage loss.

4.2 mmWaves solution for 5G

The transmission rates of massive systems are increasing day by day. The needs of modern industries, including healthcare systems, reach several gigabits per second. The use of previously unaffected frequencies, in particular the millimeter wave spectrum, can be a technical and financial solution to the problem of lack of bandwidth. Millimeter wave carrier frequencies allow optimal bandwidth distribution, which guarantees high communication speeds. The increase in speed entails a significant increase in the information limit as well as a reduction in downtime. Millimeter waves at their high frequencies make it possible to apply new strategies of polarization, spatial processing, universal beamforming technologies, and Multiple Input Multiple Output systems (MIMO) [56].

Given the new bandwidth and data pumping, the base station (BS) and backhaul connections between them will have sufficient bandwidth to handle numerous devices in a densely populated area. In addition, the 5G network will be based on a MIMO base station serving small cells, usually up to 200 in a radius, which breaks the stereotypes that rain and other climatic conditions weaken the millimeter wave range for universal communication. Short wavelengths and advances in low-power complementary metal oxide semiconductor (CMOS) circuits make it possible to use small antennas. Such antennas can be used to form an array with a high reception level, on the surface of a mobile device, or even inside a microcircuit. This is undoubtedly a huge advantage when building portable, energy-efficient transceivers.

Despite all the advantages for the full use of mmWaves, it is necessary to create systems that operate on the basis of the propagation characteristics of these waves, which differ from the spectrum characteristic of traditional systems. The mmWave specifications are given below.

4.2.1   Path loss

It is known that losses during transmission of electromagnetic waves depend on the carrier frequency f_c. A high carrier frequency means a decrease in the size of the antenna of the device. Therefore, the effective aperture of the antenna increases by a factor of $\lambda^2/_{4\pi}$, and also the loss during signal transmission through spaces increases by a factor of f_c^2. Making simple calculations, you can see that when using a 30 GHz carrier instead of the traditional 3 GHz, we get an additional 20 dB power loss along the path, regardless of the source and the receiver location distance. This problem is solved by maintaining a constant aperture on the transceivers. Studies have shown that a constant aperture on one side of the data exchange channel allows maintaining the level of power loss and does not add additional antennas, and a constant aperture on both sides of the data exchange channel allows reducing losses by a factor of f_c^2 [57].

4.2.2   Blockage

In the chronology of the frequency spectrum of electromagnetic waves, with decreasing wavelength, the frequency increases. So, for example, microwave waves have a lower frequency than millimeter waves, which means that microwave waves having a lower frequency are more prone to diffraction than millimeter waves. However, millimeter waves propagate prismatically, are less diffracted, and therefore more susceptible to clogging. Recent studies have shown [57] that as the distance between the transmitter and the receiver increases, the loss increases by 20 dB for each 10 m in case of visibility, by 40 dB in indirect visibility loss with the addition of 15–40 dB of attenuation due to blocking. These data show that blockage and interference are huge disadvantages that have been addressed with large scale anti-diversity measures.

4.2.3   Atmospheric and rain absorption

As mentioned above, millimeter waves having a short wavelength are very easily absorbed by objects. Specifically, absorption by foliage, rain, and oxygen in the atmosphere is a major obstacle to the use of millimeter waves. Absorption by heavy rain or oxygen in the atmosphere reaches 10–20 dB per km; the higher the frequency, the higher this value. According to [58] on studies at a wave frequency of 60 GHz, the absorption by oxygen is on the order of 15 dB/km. However, 5G implies the construction of a network based on small cells with powerful base stations that compensate for the absorption of millimeter waves.

The main characteristics of millimeter waves are given in Table 7. According to the data from the table, we can assume that increase in the frequency leads to LOS and

Table 7 Characteristics of millimeter waves.

Frequency band	PLE		Rain attenuation for 200 m		Oxygen absorption for 200 m
	LOS	NLOS	5 mm/h	25 mm/h	
28 GHz	1.8–1.9	4.5–4.6	0.18 dB	0.9 dB	0.04 dB
38 GHz	1.9–2.0	2.7–3.8	0.26 dB	1.4 dB	0.03 dB
60 GHz	2.23	4.19	0.44 dB	2 dB	3.2 dB
73 GHz	2	2.45–2.69	0.6 dB	2.4 dB	0.09 dB

NLOS channels increase. This is also true for rain attenuation with intensities of 5 mm and 25 mm per hour. However, oxygen wave absorption is highest at 60 GHz frequencies [58].

4.2.4 Foliage loss

Foliage loss is the phenomenon of wave absorption and obstruction caused by the presence of vegetation and trees. Unlike low-frequency millimeter waves, foliage loss has a significant impact and may limit its use in some environments. So, for example, at a frequency of 80 GHz, the attenuation when passing through the foliage reaches 2.5 dB for each meter of penetration. For comparison, under the same conditions, the attenuation for the 3 GHz frequency is 0.8 dB per meter [59].

4.3 mmWaves enabling technologies

In this section, we will look at the key methods for providing mmWave connectivity for 5G networks. The operation of a millimeter wave system, including the performance of a wireless system, depends on several factors, subproblems, and approaches to a solution, such as the transmission scheme, access strategy, how the waveform structure is designed, and the channel identification method.

One of the promising technologies to improve the performance of the system is MIMO. Usually, conventional digital beamforming (DB) is used to ensure the operation of MIMO systems at channel damage. This approach is valid for most wireless systems, but due to parametric differences, it is ineffective when using millimeter waves. DB implies allocating one radio frequency (RF) chain to each antenna while traditional systems can use multiple antennas, so DB is a realistic approach to wireless system design. However, when using millimeter waves, multiple antenna arrays are required, making it impossible to allocate RF for each individual string. For this reason, MIMO systems based on millimeter waves are formed using hybrid beamforming (HB) [60].

Based on the aforementioned properties, millimeter waves are able to provide deployments of many antennas (from 100 to 1000) and they also operate in very high-frequency ranges, which means they provide large bandwidth. This facilitates the implementation of spatial multiplexing of wave channels, which ensures high channel performance [61]. Spatial multiplexing provides increased transmission capacity by splitting the transmission stream into multiple portions and transmitting each individual stream with a separate antenna in parallel.

The efficiency of spatial multiplexing and beamforming is measured by the amount and quality of channel state information (CSI). Effectively performing CSI detection determines the quality of the bandwidth. Detection of CSI requires MIMO study; however practical channels have a limited coherence time, so the study period is limited. Another important factor influencing performance at the link layer is the waveform of the signal [62]. Various signal designs contribute to the disassembled system performance in terms of beamforming and channel estimation.

The strategy for accessing the wireless channel is an important factor in improving the performance of the link layer in systems using mmWave. To provide it, the method of superimposed small cells is used. For example, in 5G, control planes must be separated from the data planes so that critical control data are transmitted over reliable microwave links and high-speed data transmission between devices occurs through millimeter wave systems [63]. Thus, it becomes possible to use a reliable channel at high data rates.

5 Leveraging mmWaves and D2D in healthcare

5.1 D2D in healthcare

As mentioned in the previous sections, the modern healthcare system is patient-centered and the main task is to personalize services. Personalization of services today is provided through the WBAN. As the number of users increases, the likelihood of Internet working conflicts or WBAN conflicts increases. This is the process of affecting data transmission within a WBAN on transmissions in another WBAN located in the vicinity and operating in the same frequency channel. Such impacts usually affect the QoS performance as well as lead to reduced transmission reliability, reduced throughput, increased end-to-end latency, etc. Based on the health system requirements outlined in Section 2, it can be argued that QoS decreases in healthcare are not acceptable. Collisions between WBANs and WBAN conflicts can be resolved through the use of D2D communications [64]. With D2D, devices can send end-to-end data to each other without using base stations. This end-to-end transmission potentially reduces channel distance and also reduces the quantity of required transmissions from two to one unit of information. D2D communication has the potential to improve communication efficiency for the healthcare system.

Cellular-assisted D2D—D2D in a distributed mode, provides protection against WBAN collisions. However, this increases the number of nodes loading the base station, such as medical sensors, WBAN concentrators, and typical cellular users. In such scenarios, the transmissions between sensors and their hubs (D2D) can be performed in parallel with the transmissions of cellular communications between cellular users and the base station to efficiently allocate spectrum. However, this scenario does not always suit mobile operators because the interference created by D2D can affect the quality of communication of cellular subscribers, which are the operator's main source of income [65]. This problem is easily solved by simple algorithms for controlling the transmission power of both D2D and cellular users, which makes it possible to provide maximum bandwidth for cellular users and the same communication channel is not assigned to neighboring WBAN.

Research on the use of D2D in healthcare is a priority area of modern science. But in most cases, the concepts of BCH and healthcare are considered separately from D2D. So work on the use of D2D communications in healthcare, and in particular WBAN for healthcare monitoring, is limited. The work in [66] where D2D is considered a connection scenario in mobile hospitals can be referred to a small number of works. In [67], the studies carried out show that when transmitting D2D data, the power consumption of wearable medical sensors is reduced by as much as 50% compared to a direct connection to a base station.

D2D in most cases is used to organize networks to ensure continuous monitoring of the patient's condition. For example, in [68] with the help of ZigBee, a WBAN is formed to monitor the heart rate, where D2D successfully copes with the problem of WBAN collisions. In addition, single and multilink D2D avoids overloading the base station by unloading communication traffic in healthcare, as shown in [69]. The authors of [70] proposed a ZigBee-based access control scheme to detect and resolve collisions between WBANs.

As you can see from the use of D2D, one of the main problems of its application is the collision of WBANs. One of the solutions to this problem is to shift the start time of the frame to control access to the medium as well as adjust the time of transmission of the beacon of the transmitting node. Another factor in the success of using D2D in healthcare is the mechanisms for protecting information during storage and processing in wearable devices. The authors of [71] investigated the problem of the weakening of the secrecy of the physical layer that occurs when passively listening to D2D broadcasts. These works indicate and prove the high efficiency of the implementation of D2D in the healthcare system.

5.2   mmWaves in healthcare

Virtually any technology can be used to maintain communication between transmitter and receiver devices. However, not every technology can handle the increasing demand for bandwidth. mmWaves are an ideal candidate for building corporate healthcare networks where high-speed diagnostic systems must be connected to a central server. Because millimeter waves are reflected from the surface of the human body, they have little radiation; however, they are not applicable to implant sensors.

By far the main factor in the widespread use and interest in millimeter waves is associated with the enormous and constant bandwidth. One of the applications of millimeter waves is high-speed video streaming in telemedicine. The study [72,73] showed excellent results for the implementation of BAN for in-body and out-of-body applications based on 60 GHz radios. In addition, these studies have shown that the presence of a body cannot in any way affect the impedance matching and gain of the antenna. The application of millimeter waves in healthcare is a very complex process. It is used in conjunction with other wireless access technologies, especially as a fundamental link of 5G, as given in Fig. 6.

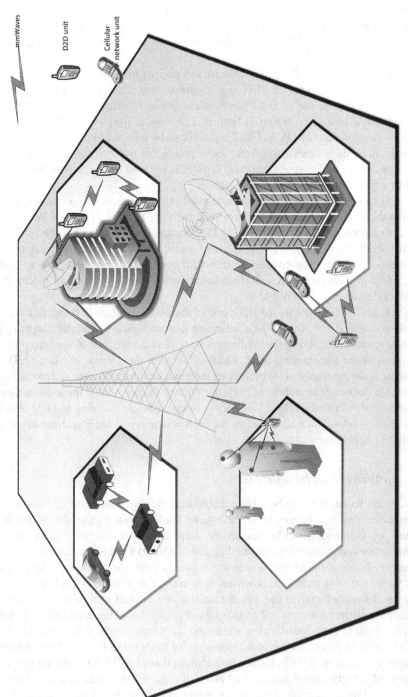

Fig. 6 D2D and mmWaves in healthcare.

mmWaves

D2D unit

Cellular network unit

6 Conclusion

Healthcare informatics places huge demands on telecommunication networks. Basically, these requirements are associated with ensuring high data rates and providing quality service. Telecommunications networks are responding by offering next-generation 5G technology to deliver the desired performance. However, the concept of 5G should be considered comprehensively because it relies on many additional solutions to ensure its functions. In this chapter, we have looked at several of these solutions such as D2D communications and millimeter waves.

D2D technologies support multiple modes and have a variety of architectures and build configurations. The selected configuration depends on the purpose of the application. In particular, for use in healthcare informatics, D2D devices must be controlled by a 5G base station because in this case, network adaptability is improved and interference is reduced. Additionally, D2D requires the use of a licensed spectrum because the use of unlicensed spectra violates one of the most important requirements of healthcare informatics—reliability. In addition, sharing the spectrum with cellular devices increases the potential for interference and noise. For this reason, it is advisable to use the separately allocated spectrum mode.

Millimeter waves provide a huge previously unused bandwidth for healthcare applications. However, as this technology is at an early stage of development, research is required to increase the efficiency of millimeter waves, reduce operating costs, and improve signal transmission.

References

[1] R. Raghu, Seminar Report on Millimeter wave mobile communication for 5G cellular, 2020. *http://www.slideshare.net/raghubraghu/mmwave-3-140920062222/>*. accessed 10.10.2020.
[2] F. Jameel, Z. Hamid, F. Jabeen, S. Zeadally, M.A. Javed, A survey of device-to-device communications: research issues and challenges, IEEE Commun. Surv. Tutor. 20 (2018) 2133–2168.
[3] A. Ahad, M. Tahir, K.-L.A. Yau, 5G-based smart healthcare network: architecture, taxonomy, challenges and future research directions, IEEE Access 7 (2019) 100747–100762, https://doi.org/10.1109/ACCESS.2019.2930628.
[4] R. Gupta, S. Tanwar, N. Kumar, Secrecy-ensured NOMA-based cooperative D2D-aided fog computing under imperfect CSI, J. Inform. Sec. Appl. 59 (2021) 102812, https://doi.org/10.1016/j.jisa.2021.102812.
[5] S. Mumtaz, J. Rodriguez, Smart Device to Smart Device Communication, Springer, 2014.
[6] Q. Wang, B. Rengarajan, Recouping opportunistic gain in dense base station layouts through energy-aware user cooperation, in: International Symposium and Workshops on a World of Wireless, Mobile and Multimedia Networks (WoWMoM), 2013, pp. 1–9.
[7] P. Mach, Z. Becvar, T. Vanek, In-band device-to-device communication in OFDMA cellular networks: a survey and challenges, IEEE Commun. Surv. Tutor. 17 (4) (2015) 1885–1922.
[8] I. Budhiraja, S. Tyagi, S. Tanwar, N. Kumar, J.J.P.C. Rodrigues, DIYA: tactile internet driven delay assessment NOMA-based scheme for D2D communication, IEEE Trans. Ind. Inform. 15 (12) (2019) 6354–6366, https://doi.org/10.1109/TII.2019.2910532.

[9] G. Fodor, E. Dahlman, G. Mildh, S. Parkvall, N. Reider, G. Miklós, Z. Turányi, Design aspects of network assisted device-to-device communications, IEEE Commun. Mag. 50 (3) (2012) 170–177.

[10] Y. Pei, Y.-C. Liang, Resource allocation for device-to-device communications overlaying two-way cellular networks, IEEE Trans. Wirel. Commun. 12 (7) (2013) 3611–3621.

[11] B. Zhou, H. Hu, S.-Q. Huang, H.-H. Chen, Intra cluster device-to-device relay algorithm with optimal resource utilization, IEEE Trans. Vehic. Technol. 62 (5) (2013) 2315–2326.

[12] J.B. Misic, V.B. Misic, Adapting LTE/LTE-A to M2M and D2D communications, IEEE Network 31 (3) (2017) 63–69.

[13] A. Virdis, C. Vallati, G. Nardini, G. Tanganelli, G. Stea, E. Mingozzi, D2D communications for large-scale fog platforms: enabling direct M2M interactions, IEEE Vehic. Technol. Magaz. 13 (2) (2018) 24–33.

[14] E. Yaacoub, O. Kubbar, Energy-efficient device-to-device communications in LTE public safety networks, in: 2012 IEEE Globecom Workshops, 2012, pp. 391–395.

[15] K. Ali, H.X. Nguyen, P. Shah, Q.T. Vien, N. Bhuvanasundaram, Architecture for public safety network using D2D communication, in: 2016 IEEE Wireless Communications and Networking Conference Workshops, 2016, pp. 206–211.

[16] K. Ali, H.X. Nguyen, Q.T. Vien, P. Shah, Z. Chu, Disaster management using D2D communication with power transfer and clustering techniques, IEEE Access 6 (2018) 14643–14654.

[17] V. Raghavan, A. Partyka, L. Akhoondzadeh-Asl, M.A. Tassoudji, O.H. Koymen, J. Sanelli, Millimeter wave channel measurements and implications for PHY layer design, IEEE Trans. Antennas Propag. 65 (12) (2017) 6521–6533.

[18] R. Gupta, S. Tanwar, S. Tyagi, N. Kumar, Tactile internet and its applications in 5G era: a comprehensive review, Int. J. Commun. Syst. 32 (2019), https://doi.org/10.1002/dac.3981.

[19] N. Bahadori, N. Namvar, B. Kelley, A. Homaifar, Device-to-device communications in the millimeter wave band: a novel distributed mechanism, in: 2018 Wireless Telecommunications Symposium (WTS), 2018, pp. 1–6.

[20] E. Reypnazarov, N. Akhmedov, D. Khasanov, Blockchain for 5G Healthcare architecture, in: 2020 International Conference on Information Science and Communications Technologies (ICISCT), Tashkent, Uzbekistan, 2020, https://doi.org/10.1109/ICISCT50599. 2020.9351398.

[21] R. Gupta, S. Tanwar, F. Al-Turjman, P. Italiya, A. Nauman, S.W. Kim, Smart contract privacy protection using AI in cyber-physical systems: tools, techniques and challenges, IEEE Access 8 (2020) 24746–24772, https://doi.org/10.1109/ACCESS.2020.2970576.

[22] M. Khan, M. Alam, Y. Moullec, E. Yaacoub, Throughput-aware cooperative reinforcement learning for adaptive resource allocation in device-to-device communication, Future Internet 9 (4) (2017) 72.

[23] O. Bello, S. Zeadally, Intelligent device-to-device communication in the internet of things, IEEE Syst. J. 10 (3) (2014) 1172–1182.

[24] Y. Li, Y. Liang, Q. Liu, H. Wang, Resources allocation in multicell D2D communications for internet of things, IEEE Internet Things J. 5 (5) (2018) 4100–4108.

[25] S. Tanwar, J. Vora, S. Tyagi, N. Kumar, M. Obaidat, A systematic review on security issues in vehicular ad hoc network, Security Privacy 1 (2018) 1–26, https://doi.org/ 10.1002/spy2.39.

[26] R. Gupta, S. Tanwar, N. Kumar, Blockchain and 5G integrated softwarized UAV network management: architecture, solutions, and challenges, Phys. Commun. 47 (2021), https:// doi.org/10.1016/j.phycom.2021.101355. ISSN 1874-4907.

[27] K. Kushalad, M. Sarkar, P. Patel, Asynchronous device discovery and rendezvous protocol for D2D communication, in: Conference on Computer Communications Workshops, 2016, pp. 199–200.

[28] X. Lin, L. Jiang, J.G. Andrews, Performance analysis of asynchronous multicarrier wireless networks, IEEE Trans. Commun. 63 (9) (2015) 3377–3390.

[29] H. Khujamatov, E. Reypnazarov, D. Khasanov, N. Akhmedov, IoT, IIoT, and cyberphysical systems integration, in: K.K. Singh, A. Nayyar, S. Tanwar, M. Abouhawwash (Eds.), Emergence of Cyber Physical System and IoT in Smart Automation and Robotics, Advances in Science, Technology & Innovation (IEREK Interdisciplinary Series for Sustainable Development), Springer, Cham, 2021, https://doi.org/10.1007/978-3-030-66222-6_3.

[30] K. Wang, X. Mao, Y. Liu, BlindDate: a neighbor discovery protocol, IEEE Trans. Parallel Distrib. Syst. 26 (4) (2015) 949–959.

[31] Z. Li, COAST: a connected open platform for smart objects, in: 2nd International Conference on Information and Communication Technologies for Disaster Management (ICT-DM), IEEE, 2015, pp. 166–172.

[32] H.-B. Li, R. Miura, F. Kojima, Channel access proposal for enabling quick discovery for D2D wireless networks, in: International Conference on Computing, Networking and Communications (ICNC), IEEE, 2017, pp. 1012–1016.

[33] C. Campolo, A. Molinaro, A. Vinel, N. Lyamin, M. Jonsson, Service discovery and access in vehicle-to-roadside multi-channel VANETs, in: International Conference on Communication Workshop (ICCW), IEEE, 2015, pp. 2477–2482.

[34] A. Prasad, K. Samdanis, A. Kunz, J. Song, Energy-efficient device discovery for social cloud applications in 3GPP LTE-advanced networks, in: Symposium on Computers and Communication (ISCC), IEEE, 2014, pp. 1–6.

[35] C. Xu, C. Gao, Z. Zhou, Z. Chang, Y. Jia, Social network-based content delivery in device-to-device underlay cellular networks using matching theory, IEEE Access 5 (2017) 924–937.

[36] R. Wang, H. Yang, H. Wang, D. Wu, Social overlapping community-aware neighbor discovery for D2D communications, IEEE Wirel. Commun. 23 (4) (2016) 28–34.

[37] A. Orsino, M. Gapeyenko, L. Militano, D. Moltchanov, S. Andreev, Y. Koucheryavy, G. Araniti, Assisted handover based on deviceto-device communications in 3GPP LTE systems, in: 2015 IEEE Globecom Workshops (GC Wkshps), 2015, pp. 1–6.

[38] H.Y. Chen, M.J. Shih, H.Y. Wei, Handover mechanism for device-to-device communication, in: Conference on Standards for Communications and Networking (CSCN), 2015, pp. 72–77.

[39] R. Gupta, S. Tanwar, N. Kumar, S. Tyagi, Blockchain-based security attack resilience schemes for autonomous vehicles in industry 4.0: a systematic review, Comput. Electr. Eng. 86 (2020), https://doi.org/10.1016/j.compeleceng.2020.106717.

[40] W. Wang, K.C. Teh, K.H. Li, Enhanced physical layer security in D2D spectrum sharing networks, IEEE Wireless Commun. Lett. 6 (1) (2017) 106–109.

[41] L. Wan, G. Han, J. Jiang, C. Zhu, L. Shu, A DOA estimation approach for transmission performance guarantee in D2D communication, Mobile Networks Appl. 22 (2017) 1–12.

[42] G. Geraci, H.S. Dhillon, J.G. Andrews, J. Yuan, I.B. Collings, A new model for physical layer security in cellular networks, in: International Conference on Communications (ICC), IEEE, 2014, pp. 2147–2152.

[43] L.Y. Paul, G. Verma, B.M. Sadler, Wireless physical layer authentication via fingerprint embedding, IEEE Commun. Mag. 53 (6) (2015) 48–53.

[44] W. Hou, X. Wang, J.-Y. Chouinard, A. Refaey, Physical layer authentication for mobile systems with time-varying carrier frequency offsets, IEEE Trans. Commun. 62 (5) (2014) 1658–1667.

[45] J. Hathaliya, S. Tanwar, An exhaustive survey on security and privacy issues in healthcare 4.0, Comput. Commun. 153 (2020), https://doi.org/10.1016/j.comcom.2020.02.018.

[46] P. Huang, X. Wang, Fast secret key generation in static wireless networks: a virtual channel approach, in: INFOCOM, 2013 Proceedings IEEE, IEEE, 2013, pp. 2292–2300.

[47] Y.-W.P. Hong, L.-M. Huang, H.-T. Li, Vector quantization and clustered key mapping for channel-based secret key generation, IEEE Trans. Inform. Foren. Sec. 12 (5) (2017) 1170–1181.

[48] A. Zhang, L. Wang, X. Ye, X. Lin, Light-weight and robust security-aware d2d-assist data transmission protocol for mobile-health systems, IEEE Trans. Inform. Foren. Sec. 12 (3) (2017) 662–675.

[49] S. Wen, X. Zhu, Z. Lin, X. Zhang, D. Yang, Optimization of interference coordination schemes in device-to-device (D2D) communication, in: 7th International ICST Conference on Communications and Networking in China (CHINACOM), IEEE, 2012, pp. 542–547.

[50] L. Su, Y. Ji, P. Wang, F. Liu, Resource allocation using particle swarm optimization for D2D communication underlay of cellular networks, in: Wireless Communications and Networking Conference (WCNC), IEEE, 2013, pp. 129–133.

[51] Y. Liu, R. Wang, Z. Han, Interference-constrained pricing for D2D networks, IEEE Trans. Wirel. Commun. 16 (2016) 475–486.

[52] A.H. Sakr, H. Tabassum, E. Hossain, D.I. Kim, Cognitive spectrum access in device-to-device-enabled cellular networks, IEEE Commun. Mag. 53 (7) (2015) 126–133.

[53] H. Elsawy, E. Hossain, M.-S. Alouini, Analytical modeling of mode selection and power control for underlay D2D communication in cellular networks, IEEE Trans. Commun. 62 (11) (2014) 4147–4161.

[54] G. Zhang, J. Hu, W. Heng, X. Li, G. Wang, Distributed power control for D2D communications underlaying cellular network using Stackelberg game, in: Wireless Communications and Networking Conference (WCNC), IEEE, 2017, pp. 1–6.

[55] K. Khujamatov, D. Khasanov, E. Reypnazarov, N. Akhmedov, Existing technologies and solutions in 5G-enabled IoT for industrial automation, in: S. Tanwar (Ed.), Blockchain for 5G-Enabled IoT, Springer, Cham, 2021, https://doi.org/10.1007/978-3-030-67490-8_8.

[56] F. Rusek, D. Persson, B. Lau, E. Larsson, T. Marzetta, O. Edfors, F. Tufvesson, Scaling up MIMO: opportunities and challenges with very large arrays, IEE Signal Process Mag. 30 (1) (2013) 40–60.

[57] I. Mistry, S. Tanwar, S. Tyagi, N. Kumar, Blockchain for 5G-enabled IoT for industrial automation: a systematic review, solutions, and challenges, Mech. Syst. Signal Proc. 135 (2020), https://doi.org/10.1016/j.ymssp.2019.106382.

[58] T.S. Rappaport, S. Sun, R. Mayzus, H. Zhao, Y. Azar, K. Wang, G.N. Wong, J.K. Schulz, M. Samimi, F. Gutierrez, Millimeter wave mobile communications for 5G cellular: it will work! Access, IEEE 1 (2013) 335–349.

[59] F. Khan, Z. Pi, mmWave mobile broadband (MMB): unleashing the 3–300 GHz spectrum, in: Proceedings of IEEE Sarnoff Symposium, 2011, pp. 1–6.

[60] O.E. Ayach, S. Rajagopal, S. Abu-Surra, Z. Pi, R.W. Heath, Spatially sparse precoding in millimeter wave MIMO systems, IEEE Trans. Wirel. Commun. 13 (3) (2014) 1499–1513.

[61] C. Sheldon, M. Seo, E. Torkildson, M. Rodwell, U. Madhow, Four-channel spatial multiplexing over a millimeter-wave line-of-sight link, in: Proceedings of IEEE International Microwave Symposium Digest (MTT-S), 2009, pp. 389–392.

[62] H. Khujamatov, E. Reypnazarov, N. Akhmedov, D. Khasanov, Industry digitalization consepts with 5G-Based IoT, in: 2020 International Conference on Information Science and Communications Technologies (ICISCT), Tashkent, Uzbekistan, 2020, https://doi.org/10.1109/ICISCT50599.2020.9351468.

[63] K. Zheng, L. Zhao, J. Mei, M. Dohler, W. Xiang, Y. Peng, 10 Gb/s HetSNets with millimeter-wave communications: access and networking challenges and protocols, IEEE Commun. Mag. 53 (1) (2015) 86–92.

[64] P.-Y. Kong, Multicell D2D communications for hierarchical control of microgrid system, IEEE Syst. J. 15 (2020) 1929–1938.

[65] M. Noura, R. Nordin, A survey on interference management for device-to-device (D2D) communication and its challenges in 5G networks, J. Netw. Comput. Appl. 71 (2016) 130–150.

[66] D. Lin, Y. Tang, A.V. Vasilakos, User-priority-based power control in D2D networks for mobile health, IEEE Syst. J. 12 (4) (2018) 3142–3150.

[67] B.K.-P. Koh, P.-Y. Kong, Performance study on ZigBee-based wireless personal area networks for real-time health monitoring, ETRI J. 28 (4) (2006) 537–540.

[68] N. Shakhakarmi, Next generation wearable devices: smart health monitoring device and smart sousveillance hat using device to device (D2D) communications in LTE assisted networks, WEAS Trans. Commun. 14 (2015) 241–255.

[69] H. Huang, W. Xiang, Y. Tao, B. Liu, H. Min, Relay-assisted D2D transmission for mobile health applications, Sensors 18 (12) (2018) 1–19.

[70] K. Khujamatov, D. Khasanov, E. Reypnazarov, N. Akhmedov, Networking and computing in Internet of Things and cyber-physical systems, in: The 14th IEEE International Conference Application of Information and Communication Technologies, 07-09 October, 2020, https://doi.org/10.1109/AICT50176.2020.9368793. Tashkent, Uzbekistan (Scopus).

[71] C. Ma, J. Liu, X. Tian, Y. Hui, Y. Cui, X. Wang, Interference exploitation in D2D-enabled cellular networks: a secrecy perspective, IEEE Trans. Commun. 63 (1) (2015) 229–242.

[72] N. Chahat, M. Zhadobov, L.L. Coq, S.I. Alekseev, R. Sauleau, Characterization of the interactions between a 60-GHz antenna and the human body in an off-body scenario, IEEE Trans. Antennas Propag. 60 (12) (2012) 5958–5965, https://doi.org/10.1109/TAP.2012.2211326.

[73] G. Valerio, N. Chahat, M. Zhadobov, R. Sauleau, Theoretical and experimental characterization of on-body propagation at 60 GHz, in: 2013 7th European Conference on Antennas and Propagation (EuCAP), 2013, pp. 583–585. http://www.research.philips.com/initiatives.

Blockchain-based privacy approaches for 5G healthcare informatics

10

B.L. Sandeep, Vibhavari B. Rao, K. Aditya, S.R. Mani Sekhar, and G.M. Siddesh
Information Science and Engineering, Ramaiah Institute of Technology (Affiliated to VTU), Bangalore, Karnataka, India

1 Introduction to blockchain-based smart healthcare systems

In today's world, with the growing healthcare industry dealing with copious amounts of data, it has become imperative to integrate the concept of smart healthcare in health facilities and institutions. Healthcare that makes use of technology such as big data, the Internet of Things (IoT), the cloud, and artificial intelligence (AI) relies on innovative technologies to transform the modern medical system [1]. Although from a macro level these technologies show a massive improvement in the healthcare ecosystem in terms of speed, latency, and convenience, the underlying communication network poses many drawbacks, one of which is reliability. Communication networks such as 4G/5G are very promising in offering seamless high-quality interconnection between devices. However, they lack privacy protection due to the involvement of third-party network controllers who could access even the most sensitive and confidential information shared through the network. In recent times, telemedicine services have played a major role in connecting patients with doctors. In such a use case, it is vital to keep the information shared during the telemedicine session very confidential but because it is bound by a centralized infrastructure, it is exposed to security and privacy vulnerabilities [2,3]. It is essential to develop robust health monitoring networks. The future intelligent healthcare networks, which will increase spectrum performance and allow high-speed communications, are defined by health management provided by cloud computing, edge computing, and 5G [4].

Several key IoT issues have paved the way for blockchain's inclusion in 5G-based IoT, including architecture, scalability, large-scale deployment, interconnectivity, thick heterogeneous networks (HetNets), concerns with respect to security and privacy, network functions virtualization (NFV) and software defined networks (SDN) queries, and multidevice networking [5]. In healthcare, privacy largely relates to who has access to a patient's records and data, but it also refers to data that may be collected, utilized, and made public by anybody who is not specifically authorized to do so [6]. Blockchain technology, one of the world's largest transformation technologies, strives to provide a massively transparent, unchanging, stable

Blockchain Applications for Healthcare Informatics. https://doi.org/10.1016/B978-0-323-90615-9.00020-7
Copyright © 2022 Elsevier Inc. All rights reserved.

mechanism that replaces the current focused infrastructure. Public health administration, statistical health history, electronic claim adjudication, remote patient tracking, patient information, user-oriented diagnostic analysis, fraudulent pharmaceutical products, clinical testing, and precision medicine are just a few of the technologies used in healthcare [7]. Distributed ledger technology (DLT) enables the seamless transmission of patient medical information, controls the drug supply chain, and assists healthcare experts in deciphering the genetic code [8]. Because the blockchain is incorruptible, decentralized, and open, it is a technology ready for data security applications. Furthermore, while blockchain is open, it is also confidential, concealing any individual's identity with complicated and protected codes capable of protecting the sensitivity of medical details. Smart contract-based privacy-preserving databases are a promising tool for protecting privacy and distributed data on the blockchain [9]. The technology's decentralized architecture further enables patients, physicians, and healthcare professionals to share the same information in a timely and secure manner. Hathaliya et al. [6,10] investigated various blockchain-based technologies for strengthening healthcare systems' existing shortcomings. A Hyperledger-based access management policy algorithm is being introduced to improve data accessibility between healthcare professionals.

1.1   Transition from Healthcare 1.0 to Healthcare 4.0

Similar to the transition witnessed in manufacturing sectors, healthcare delivery too has evolved substantially. These evolutions are summarized and grouped as four stages, described below:

1.1.1   Healthcare 1.0

This first stage, Healthcare 1.0, is the fundamental patient-doctor interaction. In this scenario, a patient would typically visit a clinic and meet their preferred doctor and team. Through initial diagnosis during this visit, the doctor and team would conduct initial testing and provide a prescription mentioning the required medication, adequate doses, and other necessary instruction. This has been popular in the healthcare sector for centuries.

1.1.2   Healthcare 2.0

Healthcare 2.0 primarily describes performing complex diagnoses and producing better test results. Along with the immense growth in healthcare, life sciences, and biotechnology, more innovative medical gadgets that have been created and evaluated are being utilized in the healthcare system. For example, magnetic resonance imaging (MRI), ultrasound imaging, computed tomography (CT), arterial line, surgical equipment, and other life support appliances are increasingly being utilized in hospitals and other medical institutions for diagnosis, treatment, and monitoring.

1.1.3   Healthcare 3.0

Healthcare 3.0 describes the use of computer technology to automate manual tasks in the hospital. Electronic medical records (EMR) or electronic health records (EHR) have been used to handle patient requests, conditions, and other data across various healthcare institutions. Technology has significantly improved the operational processes of a healthcare business. The use of time-stamping and EMR records has enabled the automation/computerization of many manual tasks (e.g., order input in computerized provider order entry [CPOE] and digitalization, e.g., electronic after visit summary [AVS]).

A manual visit in the past has been replaced by telehealth and/or the use of computer networks to make visits more accessible.

1.1.4   Healthcare 4.0

There are two very important aspects of Healthcare 4.0. The first is smartness, which is achieved through AI technology to improve diagnosis, treatment, coordination, and communication among patients, doctors, and other stakeholders to achieve individualized and patient-centered smart healthcare management. The second is interoperability, which is achieved through communication among patients, doctors, and other stakeholders. Not only do we need information connection in each aspect, but we also demand information integration across the whole patient experience at all phases. Security and approval of information sharing across stakeholders may result in substantial advances in the delivery of healthcare services to patients. As a result, blockchain, via its interoperability, has the potential to improve access to patient medical data, ensure the safe monitoring of devices, and, as a result, fulfill the necessary privacy standards.

2   Transformative ecosystem: 5G

Complex healthcare processes require communication and delivery of heterogeneous patient records as well as efficient resource utilization and logistical management. The current cellular systems (3G, 4G, and WiMAX) use macrocells to offer a broader spectrum suited for lower data speeds. These items are appropriate for smart health surveillance systems, social interactions, and activity tracking. For medical services such as remote surgery, heterogeneous wireless technology that can operate on various frequency ranges while also delivering a high data speed with very low latency is required. 5G may be the ecosystem that revolutionizes healthcare systems [11]. It is designed not only to expand capacities but also allows the smallest devices to conduct high-level calculations and connect rapidly with system-wide computing power, which is available through a licensed common bandwidth and an unlicensed bandwidth [12].

2.1   Communication technologies for smart healthcare

Smart healthcare services for a rapidly evolving healthcare system have now become the dire need of this century. This involves the smart monitoring of patient status in a noninvasive way, at any point of time, making the traditional way of monitoring obsolete. This has been considerably influenced by and pivoted around some of the in-demand information technologies such as IoT, big data, SDN, NFV, network slicing and cloud computing, thus enhancing the availability, efficiency, reliability, and convenience of healthcare [13]. The underlying communication technologies enabling IoT have also been the subject of expeditious research and development over the past decade. Currently, in healthcare systems, mainstream wireless networking devices such as Bluetooth, cellular networks, and WiFi are included [14,15]. These technologies will not serve the growing needs of future generations, considering the significant potential growth in healthcare industries and their consequent generation of big data [13,15,16]. Such extremely voluminous and diverse data should be processed solely in order to ensure that delays, bandwidth, latency, and other attributes are taken into account [14]. 5G networks have now come to the fore to address the complex needs of networking in healthcare.

The prevalence of information and communication technology (ICT) in the healthcare industry is widely impacting the enhanced provisioning and utilization of healthcare resources along with operational efficiency and security. Typically, smart healthcare services should be extremely reliant on correspondence ranges such as short-range and long-range servers and devices. The most commonly employed wireless devices for smart-health treatment, such as the body area network (BAN), include Bluetooth, ZigBee, and WiFi.

2.1.1   Short-range technologies

Personal area network (PAN): A wireless personal area network (WPAN) is a network that covers narrow areas, such as a home, and allows adjacent devices to communicate and share data with one another. The following are some of the innovations of WPAN [17].

- **Near field communication (NFC)**: This contactless communication technology allows the exchange of data between devices in close proximity of 10 cm. This helps with encrypted purchases, digital material sharing, and connecting electronic devices with a single click. Because transfers take place over a short distance, both devices must have NFC chips. It supports a data rate of about 100–400 kbps and a frequency of 13.56 MHz. It has very low power usage. Due to the quick transmission between devices, it significantly reduces the chance of human error. NFCs are well-known today as the technology that allows users to pay for goods and services using their phones. NFC has paved the way for innovation in the healthcare sector as well as other sectors. NFC-enabled wristbands help in tracking and monitoring a patient. By tapping the wristband on a tablet or phone, the health data are directly transmitted to the doctor's office. Hospital staff can further track the real-time status of the patient and then decide on the right medication [18].
- **Bluetooth 4**: In addition to traditional Bluetooth protocols, such as Classic Bluetooth, Bluetooth High Speed, and Bluetooth Low Energy, the newest generation of Bluetooth protocols are also

utilized with Bluetooth Smart. The 0.1 km proximity radius, 1 Mbps data throughput, and 2.4 GHz frequency make it perfect for mobile applications. It is also fuel-efficient. It was built for use in low-power applications that are powered by a coin battery in contrast to previous versions that used the Bluetooth standard protocols. This is all backed up by the fact that the chip designs allow dual mode, single mode, and previous model upgrades. Although only a low-energy protocol stack is introduced in single mode, the original Classic Bluetooth controller is enhanced with Bluetooth Smart features in dual mode. The software in Bluetooth 4.1 and 4.2 models was enhanced even further, with additional capabilities for the IoT.

- **Bluetooth 5**: This improved version of Bluetooth 4 supports a higher data rate of 2 Mbps and a proximity range of 0.25 km. It again consumes very low power. It is the most recent Bluetooth networking protocol edition. Wireless speakers and other audio hardware as well as wireless keyboards, mice, and game controllers have all benefited from it [19]. It also plays an important role in the collaboration between smart homes and IoT users. It has dual audio support, allowing you to listen to music on two separate platforms at the same time. Two separate audio sources may be streamed to two varied audio devices at the same time. Compared to Bluetooth 4.2, Bluetooth 5.0 can transmit eight times more data, at twice the speed, across four times the range. Walls and other obstacles, on the other hand, can slow you down [20].
- **ISO/IEC 15693**: It is an ISO standard for proximity cards that can be read from farther away than proximity cards. It runs at a frequency of 3.56 MHz and has a data rate of 6.6–26 Kbit/s. Its proximity scale is 1–1.5 m. It uses very little energy. Members may hold this proximity card in their purse or pocket, and when they bring it near a terminal unit, they obtain access to locations, products, or facilities. An alternating current field generated in the reader, also known as a coupler, couples power to the proximity card. The powering area uses a frequency of 13.56 MHz, which is one of the industrial, science, and medical (ISM) frequencies that can be used anywhere in the world. Vicinity cards without a power supply can be energized from a coupler that can only relay power under the limitations set by international radio frequency (RF) regulations.

Local area network (LAN): This is a network generally used in places requiring limited coverage such as schools, hospitals, libraries, etc. The below-listed communication technologies are a type of LAN.

- **ZigBee**: It is one of the well-suited high-level communication protocols for IoT networks operating over a frequency of 2.4 GHz. It has a high data rate of 250 kbps and a range of 10–100 m. It consumes very little electricity. ZigBee was created to communicate in noisy RF environments such as those used in commercial and industrial settings. New tracking and control functions from devices such as smart phones and tablets on a wide area network (WAN) or LAN are opened up by linking Zigbee 3.0 networks to the IP domain, taking the real IoT to fruition. It may be the design of the whole network, from simple point-to-point connections to multipoint links to mesh networking. It has less latency and a single charge lasts for a long time [21].
- **Z-Wave**: The Z Wave Protocol is a wireless and RF interoperable networking technology. It is one of the upcoming new communication standards in the world of IoT. It operates over a range of frequencies between 908 MHz and 968 MHz and supports a data rate of 100 kbps with a proximity range of up to 100 m. Here, power consumption is incredibly poor. Z Wave was created with tracking, surveillance, and status reading in mind in both residential and light commercial settings. Because all Z Wave devices are compatible with one another, it can mix and match devices from multiple vendors. Another benefit is that there is less congestion and fewer disconnections than in Bluetooth and other WiFi networks (http://www.safety.com/2021) [22].

- **Radio frequency identification (RFID)**: RFID is, in essence, a technology that allows you to track things. Radio waves are used to collect the digital data stored in RFID tags or smart labels. It is part of the automated identification and data capture (AIDC) technology community, which is known for automatically identifying items, collecting data about them, and entering the data into computer systems with little to no human interference. It deploys electromagnetic fields to automatically identify objects by tagging them with RFID tags. It operates on a frequency range of 13.56 MHz–2.45 GHz with a data rate of 40–640 kbps and a proximity range of 1–100 m. It has low power usage. RFID systems are made up of three major parts: an RFID tag or smart mark, an RFID scanner, and an antenna. The RFID tag's integrated circuit and antenna assist in transmitting data to the RFID scanner, which transforms radio waves into a more usable medium of data [23].
- **Thread**: It is a low-power mesh networking technology for IoT products, operating on the 2.4 GHz frequency and supporting 250 Kbits/s of data rate within 10–100 m of proximity. It allows quick and safe interconnections between several users as well as cloud addressability through the use of actual Internet protocols in a low-power wireless mesh network. It provides banking-class encryption to close security gaps found in previous standards. The thread IoT concept has been designed to offer low power levels. The key concept of thread is to provide reliability in device communications. Latency is also reduced to 100 ms for typical interactions [24].
- **WiFi**: It belongs to the family of wireless networks that offers an interface between computers or phones and the Internet. It operates between 2.4 GHz and 5 GHz frequencies. It supports a rate of about 1 Gbps of data within a proximity of 50 m. The power usage can vary between low and high. WiFi is used mostly in smart phone applications because consumers tend to utilize WiFi rather than mobile networks because they have a higher rate of data and secure indoor access at a reduced cost. Wireless Internet access is one of the most common technological wireless connectors and carriers of IP traffic, including email, audio, pictures, and videos. The explanation for wired Ethernet's popularity is the additional versatility [25].

2.1.2   Long-range technologies

Wide area networks: A WAN is a network that has broad geographical reach and connects small regional and university networks to a central distributed network at various locations. The below-stated technologies are classified under WAN

- **WiMAX**: This serves for creating metropolitan area networks (MANs). It is very much like Wi-Fi except that it supports a far greater range of coverage. It supports a high-frequency range of 10–66 GHz, a data rate of 11–100 Mbs, and a proximity range of 50 km. It has a potentially high power usage. WiMAX systems are classified into fixed and mobile types, respectively. Fixed-wireless enables point-to-point connections to stationary and nomadic customers, whereas mobile WiMAX gives mobile cell-type connectivity. As long as we have cheap Internet access and plenty of data, we can support a lot of different TV options [26].
- **LoRa**: It is a low-power, high-frequency network supporting a frequency range of 868/915 MHz and a data rate of 50 kbps. The proximity range for LoRa is about 25 km. The LoRa modulation is obtained from the chirp spread range, allowing for the use of low-quality oscillators in the end system as well as quicker and more accurate synchronization. Thanks to its good coverage and low power consumption, LoRa seems to be a promising technology to be leveraged in all IoT applications. LoRa operates on three layers, namely, the physical layer, the data link layer, and the network architecture wiring star-of-stars architecture is

commonly used in LoRaWANs, which include gateways between end devices and the network server [27].

- **SigFox:** This technology belongs to the LPWAN family of technologies, operating at either 868 or 915 MHz. It offers a data rate of 300 bps and a net coverage of 50 km. While data transfers are minimal, a large range of transmission capacity is available, and little power is used; IoT development favors relatively low-power communication schemes. The D-BPSK modulation provides superior efficiency and is straightforward to apply because of it. A low bit rate enables the use of low-cost components in the transceiver part. The SigFox communication technology can additionally connect great spans of land, of the order of tens of kilometers in the countryside and a few kilometers in urban areas due to its effortless coverage of a large area [28].

- **4G:** The 4th generation of wireless coverage is an improvement over the 3rd generation and is now the most extensive, ubiquitous, fast, and high-speed wireless service. It is designed to deliver high speeds irrespective of the technology that drives 4G. The fourth generation of cellular communications offers a considerably high data rate of up to 12 Mbps at frequencies of 700, 1700, 2800 MHz. It has a network coverage of up to 10 km. Presently, 4G is available only in limited regions. Some of the key characteristics of 4G services of user interest include application adaptability and high dynamism, which essentially means that different services can be delivered and made available to users' personal preferences while supporting the user traffic, air interfaces, quality of service, and radio environment. Currently, 4G is used in very few regions [29].

- **5G:** It is a new global wireless standard that is the successor to 4G networks. At low-frequency bands, it was designed to provide a high data rate of up to 3.6 Gbps with a proximity range of up to 10 km and at high-frequency bands, it provides a data rate of about 10 Gbps with a proximity range less than 1 km. This certainly will consume high power. If operated at high-frequency bands, the data rate that will be provided will be about 10 Gbps with the network coverage being less than a kilometer [6]. Compared to the existing 4G technology, which uses frequencies below 6 GHz, 5G networks support an extremely higher frequency that ranges from 30 to 300 GHz [30]. Currently, 5G has been deployed in Australia, the United States, the United Kingdom, and China to support a large and diversified range of requirements [31].

- **Narrowband-IoT (NB-IoT):** A type of WAN that offers up to 245 kbps at 850 MHz and a coverage of about 35 km. It enables a wide range of new services. This radio access technology is standardized by the 3GPP to bolster a wide range of use cases for massive machine-type communications (mMTC). Contrary to human-oriented 4G technologies, in terms of coverage, improved power-saving, and fewer functions, NB-IoT combines important design characteristics, thereby allowing higher coverage, greater power savings, and decreased complexity of devices in difficult locations, increasing the connection of such devices and enhancing battery life.

- **Extended coverage-GSM-Internet of Things (EC-GSM IoT):** EC-GSM is a potential solution for the billion-device cellular IoT because it provides comparable coverage and battery life as NB-IoT (cIoT). These cellular systems allow low power and minimal complexity such as IOT connectivity. They bear frequency of 890 MHz while supporting data rate up to 140 kbps with a network coverage ranging up to 100 km. Currently, cellular IoT (cIoT) devices utilize GPRS/EDGE to connect to the Internet because it results in a 20 dB coverage increase and better energy efficiency. The recommended maximum coupling loss for EC-GSM IoT is 164 dB and the minimum battery life is 10 years [32].

- **LTE-M (M1):** It is a novel cellular radio access technology that coexists with NB-IoT as well as nonstandardized LPWA technologies such as SigFox and Lo-Ra. The 3rd Generation Partnership Project 4G LTE Standard is based on the LTE mobile data network standard, which has the capacity to supply reliable and flexible Internet protocol (IP) technology for worldwide coverage as well as fast connection speeds, mobility options, prioritization mechanisms, and heightened security. It operates at frequencies of 700, 1450–2200, and 5400 MHz, offering a data rate of 0.144 Mbps and network coverage of 35 km. It is supposed to consume high power. This kind of device is utilized in many applications with frequencies and latencies that vary greatly. For IoT applications that need greater data speeds, low latency, complete mobility, and voice in normal coverage conditions, it is an excellent solution to use a low-power wide-area network technology [33].

2.2   Advances in 5G spectrum usage

5G, which stands for the fifth generation telecommunications network, is predominantly used in expanded mobile broadband, mission-critical communications, and large IoT implementations. It surpasses 2G, 3G, and 4G communication platforms in terms of speed and latency. Its apt and flexible design has the capability of taking over future generation services that are unknown to us today. To be able to serve such cost- and energy-efficient capabilities, large quantities of millimeter wave (mmWave) bands of the radio spectrum have been allotted to 5G. Although the frequency range 3.3–3.8 GHz has been widely used in the majority of the commercial 5G networks, in order to accommodate large data speeds, the spectrum of frequency ranges used by mobile communications would need to be expanded. This will involve the radio spectrum below 6 GHz as well as a higher frequency spectrum. In the frequency spectrum, a higher frequency would imply a faster decay irrespective of the technology used. This is because of the law of physics that states for an antenna of constant height, configuration and power, the coverage area will have to decrease with the increase in frequency. On the contrary, a lower frequency indicates that there are more users in a given cell, implying that each consumer has a low throughput. A higher frequency, on the other hand, can be mirrored by walls and have low penetration. Walls attenuate a lower frequency, but it nevertheless penetrates.

As a result, if 5G has to be ubiquitously available everywhere, there needs to be a three-pronged approach to the spectrum: the coverage layer that is the low-frequency band and is below 1 GHz, the capacity layer that uses a frequency between 1 and 6 GHz and provides a slightly higher throughput, and the high-throughput layer operating between frequencies 6–100 GHz (Fig. 1).

It is also important to note that all 5G deployments today are known as nonstandalone (NSA) 5G networks, where LTE is deployed as the master node and 5G as the secondary node. In other words, they reform the existing frequency bands. Now, as we elaborate on the three different spectrum bands, we have

- **Low band spectrum**: This is the sub-1 GHz spectrum, which is commonly used by US carriers for 3G and LTE, and delivers a wide coverage area along with good building penetration. The data rate, however, peaks at around 100 Mbps. This spectrum is soon to be reclaimed primarily by 5G. From the observed digital trends, it has been identified that T-Mobile, which is one of the biggest players in the low-band spectrum space, is rolling out 5G in the 600 MHz band, which is already being used for 4G. As this is an NSA 5G deployment, T-Mobile will have to use a chunk of spectrum for 4G and another for 5G,

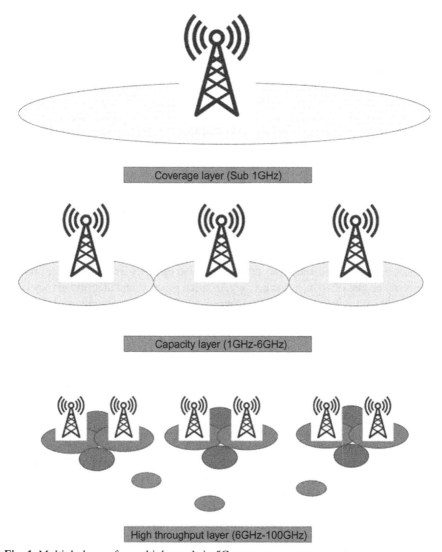

Coverage layer (Sub 1GHz)

Capacity layer (1GHz-6GHz)

High throughput layer (6GHz-100GHz)

Fig. 1 Multiple layers for multiple needs in 5G.

in which way it can reach everywhere. Using the carrier aggregation of 4G, it will continue to provide high speeds but it will not be different from 4G until they add a new capacity-layer 5G spectrum.
- **Mid-band spectrum**: This spectrum has greater throughput and reduced bandwidth than the low-band spectrum. The transmissions are less ideal for entry into buildings here, and overall data rates are about 1 Gbps. It also provides more capacity to the network. Typically, massive multiple-input-multiple-output (MIMO) and beamforming antenna technologies are leveraged to enhance penetration and coverage areas of this spectrum. This technology has all antennas aggregated in one cell tower and improves performance, as they will not be transmitting in directions where the signal is not needed, tending to reduce unnecessary collisions.

- **High-band spectrum**: This spectrum is usually referred to by most people as 5G. It is also referred to as mmWave or FR2 in the industry, enabling speeds in the tens of Gbps range at a really low latency. The only drawback is the limited high band coverage area and poor building and rain penetration. Thus, this is not suited for providing wide-area network coverage but instead is most likely to be used in areas with the highest demand from mobile phone users—the so-called "hotspots." Major mobile devices using mmWave will need an antenna technology that can dynamically steer and form the radio beam to and from the cell tower. Because these mmWaves are crucial to attain high speed and low latency targets, efforts are made by companies to overcome propagation challenges. Carriers can depend on LTE when overlaying networks to enable 5G as 5G begins to use the high-band spectrum. One way to improve coverage would be the construction of small cells, such as low-power base stations to protect small regions.

2.3   Privacy issues in 5G technologies in healthcare

Although the introduction of 5G paved the way toward revolutionizing communication technologies in terms of bandwidth, connectivity, distribution, and mobile experiences, it sure has posed numerous data privacy and integrity issues. The user privacy can broadly be classified into data privacy, location privacy, and identity privacy [34]. In the healthcare industry, especially where we see massive amounts of data being shared in real time among IoT devices, data privacy could potentially be violated. Personal and sensitive information such as heart rate or insulin level, which are being monitored and transmitted by wearable devices and smart healthcare applications, can be at risk of cyberattack, which would account for either data loss or inaccurate data transmission. The biggest target has been the information theft of health records in hospitals, which often contain personal information such as a patient's name, Social Security number, and address. This is a consequence of ineffective government policies and insufficient security measures [35]. With the introduction of 5G, location-based networks would become more prevalent. They have gained popularity in the IoT sector as they possess real-time tracking and positioning capabilities. However, with these features it becomes convenient for network operators to have access to a consumer's location and violate location privacy. Alternatively, when it comes to identity privacy, in order to access or provide services, any computer would be assigned an identity, and this identity information may include user personal information, necessitating aggressive privacy management.

As the future of healthcare will largely encompass the strategies used by 5G networks, it is expected that 65% of the world would have access to 5G with 45% of data traversing 5G networks. Some of the prevailing privacy issues predominantly originating from cloud concepts are:

1. **End-to-end data privacy**: Because 5G has a small coverage area, it has many cellular towers clustered within a small radius, giving mobile operators and different stakeholders in the 5G ecosystem unnecessary access to the user's personal data and location, which can further be mishandled. With the advancement of IoT capabilities in healthcare, smart health monitoring has come to the fore where IoT devices can be left running without having to be monitored. That could potentially turn out to be a surveillance nuisance in the future. Thus, hard efforts should be made to ensure the point-to-point data confidentiality.

2. **Responsibility ambiguity**: This results in the sole loss of data ownership. Privacy-activated service arrangements must be negotiated because there are multiple network carriers, cloud service providers, and third-party device developers who are engaged.

3. **Law conflict or location of legal disputes**: The projection of user data is determined by the hosting country's laws in compliance with different relevant jurisdictions. The offender's address, the victim's location, and the service provider's location are the three options.

4. **Shared environment**: With the virtualization of internetworking resources and the similar infrastructure being shared among different network service users, it will be prone to unauthorized user data attacks, ranging from exploitation of bugs in hypervisors to distributed denial of service (DDOS) attacks. This could compromise user privacy and extend its influence over other virtual machines in the process.

5. **Varied objectives of trust**: Although different participating entities such as infrastructure providers, mobile virtual network operators (MVNOs), mobile virtual network enablers (MVNEs), and communication service providers could collaborate, their security priorities may differ from each other. As a result, all security and privacy aspects will not be covered.

6. **Loss of control**: When a mobile operator transfers a section of network to the cloud, some of the control and responsibilities will be taken over by the cloud service provider (CSP). This transition to cloud administration will result in a loss of direct network management for the mobile operator, who will have to cooperate with CSP to carry out responsibilities and activities spanning both parties.

7. **Visibility**: The mobile operator is completely dependent on the CSP to be well aware of the latter's privacy measures but sometimes those details are not disclosed. This makes it harder for the mobile operator to define its privacy management, and they will lose full visibility of their networks.

8. **Transborder data flow**: With superwide global connectivity, it becomes crucial to keep track of how the data are stored, processed, and transferred between country borders. The data privacy mechanisms differ from country to country. For instance, the law enforcement agencies in some countries are permitted to intercept data while this is strictly prohibited in others. Different legislation can also be a factor toward differences in data privacy values. The use of public clouds will hinder network operator freedom to control the storage of data's physical boundaries. The new routing calls are designed for maximum reliability and flexibility, and once the destination IP is created, there will be no limits on how it reaches the destination, theoretically allowing it to cross countries.

9. **Hacking**: Recent telecommunication networks, such as LTE and 5G, are vulnerable to a wide variety of IP and web-based threats, including hacking, as a result of the evolution of open IP-based open architecture. The user's privacy issues would be exacerbated by cloud technology's high reliability.

10. **Leaking information to third parties**: Third-party application developers enjoy their privilege of access to 5G systems and can sell or share the sensitive information with other parties. The cloud's information-sharing capabilities as well as the possibility for private data to be used for future uses could pose privacy issues. Third-party device configurations and permission lists should be kept up to date. Newly created access privileges should also be thoroughly validated to prevent discrepancies, which may lead to privacy-threatening vulnerabilities.

11. **IoT privacy**: IoT can have many loopholes with respect to security, as its design often does not include security. According to research, 20% of IoT designers leave security measures out of their designs, and more than 40% of developers do not encrypt their interactions due to cost constraints. The information stored in these devices can be personal and highly sensitive, and it will be highly risky if it ends up in the wrong hands (such as criminals).

3 Blockchain-based healthcare informatics with 5G support

Special communication criteria, such as high reliability, low latency, versatility, and security, characterize industrial IoT. Because 5G technology is the only one that can deliver these, it is a strong contender for supporting commercial IoT. The use of 5G in healthcare informatics will improve the quality of healthcare received by hundreds of millions of patients and will make significant alterations in how healthcare services are delivered. As 5G promotes information collection, information transmission, and big data analytics, it will be a major ingredient of the transition to a "value-based" healthcare system. Some areas in healthcare that will be heavily impacted by 5G include continuous monitoring, predictive analytics, diagnosis and imaging, and improved state of the art. Owing to its key properties, 5G enables a vast network of connected "things"—devices and machines that can interact with other devices and machines implicitly with or without human intervention. When it comes to the Internet of Medical Things (IoMT) such as medical devices, wearables, and remote sensors, 5G acts as a remarkably effective catalyst. The technologies associated with 5G do far more than just transfer bits of data at ever-faster rates; they also allow apps to easily process information and deliver a near real-time and highly sensitive experience [36]. 5G is ubiquitous as it is not a mere extension of 3G or 4G networks. This ubiquity bolsters the proliferation of connected devices and enables many healthcare services such as the continuous monitoring of patients. It is crucial that the security and integrity of the information are safeguarded by 5G's security properties, consequently lowering a critical barrier to the dissemination and harnessing of information.

3.1 Issues related to 5G support for healthcare

Besides the various advances made by 5G in healthcare, the adoption of 5G for smart healthcare faces various obstacles and open testing problems. Some of the main threats and drawbacks are mentioned below:

- *Achieving interoperability*: The ability to link two or more separate computers and networks to share information is known as interoperability. Smart healthcare is made up of a variety of IoT devices and HetNets that cover a variety of areas, including digital health control, remote surgery, and electrocardiograms (ECGs). As a result, interoperability is critical in offering a shared interface for connecting multiple devices using various communication technologies. Interoperability across different domains is, however, a major roadblock to IoT performance due to the absence of a common standard in communications technology. As a result, it is critical to test for interoperability at various stages, allowing millions of computers in the network to connect with one another. To solve the interoperability problem, different organizations, oneM2M and FIWARE, are collaborating with numerous standardizations, ETSI, OMA, and 3GPP, to sort out the interoperability issue.
  Key requirements to achieve interoperability: Universal and integrated models that are adaptable to the rest of the technology, are needed for communication, such as Constrained Application Protocol (CoAP) and Internet Protocol (IP) for IoT devices.

• *Big data analysis*: Nowadays in smart healthcare, big data analytics is a predominant area of research. In the healthcare ecosystem, the exponential growth of Internet technologies has resulted in the availability of large amounts of medical data. To be able to handle big data by paying heed to security and privacy issues simultaneously is a growing concern. Despite the fact that the Internet has the potential to popularize and intelligently improve medical services, the privacy of patients, physicians, nurses, and healthcare professionals remains a concern [16]. These data could potentially contain private information, which could also include surrounding information such as the heartbeat rate and ECG results. As a result, to protect sensitive data provided by local devices, intelligent approaches must be used. The key areas of concern are:

o Data analysis protection for consumer data must be provided.

o A sufficient level of confidentiality must be established for private data.

o A well-defined architecture for data collection and processing must be developed.

o Computation power must be provided for user data extraction.

Research challenges include the limitation of useful tools to be able to process heavy data generated by IoT devices in the network. Also, the lack of centralized and distributed resources poses a roadblock.

Key requirements: Centralized big data center for processing the data received from IoT devices.

• *Performing IoT connectivity*: A smart healthcare network will potentially be used for connecting millions of devices in the future. This concept will succeed only if every single device in the network receives connectivity. There are many obstacles to ensuring access to each system in the smart healthcare network, including:

o Assuring decent network access to users of high mobility (moving patient or high-speed ambulance).

o Providing both long range and connectivity to the devices in the network.

Regarding the research challenges involved in overcoming this issue, it is necessary to optimize the resources in an ultrahigh dense network. It is necessary to assess the means to meet the energy-efficiency requirements in an ultrahigh dense network. It is essential to assure the connectivity of various devices from different domains in high mobility.

Key requirements: Efficient techniques are required for the usage of the 5G spectrum for the IoT devices in the healthcare system to communicate with each other. There should be smart algorithms that ensure constant connectivity of different devices because the health-related data of the patient are monitored all the time. This also makes an efficient clustering technique necessary to support a mixed workload and to improve resource availability to avoid deadlock conditions while dealing with the patient's health-tracking devices.

• *Achieving security, privacy, and trust*: The IoT is made up of an ecosystem of devices that are able to exchange information with one another via the Internet. 5G, due to its quick speed and ability to transmit large packets of data, is expected to change the foundation of the IoT. In healthcare, the IoT ecosystem, sometimes dubbed the Internet of Medical Things (IoMT), includes a plethora of gadgets ranging from Internet-connected medical devices to other necessary equipment and wearables, all of which pave the way to constantly and remotely monitor patient health. This connection of devices and machines to one another is greatly complemented by the use of 5G, as it brings together all these devices and applications that are dependent upon lots of data moving from one device to another very quickly and basically in a real-time environment. The problem is that by connecting these devices to one another, we widen the possible attack surface that a hacker can target to gain access to an establishment's network. Attackers leverage greater speed and lower latency to intrude into the network. Once they attack the network, they can get access to more data due to the hyperconnectivity of devices. We may assume that the number of computers connecting to each another and exchanging data represents access points that can be targeted and hacked to gain access to the network. IoT devices, in particular, are more vulnerable to threats because most of these compact devices have little computing capacity, making them incapable of handling complex encryption algorithms. As a result, data in transit would be transmitted without encryption. As a result, strong mechanisms will be needed to encrypt and protect certain bare communications. Similarly, if the company uses cloud-based IoT computers for outsourced computing and computation, there would be certain protection and privacy issues. 5G networks must account for and overcome these concerns for this vision to become a reality. Some of the generalized concerns that 5G has to overcome include:

o Secure communication should be delivered between the cloud database center and smart healthcare devices for data integrity and authenticity.

o When a new user is allowed, a strict privacy policy should be established.

o To detect present as well as upcoming attacks, for risk management a well-defined approach needs to be developed.

Research challenges in this regard include the necessity to securely deploy and integrate cloud-based services at both the device and network levels. There is also the need to detect threats and device/network hackers at both the inside and outside levels before executing any task.

Key requirements: The need to be able to collect data that serve as proof of vulnerabilities in the healthcare ecosystem, which in turn will be points of entry for different attackers.

3.2 Blockchain and 5G integration

While people's understanding of 5G is that it is a quicker Internet, it really reflects a more secure connection to huge artifacts and medical devices with greater range, bandwidth, and functionality than what is found with today's 4G LTE networks [37]. It may also assist networks with ultralow latency requirements. With the significant growth in 5G capacities and the latest breakthroughs in blockchain technologies, blockchain-based 5G networks have gained great significance for reaping potential benefits. Because of its intrinsic superior properties such as immutability, decentralization, openness, traceability, stability, and protection, blockchain has the capacity to be incorporated with 5G architectures, effectively addressing the existing problems of 5G [13,38].

Because 5G networks will connect many aspects of society such as self-sufficient resources, ubiquitous networking, reliable content-based storage, and intelligent data management, blockchain is predicted to greatly benefit from 5G networks. The aforementioned technologies and 5G applications include cloud networking, edge computing, SDN, NFV, network slicing, and device-to-device (D2D) communications, among others.

The infrastructure built and supported by software uses NFVs to perform necessary network functions. These network functions promote IoT interaction, whereas cloud computing facilities support the quick delivery and accessibility of healthcare. This facilitates the early examination of a patient's health condition, which ensures better chances for the patient. Fig. 2 depicts the layered blockchain paradigm over the 5G

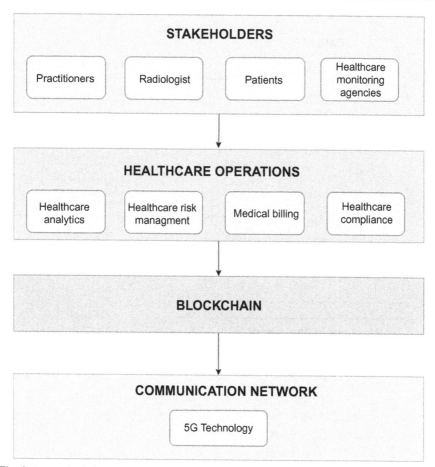

Fig. 2 Image depicting the layer dependency of healthcare operations.

network as well as various healthcare-related applications. Practitioners, radiologists, patients, and healthcare monitoring service providers will be among those involved.

In these 5G healthcare scenarios, we require the patient's data being transmitted and shared with the necessary professionals to be delivered safely. For this purpose, blockchain technology is used to create a peer-to-peer storage infrastructure capable of recording and validating transactions. These transactions include the healthcare request from the patient and the patient transferring the necessary data regarding their current health condition. Another requirement from the peer-to-peer database is for it to be able to store the data immutably in preferably decentralized ledgers. This again is one of the main domains of blockchain and can be carried out by blockchain efficiently. By doing so, the transaction blocks that store the data are visible to all the healthcare network members. Data sharing will be accelerated, in a more secure way, to doctors, patients, and clinicians during the treatment process.

A potential system architecture connecting the IoT with blockchain and 5G is used for remote patient monitoring, as shown in Fig. 3.

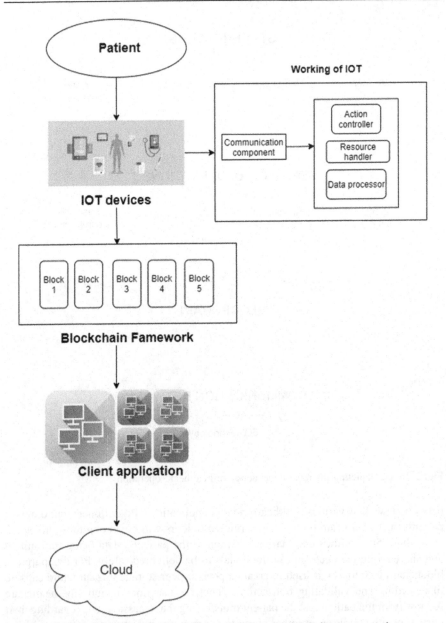

Fig. 3 System architecture using blockchain with 5G-enabled IoT for remote patient monitoring.

This kind of design integrates IoT devices into a remote medical monitoring system. These gadgets can determine the patient's overall well-being, including heart rate, sleep patterns, stress, and glucose levels. The collected data are subsequently kept in the cloud by blockchain. To properly process incoming data, it must be validated by an authorized device. Patients can make this data available to other healthcare facilities. An agreement written into the blockchain to safeguard transactions is called a smart contract. Here, patients, clouds, hospitals, and institutions are all participants in this model. Patients are given unique IDs, and all transactions concerning them are kept in the cloud. Privacy protection is assured via the use of encryption technology. Once 5G is used, the encrypted information is sent to other parties. However, to see this registration form, a password is needed, and therefore healthcare providers must be authenticated prior to doing so. In order to access a patient's medical data, hospitals and institutions must first prove their identification to the patient. Patients utilize algorithms to create keys and provide other parties with safe access to these keys, and they use this approach to exchange records. Patient identification is a difficult problem in the healthcare industry because patients may register to the same hospital many times using various accounts. This may result in fragmentation. Key custody technology is utilized to address the issue of accessing the registry when the patient fails to react. This record will be saved and stored as patient identification, medical record identification, record hash, file identification, date, doctor identification, disease identification, and parent identification hash and structured as patient ID, health data, hash field, and file ID. The record structure of a hospital/doctor is {ID, key}. Each record transaction will have patient address, service provider access, record hash, file identity, patient consent, time-stamp, and signature. The key transaction (user/patient) is hospital/patient address, public key, time-stamp, and signature.

4 Applications that use 5G technology in healthcare systems

4.1 Remote patient monitoring

Through wearables, electronic health devices, and sensors, patient details and attributes can be collected and subsequently analyzed without the patient needing to travel to a clinic or hospital and go through the hassle of a face-to-face appointment with a medical professional.

Such remote patient monitoring systems are seen as a key element for more efficient delivery of healthcare services. These services are expected to use 5G technology, which will enable them to function at scale in comparison to other connectivity techniques through the assurance of:

- Having an increased capacity of the number of connected devices.
- Increased security and reliability of the service.
- In-home solutions for connectivity, such as WiFi.

4.2 Connected ambulance services

A connected ambulance collects and transfers information on a patient's condition to the hospital while the patient is being transported to the hospital. The ambulance's crew collects data using sensors, wearable devices, or streaming high-definition (HD) video of the patient's condition. This way, doctors and the hospital staff will have prior knowledge of the patient's condition before arrival. In extreme situations, specialists can help paramedics through certain diagnostic assessments and procedures without the need to travel to the hospital. Emergency services have very stringent targets. With the technology and services provided by a connected ambulance, healthcare can meet its targets and improve overall patient outcomes.

Connected ambulance technology can be implemented only with the use of 5G technology. This is because:

- Lower latency obtained using 5G—The video and data from the ambulance must be sent to the hospital or clinic in real time. In emergency situations, split-second decisions might have a major impact.
- High security and reliability from 5G is crucial when transferring confidential and important patient data.
- With 5G's network slicing, if needed emergency services can have their own private "slice."
- 5G has high bandwidth compared to other networks. This will enable live video streamed from the ambulance to be delivered without buffering or any loss in quality.

4.3   HD virtual consultations

In this method, two-way HD video is used for communications between the patient and his/her medical professional to conduct routine check-ups, screening assessments, therapy and/or rehabilitation sessions, and diagnosis. This is highly visual, such as identifying the patient's dermatological conditions and symptoms. These appointments, which are done virtually, prevent patients from traveling to clinics or hospitals to meet the medical professional.

Due to its high bandwidth and low latency, 5G services can enable virtual appointment services to occur smoothly and without any network issues. 5G also brings increased reliability and security, therefore ensuring the patient's privacy and data security.

4.4   Augmented reality and virtual reality healthcare assistance for the visually challenged

The visually challenged find it harder to perform some necessary medical tasks that are relatively simple for a normal person. By using an augmented reality (AR)/virtual reality (VR) headset with 5G enabled or a set of video streaming glasses, a doctor can be connected to a visually impaired patient. That doctor can then guide the patient through some medical activities in their daily life. For instance, a company called Aira is looking to provide such services to visually impaired patients.

5G technology is crucial for the smooth operation of such services for the following reasons:

- The lag and jitter, associated with slow networks, while using AR/VR headsets could cause the patient to feel seasick. To overcome this issue, low latency of 5G networks is highly desirable.
- The mobility provided by 5G networks allows patients to use AR/VR headsets on the move and even at times when there is no WiFi connectivity.

4.5   High throughput real-time computational processing

In the healthcare industry, there will be many high-resolution files and images involved. For diagnostics and design, these files and images require high-throughput computational processing. Some of the examples where 5G technology is used in real-time processing include:

- Once a CT scan or MRI is received, these images will be sent to the respective department to be analyzed and produce a diagnosis. This is happening in real time and it is possible to operate this smoothly with the use of 5G.
- To produce a more effective drug, the pharmaceutical industry is using in silico high-throughput screening for better drug design. In this regard, 5G technology enables the sending and analysis of the structure and molecular models to the cloud. This is done to make use of the high graphic processing and computational power of the cloud resources, which are also cheaper to use than the necessary desktop computers.

5   Data privacy approaches in healthcare and open research areas in the domain

5.1   Objectives for privacy protection

Because maintaining protection of privacy in 5G networks is a major priority, a list of objectives has been identified to ensure privacy. These objectives are based on the regulatory objectives of those in cloud computing and also generic regulatory objectives. These objectives are summarized below:

(i) **Promotion of the digital single market**: It is critical to ensure all digital services are protected on a worldwide basis. All necessary directives and legislative instruments must be supported to allow for cross-border policies and regulations.

(ii) **To balance the interests of different nations**: Because privacy and technology services are global issues, it is important to have rules that balance the interests of various nations in preserving privacy and enabling the use of technological services internationally. All nations have to completely understand the advantages of novel technologies and should be able to incorporate these technologies in their respective countries.

(iii) **Legislation of privacy in a global view**: Privacy legislation must be used globally and cohesively between nations to ensure that they are compatible with emerging innovations. The various jurisdictions of various nations have to cooperate with each other to be able to develop privacy requirements that are interoperable. This facilitates the flow of information between different nations with the level of privacy protection required for a particular technology or operation. For example, the "Safe Harbor" pact established among the United States as and European Union governments requires all US companies to obey EU regulations regarding data privacy and storage so that EU companies are able to safely store and process the data in the data centers present in the United States.

(iv) **Portability of data and fostering interoperability**: This objective allows for technology used in different parts of the world to be neutral. This essentially means avoiding the mandated standards and/or preferences that could make the technology interoperable. One of the major reasons for this objective is the need to promote the ongoing efforts in the industry to allow technologies dealing with data to be interoperable, which is essential to define uniform and global privacy policies.

(v) **Defining a simple, straightforward, and applicable law**: Another main objective is to define and enact comprehensive data protection legislation. These laws should be applicable over country borders between different nations. It has to be simple and easy to set up across the globe for convenience. An important criterion with these laws is the framework on which the law is established to enable individuals and groups to keep track of their progress in areas in which they choose to become accountable. Another constraint is for these laws to support various self-regulatory codes.

(vi) **Amendment to execute the right of an individual to erase and rectify private data**: Every individual has the right to request the correction of wrong or incomplete private/personal data. This is also applicable to individuals who want to erase their personal information from various digital locations such as social media and blogs. This raises a concern regarding how companies, operating with their users digitally via the Internet, handles the data of users who are deceased. It is essential even for deceased individuals to keep their data private. Therefore, it is necessary for these companies to have a way to handle the data of deceased individuals and ensure that their privacy in the digital world is protected.

(vii) **Efforts to increase the sense of responsibility and accountability**: The entities handling a user's private data must be evaluated thoroughly by both the company handling this task and the cybersecurity forces. It is essential to increase the responsibility of these entities and make sure that they realize the importance of the private data they are dealing with. They should realize that they will be held accountable if there is any misconduct with the data. Companies must ensure that there are rules and regulations to audit and punish these entities if they are involved in something illegal. This objective also covers the fact that there must be transparency between the company's policies and the user to ensure that the users understand how their private data are used and the outcomes following it.

5.2 Security and privacy requirements of blockchain

Healthcare is a sector that deals with enormous amounts of confidential data, raising concerns about personal safety and network reliability issues. Such a data-driven domain lays importance on access control, provenance, data integrity, and interoperability [39]. Healthcare companies now utilize a multitude of attack surfaces in their information systems. Triage, wellness problem-solving, professional decision-making, implementation, and evaluation of evidence-based programs are all required to meet the goal of producing the desired clinical result, and the healthcare sector has been divided into these several categories. Thus, various healthcare institutions must work together and conduct actions that call for data transfer across institutional boundaries to meet the above need. At the same time, healthcare providers must keep confidential information that patients choose to reveal private. Because securing electronic health records (EHRs) and associated personal details is a top priority in the healthcare industry, emerging blockchain technology can offer security and privacy solutions to the healthcare ecosystem. The use of private and public keys is a critical feature of blockchain encryption. Asymmetric cryptography is typically used by blockchain to secure transactions between members. It is theoretically impossible for a user to figure out another user's private key by knowing their public key. This safeguards blockchain data from potential attacks and eliminates concerns around data leakage.

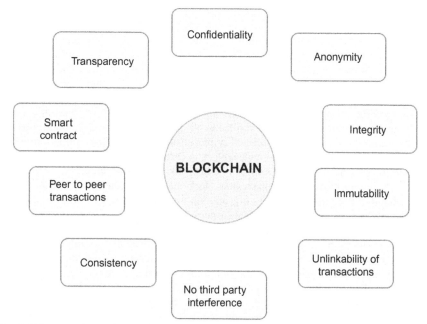

Fig. 4 Privacy and security requirements of blockchain.

Some of the key privacy and security requirements of blockchain are shown in Fig. 4 and are also explained below:

1. **Availability/transparency**: Because there are several versions of data accessible at various locations, tampering with a node's data would have little impact on the aggregate health data [40]. This provides the ability to withstand outages and attacks. The ledger's transaction data should be viewable by members of the blockchain network at all times. This implies that there should be availability at both the device and transaction levels. At the device stage, the system should be able to function efficiently except in the case of a network attack. Alternatively, at the transaction stage, transaction details may be viewed by only authenticated users (as in a permissioned blockchain) without being inaccessible, inconsistent, or compromised. In its working condition, the system should have the capacity of handling high loads.

2. **Confidentiality**: Transactions as well as the identity of the participating notes of the blockchain network are protected. To achieve this requirement, the system must include:
   * Anonymity and privacy must be maintained with any blockchain exchange to avoid any fraud and to keep the number of alternate parties to a trade a secret.
   * A person must be trusted to use it only as long as they continue to have access to their participants and do not otherwise want to gain private knowledge of the information of the deal.

3. **Anonymity**: Public blockchain is typically designed around the idea of anonymity. This is provided through cryptographic functions such as public-private key [41] cryptography to hide the true identity of the participants. Rather, each user is identified by a dynamic key [42]. Thus it becomes a trustless network as the participants need not know each other.

4. **Integrity**: To ensure the security of transactions, the mechanism must guarantee their legitimacy and avoid tampering. It is essential that only known people have access to the data, or they would be able to impersonate other users and use it to store their own private information. Even though blockchain is a distributed network, all the information and data remain the same for all nodes of the network, ensuring integrity. The information is redundant among all the nodes of the network, increasing the reliability of the network. Further, the application of cryptographic functions to validate the transactions increases the level of integrity.

5. **Immutability**: It is known as a blockchain ledger's capacity to hold transaction details immutable over time. After being verified by the blockchain network, the transactions are then included in a block that is secured cryptographically by a hashing process. It links to and incorporates the hash of the previous block. A chronological chain is built by connecting multiple blocks together. Specifically, the hashing process of a new block always contains the metadata of the hash value of the previous block, making the data strongly unalterable.

6. **Unlinkability of transactions**: An organization would have to make sure that all transactions pertaining to a certain user are not connected in such a way that inference of additional information is made about the user. Adversarial parties may determine the actual identify of the user with the assistance of both transactional and account data as well as some information about the individual. The speculation is that this feature will assist to minimize the danger of pseudonymous accounts being linked to the actual person's identity. Instead of the publicly visible blockchain, this encourages need-to-know-based sharing [43].

7. **Lack of trusted third parties**: Because the blockchain framework promotes decentralization at its core, it does not encourage any trusted third parties having complete control over the network. Instead, the control and responsibility of the network are shared between the different nodes of the network. It should have multiple nontrusting writers to validate the transactions.

8. **Consistency**: There should be a consistency of the ledgers across different health institutions [44]. Because blockchain is primarily used for EHR systems in healthcare, there should be a clear format by which all the transactions are stored in the ledger. For example, the "transaction ID, patient ID, medicine name" use case. Thus all the nodes should have the same ledger at the same time.

9. **Peer-to-peer transactions**: The transactions should occur peer to peer without being governed or influenced by any central authority. This prevents even root users or administrators from accessing any sort of sensitive information. This is one of the main requirements to establish security and privacy in blockchain.

10. **Smart contract**: A smart contract is similar to a script used to execute transactions automatically based on predefined rules such as sender and receiver hashes, process type, and transaction date [45]. It gives the data provenance rights to users as a part of its privacy service. With the capabilities provided by this feature, business owners are empowered to manage who gets to see their data, particularly by implementing access restrictions on self-executing smart contracts, thereby safeguarding data owners' privacy and equity. Smart contracts are more cost-effective, flexible, and reliable alternatives to conventional contracting schemes in which contract terms are often strictly implemented by a central authority or control structure.

5.3   Opportunities brought by blockchain to 5G

One of the most significant problems facing 5G networks is ensuring a free, transparent, and stable infrastructure across the massive amount of capital and smartphone users. Given the performance expectations for 5G systems, it is predicted that blockchain will be able to meet the aforementioned requirements for data privacy, security, transparency, and immutability for the storage of 5G heterogeneous data. It keeps operating expenses and administration expenditures to a minimum. The advantages that blockchain technology offers to 5G networks and services include:

- **Security enhancements**: The key advancements in 5G are decentralization, privacy, immutability, traceability, and openness. This improves confidence in the system' considerably by removing centralized network design and single-point failure bottlenecks, even while it relies on third-party authorities and a network topology that is not subject to central authority. The data stored on each D2D computer are used as a blockchain node, and to maintain a second copy that also allows for better database stability and transparency, due to blockchain's peer-to-peer network. The core benefit of blockchain and smart contracts over traditional database administration is that they will ensure device control validation through a decentralized validation process that utilizes the resources of all legitimate network users, making 5G services such as spectrum exchange, data sharing, and resource distribution extremely resistant to changes in data. When using blockchain, spectrum licenses and band managers are removed and spectrum allocation is done via a distributed network of peers. The third point is that blockchain helps maintain the trustworthiness of all the parties involved in the transaction while at the same time providing a mechanism to monitor and execute transactions. Additionally, it uses powerful encryption methods that rely on public-private key pairs to enhance the security of participants. Contracts can accomplish user authentication, detect risks, and identify and reject malicious network access in an automated way. This second step provides a certain level of data security by uploading the user's data to the ledger, where the data are represented by hash functions and added immutably to blocks.
- **System performance improvements**: In this regard, blockchain has tremendous potential, thanks to its capacity to offer superior data storage and management services with low latency and data retrieval. Using decentralized blockchain nodes, together with sophisticated smart contracts, a wide range of requests, including data access, may be validated without going via a centralized authority. By using blockchain, 5G service providers may connect directly with mobile consumers, substantially lowering the cost of administration. As a result, 5G ecosystems will need a data delivery architecture that is considerably more flexible and efficient to satisfy rigorous security standards. In theory, this decentralized approach may decrease the cost and delay of transactions as well as the geographic restrictions on user accessibility, thus improving the system performance as a whole. No single-point failure vulnerabilities for better security are enforced via distributed consensus on distributed ledgers, which means that when an entity is compromised by malicious attacks or threats, the overall operation of the involved network is still handled and maintained via agreement on distributed ledgers.
- **Network simplification**: Blockchain facilitates the development of 5G networks because of its decentralized design. There are no issues with the creation of centralized servers because blockchain runs on a peer-to-peer network. On the decentralized ledgers among network participants, including service providers and mobile users, it is possible to integrate all three aspects of 5G service delivery: user access, service replies, and service trading. Each entity has equal access to all the various 5G service transactions such as data sharing and spectrum sharing, which are all under the same blockchain. Blockchain exploits the participants' resources to maintain and manage the network, thus facilitating network simplification, user interface, and service transaction.

5.4 Data privacy management and security solution

The architecture of the healthcare industry consists of a large variety of interconnected computers and software programs that interact with other IT processes. Blockchain will greatly impact such an infrastructure by providing both security and privacy of data. There are a variety of blockchain infrastructures and architectures that can help the healthcare sector deliver better treatment. When blockchain and IoT systems are combined, healthcare facilities will provide more reliable and precise data keeping, which is important. In this case, smart contracts that have a membership-based environment significantly aid in expanding the capabilities of Bitcoin-like blockchains that only accept pure crypto currency transactional data to a more sophisticated and versatile logic that governs the transfers of abstract data and data structures, thus offering nonrepudiation of such transactions. It guarantees that knowledge can only be exchanged by users of the permissioned blockchain, such as healthcare professionals.

With regard to the electronic medical history of patients, blockchain has been used as a framework to hold all the various components involved. The three contracts used in the arrangement are the registrar contract (RC), the patient-provider relationship contract (PPR), and the summary contract (SC). The corresponding RC for each participant's identity is created using RC. The PPR, which is created between two nodes in a framework, is used to store and manage the statement's medical records. SC retrieves a patient's medical record history and displays all the participant's past and current interactions with other device nodes.

Another notable mention of healthcare is that the blockchain framework combines health organizations, institutions, and patients, and maintains the exchange of health information. This unique framework enables a very secure network infrastructure through the following ways:

- Information may be directed to the blockchain by health organizations: Clinical data are monitored and saved in current health IT systems whenever healthcare institutions offer services to patients. Different application programming interfaces (APIs) are used to redirect the patient's public ID to the blockchain. Each patient's public ID is a nonidentifiable key.
- Transactions are completed and uniquely identified: Smart contracts verify the incoming transactions and complete them. Once a transaction is made, the personal patient data are recorded on the blockchain with the patient's public ID.
- Health organizations can directly query the blockchain: These queries are mainly submitted through APIs, after which nonidentifiable patient information such as age, gender, and illness is viewable. Such data provide valuable insights to the institutions, accelerating and smoothening the analysis.
- Patients can further share their identity with health organizations: Each patient has a unique private key that is used to connect patient identification to blockchain data. This key uncovers patient data from the blockchain. Hence, if the patient shares this key with a health organization, the latter will be able to retrieve the specific patient's health data. For people without the key, the data remain nonidentifiable. This infrastructure often includes a provable method of identifying and authenticating each participant as well as a standardized representation of permission to access EHRs. This prevents unauthorized and untrusted people from having access to patient's private data.

A healthcare practitioner's data, like that of patients, is vulnerable to protection and privacy breaches. Patients are only consumers of healthcare services; healthcare professionals, on the other hand, have many more regulatory liabilities and commitments that they must accept prior to and through their work. They must keep up-to-date and valid certificates or permits as well as comply with all mandatory immunization and vaccine standards at prescribed times to ensure a healthy atmosphere for all patients and coworkers. The licensure and enforcement data associated with each practitioner's work, similar to how patient data are often soiled within a healthcare institution, often face data transmission and sharing problems, particularly as healthcare practitioners transition to a new healthcare workplace. Aside from delaying such practitioners' careers, the delayed dissemination of knowledge may often cause significant financial hardship for patients and insurance providers. This problem can be solved using blockchain technology, which provides a full decentralized ledger as a public provider repository that contains up-to-date details while also restoring network consistency and immutability. The list could also retain records on licensure and/or immunization enforcement, easing the pressure on healthcare providers to keep up with employment-related details.

The popularity of blockchain is due to a functioning process known as proof of work (PoW), which is basically a cryptographic puzzle implemented as a security mechanism. Blockchain makes significant contributions to healthcare, especially when it comes to precision medicine and clinical trials that use distinct layers of blockchain made up of distributed and concurrent computing, storage management, anonymous identity management, and data interchange management. Other notable contributions are the healthcare data portal smart phone app, which was designed to let people retain safe and personalized access to healthcare information while also facilitating multiparty analysis of that data.

Because transactional secrecy is one of the most difficult challenges for blockchain technology, many approaches for improving blockchain anonymity have been suggested. Mixing services, a transactional privacy process, transfers money from the N input addresses to the M output addresses, thereby making it unnecessary for customers to utilize the same account for each transaction. Mixcoin, which uses the same methodology, can identify deceptive activity patterns as well. Coinjoin, on the other side, shuffles output addresses with the help of a third party. Alternatively, in the case of Zerocoin, transactions and coin root are unlined, and miners verify operations using zero-knowledge proofs.

6 Case study—Telemedicine: A blockchain-based smart healthcare system

The introduction of EHRs, cloud-based storage, and laws for patient data privacy have all seen fast development in smart healthcare. The ability to access and share personal health data provides new possibilities for healthcare data management. Blockchain, with its three superior qualities of decentralization, immutability, and security, can profoundly impact the telemedicine field, a modern technology that uses telecommunication to assist doctors to connect with their patient virtually. Through telemedicine, real-time resources can be shared with the doctor or any hospital in the world. Telemedicine also requires a network that provides real-time support, enabling good quality, speed, reliability, and latency in communication. Thus, 5G integration in the existing infrastructure is crucial to enable faster transmission of images, documents, and videos, along with video-based consultations in real time. The biggest concern in telemedicine is the risk of data breach, and this is resolved with the help of blockchain. When healthcare providers use a blockchain with 5G, it provides a highly secure network that empowers them to access data in a decentralized ledger. The functionality of this tool also allows for the restriction of sensitive patient information, so patients may get access to their medical records when necessary and communicate this information with their medical consultant in a safe manner. Blockchain technology stores information in a fragmented system, thus promoting the storage of a patient's vast historical data and securely encrypted medical records.

The following illustration in Fig. 5 shows the framework of the integration of 5G and blockchain in telemedicine.

Integrating blockchain technology with IoT capable of 5G has a few limitations. A large number of problems, including those related to energy consumption, scalability, slowness in data transfers, the absence of standards, limited storage capacity, and poor computing power, exist. Various studies show that there has been an increase in the number of IoT devices, resulting in an increase in the battery power and energy required for processing. The computational and energy costs of block mining in blockchain technology are extremely high. More storage space and more computing power are required due to the use of blockchain technology for data storage. More than a difficulty, this is one of the pitfalls of IoT devices. Two security concerns in blockchain technology are the assaults that occur when nodes collaborate, and the lack of trust between them. In Internet of Vehicles, personal information and other data must be transmitted due to anonymity in blockchain technology. For blockchain-enabled IoT applications, the problem is of little significance. Device communication across ledgers is considerably more challenging due to the absence of standards.

7 Conclusion

Among the various blockchain solutions in healthcare, the blockchain-based EHR system was found to be the most impactful. It allows medical units (MUs) to function anonymously while still validating transactions via mining processes. MUs may also grant the hospital permission to track and recover their health status as reported by healthcare data transactions. This ensures privacy as other MUs and potential attackers will not be able to obtain the encrypted private information. From institution-driven interoperability to patient-centered interoperability, there is a transition period. Patients are able to choose guidelines for how and for how long particular researchers are able to access their medical data. As a result, medication sourcing as well as vendor and distributor information may be tracked throughout the supply

- Patient data is collected using IOT sensors
- The right measurement of patient data is chosen

- IOMT(Internet of Medical Things) is attached to the patient's close to the body to generate large real-time health data
- A relevant analysis is made on this data to provide better treatment.

- The gathered data is stored in a storage point treated as a database of patient data.
- This data is later stored in blocks in the decentralized ledger provided by blockchain technology, securing sensitive information.
- Secured data is forwarded to healthcare providers using high transmission 5G, increasing the efficiency of the healthcare system.

- Healthcare providers provide healthcare services to patients based on their shared health data.

Fig. 5 Framework of integration of 5G and blockchain in telemedicine.

chain instantly, enabling end-to-end visibility. The distributed ledger of blockchain enables healthcare managers and doctors to validate and authenticate vendor credentials. It will be possible for pharmacies and healthcare professionals to help guarantee that genuine medicines keep getting to people who need them the most. When it comes to creating a trustworthy network, blockchain technology offers tremendous potential. Additionally, the long-term continuous monitoring of medical cases of MUs is supported. However, traditional encryption algorithms can be calculative as well as energy-intensive, further preventing the blockchain growth of electronic systems. Energy-efficient frameworks must also be built to function in environmentally friendly settings. Despite some work being done on smart contracts and permissioned blockchains, development is still continuing to satisfy regulatory requirements for medical data and patient protection.

References

[1] S. Tian, W. Yang, J.M. Le Grange, P. Wang, W. Huang, Z. Ye, Smart healthcare: making medical care more intelligent, Global Health J. 3 (3) (2019) 62–65.

[2] Y. Siriwardhana, G. Gür, M. Ylianttila, M. Liyanage, The role of 5G for digital healthcare against COVID-19 pandemic: opportunities and challenges, ICT Exp. 7 (2021) 244–252.

[3] A. Darkins, P. Ryan, R. Kobb, L. Foster, E. Edmonson, B. Wakefield, A.E. Lancaster, Care coordination/home telehealth: the systematic implementation of health informatics, home telehealth, and disease management to support the care of veteran patients with chronic conditions, Telemed. e-Health 14 (10) (2008) 1118–1126.

[4] P. Dong, Z. Ning, M.S. Obaidat, X. Jiang, Y. Guo, X. Hu, B. Sadoun, Edge computing based healthcare systems: enabling decentralized health monitoring in internet of medical things, IEEE Netw. 34 (5) (2020) 254–261.

[5] P. Varga, J. Peto, A. Franko, D. Balla, D. Haja, F. Janky, L. Toka, 5g support for industrial iot applications–challenges, solutions, and research gaps, Sensors 20 (3) (2020) 828.

[6] J.J. Hathaliya, S. Tanwar, An exhaustive survey on security and privacy issues in Healthcare 4.0, Comput. Commun. 153 (2020) 311–335.

[7] F. Casino, T.K. Dasaklis, C. Patsakis, A systematic literature review of blockchain-based applications: current status, classification and open issues, Telematics Inform. 36 (2019) 55–81.

[8] A.F. Hussein, N. ArunKumar, G. Ramirez-Gonzalez, E. Abdulhay, J.M.R. Tavares, V.H. C. de Albuquerque, A medical records managing and securing blockchain based system supported by a genetic algorithm and discrete wavelet transform, Cogn. Syst. Res. 52 (2018) 1–11.

[9] K.M. Hossein, M.E. Esmaeili, T. Dargahi, Blockchain-based privacy-preserving healthcare architecture, in: 2019 IEEE Canadian Conference of Electrical and Computer Engineering (CCECE), IEEE, 2019, pp. 1–4.

[10] A.S. Ahuja, The impact of artificial intelligence in medicine on the future role of the physician, PeerJ 7 (2019) e7702.

[11] S. Latif, J. Qadir, S. Farooq, M.A. Imran, How 5g wireless (and concomitant technologies) will revolutionize healthcare? Future Internet 9 (4) (2017) 93.

[12] D.M. West, How 5G technology enables the health internet of things, Brookings Center Technol. Innov. 3 (2016) 1–20.

[13] D.C. Nguyen, P.N. Pathirana, M. Ding, A. Seneviratne, Blockchain for 5G and beyond networks: a state of the art survey, J. Netw. Comput. Appl. 166 (2020) 102693.

[14] A. Ahad, M. Tahir, M. Aman Sheikh, K.I. Ahmed, A. Mughees, A. Numani, Technologies trend towards 5G network for smart health-care using IoT: a review, Sensors 20 (14) (2020) 4047.

[15] L. Liu, M. Han, Privacy and security issues in the 5g-enabled internet of things, in: 5G-Enabled Internet of Things, CRC Press, 2019, pp. 241–268.

[16] Z. Lv, L. Qiao, Analysis of healthcare big data, Futur. Gener. Comput. Syst. 109 (2020) 103–110.

[17] P. Zhang, M.N.K. Boulos, Blockchain solutions for healthcare, in: Precision Medicine for Investigators, Practitioners and Providers, Academic Press, 2020, pp. 519–524.

[18] C. Tardi, K. Khartit, Near-Field Communication (NFC), Investopedia, 2020.

[19] L. Feltrin, G. Tsoukaneri, M. Condoluci, C. Buratti, T. Mahmoodi, M. Dohler, R. Verdone, Narrowband IoT: a survey on downlink and uplink perspectives, IEEE Wirel. Commun. 26 (1) (2019) 78–86.

[20] C. Hoffman, Bluetooth 5.0: What's Different, and Why It Matters, How, How-To Geek (31 Aug) (2018). https://www.howtogeek.com/343718/whats-different-in-bluetooth-5.0/.

[21] Digi, Zigbee Wireless Mesh Networking, Retrieved March 31, 2021, from https://www.digi.com/solutions/by-technology/zigbee-wireless-standard.

[22] Safety.com, What Is Z-Wave? March 11 2021, Retrieved March 31, 2021 from https://www.safety.com/z-wave/.

[23] American Barcode and RFIT (ABR), What Is RFID and How Does RFID Work? Retrieved March 31, 2021, from https://www.abr.com/what-is-rfid-how-does-rfid-work/.

[24] Electronics Notes, Thread IoT Wireless Technology, Retrieved March 31, 2021 from https://www.electronics-notes.com/articles/connectivity/ieee-802-15-4-wireless/thread-wireless-connectivity.php.

[25] K. Pahlavan, P. Krishnamurthy, Evolution and impact of Wi-Fi technology and applications: a historical perspective, Int. J. Wirel. Inf. Netw. 28 (1) (2021) 3–19.

[26] O. Issa, W. Li, H. Liu, WiMAX TV: possibilities and challenges, in: International Conference on User Centric Media, Springer, Berlin, Heidelberg, 2009, pp. 127–136.

[27] J. Petäjäjärvi, K. Mikhaylov, M. Pettissalo, J. Janhunen, J. Iinatti, Performance of a low-power wide-area network based on LoRa technology: doppler robustness, scalability, and coverage, Int. J. Distrib. Sens. Netw. 13 (3) (2017). 1550147717699412.

[28] A. Lavric, A.I. Petrariu, V. Popa, Long range sigfox communication protocol scalability analysis under large-scale, high-density conditions, IEEE Access 7 (2019) 35816–35825.

[29] A. Kumar, A. Aswal, L. Singh, 4G wireless technology: a brief review, Int. J. Eng. Manag. Res. 3 (2) (2013) 35–43.

[30] I. Mistry, S. Tanwar, S. Tyagi, N. Kumar, Blockchain for 5G-enabled IoT for industrial automation: a systematic review, solutions, and challenges, Mech. Syst. Signal Process. 135 (2020) 106382.

[31] Y. Wu, H.N. Dai, H. Wang, K.K.R. Choo, Blockchain-based privacy preservation for 5g-enabled drone communications, IEEE Netw. 35 (1) (2021) 50–56.

[32] S. Lippuner, B. Weber, M. Salomon, M. Korb, Q. Huang, EC-GSM-IoT network synchronization with support for large frequency offsets, in: 2018 IEEE Wireless Communications and Networking Conference (WCNC), IEEE, 2018, pp. 1–6.

[33] S.R. Borkar, Long-term evolution for machines (LTE-M), in: LPWAN Technologies for IoT and M2M Applications, Academic Press, 2020, pp. 145–166.

[34] M. Liyanage, J. Salo, A. Braeken, T. Kumar, S. Seneviratne, M. Ylianttila, 5G privacy: scenarios and solutions, in: 2018 IEEE 5G World Forum (5GWF), IEEE, 2018, pp. 197–203.

[35] G.G. Dagher, J. Mohler, M. Milojkovic, P.B. Marella, Ancile: privacy-preserving framework for access control and interoperability of electronic health records using blockchain technology, Sustain. Cities Soc. 39 (2018) 283–297.

[36] D.J. Teece, 5G mobile: impact on the health care sector, in: Working Paper, Haas School of Business, 2017, pp. 1–17.

[37] D. Li, 5G and intelligence medicine—how the next generation of wireless technology will reconstruct healthcare? Precis. Clin. Med. 2 (4) (2019) 205–208.

[38] I. Abu-Elezz, A. Hassan, A. Nazeemudeen, M. Househ, A. Abd-Alrazaq, The benefits and threats of blockchain technology in healthcare: a scoping review, Int. J. Med. Inform. 142 (2020) 104246.

[39] A. Hasselgren, K. Kralevska, D. Gligoroski, S.A. Pedersen, A. Faxvaag, Blockchain in healthcare and health sciences—a scoping review, Int. J. Med. Inform. 134 (2020) 104040.

[40] P. Pandey, R. Litoriya, Implementing healthcare services on a large scale: challenges and remedies based on blockchain technology, Health Policy Technol. 9 (1) (2020) 69–78.

[41] F.J. de Haro-Olmo, Á.J. Varela-Vaca, J.A. Álvarez-Bermejo, Blockchain from the perspective of privacy and anonymisation: a systematic literature review, Sensors 20 (24) (2020) 7171.

[42] A. Al Omar, M.Z.A. Bhuiyan, A. Basu, S. Kiyomoto, M.S. Rahman, Privacy-friendly platform for healthcare data in cloud based on blockchain environment, Futur. Gener. Comput. Syst. 95 (2019) 511–521.

[43] R. Zhang, R. Xue, L. Liu, Security and privacy on blockchain, ACM Comput. Surv. 52 (3) (2019) 1–34.

[44] A. Farouk, A. Alahmadi, S. Ghose, A. Mashatan, Blockchain platform for industrial healthcare: vision and future opportunities, Comput. Commun. 154 (2020) 223–235.

[45] F.A. Khan, M. Asif, A. Ahmad, M. Alharbi, H. Aljuaid, Blockchain technology, improvement suggestions, security challenges on smart grid and its application in healthcare for sustainable development, Sustain. Cities Soc. 55 (2020) 102018.

Security- and privacy-preserving ML/DL paradigms for 5G communication technology in smart healthcare

11

Poorvika Singh Negi, Aditya Garg, and Roshan Lal
Amity School of Engineering & Technology, Amity University, Noida, Uttar Pradesh, India

1 Introduction

In present times, the development of technology has become the key strategic component in conglomerates, such that the effects (social, economic, political, or environmental) have exceeded the number of technologies themselves [1]. Even though the traditional healthcare systems were giving substantial outcomes, but due to their limitation, they are unable to maintain proper communication between the patient-health service provider, and different health service providers as well as the timely availability of data (e.g., previous medical records) [2]. With the beginning of health information systems (HIS) in 1990, many countries adopted telehealth policies and eHealth, integrated with improved access to electronic health records (EHRs) [3]. Incorporating technology in different sectors of healthcare has great potential. It helps reduce the organizational costs and the cost of treatment while also educating patients or users about their medical status [2,4]. From the point of view of the patient, it empowers them to self-manage an emergency and makes them health aware. On the other hand, it helps doctors and health workers to offer their services over any geographical barrier.

Implantable and wearable medical devices (IWMDs) are the central components of modern healthcare systems. These transformative technologies facilitate noninvasive prevention and are used to monitor and diagnose several medical conditions, thereby providing continuous treatment and improving the quality of life [5,6]. As the devices have decreased in size in recent years, the energy capacity, computational power, and network ability have improved significantly. Embedding micromechanical and microelectrical sensors (gyroscopes, accelerometers, image sensors [7]) to IWMDs gives them capabilities such as motion, physiological, and biochemical sensing [8]. To further enhance the healthcare system, the confluence of the Internet of Things (IoT) and machine learning (ML) with IWMDs is evidently taking medical management and assistance to the next level. Applications of such emergent technologies include gathering and processing data with the help of the Healthcare Internet of Things (H-IoT) and using the gathered data to make accurate predictions with ML algorithms [9].

Blockchain Applications for Healthcare Informatics. https://doi.org/10.1016/B978-0-323-90615-9.00010-4
Copyright © 2022 Elsevier Inc. All rights reserved.

Even though ML and DL techniques display a superior performance for many healthcare applications, there still exist issues of security and privacy, considering their recent vulnerability to attack [10,11]. Hence, establishing and maintaining the security and integrity of ML/DL models as well as that of data are of chief importance in the healthcare industry.

1.1 Current medical scenario: Case study on COVID-19

The first size estimate of the 2019 novel coronavirus or COVID-19 was published on January 17, 2020. It suggested that the coronavirus disease caused by SARS-CoV-2 had infected a considerably larger amount of people than had been confirmed at the time. Soon, on January 30, 2020, the World Health Organization (WHO) declared COVID-19 a global health emergency requiring international concern.

Many research institutes are collaborating with technologically equipped companies to issue a call to action for artificial intelligence (AI) researchers to develop data-mining techniques so that research related to COVID-19 can be assisted efficiently. Data from all over the world is continuously being documented. Simultaneously, this is being worked on for prediction, thereby showcasing real-time outputs. It is then being integrated and analyzed with the help of ML techniques to understand the spread of the virus and its impact on patients on a global level. Furthermore, using the results, we are one step ahead to improve the accuracy and speed of effective therapeutic methods for the relief of those been exposed to the coronavirus. It also gives us a potential method to identify the susceptible pool of people based on geography, physiological characters, personalized genes, and other probable factors.

In this report, we discuss the underpinning scientific principles of different features of the response to the pandemic, including epidemiological modeling, pandemic economics, behavioral science, and the role and impact of healthcare systems. People around the globe are panic-stricken with the unexpected situation at hand and anticipate that the only solution is social distancing, but that is not true. The spread of the virus follows certain rules of mathematics and statistics, and therefore this can be used to get a better grasp. Presently, there is no way to curb or eradicate the novel coronavirus in the traditional healthcare facilities and institutes that exist in many parts of the world. However, due to constant enhancements in information and communication technology (ITC), traditional healthcare systems are being replaced by smart healthcare systems. This gives us hope that with the help of smart devices, IoT, and the confluence of ML/DL techniques in healthcare facilities, the effects of COVID-19 can be slowed if not eliminated.

1.2 Glossary for COVID-19

1.2.1 Virus

Viruses are microscopic parasites made of DNA or RNA. They bind to a living cell's resource and multiply. They can only reproduce inside the living cell. Outside the cell, they are known as virions and behave like inert, unaffecting dust particles.

1.2.2 Epidemic

An epidemic is a disease that may affect many people at the same time. It tends to be spread in a place where it is not permanently prevalent. It occurs at a region or community level.

1.2.3 Pandemic

With comparison to an epidemic, a pandemic is more widespread, prevailing through-out an entire country, continent, or the whole world. On March 11, the WHO declared COVID-19 a pandemic because of the severity of the spread.

1.2.4 Novel coronavirus SARS-CoV-2

This is the latest strain of the coronavirus. A coronavirus belongs to the family of viruses that causes the common cold and other respiratory infections. Other diseases of the same family seen before were Middle East Respiratory Syndrome coronavirus (MERS-CoV) and Severe Acute Respiratory Syndrome (SARS-CoV). The novel coronavirus that caused COVID-19 is named SARS-CoV-2. Coronavirus is zoonotic in nature, that is, it can be transmitted from animals to humans.

1.2.5 COVID-19

COVID-19 was coined by WHO, and it stands for "coronavirus disease 2019." It is a pandemic disease. It is caused by SARS-CoV-2 and was first seen in Wuhan, China. Some common symptoms of COVID-19 are fever, cough, and difficulty breathing. However, as the infection is spreading throughout the masses, recorded symptoms have also shown change. New strains are coming into existence. It has become more difficult to identify and diagnose these new COVID-19 strains. It can be spread through contact from an infected person or surface that was in contact with the infected person.

1.2.6 Physical distancing

As per the guidelines of WHO (World Health Organization) and MoHFW (Ministry of Health and Family Welfare, Government of India), there is a safe distance between two individuals to limit the spread of COVID-19. It refers to keeping at least 2 m of space between you and other people. Guidelines also sternly focus on avoiding crowded places and mass gatherings. These are the best tools to prevent coronavirus that can be followed by everyone. Physical distancing, however, does not mean that one must socially isolate themselves. It is important to connect with friends and family through social media platforms to sail through tough times. Therefore, experts have stopped using the term social distancing.

1.2.7 Symptomatic and asymptomatic persons

Individuals that have become infected with coronavirus and are showing visible symptoms of COVID-19 are known as symptomatic persons.

Individuals that have been infected with coronavirus but are not displaying any visible symptoms are known as asymptomatic persons. Even though their chances of infecting other people are relatively lower, they are still capable of transmitting COVID-19 to other people.

1.2.8 Herd immunity

Herd immunity is where a large community of people becomes immune to an infectious disease, therefore stopping the spread of disease. This can be attained by either naturally building an immune response against the disease or getting vaccinated against it.

1.2.9 Flattening the curve

This refers to slowing down the rate of increased positives of those being tested for the disease.

1.2.10 Quarantine

Quarantine refers to restrictions on people moving who were exposed to a contagious disease to see if they have caught the disease.

1.2.11 Isolation

Isolation is also referred to as restricting the movement of people. However, instead of imposing it on people exposed to the disease, it is for people who have already been infected by it. It is a way to keep the infected people away from the uninfected people.

1.2.12 Incubation period

The time period from when an individual contracts a virus to the time when the symptoms appear is known as the incubation period. In COVID-19, the incubation period ranges from 2 to 14 days after exposure to the virus. However, it may be different from person to person.

1.2.13 Mortality rate

The ratio of the total number of recorded deaths due to the viral infection to the total number of confirmed cases that tested positive for the infection is known as the mortality rate.

1.3   COVID-19 vs. other diseases

The current problem with the coronavirus is to get a better grip on how lethal this virus is and the total population it will infect. The current problem with the coronavirus is to get a better grip on how lethal this virus is and the total population it will infect. It is a time-consuming process to calculate the lethalness of newborn viruses because whether the diagnosed patient will survive the infection or not is still unknown. The only way the predictions can be accurate is by trying to cover all factors so that the prediction is as close as it can get with minimum casualties in terms of death cases. If all the infections that mankind has yet seen are put in a pyramid, COVID-19 will be on top, making it the most severe infection that has been encountered (Fig. 1).

The epidemic doubled in size every 5 days when it was first seen and identified in China, followed by the rest of the world in about a month and a half. The severity depended on how well connected people had been in recent days. There have been cases where the person infected traveled from China to other parts of the world, hence continuing the trail of infection. Community transmission was also on the rise during that time, so health guidelines were published and put into strict action. However, experts and research teams noted that it is very hard to fully curb and control COVID-19, which further evolved to be a pandemic, just as the SARS epidemic that happened in 2002.

1.4   How mathematical modeling informs policy and government response

The health guidelines that are being followed mainly include physical distancing and wearing masks. India has also approved its vaccines, Covaxin and Covishield. These practices have been efficient and have decreased the rate of infection; however, this is

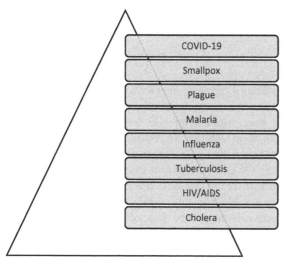

Fig. 1 Top 10 epidemics to hit the world.
https://www.mphonline.org/worst-pandemics-in-history.

not the only way through which policies and frameworks are constructed. Statistical and mathematical analysis of the data is the key for the same. It is nonetheless important to note that data acquired might be very noisy and limited to the outbreak. The uncertainty can be very high because we are dealing with an infection we have never encountered before. In a general sense, we have marked the incubation period from 2 to 14 days, but the SARS-CoV-2 has been mutating into newer strains by the day. This has led to newer and undetected symptoms in patients. The estimation is hence done with the help of statistical tools and models.

Even though there is uncertainty in the predictions and results being generated, the policymakers must have a set of numbers that can be the basis of the framework and health plan. The uncertainty gives them confidence in the estimate that has been calculated. For example, if the ratio of people who might now be able to survive the infection is varied from one in 1000 to one in 10, it can still be interpreted that the estimate may be 1%, 0.5%, or 2%. And so, the range is still a useful estimate. This prepares the government for what's called a reasonable worst-case scenario. If the preparedness effort is small in terms of the public health impact, which includes hospital beds occupied, severe illness, medical facilities, and death, the country and eventually the global economy might take a drastic hit [12].

1.5 COVID-19 world trend

The COVID-19 pandemic initially began as a global health crisis, first being discovered in China and eventually spreading all over the world. Countries have taken strong measures such as lockdowns, curfews, social distancing, etc., to minimize the effect of this hit; however, a global economic crisis could not be avoided.

The first recorded case outside China was in Thailand on January 13, 2020. By the end of January, the number of confirmed cases worldwide was reported to be 7818 in 18 countries outside China. By April 8, 2021, the recorded number of confirmed cases and deaths were 131,103,4851 and 2,887,278, respectively (Fig. 2).

2 Smart healthcare

Smart healthcare promotes and creates a sphere of interaction among the patient, the healthcare service provider, and the services required by the patient. It aims to give a real-time diagnosis. Patients use smart wearable mobile devices to always monitor their levels, without the constant medical tests that are carried out in hospitals or medical facilities. Through the smart device, they can seek medical assistance virtually, which is generally followed by clinical guidance on how to improve their health [8].

In a smart healthcare framework, there are five tasks that can be carried out: daily prevention, daily and clinical diagnosis, and clinical and daily treatments (Fig. 3) [13].

Daily prevention consists of activities that can be done before the disease or sickness occurs. Fitness check-ups, disease prediction, and emotion analysis are some of the techniques included in this component. Daily diagnosis is based on the data from

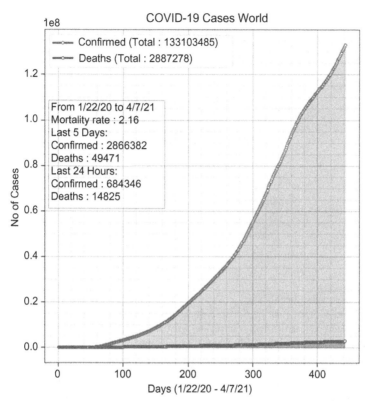

Fig. 2 COVID-19 confirmed and death cases [original].

Wearable Medical Sensors (WMS). This is often used to carry out the diagnosis of vitals from the data stream obtained from smart mobile devices. Although, in clinical healthcare, the diagnosis is personalized and is in a clinical setting. It also includes a reduction of the physician variance. Clinical treatment is plan-based. The treatment method is evaluated, and the patient is monitored [13].

2.1 Applications of smart healthcare

There are several applications of smart healthcare, the first and foremost being its use in assisting with diagnosis and treatment. The accuracy of smart healthcare exceeds that of traditional healthcare systems by a huge margin [5]. This reduces the chance of misdiagnosis and the potential casualties that can cause. With the help of smart healthcare, patients can have their own personalized treatment. The more accurate the symptoms and the description of the patient's condition, the more accurate the smart diagnosis will be. This has been evident in tumor diagnosis and prostate cancer detection [14].

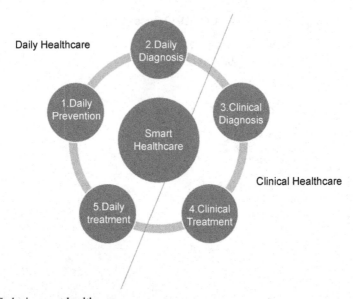

Fig. 3 Tasks in smart healthcare.
Modified from M. Zhang, H. Li, S. Pan, J. Lyu, S. Ling, S. Su, Convolutional neural networks based lung nodule classification: a surrogate-assisted evolutionary algorithm for hyperparameter optimization, IEEE Trans. Evol. Comput. 25 (5) (2021) 869–882.

Apart from diagnostics, smart healthcare is helping patients with chronic diseases by providing a health management system. In remote areas, especially where medical facilities are not easily available, wearable/implantable devices connected with a cloud server can help keep track of a patient's health data [8]. These systems can often monitor physiological indicators of patients such as heartbeat, blood pressure, cell count, etc., with comfort and great portability of their devices. This is a helpful application for the elderly and disabled as well.

Aside from these, smart healthcare has been seen to play a major role in assisting drug research (drug excavations and clinical trials), reducing medical costs, and with virtual medical assistants.

2.2   Advantages of smart healthcare

The main advantages of smart healthcare are:

- Real-time remote patient monitoring.
- Disease prevention and risk monitoring.
- Lowering the cost of medical services for patients.
- Improved accuracy of diagnosis.
- High research potential.
- Improved treatment and healthcare management.

2.3   Disadvantages of smart healthcare

The main disadvantages of smart healthcare include:

- Security and privacy issues.
- Risk of failure of the hardware or software components in the smart system.
- Cost of implementation and staff training is high.

3   Machine learning in healthcare

The concept of "learning" can simply be defined as "A computer program is said to learn from experience (E) with respect to some class of task (T) and its performance measure (P), if its performance at tasks in T, as measured by P, improves with E" [15]. The major techniques of ML/DL that are used in healthcare are supervised learning, unsupervised learning, and reinforcement learning. These procedures require different levels of supervision in the training stage of the data.

3.1   Supervised learning in 5G and wireless communication technology for healthcare

This is the most-used learning applied in medical systems. In supervised learning, there are labels. Training data are fed to the respective labels. With the subsequent learning, the main aim is to design a model that can take in a sample problem with known optima and recognize optimal solutions of new samples (Fig. 4).

These methods map associations between the output and input using the training data. If the output is of a continuous nature, the task is known as regression. On the other hand, if the output is categorized, it is known as classification. Some classic examples of this method in healthcare applications include medical image recognition [16] and the classification of types of lung diseases [17]. A prime challenge while carrying out supervised learning is that the model should work properly on testing data points. The ability of a model to do so is known as generalization. Overfitting and underfitting are also some important challenges that are to be taken care of in supervised learning. Overfitting occurs when the training error and testing error have a substantial difference, whereas underfitting occurs when the model obtains a significant error rate on the training data. A model that generalizes well is one that will neither overfit nor underfit (Table 1).

Fig. 4 Supervised learning.

Table 1 Supervised learning and its applications using mobile and wireless communication.

ML technique	Algorithm/ learning model	Healthcare component	Application using mobile and wireless communication
Supervised learning	Linear regression, Support vector machine (SVM)	Anomaly detection	Used to classify abnormal instances in the incoming wireless sensor as well as predict abnormal instances to determine whether the patient is entering a critical stage, or the sensor is reporting a faulty reading [18].
	Decision tree, K-nearest neighbor, naïve Bayesian	Analysis of ECG and blood pressure	Evaluation and classification of data acquired while doing different physical activities done by patients using microacceleration systems [19].
	SVM, decision tree, random forest, multilayer perceptron (MLP)	IoT-based behavioral and physiological monitoring system	Monitor's health status of students in an IoT-based environment and classifies health function to achieve optimal predictions [20].

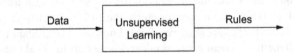

Fig. 5 Unsupervised learning.

3.2 Unsupervised learning in 5G and wireless communication technology for healthcare

In unsupervised learning, an unlabeled collection of features is used to train the data and the model aims to categorize them into small groups with similar characteristics without any external guidance (Fig. 5).

This learning revolves around utilizing unlabeled data. The clustering technique is the most popularly used ML application. Algorithms such as dimensionality reduction and feature learning are some of the most widely used algorithms that are carried out with the help of autoencoders (AE) [21]. When AE is incorporated as an end-to-end optimized task in the physical layer of a communication system, the input within a neural network can be considered a special case of AE [22]. K-means clustering is yet another unsupervised learning algorithm. There has been research that a

Fig. 6 Reinforcement learning.

combination of optimized k-means clustering, the Gaussian mixture model, and the expectation maximization (EM) algorithm works better than an energy vector-based algorithm in a wireless network system [23].

3.3 Reinforcement learning in 5G and wireless communication technology for healthcare

Reinforcement learning or approximate dynamic learning is award-based learning where the methods learn with the aid of given observations. A reward is awarded if the response to the action that has taken place falls into the correct class. This process is repeated to train the model. Reinforcement learning has numerous applications in the healthcare sector. Some of the sectors include treatment regimens in critical healthcare, chronic diseases, and automated medical diagnosis from clinical data (Fig. 6) [24].

4 Deep learning in healthcare

Deep learning has made great strides in recognition, prediction, and diagnosis in healthcare, including nuclear segmentation as well as tumor and cancer detection [25,26]. DL models and neural network models are often the best solutions when it comes to imaging datasets.

As there are many types of cells present in a human body, each has its unique structure and form. The use of classical forms of segmentation techniques becomes tedious and difficult. This issue was solved by applying DL techniques, which can be utilized to design neural networks that can look past the morphological shape of a cell and focus on the concentrated nucleus, thereby performing localized segmentation over multiple regions of interest in the image.

4.1 Image processing in a medical setup

As humans are in the midst of an era of technology, it is no surprise that the amount of data being generated is increasing exponentially. Primarily in the healthcare industry, most of the diagnoses are based on data collected from the human body. MRIs, CAT scans, and PET scans are a few imaging data examples. Image processing is an important concept frequently used in medical facilities and hospitals. It fundamentally amplifies the features of the image that are significant to the diagnosis.

Technological advances have taken this to another level where the involvement of doctors has been reduced to a minimum, and the machines themselves can give accurate diagnoses. With the help of machine learning, this has been taken to a new level, with the support of a generative adversarial network (GAN) [16], it is possible to generate artificial data/images for scenarios where data are limited, and these then act as baseline datasets to help identify them.

Image processing consists of various steps applied to the image as per the requirement and is thus referred to as an image processing pipeline [23]. The first step is carrying out preprocessing. This involves taking information from the image data and transforming it into a matrix. This makes it easier for the further application of filters on the image. When applying a filter, the purpose is to accentuate the desired features and prepare the image for segmentation. This can be done by adjusting the contrast, saturation, and histogram of the image. There are hundreds of algorithms available for segmentation, each developed based on the requirement of the dataset. These algorithms include simple mathematical calculations based on complex neural networks outside the context of human reasoning [4].

4.2   Deep learning in applications

There are several models that are widely used for image segmentation. Some of these include convolutional neural networks (CNNs), recursive neural networks (RNNs), long short-term memory (LSTM), encoder-decoders, and GANs.

Though DL comes with drawbacks, there are cases when it can be developed from scratch. But this applies to scenarios where labeled data are abundant. Then there are scenarios where transfer learning is applicable. With the help of transfer learning, old models can be repurposed and used on newer datasets. This is possible by adapting parts of older models and adjusting them according to our scenario. The basic idea is that the pretrained model is capable of capturing the semantic detail and information from the image necessary for segmentation [4,23].

Given below are some deep neural networks and their application in healthcare for image segmentation as well as other medical spheres (Table 2).

Table 2 Deep learning architectures and applications in healthcare.

S. no.	Model	Description	Application	Reference
1.	Convolutional neural network (CNN)	CNN has the ability to take in various images and assign weights and other parameters to them based on their importance, thus helping differentiate them from one another. It is a deep model with supervised learning.	Ailment of brains, breasts, and lungs.	[27]

Table 2 Continued

S. no.	Model	Description	Application	Reference
2.	Recursive neural network (RNN)	RNN's main application is with data dependent on previously used data (inbuilt memory that updates neurons) at any time stamps or positions. The main restriction with RNN is they are not able to store past dependencies after a certain limit due to memory restrictions.	Brain (MRI)	[28]
3.	Fully connected convolutional network (FCN)	FCN was able to take an arbitrary size image to produce a segmentation map for the image, thus producing a convolutional map instead of a classification score as usual.	Full-body X-rays	[16]
4.	Graphical convolutional models	This method performs operations by learning the features by examining the neighbor nodes (unordered) in the model.	For effective modeling of electronic health records	[29]
5.	Encoder-decoder models (e.g., U-Net-based CNN)	This model consists of a combination of two RNNs, where one is known as the encoder and the other is the decoder. The former aims to encode the input and the latter decodes the input.	Coding death certificates and statistical translation	[30]

4.3   Case study: Fluorescence microscopy using deep learning

Gene therapy is a field of medical science where organisms are studied at a cellular level. It revolves around how medicine alters genes. As various chemicals react differently while producing a different form of fluorescence, it is easy to detect changes that occur in the genes and at the molecular level. The aim of the case study is to identify and segment nuclei in input images, which is known as nuclear segmentation [16].

The models considered for the study are CNN, U-Net-based CNN, U-Net with ResNet-based CNN, and masked RCNN (M-RCNN). The former two were discussed in the previous sections. U-Net with ResNet-based CNN has a quality that makes it stand out from other CN models. It is created from residual blocks (ResBlocks) alongside skip connections. M-RCNN is differentiated from RNN as there exists an additional predicted segment mask at pixel level in the output. The results of these models are given in Figs. 7–10.

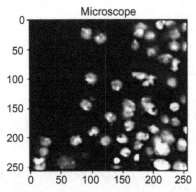 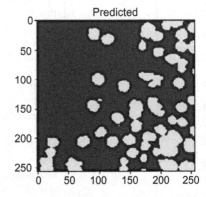

Fig. 7 Results: CNN model.

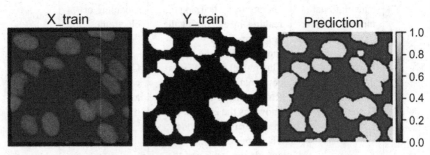

Fig. 8 Result: U-Net-based CNN.

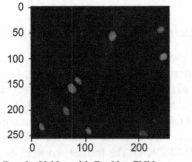 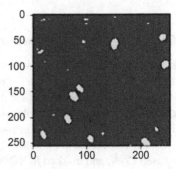

Fig. 9 Result: U-Net with ResNet CNN.

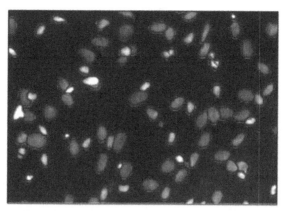

Fig. 10 Result: M-RCNN with instance segmentation.

5   Clinical workflow using ML/DL

The initial step to design a healthcare ML workflow is to analyze the problem and create a formal definition for the problem that the system aims to tackle. The specification of the functional requirements is penned down as they shape the mainframe deployment of the system. There are only three overarching categories in the healthcare sphere—diagnosis, prediction, and recommendation. The most common application in the healthcare industry is diagnosing, which is also known as classification. This supervised learning approach is based on the given set of features that describes the symptoms of a specific diseases. Like diagnosis, prediction is also a supervised learning approach where the system tries to fit the training dataset to give continuous outputs related to likelihood and quantity. A recommendation suggests the best plan of action to be followed, taking into consideration the patient's symptoms, prior medical reports, and circumstances.

When the problem statement and functional specifications have been outlined, the second step is to collect the appropriate data. Clinical data accessed by healthcare reports is the staple resource for medical research. Test results, diagnoses, clinical observation reports, current medical issues, the medications prescribed to the patient, and the procedures that the patient underwent are some parameters that are included in EHRs. Aside from these, medical images, physician notes, and medical scans also play an important role in DL medical applications. This is a key step as the medical ecosystem is complex and robust in terms of the data it accumulates. A patient's medical data that is to be accessed should be anonymized to appropriately preserve the privacy of the data. To develop efficient neural diagnostic solutions that take advantage of big data, accurately labeled data and annotated data are musts.

The following phase is the model development phase, which requires a lot of trial and error. The model should have a balance between efficiency and complexity. Some models that are used include CNN, LSTM, GAN, etc. Once model development has taken place, an algorithmic audit is done where the experts are engaged to test and improve the performance of the developed ML/Dl system. The next step is model

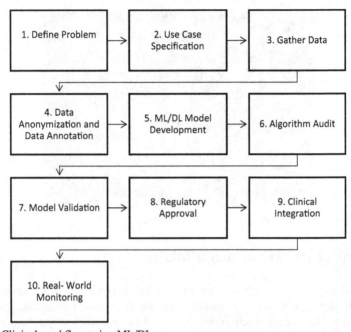

Fig. 11 Clinical workflow using ML/DL.
Modified from A. Qayyum, J. Qadir, M. Bilal, A. Al-Fuqaha, Secure and robust machine learning for healthcare: a survey, IEEE Rev. Biomed. Eng. 14 (2021) 156–180. https://doi.org/10.1109/RBME.2020.3013489.

validation. It is a one-time iterative process that takes place right after model development. During this phase, the outputs of the model are checked to ensure that they are performing as expected in terms of design objectives and business use. Before the system is deployed in an actual medical environment, it must be approved by the regulatory authorities. It is often given a trial run to see its acceptance based on the opinion of the end users. It is then deployed in the real world, with regular checks to improve the system and identify potentially needed features (Fig. 11).

6   Security, privacy, and federated learning in healthcare

The world as we know it has evolved and changed due to the introduction of AI intelligence technology in all sectors. The application of ML techniques with the confluence of computer vision [31], especially DL techniques, has increased accuracy in medical science. The key for progress is the existence of large corpora of images. It is because of these that we can design and facilitate learning models with a wide range of applications in cancer detection, tumor detection [25], genetic replacement [32] and characterization, risk prediction and quantification [26], X-ray analysis, etc. Even though there exists a large database of medical data, there remains a large barrier to transform that data for use in a manner that can answer significant questions.

The prime reason is the paucity of standardized electronic medical records (EMRs). Storing and managing electronic patient data is expensive [32]. Medical health centers and hospitals in underdeveloped and developing regions are unable to maintain records or participate in studies requiring then. This is a potential and unintentional reason that perpetuates issues of fairness and bias. In the area of medical imaging, digital imaging and communications in medicine (DICOM) [33] is the universal standard for communication, management, and transmission of image data format. Digital imaging data have advantages such as permanent storability, remote access, and easy shareability.

Another issue that persists during patient trials and medical record collection is the regulation of patient medical data and the need for protection. The Health Insurance Portability and Accountability Act (HIPPA) [34] was created in 1996 to introduce a modern solution to the chain of healthcare information. It laid down how patient records are to be maintained by medical facilities to protect them from fraud or theft. Similarly, the European General Data Protection Regulation (GDPR) [35] also placed strict directives about storing and exchanging patient data that require authentication and authorization. Apart from this, GDPR provides facilities such as interpretability, data handling, and governance with an application of AI [3].

The use of AI in medical imaging has brought about an immense transformation. Privacy-preserving AI is providing solutions and methods that are can be used to protect data, along with use for clinical analysis. It allows data processing in such a manner that data are not revealed in the process. Secure AI, on the other hand, deals with methods that are concerned with safeguarding or protecting algorithms. When these two are effectively put into use together, they provide systems that have structured transparency (Fig. 12). These systems can counter attacks against datasets [36], attacks on computational processes [37], and feature reidentification [38,39].

The most popularly used techniques for privacy preservation in healthcare are anonymization and pseudonymization [40], collectively known as the deidentification of data. Data anonymization is a processing technique that removes the identifiable information of a patient from the medical records so that the data remain anonymous. However, in pseudonymization, instead of eradicating data, the subject is replaced by identifiers or pseudonyms. This denotes that the individual from the medical records can still be identified by indirect means and that the pseudonymized data are still in the scope of GDPR. But anonymized data cannot be restored and therefore are out of scope. The main reason why these techniques are widely used is because of their simplicity. Keeping the pros of simple implementation aside, these techniques are prone to attacks. Moreover, there is always a scope for technical error that can affect the protection of the dataset. Deidentification of data usually takes place before sharing or transferring data; the process is highly dependent on the different image datasets (Fig. 13) [41].

Reidentification attacks [42] are more prone to data in tabular form [43] as well as images. Therefore, records and data that are prone to identification (for example, removing the skull region from input images) should be processed rigorously. In a nutshell, to increase the level of data protection, more measures must be taken [44]. Reidentified medical records are major targets for insurance companies that want

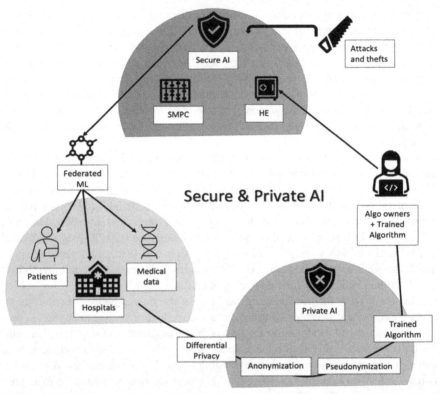

Fig. 12 Security architecture of smart healthcare.

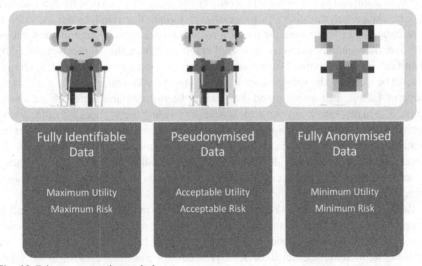

Fig. 13 Privacy prevention techniques.

to decrease financial risk by discriminating against patients with specific disorders and diseases. These datasets are also seen as business models for data analytic companies. The applications of ML in privacy and security are vast. They have provided major transformations in the computational structure of models, with the only requirement being complex system architectures and the data to feed it. Centralized data storage solutions increase the computational requirement exponentially, and therefore the use of distributed systems is preferred. Distributed ML has high real-world applicability and goes beyond parallel computing power. Federated learning proposes the idea of training locally stored data (nodes), with the help of available local computational power (for example, updating neural net weights during performing local iterations) while protecting patient privacy [45]. The federation topology allows the flexible sharing of models among the nodes. Thus, this approach has gained popularity in next-generation privacy preservation and medical applications.

Federated ML provides an easy solution for the governance of data, but that does not itself give an assurance to security and privacy of the medical data. Encryption is important during the process to defend data against attacks that intend to steal identifiable patient information straight from nodes. If the data in consideration are manageable in size, this can easily be done. As the volume of data increases, it requires more computation power and highly observant experts, making the whole process tedious. This can also result in data leaks, stolen data, and data hampering, thus compromising the quality of results. Although federated learning offers safety in terms of infrastructure, it is insufficient against interference. This, from the view of patent restrictions and asset protection, is unacceptable.

To further increase the scope of privacy and security, methods that work on data with the property of systematic randomization are applied. This helps in reducing the information needed for computation while retaining the global statistical reasoning of the system. This methodology to maintain the statistical outputs of a model while decreasing individual recognizability in the input data is known as differential privacy (DP) [46]. It can solve issues when companies want to release statistical data based on medical patient records and there are adversaries present who want to uncover the sensitive records. This method works very efficiently with tabular data, but its implementation in imaging data still has unclear results. The results hold the potential of unpredictability and inefficiency (Fig. 14).

Encryption techniques are extensively used in data security and privacy. They can be applied on data as well as algorithms. Under the homomorphic encryption (HE) scheme, systems are allowed to perform computations on encrypted data as if they were plain text. In this approach, the structure is preserved throughout the computation, as the word "homomorphic" (addition and multiplication operations) suggests. HE has been deemed to be successful when applied to ConvNets [47] and in scenarios where ML works as a service [48]. Moreover, systems can be further secured using secure multipart computation (SMPC) [49]. When no single company has sole hold on the data, the computation can be extended to multiple parties. For instance, ML-assisted medical image services can be presented given that the data are protected from malicious use or theft.

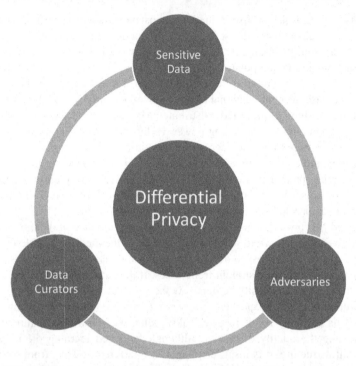

Fig. 14 Differential privacy solves problems with these three parts.

7   Conclusion

To sum up, it can easily be seen that the prospects for smart healthcare are vast. Machine learning and deep learning solutions in healthcare provide timely medical services with better accuracy and efficiency. The more detailed the symptoms and physiological characteristics of the patients, the easier is it to get a smart diagnosis with a personalized healthcare management system. The major tasks carried out in a healthcare system are prevention, diagnosis, and treatment. However, while setting up a smart healthcare system, the issue of security and privacy of patient medical records may arise. For safe use of data, regulations such as DICOM, HIPPA, and GDPR have been set in motion that protect and monitor the integrity and privacy of data. Apart from these regulations, privacy-preserving techniques such as anonymization and pseudonymization are widely being used in healthcare facilities. With the help of distributed infrastructure and federated machine learning, healthcare systems can easily be set up without having to deal with a lack of computation power. This chapter also discussed the different types of learnings and their application in wireless communication systems. Lastly, we discussed the clinical workflow that is followed in any conventional smart healthcare set-up.

References

[1] M. Esmaeili, A.T. Eshlaghi, A.P. Ebrahimi, R. Esmaieli, Study on feasibility and acceptance of implementation of Technology Acceptance Model of Davis in staff of Shahid Beheshti University of Medical Sciences, Pajoohandeh J. 18 (1) (2013) 40–45.
[2] A. Garavand, M. Mohseni, H. Asadi, M. Etemadi, M. Moradi-Joo, A. Moosavi, Factors influencing the adoption of health information technologies: a systematic review, Electron. Physician 8 (8) (2016) 2713.
[3] GDPR, Intersoft Consulting, 2016. https://gdpr-info.eu.
[4] S. Minaee, Y.Y. Boykov, F. Porikli, A.J. Plaza, N. Kehtarnavaz, D. Terzopoulos, Image segmentation using deep learning: a survey, in: IEEE Transactions on Pattern Analysis and Machine Intelligence, 2021, p. 1.
[5] H. Yin, A.O. Akmandor, A. Mosenia, N.K. Jha, Smart healthcare, Found. Trends Electron. Des. Autom. 12 (4) (2018) 401–466.
[6] H. Ghayvat, J. Liu, S.C. Mukhopadhyay, X. Gui, Wellness sensor networks: a proposal and implementation for smart home for assisted living, IEEE Sensors J. 15 (12) (2015) 7341–7348.
[7] P.S. Negi, P. Kumar, An analytical study on gesture recognition technology, in: Proceedings of the Third International Conference on Computational Intelligence and Informatics, Springer, Singapore, 2020, pp. 857–867.
[8] H.C. Koydemir, A. Ozcan, Wearable and implantable sensors for biomedical applications, Annu. Rev. Anal. Chem. 11 (2018) 127–146.
[9] H.K. Bharadwaj, A. Agarwal, V. Chamola, N.R. Lakkaniga, V. Hassija, M. Guizani, B. Sikdar, A review on the role of machine learning in enabling IoT based healthcare applications, IEEE Access 9 (2021) 38859–38890.
[10] S.G. Finlayson, J.D. Bowers, J. Ito, J.L. Zittrain, A.L. Beam, I.S. Kohane, Adversarial attacks on medical machine learning, Science 363 (6433) (2019) 1287–1289.
[11] K. Papangelou, K. Sechidis, J. Weatherall, G. Brown, Toward an understanding of adversarial examples in clinical trials, in: Joint European Conference on Machine Learning and Knowledge Discovery in Databases, Springer, Cham, 2018, September, pp. 35–51.
[12] R. Gupta, A. Kumari, S. Tanwar, N. Kumar, Blockchain-envisioned softwarized multi-swarming UAVs to tackle COVID-19 situations, IEEE Netw. (2020), https://doi.org/10.1109/MNET.011.2000439.
[13] H. Yin, O. Akmandor, A. Mosenia, N.K. Jha, J.-B. Raclet, P. Reinkemeier, A. Vincentelli, W. Damm, T. Henzinger, K. Larsen, Smart Healthcare, 2018, pp. 401–466, https://doi.org/10.1561/9781680834413.
[14] A. Qayyum, J. Qadir, M. Bilal, A. Al-Fuqaha, Secure and robust machine learning for healthcare: a survey, IEEE Rev. Biomed. Eng. 14 (2021) 156–180, https://doi.org/10.1109/RBME.2020.3013489.
[15] T.M. Mitchell, Machine learning and data mining, Commun. ACM 42 (11) (1999) 30–36.
[16] Z. Yan, Y. Zhan, Z. Peng, et al., Multi-instance deep learning: discover discriminative local anatomies for bodypart recognition, IEEE Trans. Med. Imaging 35 (5) (2016) 1332–1343, https://doi.org/10.1109/tmi.2016.2524985.
[17] M. Zhang, H. Li, S. Pan, J. Lyu, S. Ling, S. Su, Convolutional neural networks based lung nodule classification: a surrogate-assisted evolutionary algorithm for hyperparameter optimization, IEEE Trans. Evol. Comput. 25 (5) (2021) 869–882.
[18] S. Ifzarne, H. Tabbaa, I. Hafidi, N. Lamghari, Anomaly detection using machine learning techniques in wireless sensor networks, J. Phys. Conf. Ser. 1743 (1) (2021) 012021.

[19] L.C. Jatobá, U. Grossmann, C. Kunze, J. Ottenbacher, W. Stork, Context-aware mobile health monitoring: evaluation of different pattern recognition methods for classification of physical activity, in: Annual International Conference of the IEEE Engineering in Medicine and Biology Society. IEEE Engineering in Medicine and Biology Society. Annual International Conference, 2008, 2008, pp. 5250–5253.

[20] A. Souri, M. Ghafour, A. Ahmed, F. Safara, A. Yamini, M. Hoseyninezhad, A new machine learning-based healthcare monitoring model for student's condition diagnosis in Internet of Things environment, Soft. Comput. 24 (2020), https://doi.org/10.1007/s00500-020-05003-6.

[21] H. Bourlard, Y. Kamp, Auto-association by multilayer perceptrons and singular value decomposition, Biol. Cybern. 59 (4–5) (1988) 291–294.

[22] T. O'Sheaand, J. Hoydis, An introduction to deep learning for the physical layer, IEEE Trans. Cogn. Commun. Netw. 3 (4) (2017) 563–575.

[23] G.C. Sobabe, Y. Song, X. Bai, B. Guo, A cooperative spectrum sensing algorithm based on unsupervised learning, in: Proceedings of the 10th International Congress on Image Signal Processing, Biomedical Engineering and Informatics (CISP-BMEI), vol. 1, October 2017, pp. 198–201.

[24] C. Yu, J. Liu, S. Nemati, Reinforcement Learning in Healthcare: A Survey, 2019. arXiv preprint arXiv:1908.08796.

[25] S.M. McKinney, et al., International evaluation of an AI system for breast cancer screening, Nature 577 (2020) 89–94.

[26] B. Varghese, et al., Objective risk stratification of prostate cancer using machine learning and radiomics applied to multiparametric magnetic resonance images, Sci. Rep. 9 (2019) 1570.

[27] D.R. Sarvamangala, R.V. Kulkarni, Convolutional neural networks in medical image understanding: a survey, Evol. Intell. (2021), https://doi.org/10.1007/s12065-020-00540-3.

[28] Y. Yang, J. Sun, H. Li, Z. Xu, Deep ADMM-Net for compressive sensing MRI, in: Proceedings of the 30th International Conference on Neural Information Processing Systems, 2016, December, pp. 10–18.

[29] E. Choi, Z. Xu, Y. Li, M. Dusenberry, G. Flores, E. Xue, A. Dai, Learning the graphical structure of electronic health records with graph convolutional transformer, in: Proceedings of the AAAI Conference on Artificial Intelligence, vol. 34, no. 01, 2020, April, pp. 606–613.

[30] E. Tutubalina, Z. Miftahutdinov, An Encoder-Decoder Model for ICD-10 Coding of Death Certificates, 2017. Preprint arXiv:1712.01213.

[31] H.J.W.L. Aerts, et al., Decoding tumour phenotype by non-invasive imaging using a quantitative radiomics approach, Nat. Commun. 5 (2014) 4006.

[32] H. Lu, et al., A mathematical-descriptor of tumor-mesoscopic-structure from computed-tomography images annotates prognostic- and molecular- phenotypes of epithelial ovarian cancer, Nat. Commun. 10 (2019) 764.

[33] S.J. Wang, et al., A cost-benefit analysis of electronic medical records in primary care, Am. J. Med. 114 (2003) 397–403.

[34] DICOM reference guide, Health Devices 30 (2001) 5–30.

[35] hhs.gov, HIPAA, US Department of Health and Human Services, 2020. https://www.hhs.gov/hipaa/index.html.

[36] A. Theodorou, V. Dignum, Towards ethical and socio-legal governance in AI, Nat. Mach. Intell. 2 (2020) 10–12.

[37] C. Dwork, A. Smith, T. Steinke, J. Ullman, Exposed! A survey of attacks on private data, Annu. Rev. Stat. Appl. 4 (2017) 61–84.
[38] K. Kurita, P. Michel, G. Neubig, Weight Poisoning Attacks on Pre-Trained Models, 2020, Preprint at https://arxiv.org/abs/2004.06660.
[39] V. Bindschaedler, P. Grubbs, D. Cash, T. Ristenpart, V. Shmatikov, The tao of inference in privacy-protected databases, Proc. VLDB Endow. 11 (2018) 1715–1728 (ACM).
[40] H. Surendra, H.S. Mohan, A review of synthetic data generation methods for privacy preserving data publishing, Int. J. Sci. Technol. Res. 6 (2017) 95–101.
[41] J. Hathaliya, S. Tanwar, An exhaustive survey on security and privacy issues in healthcare 4.0, Comput. Commun. 153 (2020), https://doi.org/10.1016/j.comcom.2020.02.018.
[42] K. El Emam, E. Jonker, L. Arbuckle, B. Malin, A systematic review of re-identification attacks on health data, PLoS One 6 (2011) e28071.
[43] Y.A. de Montjoye, L. Radaelli, V.K. Singh, A.S. Pentland, Identity and privacy. Unique in the shopping mall: on the reidentifiability of credit card metadata, Science 347 (2015) 536–539.
[44] D. Abramian, A. Eklund, Refacing: reconstructing anonymized facial features using GANs, in: 2019 IEEE 16th International Symposium on Biomedical Imaging, IEEE, 2019, https://doi.org/10.1109/ISBI.2019.8759515.
[45] B. McMahan, E. Moore, D. Ramage, S. Hampson, B. Agüera-y-Arcas, Communication-efficient learning of deep networks from decentralized data, in: Proceedings of the 20th International Conference on Artificial Intelligence and Statistics, AISTATS 2017, vol. 54, 2017.
[46] A. Roth, C. Dwork, The algorithmic foundations of differential privacy, Found. Trends Theor. Comput. Sci. 9 (2013) 211–407.
[47] E. Hesamifard, H. Takabi, M. Ghasemi, CryptoDL: Deep Neural Networks over Encrypted Data, 2017, Preprint at https://arxiv.org/abs/1711.05189.
[48] N. Dowlin, et al., CryptoNets: applying neural networks to encrypted data with high throughput and accuracy, in: Proceedings of the 33rd International Conference on Machine Learning, vol. 48, PMLR, 2016, pp. 201–210.
[49] C. Zhao, et al., Secure multi-party computation: theory, practice and applications, Inf. Sci. 476 (2019) 357–372.

Further reading

U. Bodkhe, S. Tanwar, A. Ladha, P. Bhattacharya, A. Verma, A survey on revolutionizing Healthcare 4.0 applications using blockchain, in: International Conference on Computing, Communications, and Cyber-Security (IC4S 2020), Lecture Notes in Networks and Systems, 12-13th October, Springer, Chandigarh, India, 2019, pp. 1–16.

BEST: Blockchain-Enabled Secure Technology in a healthcare management system

Harsha Aggarwal[a], Rahul Johari[b], Deo Prakash Vidyarthi[c], Kalpana Gupta[d], and Arun Arora[b]

[a]Dream Technology, Delhi, India, [b]SWINGER (Security, Wireless IoT Network Group of Engineering and Research) Lab, USIC&T, GGSIP University, New Delhi, India, [c]Parallel and Distributed System Lab, School of Computer and Systems Sciences, JNU, New Delhi, India, [d]Centre for Development of Advanced Computing (C-DAC), Noida, India

1 Introduction

A hospital is a medical management organization that provides diagnoses and looks after the sick and injured through specialized staff and technology. Good technologies and hospital architecture lead to the best services. The medical industry has evolved from Healthcare 1.0 to Healthcare 4.0, as shown in Fig. 1. Blockchain-based architecture can play an important role in the healthcare industry. With the help of blockchain, a user can add more data through extra blocks. All previously stored data are to be permanently kept and can't be altered with the help of this architecture. The technology ensures a quick and easy way to perform validation on a transaction and writing a new transaction. The adoption of blockchain technology ensures safe, secure, integrity-based and transparency-driven healthcare data management. A patient can be sure that the data they fetch is unaltered since the time it was recorded. Blockchain facilitates better healthcare by data sharing. Blockchain assists in humanized and reliable health service by combining the complete real-time medical data of a patient's health while ensuring a secure health set-up. Health information is viewed as the most sensitive data related to a person. Although various approaches, rules, and consistency necessities are set up to defend health data, protection and security remain the main points of contention for electronic medical service frameworks. The objective of this chapter is to examine how our proposed system addresses safety concerns in Healthcare 4.0.

1.1 Research contribution

The primary contributions of this chapter are detailed as follows:

- The ages of Blockchain 1.0 to Blockchain 4.0 in the health sector are examined and shown in Fig. 1.
- The pros and cons of Blockchain 4.0 are discussed.

Blockchain Applications for Healthcare Informatics. https://doi.org/10.1016/B978-0-323-90615-9.00013-X
Copyright © 2022 Elsevier Inc. All rights reserved.

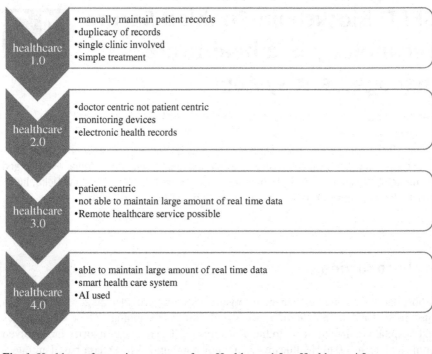

Fig. 1 Healthcare feature improvement from Healthcare 1.0 to Healthcare 4.0.

- A blockchain-based approach for electronic health records (EHR) is suggested.
- The safety difficulties of the conventional medical services are discussed, including how blockchain overcomes these issues.
- How to use blockchain to write a smart contract for a hospital management system is also discussed.
- The application of blockchain in the health sector is presented. A healthcare smart contract system for clinical data management is proposed in this chapter.

The organization of this chapter is as follows. Section 2 presents a literature review on the health domain. Section 3 highlights the characteristic features of blockchain technology. Section 4 discusses the security and privacy concerns in the healthcare system besides the blockchain applications in the healthcare sector. Section 5 illustrates the technological advantages of blockchain. Section 6 is a problem statement. It also describes the concept of a smart contract. Section 7 presents the system architecture in terms of its design and implementation on REMIX IDE. Section 8 describes the proposed methodology and snapshots of the smart contract. Section 9 concludes the chapter.

2 Literature review

Blockchain's healthcare technology is a commitment that ensures the greatest level of privacy. Blockchain can solve many real-life problems such as public safety mapping, centralized clinical results, reducing costs, integrated medical data, etc. [1]. Numerous researchers have done accomplished work in blockchain-based medical care. A few related recent works are listed in this section.

Nguyen et al. [2] proposed an EHR framework utilizing Ethereum blockchain that helps specialists and patients to share information in a safe way. The EHR framework protected the sensitive data of patients from network assaults. Siyal et al. [3] noted that keeping track of medical records is a critical task. Data can be lost or altered. All these problems can be solved by blockchain. They also explained the role of smart contracts and the application of blockchain in the health sector. Chattu et al. [4] examined the role of blockchain in an illness observation framework. They likewise clarified how blockchain is helpful at distinguishing danger ahead of time and can send a report to the medical service association for taking preventive measures.

Zheng et al. [5] talked about different sorts of safety limitations and the secure verification of smart contracts in a blockchain. They likewise clarified two conventions for confirmation and sharing of medical information. Uddin et al. [6] conceptualized the framework that continuously monitors a patient using a patient-centric agent. This framework counters network attacks. Fan et al. [7] worked on a consensus algorithm to raise the safety and privacy of a patient. Rifi et al. [8] described the benefits of blockchain in sharing patient information. They also illustrated the issues faced by traditional medical services such as extendibility and information sharing. Wang and Song [1] used smart contracts for sharing patient data so that the data retain integrity and are easily traceable.

Griggs et al. [9] described the private blockchain-based smart contracts for the remote patient monitoring system. This smart contract upholds the continuous monitoring of a patient and settles numerous security weaknesses. Srivastava et al. [10] portrayed how blockchain is useful for remote patient monitoring systems. They also used smart contracts for investigating data related to patient well-being.

Shen et al. [11] worked on blockchain to exchange healthcare data from different networks. They also described the mechanism through which patient data may be generated using various apps or other sources. Khezr et al. [12] mentioned different problems of the health system encountered by patients, doctors, etc. They also explained how blockchain is useful in the health sector. Litchfield et al. [13] talked about how blockchain helps overcome the problem of safety and solitude of data faced by patients and doctors. Vora et al. [14] talked about blockchain mechanisms to deal with EHRs. The primary thought process of their work is to show how the blockchain framework fulfills the needs of patients and doctors.

Zhang et al. [15] wrote about the significant role of blockchain in the healthcare system. Rouhani et al. [16] talked about blockchain mechanisms to handle EHRs. They also listed the pros and cons of blockchain in healthcare management. Anurag et al. [17] discussed blockchain mechanisms to handle EHRs to make patient data secure and private. They talked about the merits and demerits of blockchain. Gordan and Catalini [18] monitored blockchain innovation in medical services. They also explained that with blockchain apps, patients would be able to digitally access their data anywhere and anytime. Kumar et al. [19] explained the uses of blockchain in secure healthcare management. They also discussed the pros and cons of blockchain. Rahmadika et al. [20] worked on individual medical information systems to make the data available to the shared database. Personal Health Information (PHI) structure means that healthcare companies and patients have collectively been incorporated into the same blockchain channel. Zhang et al. [21] depicted the system for sharing PHI that assists with diagnosing well-being and upgrading security and protection. They likewise discussed how agreements are able to address the issues noted by medical care and the advancement of blockchain-based applications. Hoy et al. [22] described the implementation of blockchain in medicine that can eliminate fake drugs while increasing the quality of medicines and maintaining secure patient records.

3 Characteristics of blockchain technology

Blockchain was first proposed by Satoshi Nakamoto in 2008 [23]. It is seen as a technological fourth revolution. Blockchain is a peer-to-peer (P2P) network that manages distributed technology [24,25]. Blockchain outlines the problems of data uniformity, information sharing, encryption, stability, confidentiality, and accessibility to medical records. The blockchain data structure is a list of data blocks secured by cryptographic methods using hash techniques. Due to this, immutability [26] is attained in this innovation. Data added to the blockchain cannot be altered. Blockchain, which consists of blocks, represents a set of transactions for each block. Each block has a hash value that can be used to check the accuracy of the transaction [27]. The hash of the following block depends on the hash of the preceding block. These blocks are linked by handing out leads to understand and monitor the information [28,29].

There are three kinds of blockchain: private, public, and consortium, as shown in Fig. 2. Different generations of blockchain are shown in Fig. 3.

Medical care is improving daily with the help of blockchain. Smart contracts use blockchain technology in healthcare systems. The hash of a previous block binds the blockchain and does not permit any tampering or insertion. Blockchain offers a broad range of datasets used by medical researchers and doctors and helps them to accelerate treatment, in addition to drug development. Blockchain also helps in the development of healthcare provider apps. Datasets created during the clinical phase assist in maintaining the electronic health system, remote patient monitoring, and public health

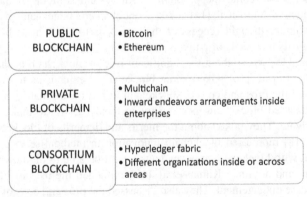

Fig. 2 Types of blockchain.

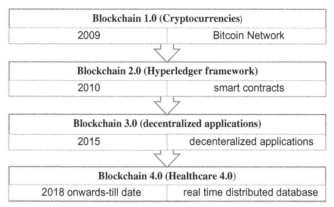

Fig. 3 Generations of blockchain.

devices. Medical services include medical details that are not accessible to any untrusted third party because of health problems and expertise deception [30]. Health records create utilities for patients, claims payment management, analyze data, and exchange for financial auditing and transparency [31]. The EHR system maintains the medical history of a patient; sometimes patients hesitate to disclose this with doctors or they forget to convey the information to the doctor (Fig. 4).

4   Security and privacy concerns in healthcare

With innovations in information science and data, patient security is the main worry for medical service associations. Blockchain with medical care information gives some security features [32]. Still, security and protection remain the chief worries in blockchain-based medical services and require substantial security arrangements. Security and privacy policies must be developed and coordinated publicly. Despite these challenges [33], many technologies have already been implemented by the medical field. Numerous privacy and security frameworks are already in place and we must leverage the existing process to utilize these standards in healthcare information technology (IT). Fig. 5 presents an overview of security and privacy issues and Fig. 6 discusses the prominent Issues related to data management. The dangers and expenses related to information security breaks are excessively high while the private

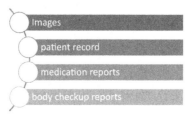

Fig. 4 Role of electronic health records.

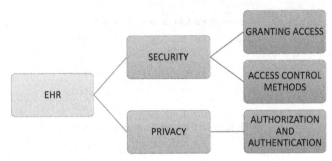

Fig. 5 Security and privacy issues.

Fig. 6 Prominent problems related to data management.

information of millions is in danger. This makes information security medical care's greatest concern today and an issue for which advancement and correspondence are absolutely critical.

The accompanying security issues ought to be taken care of appropriately in any medical services element while getting to or executing EHR.

4.1 Application of blockchain in healthcare

In building up many areas of healthcare, such as device tracking, medical device assets, medical trials, drug tracing, and health insurance, blockchain plays important roles. These are listed as follows.

4.1.1 For device tracking

Blockchain behaves like a spy-cam. Smart contracts are written in blockchain that support tracking fake drugs and identifying pills boxes using radio frequency identification (RFID).

4.1.2 Within clinical trials

Blockchain promotes integrity, solves the problem of false results and data removal, and keeps immutable logs that help the pharmaceutical industry to improve its efficiency and increase transparency and audibility.

4.1.3 For drug tracking

RFID is used so that genuine medicines reach patients. RFID allows monitoring the whole custody chain to ensure that medicines are purchased from authentic sources in the hospital. If by using blockchain it is found that drugs were modified or tampered with at the point of production, then fake medicines are removed from the supply chain entirely.

4.1.4 Management of claims and charges

Blockchain helps to reduce problems that patients face during processing claims and payments. Blockchain permits sharing a contract with all parties of a single copy and documents related to billing. The healthcare sector continues to have high levels of medical billing fraud. Some common healthcare fraud involves providers claiming charges for services that are not done and unnecessary medical services.

4.1.5 Maintaining medical history

Sometimes patients cannot visit the hospital frequently, so the hospital does not maintain such patient records. Due to the unavailability of medical and laboratory records, the patient may have to repeat the same tests, resulting in recurring costs potential harm to the patient. This problem is solved by blockchain. Blockchain helps to preserve patient records.

4.1.6 Billing/payers

The billing process requires more resources, takes a longer time to clear claims, and results in delays in receiving bills. Many times, billing-related fraud also takes place. Further, sometimes it takes more than a week for bill claims when an insurance company participates in the payment procedure. Blockchain-based payment makes the billing process much easier and fraud-free. In addition, the insurance claims can be faster and resources, time, and cost can be reduced [34,35].

5 Technological advantages of blockchain

The benefits of blockchain technology are as follows.

5.1 Durability

Blockchain enables all parties to provide transactions without human or computer errors. These are maintained in the central register and connected through the distributed registry system. These are secured by a validation process, which is adoption of the hashing technique.

5.2 Transparency

All transactions work in a real-time environment in blockchain. A copy of every transaction is known as a node so a user can always audit and inspect data.

5.3 Immutability

In the blockchain environment, a block cannot be modified when a transaction has been made. This is because each authorized user has been sent a copy of that transaction.

5.4 Process integrity

This consists of maintaining and ensuring the accuracy and coherence of data over the entire life.

6 The problem statement

The sharing of healthcare data among various institutions, hospitals, and healthcare providers is complex. It is likely to increase clinical research and efficiency significantly [36]. Data sharing faces many problems, including:

Security
   Securing electronic medical records is a challenging task [37]. During data sharing, the main focus is on privacy and confidentiality. Privacy for patients is not only a moral responsibility, but a legal requirement as well [38]. Data confidentiality is a way through which only a summary or partial information is shared.
Framework
   Data sharing traditionally involves a centrally controlled dataset that increases the security risk and requires confidence in a centralized data source.
Interoperability
   Data should be shared so that the structure and meaning can be comprehended by all parties.

6.1 Smart contract in blockchain

Smart contracts were first proposed in 1994 by Nick Szabo, an American computer researcher who created a virtual money called "Spot Gold" in 1998. This was 10 years before the creation of Bitcoin. It is a type of Ethereum account. The concept of a smart contract is shown in Fig. 7 and its advantages are shown in Fig. 8. It is an assortment of code and information that dwells at a particular location on the Ethereum blockchain. Solidity language is widely used to write smart contracts. Solidity checks the program at runtime.

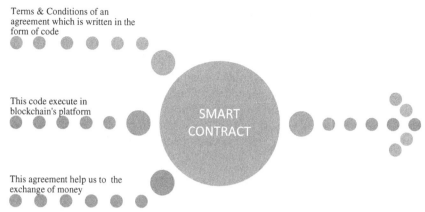

Fig. 7 Smart contract concept.

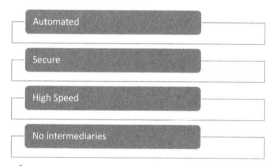

Fig. 8 Advantages of smart contract.

7 The system architecture: Ethereum—Remix IDE

Ethereum designers use truffle integrated, development and environment (IDE) that incorporates aggregation, testing, and organization of smart contracts. The developers can design DApps utilizing truffle that works with the smooth and consistent turn of events. DApps would be able to detect abnormalities, unauthorized data, and lack of data. The smart health (DASH) DApps offer an online gateway to patients to access, update, and present records. DApps also provides the option of reviewing patient authorization data.

The main elements of smart contracts are written in the Solidity programming language. Remix IDE has been used to deploy the smart contract. The supply chain system was implemented and used by Remix IDE [39]. For online debugging, analysis, and deployment, Remix is a very useful tool.

8 The proposed methodology

In the proposed framework, when the patient visits the hospital for the first time, she/he must register. Thereafter, the patient is directed to a doctor for the ailment. The physician uploads the patient's information and sends it to all departments such as third-party administrator (TPA), laboratory, blood bank, medicine, etc. Blockchain will assist the specialist in prescribing the right medication after looking at the patient history. Fig. 9 represents a smart contract-based framework of a hospital for better clarity and communication. Fig. 10 showcases the flowchart of the proposed model.

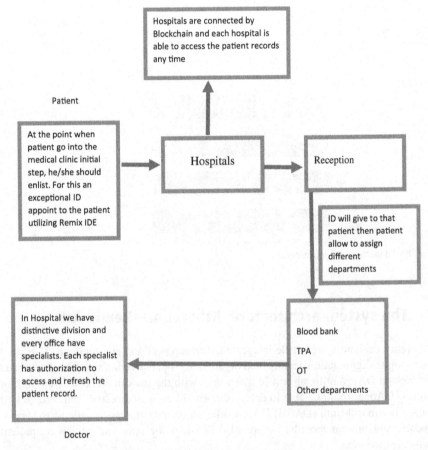

Fig. 9 Smart contract-based framework of the hospital.

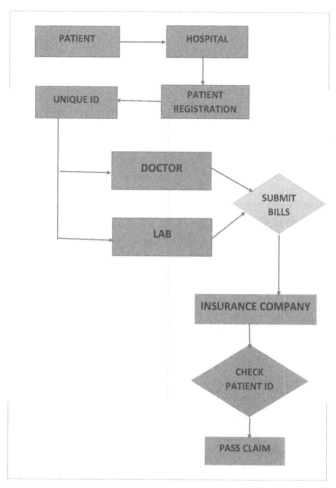

Fig. 10 Flowchart of the proposed model.

8.1 Pseudocode to create a smart insurance contract

The pseudocode for the proposed smart contract is as follows.

```
contract PatientInsurance {
  address Ow;
  struct patient {
    bool uid;
    string patientname;
    uint amtInsured;
  }
  mapping(address =>patient)public patientmapping;
  mapping(address =>bool)public doctmapping;
  constructor(){
    Ow=msg.sender;
  }
  modifier onlyOw() {
```

```
require (Ow==msg.sender);
;
}
function setDoct(address _address)onlyOw{
require(!doctmapping[_address]);
doctmapping[_address]=true;
}
function setPatientData (string _patientname, uint _amtInsured)
returns(address) {
address uniqueId=address(sha256(msg.sender,now));
require (!patientmapping[uniqueId].uid);
patientmapping[uniqueId]. uid=true;
patientmapping[uniqueId].patientname=_patientname;
patientmapping[uniqueId]. amtInsured =_amtInsured;

return uniqueId;
}
function  useInsurance  (address  _uniqueId,  uint  _amtUsed)
returns(string){
// require(doctmapping[msg.sender]);
if(patientmapping[_uniqueId].amtInsured< _amtUsed) {
throw;
}
patientmapping[_uniqueId].amtInsured-=_amtUsed;
return "Insurance has used successfully";
}
}
```

The above pseudocode represents a smart contract that would assist hospitals in receiving money from an insurance company on behalf of patients. To achieve it, the following steps are executed in the design of the smart contract.

1. A structure named as a patient is declared in which variables such as unique ID, patient name, amount to be insured, etc., are declared.
2. Every time a patient files for insurance in the company, the company using a bool variable checks the existence of the unique ID.
3. Mapping function: Every time a patient applies for insurance, a unique ID is generated that checks whether a patient is registered.
4. A constructor is defined and invoked.
5. Modifiers put conditions on any function that we use and restrict that access function.
6. Function setdoct: This function takes the address as an argument to check whether an address of a doctor exists.
7. **Function setpatientdata:** This function sets the citizen data into data mapping and generates the unique ID with the SHA 256 hashing technique. The ID generated after "set patient data" copies the unique ID generated by hashing techniques. In the console window, "ID" come sunder head deploy output. After that, the address is copied and pasted into citizen mapping.
8. **Function useinsurance:** This function takes two arguments: a doctor's unique ID and the expenditure incurred in treating the patient. Using the **require** method, it checks that the person in the **doctor mapping** module is an authorized doctor.
   The **execute and check** module checks whether the expenditure incurred in treating the patient is more than the insured amount; if so, it flashes an error. If the condition is true, it

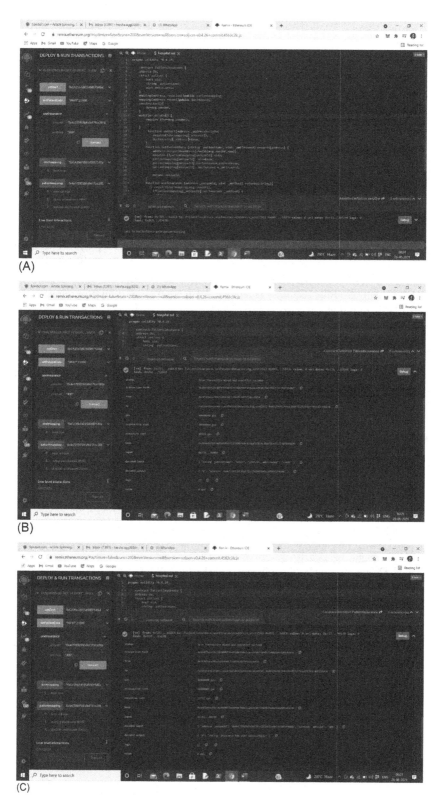

Fig. 11 (A)–(C) Snapshots of the smart insurance contract on REMIX IDE.

generates an error message; otherwise, the amount incurred is deducted from the amount insured and a successful transaction message is displayed. Fig. 11A–C show sample snapshots of a smart insurance contract designed and developed using Solidity on REMIX IDE.

9 Conclusion

With new headways in web and organization advancements, there is a reasonable requirement to handle and upgrade the clinical and well-being administration in hospitals. There are various data management and security inadequacies in the current medical care framework. These inadequacies have been well addressed by blockchain. Blockchain has written a new chapter in the healthcare sector as it plays an important role in keeping online healthcare information safe and secure. To exchange, monitor, and check patient data, the smart intelligent insurance contract was designed and developed using Solidity. Solidity is an intelligent contract writing programming language that is highly contract-oriented. Blockchain features help to overcome issues such as health sector' data security and privacy challenges.

In the COVID-19 pandemic, blockchain may assume a vital part. With the assistance of blockchain, numerous clinics may interface with each other to assist specialists in directly facing patients and remotely monitoring patients. By utilizing this innovation, all clinics can interface and update a patient's records simultaneously while more accurately dealing with all the basic circumstances.

References

[1] H. Wang, Y. Song, Secure cloud-based EHR system using attribute-based cryptosystem and blockchain, J. Med. Syst. 42 (8) (2018) 152.
[2] D.C. Nguyen, P.N. Pathirana, M. Ding, A. Senevirantne, Blockchain for secure EHR sharing of mobile cloud based e-health systems, IEEE Access 7 (2019) 66792–66806.
[3] A. Siyal, A.Z. Junejo, M. Zawish, K. Ahmed, A. Khalil, G. Soursou, Applications of Blockchain technology in medicine and healthcare: challenges and future perspectives, Cryptography 3 (1) (2019) 3.
[4] V.K. Chattu, A. Nanda, S.K. Chattu, S.M. Kadri, A.W. Knight, The emerging role of Blockchain technology applications in routine disease surveillance systems to strengthen global health security, Big Data Cogn. Comput. 3 (2) (2019) 25 (online).
[5] R. Zhang, R. Xue, L. Liu, Security and privacy on Blockchain, ACM Comput. Surv. 52 (3) (2019) 1–34. abs/1903.07602 (Online).
[6] M.A. Uddin, A. Stranieri, I. Gondal, V. Balasubramanian, Continuous patient monitoring with a patient centric agent: a block architecture, IEEE Access 6 (2018) 32700–32726.
[7] K. Fan, S. Wang, Y. Ren, Y. Yang, Medblock: efficient and secure medical data sharing via Blockchain, J. Med. Syst. 42 (8) (2018) 136.
[8] N. Rifi, E. Rachkidi, N. Agoulmine, N.C. Taher, Towards using Blockchain technology for eHealth data access management, in: Proceedings of the 4th ICABME October, 2017, pp. 1–4.
[9] K.N. Griggs, O. Ossipova, C.P. Kohlios, A.N. Baccarini, E.A. Howson, T. Hayajnesh, Healthcare Blockchain system using smart contracts for secure automated remote patient monitoring, J. Med. Syst. 42 (7) (2018) 1–7.

[10] G. Srivastava, A.D. Dwivedi, R. Singh, Automated remote patient monitoring: data sharing and privacy using Blockchain, ArXiv (2018). vol. abs/1811.03417.

[11] B. Shen, J. Guo, Y. Yang, Medchain: efficient healthcare data sharing via Blockchain, Appl. Sci. 9 (2019) 1207.

[12] S. Khezr, M. Moniruzzaman, A. Yassine, R. Benlamri, Blockchain technology in healthcare: a comprehensive review and directions for future research, Appl. Sci. 9 (2019) 1736.

[13] A.T. Litchfield, A. Khan, A review of issues in healthcare information management systems and Blockchain solutions, in: CONF-IRM, 2019.

[14] J. Vora, A. Nayyar, S. Tanwar, S. Tyagi, N. Kumar, M.S. Obaidat, J.J. Rodrigues, BHEEM: a blockchain-based framework for securing electronic health records, in: Proceedings of the 2018 IEEE Globecom Workshops (GC Wkshps), Abu Dhabi, UAE, 9–13 December, 2018.

[15] P. Zhang, D.C. Schmidt, J. White, G. Lenz, Blockchain technology use cases in healthcare, in: Advances in Computers, vol. 111, Elsevier, Amsterdam, The Netherlands, 2018, pp. 1–41.

[16] S. Rouhani, L. Butterworth, A.D. Simmons, D.G. Humphery, R. Deters, MediChainTM: a secure decentralized medical data asset management system, in: Proceedings of the 2018 IEEE International Conference on Internet of Things (iThings) and IEEE Green Computing and Communications (GreenCom) and IEEE Cyber, Physical and Social Computing (CPSCom) and IEEE Smart Data (SmartData), Halifax, NS, Canada, 30 July–3 August, 2018.

[17] A.A. Vazirani, O. O'Donoghue, D. Brindley, E. Meinert, Implementing Blockchains for E_client health care: systematic review, J. Med. Internet Res. 21 (2019), e12439.

[18] W.J. Gordon, C. Catalini, Blockchain technology for healthcare: facilitating the transition to patient-driven interoperability, Comput. Struct. Biotechnol. J. 16 (2018) 224–230.

[19] T. Kumar, V. Ramani, I. Ahmad, A. Braeken, E. Harjula, M. Ylianttila, Blockchain utilization in healthcare: key requirements and challenges, in: Proceedings of the 2018 IEEE 20th International Conference on e-Health Networking, Applications and Services (Healthcom), Ostrava, Czech Republic, 17–20 September, 2018.

[20] S. Rahmadika, K.-H. Rhee, Blockchain technology for providing an architecture model of personal health information, Int. J. Eng. Bus Manage. (2018), https://doi.org/10.1177/1847979018790589.

[21] A. Zhang, X. Lin, Towards secure and privacy-preserving data sharing in e-health systems via consortium Blockchain, J. Med. Syst. 42 (8) (2018) 140.

[22] M.B. Hoy, Introduction to the Blockchain and its implications for libraries and medicines, Med. Ref. Serv. Q. 36 (3) (2017) 273–279.

[23] S. Nakamoto, Bitcoin: A Peer-to-Peer Electronic Cash System, Tech.Bitcoin.Org, 2008.

[24] K.V.O. Rabah, "Challenges & opportunities for Blockchain-powered healthcare systems". A review, Mara Res. J. Med. Health Sci. 1 (2017) 45–52.

[25] M. Holbl, M. Kompara, A. Kamisalic, L.N. Zlatolas, A systematic review of the use of Blockchain in healthcare, Symmetry 10 (2018) 470.

[26] M. Swan, Blockchain: Blueprint for a New Economy, O'Reilly Media, Inc., Sebastopol, CA, USA, 2015.

[27] A. Ovais, Block Chain Technology: Concept of Digital Economics, University Library of Munich, Munich, Germany, 2017.

[28] X. Yue, H. Wang, D. Jin, W. Jiang, Healthcare data gateways: found healthcare intelligence on Blockchain with novel privacy risk control, J. Med. Syst. 40 (2016) 218.

[29] N.J. Witchey, Healthcare Transaction Validation via Blockchain, Systems and Methods, U.S. Patent No. 10,340,038, 2019.

[30] H.M. Hussien, S.M. Yasin, S. Udzir, A.A. Zaidan, B.B. Zaidan, A systematic review for enabling of develop a Blockchain technology in healthcare application: taxonomy, substantially analysis, motivations, challenges, recommendations and future direction, J. Med. Syst. 43 (10) (2019) 320.

[31] P. Zhang, M.A. Walker, J. White, D.C. Schmidt, G. Lenz, Metrics for assessing Blockchain-based healthcare decentralized apps, in: Proceedings of the 2017 IEEE 19th International Conference on e-Health Networking, Applications and Services (Healthcom), Dalian, China, 12–15 October, 2017.

[32] A. Azaria, A. Ekblaw, A. Lippman, T. Vieria, MedRec: using Blockchain for medical data access and permission management, in: International Conference in open and Big Data, IEEE, Vienna, Austria, 2016, p. 2530.

[33] C.A. Gunter, Building a smarter health and wellness future: privacy and security challenges, in: ICTs and the Health Sector: Towards Smarter Health and Wellness Models, OECD, 2013, pp. 141–157.

[34] E. Clauson, A. Mark, Hitching healthcare to the chain: an introduction to Blockchain technology in the healthcare sector, Technol. Innov. Manage. Rev. 7 (10) (2017).

[35] M.N.K. Boulos, J.T. Wilson, K.A. Clauson, Geospatial Blockchain: promises, challenges, and scenarios in health and healthcare, Int. J. Health Geogr. 17 (1) (2018) 1–10.

[36] Y. Ge, D.K. Ahn, H. Bhagyashree Unde, D. Gage, J. Jeffrey Carr, Patient-controlled sharing of medical imaging data across unaffiliated healthcare organizations, J. Am. Med. Inform. Assoc. 20 (1) (2013) 157–163.

[37] R.C. Barrows, P.D. Clayton, Privacy, confidentiality, and electronic medical records, J. Am. Med. Inform. Assoc. 3 (2) (1996) 139–148.

[38] Centre for Disease Control, Prevention, et al., HIPAA privacy rule and public health. Guidance from CDC and the US Department of Health and Human Services, MMWR Morb. Mortal. Wkly Rep. 52 (Suppl. 1) (2003) 1–17.

[39] M. Di Angelo, G. Salzer, A survey of tools for analyzing ethereum smart contracts, in: 2019 IEEE International Conference on Decentralized Applications and Infrastructures (DAPPCON), IEEE, 2019, pp. 69–78.

Amalgamation of blockchain, IoT, and 5G to improve security and privacy of smart healthcare systems

13

M. Kumaresan[a], R. Gopal[b], M. Mathivanan[c], and T. Poongodi[d]
[a]Department of Computer Science and Engineering, Jain Deemed-to-be University, Jakkasantra Post, Kanakapur Taluk, Ramanagar, India, [b]Information and Communication Engineering, College of Engineering, University of Buraimi, Al Buraimi, Sultanate of Oman, [c]Department of Electronics & Communication Engineering, ACS College of Engineering, Bangalore, India, [d]School of Computing Science and Engineering, Galgotias University, Greater Noida, Delhi, NCR, India

1 Introduction

Advances in technology over the past decades have revealed developments as well as disasters. Every new innovation shows interest in improvements in science and engineering, which will help in many ways where people struggle in their lives. Healthcare monitoring is also one of the domains that is developing very fast in many ways, including helping to identify diseases in early stages, taking different types of scans of internal and external parts, monitoring patients in each stage, curing diseases, and retaining the patient health condition. Healthcare monitoring has been categorized into Healthcare 1.0 through Healthcare 4.0, beginning in the 1800s and continuing through today.

This chapter deals with monitoring and taking care of patients affected by normal to dangerous diseases using 5G technology. So, the identification of diseases using artificial intelligence (AI), machine learning (ML), etc., is differentiated into various types [1]. In this regard, the collective measures of cleanliness, germ control, vaccination, and epidemiology formed a better atmosphere for a healthy life. Past days of Healthcare 1.0 in which main health problems were determined with smart public health methods.

Famed pharmaceutical companies were formed a few years before the end of the 19th century. With the support of industrial mass manufacturing technology, some antibiotics were introduced to the market after that period. Hospitals were larger and had more staff while doctors were trained for specialties to deal with more patients and the complicated conditions of the 19th century were cured. That was Healthcare 2.0.

Blockchain Applications for Healthcare Informatics. https://doi.org/10.1016/B978-0-323-90615-9.00015-3
Copyright © 2022 Elsevier Inc. All rights reserved.

With the latest technology, tomography leaped from single images to reassembled images, allowing doctors to scrutinize lesions with extra information and recognize diseases earlier. Most medical literature can be transferred from e-libraries. Information technology comprises the basis of healthcare Healthcare 3.0.

Today, the industrial revolution [2–5] has transformed to its next version called as Healthcare 4.0 with the help of computerization and data interchange techniques. The accuracy medicine monitors the treatment by using additional complete molecular diagnoses. Telemedicine will brand be seeing or being seen cooler, and of course it is not possible without IoT. The new indicators include automaton, minilaboratories, wearable devices, personalized materials, etc.

1.1 Motivations

Wireless innovations have been rapidly advancing all over the world in recent years. Fifth-generation (5G) wireless technology has emerged as a particularly challenging and intriguing subject in wireless science. The Internet of Things (IoT) will be a game changer in the 5G era. It will pave the way for innovative wireless architecture and intelligent services. The existing 4G cellular network is not adequate or effective enough to fulfill the challenges of multiple users. Device compatibility and fast data rates as well as additional bandwidth, low latency service quality, and low interruption are all advantages to deal with these challenges. We believe 5G is the most exciting technology. 5G IoT networks will also provide a comprehensive description of the problems and visions of different communication industries while giving a systematic review of evolving and supporting technologies for the 5G framework, which enables IoT [1,2,4–6].

In IoT-based 5G wireless networks, fast data, low latency, efficient spectrum utilization, and coexistence of different network technologies are all important factors. AI must be used to make efficient decisions based on the vast amounts of data provided by the large number of IoT devices to meet the above requirements [7]. AI methods examine data to extract patterns and develop a sense of them so that end devices can take action. We begin by providing an overview of 5G and IoT technologies as well as IoT-based 5G enabling technologies, then meet the issues and relevant solutions.

As shown in Fig. 1. IoT in a 5G context consists primarily of a five-layered architecture [8–11] and data collection, processing, analysis, and exchange of information between systems and communication networks.

(i) *Sensor layer*: It interacts with the network layer and basically contains a physical layer structure such as sensors.
(ii) *Network layer*: CARP, 6LoWPAN, Sigfox, LoRa, RPL, and ZigBee are examples of this layer in IoT.
(iii) *Communication layer*: This is the foundation of IoT architecture, and it performs data transfer between the different layers.
(iv) *Architecture layer*: This is layer stores and processes the huge amounts of data.
(v) *Technology/application layer*: Smart applications such as factories, houses, agriculture, transportation, and other IoT applications can be realized. It connects all other smart devices and data to the Internet through wireless connectivity.

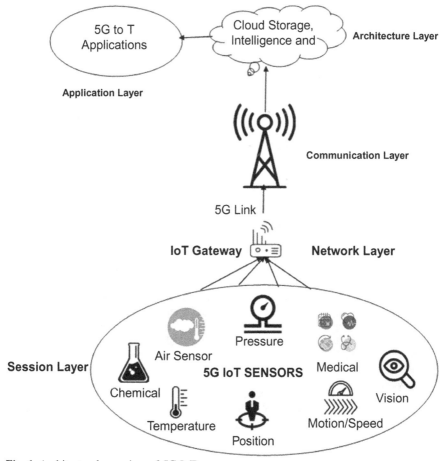

Fig. 1 Architectural overview of 5G IoT.

A wide variety of applications are available with 5G Machine-Type Communication (MTC). Future wireless technology would enable machines and devices to communicate without being interrupted by humans [12]. Higher data rates, latency, speed, and multiple device connectivity are all technologies that should be considered in wide areas of application [8,13].

The different level applications are shown in Fig. 2 [2,3,10,14–18], and include:

(i) *Smart cities:* The world is coming closer to anywhere, anytime connectivity. Future wireless technology would have a data speed of up to 2GB/s, which is 10 times faster than current technology, allowing for smart communications between devices as well as high-speed Internet access. A smart city provides efficient service based on public resources. Create smart cities and use MTC's multitier technologies, which include smart buildings, grids, transportation, garbage collection and management, and smart lighting, and all these applications work together [8,9].

Fig. 2 Applications of 5G IoT.

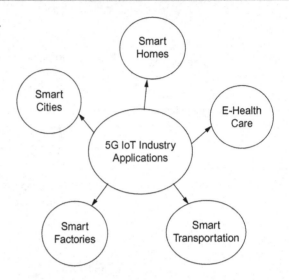

(ii) *Smart homes:* Wireless technology enables household appliances to communicate with one another. 5G technology enables computers and devices to communicate without being interrupted by humans. Refrigerators, air conditioners, televisions, and other electronic devices are all enabled with the Internet for smart and effective operation.

(iii) *E-Healthcare:* Considering the adage "health is wealth," telemedicine is a term that refers to providing improvements in the medical field. Connectivity via a 5G link allows the medical field to be smarter. The 5G telemedicine system provides remote areas with effective patient monitoring. Via the 5G communication connection, patient health signs such as ECG, body temperature, and pressure are transmitted from remote hospitals to well-equipped hospitals.

   Doctors can diagnose based on healthcare records. Finally, 5G connections would be a full-duplex communication device, with care taking place in remote hospitals based on diagnosis reports sent from major hospitals. For smooth operation, hospitals are equipped with high-speed Internet connectivity as well as contact between hospitals, physicians, pharmacies, and administration.

(iv) *Smart transportation*: Another popular application of 5G IoT is smart transportation, also known as ITSs. Every vehicle will have smart sensors and a control unit to track and control the vehicle in future transportation systems. This will be safe, effective, and efficient.

(v) *Smart factories*: Another significant IoT application is the smart factory. This is referred to as the fourth Industrial Revolution, where all operations are governed by digital technology. Smart factories with modern technology that implement and communicate through advanced LPN protocols, software's and an industrial method. Bringing the fourth Industrial Revolution necessitates critical processes such as cooperation between businesses, governments, and institutions. The cyberphysical system (CPS) is critical to the IoT industry's effective implementation because it saves money on manpower, technicians, and engineers. The following major technological trends are needed for smart factories:

   (a) Smart sensor applications.
   (b) Artificial intelligence.
   (c) Cloud-based robotics concepts.
   (d) Intellectual robotic Internet.

1.2   Contributions

Cryptographic concepts are used to protect and connect each of these blocks of data (i.e., block, chain). The chain is formed inexorably, and new squares are added in ways that few might imagine, with each new square containing a reference (i.e., a hash value) to the substance of the previous square. Financial experts, who are often referred to as blockchain hubs, work together in a distributed peer-to-peer (P2P) organization. Each hub in the association is responsible for two keys: a public key for encoding messages sent from a hub and a private key for unraveling the messages and allowing a hub to receive them. The public key encryption instrument is used = to ensure a blockchain's consistency, irreversibility, and nonreputability. The indicated hash, which is created using a cryptographic single bearing hash work, is used to connect all the squares in the blockchain (e.g., SHA256). The fact that blockchain is much more stable than its competitors is a factor that works in its favor. In this age of data and knowledge, immutability is something that more and more businesses are seeking. With its wide range of future applications, blockchain is ready to become a part of our everyday lives.

1.3   Organization

The smart healthcare systems nowadays have interlink of the following areas. In Chapter 2, 5G-based smart healthcare technologies are discussed. This includes the architecture, taxonomy, and the way to implement the latest applications; this includes discussions about COVID-19. Chapter 3 contains security and privacy issues in smart healthcare. Here, different types of security and privacy of important data are discussed. Chapter 4 has security concerns in healthcare data. Chapter 5 contains a comparative analysis for healthcare data using IoT and blockchain technology. After that, open research challenges and future directions are discussed in Chapter 6. Finally, in Chapter 7 the contextual investigation of the IBM blockchain healthcare drive is explained in detail.

2   5G-based smart healthcare technologies

Traveling when sick can be difficult and time-consuming for people who live in remote areas with doctors who are many miles away. We could, however, receive treatment from the comfort of our own homes, thanks to the development of telehealth and remote home monitoring systems. Doctors may make suggestions and even send medication requests after a brief video call. However, remote monitoring, in combination with sophisticated imaging equipment, will put additional pressure on healthcare industry business networks. This often causes network congestion and slows network speeds, especially for healthcare providers who can interact with hundreds of patients every day. The lag is not only inconvenient for those who use it, but the low quality can cause delays in patient care, potentially harming long-term outcomes. The amount of data on networks is expected to expand even further as the use of IoT technology continues to grow. 5G technologies can assist in the resolution of these issues. Here are a few examples of how 5G technology [19] can assist healthcare organizations in meeting the rising demands of digital transformation.

Objectives for Smart Healthcare

• Optimization of resources
• Enhancing the quality of service
• Reducing the difficulties of patients

Enhancing the efficiency of treatment using the latest technologies, 5G networks allow the development of novel network services established through various network functions in comparison to current 4G networks. Depending on the application requirements, these networks may be hosted on Internet cloud servers and with the operator offices, or at the user end. MEC servers, which are fitted with storage and processing capacity and are located at the radio network's edge, would be an ideal platform for hosting these applications. Because of recent techniques, the introduction of such applications in 5G networks would be more versatile. Bringing NFs closer to the edge reduces reliance on infrastructure outside the end user and makes applications more reliable. Because the network is programmable, increasing the convenience of the 5G network is far simpler. 5G networks can implement network slices to build logical networks that cater to services with identical specifications, such as IoT-based applications and low latency, ensuring that applications are served with assured service levels.

2.1 5G design criteria and its impact on healthcare

Diabetes patients are constantly assessed and monitored by a health monitoring system that uses 5G technology with IoT. Wearable IoT devices enable various smart healthcare applications on smartphones using the latest WSN as well as the support of 5G and an IoT-based solution for continuously checking chronic patients. For continuous health tracking, wearable devices and sensors capture different data such as heartbeat rate, time taken for sleeping, and the bodily movement activities of the patients. Smart assistance in the mobile health system helps continuous monitoring of chronic patients, and has been suggested using IoT mobile gateways [20–22]. IoT is applied for many medical applications, such as remote monitoring of chronic disease patients. Wearable devices have been suggested to facilitate contact between wearables and cloud servers, which are virtual servers that operate in a cloud atmosphere and are used to retrieve data distantly over the Internet. Typically, wearable devices capture data from different sensors and send the pulse rate, ECG readings, and various health conditions to a cloud server via the Internet to the doctors. The use of smart healthcare technologies could be boosted by 5G and IoT. Smart healthcare applications are expected to benefit from the new 5G network, which is expected to meet most of the specifications, including very low latency, more bandwidth, more reliability, high density, and high energy consumption. In the future, smart healthcare-based networks are expected to be made up of a mix of 5G with the latest IoT devices that will improve mobile range coverage and base station network capacity while resolving security concerns.

2.1.1 Role of 5G network

The main concept of IoT is supported by 5G technology in mobile networks. This will encourage the use of a large number of smart devices to improve supply chain performance. Industry demands an improved way to incorporate sensors, actuators, and robotics in the 5G network, allowing for a smart manufacturing infrastructure. The mmWave 5G small cells arranged for indoor cases will allow appropriate network connectivity for medical-related sensors, actuators, and miniaturized robots in industrial areas. As a result, 5G communications represent a standard change from current mobile networks in terms of delivering ubiquitous high-rate access and a consistent user experience.

2.2 5G smart healthcare architecture and taxonomy

The healthcare industry is divided into two categories: private services that compete with each other, and mandatory services that are given to all. Also, hospitals, which provide essential care, are evolving into strategic entities. Because several different forms of health problems are growing with the patient population, the majority of the hospitals in the world are privately owned. Hospitals, nursing homes, and retirement homes are also part of the healthcare industry. The usage of IoT devices, smartphones, wearable tags, and other similar devices is the capabilities of e-healthcare systems all over the world. In this case, information and communication technology (ICT) improves [23,24] the management of healthcare applications that manage patient medical information and data in the server.

(i) *5G Architecture*:

Small cells used in the network are less-powered wireless contact nodes with a distance of a few meters to a mile. Small cells come in a variety of shapes and sizes, and they can be useful in a variety of 5G smart healthcare applications. Small cells are one option for applications that demand high data rates. Heterogeneous networks refer to cellular networks that include macro, micro, pico, and femto base stations (HetNets). These are used to achieve spectral quality and versatile coverage.

Performance enhancement of 5G

- Peak data speeds of up to 10 gigabits per second (Gbps) are possible, and 20 gigabits per second is possible under some conditions and scenarios.
- Services with ultralow latency requirements may be provided.
- The network can achieve high mobility.
- Allows massive machine-to-machine communication while maintaining a high-density network.

(ii) *Communication technologies for smart healthcare*:

To pass data between devices and servers, smart healthcare relies on a variety of short- and long-range communication technologies. Wi-Fi, Zig-Bee, Bluetooth, and WiMAX are the most popular short-range wireless technologies, and they are mainly used for small connectivity in smart healthcare applications. In smart healthcare, a variety of technologies such as GPRS, Edge, LTE, and LTE advanced are used to transfer data from a local server to a base station.

(iii) *Telehealth facilities for patients*:

Telehealth facilities for patients is the method [20]. Remotely associated clinical healthcare, health-oriented education, public awareness for health, and fitness-related administration are examples of these facilities, which define a wider spectrum of services. Telemedicine is a term used to describe remote experimental facilities such as healthcare distribution, analysis, consultation, and treatment, in which a healthcare supplier uses communication technology to provide care to the patient at a distant location.

2.3   5G-based healthcare options for COVID-19

The pandemic initiated by the new coronavirus is currently posing the greatest global public health threat. According to the most recent survey of the World Health Organization (WHO), the number of COVID-19 cases surpassed 31 million as of September 2020, with an estimated 960,000 deaths [18]. The motive of this chapter is to evaluate the role of IoT-related technologies in COVID-19 for finding patients and controlling spread as well as examining the current architectures, frameworks, medical-based applications, and industrial facility for IoT based explanations for fighting COVID-19 in three different phases as early time diagnosis, quarantine to avoid spreading, and recovery of infection. Initial identification and diagnosis will result in fewer infections and better healthcare treatment for those who are diseased. Separating infected persons from others, isolating established or suspected cases, and executing lockdowns will help reduce the number of people affected by COVID-19. Following up on COVID-19 patients after they have recovered can aid in observing the recurrence of signs and infections in these improved cases.

(i) *Role of IoT in COVID-19*:

Wearable technologies are described as a mixture of electronics and everything that can be worn on the body. Healthcare systems which is application oriented obtain and process input while being damaged or stuck to the body, such as bands, glasses, and watches, according to Juniper Research's description. These smart wearables were created for a variety of uses in fields such as healthcare, wellness, and lifestyle. Smartphone applications are pieces of software that are programmed to perform specific tasks on a mobile device such as a smart phone [25]. These applications are very active in various fields such as healthcare, marketing, and farming, given that there will be 3.5 billion active smart phones in 2020. Many smart phone applications for the healthcare industry have been developed, and some have been used in response to COVID-19.

In order to implement the suggested solutions, many problems in the areas of security and privacy, scalability, restricted access, social concerns, and legal aspects must be addressed. Engineers, technology managers, healthcare staff, government officials, academics, and the overall public, among others, are confident that the proposed groundbreaking 5G and IoT-based technologies would allow them to perform their normal duties and functions. However, the lack of widely accessible 5G communication networks currently limits the pace at which proposed technology can be adopted. It is worth noting, however, that 5G networks are increasingly being deployed all over the world.

3 Security and privacy issues in smart healthcare

3.1 IoT-enabled health trackers in healthcare

The IoT extends seamless connectivity to all embedded devices such as wearables, electrical appliances, and so on. It enables each device to be able to be accessed with unique identifiers to perform functions in a variety of industries. The IoT has revolutionized the healthcare industry by enabling autonomous monitoring and diagnoses of patients using continuous health tracking services [11]. Patients are no longer required to exclusively visit hospitals to analyze their health conditions. They can easily access medical treatments and consultations remotely from their home. The availability of complete real-time health data of the patients enables quicker and more efficient diagnoses by the physicians.

3.1.1 Remote treatment with IoT-enabled health devices

The IoT enables the health data measured in smart wearables to be automatically transferred to an intelligent server that can alert the patient or physician in case of any observed abnormalities. Some of the smart health tracking devices available are smart clothes, fitness bands, smart medicine bottles, smart glasses, pulse oximeters, machine vision technology, fitness trackers, automated stethoscopes, moodables, wired football helmets, hearables, and other wearables. The ability of doctors to ensure patient compliance is a key benefit of using IoT in connected devices. Physicians may use linked medical devices to track whether patients are adhering to dosing schedules while prescribing medications and related dosing schedules.

3.1.2 IoT-based healthcare devices

* Automatic temperature monitoring for vaccinations
* Air supervision/quality sensors
* Patient sleep monitoring
* Child sleep monitoring device
* Medical data transfer tools
* Tracking of drug effectiveness
* Symptoms for data capturing and recording

3.1.3 IoT-enabled telemedicine

The immediate availability of real-time health data enables remote monitoring and diagnoses of patients by physicians. It is particularly helpful in rural areas where access to the best healthcare facilities is not available in practice. In addition, it would also be helpful for elderly patients who find it difficult to regularly visit the physician for medical advice due to their health conditions. Instead, their physician could remotely monitor their health and prescribe the required medication. Telemedicine enables access to state-of-the-art healthcare for patients just being in their home. They could also use voice assistant smart solutions such as Alexa to order their medication from the pharmacy, who could in turn consult the physician for the appropriate medications.

3.1.4   Challenges of IoT-powered telemedicine

Data authentication, secure and reliable data transfer, data protection, and the adoption of smart health tracking devices are the major challenges facing IoT in healthcare. Advanced sensors are currently in place to track the health parameters of patients. So, now special attention is being provided in the research and development of sensors to make them easier to be used by patients. In addition, sophisticated trainings are also provided to healthcare specialists for the successful adoption of smart health devices. To add to that, doctors are now providing patients with live online coaching. Next-generation IoT devices are being developed with ease-of-use wearables for capturing and storing patient vitals, which can then be readily accessed by their physician. This makes sure that patient data are available in a secure manner. Physicians can monitor various health-related parameters such as pulse rate, blood pressure, sleep schedule, body temperature, daily physical activities, and other medical conditions using IoT-powered telemedicine.

3.1.5   The IoT is being used in remote patient monitoring

IoT has made it possible to remotely track patients all over the world. A patient's health is constantly tracked using home-based sensors and smart sensor technology, allowing for the prompt treatment of emergency health issues. Health awareness will improve among patients as a result of IoT, which would improve their daily physical activities. With the aid of fitness bands and other health trackers, patients will be inspired to develop and preserve their personal health, thereby reducing the burden on the healthcare system.

3.1.6   The most significant benefits of IoT in healthcare

*   *Quicker diagnosis*: Patients are constantly tracked by IoT-enabled monitoring systems, which aids in the early diagnosis of diseases or health problems.
*   *Decrease in Medical Expenses*: With the availability of remote healthcare, patients get access to cutting-edge healthcare from their home without the need to visit hospitals. In addition, constant monitoring of health parameters and self-health awareness due to the immediate availability of health data lead to reductions in the need for hospitalization, which would lead to a significant decrease in medical expenses.
*   *Better access to rural healthcare*: In the developing world, most rural areas do not have access to good healthcare in their immediate vicinity. They are required to travel to cities for any health problem. IoT-powered telemedicine would significantly improve this with access to start-of-the-art healthcare from their home.
*   *Elimination of manual errors*: In traditional healthcare, manual errors are always a concern. However, with IoT-enabled healthcare, the complete health data collection process is automated, which significantly reduces manual errors. This in turn results in significant improvements in the quality of diagnostics.

- *Better medical treatment*: The immediate availability of a patient's real-time health vitals could enable specialized treatment. In addition, the effects of each prescribed medication could be directly checked by physicians, which also results in an efficient follow-up process after treatment.
- *Efficient management of medical equipment*: The handling of medical equipment can be improved with IoT by enabling automation, which results in the reduction of manual errors.
- *Identification of side effects at early stages*: The use of next-generation technology aids in the early detection of drug side effects, which benefits both the practitioner and the patient. The earlier identification helps the doctor represcribe alternate medications before the situation becomes worse.
- *Benefits to health insurers*: Prevention is better than a cure. The use of IoT devices aids in the prevention of serious diseases, which in turn offsets the costs for health insurers. So, insurers pass on these benefits to policy holders by providing incentives to those who adopt IoT devices and to those who follow medical recommendations provided by a physician. The use of IoT devices also helps with medical claims being processed in a fair and transparent manner.

The adoption of IoT-powered telemedicine provides a preventative and proactive healthcare infrastructure instead of a reactive treatment when the health condition becomes worse. This aids the healthcare system in focusing on disease prevention so that patients are not required to bear the effects of their illnesses. Smart health monitoring systems aid in the early detection and treatment of health abnormalities. Furthermore, with the aid of IoT-enabled software, patients can obtain customized care because physicians can get a good picture of their lifestyle and case history. This is beneficial to the whole society, including doctors, patients, and insurers, because it improves the overall situation.

3.2 Observing patients using smart contracts

Many healthcare technologies have been created in recent years to improve the healthcare industry. Electronic healthcare science and industry have been transformed by recent advances in information technology (IT) and blockchain technology. The healthcare system has been strengthened and protected thanks to the creation of miniaturized sensors for following up on patient vital signs. The proliferation of portable hand-held health devices has improved the uniformity of health surveillance status, both at the activity and fitness level of health status screening as well as at the medical level. This is done by giving doctors more data as well as the potential for earlier research and follow-up. The interaction and compilation of electronic health records (EHR) include data protection and comfort when exchanging personal medical information. Present systems, on the other hand, struggle to fulfill these criteria due to inconsistencies in security protocols and access control frameworks. The data access should be enhanced with new technologies. The reliability of medical data should be ensured through security and privacy standards by the government. Blockchain opens the door to a revolution in conventional pharmaceuticals, with advantages such as data transparency and privacy.

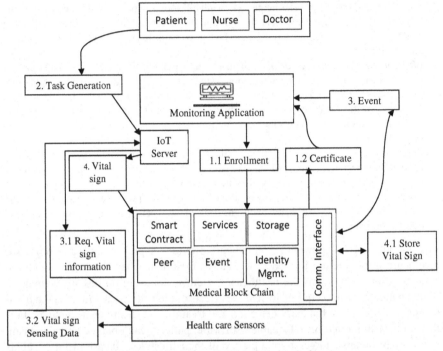

Fig. 3 Workflow of the proposed healthcare IoT blockchain platform.

A new platform is to track patient vitals using smart contracts based on blockchain technology. The design and implementation of the proposed system have been done by using the Hyperledger fabric architecture. The Hyperledger fabric architecture is an enterprise-distributed ledger architecture to design blockchain-oriented applications. Patients benefit from a lengthy, immutable history log as well as comprehensive access to medical information at all times and from any place. To collect physiological data, the Libelium e-Health toolkit is used. The efficiency of the developed system is measured in terms of transactions per second, transaction latency, and resource usage. Hyperledger Caliper, a benchmark method, is used to measure the efficiency [26].

3.3 Blockchain technology solution to healthcare IoT devices

The execution of the proposed blockchain technology solution to healthcare IoT devices is illustrated in Fig. 3. This proposed system incorporates an infrastructure that discloses the distributed ledger (DL) and smart contract through a user service platform. To preserve the homogeneity of the distributed ledger, the medical blockchain model comprises a constant lawful peer where every peer holds a copy of a record of the blockchain network.

The DL is made with a set of blocks for storing unchangeable transactions. To maintain the medical data collected from sensors and various network participants, a data lake is used. The blockchain network serves as a transaction log for the data lake, recording and maintaining all changes. The data lake serves as a database for storing patient information such as modified vital sign values, healthcare device information, and so on. This database is also used for analytic purposes and all healthcare-related services. These healthcare-related services comprise emergency care and preventive care. Transaction requests such as user and device registration and task generation can be handled by REST API by the client framework. Before submitting a transaction, each participant must first register on the blockchain.

A private key is included in the enrollment certificate and is used to sign the transaction. A transaction in the blockchain network consists of read and write from the DL. The participant (patient, nurse, or doctor) may initiate a transaction to the IoT server to newly create a task or receive a reply from an earlier created task. The healthcare IoT (HIoT) server instructs the blockchain network to respond to the request. Next, the healthcare IoT server handover task is created by the user to retrieve the patient's real-time data. These collected data and the patient data are stored in the ledger. Finally, after a satisfactory transaction, a message is sent to the concerned participant [27].

The execution of the healthcare IoT blockchain platform and use case deployment for secure monitoring of a patient's vital signs are presented in Fig. 4. Here, the patient has different vital sign-sensing devices by using a technology based on blockchain. A communication is made among the IoT resources, HIoT, and the blockchain network. An IoT gateway is established by using Raspberry Pi, which routes the vital data to the HIoT server. The HIoT server processes the request and provides the

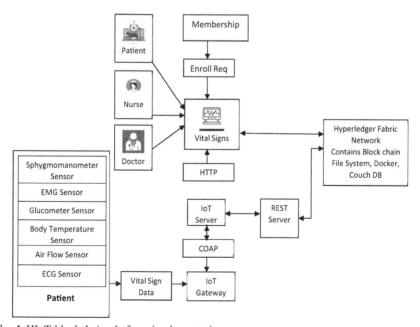

Fig. 4 HIoT blockchain platform implementation.

required data to the client. While processing the request, it filters the data, checks for abnormalities in the vital signs, and provides data in the format prescribed by the client. The Hyperledger fabric framework is used to establish the four-peer blockchain network where each peer is working as an image in a docker container. In this proposed blockchain network, every peer handles the smart contract and data storage to update the transaction to the ledger. REST API is used to access the services given in a smart contract. Using a web socket, the notification to the client is given [26].

4   Security concerns in healthcare data

4.1   *Framework and risk model of smart healthcare*

In recent years, the impact of IoT in the healthcare industry has been more promising, which leads the healthcare system to be more autonomous and robust to environmental conditions. Various frameworks have been developed for the smart healthcare system. The most prominent frameworks used in healthcare are application, efficiency, and security domains. These frameworks are used to design and implement the entire system. They also include the addresses of the data communication, storage and flow, infrastructure needed, and technologies used. The security and data privacy in healthcare are achieved by the use of blockchain technologies in the IoT environment. In the application domain, a list of frameworks has been proposed that follows the design of remote patient monitoring through the distributed system architecture. In the security domain, the privacy of the EHR as well as the location and privacy during data in motion and at rest are considered, and frameworks are designed based on it.

The basic framework model for the smart healthcare system using IoT and blockchain is shown in Fig. 5. The framework consists of various components such

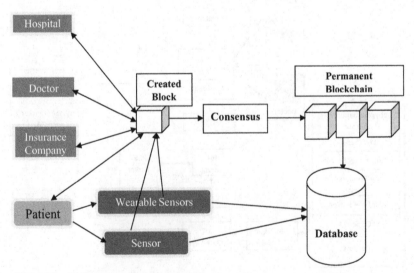

Fig. 5 Framework for a smart healthcare system.

as sensors, stakeholders, transaction management, and blockchain [28]. The sensor component is the IoT part of the smart healthcare system, in which the sensors are implemented. The various types of biosensors are implemented according to patient conditions. The healthcare center which consists of the doctor, the various department of the hospital who are involved in the patient health. The insurance company is also one of the stakeholders in the smart healthcare system, and is related to patients for financial constraints. The stakeholders will generate a block when they want to make a transaction of storing the information related to the patient health record. A database will be maintained to record all the sensor-fetched information along with the created blockchain.

The information will be fetched from sensors that monitor the environment. The sensor can be either wearable or placed in the patient's environment. Wearable sensors will monitor the health parameters in real time in an environment outside the healthcare center and provide recommendations to the patients or communications to the healthcare center in emergency needs. Wearable sensors such as those for heart-beats, breathing and sleep monitoring, and blood pressure can monitor patients con-tinuously and generate data. The data which is obtained from the sensors are measured by using the electrochemical, photoelectric, electromagnetic, and electroacoustic properties and has mobility types as stationary, mobile which in turn classified as in-body, on-body, and transportable.

Wearable sensors [29] provide more accurate data about patient health parameters than traditional testing. Hypoglycemic events can be detected using glucose monitor-ing sensors, as they are not detected in normal blood tests. A more detailed patient status can be obtained by using biosensors that can provide more personalized and patient-centric healthcare solutions and assistance. It is necessary to implement bio-sensors if the patient is bedridden and more assistance is needed. Sensors generate a huge amount of patient data to be analyzed or processed by the clinician. Thus, this data will be stored in the database and access to this database by another stakeholder is managed by the blockchain network.

Stakeholders such as the clinician and hospital are also involved in the smart healthcare system. Based on the patient information collected by the sensors, the doc-tor can diagnose the patient. Once the diagnosis is completed, the details are to be stored in the blockchain. The hospital [30,31], which includes the pharmacy, imaging departments, and more will provide a report and medicine will be given to the patient. All this information is to be secured by the consensus made by the stakeholders before it can be stored in the database. The patient's health status, diagnosis report, medicine provided, and test report will be stored in the database for future reference. A new block will be created and broadcast to the stakeholder for agreement.

Once the stakeholders reach a consensus on the block created, then it will be stored in the database. This database can be a centralized or distributed database in which each stakeholder maintains their own blockchain database. The insurance company will be involved in the healthcare system when the patient raises a claim and the insur-ance company will validate the details provided by the patient from the blockchain created to complete processing the claim. A consensus can be obtained by using var-ious types of algorithms implemented in blockchain such as proof of work, proof of stake, practical Byzantine fault tolerance (PBFT) [32], and many more. For each block created, a hash value will be generated and the hash value of the previous block will be stored as a reference to validate the previous blocks created. A Merkle root, also known as a binary hash tree, is a data structure used to preserve the privacy in the blockchain by calculating a single hash chain from the blockchain created. Any change in the block created will make a change in the Merkle root or the root hash value.

The environment for blockchain in the healthcare system starts with the healthcare center joining the blockchain system. Each healthcare center needs at least one node, which may be a computer, to join the blockchain system. The node which is present in the healthcare center will create the starting block, known as the genesis block, to the blockchain and a secure connection with server outside the healthcare center and with the internal firewall and create a database to receive the information from other healthcare center. A blockchain [33] account will be created for the system administrator, who in turn will create the blockchain account for the doctors, patients, and other stakeholders. When a patient goes to the healthcare center for the first time, he/she will be registered into the blockchain system with a new account and a new unique global ID will be created in the blockchain system. Then, the system administrator will record the personal information of the patient and relate it to the global ID created for the patient. Also, the biometric characteristics of the patient are recorded as indexing parameters for identification in future cases. The patient will have an individual ID for different healthcare centers. The patient owns their information regarding the various healthcare centers visited before. The system administrator will create the doctor ID in a particular healthcare center. Table 1 shows the various lists of framework models in a smart healthcare system using blockchain [34], along with their merits and demerits. A different framework provides a different way of preserving data privacy in the healthcare system.

The emerging smart healthcare system with IoT and blockchain technologies makes it the most suitable model for the revolution of the healthcare industry. The traditional process of healthcare [35,36] is changed with the application of biosensors that can be implantable, wearable, or placed in the patient environment for continuous health monitoring. The sensor part or the IoT part of the healthcare system will consist of sensors, controllers, and actuators. The sensor will gather health information about the patient and forward that to the controller for further processing. Upon receiving the data from the sensor, the controller will either analyze the data by itself or forward the data to a central data center with a high-performance device for processing. The processing response will be sent back to the controller.

The controller in either case will have a response of what to do and will instruct the actuators to perform a certain task. In a healthcare system, this is the point of vulnerability for attacks. The intruder will breach the IoT network because of its open environment and the IoT devices used. Sensors will generate a massive amount of information about the patients and this information will be used by doctors to diagnose patients. Also, the data generated by sensors is to be shared with the healthcare center for further analysis by a doctor. If these data are hacked or modified before they reach the healthcare center, then the doctor might wrongly diagnose the patient. So, it is

Table 1 Framework models in a healthcare system using blockchain.

Reference	Framework model	Merits	Demerits
Xia et al.	Data sharing framework based on blockchain in cloud environment	Authentication is done based on the identity and agreement protocol based on key for access control	No complete investigation of communication and authentication protocol.
Xia	Framework for medical data sharing among untrusted parties using blockchain	During sharing of patient medical data, the data provenance is provided	No complete investigation of generation of key and replacement.
Dubovitskaya et al.	Healthcare data management framework using blockchain	Medical data of the patient can be shared with more security and privacy	Diverse medical data handling and legal issues are not investigated
Al Omar et al.	Framework for patient's health data privacy using blockchain	Cryptographic-based healthcare management system framework in patient-centric system	No complete investigation of generation of key
Liang et al.	Framework for healthcare data sharing using permissioned blockchain	Patient-centric model with data integrity and ownership	No complete investigation of smart contracts
Fan et al.	Framework for medical data sharing using blockchain for EMR system	Access control and cryptographic protocol are used to preserve data privacy	No complete investigation of PBFT consensus

important to apply security procedures while transmitting the collected data to the cloud server or to the healthcare center server. Also, IoT has resource limitations such as power and scalability. Also, when implemented through cloud storage, then infrastructure availability and performance monitoring will be a risk.

4.2 Targets to preserve privacy

In the usage of blockchain in a smart healthcare system, the patient can access his or her sensitive information in public network places such as hospitals, clinics, in the available network during the mobility which are not secured and will be an issue to the data privacy and security. Lack of data privacy [37] in the smart healthcare system has its root in the IoT network, where numerous devices are implemented and connected through the Internet or any available network. IoT devices are more vulnerable to attacks. According to a recent study by Gartner, 20% of organizations have come across at least one IoT attack in the last 3 years. The security and data privacy issues are by "privacy by design." Privacy by design requires full functionality to provide security and privacy, robustness, privacy embedded, proactive such that it prevents threats rather than react to it, data life cycle means privacy from starting till end in the system, visibility, and transparency. The transmission of data should be secured, the protocols used in the system should be secured, the communication medium should be secured, and encryption standards should be applied to the data during motion and at rest.

The various security requirements of the healthcare system are as follows:

1. Confidentiality
2. Integrity
3. Ownership
4. Auditing
5. Nonrepudiation
6. Privacy
7. Availability
8. Authenticity
9. Anonymity
10. Secure data transmit
11. Data freshness
12. Access control

The gathered raw information is to be aggregated in the IoT network to get information and the obtained information will be further analyzed to get meaningful information. So, in the IoT network, devices are connected to the gateway and the hardware used in the IoT network has constrained resources. This allows attackers to attack these devices easily. In the IoT architecture, the physical layer, the network layer, and the application layer can be attacked, and these layers are vulnerable to data privacy issues. Table 2 shows the various types of attacks based on IoT layers [38,39]. All devices in the network should be authenticated to prevent unauthorized access to network resources. The data stored in the network should be more secured and cryptography protocols and secure database techniques should be implemented. Trust in the healthcare system is mandatory as the health-related data are shared and stored in the system by the patient where the data might be accessed by several users or participants of the system.

The device layer in the IoT network consists of all things of the IoT network that will collect the data and forward it to the higher layer. Security should be provided to this layer to prevent various malicious attacks such as whitelisting, secure booting, and

Table 2 Layer-wise security issues in IoT.

Layer	Attacks
Physical Layer	Node capture, replay, side channel, eavesdropping, false data injection
Network Layer	Sinkhole, DoS, man in the middle, unauthorized access, spoofing
Application Layer	Trust management, authentication, policy enforcement, phishing, malicious scripts

sandboxing. The communication layer is where all the devices communicate with each other to share the data collected using a wired or wireless network. Different protocols will be implemented in this layer. Even the blockchain suffers from privacy issues by attacks such as a 51% attack, malicious smart contracts, double spending, record hacking, wallet-based attacks, ledger-based attacks, eclipse attack, Sybil attack, Finney attack, mining malware, selfish mining attack, time jack attack, race attack, and DAO attack. Errors in blockchain are more costly and reverting to the same is impossible. So, security measures are implemented before deployment of the system in all processes.

4.3 Different security and privacy issues in healthcare

* *Security problem in RFID*: Issues can be raised by hackers such as eavesdropping, DOS, cloning, and spoofing.
* *Key management and maintaining confidentiality*: Security key issues and data integrity need to be addressed.
* *Issue in secure communication*: Sniffing can be done by intruders.
* *Security policy*: Cybersecurity, access authorization, inner-device authentication, and data authentication over the cloud need to be maintained.

4.4 Solution for security and privacy issues in healthcare

The importance of chosen architecture and device security protocols buying cost of wearable devices, ease of maintainability, device adoptability through several environment and good reliability and better Fault tolerance.

To provide the required knowledge to the people in cyber security to prevent the patient data and give the access only by multifactor authentication and control the data such as copying to external source. Monitor access by logging information to keep track of user activities. Encryption plays the major role in storing the patient data for security and concentrate on device security such as updated OS, application, locking the stolen device in remotely, encrypt the data while transit, monitoring the email attachments to prevent malware, and ensure the device having security solutions and monitoring [40,41].

5 Comparative analysis of healthcare data using IoT and blockchain

In smart healthcare systems, the security and data privacy of EHRs [16,17] are vital as these contain sensitive information about a patient. A provider can make decisions about patient healthcare based on the evidence gathered through the automated streamline provider. According to Gartner, organizations using smart contracts will increase the data quality by 50%. In blockchain, various standards and protocols are used to maintain the healthcare data in the system. One is the open EHR, which is an open standard to represent healthcare data or information that also describes the storage, retrieval, management, and sharing of healthcare data. This standard is vendor-independent and it consists of information, clinical workflow, demographics, and archetype paradigm.

The fast healthcare interoperability resources (HL7 FHIR) [42] developed by Health Level 7 is a standard that describes an application programming interface, elements, and data formats for the healthcare data exchange. FHIR-based EHR creates a huge market share in the healthcare data system. The Health Insurance Portability and Accountability Act (HIPAA) is a standard used for data privacy and security in the healthcare data system. Without patient consent, healthcare information should not be shared. It consists of five major rules: the privacy rule, the security rule, the transactions rule, the identifiers rule, and the enforcement rule. Other standards are general data protection regulation (GDPR); integrating the healthcare enterprise (IHE); the International Organization for Standardization (ISO): ISO/IEEE 11073 and ISO 14721; systematized nomenclature of medicine (SNOMED), digital imaging and communications in medicine (DICOM), health information exchange (HIE) and personally identifiable information (PII).

The EHR structure is divided into three types: time-oriented, source-oriented, and problem-oriented. In time-oriented medical records, the chronological order is followed to represent the health data. In the source-oriented medical record, the data are recorded based on the way they are gathered. Example of data gathered are blood pressure tests, blood tests, laboratory reports, and visit notes. In each section, the data will be ordered chronologically. The various types of EHRs are hospital EHR, departmental EHR, interhospital EHR, interdepartmental EHR, digital medical records, personal health records, virtual EHRs, and population health records [43,44].

The healthcare data consists of different types of sensitive information about patients. They are linked into the blocks of the blockchain represented using various data types and data structures and standards. The healthcare data will be both structured and unstructured. The structured data types are classified into common data types and emerging data types and in which the users can select only the predefined values following a data model and value set. Some common data types extracted from healthcare data are demographics, medications, vital signs, problem lists, allergies, family history, reports, immunizations, utilization events, procedures, patient identifiers, laboratory results, and diagnoses. The various emerging data types are free text, geospatial, social data, biosample data, genetic information, patient generated, surveys, community, and other data types.

Age, race, ethnicity, and gender are information considered to be demographics data. This information is vital for clinical treatment and the accuracy of this information is important. But the accuracy of the demographics data may be affected by measurements, human error, and conversion types. Nonessential demographic information includes education, nationality, marital status, employment status, and income. Medication data types are used to know about the effect of the treatment and for safety purposes. Medication information is used during the claim made by the patients. Vital signs include physiological variables such as body mass index, blood pressure, temperature, height, pulse rate, weight, and respiratory rate. Vital sign data follow the logical observation identifiers names and code (LoINC) coding standard.

A problem list is a data type that holds information about the diagnoses that are both active and resolved. Allergy data types have information about the various allergies of the patient based on food and medicine. Pathology, surgery, and laboratory information consists of the procedure data types. Procedure data types are local to the EHR type and are used only within the provider premises. The information from lab reports and lab orders comes under the laboratory data type. The LoINC standard, the systematized nomenclature of medicine standards, and current procedural terminology standards are used. Utilization data types are used when the insurance claims made by the patient are unavailable.

It includes the hospitalization, ICU admission, and other healthcare events and it follows the claim submission policies. Data prepared by performing various surveys are the information collected by the questionnaires and the patient-reported outcomes measurement information systems (PROMIS), life event checklist, health risk assessments standards are used and information such as the housing condition, smoking status, and individual behaviors are recorded. Patient-generated data types covers a variable domain values such as sleeping pattern, activities related to health such as exercise, walking, and the symptoms informed by the patients. This type of data is more inconsistent and collected by using wearable devices and using various mobile health exchange applications.

6 Open research challenges and future directions

The IoMT is widely adopted in healthcare in our current connected world, and this enables quicker and more efficient diagnoses for patients. However, the issues of data privacy and security are still a concern. So, various research is being pursued to enable blockchain methodologies in IoMT that would mitigate security concerns. However, the existing blockchain solutions still require huge computational power, which restricts their commercial adoption in healthcare. So, future work could focus on providing a hybrid blockchain solution adapted to healthcare that would be commercially viable. In addition, the research could also focus on the application of blockchains to varied healthcare applications, that is, diagnostics, continuous remote monitoring of patients, anonymous and distributed storage of healthcare data, and automated medical advice.

7 Contextual investigation of the IBM blockchain healthcare drive

IBM reported its community-oriented blockchain drive with significant medical service players, including Aetna (procured by drug store and well-being plan supplier CVS Well-being), Anthem (well-being plan supplier), Health Care Service Company (the biggest client claimed healthcare coverage supplier in the United States), and PNC Bank [45]. IBM has been looking for new freedoms by utilizing the potential of blockchain and endeavoring to develop an exceptional organized medical services biological system. Over the most recent couple of months, well-being associations, medical services suppliers, new companies, and innovation organizations participated in this drive to develop the Health Utility Organization, of which Cigna and Sentara Healthcare are members. The point is to drive computerized change by giving better straightforwardness and interoperability. Members may receive rewards from building, sharing, and conveying answers for officeholder challenges in the medical care setting. Significant issues and potential blockchain use cases are listed as follows.

7.1   Provenance and discernibility of drug inventory network

Fake medications could be irksome and risky as medication provenance is hard to follow in a cross-line setting. An enormous number of handovers from producers, transporters, wholesalers, retailers, and drug stores may cause errors and questions in clinical conveyance activities. Fake medications with inappropriate ingredients and doses may imperil patients and even raise lawful questions among makers, providers, and clients. With permanent, sealed, and identifiable attributes, blockchain may give answers for the genuineness and detectability of drugs alongside auditable and secure exchange records among partners. For instance, in a private medication blockchain, drug enlistment by drug organizations may allow a more significant level of dependability and credible evidence. These organizations, going about as dominators, could allot the parts of the entertainers; some of them may have the rights for enlistment while others may lead check of exchanges. The record of medications can be guaranteed through confirmation measures with related assembling or personality data when annexed on-chain, making it simple to be followed.

7.2   Information stored during clinical preliminaries

Clinical preliminaries are carried out and various information is created by various gadgets through the activity of clinical staff. How this information is stored, sent, shared, and used for clinical treatment or activities is basic to existing manual frameworks. Blunders and extortion during clinical preliminaries could happen by means of malignant adjustments or accidental botches. Normal blemishes could happen when preliminary techniques are erroneously planned by one-sided expectations from entertainers or then again conflicting records and reactions from patients' transformative clinical reports. Blockchain could provide evidence of presence to any type of documentation. The data should be confirmed by means of the assent of the partaking hubs and not under a solitary substance's control. Adjusting or changing data would be cryptographically hard to direct among a greater part of network players, hence making documentation profoundly trusted.

7.3   EMR and EHR

Based upon the clinical records are concerned, a test is that singular clinical information is not effectively gotten to by diverse clinical foundations or centers. While clinical data are stored dissimilarly in different datasets or frameworks, it is hard to convey appropriate prescription and care administration in a customized setting. Touchy information can likewise impede transmission effectiveness among clinical associations. The most effective method to access, share, and use a comprehensive clinical treatment history in a safe manner stays a testing issue in unified EMR frameworks. In any case, with the assistance of dispersed record innovation, blockchain may have potential with respect to the control and access of such EHR and EMR frameworks. Blockchain stages can be joined with existing EHR and EMR frameworks, either in the distributed computing climate or something else, using Oracle and information doors. Patients can share their clinical records, with or without consent, to enlisted clients or partners on a clinical blockchain. Decision can be made by the patients to choose the degree of data revelation through savvy contract settings to explicit clients, along these lines getting compensations from the blockchain framework, in such as manner. As per the discussion made above, blockchain could work with the sharing and the board of EHRs and EMRs among market interest elements. Related information examination and awards from sharing might advance the cooperation of the clinical local area and, thus, influence an organizational impact.

In medical care, significant shortcomings can emerge from clinical tasks, managerial preparing, and contacts among different frameworks. Trouble spots which are identified have diminished the general execution and have prompted helpless client encounters in respect to officeholder clinical and medical services frameworks and administrations. The demonstration of consolidating significant players through blockchain-based frameworks and administrations in medical services may help to create a solid, open-arranged, and community-oriented environment.

Blockchain empowerment cooperation expects to address the previously mentioned difficulties by seeking after diminished authoritative blunder, alleviated framework contacts, smoothed out cases and installment exchanges, and proficient data trade. Iansiti and Levien extended Moore's biological system see furthermore, proposed the methodologies that organizations may receive to position themselves in the business biological system. The essential jobs incorporate cornerstones, specialty players, and physical dominators. The cornerstone in the business environment gives a stage to which specialty players add worth and contributions. Account of the specialty players account for the mass extent of the environment and are mindful for esteem creation and advancement. The physical dominator straightforwardly controls most of an organization through even or vertical coordination. In an IBM blockchain biological system, the major players' jobs and relating capacities are shown in Table 3 and are summed up as follows:

1. *IBM*: Cornerstone—blockchain stage supplier and facilitator.
2. *Aetna of CVS*: Specialty player—improves information precision and medical care framework activity.
3. *Hymn*: Specialty player—clinical data trade.
4. *Medical Care Service Corporation*: Physical dominator—decreases data discontinuity and improves claims methodology and medical service framework association.
5. *PNC Bank*: Specialty player—works with installment exchanges and upholds clinical money.

Table 3 Significant players' jobs and impacts in a blockchain-based medical services biological system.

Type	Significant players	Jobs	Impacts on the environment
Key	Stage supplier in the biological system Intend to set out open doors for specialty players and support the activity of the entire framework	Stage supplier in the biological system Plan to set out open doors for specialty players and support the activity of the entire framework	Empower the foundation of a sound climate, which prompts an association's endurance and success Convene adherents to accomplish variety
Physical dominator	Medical care service corporation or other medical care specialist organizations	Integrators in the biological system Integrators straightforwardly possess and deal with an enormous extent of an organization by utilizing vertical or flat measures	Give most items and administrations to meet clients' needs endeavor their situations to assume control over the organization and remove the made worth
Niche player	Aetna of CVS, Anthem, or PNC Bank	Worth makers and trend-setters in the environment Spotlight all expected undertakings on improving them thin space of ability	Influence corresponding assets from others to make separated worth Rivalry and collaboration of specialty players support the coevolution of the environment

Blockchain innovation is not the advantage of this drive. Contenders putting forth comparative attempts, for example, Change Healthcare, Hashed Health, Guardtime, Gem, and Simply Vital Health, have likewise collaborated to dispatch a blockchain pilot—Intelligent Healthcare Network with Blockchain Cycles—in the domain of medical care. Other contending projects with a pretty much extraordinary center have additionally prompted consortia contest. Conspicuous models incorporate Synaptic Health Partnership, focusing on supplier indexes and information compromise, what's more, ProCredEx, zeroing in on capacity and sharing of clinical certifications. PNC Bank, going about as an accomplice of interdisciplinary partnership, remains in a public position and contributes its edge to work with exchanges among patients, payers, and suppliers in both homegrown and cross-line settings.

7.3.1 Business ecosystem with evolutionary life cycle

Blockchain, as an arising advancement, has given freedoms to medical service partners. Concerning the IBM case, a joint effort of medical service accomplices has brought about another environment. Its like transformative stages have framed a business biological system focal point; these stages are summed up in Table 4.

Table 4 The transformative way of a blockchain-medical care biological system: The IBM case.

Stage	Cooperative difficulties	Competitive difficulties
Birth	Partners make new incentives of blockchain-based environments and characterize their jobs when working with providers also, clients Players take advantage of lucky breaks Model: IBM blockchain-medical services environment	Ensure thoughts against contenders with comparable contributions Pilot cases with comparative highlights Models: Change Healthcare's Intelligent Healthcare Network with blockchain measures, Synaptic Health Alliance, and ProCredEx
Extension	Bring new developments (i.e., items or administrations) to market to expand the piece of the pie or inclusion Methodology: improve stage usefulness, assimilate reciprocal medical services individuals, and recognize and address changing requests from clients	Contend with and rout rival executions Expand portion of the overall industry by building up market or specialized principles Procedure: develop specialized or modern norms and extend the selection of blockchain-based applications
Administration	Make future possibilities and urge accomplices to venture forward Measure: incorporate with other disturbing advances (e.g., AI, man-made reasoning, portable and omnipresent wellbeing, wearables, and web of things)	Keep up bartering power against biological system players Measures: keep clients fulfilled and fortify the client relationship the board; utilize in reverse incorporation, search various providers, increment profile, and lead market instruction
Self-restoration or demise	Adapt to trailblazers to create or take advantage of new lucky breaks or be supplanted by elective standards	Fabricate significant degrees of section hindrances and client changing expenses to forestall being supplanted by elective environments

At the birth stage, the IBM blockchain–medical services pilot faced consortia contests from different partners. Even though the centered business sectors may be somewhat not the same as pilot to steer, comparable endeavors and normal goals for driving advanced change in the medical care industry are something similar. IBM, as a perceived driving undertaking blockchain supplier, has a profitable edge against contenders. During the extension stage, the key center is to bring new developments to market to build the share. It is performed by convincing providers and clients to finish sound. Moreover, to beat rival biological systems, it is vital to develop specialized or mechanical principles as far as serious methodology [46]. During the initiative stage, the main biological system may zero in on future possibilities for supporters. This could be carried out by convincing providers and clients to finish sound dreams; for instance, joining with other problematic advances, for example, AI, man-made brainpower, versatile and omnipresent wellbeing, wearables, and web of things (IoT). To keep pressure from expanded haggling power, activities such as utilizing in reverse joining, looking various providers, expanding profile, and directing business sector instruction are required. At the last stage, the blockchain–medical services environment may venture toward self-restoration or demise. This may rely exceptionally upon capacities that the current biological system may have; it can either advance or be supplanted with elective biological systems or ideal models [47].

Similar analysis of the existing system and the future ecosystem blockchain applications in the well-being area have been getting expanded consideration and possibilities. We have summed up the current medical care administration problem areas and featured the capability of blockchain in reshaping customary practice and tasks. Scientists have directed writing audits to report on the current difficulties [48,49]. The significant issues with relating the possible impacts of blockchain are shown in Table 5.

Table 5 Medical care administration trouble spots and the possible impacts of blockchain in the medical services biological system.

Issue	Medical care administration problem areas	Possible impacts of blockchain influence
Clinical information stockpiling Misrepresentation and credibility	Profoundly different information sources across singular facilities or well-being care-related foundations. Malevolent endeavors or human mistakes may cause extortion, modifications, or clinical questions. Specialists are needed for trust working among partners. Significant issues incorporate medication duplicating and provenance	Decentralized information stockpiling permits copy and changeless well-being records in the well-being organization. Keeping basic things (i.e., clinical exchanges or records) on blocks and forever recording procedure on-chain moderating the altering issue by means of the confirmation and agreement Engineering

Table 5 Continued

Issue	Medical care administration problem areas	Possible impacts of blockchain influence
Archive type	Paper-based and manual preparing causes challenges in information conglomeration	Supporting digitalized well-being archives conveyed on shared record
Interoperability	Siloed information structures upset interoperations across various datasets.	Blockchain-based organizations empower cooperation among medical service partners.
Well-being cases and exchanges	Failures that exist in clinical and authoritative strategies and erosions among particular well-being frameworks have caused helpless activities.	Interaction robotization worked with by blockchain-based savvy contracts empowers smoothed out cases and exchange strategies.
Exploration information access and adaptation	Difficulties in accumulating, enrolling, and holding information among clinical gatherings and challenges in adaptation	Clinical empowerment preliminary information sharing and worth added investigation to make information use and adaptation
Data sharing and transmission	Manual handling increases operational expenses and consumption. Weakness and vulnerabilities from cyberattack or framework breakdown	Blockchain is appropriated ascribes permit shared data in the medical care organization. Agreement component with sealed highlights could lessen security and protection concerns.
Clinical inventory network discernibility	Vulnerabilities during handovers among participating parties.	The shared records take into account better straightforwardness and observing on store network discernibility. Keen agreements can work with warnings of state changes

8 Conclusion

As per the Gartner statistics, the global smart healthcare market size is expected to reach $81.5 billion by 2022 from $69 billion in 2020. In addition, the widespread adoption of smart wearables together with 5G, which provides ultra-reliable and low latency communication, will further fuel the growth of the smart home healthcare market. It enables IoT-enabled smart wearables and helps in the automated collection and storage of patient medical data. However, it opens new challenges too, such as data privacy and security concerns. Due to their intrinsic characteristics such as distributed and anonymous data storage, existing blockchain technologies have the potential to be a game changer in the smart healthcare industry by providing a service-oriented approach. It would also enable patient-centric medical data access, which could be used to provide automated medical verification instead of always seeking professional medical advice. However, the main challenge that still needs to be answered is the resource constraints of IoT devices.

References

[1] C. Chen, E.-W. Loh, K.N. Kuo, K.-W. Tam, The times they are a-Changin'—Healthcare 4.0 is coming! J. Med. Syst. 44 (40) (2020), https://doi.org/10.1007/s10916-019-1513-0.

[2] J. Li, P. Carayon, Health Care 4.0: a vision for smart and connected health care, IISE Trans. Healthcare Syst. Eng. (2021), https://doi.org/10.1080/24725579.2021.1884627.

[3] J. Hathaliya, P. Sharma, S. Tanwar, R. Gupta, Blockchain-Based Remote Patient Monitoring in Healthcare 4.0, in: 9th IEEE International Conference on Advanced Computing (IACC), Tiruchirappalli, India, December 2019, pp. 87–91.

[4] R. Gupta, S. Tanwar, S. Tyagi, N. Kumar, M.S. Obaidat, B. Sadoun HaBiTs, Blockchain-Based Telesurgery Framework for Healthcare 4.0, in: International Conference on Computer, Information and Telecommunication Systems (IEEE CITS-2019), Beijing, China, August 28–31, 2019, pp. 6–10.

[5] S. Tanwar, K. Parekh, R. Evans, Blockchain-based electronic healthcare record system for Healthcare 4.0 applications, J. Inform. Security Appl. 50 (2019) 1–14.

[6] P. Bhattacharya, S. Tanwar, S. Tyagi, N. Kumar, BINDaaS: Blockchain integrated deep-learning as a Service in Healthcare 4.0 applications, in: IEEE Transactions on Network Science and Engineering, 2019, pp. 1–14.

[7] R. Gupta, A. Shukla, S. Tanwar, AaYusH: A Smart Contract-based Telesurgery System for Healthcare 4.0, in: IEEE Conference on Communications (IEEE ICC-2020), Dublin, Ireland, 07-11th June, 2020, pp. 1–6.

[8] L. Chettri, R. Bera, A comprehensive survey on Internet of Things (IoT) toward 5G wireless systems, IEEE Internet Things J. 7 (1) (2019) 16–32.

[9] Z. Dawy, W. Saad, A. Ghosh, J.G. Andrews, E. Yaacoub, Toward massive machine type cellular communications, IEEE Wirel. Commun. 24 (1) (2016) 120–128.

[10] A. Zanella, N. Bui, A. Castellani, L. Vangelista, M. Zorzi, Internet of things for smart cities, IEEE Internet Things J. 1 (1) (2014) 22–32.

[11] T. Gea, J. Paradells, M. Lamarca, D. Roldan, Smart cities as an application of internet of things: Experiences and lessons learnt in Barcelona, in: Seventh International Conference on Innovative Mobile and Internet Services in Ubiquitous Computing, 2013, pp. 552–557.

[12] U. Bodkhe, S. Tanwar, A. Ladha, P. Bhattacharya, A. Verma, A survey on revolutionizing Healthcare 4.0 applications using blockchain, in: International Conference on Computing, Communications, and Cyber-Security (IC4S 2020), Lecture Notes in Networks and Systems, Springer, Chandigarh, India, 12–13th October, 2019, pp. 1–16.

[13] J. Lin, W. Yu, N. Zhang, X. Yang, H. Zhang, W. Zhao, A survey on internet of things: architecture, enabling technologies, security and privacy, and applications, IEEE Internet Things J. 4 (5) (2017) 1125–1142.

[14] H. Wang, A.O. Fapojuwo, A survey of enabling technologies of low power and long-range machine-to-machine communications, IEEE Commun. Surv. Tutor. 19 (4) (2017) 2621–2639.

[15] P.A. Laplante, N. Laplante, The internet of things in healthcare: potential applications and challenges, IT Prof. 18 (3) (2016) 2–4.
[16] M. Centenaro, L. Vangelista, A. Zanella, M. Zorzi, Long-range communications in unlicensed bands: the rising stars in the IoT and smart city scenarios, IEEE Wirel. Commun. 23 (5) (2016) 60–67.
[17] M. Condoluci, M. Dohler, G. Araniti, A. Molinaro, K. Zheng, Toward 5G densenets: architectural advances for effective machine-type communications over femtocells, IEEE Commun. Mag. 53 (1) (2015) 134–141.
[18] E. Hossain, M. Rasti, H. Tabassum, A. Abdelnasser, Evolution toward 5G multi-tier cellular wireless networks: an interference management perspective, IEEE Wirel. Commun. 21 (3) (2014) 118–127.
[19] A. Ahad, M. Tahir, K.L.A. Yau, 5G-based smart healthcare network: architecture, taxonomy, challenges and future research directions, IEEE Access 7 (2019) 100747–100762.
[20] Y. Siriwardhana, G. Gür, M. Ylianttila, M. Liyanage, The role of 5G for digital healthcare against COVID-19 pandemic: opportunities and challenges, ICT Expr. 7 (2) (2021) 244–252.
[21] R. Gupta, A. Kumari, S. Tanwar, Fusion of Blockchain and AI for secure drone networking underlying 5G communications, Trans. Emerg. Telecommun. Technol. 32 (2020), https://doi.org/10.1002/ett.4176.
[22] I. Mistry, S. Tanwar, S. Tyagi, N. Kumar, Blockchain for 5G-enabled IoT for industrial automation: a systematic review, solutions, and challenges, Mech. Syst. Signal Process. 135 (2019), https://doi.org/10.1016/j.ymssp.2019.106382.
[23] V. Thayananthan, Healthcare management using ICT and IoT based 5G, Int. J. Adv. Comput. Sci. Appl. 10 (2019) 305–312.
[24] M. Nasajpour, S. Pouriyeh, R.M. Parizi, M. Dorodchi, M. Valero, H.R. Arabnia, Internet of Things for current COVID-19 and future pandemics: an exploratory study, J. Healthcare Inform. Res. (2020) 1–40.
[25] Y. Siriwardhana, C. De Alwis, G. Gür, M. Ylianttila, M. Liyanage, The fight against the COVID-19 pandemic with 5G technologies, IEEE Eng. Manag. Rev. 48 (3) (2020) 72–84.
[26] F. Jamil, S. Ahmad, N. Iqbal, D.H. Kim, Towards a remote monitoring of patient vital signs based on IoT-based blockchain integrity management platforms in smart hospitals, Sensors 20 (8) (2020) 2195.
[27] M. Picone, S. Cirani, L. Veltri, Blockchain security and privacy for the Internet of Things, Sensors 21 (3) (2021) 892, https://doi.org/10.3390/s21030892.
[28] S. Chakraborty, S. Aich, H.C. Kim, A secure healthcare system design framework using blockchain technology, in: 21st International Conference on Advanced Communication Technology (ICACT), 2019, pp. 260–264.
[29] M. Marschollek, M. Gietzelt, M. Schulze, M. Kohlmann, B. Song, K.H. Wolf, Wearable sensors in healthcare and sensor-enhanced health information systems: all our tomorrows? Healthcare Inform. Res. 18 (2) (2012) 97.
[30] M. Kubendiran, S. Singh, A.K. Sangaiah, Enhanced security framework for e-health systems using blockchain, J. Inform. Process. Syst. 15 (2) (2019) 239–250.
[31] T. Alam, mHealth communication framework using blockchain and IoT technologies, Int. J. Sci. Technol. Res. 9 (6) (2020) 1–6.
[32] P.P. Ray, D. Dash, K. Salah, N. Kumar, Blockchain for IoT-based healthcare: background, consensus, platforms, and use cases, IEEE Syst. J. 15 (1) (2020) 85–94.
[33] H. Zakaria, N.A.A. Bakar, N.H. Hassan, S. Yaacob, IoT security risk management model for secured practice in healthcare environment, Proc. Comput. Sci. 161 (2019) 1241–1248.

[34] N. Tariq, A. Qamar, M. Asim, F.A. Khan, Blockchain and smart healthcare security: a survey, Proc. Comput. Sci. 175 (2020) 615–620.

[35] F.I. Salih, N.A.A. Bakar, N.H. Hassan, F. Yahya, N. Kama, J. Shah, IoT security risk management model for healthcare industry, Malays. J. Comput. Sci. (2019) 131–144.

[36] R.M.A. Latif, K. Hussain, N.Z. Jhanjhi, A. Nayyar, O. Rizwan, A remix IDE: smart contract-based framework for the healthcare sector by using Blockchain technology, Multimed. Tools Appl. (2020) 1–24.

[37] C. Butpheng, K.H. Yeh, H. Xiong, Security and privacy in IoT-cloud-based e-health systems—a comprehensive review, Symmetry 12 (7) (2020) 1191.

[38] B.K. Mohanta, D. Jena, S. Ramasubbareddy, M. Daneshmand, A.H. Gandomi, Addressing security and privacy issues of IoT using blockchain technology, IEEE Internet Things J. 8 (2) (2020) 881–888.

[39] K. Häyrinen, K. Saranto, P. Nykänen, Definition, structure, content, use and impacts of electronic health records: a review of the research literature, Int. J. Med. Inform. 77 (5) (2008) 291–304.

[40] J. Hathaliya, S. Tanwar, An exhaustive survey on security and privacy issues in Healthcare 4.0, Comput. Commun. 153 (2020), https://doi.org/10.1016/j.comcom.2020.02.018.

[41] J. Ranjith, K. Mahantesh, Privacy and security issues in smart Health Care, in: 2019 4th International Conference on Electrical, Electronics, Communication, Computer Technologies and Optimization Techniques (ICEECCOT), 2019, pp. 378–383, https://doi.org/10.1109/ICEECCOT46775.2019.9114681.

[42] F. Ghavimi, H.H. Chen, M2M communications in 3GPP LTE/LTE-A networks: architectures, service requirements, challenges, and applications, IEEE Commun. Surv. Tutor. 17 (2) (2014) 525–549.

[43] Y. Sharma, B. Balamurugan, Preserving the privacy of electronic health records using blockchain, Proc. Comput. Sci. 173 (2020) 171–180.

[44] A.H. Mayer, C.A. da Costa, R.D.R. Righi, Electronic health records in a blockchain: a systematic review, Health Informatics J. 26 (2) (2020) 1273–1288.

[45] Aetna, Anthem, Health Care Service Corporation, PNC Bank and IBM announce collaboration to establish blockchain-based ecosystem for the healthcare industry, in: IBM News Room, 2019 Jan 24. *https://tinyurl.com/y3tej8x7.*

[46] K. Rong, Y. Lin, Y. Shi, J. Yu, Linking business ecosystem lifecycle with platform strategy: a triple view of technology, application and organisation, Int. J. Technol. Manag. 62 (1) (2013) 75, https://doi.org/10.1504/ijtm.2013.053042.

[47] S.E. Chang, Y. Chen, Blockchain in health care innovation: literature review and case study from a business ecosystem perspective, J. Med. Internet Res. 22 (8) (2020), https://doi.org/10.2196/19480, e19480.

[48] E. Chukwu, L. Garg, A systematic review of blockchain in healthcare: Frameworks, prototypes, and implementations, IEEE Access 8 (2020) 21196–21214, https://doi.org/10.1109/access.2020.2969881.

[49] A. Hasselgren, K. Kralevska, D. Gligoroski, S.A. Pedersen, A. Faxvaag, Blockchain in healthcare and health sciences—a scoping review, Int. J. Med. Inform. 134 (2020) 104040, https://doi.org/10.1016/j.ijmedinf.2019.104040 (Medline: 31865055).

Reliability of 5G in human health monitoring using blockchain technology

14

K. Raghavendra and Deepti Kakkar

Department of ECE, Dr. B.R Ambedkar National Institute of Technology, Jalandhar, India

1 Introduction

Communication innovations have increased from 1G to 5G. In this change, there have been various points and objectives to accomplish for every era [1]. For example, 1G and 2G networks were mostly related to voice where 3G was a mix of voice and data services. 4G was LTE-based, and is mostly a data-centric technology where data rates of up to 400–500 Mbps are achieved [2]. As of now, 5G is in the commercial rollout stages in many developing economies. For example, in Australia, the United States, Japan, Korea, China, the Middle East, and in many parts of Europe, 5G is in the initial deployment state. But what we need to emphasize is that going from 4G to 5G means a huge shift in terms of both technology and the impact it will have on our lives.

5G means to provide three basic uses:

1. eMBB ➜ Enhanced multimedia broadband.
2. URLLC ➜ Ultrareliable low latency communication.
3. MMTC ➜ Massive machine tap communication.

These are the three areas that will provide a massive shift from 4G to 5G (Fig. 1).

eMBB: In eMBB, high Gbps data rates are possible for vehicles traveling at 500 km/h. Person traveling in a fast moving train supposed to travel with 5G communication unit for experiencing high quality streaming. In LTE, the vehicular speed is around 150–200 km/h whereas in 5G, a multimedia experience can be achieved in vehicles traveling at a speed of 500 km/h.

URLLC: This technique is implemented on automated vehicles, virtual reality and augmented reality applications. In automated vehicles, the connection is established between the vehicles in order to transfer information. So, the amount of time it takes for information to travel from a car to a base station or any remote relay and returns to the car, called latency, should be much less. Second, the processing capability should be present on the edge. The edge means a relay node so edge computing is essential in 5G.

MMTC: This part centers around expansive inclusion and the broadened battery life season of sensors, actuators, cameras, and so forth so essentially this is named as an augmentation of IoT into MMTC, while the entirety of our gadgets are associated in urban communities (named as brilliant urban communities, keen homes) fundamentally as far as detail 5G hub ought to have a million connections which are kept as a point in R-16 and R-17 indicated

Blockchain Applications for Healthcare Informatics. https://doi.org/10.1016/B978-0-323-90615-9.00012-8
Copyright © 2022 Elsevier Inc. All rights reserved.

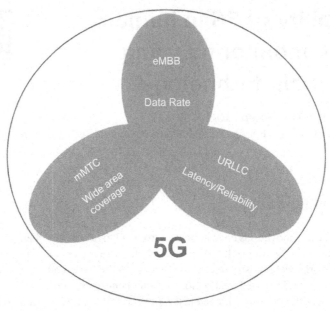

Fig. 1 Basis of 5G [2].

by 3GPP, where the primary stage for example Release 15 (R-15) is generally identified with eMBB part.

5G works on an Internet of Things (IoT) platform where the transformation goes from machine to machine (M2M) (Table 1).

1.1 Evolution of 5G

The evolution of wireless technology started with the transmission of analog signals over long distances. Improvements and the speed of data transmission in each generation are discussed as follows:

Table 1 Frequency partition in 5G [3].

Frequency range	Application	Remarks
Less than 6 GHz	Basic Internet of Things (IoT)	Data transmission for maximum distances with fewer investments
1–6 GHz	IoT, high-capacity data transfer	The availability of bandwidth is greater but short range and less effective compared with HF
Beyond 6 GHz	High data transfer rates	Latency time is reduced, short range with high-speed data transmission

1G Technology: It is the original remote correspondence where simple signs were utilized to send information. It was presented in the United States in the mid-1980s and planned only for voice correspondence. It worked with a speed of 2.4 Kbps and had poor voice quality. The telephones were large and had a restricted battery life. The information security was low [4]. **2G Technology**: This was the second era of remote portable communication that utilized advanced signals. 2G first began in Finland in 1991 and groupie special module (GSM) was utilized. GSM was later named the global system for mobile communication. Voice correspondence utilizing computerized signals was done in 2G. The data speed was up to 64 kbps and text and media informing were conceivable. When GPRS was presented, it empowered web browsing, email administration, and quick transfer/download speeds. 2G +GPRS was called 2.5G. Later came 2.75G, where enhanced data rate for GSM (EDGE) development began; the information speed was 90–120 kbps [5]. **3G Technology**: This technology provided significant impact on the data rate. The higher data rate is utilized for 3D gaming, multimedia email, and video conference. The 3G framework is named the universal mobile telecommunication system (UMTS). In 3.5G with the high-speed downlink packet access (HSDPA), greater information rates were accomplished [6]. **4G Technology**: Keeping up the trend of a new wireless generation every decade, 4G technology came into existence in 2011 with advancements in Long Term Evolution (LTE) technology where the data speed is 1 Gbps under stationary object conditions and a data speed of 100 Mbps when the object is under motion is achieved and this enabled us for high definition mobile TV, mobile web access, cloud computing, IP telephony. The basic term used to describe 4G is "MAGIC" where M represents mobile multimedia, A represents any time anywhere, G represents global mobility support, I represent integrated wireless solution, and C represents customized personal services. The major challenges of 4G technology such as short bandwidth and high energy consumption remain unsolved [7]. **5G Technology**: It is highly supportable for the wireless world wide web (WWWW). The major benefits of this technology are providing large data broadcasting in Gbps [8]. Highdefinition television transmission and multimedia-based newspapers require faster data transfer and it can be achieved using the 5G technology. In 5G, higher bands not previously utilized called millimeter (mm) bands are used. In these bands, the amount of bandwidth is extremely high, but the propagation is not very good, so there is a need for much closer cell sites to the user. It allows us to be far more precise in terms of transmitting to a given user. In 5G technology, adaptive beam switching is needed where the user has to switch back and forth between multiple beams [9], as shown in Fig. 4. In Table 2, various factor comparisons from 1G to 5G are mentioned.

1.2 Network architecture of 5G

In LTE, the core network is the evolved packet core (EPC) and it consists of a software gateway (SGW) and a mobility management entity (MME). SGW handles the user plane whereas MME handles the control plane. In 5G, the core part is named the next generation core (NGC), which consists of two logical block entries named the user plane function (UPF) and the access and mobility management function (AMF). UPF deals with user-plane functionalities whereas AMF deals with access and mobility functionalities and handles the control plane (Fig. 2).

Table 2 Various factors comparisons from 1G to 5G [10].

Parameter	1G	2G	3G	4G	5G
Technology started	1970	1980	2000	2011–15	Yet to come
Bandwidth used/needed	1.5–2 Kbps	64 Kbps	1–2 Mbps	1 Gbps	More than 1 Gbps
Technology used	Analog	Digital	CDMA, UMTS, EDGE, HSDPA, HSPA+	WiFi, Wi-Max, LTE	WWWW
Multiplexing technique used	FDMA	TDMA	CDMA	CDMA	OFDM
Major impairments	Mobility	Security	Internet experience in a better way	High-speed Internet, low latency	Fast transmission with low latency. High performance with high rate
Switching used	Circuit switching	Circuit switching	Packet switching	All packet switching	All packet switching
Applications	Analog telephony	Digital telephony	Messaging, Internet telephony	IP services	High-speed video calling and high-speed broadband applications

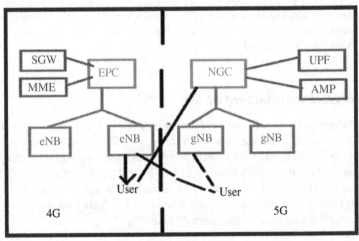

Fig. 2 Basic differences between LTE network and 5G Network [11].

When the radio part is concerned, the BTS is named e node B (eNB) whereas in 5G BTS is named g node B (gNB). Major specifications of 5G give users capability to attach to the LTE network as well as the 5G network, which is called multi-connectivity [12]. The detailed architecture of 5G is shown in Fig. 3.

The client plane availability in 5G is called the protocol data snit (PDU) session. PDU meetings are interesting to the gadget. Inside the PDU meeting, the quality of service (QoS) is accomplished by making separate QoS streams that are remarkably related to the QoS stream ID. AMF plays a critical job in security, registration, and validating the supporter inside the organization. AMF will likewise furnish the gadget with an impermanent character that can be utilized at whatever points it flags the organization; a transitory ID is utilized in paging also [12–15].

The session management function (SMF) in 5G arrangements with strategy control function (PCF) is used for interaction under information Network Profile. It is straightforwardly associated with the foundation of genuine PDU meeting availability. It chooses the necessary client plane capacity. Additionally, assuming the information meeting is the IP base, SMF will allocate IPv4 or IPv6 addresses.

UPF is an anchor point for NG-RAN versatility. In the radio access network, UPF will act as center point in the network, such that the client plane availability will be running from gNB to UPF in the center organization and because the UPF is straightforwardly positioned on the client plane its an ideal highlight authorize QoS and furthermore strategy authorization.

UDM gives access authorization, registration/portability to executives, and data network profiles.

The functions of the policy control function (PCF) are making dynamic policy decisions based on conditions and ability to alter both mobility and session-related service aspects [16–20].

1.3 Overview of blockchain technology

Blockchain permits a common record with safe administration, in the organization every exchange is put away, what's more, confirmed with no focal power. Blockchain is safer when an exchange of a block is recorded. The blockchain has an assortment of

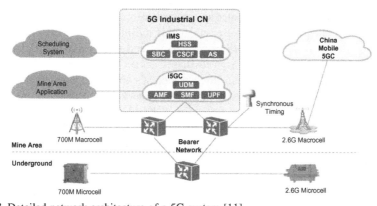

Fig. 3 Detailed network architecture of a 5G system [11].

blocks kept in a chain module. Each chain module is safer by cryptographic hash work. A block is added after confirming with every one of the blocks from the blockchain. After approval, another block is added. Blockchain is classified in four categories: private, public, consortium, and permission-based. The benefits of blockchain are stamping, expanded limit, security, changelessness, quicker settlement, and decentralized framework. The center parts of blockchain innovation are the hub, exchange, block, chain, diggers, and agreement. The significant key parts of blockchain are data block, distributed record, consensus algorithm, flexible smart contracts, and security in an enhanced form.

Data blocks are records of digital currency exchange information where blocks are connected to one another to frame a blockchain. These are represented in a sequential way. Cryptographic tags have been enabled for each block.

In a distributed record, every dataset is shared and recreated in a shared network. Every exchange is recorded by a disseminated record, which is the way toward trading information among network members. Inside the blockchain system, the dataset is shared for every one of the members in the network. With the assistance of an agreement system, every member in the network can accomplish this with the arrangement. No outcast is needed to play out the exchanges in a conveyed climate. In the model, if an individual joins in bitcoin applications, he ought to keep every one of the principles and guidelines of the bitcoin application programming code. Any exchanges can be traded with different individuals naturally with no outsider communication. Each record has an exceptional secured mark with a time stamp in the circulated record. This cryptographic mark makes the record unchanging but auditable.

The mechanism of how a single data block is processed among numerous temperamental nodes is done through a consensus algorithm.

Data corruption is avoided here because before adding the particular transaction, each node is properly verified and based on the validation, it is placed in the record or ledger. As the central authority process is completely eliminated, then a change of attributes based on their benefits is not possible so enhanced security is an added advantage [21,22].

1.4 Blockchain for 5G-empowered IoT applications

Today, more IoT gadgets are associated and move data through the correspondence channel without any client collaboration. Because of this, the information shared is less secure, leading to potential issues of data loss, network issues, and so on. This type of connectivity problem is settled by 5G. 5G IoT design also has issues such as versatility, security, executive networking, validation, personality, absence of norms, and interoperability [22]. Among these, a few security issues are tackled by blockchain. Under 5G, blockchain is interconnected with more IoT devices to give all the more new opportunities to accomplish more help and applications in new innovation [23]. This segment has examined blockchain for 5G IoT applications (Fig. 4). The blockchain will uphold numerous applications such as smart medical services, smart cities, smart banking, advanced vehicular transportation, smart matrix, smart home, manufacturing industry, the Internet of Vehicles, supply chain, smart agriculture, smart schools, virtual reality, and smart contracts, which will be examined in Fig. 2.

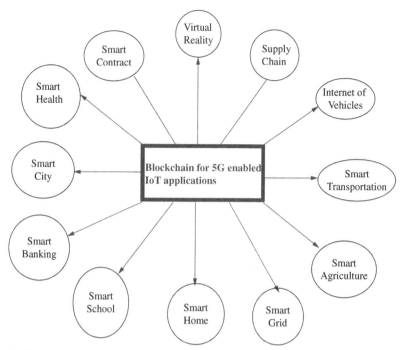

Fig. 4 Blockchain for 5G-enabled IoT applications.

1.5 Smart healthcare

Medical care is a mechanical area where affiliations and clinical associations give restorative administrations organizations, clinical gear, and clinical service to urge social protection movement to patients. The joining of blockchain with 5G innovation can drive the current medical care framework and give more benefits such as smart health and virtual reality. The software-based structure can perform smart works through NFVs, which advance IoT correspondence, while appropriated figuring can reinforce fast friendly protection movement networks for early recognizable proof of patient prosperity conditions [24–27].

Blockchain is used to fabricate a conveyed information base structure that can support and record all trades (for instance, friendly protection interest, getting data) and store them constantly in decentralized records. The work caried out under blockchain is to oversee prosperity data interoperability and security issues, for instance, enabling incredible endorsed collaboration among patients and social protection providers (trained professionals, protection organizations), and passing on industrious data securely to a combination of affiliations and devices [28–32].

Medical information ought to be safer and more protected. This information ought to be limited from change and destruction of stored information. On the off chance that an unapproved individual gets the information, the information will be sold or abused. In 5G, the size of the medical care information increases, so the security instruments to ensure the information ought to be likewise constrained should also increase.

2 Existing approach

5G has shown plenty of advantages in different applications. One of the significant applications is medical services. The medical systems can be far off, remotely observing patients. The patient data will be sent to the overseer immediately. This 5G innovation conveys the data with high speed without diminishing inactivity. This proposed system examines how to get the information with security, which is a change from patient to medical care suppliers by utilizing blockchain in 5G.

The information is produced from the patient and the specialist association. The essential information has a clinical history and recent concerns about the patient [33]. The essential information has the medication history, nursing care, and reports about the patient. In the alternative method with respect to client access, it offers an inclination to the proprietor to get to the data. In the event that the information is changed by unapproved clients, the clinical idea and medications proposed by specialists could cause poisoning, death, etc. To stay away from this issue, greater security is required while sending and getting the information [34–39]. This research work concentrates on the communication and transferring information between the doctor and patient (Fig. 5).

More calculations have been effectively proposed for getting the well-being information utilizing blockchain procedures. The final approach is to calculate the medical service information and provide it to the authorized person.

3 Proposed system

In 5G, a large number of IoT devices are associated together and moving the information to another. On the off chance that more information is moving from one device to other, it might prompt less secure transmission. So, greater security is proposed. This proposed system examines how information transmission is done utilizing blockchain in medical service applications. Medical service information ought to be safer and protected. Security implies that the individual ought to reserve the privileges to get to or uncover individual data. Security determines who ought to be permitted to get to the information. Specifically, the targets are:

1. To diminish the calculation time and encryption time.
2. To plan verification convention for securing data move with less capacity.

3.1 Model of proposed system

In this system, the patient is observed distantly utilizing medical care IoT-based devices that monitor pulses, sleeping conditions, pressure, glucose level, and so forth.

Fig. 5 Model of existing system.

This information is checked by specialists and stored in the cloud utilizing blockchain. The information ought to be checked from the approved gadget. The patient can impart this information to different clinics. Smart contracts are utilized to exchange data, which are stored in the blockchain. In the system graph, the elements utilized show restraint, cloud, hospitals, and organizations. Every patient is allocated with the patient ID, and the information is processed and transferred to the cloud for later access. With the assistance of keys, the record can be gotten to by medical care suppliers. This proposed framework centers around how the information is stored safely and how it is accessed safely, as shown in Fig. 6.

Security is accomplished by storing records in a scrambled configuration. The hospitals/agencies that wish to peruse the well-being record should move toward the patient with their character. The patient creates the key utilizing calculation and safely shares the key with the outsider to offer the record. Patient health is a concern in the medical services, as a patient may be enrolled on numerous occasions with various records at the same or various emergency clinics. This prompts discontinuity.

In this step, the patient health information is processed and the highlight information is compared with the threshold value and provides a solution.

Here, the record includes the patient name, register ID, doctor giving treatment, disease name, and its ID. The record transaction denotes the patient address, billing details, time of appointment, and visits made. The key transaction includes hospital address, patient address, billing signature, time stamp, etc.

3.2 Connection establishment flow between patient to cloud and vice versa

The patient information ought to be stored in the cloud by utilizing smart contracts. All the information is stored in cloud. The filtered information is passed to the cloud. A health access record is sent to the patients based on their request once it has been approved by the consulting doctor.

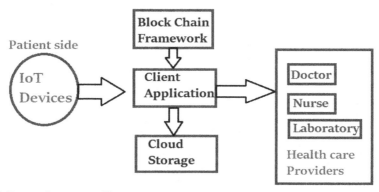

Fig. 6 Proposed system architecture.

3.3 ECC algorithm

In this proposed method, an ECC algorithm is utilized to accomplish security in a blockchain utilizing two parties, A and B. It has two focuses, P and Q.

- The parties contain the keys P and Q.
- A sends a solicitation message to B (message consists of its key P or Q).
- B acknowledges the message from A.
- Computes the value δ where $\delta = Y_Q - Y_P/Z_Q - Z_P$.
- B computes the C value δ.
- B sends the message to A, which consists of an ID and C value.
- The value of C is computed as $\begin{aligned} Z_C &= \delta^2 - Z_P - Z_Q \\ Y_C &= (\delta Z_P - \delta Z_C) - Y_P \end{aligned}$
- A checks the C value.
- If it is equal then A sends data to B.

4 Results

The following table shows the experimental results for the proposed system. Communication and computation overhead metrics are considered in the proposed system. The number of messages and the complete information that should be traded are determined in the correspondence overhead.

Parameter	Value
Total number of patients	1000
Record size in total	3 GB
Average patient record size	100 KB
Key generation algorithm	ECC
Blockchain size	700 GB

The proposed method is made in comparison with two techniques mentioned earlier, RSA and Diffie-Hellman. ECC calculation is done in this proposed method. ECC calculation has fewer messages that are exchanged, as represented in Fig. 7. The quantity of messages exchanged is seven in the proposed system. In any case, in RSA and Diffie-Hellman more messages are exchanged compared to ECC, as shown in Fig. 8. The measure of information utilized in the proposed method utilizes two bytes for the message, A has 20 bytes, the elliptic bend point has 20 bytes, identification has 20 bytes, and the time stamp has five bytes. The proposed method reduces the number of messages and the measure of information needed to be exchanged is less when compared with other schemes, as represented in Fig. 9.

The calculation overhead is the time needed for the 5G hub to process the necessary capacities that are utilized in the verification methodology, which diminishes the clog in the center network and decreases security hazards (Fig. 10).

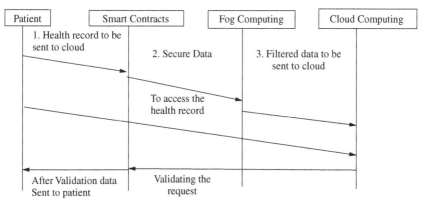

Fig. 7 Connection establishment flow between patient to cloud and vice versa.

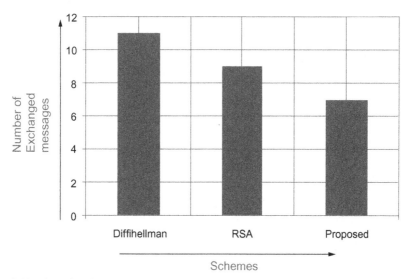

Fig. 8 Number of exchanged messages.

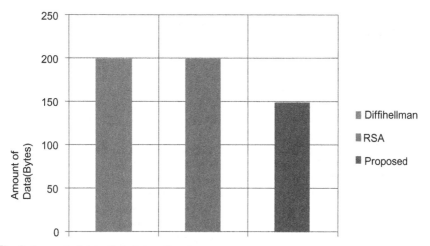

Fig. 9 Amount of data (bytes) transferred.

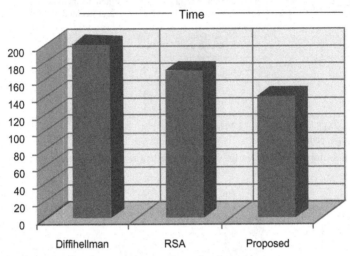

Fig. 10 Result graph related to computational overhead.

5 Conclusion

In a 5G network, more IoT devices are interrelated. Blockchain is a new innovation utilized in more fields such as digital payments, medical care, smart homes, and so on. Broadening blockchain to the IoT can have more benefits. The significant issue in 5G innovation is security. This information ought to be safer utilizing blockchain. The proposed method is to have the utmost security in the application of medical care utilizing blockchain and ECC algorithm under a 5G network. The proposed approach is compared with present models such as RSA and Diffie-Hellman. In the proposed system, two parameters are considered and a performance comparison between the existing and proposed systems is made under these considered parameters. This proposed method is more secure by comparison.

References

[1] H. Hui, Y. Ding, Q. Shi, F. Li, Y. Song, J. Yan, "5G network-based Internet of Things for demand response in smart grid: a survey" on application potential, Appl. Energy 257 (August 2019) (2020) 113972, https://doi.org/10.1016/j.apenergy.2019.113972.
[2] A. Rahim, P.K. Malik, Analysis and design of fractal antenna for efficient communication network in vehicular model, Sustain. Comput.: Inform. Syst. 31 (2021) 100586, https://doi.org/10.1016/j.suscom.2021.100586.
[3] M. Crosby, P. Pattanayak, S. Verma, V. Kalyanaraman, et al., Blockchain technology: beyond bitcoin, Appl. Innov. 2 (6–10) (2016) 71.
[4] A. Rahim, P.K. Malik, V.A. Sankar Ponnapalli, State of the art: a review on vehicular communications, impact of 5G, fractal antennas for future communication, in: P. Singh, W. Pawłowski, S. Tanwar, N. Kumar, J. Rodrigues, M. Obaidat (Eds.), Proceedings of First International Conference on Computing, Communications, and Cyber-Security

(IC4S 2019), Lecture Notes in Networks and Systems, vol. 121, Springer, Singapore, 2020, https://doi.org/10.1007/978-981-15-3369-3_1.

[5] K. Kitao, A. Benjebbour, T. Imai, Y. Kishiyama, M. Inomata, Y. Oku-mura, 5G system evaluation tool, in: 2018 IEEE Int. Work. Electromagn. Appl. Student Innov. Compet. iWEM 2018, 2018, pp. 1–2, https://doi.org/10.1109/iWEM.2018.8536617.

[6] U. Kujur, R. Shukla, Features analysis and comparison of 5G technology: a review, Int. J. Adv. Res. Comput. Eng. Technol. 7 (5) (2018). 2278–1323.

[7] F. Sindico, Seminar report, Int. J. Water Resour. Dev. 26 (4) (2010) 715–718, https://doi.org/10.1080/07900627.2010.524431.

[8] R.N. Mitra, D.P. Agrawal, 5G mobile technology: a survey, ICT Express 1 (3) (2015) 132–137, https://doi.org/10.1016/j.icte.2016.01.003.

[9] A. Rahim, P.K. Malik, V.A. Sankar Ponnapalli, Fractal antenna design for overtaking on highways in 5g vehicular communication ad-hoc networks environment, Int. J. Eng. Adv. Technol. 9 (1S6) (2019) 157–160. ISSN: 2249–8958.

[10] M. Nesterova, S. Nicol, Y. Nesterova, Evaluating power density for 5G applications, in: IEEE 5G World Forum, 5GWF 2018 – Conf. Proc., 2018, pp. 347–350, https://doi.org/10.1109/5GWF.2018.8517003.

[11] A.A. Labade, G.V. Lohar, P.R. Dike, N.N. Pachpor, Spectral efficiency enhancement through Wavelet Transform (WT) for 5G, in: Proc. – 2014 18IEEE Glob. Conf. Wirel. Comput. Networking, GCWCN 2014, 2015, pp. 268–272, https://doi.org/10.1109/GCWCN.2014.7030892. no. December 2014.

[12] Z.U. Khan, A. Alomainy, T.H. Loh, Empty substrate integrated waveguide planar slot antenna array for 5g wireless systems, in: 2019 IEEE Int. Symp. Antennas Propag. Usn. Radio Sci. Meet. APSURSI 2019 – Proc., 2019, pp. 1417–1418, https://doi.org/10.1109/APUSNCURSINRSM.2019.8888861.

[13] I. Ahmad, T. Kumar, M. Liyanage, J. Okwuibe, M. Ylianttila, A. Gurtov, Overview of 5g security challenges and solutions, IEEE Commun. Stand. Mag. 2 (1) (2018) 36–43.

[14] International Telecommunication Union, Setting the scene for 5G: opportunities & challenges, 2018.

[15] S. Li, L. Da Xu, S. Zhao, 5g internet of things: a survey, J. Ind. Inform. Integr. 10 (2018) 1–9. 0 50 100 150 200 250 Time (ms) Diffie-Hellman RSA Proposed Algorithm.

[16] A. Tabassum, M.S. Mustafa, S.A. Al Maadeed, The need for a global response against cybercrime: Qatar as a case study, in: 2018 6th International Symposium on Digital Forensic and Security (ISDFS), 2018, pp. 1–6.

[17] A. Rahim, P.K. Malik, Analysis and design of planner wide band antenna for wireless communication applications: fractal antennas, Design Methodologies and Tools for 5G Network Development and Application, IGI Global, 2021, pp. 196–208.

[18] A.A. Zaidi, et al., OFDM numerology design for 5G new radio to support IoT eMBB and MBSFN, IEEE Commun. Stand. Mag. 2 (2) (2018) 78–83.

[19] S. Shinjo, et al., A 28GHz-band highly integrated GaAs RF frontend Module for Massive MIMO in 5G, in: 2018 IEEE MTT-S Int. Microw. Work. Ser. 5G Hardw. Syst. Technol. IMWS-5G 2018, 2018, pp. 1–3, https://doi.org/10.1109/IMWS-5G.2018.8484564.

[20] M.A.B. Abbasi, H. Tataria, V.F. Fusco, M. Matthaiou, On the impact of spillover losses in 28 GHz Rotman lens arrays for 5G applications, in: 2018 IEEE MTT-S Int. Microw. Work. Ser. 5G Hardw. Syst. Technol. IMWS-5G 2018, 2018, pp. 1–3, https://doi.org/10.1109/IMWS5G.2018.8484443.

[21] M. Simkó, M.O. Mattsson, 5G wireless communication and health effects: a pragmatic review based on available studies regarding 6 to 100 GHz, Int. J. Environ. Res. Public Health 16 (18) (2019) 1–23, https://doi.org/10.3390/ijerph16183406.

[22] S.A. Busari, K.M.S. Huq, S. Mumtaz, L. Dai, J. Rodriguez, Millimeter wave massive MIMO communication for future wireless systems: a survey, IEEE Commun. Surv. Tutorials 20 (2) (2018) 836–869, https://doi.org/10.1109/COMST.2017.2787460.

[23] GSMA, G. Intelligence, Understanding 5G: perspectives on future technological advancements in mobile, in: GSMA Intell. Underst. 5G, 2014, pp. 3–15. no. December.

[24] D. University College, IEEE Microwave Theory and Techniques Society, European Microwave Association, Institute of Electrical and Electronics Engineers, 2018 IEEE MTT-S International Microwave Workshop Series on 5G Hardware and System Technologies: 30th–31st August 2018, UCD, Dublin, Ireland, vol. 1, 2018, pp. 1–3. no. c.

[25] K.N. Griggs, O. Ossipova, C.P. Kohlios, A.N. Baccarini, E.A. Howson, T. Hayajneh, Healthcare blockchain system using smart contracts for secure automated remote patient monitoring, J. Med. Syst. 42 (7) (2018) 130.

[26] A.D. Dwivedi, G. Srivastava, S. Dhar, R. Singh, A decentralized privacy-preserving healthcare blockchain for iot, Sensors 19 (2) (2019). [Online]. Available from: http://europepmc.org/articles/PM C6 359727.

[27] A. Reyna, C. Martín, J. Chen, E. Soler, M. Díaz, On blockchain and its integration with iot challenges and opportunities, Future Gener. Comput. Syst. 88 (2018) 173–190.

[28] Y. Yang, M. Ma, Conjunctive keyword search with designated tester and timing enabled proxy re-encryption function for E-health clouds, IEEE Trans. Inform. Forensics Secur. 2 (2016) 746–759.

[29] M. Li, S. Yu, Y. Zheng, Scalable and secure sharing of personal health records in cloud computing using attribute-based encryption, IEEE Trans. Parallel Distrib. Syst. 24 (1) (2013) 131–143.

[30] J. Sun, X. Wang, S. Wang, L. Ren, A searchable personal health records framework with fine grained access control in cloud fog computing, PLoS One 13 (11) (2018), https://doi.org/10.1371/journal.pone.0207543, e0207543. PMID: 30496194.

[31] J. Sun, L. Ren, S. Wang, X. Yao, A blockchain-based framework for electronic medical records sharing with fine-grained access control, PLoS One 15 (10) (2020), https://doi.org/10.1371/journal.pone.0239946, e0239946.

[32] R. Gupta, S. Tanwar, F. Al-Turjman, P. Italiya, A. Nauman, S.W. Kim, Smart contract privacy protection using AI in cyber physical systems: tools, techniques and challenges, IEEE Access 8 (2020) 24746–24772, https://doi.org/10.1109/ACCESS.2020.2970576.

[33] U. Bodkhe, D. Mehta, S. Tanwar, P. Bhattacharya, P.K. Singh, W. Hong, A survey on decentralized consensus mechanisms for cyber physical systems, IEEE Access 8 (2020) 54371–54401, https://doi.org/10.1109/ACCESS.2020.2981415.

[34] J. Hathaliya, S. Tanwar, An exhaustive survey on security and privacy issues in healthcare 4.0, Comput. Commun. 153 (2020), https://doi.org/10.1016/j.comcom.2020.02.018.

[35] S. Huh, S. Cho, S. Kim, Managing iot devices using blockchain platform, in: Advanced Communication Technology (ICACT), 2017 19th International Conference on IEEE, 2017, pp. 464–467.

[36] A. Dorri, S.S. Kanhere, R. Jurdak, P. Gauravaram, Blockchain for iot security and privacy: "The case study of a smart home", in: Pervasive Computing and Communications Workshops (PerCom Workshops), 2017 IEEE International Conference on IEEE, 2017, pp. 618–623.

[37] A. Rahim, K. Raghavendra, Fractal antenna design for various multiband application, Int. J. Eng. Adv. Technol. 8 (6 Special issue 3) (2019) 1813–1816.

[38] A. Rahim, P.K. Malik, V.A. SankarPonnapalli, Design and analysis of multi band fractal antenna for 5G vehicular communication, Test Eng. Manage. 83 (2020) 26487–26497.

[39] R. Gupta, S. Tanwar, S. Tyagi, N. Kumar, Tactile-Internet-based telesurgery system for healthcare 4.0: an architecture, research challenges, and future directions, IEEE Network 33 (6) (2019) 22–29, https://doi.org/10.1109/MNET.001.1900063.

The importance of 5G healthcare using blockchain technologies

Bela Shrimali and Shivangi Surati
LDRP Institute of Technology and Research, Kadi Sarva Vishwavidyalaya, Gandhinagar, India

1 Introduction

The increased use of networks for mobile communication and the Internet-of-things (IoT) have enabled billions of objects to communicate with each other at any time and at any place. The affecting performance parameters are data transfer rate, available bandwidth, processing power of devices, communication ranges of available networks, etc. With the growth of networks and industry revolution to improve these parameters, the healthcare industry has also grown from Healthcare 1.0 to 4.0 [1]. The evolution originated with Healthcare 1.0, which was doctor centric. It was followed by Healthcare 2.0, the beginning of industrialization and hospitals with equipments. Then came Healthcare 3.0, in which the technology became patient centric. Next, Healthcare 4.0 was equipped with advanced digital technologies such as IoT, cloud computing (CC), and fog computing (FC) for sharing or communicating the data between various stakeholders such as doctors, patients, laboratories, nurses, relatives/caretakers, etc.

Modern technology such as telehealth and telemedicine are cultivated that utilize the features of this healthcare development. Telemedicine takes advantage of telecommunication. Through this technology, doctors can check patients virtually by means of: (1) real time or live video, (2) high-quality images of disease, and (3) images of clinical reports shared via electronic media (e-mail or text message). Similarly, the detection of disease, treatments, and follow-up can also be suggested to patients virtually depending on the diagnosis. Apart from these, data, records, and resource management at hospitals or with doctors can be achieved effectively using telemedicine. However, time and distance are two major factors that affect the efficiency of telemedicine [2]. In addition, improved healthcare services are provided in connection with information technology (IT) filed by means of the Internet of medical things (IoMT), which is also known as healthcare IoT [3].

5G networks [4] are efficient in reducing these time and distance factors by providing faster means of communication and remote monitoring. 5G will not only improve telemedicine, but will also help many existing challenges in healthcare and in current technologies used, including remote examination and operations of patients. The major advantages proposed in 5G healthcare are low latency (end-to-end), reliable communication, remote monitoring at distant locations, remote

Blockchain Applications for Healthcare Informatics. https://doi.org/10.1016/B978-0-323-90615-9.00007-4
Copyright © 2022 Elsevier Inc. All rights reserved.

surgeries, immediate notifications and treatments through live sharing of high-quality digital records, etc. In addition, the emerging technologies that play vital roles in healthcare transformation as well as real-time data management are as follows [5]:

- 5G new radio interface and access;
- federated network slicing;
- radio access network (RAN) virtualization and distributed cloud;
- augmented reality (AR), virtual reality (VR), and spatial computing;
- artificial intelligence (AI) and machine learning (ML);
- Internet of things (IoT); and
- big data analytics.

Despite these advantages, the major challenge for current 5G technology is the need to assure an open, reliable, transparent, regulated, and especially secure system among the extraordinary, heterogeneous huge number of resources and mobile users.

1.1 Motivations

The records of patients are accessible to different stakeholders in healthcare and hence, the identity and authentication of stakeholders are critical parameters before sharing these sensitive records. Thus, the proposed 5G methodologies are not bound only to the management and transfer of data when applied for healthcare. They should be able to guarantee the highest level of security and trust management among the involved humans/devices. In addition, the access and reuse of medical records must also follow the governing regulations and should not be influenced by third parties. Hence, it is envisioned that the 5G healthcare architectures and platforms must be equipped with a middleware layer to provide secure and trustworthy communication.

As per our observations, Blockchain with its distributed and decentralized nature of data sharing and processing can facilitate a high level of data transparency, privacy, security, and immutability for 5G heterogeneous data [6, 7]. Thus, Blockchain is expected to satisfy the performance expectations for 5G healthcare with lower storage and operational costs [8]. The Blockchain layer can be implemented as a middleware layer between the healthcare applications and 5G technologies to provide the security and privacy execution of the appropriate Blockchain technology. Hence, the motivations behind this chapter are to describe the secure and immutable collaboration and communication of various healthcare stakeholders using Blockchain (Fig. 1).

1.2 Contributions

The contributions in this chapter are as follows:

- Discussion about 5G healthcare: The 5G healthcare, its technological evolution, advantages, and issues are discussed in detail.
- A secure and reliable 5G healthcare using Blockchain: The emergence of 5G healthcare with Blockchain is explained in detail to create a secure and reliable 5G healthcare system. Moreover, the technical aspects of how security, privacy, and immutability are maintained through Blockchain in 5G healthcare are also discussed.

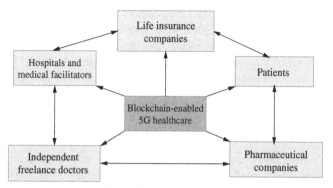

Fig. 1 Representation of stakeholders of Blockchain-based 5G healthcare ecosystem.

- An architecture of Blockchain-based 5G healthcare: The opportunities and scope of Blockchain in the healthcare domain are discussed. In addition, two types of architectures of Blockchain-based 5G healthcare are proposed: layered architecture and conceptual architecture.
- The applicability of 5G healthcare using Blockchain: The case studies/applications where this emergence of two technologies can be utilized efficiently are discussed. In addition, the importance of implementing Blockchain in 5G healthcare are presented.
- The comparative study of 5G healthcare with and without Blockchain is presented.
- Lastly, the research directions of the integration of Blockchain and 5G networks are highlighted with the aim to help researchers and organizations make enhancements in these emerging fields.

1.3 Organization

The main features of 5G healthcare and the use of Blockchain in it are discussed in Section 2. In addition, how Blockchain can be adopted in 5G healthcare is explained by exploring issues in 5G healthcare and the opportunity and scope in it through Blockchain in Section 3, followed by a discussion of the importance of Blockchain in 5G healthcare and various case studies/applications of it in Section 4. Next, in Section 5, research directions are discussed along with conclusion in Section 6.

2 Background

The evolution and background knowledge of 5G healthcare are discussed in detail in this section. In addition, a general overview of Blockchain and its technical aspects are explored in order to understand their usefulness in the domain.

2.1 5G healthcare

The current healthcare system is not fully utilized due to the mandatory requirement of physical visits of patients or doctors and analysis and follow-up of biomedical data and clinical reports. Instead, by using advanced technologies such as telehealth, remote monitoring, and telemedicine [2], the virtual visits of patients and doctors are possible by using real-time video, images, electronic reports, and sharing of patients' reports generated/transferred via electronic media. This development is the result of overcoming the limitations of time and distance by means of healthcare using 5G networks. The evolution of 5G healthcare, the advantages/characteristics, and application use cases are discussed in this section.

2.1.1 5G healthcare evolution

The industry evolution [1] and web evolution [9] as per the requirements and limitations of different eras also led to the development of the healthcare domain (Fig. 2) and the relations between various stakeholders of healthcare as follows [10]:

1. *Healthcare 1.0*: The doctor-centric Healthcare 1.0 followed the classical method of physical visits/travels of patients or doctors even at distant places and the treatment was according to test reports and other evidence from patients. The consultation was through one-to-one communication and followed predefined practices and treatments that were nonexperimental and recorded on paper. The treatments and prescriptions were based on past experiences, healthcare domain knowledge and experience, or sometimes by taking help from expert doctors. The survivability of the patients using known scientific techniques was the main focus of medical personnel. The disadvantages were the high cost of treatments, limited awareness among people, additional test reports for diagnosis, and lack of communication between stakeholders.
2. *Healthcare 2.0*: With the growth of industrialization, Healthcare 2.0 concentrated on hospital and medical instrument development, social software tool development, and collaboration between hospitals. The patient care services were integrated socially and the patients started participating in decisions related to their health.

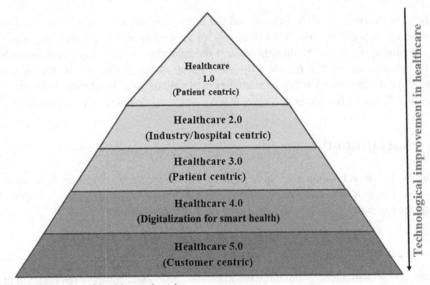

Fig. 2 Evolution of healthcare domain.

3. *Healthcare 3.0*: It adopted a patient-centric approach with digitalized records and remote care of patients. The communication and interaction between patients and doctors were increased by incorporating virtual tools. The motive was to automate the health domain by applying enterprise resource planning, automated patient check-ins, and the use of information communication technologies.

4. *Healthcare 4.0*: Advanced digital technologies such as the IoT, CC, AI, ML, sensor networks, and FC emerged with healthcare (Healthcare 4.0) for sharing or communicating data between various stakeholders such as doctors, patients, laboratories, nurses, relatives/caretakers, etc. This growth in healthcare introduced electronic health (eHealth) and mobile health (mHealth) for the collection, storage, processing, remote monitoring, and analysis of patient data on a larger scale. However, the use of these digitalized technologies emphasized large amounts of data and an additional load on the existing networks, resulting in lower speed, poor quality, and network congestion. These can lead to delays in patient treatment (even those who are in queue) that may not be acceptable in case of life-threatening situations.

5. *Healthcare 5.0*: 5G technologies have the capabilities to overcome these issues and challenges due to their characteristics such as lower latency, lower power consumption, multimedia support, higher data rate, etc. Nowadays, smart health (sHealth) is developed in Healthcare 5.0 with an aim to concentrate not only on the patients, but also on the customers (other than patients) for their wellbeing, quality and comfort of life, and city sustainability [11]. The development of sHealth is feasible with the use of advanced features provided by 5G networks.

Thus, 5G completely enhanced healthcare with new perspectives and directions that allow the stakeholders of healthcare to be connected with each other virtually by live chat or video processing in real time [12, 13]. The patients with acute situations who are unable to leave their homes to visit doctors can also be monitored by doctors from distant locations in 5G healthcare. Even the hospitals are converted to smart hospitals and any stakeholder can contact other stakeholders through this updated healthcare. A summary of this technological shift in healthcare is shown in Table 1.

2.1.2 Advantages of 5G healthcare

5G healthcare offers various advantages that meet the requirements of digital technologies and transformations as follows [2, 5]:

- *Healthcare to homecare transformation*: The treatment, monitoring, and follow-up of patients can be implemented from distant locations (even though the patient is at home).
- *Distributed and decentralized treatment*: The stakeholders can contact each other for online data and treatment management in the decentralized environment, even though they are at geographically distributed locations.
- *Rapid transmission of large files and videos*: The medical treatments generate various reports with larger size such as MRI reports, live online videos, and other images to be sent to doctors for treatment. The quick and reliable transmission of these data files will hasten decisions in treatment, resulting in the improved care of patients, especially in emergency situations.
- *Improved telehealth and telemedicine*: The availability of specialist doctors and other patient caretakers as well as their collaboration and coordination are important challenges in the healthcare domain, especially in rural and remote areas. Telepath and telemedicine have

Table 1 The technological shift in healthcare.

Characteristics	Healthcare 1.0	Healthcare 2.0	Healthcare 3.0	Healthcare 4.0	Healthcare 5.0
Focus	Doctor-centric	Industry-centric	Patient-centric	Digitalization for smart health	Personalization (customer-centric)
Treatment	Test reports and evidence-based, past experiences, and expertise in domain	Quality care using medical instruments, devices, and social software tools, emergence of clinics, and hospitalization	Automated treatments, operating, and value-based models	Preventive and proactive care using artificial intelligence, sensors, machine learning, three-dimensional printing, etc., continuous monitoring and predictions about growth of disease	Online consultations using sensors and other physical devices, digital wellness for physical, mental, and emotional well-being of customers
Communication technology	Physical, one to one	Between all stakeholders by sharing records and integration of patient care services	Information communication technologies, telehealth, and remote care via networks	Through networking and technology such as IoT, distributed networks, image processing, CC	Remote access using 5G networks, augmented reality, virtual reality, and robotics
Record keeping	On paper	Electronic health records (EHR)	Database development and analysis, digitized records	EHR repositories, data sharing at any location, eHealth, eMedical, and mHealth	EHR, at centralized servers such as cloud
Strategic differentiator	Survivability of patients	Responsiveness by stakeholders, including patients	The lower cost and higher efficiency of treatments, easy access to health services	Uniqueness of services provided	Lifelong relationships, qualitative, and comfortable life

requirements of higher speed, improved bandwidth, and lower latency time to manage appointments and the transmission of high-quality video in real time. This can be achieved via 5G healthcare across the world.

- *R3 characteristics*: 5G healthcare offers R3 (real time, remote, and reliable) monitoring as well as treatment of patients. The doctors can receive patient-related information on time due to lower latency and can suggest the line of treatment immediately, therein treating more patients. The remote monitoring has become feasible due to the increased capabilities of 5G networks. The unnecessary delays, slow network speed, and packet loss issues are also addressed in 5G, hence, improving the reliable transfer of data.
- *Invention of new sensors*: Depending on the patient needs and relevant treatment, more accurate and multipurpose sensor devices are invented to gather the data of patients. This improves the personalized treatment and care of patients through the IoMT.
- *Support of multimedia through AR/VR*: With the use of AR and VR, doctors can deliver innovative lectures and efficient operative guidance in live environments.

2.2 Role of Blockchain in 5G healthcare

With the arrival of 5G, higher bandwidth, and low latency, a new vision for to healthcare industry has arisen. It contributes to remote and better diagnosis, high-quality medical resources, and prompt triage. Though, 5G healthcare fails to ensure security and privacy of stakeholders due to its centralized or decentralized implementation environment. This section discusses the possible issues in 5G healthcare and their solutions through Blockchain with required technicality.

2.2.1 Problems and its solutions through Blockchain

1. The secure exchange of information between healthcare stakeholders: The 5G network provides the heterogeneous environment of communication and hence, the secure exchange of information becomes essential. Also, the identity of stakeholders is important. For example, patients' private sensitive medical information should be shared between stakeholders securely with full privacy. In a 5G network, that becomes a big challenge. Here, the use of Blockchain can resolve the issue.

   Solution: Asymmetric cryptography or public-key cryptography is an essential component of Blockchain technology. These advanced cryptographic techniques ensure that the source of communication is legitimate and that intruders cannot steal a message.

   Here is an example of how public-key cryptography can be used in 5G healthcare. Let us consider a scenario where all stakeholders are part of Blockchain. A basic example is where patients want a medicine prescription at regular intervals from doctors and that prescription is forwarded to the pharmacy. The doctor sends the prescription to the patient over an unreliable, unsecured, and heterogeneous network of communication such as the Internet and mobile networks. The doctor could use public-key cryptography by generating a set of public and private keys. He then posts his public key to the patient. Now, whenever he wants to communicate with the patient, he can add a digital signature to his message by using his private key. This would prove that he is the creator of the message. The patient can verify the same using the message he received and the doctor's public key. Similarly, the pharmacy verifies the patient. A digital signature is used for the authentication of every

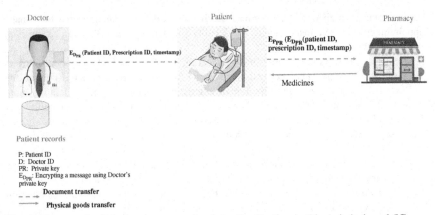

Fig. 3 The use of public key cryptography for authentication in Blockchain-based 5G healthcare.

stakeholder. Every communication has a different digital signature that depends on the private key of the stakeholders. This is shown in Fig. 3.

2. Fraud in the medicine supply chain, medical prescriptions, fund transfers, and sensitive data: The medical data of patients can be easily hacked in a heterogeneous network of communication. Also, fraud in the medicine supply chain, medical prescriptions, and fund transfers is easily possible in a centralized environment.

   Solution to fraud and tampering: The medical data of patients are very sensitive and hence, its storage should be tamper-proof. These sensitive data are prime targets for cyberattacks. Its security is a major concern. Also, the access control over the sensitive data should be managed and controlled by patients. Therefore, sharing and accessing the control of patients' healthcare data is another important concern. Blockchain technology is very robust against failures and attacks due to its distributed peer-to-peer network environment. Also, it provides different methods of access control in heterogeneous communication environments [14]. Therefore, Blockchain is most suitable for 5G healthcare. It facilitates secure storage for various sensitive data such as drug descriptions and supply chain data. It also supports effective access control, data sharing, and managing of an audit trail of medical activities. Data in Blockchain are stored in a block. "SHA256 Hash Function" is used to make block tempered-proof.

   A transaction is only included in the block if it is validated using the cryptographic algorithm by every participating peer and if it is received from the other maximum number of peers. Once the block is filled by the transaction with its predefined limits along with all the details of validated transactions, a timestamp, a cryptographic hash (a mathematically generated alphanumeric string) of the data, and the hash of the previous block, it is introduced at the end of Blockchain after the mutual agreement of every peer. This process of including block to Blockchain is called mining and 256 Hash Function miner gets rewarded for the introduction of every block.

   Every block in the Blockchain is securely linked to its previous (preceding) block using the hash. Malicious changes of the data of the block change the hash of the current block. So, this hash change needs to be reflected in all the succeeding nodes. This way, immutability is maintained in the Blockchain. The blocks and their connections are shown in Fig. 4.

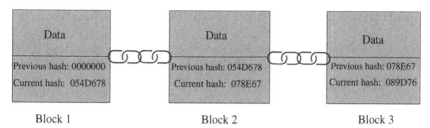

Block 1   Block 2   Block 3

Fig. 4 The immutability through blocks and Blockchain.

The overall operation of Blockchain is shown in Fig. 5. Here, peer A transfers some amount to peer B. So, this is called a transaction between peers A and B. In Blockchain, this transaction will be verified by all the other participating peers using asymmetric key cryptography that verifies the double spending as well as authenticity. Once the transaction is verified, it will be executed and added to the block. All the nodes of the network, that is, A, B, C, D, need to solve the mathematical puzzle (in case of a proof of work mechanism) to introduce a block in the Blockchain. The one who solves the puzzle is allowed to include the block in the Blockchain.

With this background knowledge, how secured transactions offered by Blockchain can be incorporated in 5G healthcare for security concerns is discussed in the next section.

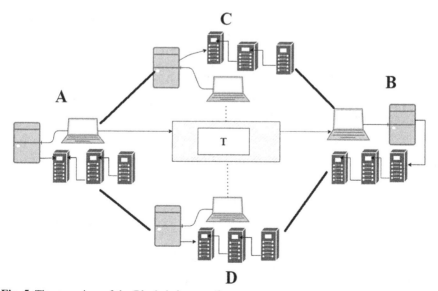

Fig. 5 The overview of the Blockchain operation.

3   Adoption of blockchain technology in 5G healthcare

The various issues and challenges related to 5G healthcare are presented in this section. Also the opportunities and scope of Blockchain to overcome these challenges are discussed and the required architecture is proposed for the same.

3.1   Issues in 5G healthcare

The changes required in the existing technologies/networks to accommodate the features of 5G and relevant issues are as follows [5, 15]:

- *Transformations of network*: The communications, data transmission, and real-time decisions in 5G healthcare demand network conversions and a supportive networking infrastructure that is reliable and agile.
- *Transformations of stakeholders*: The hospitals should be able to store and manage the data and medical records of patients similar to the data centers. Not only that the doctors and the other supportive staff are required to learn the use of applications and technologies similar to data scientists.
- *Coordination and collaboration between stakeholders*: The practice and applicability of new technologies raise the requirements to learn new updates, take new responsibilities precisely, and the timely coordination between all stakeholders for the smooth effective care of patients.
- *Reliability*: Though 5G networks offer high-speed data transfer, thereby decreasing the delay time, devices such as patients' and doctors' smartphones cannot rely merely on connectivity. The parameters such as battery life, communication range, and processing power of the devices also affect the reliability of healthcare procedures. In addition, procedures such as remote robotic surgeries happening today still require the physical presence of a surgeon.
- *High-quality resources*: For live video sharing, high-quality cameras and minimum connectivity requirements are issues in the rural areas of developing countries.
- *Security and privacy*: 5G networks have brought some level of security through encryption techniques, but still a higher level of security and privacy is required for critical data related to patients, their diseases, and treatments. Hence, additional cybersecurity measures for the healthcare domain are necessary to identify different types of threats and attacks.

Thus, 5G networks are efficient for real-time applications, yet the requirements of 5G healthcare are even higher.

3.2   Opportunity and scope in 5G healthcare through Blockchain

The healthcare sector is an industry where health institutions and organizations provide health insurance, medical services, and equipment to facilitate efficient healthcare services for patients. The use of new promising technologies in healthcare fulfills the requirements such as trust, quality of service (QoS), security, and privacy. 5G technologies in healthcare applications facilitate prerequisites such as essential levels of connectivity, improved QoS, better density, ultrahigh reliability, convenience, and accuracy. However, to provide the full potential of 5G networks in the healthcare industry, network security and data privacy are paramount.

5G healthcare with Blockchain can uplift the existing healthcare systems and facilitate higher performance benefits through decentralization, security, privacy [15, 16], service efficiency, and system simplification [17]. There are many services that 5G incorporates in healthcare such as healthcare networking and computing services, home-based healthcare services, and flexible diversified computation services. The role of Blockchain in 5G healthcare services is to manage the security and interoperability issues of sensitive health data such as effectual authorized interactions between patients and healthcare providers such as doctors, healthcare workers, and health insurance companies, as well as the transmission of patients' sensitive data securely to these stakeholders. To facilitate the mentioned properties, Blockchain can integrate with various 5G technologies such as softwarization, device to device (D2D) communications [18], mobile edge computing (MEC) [19], and cloud/edge/FC. The network functions are carried out by softwarized infrastructure using network functions virtualizations (NFV) [20] that promote IoT communication while cloud/edge/FC is used for prompt medical services for the prestage detection of patients' health conditions [21]. In such a scenario, Blockchain is deployed to implement a peer-to-peer distributed database system in the form of a distributed shared ledger that can validate, record, and maintain all transactions such as patient data and healthcare requests. All the transactions of the shared ledger are visible to all the healthcare stakeholders such as doctors, nurses, clinicians, and patients to speed up data sharing during medical treatment and medication processes [21].

The integration of both the technologies is explained previously to discuss the opportunity and scope through it. Blockchain provides the capability of controlling, storing, and managing 5G data through its secure, tamper-proof shared distributed ledger. Mainly, Blockchain provides lots of features such as immutability, decentralization, transparency, and privacy, all of which assure handling security issues of current 5G networks effectively. Thus, the important points of Blockchain are its capabilities to support security, privacy, transparency, and network management for 5G networks [21]. In the following, the opportunities and scope in 5G healthcare from Blockchain integration are presented.

- *Security enhancement*: By providing many technical facilities such as decentralization, immutability, traceability, and transparency, Blockchain enhances the security and privacy of 5G healthcare. Blockchain integrated with different 5G suitable network technologies such as cloud/edge computing, D2D communication, and software defined networks (SDN)-based healthcare networks, helps to achieve secure data exchange between the devices in the network. All patients' sensitive information and medical test results can be stored and managed by Blockchain. Every stakeholders' authentication and validation are handled by Blockchain before any medical process is performed such as medical tests, virtual medical remote surgeries, or remote medical advice [22].
- *System performance enhancement*: Blockchain with 5G healthcare improves the performances of systems. In comparison to traditional centralized databases, Blockchain provides better data storage and management services with low latency data retrieval. For example, in 5G healthcare, Blockchain can help to establish secure peer-to-peer communication among all stakeholders without third-party intervention. This would improve communication latency and traceability as well as facilitate global accessibility for all users that will enhance the overall healthcare system performance. Due to the distributed property and environment

of Blockchain, an intruder's attack or threat would not affect the overall network operations [21].

- *Simplified network*: Blockchain with a 5G healthcare network simplifies the network deployments due to its distributed and decentralized architectures. This network removes third-party intervention. Hence, the healthcare system's stakeholders have no worries about the establishment of a connection with the centralized control servers. These peer-to-peer networks promise data availability in any case of single node failure.
- *Privacy management*: Blockchain with a 5G healthcare network provides anonymity and privacy through Blockchain's cryptographic techniques. In the healthcare system, the patients' sensitive health data need to be secured. Blockchain would ensure secure data storage by storing the information to a distributed shared ledger that is maintained by all the stakeholders of the system.
- *Transparency*: Because Blockchain manages the distributed shared ledgers with healthcare stakeholders, it facilitates patients taking control of their own medical information during medical treatments, clinical tests, doctor visits, and moving to other labs and hospitals.

3.3 Architecture of Blockchain-based 5G healthcare

The architecture of Blockchain-based 5G healthcare using two different approaches is discussed in this section. First, the layered architecture that depicts the Blockchain-based 5G healthcare system from the users' perspective is discussed. After that the conceptual architecture to describe the transmission and control of the data along with the role of technologies and stakeholders in Blockchain-based 5G healthcare systems is presented in detail.

3.4 Layered architecture

The layered architecture of Blockchain-based 5G healthcare is shown in Fig. 6. The operation of a computing system is split into four different abstraction layers: the stakeholder layer, healthcare application layer, Blockchain layer, and the 5G network technology layer. The description of each layer follows:

1. *Healthcare stakeholder layer*: This lowest layer is concerned with the multiple healthcare stakeholders of the system and their intercommunication and interaction with the upper layers through IoT. The IoT devices pass the electronic health data (EHD) to the upper layer. This layer defines the beneficiary of the system.
2. *Healthcare application layer*: The second-lowest layer of the architecture is a healthcare application that describes operations carried out by the system such as data management, supply chain operations, and the IoMT. This layer is responsible for the collection, management, and control of data.
3. *Blockchain layer*: The upper layer is the Blockchain layer that is responsible for the privacy, security, transparency, availability, and reliability of data. It describes the Blockchain-based storage and computing of data. This layer describes the suitable implementation of Blockchain technology such as permissioned, permissionless, and hybrid Blockchain. It enables multiple stakeholders to benefit from healthcare applications.
4. *5G technologies layer*: The uppermost layer is the 5G network technologies layer that defines the available 5G network technologies such as D2D, NFV, cloud/edge, network slicing, and V2V for fast and interruptless communication. This layer is responsible for and

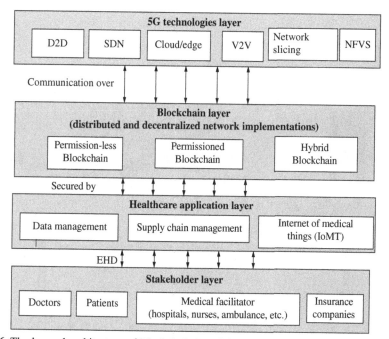

Fig. 6 The layered architecture of Blockchain-based 5G healthcare.

describes how these various technologies will be used to fulfill the needs of various diverse applications from the continuous traffic of connected heterogeneous devices [21].

3.5 Conceptual architecture

A conceptual diagram of the integration of Blockchain in 5G healthcare is shown in Fig. 7. The three-part conceptual architecture is shown here.

1. *Healthcare user service*: A Blockchain-based 5G healthcare scenario is considered where users' (patients, doctors, medical facilitators, healthcare insurance companies, etc.) EHD are gathered through IoT devices and local networks. EHD may include personal information and medical history provided by patients or doctors.
2. *5G network*: As shown in Fig. 7, 5G networks are going to be hugely distributed and will require the inclusion of several new technologies such as SDN, edge computing, NFV, cloud, and D2D. It may be possible that the complexity of 5G networks will exceed the capability of a single admin to manage the end-to-end network.
3. *Blockchain*: Blockchain, specifically the hybrid or private Blockchain, is perfectly poised to solve these issues in 5G networks. Blockchain is a distributed and decentralized peer-to-peer network that can work perfectly in a distributed network such as 5G. Because multiple stakeholders in a network are involved, it is difficult to build trust and transparency while also guaranteeing security, privacy, and immutability. With Blockchain, all data will be available and transparent to everyone. The allocation and deallocation of resources are performed using smart contracts when all the stakeholders are agreed on service-level agreement (SLA). Smart contract-based operations are carried out between the stakeholders. Hence,

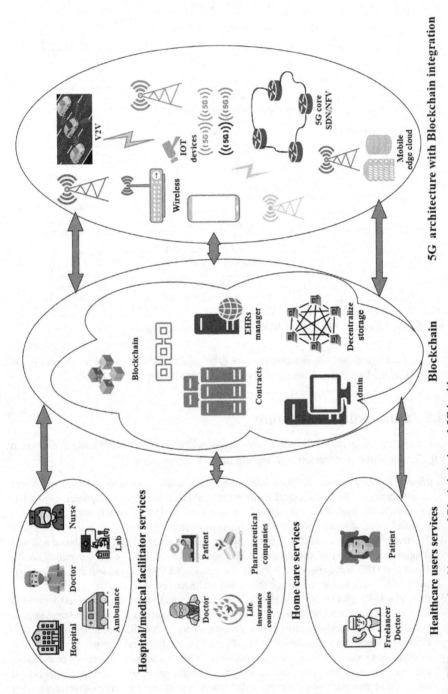

Fig. 7 The conceptual architecture of Blockchain-based 5G healthcare.

The importance of 5G healthcare using blockchain technologies

the entire process will be transparent to all stakeholders, providing a secure, reliable, and auditable trail of transactions on the Blockchain.

In Ref. [23], a 5G and Blockchain-based sensor architecture is proposed for continuous and remote monitoring. This proposed data architecture consists of five layers: the data gathering layer, the data processing layer, the 5G network layer, the data preservation layer, and the application layer. The data architecture describing the general layers and their responsibilities in data transfer in the system is discussed here.

4 Discussion

After discussing the collaboration Blockchain with 5G healthcare to create a secured and reliable architecture for the same, the importance and case studies/applications showing the future of healthcare are explored in this section.

4.1 Importance of Blockchain in 5G healthcare

5G healthcare brings lots of opportunities in healthcare services using prompt mobile networks that fulfill the increasing demands for performance enhancement, portability, availability, and energy efficiency posed by the ever-growing network services. In the case of healthcare industries, all kinds of medical healthcare procedures, such as preventive, diagnostic, rehabilitation, etc., demand continuous monitoring of data to detect symptoms for early diagnosis, logging private medical history, sharing securely medical documents, etc. In such cases, the privacy and security of sensitive data are essential. Blockchain can provide trusted and secure medical automation systems for monitoring, treatments, and healthcare data access control [24].

From the previous analysis, there are three core importances of Blockchain in 5G healthcare:

1. The integration of Blockchain with 5G healthcare provides reliable data storage and program execution in a distributed manner that also satisfies the needs of the computation and computation loads. The communication delay of Blockchain is relatively high because of the decentralization property, but that can be managed by the 5G network.
2. The implementation of the 5G network brings out a strong and powerful communication ability with higher bandwidth and lower latency compared to the existing 4G-based wireless networks. However, these 5G devices for mentioned healthcare systems such as movable vehicles, communication base stations, smart phones, or even wearable devices have relatively low storage and computation capabilities that may lead to unreliable data storage and transmission. This problem of unreliable communication and the security of data can be achieved using Blockchain implementation. Large-scale and people-centric interconnections, D2D communications, and IoT networks can be attained using peer-to-peer concepts of Blockchain nodes without being changed or modified. Blockchain enables strong immutability for 5G services and different operations such as data sharing, spectrum sharing, virtualized network resource provisions, etc. [21].
3. Transparency and anonymity are the much-needed requirements of healthcare, especially when data are communicated through a network. The sensitive data of a patient's diagnosis,

medication, or critical surgeries requires anonymity and transparency. Both these properties along with security and privacy can be achieved through Blockchain. The distributed shared ledger of Blockchain spreads across a large network for public verifiability. This enables all the stakeholders to fully access, verify, and track transaction activities over the network with equal rights [21].

Blockchain-based 5G healthcare gains secure, reliable, trustworthy, and privacy-preserving contact tracing with high efficiency and low latency. More specifically, the reliability of Blockchain and high speed with low latency of the 5G network will eliminate the deficiencies brought from using either of them alone. 5G healthcare and Blockchain-integrated 5G healthcare are discussed and compared in Table 2. Both the systems are compared in terms of various characteristics such as immutability, security, privacy, trust, transparency, and decentralization. The notifiable features lacking

Table 2 Comparison of 5G healthcare system with and without Blockchain integration.

Characteristics	5G healthcare	Blockchain-enabled 5G healthcare
Decentralization	5G healthcare requires a trusted external authority to perform transactions/operations [25]	Decentralizing 5G networks eliminates the need for a trusted external authority to perform transactions/operations. Stakeholders have full control over their own data [24]
Security	5G connects critical infrastructure with the use of recent technologies such as NFV and SDN, bringing lots of security threats and safety issues for the network [26]	Blockchain secures 5G networks by providing distributed trust models with high access authentication to ensure data privacy. By storing the information of data (i.e., IoMT metadata) across a network of computers in the form of a shared ledger makes data tampering more difficult for hackers. Blockchain provides authentication, user verification, and preservation of 5G healthcare resources
Privacy	5G networks have different communication systems such as virtual mobile network operators (VMNOs), communication service providers (CSPs), and network infrastructure providers.	Blockchain has a decentralized, distributed, peer-to-peer network with a public-key cryptography mechanism for privacy and security. Hybrid Blockchain implementation for 5G

Table 2 Continued

Characteristics	5G healthcare	Blockchain-enabled 5G healthcare
	All these systems have different priorities for privacy. Communication over the various communication systems brings privacy issues due to their different privacy policies. Hence, privacy becomes a major concern for the 5G healthcare network in terms of users' data, location, and identity [26, 27]	healthcare allows the data to remain strongly private and secure
Immutability	It is very difficult to maintain immutability in 5G healthcare with a heterogeneous centralized system and communication systems	It is very difficult to modify or change the data recorded in the Blockchain due to its peer-to-peer networks of the ubiquitous Blockchain environment [21]
Trust	Trust between the many 5G technology service providers is tough to maintain due to their different privacy and security policies. Hence, trust in 5G healthcare is the main concern	Blockchain facilitates the immutable and transparent system through its distributed shared ledger that brings trust between stakeholders of the healthcare system [21]
Transparency	5G healthcare may not provide transparency to its stakeholders	All information of transactions on Blockchain (i.e., public ledgers) is viewable to all stakeholders based on their role in the Blockchain network. So, transactions/operations in Blockchain are transparent to all its stakeholders

in the 5G healthcare system are highlighted, followed by how Blockchain-enabled 5G healthcare resolves the issues.

4.2 Use case scenarios and case studies/applications

5G has increased the scope of healthcare of hospitals and clinics. The consultation of patients, the diagnosis of diseases, medicine prescriptions, continuous monitoring, and follow-up—all these medical scenarios can be administrated through 5G healthcare. Various area/use cases in healthcare that make use of this modern technology are as follows [5].

4.2.1   Patient-related applications

Application 1: Remote patient monitoring:

Remote patient monitoring can be considered a fundamental application to verify the practical efficiency of healthcare services and chronic disease management using Blockchain. Patient-related information and required parameters can be collected and analyzed using various wearable and eHealth devices and body sensors without the need for patients to travel physically to primary care facilities and one-to-one communication with medical professionals. Blockchain plays a vital role in securing these collected data. A study to improve the remote surveillance of patients and to provide teleguidance to patients through continuous monitoring of patients is presented [28]. It utilized IoT-connected devices and the layered model of Blockchain-enabled IoT in 5G healthcare is proposed that can be effectively applied to patient remote monitoring. A clustering-based sensor network is constructed with cluster head's responsibilities of exchanging data with the base station. The SHA-256-based securing technique is implemented to update the ledger in distributed networks.

Another sensor network for remote and consistent data monitoring is proposed in Ref. [23] that is based on 5G networks and Blockchain. Two use cases are considered using the proposed architecture for continuous and remote monitoring—(1) monitoring of chronic diseases and (2) monitoring of back pain.

Application 2: High definition (HD) virtual consultations:

The patients and healthcare professionals can communicate virtually by means of two-way HD video for (1) virtual consultation, (2) initial screening and analysis, (3) physical or visual observation and diagnoses such as dermatological symptoms, (4) follow-up such as routine activities of Parkinson's patients, and (5) rehabilitation therapy. Again, the discussion, treatments, and follow-up can be applied over the Internet without physical communication. This is useful especially to patients suffering from diseases, elderly patients that are unable to move outside, or patients requiring continuous follow-up. The Blockchain architecture is useful in such HD video consultations to maintain the privacy and security of patients' data streaming over the 5G networks.

Case study 1: COVID-19 pandemic:

The B5G framework for detecting COVID-19 using 5G healthcare through Blockchain is proposed in Ref. [29]. This framework is developed to detect COVID-19 using chest X-ray or CT scan images via the 5G network's low latency and high bandwidth characteristics. In addition, a mass surveillance system is integrated in the proposed architecture to observe previous movements of patients identified as COVID-19 patients. The detection of social distancing detection and mask wearing as well as monitoring body temperature are the vital parameters measured by mass surveillance systems. The patient suspecting symptoms of COVID-19 can record and send vital signs to doctors/hospitals. Next, three deep leaning (DL) models (ResNet50, Deep Tree, and Inception v3) are investigated in the framework and experiments are carried out with three types of approaches: (1) a local mobile approach, (2) a local mobile with edge approach, and (3) a local mobile with cloud approach. The experimentation was conducted using the fivefold validation method on the training set with 2000 healthy samples, 2000 pneumonia samples (non-COVID-19), and 200

COVID-19 samples while the testing set consisted of 200, 200, and 50 samples, respectively. The deep tree model was found to be more suitable in the proposed framework compared to the other two.

In addition, the roles of 5G and Blockchain in the COVID-19 pandemic are explored in Ref. [3]. The applicability of IoMT and unmanned aerial vehicle (UAV) (such as drones) technologies in COVID-19 are identified as: (1) smart thermometers, (2) battery-operated IoT buttons, (3) surveillance of crowds, (4) mass screening, (5) spraying disinfectants, and (6) delivery of healthcare essentials and medicines. Based on these, various governments and companies have developed apps using Blockchain to integrate and continuously validate the dynamic data in a secure manner. Two Blockchain-based applications are discussed in this review as follows:

(1) *CIVITAS*: An app known as Civitas was developed by a Canadian start-up based on Blockchain that checks the permission of persons to leave home. In addition, doctors can keep track of COVID-19 patients' symptom and offer advice about treatments and medicines using telemedicine functionality.

(2) *MiPasa*: This is an app that works on streaming of data provided by medical associations or stakeholders. These data are secured using IBM Blockchain to help hospitals and other medical organizations make decisions about future action plans and resource allocation.

Another case study to fight COVID-19 is presented in Ref. [30] that proposed IoT-based healthcare using Blockchain. A cognitive engine is developed that manages the user commands and represents various dashboards related to COVID-19 document management to the users. The dashboards are related to COVID-19 test certificates, verification of antibody testing, modeling and analysis of the virus, and information related to medical development. In addition, the proposed architecture helps in determining social distancing, prediction of the number of infected and cured cases, pattern mining, and genetic-based analysis. Blockchain technology is used to secure documents and vaccination-related information in this architecture.

Case study 2: Tactile robotic telesurgery:

The architecture toward 5G-enabled tactile robotic telesurgery (T5ET) with haptic feedback is proposed in Ref. [31] that shows progress in surgeries. Two types of links are used: (1) a forward link to control the motion of robotic arms as well as the master console command, and (2) a feedback link based on sensors to observe the patient's heartbeat and blood pressure by other medical supporting staff. The performance parameters (jitter, throughput, delay) were improved in 5G as discussed in the experimental results.

4.2.2 Hospital-related applications

Application 3: Smart and connected ambulance:

The ambulances play an important role in transporting patients demanding emergency treatment. Smart and connected ambulances can be developed by the following two scenarios:

· While the patient is being transferred to a hospital in case of emergency, the records and information of the patient can be transferred to hospital stakeholders through wearable devices/sensors/HD live videos. In this way, hospital stakeholders can get the information in advance and can prepare the line of treatment before the patient arrives. In addition, the preliminary treatments/procedures to be given inside the ambulance can be suggested to the paramedics.

- Smart ambulances can be maintained to give emergency treatment if the service request is generated by the nearby patient. The medical professionals in these ambulances can start the treatment of the patient based on his history and the patient can be saved from life-threatening health attacks.

In both these scenarios, the records and information of the patient can be managed and transferred using security aspects of the Blockchain.

Application 4: Collaboration at remote locations in telesurgery:

The higher quality and accurate healthcare surgical services as well as required collaboration at distant or remote locations can be provided through telesurgery (TS). An approach named AaYusH is proposed in Ref. [32] that utilized Ethereum smart contract (ESC) and an IPFS-based TS system to resolve security and privacy issues in TS. The components used in this approach are: (1) surgeon layer initiates and controls the surgical procedures by passing the commands over a 5G network, (2) transmission layer: the network layer as the communication path between the surgeon and patient layer using ESC and peer-to-peer distributed off-chain IPFS to certify the surgeons to allow TI, and (3) patient layer: teleoperator that executes the commands using tactile haptic devices and takes feedback from the patient. The latency and data storage costs are improved compared to traditional approaches.

Another Blockchain-based flawless and secure interoperable telesurgery framework, HaBiTs, is proposed in Ref. [33] to achieve immutable and interoperable security by smart contracts. The framework utilizes three domains: (1) master domain that includes surgeons (human operators) to pass the commands, (2) slave domain to receive and transmit commands from surgeons, and (3) network domain to provide a smart communication path between the first two domains. The Blockchain is integrated in the framework to provide a secure and efficient telesurgery system without third-party intervention.

4.2.3 Medical data management

Application 5: Efficient data management:

An efficient and secure decentralized healthcare data sharing framework, MedChain, is proposed in Ref. [34] to manage various information related to healthcare. The framework connects all healthcare providers through super peer and edge peer nodes. The super peer includes three modules: (1) Blockchain service executed on the Blockchain server to maintain a complete Blockchain, (2) a directory service that manages the mutable information related to healthcare records, and (3) a healthcare database to manipulate patient data in the Blockchain. This digest chain session-based data-sharing structure shows improvement in the data-sharing environments.

Case study 3: Path recommendation for pandemic situations and health insurance recommendations:

Two Blockchain-based case studies in healthcare—path recommendation for pandemic situations and health insurance recommendations—are presented in Ref. [30]. In the first case study, the user can send voice commands to the cognitive engine for recommending a safe path from the source to the destination. The microservices interpret the commands and set the goals (safe path) and then fetch three smart contracts (the user-medical-records-contract, geographic-information-system-contract, and the mass-surveillance-system-contract) implemented using Blockchain based on the user's medical records. Finally, a low-risk path is suggested to the user based on the fetched information. In the second case study of insurance recommendations, each user's information including environmental information (sensed by IoT sensors) is stored based on the unique identifier in the Blockchain. Again, based on the user's commands, the cognitive engine and microservices fetch the smart contracts related to the user's medical records, DNA, and allergy information, doctor's prescription, and other clinical parameters of the user (Phase 1). In Phase 2, the respective microservices are called and in the third phase, the best insurance package can be suggested to the user after calculating discounts for the insurance packages.

5   Research directions

Our research studies on the integration of Blockchain and 5G networks motivated us to highlight the following possible research directions.

- Integrating ML with Blockchain-based 5G healthcare: The rapid developments in IoT, network technologies and Blockchain technology are inviting new opportunities for AI-based applications. The revolution of ML technology can be applied to current Blockchain-based 5G healthcare services to learn from healthcare data and provide data-driven perceptions, predictions, and decision support. These features of ML would be helpful for data analytics not only limited to patients' data but also to assist with network changes and to predict possible security attacks [21]. A secure and intelligent architecture for 5G networks by integrating Blockchain and AI into the wireless network is proposed in Ref. [35]. The suitable architecture to utilize advanced deep reinforcement learning to design a caching scheme for maximizing caching resource utilization is introduced in it. On the other side, a Blockchain-based secure-federated learning framework to create smart contracts and prevent malicious and unreliable participants in the network is proposed in Ref. [36]. In this model, the central aggregator identifies the malicious and unreliable participants by automatically executing smart contracts to defend against poisoning attacks.
- Big data management for 5G healthcare: In the age of digitization, big data has become an interesting research topic in 5G. A large amount of healthcare data generated from ubiquitous 5G IoMT devices can be exploited to enable healthcare applications. For example, data storing, data analytics, and data extraction empowered by AI solutions can be applied to these IoMT data for further decision making. Different big data technologies such as Hadoop [37], cloud technology [38], TensorFlow [39], Beam [40], and Docker [41] can offer high storage capabilities to cope with the expansion of the quantity and diversity of IoMT data.
- Robotic surgeries: The surgical procedures done using robotic systems (robotically assisted) will improve the physical scope of surgeries across the world. By means of secured and efficient networks, surgeons can guide the robots in performing live surgeries via video transmission in a timely manner.

6 Conclusions

5G promises a better network for the healthcare industry through fast communication and high connectivity. However, security, privacy, and fault tolerance remain the main concerns in 5G healthcare. The evolution of Blockchain technology can resolve these issues. The use of Blockchain can trigger strength in the form of security, privacy, transparency, immutability, and trust. It can resolve many issues related to security and network performance improvements. In this chapter, the need of Blockchain in 5G healthcare is highlighted and the opportunities brought by Blockchain to empower 5G healthcare systems are explored. Further, the issues of 5G as well as the opportunities and scope through Blockchain in 5G healthcare are explored in detail. Moreover, the conceptual and layered architecture of Blockchain-based 5G healthcare is also proposed along with the discussion of the roles and responsibilities of stakeholders, Blockchain, and the 5G network. Lastly, the importance of Blockchain for 5G healthcare is analyzed in detail with a few successful case studies. The use of Blockchain for 5G wireless networks and its different applications along with healthcare applications are still in infancy. But, it is strongly believed that Blockchain will significantly raise the experience and form of future 5G healthcare services. Moreover, this timely study will highlight the research problems associated with Blockchain-5G healthcare integration as well as motivate interested researchers and practitioners to put more research efforts into this promising area.

References

[1] S. Surati, S. Patel, K. Surati, Background and research challenges for FC for Healthcare 4.0, in: Fog Computing for Healthcare 4.0 Environments: Technical, Societal, and Future Implications, Springer International Publishing, Cham, 2021, pp. 37–53. Chapter 2.
[2] K. Hameed, I.S. Bajwa, N. Sarwar, W. Anwar, Z. Mushtaq, T. Rashid, Integration of 5G and block-chain technologies in smart telemedicine using IoT, J. Healthcare Eng. 2021 (2021).
[3] V. Chamola, V. Hassija, V. Gupta, M. Guizani, A comprehensive review of the COVID-19 pandemic and the role of IoT, Drones, AI, Blockchain, and 5G in managing its impact, IEEE Access 8 (2020) 90225–90265.
[4] I. Mistry, S. Tanwar, S. Tyagi, N. Kumar, Blockchain for 5G-enabled IoT for industrial automation: a systematic review, solutions, and challenges, Mech. Syst. Signal Process. 135 (2020) 106382.
[5] Ericsson, 5G Healthcare: How will 5G affect healthcare?, Available from: *https://www.ericsson.com/en/reports-and-papers/5g-healthcare*.
[6] S. Surati, B. Shrimali, H. Patel, Introduction of blockchain and 5G-enabled IoT devices, in: Blockchain for 5G-Enabled IoT: The New Wave for Industrial Automation, Springer International Publishing, Cham, 2021, pp. 83–105. Chapter 4.
[7] I. Jovović, S. Husnjak, I. Forenbacher, S. Maček, Innovative application of 5G and blockchain technology in industry 4.0, EAI Endorsed Trans. Indus. Netw. Intell. Syst. 6 (18) (2019).
[8] S.V. Akram, P.K. Malik, R. Singh, G. Anita, S. Tanwar, Adoption of blockchain technology in various realms: opportunities and challenges, Secur. Privacy 3 (5) (2020) e109.

[9] H. Aziz, A. Madani, Evolution of the web and its uses in healthcare, Clin. Lab. Sci. 28 (4) (2015) 245–249.

[10] R. Jain, M. Gupta, A. Nayyar, N. Sharma, Adoption of fog computing in Healthcare 4.0, in: Fog Computing for Healthcare 4.0 Environments: Technical, Societal, and Future Implications, Springer International Publishing, Cham, 2021, pp. 3–36. Chapter 1.

[11] A. Capossele, A. Gaglione, M. Nati, M. Conti, R. Lazzeretti, P. Missier, Leveraging blockchain to enable smart-health applications, in: 2018 IEEE Fourth International Forum on Research and Technology for Society and Industry (RTSI), 2018, pp. 1–6.

[12] B. Mohanta, P. Das, S. Patnaik, Healthcare 5.0: a paradigm shift in digital healthcare system using artificial intelligence, IoT and 5G communication, in: 2019 International Conference on Applied Machine Learning (ICAML), 2019, pp. 191–196.

[13] J. Li, P. Carayon, Health Care 4.0: a vision for smart and connected health care, IISE Trans. Healthcare Syst. Eng. 11 (3) (2021) 171–180.

[14] M. Hölbl, M. Kompara, A. Kamišalić, L.N. Zlatolas, A systematic review of the use of blockchain in healthcare, Symmetry 10 (10) (2018) 470.

[15] I. Mistry, S. Tanwar, S. Tyagi, N. Kumar, Blockchain for 5G-enabled IoT for industrial automation: a systematic review, solutions, and challenges, Mech. Syst. Signal Process. 135 (2020) 106382.

[16] C. Thuemmler, C. Rolffs, A. Bollmann, G. Hindricks, W. Buchanan, Requirements for 5G based telemetric cardiac monitoring, in: 2018 14th International Conference on Wireless and Mobile Computing, Networking and Communications (WiMob), IEEE, 2018, pp. 1–4.

[17] H.L. Cech, M. Großmann, U.R. Krieger, A fog computing architecture to share sensor data by means of blockchain functionality, in: 2019 IEEE International Conference on Fog Computing (ICFC), IEEE, 2019, pp. 31–40.

[18] W. Nam, D. Bai, J. Lee, I. Kang, Advanced interference management for 5G cellular networks, IEEE Commun. Mag. 52 (5) (2014) 52–60.

[19] Y. Sun, L. Zhang, G. Feng, B. Yang, B. Cao, M.A. Imran, Blockchain-enabled wireless Internet of things: performance analysis and optimal communication node deployment, IEEE Internet Things J. 6 (3) (2019) 5791–5802.

[20] F.Z. Yousaf, M. Bredel, S. Schaller, F. Schneider, NFV and SDN—key technology enablers for 5G networks, IEEE J. Sel. Areas Commun. 35 (11) (2017) 2468–2478.

[21] D.C. Nguyen, P.N. Pathirana, M. Ding, A. Seneviratne, Blockchain for 5G and beyond networks: a state of the art survey, J. Netw. Comput. Appl. 166 (2020) 102693.

[22] K. Khujamatov, E. Reypnazarov, N. Akhmedov, D. Khasanov, Blockchain for 5G healthcare architecture, in: 2020 International Conference on Information Science and Communications Technologies (ICISCT), IEEE, 2020, pp. 1–5.

[23] A. Basholli, H. Cana, A novel sensor-based architecture using 5G and Blockchain for remote and continuous health monitoring, in: 18th International Symposium on Health Information Management Research, 2020.

[24] T.M. Hewa, A. Kalla, A. Nag, M.E. Ylianttila, M. Liyanage, Blockchain for 5G and IoT: opportunities and challenges, in: 2020 IEEE Eighth International Conference on Communications and Networking (ComNet), IEEE, 2020, pp. 1–8.

[25] M. Chen, J. Yang, Y. Hao, S. Mao, K. Hwang, A 5G cognitive system for healthcare, Big Data Cogn. Comput. 1 (1) (2017) 2.

[26] I. Ahmad, T. Kumar, M. Liyanage, J. Okwuibe, M. Ylianttila, A. Gurtov, 5G security: analysis of threats and solutions, in: 2017 IEEE Conference on Standards for Communications and Networking (CSCN), IEEE, 2017, pp. 193–199.

[27] Z. Yan, P. Zhang, A.V. Vasilakos, A security and trust framework for virtualized networks and software-defined networking, Sec. Commun. Netw. 9 (16) (2016) 3059–3069.

[28] P.N. Srinivasu, A.K. Bhoi, S.R. Nayak, M.R. Bhutta, M. Woźniak, Blockchain technology for secured healthcare data communication among the non-terminal nodes in IoT architecture in 5G network, Electronics 10 (12) (2021) 1437.

[29] M.S. Hossain, G. Muhammad, N. Guizani, Explainable AI and mass surveillance system-based healthcare framework to combat COVID-I9 like pandemics, IEEE Netw. 34 (4) (2020) 126–132.

[30] M. Vahdati, K.G. HamlAbadi, A.M. Saghiri, IoT-based healthcare monitoring using blockchain, in: Applications of Blockchain in Healthcare, Springer Singapore, Singapore, 2021, pp. 141–170.

[31] D.A. Meshram, D.D. Patil, 5G enabled tactile internet for tele-robotic surgery, Proc. Comput. Sci. 171 (2020) 2618–2625.

[32] R. Gupta, A. Shukla, S. Tanwar, AaYusH: a smart contract-based telesurgery system for Healthcare 4.0, in: 2020 IEEE International Conference on Communications Workshops (ICC Workshops), 2020, pp. 1–6.

[33] R. Gupta, S. Tanwar, S. Tyagi, N. Kumar, M.S. Obaidat, B. Sadoun, HaBiTs: blockchain-based telesurgery framework for Healthcare 4.0, in: 2019 International Conference on Computer, Information and Telecommunication Systems (CITS), 2019, pp. 1–5.

[34] B. Shen, J. Guo, Y. Yang, MedChain: efficient healthcare data sharing via blockchain, Appl. Sci. 9 (6) (2019) 1207.

[35] Y. Dai, D. Xu, S. Maharjan, Z. Chen, Q. He, Y. Zhang, Blockchain and deep reinforcement learning empowered intelligent 5G beyond, IEEE Netw. 33 (3) (2019) 10–17.

[36] Y. Liu, J. Peng, J. Kang, A.M. Iliyasu, D. Niyato, A.A. Abd El-Latif, A secure federated learning framework for 5G networks, IEEE Wireless Commun. 27 (4) (2020) 24–31.

[37] A. O'Driscoll, J. Daugelaite, R.D. Sleator, 'Big data', Hadoop and cloud computing in genomics, J. Biomed. Inf. 46 (5) (2013) 774–781.

[38] A. Oussous, F.-Z. Benjelloun, A.A. Lahcen, S. Belfkih, Big Data technologies: a survey, J. King Saud Univ. Comput. Inf. Sci. 30 (4) (2018) 431–448.

[39] J.V. Dillon, I. Langmore, D. Tran, E. Brevdo, S. Vasudevan, D. Moore, B. Patton, A. Alemi, M. Hoffman, R.A. Saurous, Tensorflow distributions, arXiv preprint arXiv:1711.10604 (2017).

[40] S.V. Kalinin, A.R. Lupini, O. Dyck, S. Jesse, M. Ziatdinov, R.K. Vasudevan, Lab on a beam—big data and artificial intelligence in scanning transmission electron microscopy, MRS Bullet. 44 (7) (2019) 565–575.

[41] M. Gupta, N. Singla, Evolution of cloud in big data with Hadoop on Docker platform, in: Web Services: Concepts, Methodologies, Tools, and Applications, IGI Global, 2019, pp. 1601–1622.

Security and privacy in cloud-/edge-/fog-based schemes

Jais Dargan, Aakash Puri, and Roshan Lal
Department of Computer Science and Engineering, Amity University, Noida, Uttar Pradesh, India

1 Introduction

The healthcare sector plays a significant role in boosting the economy of a country. In several countries of Europe, the use of smart healthcare has given a major boost to their economies. They spend approximately 10% of their gross domestic product (GDP) on only smart healthcare and they make up to 100 billion euros a year. In smart healthcare, leading roles are played by blockchain and the Internet of Things (IoT). In 2020, $117 billion was invested in the market on smart healthcare. There have been many apps launched in the market, especially in these COVID-19 times, that provide healthcare benefits from our home. But the biggest leap taken by the smart healthcare system is the introduction of 5G networks. Merging 5G with IoT and blockchain has brought a huge amount of change in the use and ease of technology in smart healthcare. There are several wearable devices in the market such as smart watches, sensors, etc. that monitor heart rate and other metrics related to health. These devices sometimes are useful in cases of chronic patients as they send a signal to cloud servers thus alerting the hospital or healthcare facility in case of any attention required immediately.

1.1 What is smart healthcare?

Smart healthcare is a set-up used by various hospitals or healthcare organizations to keep track of patients through such as smart watches and IoT. These give access to data and connect healthcare facilities to individuals. In brief, it allows access to information, then gets accurate results for individuals by tracking their daily activities. This has been a great help in the healthcare sector specifically to doctors, nurses and to differentiate between different states of chronic patients. This has reduced costs, has given results of minimum medical errors, and improved efficiency.

1.2 Architecture of IoT

When we look from a basic level, the IoT system mainly has a four-stage architecture (Fig. 1):

(1) Sensors—They collect data from the surroundings and convert them into useful information.

Blockchain Applications for Healthcare Informatics. https://doi.org/10.1016/B978-0-323-90615-9.00021-9
Copyright © 2022 Elsevier Inc. All rights reserved.

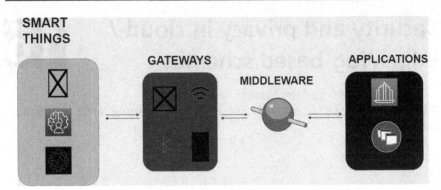

Fig. 1 Architecture of IoT.

(2) Internet gateway—The data fetched by the sensors are in an analog form, which is to be converted to digital by data acquisition systems (DAS). The Internet gateway receives these digitalized data and routes them to stage 3.
(3) Edge IT—Before moving to the cloud, edge IT preprocesses the data.
(4) Data center/cloud—The data that need more processing and the feedback are forwarded to the cloud [1].

1.3 Architecture of blockchain

A simple blockchain architecture comprises several nodes that contain a series of transactions with a particular block. The figure below depicts a simple transaction performed using blockchain that serves as a purpose to the blockchain.

Blockchain architecture is initiated by requesting a transaction. Then, the block representing the transaction is created, and then the block is sent to every node in the whole network. After this process, the nodes will help validate the transaction. They will receive a reward also for the particular work, known as proof of work. Further, the block is added to the blockchain and thus the transaction gets completed. So, this is the series of steps that shows how blockchain works (Fig. 2).

The main components of a blockchain architecture:

(1) **Node**
(2) **Transaction**
(3) **Block**
(4) **Chain**
(5) **Miners**
(6) **Consensus (protocol)**

1.4 Architecture of 5G

The 5G system consists of the main terminal and many independent autonomous radio access technologies. Each radio is considered an IP address for the Internet world. This technology is to make sure of sufficient switch information for appropriate routing of IP packets. They are built-in by user guidelines that are regulated by the government (Fig. 3).

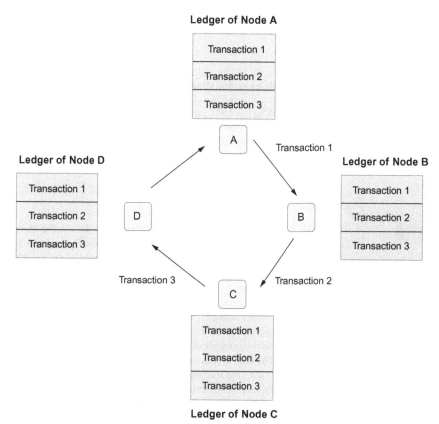

Fig. 2 Architecture of blockchain.

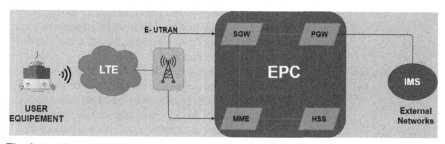

Fig. 3 Architecture of 5G.

1.5 Features of 5G

Feature	Brief explanation
Device-to-device (D2D) communication	D2D is a quick correspondence between two devices in the association without including the base station or the middle association. Significantly thick association issues can be handled through D2D correspondences. In D2D correspondence, each terminal can communicate with each other clearly to exchange information or to share their radio access affiliation.
Millimeter waves (mmWaves) communication	mmWaves have a band range between 20–30 GHz. Because of the absence of range below 3 GHz, the 5G should stretch out its recurrence to the mmWaves band, for the most part between 20–90 GHz, in light of the fact that there is a colossal measure of unused data transfer capacity. Utilizing mmWaves with little cells will lessen the highway misfortune issue, and will be valuable for a few applications including shrewd medical care. mmWaves are practical with minimal effort, and they are discovering all assortment of cutting-edge employments. The best part is that mmWaves take the weight off the lower frequencies and broaden remote correspondence in the external restriction of radio innovation.
Software-defined network (SDN)	SDN is a design that is dynamic, reasonable, adaptable, and savvy to convey the high transmission capacity needed for a few applications. SDN fuses a few kinds of organizational advancements to make the organization nimbler and more adaptable as well as to keep up the cutting-edge server farm, virtualized workers, and capacity foundation. SDN organizing characterizes a way to deal with construct, planning, and taking care of organizations by isolating organization control planes and sending planes. SDN can uphold different necessities of smart medical services in 5G. The cases that are used to be utilized is taken care through cloud on administrator side while other small issues that require quick actions are dealt at the user side itself.
Network function virtualization (NFV)	NFV is a network approach that empowers the substitution of costly committed equipment gadgets such as firewalls and switches with programming-based organization apparatuses that run as virtual machines on standard workers. 5G should empower D2D correspondence in smart medical care, due to which a monstrous measure of information is unsurprisingly produced. It is unimaginable to expect to send the entirety of the produced information

Continued

Feature	Brief explanation
Edge computing	to the concentrated server farm for preparing. Hence, some astute choices are needed to oversee information at the edge cloud and cloud workers. By utilizing NFV, information can be sent in the organization dependent on QoS necessity. This should guarantee network adaptability. Edge is an appropriated innovation plan in which information is handled at the edge of the organization, near the starting source. In future smart medical care, machines are required to make choices and reactions as per the assignment. For such reactions and choices, handled information is required by machines. By and large, continuous prepared information is fundamental. Edge processing assumes a significant part in such cases where time is more significant, particularly in 5G-based organizations.

2 Literature review

Author	Year	Description	Approaches	Technologies used
Siddique Latif, et al.	2017	As the research work predicts the current healthcare system that is emphasized by numerous activities; the rate of increment in the chronic disease; the operating model for the patients screening; the wireless technology enables communication between humans and smart healthcare systems. Further, we have featured the energizing examination and execution openings in building this 5G-	These emerging technologies such as AI/ML, IoT, blockchain, and big data will empower medical service upheaval. The IoT trend is the future generation technology that could make revolutionary changes in the whole healthcare sector.	AI/ML, IoT, blockchain, big data, EHRs, 5G

Continued

Continued

Author	Year	Description	Approaches	Technologies used
		enabled care, likewise pinpointing the considerable difficulties included and the possible entanglements.		
Min Chen, et al.	2017	The paper portrays the development and advancements in healthcare technology and the positive changes in people's living standards that make people healthier. To label this issue, a video meeting-based telemedicine framework is sent to break the impediments of clinical assets regarding existence.	In this paper, we propose a novel medical services framework dependent on a 5G cognitive system (5G-Csys). The 5G-Csys comprises an asset cognitive motor and an information cognitive motor.	5G cognitive system (5G-Csys)
Shahid Mumtaz, et al.	2018	The great accomplishment of 2G and 3G versatile organizations and the quick development of 4G, the cutting-edge portable organizations 5G were proposed expecting to give endless systems administrations ability to versatile clients. It expects to include and profit from numerous current specialized advances including the Industrial Internet of Things (IIoT).	The IIoT incorporates numerous heterogeneous organizations such as wireless sensor networks (WSNs), wireless local area networks (WLANs), mobile communication networks (3G/4G/LTE/5G), wireless mesh networks (WMNs), and wearable medical service frameworks. It is a basic plan to self-sort out and savvy conventions for heterogeneous impromptu organizations in different IoT applications.	3G, 4G, 5G, LTE, IIoT, IoT

Continued

Author	Year	Description	Approaches	Technologies used
Farah Nasri, et al.	2017	The paper plans to give proportions of physiological boundaries. The handy frameworks used in medical sector is intended to accumulate sheets.	The portable medical care framework (IoT stage) is intended to accumulate biometric data. This data can be utilized to continuously screen the condition of a patient or to get private information to be investigated for clinical conclusions, utilizing an Android application, web administration, and multiconvention units. The plan of a particular multiconvention unit is for all-inclusive availability of WBSN.	IoT, 5G, WBSN
Muhammad, Arslan, Usman, et al.	2019	The paper presents a total system for a 5G-enabled associated emergency vehicle that centers around two-way information correspondence, including general media sight and sound streams between ambulances and clinics. A conversational ward on the organization requirements of convenient clinical services are likewise given.	The model incorporates remote transmission, in view of a 5G organization, of three sorts of information. This will empower specialists to distantly guide the emergency vehicle team to give beginning clinical consideration to in- rescue vehicle patients.	5G-enabled technology

3   Security and privacy

5G will interface with pretty much every part of human existence to the Internet by utilizing billions of gadgets and sensors. This will most likely bring about different dangers to the security and protection of customer information. 5G security dangers are more genuine to medical service frameworks, as digital assaults on them can be hindering at a cultural level. Specifically, IoT gadgets will be more vulnerable to weaknesses, as a large portion of the sensors and gadgets with low computational force cannot deal with complex encryption calculations. Thus, the information on the way should be sent with no encryption. Along these lines, solid components are needed to get or scramble such exposed correspondences. Similarly, cloud-based IoT stages used for reconsidered limit and computation in view of the resource necessities of IoT sensors and devices. 5G organizations should manage the online protection dangers and security worries of clients and governments. Hence, the degree of start to finish incorporated security and privacy for 5G organizations ought to be more far reaching than in the past.

3.1   Security issues

Security is perhaps the primary structure. People have different perspectives with respect to security and hence, it is portrayed according to various perspectives. In simple words, security is a thought the success of the organization all things considered. The interchanges in sensor network applications in clinical benefits are by and large distant in nature. This may cause distinctive security risks to these structures. These hazards can create problems for the public movement of the user who is using distant sensor gadgets. On events, for example, following the space of a patient or individual whenever compromised may provoke grave results. People with malicious objectives may use private data to hurt the person. Security issues in clinical considered livelihoods sensor networks have been there for each and every situation that has been a part of the strong assessment. Generally, security issues are far off sensor networks on huge scale of investigation in the later part.

3.2   Threats and attacks

Security infiltration in the health use of sensors is of great concern. The security issues can be split into two levels: system security and information security. A separated attack may occur while coordinating the data packs in the structure. The aggressors may change the target of bundles or make controlling clashing. Similarly, in the case of aggressors, they take the data by sneaking around to the far-off correspondence media. Dynamic risks are more damaging than their inactive accomplices. Criminal may find the space of the customer by tuning in. This may provoke dangerous conditions.

3.3 Privacy issues

Privacy is among critical concerns in far-off sensor networks concerning medical applications. The protected health information (PHI) is private in nature. Security issues arise for various reasons. Well indeed, it might be close to home conviction, social what is more, social climate, and other overall population/private causes. Transferring patient information through distant media can introduce real threats to the security of an individual.

4 Healthcare industry

Now the healthcare sector employs the latest technologies for automation and content exchange on cloud platforms, big data technology, making machinery wireless and creating network systems using IoT, emerging 4G and 5G technologies, the cryptography exchange using blockchain, the use of AR (Augmented Reality) and VR (Virtual Reality) and production of the human-machine interface and at last linking essentials to the ones through the supply chain (Fig. 4).

The figure describes the evolution of the healthcare Industry from evidence-based treatment to digitalization and uniqueness in the treatment. Healthcare 4.0 comprises the latest technologies working for the welfare of society. We might frame the best out of IoT emerging with Blockchain technology making it more compatible, advance, secured, and decentralized systems which can be used for the Healthcare Industry in their major consequences. Healthcare 4.0 has designed principles that take care of any challenges in today's world.

4.1 Challenges

At the present time, medical services are chiefly worried about the expanded weight of persistent sickness and future, deficiencies of assets, administrative necessities issues,

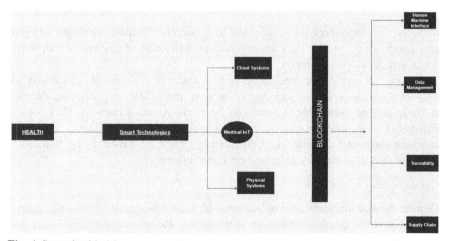

Fig. 4 Smart health 4.0.

rising patient assumptions, and required expenses. In the coming years, IoT robotization, large information investigations, distributed computing, and advanced mechanics will bring about an incredible change in medical care around the world. Numerous difficulties will emerge from this such as patient protection, network safety, and information administration issues. Essentially, a 5G-empowered incorporated, astute, and gigantic medical care framework in each city, town, and local area of the world will require huge measures of cash, time, and human capital. This is fundamentally to embrace keen, instructed, and coordinated systems to have not here from the abuse of money, time, and work.

- Electronic health records (EHRs)

EHR is a vault containing patient computerized information that is safely interchangeable with various approved clients. EHR stores audit, approaching, and concurrent data with the reason to help proficient, proceeding, and quality assistance in coordinated wellbeing. As opposed to the ideals and accomplishments of EHRs, there are different difficulties and restrictions. The absence of information sharing is a significant issue because emergency clinics and doctors are generally not associated. So, that results in the patient well-being data that has to be compelled inside emergency clinics and research facilities.

- Access to healthcare

Widespread admittance to medical care means that everyone has impartial admittance to medical care with no segregation, particularly on the ability to pay. Because of medical care administrations is restricted when a nation needs prepared medical care experts, administrations, and hardware; accessible assets are not situated in nearness, and people cannot bear the cost of administrations because there is an enormous expense. All-inclusive healthcare managements are especially difficult for developing nations, where medical assets and specialists are hard to come by. All-inclusive admittance to medical care can be accomplished by erasing the difficulties that keep individuals from reasonable and complete medical care decided at the public or worldwide level.

- Long-term chronic diseases

Infections are expanding universally and have become the most prevailing and genuine danger to the world. They are influencing individuals of any age in both developing and developed countries.

The current worldwide medical services framework is especially distressing for individuals with persistent sicknesses. Because individuals experiencing ongoing sickness depend even more intensely on the medical care framework, they use the framework even more regularly, use additional assets, visit different specialists, and have long-haul associations. Consequently, when the medical care framework falls, patients with ongoing infection are more influenced.

- Insufficiency of resources

Despite the extraordinary accomplishments of the medical care framework, general medical services administrations are still lacking. Patients need to head out from inaccessible spots to visit their healthcare workers. The issue is currently getting more intense, and the world will have an expected deficiency of millions in medical services by 2035. Along these lines, we need some genuine improvements in medical care to build the efficiency of medical experts by utilizing telemedicine and eHealth administrations.

• Constraints in informatics of healthcare systems

The progress in data correspondences innovation can possibly get a huge change in the medical care framework by interfacing clinical gadgets, robotizing monetary exchanges, and forestalling blunders to upgrade customer trust in the wellbeing framework. In any case, the medical care frameworks are exceptionally unpredictable, as they incorporate correspondence and handling of heterogeneous medical data, the ideal allotment of accessible assets, and authoritative administration at the same time. Existing remote advancements (3G/4G) abuse full-scale cells to give a more extensive territory to bring down information rates. These advancements are primarily reasonable for smart medical observing gadgets, social cooperation, and health checking applications.

• Inconsistency in healthcare

Right now, medical care situations are generally pay-based rather than based on the requirement. Individuals who need medical care are getting less access than individuals who need it least. By and large, in the United States, the rich are the greatest purchasers of medical care in spite of being more grounded than poor people. In another examination, it was discovered that individuals in the lower pay quartile are less healthy. This medical care is creating inconsistencies in healthcare across pay scales.

4.2 Solutions

In this section, we will discuss how to deal with the challenges faced by the healthcare sector. With the help of technology, we will soon be able to fix most of the current issues in the healthcare system.

The emerging technologies such as IoT and blockchain are revolutionary solutions to today's healthcare system.

• Healthcare advances with IoT

Medical services procedures, screen, and send data to a public or private cloud to collaborate with another degree of advantageous and proficient mechanization. The solutions based on IoT are successful regarding energy utilization as well as CPU and memory use. IoT trends are making systems more efficient, making them the next-generation technology.

Patient consistency with drugs and treatment by medical personnel is another conspicuous expected utilization of IoT. Moreover, IoT can be utilized to verify medications, screen drug supplies, and give productive booking of accessible assets to guarantee their best use for additional patients. In clinical IoT, different clinical sensors, gadgets, cell phones, imaging gadgets, personal assistants, and EHRs are centerpieces of the framework. These gadgets screen significant health data such as vital signs, changes in mindset and practices, and blood glucose, which can be successfully used by medical staff to improve care.

Moreover, IoT-based arrangements can possibly diminish the time for distant health arrangements and increase care by lessening costs with improved client experience.

• 5G wireless connectivity

Because of the untethered nature and cheap arrangement cost of wireless innovations are undeniably fit to give the essential network that is required between the different partners of the medical care framework. The use of wireless innovations for medical services has been investigated in different studies.

The progress in wearable automation, bio-designing, and cell phones have empowered an emotional expansion in the misuse of omnipresent and inescapable wireless advancements in the medical care framework. This pattern will probably proceed and additionally be reinforced by the improvement of 5G wireless innovation, which will give much better execution as far as throughput and inactivity contrasted with pre-5G advances.

In present times look at how wireless advancements and clinical benefits can be incorporated to give adaptable, advantageous, and practical telemedicine. These days, the quick development of wireless sensors, wireless correspondence, wearable sensors, and particularly cell phones has cleared the way to new e-Health frameworks, which are better than customary telemedicine frameworks.

Technologies such as URLLC empowered by 5G will make health interchanges stronger and will open new medical care such as distant medical procedures and far-off finding with haptic criticism. This will open some other season of advantages from improving execution in clinics to better approaches for observing the patients' wellbeing, infection movement, and individualized drug examination.

5 Cloud to fog to IoT

IoT is basically characterized by limited storage, slow processing, and various other issues. Therefore, to deal with these issues we use cloud computing with IoT, which is popularly known as the Cloud of Things (CoT) [2]. It simplifies the flow of IoT data storing and processing. In CoT, the IoT data are transported to the cloud center, where they are processed and the result is sent to specified applications. The cloud center may even store the IoT data, if required, for future decision-making. The CoT has become popular also because of the fact that it is economical. But in the era of big data, it has become very difficult to send a large quantity of information to the cloud as it swarms the cloud with IoT data. In this manner, it requires a high transfer speed. So, to solve these issues, fog computing has become an integral factor. The term "fog computing" was first presented by Cisco and it is very useful in IoT. Basically, fog computing provides data processing and storage at a local level. It is like a smart layer sitting between the cloud and IoT. Because of these countless benefits, the opportunities for research have been increasing in this area (Fig. 5).

6 Blockchain in smart healthcare using 5G

This figure displayed below shows how the healthcare industry is evolving with blockchain technology. The diagram above is blockchain architecture for healthcare applications. The blockchain involves the digitalization of medical records using wireless sensors, thus transforming them into smart contracts and storing them in cloud platforms so the patient can be monitored with ease (Fig. 6).

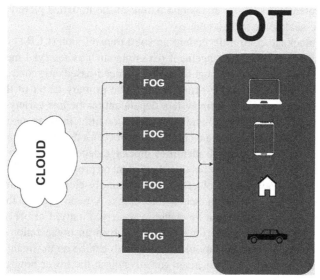

Fig. 5 Cloud to fog IoT.

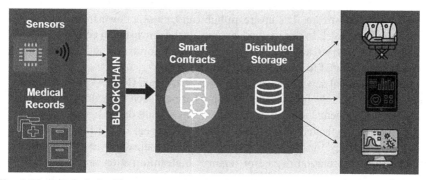

Fig. 6 Blockchain in healthcare.

There are a large number of studies on how to improve medical care applications. Some of them are briefly explained below.

6.1 Blockage control schemes

In [3], a need rate-based steering convention (PRRP) is proposed for clog switch cutting-edge small-asset transfer speed organizations, for example, remote sight and sound sensor organizations. Because of the great data transfer capacity interest for sight and sound traffic, the clog may effortlessly happen in low-asset transmission capacity organizations. The obstruct can waste meagre resources like the energy of centres, and impact application express QoS necessities, which can without a doubt achieve a lamentable realistic and sound nature of the imparted pictures, sound and video for the healthcare submission.

In [4], a blockage control dependent on solid transmission (CCRT) conspires for constant web-based media management (example such as reserved medical procedures) is proposed to get rid of clog. CCRT uses a need-based clog control instrument for dependable transmission for genuine data. The primary target of the plan is to recover QoS by a clog recognition system dependent on the line variety degree, then a line length in the society. Each bundle consumes too little, medium, or high need in a stripe, which assists with focusing on high need parcels for dependable transmission of these bundles. A beneficiary hub identifies blockage dependent on two rules.

In [5], clog control and energy balance dependent on progression (CcEbH) plots are planned to keep away from a blockage in profoundly clogged organizations with restricted assets (e.g., persistent health checking). A main goal of the plan is to upgrade the QoS by diminishing blockage in society. Firstly, CcEbH organizes the organization into progressive, from a solitary hub in an organization (e.g., a sink hub in a remote sensor organization), so every hub can be an upstream (or a hub at the upper various level), a downstream (or a center at the lower progressive level), and a comparable progressive level hub. A clog at a hub can be recognized dependent on its line size, whereby the approaching information rate is more noteworthy than the active information rate. The upstream hubs can test the cradle inhabitance (or line size) at the downstream. The upstream hub can choose a downstream center with a lower blockage level. In this method, as soon as the downstream center gets blocked, an additional downstream hub is chosen to gather information and forward bundles. CcEbH has appeared to lessen energy utilization.

In [6], a medical services advanced blockage aversion (HOCA) plot is proposed to keep away from clogs for medical care applications, such as health-related crises or observing fundamental indications of patients, as a result of the significance and criticality of communicated information. The primary goal of the plan is to improve energy proficiency by diminishing clogs in an organization. Every bundle either requires low information degree or requires high information rate. There are four belief undertakings for the sink hub (e.g., a clinical focus) to assemble info or times from hubs implanted in patients. First, the sink hub broadcasts a solicitation for information to hubs. Cutting-edge technology affected role answer to the sink hub with information and occasions by indicating a side-by-side significance. Thirdly, the sink center chooses the last hub dependent taking place at a specific degree of significance and shapes about it in a diverse method (i.e., spreading of traffic over numerous ways from source to an objective hub in the organization) and courses toward the chose hub to less down the blockage. Fourth, the chosen hub detects the occasion and creates the parcel. A high need parcel chooses the next jump from the high need table (i.e., precharacterized) to send information while the low need bundle chooses from the low need table (i.e., precharacterized). HOCA has appeared to lessen energy utilization to give a more extended lifetime and diminish start to finish delay.

In [7], a window-based rate control calculation (w-RCA) is a plan to change a source hub sending rate (the dimensions of a window of unacknowledged bundles) besides the objective hub's cradle size for accomplishing a reasonable compromise between top to mean proportion and standard deviation to streamline the QoS of audiovisual broadcasts intended for telesurgery. Edge processing empowers distributed computing skills and IT managements at the edge worker, in the remote versatile organization. Machine-based calculation (be subject to on PC programs which can get to information and use it and find out on an individual basis) are utilized to design support (i.e., transitory capacity) limits with regard to impending edges which prompts even audio-visual broadcast (for any place in the web inclusion) in 5G organizations. The proposed conspire streamlines network boundaries, including the top to-mean proportion, the standard deviation of deferral, then jitter. Various conventions (i.e., transmission control convention, user datagram convention, session portrayal convention, and so forth) are utilized on both customer and worker sides in the plan for trading video outlines. The proposed plot has appeared to diminish start to finish interruption, then jitter in the audiovisual broadcast.

6.2   Planning schemes

In a cutting-edge-based 5G wearable organizations is introduced, on the method to mend the society strength distribution then-energy proficient use [8]. The primary goal of the plan is to advance the assets and energy effectiveness of the organization by conveying software-characterized network (SDN) and network work virtualization (NFV). SDN switches both the control and information planes to give adaptable control of the organization stream subsequently. NFV disseminates the capacity of the organization into different valuable areas with the assistance of virtualization and programming. In this manner, circulated coordination of capacity, correspondence assets, and registering can be acknowledged through network cutting, which can give low dormancy necessity and decrease start to finish delay. Further, an information-driven asset is introduced, in the view of an intellectual assistance motor. The intellectual asset motor is conveyed at the foundation layer to allot assets through an artificial intelligence (AI) calculation in a proficient manner. To gain administrative information carried out by psychological assistance motor through AI calculation. The worldwide psychological motor is conveyed to acknowledge tight coupling among assets and administrations to improve usage QoE of clients and assets.

In [9], an organization administration affixing (NSC) model is introduced to deftly coordinate SDN and NFV to mechanize virtual organization gadgets, instead of utilizing manual associations, for medical care management in the 5G network. The primary goal of the plan is to upgrade QoS. A prototype works in a joint effort with the product characterized network (SDN) and organization work representation (NFV) advances. The model coordinates with both cutting edge innovations to offer quick types of assistance (i.e., lower delay) in the 5G climate with the assistance of various sorts of correspondence conventions, including a directing plan for low power misfortune organizations. Open Flow compelled application convention (CoAP) for informing and the transport layer security (TLS) worker aimed at safety improvement, to empower activity of shrewd gadgets. Also, WiFi, cell phone advances, little base stations (big scale, pico, femtocells) stay utilized to give the best quality of service to smart gadgets. Further, a protected prototype with the Kerberos (secure correspondence convention permit hub to convey another nonsecure organization safely) validation worker is introduced to get the cloudlet network from the DDoS assault. The transport layer security (TLS) convention is conveyed to the worker to give a secure correspondence between parties. The model has appeared to expand QoS by diminishing start to finish interruption with high security.

In [10], the 5G intellectual framework (5G-Csys) is proposed. The primary target of the plan is to upgrade the QoS by accomplishing super low dormancy and super high unwavering quality in the heterogeneous organization for intellectual applications (i.e., remote medical procedure). The framework comprises an asset intellectual and an information psychological motor. The intellectual knowledge in the view of the learning of organization (i.e., programming characterized network) by cognizing the assets in the organization, to accomplish that it requires super low dormancy and super high unwavering quality of the framework. The psychological motor influence machine and profound learning calculations (i.e., be subject to PC program's which can get to information and use it find out on an individual basis) is to examine medical care information, e.g., discourse feeling acknowledgment. The proposed framework has appeared to accomplish QoS by diminishing start to finish delay in the organization.

In [11], 5G-based technology, smart diabetes strategy is introduced. The fundamental aim is asset enhancement to give better QoS for continuous remote checking of patients. The plan contains three layers: the sensing layer gathers information on various assets (i.e., sensors) continuously. The customized analysis layer measures the gathered information with current AI calculations (depends on PC programs that can get the information and use it to find out on an individual basis [60]) to investigate the illness. The information-sharing layer shares the information on friendly space, then information space through the interpersonal organization utilizing the 5G organization to the specialists and family members of the patient. 5G with cell phone and wearable clinical gadgets are utilized in the plan. The plan is demonstrated to be exceptionally precise by diminishing parcel misfortune and start to finish delay.

In [12], the 5G little cell network approach is introduced to develop QoS by accomplishing a high information degree. Transmissions of clinical ultrasound video from moving emergency vehicles to emergency clinic uplinks are considered for the situation. A heterogeneous organization, containing macrocell with eNodeB existing together with a little versatile cell is a popular an answer to LTE, 5G or 4G. A signal is sent to the rescue vehicle named as a portable little cell which authorizes clients to move around and associate with the administrator's organization nearby. Its utilities are a normal radio interface method (e.g., FDMA (recurrence division numerous entrance), TDMA, CDMA, and OFDMA (symmetrical recurrence division various access)) to associate with the portion macro cell (BS) base station (eNodeB). LTE-Sim, a framework-level test system, is utilized to get the outcomes. From the outcome, it is shown that the organization improves the QoS in a period amount of time and reduce Packet Loss Rate (PLR).

6.3 Directing schemes

In [13], a delivery plan in 5G to help cell clients in D2D correspondence (G.1) at the cell edge is introduced. The primary target of the plan is diminishing impedance (O.3) by overseeing portability to limit start to finish delay (P.4) during movement of the cell. Throughout a delivery, hubs (or UEs) can change starting with one cell then onto the next and the structure D2D joins with adjoining hubs to give consistent network better channel quality. eNB is answerable for an asset board, power control, and D2D meeting foundation. The eNB produces handover choice dependent on the channel quality indicator (CQI). The handover cycle is separated into three phases. In the preparation step, UEs send data to the eNB portion identified with the channel, which decides whether to enroll the handover interaction on explicit circumstances. Now, in the execution step, the decision is made as to whether to move the conduct and data of UEs to additional cells. After that, in the fulfillment step, affirmation is divided among cells, and status is refreshed in the new cell around UEs. The plan is energy productive.

In [14], DARA for gadget-to-gadget correspondence in a multimap network is introduced. The primary target of the plan is the asset enhancement of the organization to expand the network lifetime (energy productivity). In DARA, each hub chooses the measure of information it can deal with dependent on its leftover energy and processing power. An organization utility augmentation (NUM) recipe is sent to join gadget abilities. A hub decides whether to advance info and furthermore switch on the connection for the next jump hub (planning choice). In this way, calculations have both steering and booking choices. A proving ground is utilized for execution, and the outcome shows a huge improvement in throughput when contrasted with the conventional back pressure calculation.

The fundamental target of the plan is to lessen impedance. The plan empowers the course among source and objective by utilizing hubs on the cell's edges. First and foremost, the switch sends information to introduce centers in the edges. At that point alongside the cell edge, information goes to the neutral. At that point finally, information is shipped off the objective after cell edges. To each stage, IAR devours the shortest path routing (SPR). Thus, courses in IAR are longer when contrasted with the briefest way; however, IAR has lesser impedance generally speaking. The plan is demonstrated to be energy proficient with a high information rate.

The main plan is to save away from obstruction by choosing the believed hub for information sending. At every hub, the trust is determined by depending on experience, especially the parcel's fruitful conveyance rate and the translating mistake. Every hub keeps a trust table to monitor its neighbor hubs and handpicked a next-jump hub dependent on the rested table. The trust esteems are viewed as dependent on four boundaries, to be specific, cradle limit, SNR, energy, and dependability of gadgets. The plan is demonstrated to be energy effective.

The principal aims of this plan are to improve network assets, lessen start to finish delay, and give high data transmission to the client with an assurance to stay away from blockage. The creator utilized an advanced mobile phone, wearable gadgets, and 5G organization to divide information among sensors, mobiles, and base stations. AI calculations (i.e., depends on PC programs which can get to info and use it find out on their own) having term optimal to examine the information to make a vital move. The calculation examines the information and actuate the caution if there should be an occurrence of a strange circumstance. The plan has the capacity of information assortment progressively with quick reaction. In the presented book chapter, the utilization of 4G and 5G networks are presented to combine and divide the exhibition. The outcome shows that 5G increases the amount, start to finish delay, and organization lifetime (energy efficient).

The fundamental goal of the plan is to streamline network assets to accomplish a high information degree. A body sensor network gathers information on the client from the sensors and client's cell phones, which are enlisted under a femtocell. Femtocell keeps a data set, a got information is confirmed with the data in the data set, and if an anomaly is recognized, the information is shipped off the cloud by femtocell for additional examining and access by the specialists. A Markov Chain model (a request for potential occasions, where each occasion relies just upon the state achieved in the past occasion) is utilized in the cloud to give the best arrangement. This femtocell network approach limits the utilization of the organization assets to accomplish high energy productivity and with better security when contrasted with a macrocell network.

7 Analysis of Healthcare 4.0

The graph below depicts the percentage of GDP invested by major countries in 2018, just before COVID-19. As you can see, some invested more than 10% of their GDP in their healthcare sector. This expenditure is expected to increase year by year and this gives a lot of open doors for advanced technology in collaboration with the health sector (Fig. 7 and Table 1).

The table highlights the major companies and some start-ups that are using blockchain to provide their services in healthcare. Upon analyzing and researching, we performed a common SWOT analysis and the results are as follows (Fig. 8).

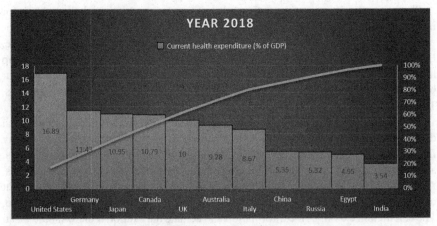

Fig. 7 Graph of expenditure on health of major countries.

Table 1 Companies providing services in healthcare using blockchain and their applications.

Company	Location	Blockchain application
BurstIQ	Colorado Springs, Colorado	It uses blockchain to share and use medical data.
Tenth aid	Kochi (India)	It uses blockchain for remote monitoring.
Medicalchain	London, England	It uses blockchain to maintain records and tries to protect patient identity. It uses double encryption.
Plenum Data	Pune (India)	It uses its own platform to record healthcare data through the integration of patient data from mobile and wearable sensors.
SimplyVital Health	Watertown, Massachusetts	It uses blockchain to create an open-source database so healthcare providers can access patient information and coordinate care.
Coral Health Research & Discovery	Vancouver, Canada	It uses blockchain technology to accelerate care, automate administrative processes, and employ smart contracts between patients and doctors.
Blockpharma	Paris, France	It has an app-based platform and uses a blockchain-based system to help prevent patients from taking counterfeit medicines.
Shivom	Chandigarh (India)	It is a start-up in India building a genomic and health data hub by combining blockchain, genomic DNA sequencing, artificial intelligence, and cryptography. Its aim is to save genome sequencing for users.

SWOT ANALYSIS

STRENGTHS	WEAKNESSES	OPPORTUNITIES	THREATS
• Decentralization • Transparency • Immutability	• Interoperability • Storage Capacity • Cost	• Lower fraud • Increase trust in patients and organisations	• Public knowledge of private information • Performance issues • Difficulty in performing analytics

Fig. 8 SWOT analysis.

8 Future work and challenges

The combination of IoT and Blockchain has received extensive exploration interest both from the scholarly community and industry. The Bitcoin-style blockchain that depends on PoW has a few qualities that make it ineffectively appropriate for some IoT situations. In view of the broad literature survey, there are challenges with blockchain-based 5G-enabled IoT applications, including:

• With the quick expansion in IoT gadgets being battery-powered (and hence asset confined), their energy necessities are restricted. Regardless, with the introduction of blockchain, where square mining is an calculation escalated task. In these situations, the energy necessities and handling season of gadgets should be investigated further.
• There are some unanswered inquiries concerning blockchain, for example, the end of specific weaknesses such as DoS assaults and the notorious 51% assault with respect to building up appropriate trust.
• Lack of appropriate normalization and no interoperability imply various records cannot straightforwardly speak with one another. However, they require elaborate partners to exceptionally bargain (going from complete information to the arrangements) to accomplish full interoperability. This requires worldwide strategies for aggregate trust and data security.
• It can interface with various partners from various locales (perhaps nations) without the requirement for any sort of legitimate consistency to follow. It is a test for both specialist organizations and producers and could be a critical hindrance to embracing blockchain in numerous business cases.
• With the coming of 5G, IoT gadgets ought to be updated to be viable with the fast organization availability.

9 Conclusions

In the time of COVID-19, the need for a healthcare system is greater than ever. There is a stupendous amount of money being invested in smart healthcare. Blockchain and IoT were already being used in healthcare and have been verified to be game changing in this industry, but the introduction of 5G has been a much bigger game changer. It is now faster and much more efficient with a higher rate of efficacy. The combination of blockchain with IoT and 5G has reduced the risks of security and privacy, but there are still some loopholes that can be worked upon in the future. The several innovations that are coming up must be taken under strict scrutiny due to security and privacy issues. So, the main issues in the smart healthcare system are security and privacy.

References

[1] A. Puri, et al., Analytical and critical review from cloud to fog to internet of things (IoT), in: International Conference on Advances in Engineering Science Management & Technology (ICAESMT)-2019, Uttaranchal University, Dehradun, India, 2019.
[2] W. Chen, Y. Niu, Y. Zou, Congestion control and energy-balanced scheme based on the hierarchy for WSNs, IET Wirel. Sensor Syst. 7 (1) (2016) 1–8.

[3] A. Kumari, S. Tanwar, Secure data analytics for smart grid systems in a sustainable smart city: challenges, solutions, and future directions, Sustain. Comput. Inform. Syst. 2210-5379, 28 (2020), https://doi.org/10.1016/j.suscom.2020.100427, 100427.

[4] A. Choudhury, D. Gupta, A survey on medical diagnosis of diabetes using machine learning techniques, in: Recent Developments in Machine Learning and Data Analytics, Springer, Singapore, 2019, pp. 67–78.

[5] Y. Hao, D. Tian, G. Fortino, J. Zhang, I. Humar, Network slicing technology in a 5G wearable network, IEEE Commun. Stand. Mag. 2 (1) (2018) 66–71.

[6] R. Chaudhary, N. Kumar, S. Zeadally, Network service chaining in fog and cloud computing for the 5G environment: data management and security challenges, IEEE Commun. Mag. 55 (11) (2017) 114–122.

[7] M. Chen, J. Yang, Y. Hao, S. Mao, K. Hwang, A 5G cognitive system for healthcare, Big Data Cognit. Comput. 1 (1) (2017) 2.

[8] I.U. Rehman, M.M. Nasralla, A. Ali, N. Philip, Small cell-based ambulance scenario for medical video streaming: a 5G-health use case, in: Proceedings of the 15th International Conference on Smart Cities Improving Quality of Life Using ICT IoT (HONET-ICT), 2018, October, pp. 29–32.

[9] A. Orsino, M. Gapeyenko, L. Militano, D. Moltchanov, S. Andreev, Y. Koucheryavy, et al., Assisted handover based on device-to-device communications in 3GPP LTE systems, in: Proceedings of the IEEE GLOBECOM Workshops, 2015, December, pp. 1–6.

[10] Y. Xing, H. Seferoglu, Device-aware routing and scheduling in multi-hop device-to-device networks, in: Proceedings of the Information Theory and Applications Workshop (ITA), 2017, February, pp. 1–7.

[11] H. Yuan, W. Guo, Y. Jin, S. Wang, M. Ni, Interference-aware multi-hop path selection for device- to-device communications in a cellular interference environment, IET Commun. 11 (11) (2017) 1741–1750.

[12] P.K. Mishra, S. Pandey, A method for network assisted relay selection in device to device communication for the 5G, Int. J. Appl. Eng. Res. 11 (10) (2016) 7125–7131.

[13] D. De, A. Mukherjee, Femto-cloud based secure and economic distributed diagnosis and home health care system, J. Med. Imag. Health Inform. 5 (3) (2015) 435–447.

[14] R. Gupta, S. Tanwar, S. Tyagi, N. Kumar, M.S. Obaidat, B. Sadoun, HaBiTs: Blockchain-based telesurgery framework for healthcare 4.0, in: International Conference on Computer, Information and Telecommunication Systems (IEEE CITS-2019), Beijing, China, August 28-31, 2019, pp. 6–10.

Interpolation-based reversible data hiding with blockchain for secure e-healthcare systems

M. Mahasree[a], N. Puviarasan[b], and P. Aruna[c]
[a]Department of Computer Science and Engineering, SRM Institute of Science and Technology (Ramapuram), Chennai, Tamil Nadu, India, [b]Department of Computer and Information Science, Annamalai University, Chidambaram, Tamil Nadu, India, [c]Department of Computer Science and Engineering, Annamalai University, Chidambaram, Tamil Nadu, India

1 Introduction

Healthcare is the backbone of any nation, through which healthy individuals contribute to the growth and welfare of a country. From a common fever to the coronavirus pandemic, the world realizes how important the proper storage and maintenance of health records are to deal with future needs. Health records are references for proper diagnosis, treatment, and prevention of diseases. This section, in particular, introduces how the technological revolution brought about a breakthrough in the healthcare industry as well as challenges in protecting healthcare records in digital form, the motivation of this work, and the proposed solution to tackle various issues in the e-healthcare platform.

1.1 Technological shift of healthcare industry

Healthcare refers to the enhancement of people's health through efficient diagnosis from patient records and suggestions of various medical treatments to prevent the worsening of the disease. This helps people and the medical team to function effectively and at ease. The functionality of the healthcare system varies from time to time with technological advancements. Such variations in healthcare evolved gradually from Healthcare 1.0 to Healthcare 4.0 [1,2].

1.1.1 Healthcare 1.0

Healthcare 1.0 began around the 1970s. It can be viewed as the traditional method of treatment in the healthcare industry, which improved patient survivability. In this, the communication was only between the doctor and the patient. Patient's medical history was stored manually in the form of paperworks. Treatment was evidence based and solely from the experience of the doctor. The use of technology was narrowed to only

Blockchain Applications for Healthcare Informatics. https://doi.org/10.1016/B978-0-323-90615-9.00005-0
Copyright © 2022 Elsevier Inc. All rights reserved.

testing and diagnostic purposes. But the major change in Healthcare 1.0 was seen as the development of biomedical machinery.

1.1.2   Healthcare 2.0

Healthcare 2.0 existed for two decades beginning in 1991. It upgraded the patient's data-sharing ability by creating communication links between other organizations and doctors. The electronic health records (EHRs) of patients were shared among researchers and healthcare professionals. It used technologies such as data analytics to enhance patient care services and gave importance to patients by allowing them to access their diagnostic medical reports. As Healthcare 2.0 allowed sharing health records, it helped governments and researchers to monitor and track the health of people in a particular region. The major five characteristics of Healthcare 2.0 were:

- Use of social network platforms for effective communication.
- Giving an important role to patients, which allows them to control access to their health information.
- Providing a third opinion using experts, technological tools, and services.
- Collaboration of patients, healthcare professionals, researchers, and the community to improve healthcare initiatives.
- Permission to the public to access health information.

1.1.3   Healthcare 3.0

The basic goal of Healthcare 3.0, which existed between 2010 and 2015, was to use the gathered health information in a semantically effective way. It provided a personalized healthcare facility using the obtained data and data sharing was permitted within a country. It increased the doctor-patient interaction through virtual reasoning expert tools, which used the data to provide enhanced healthcare facilities. It offered digital healing to patients by providing support and confirmation from others via social networking.

1.1.4   Healthcare 4.0

Healthcare 4.0 emerged in 2016 with the sole purpose of bringing advanced technologies such as artificial intelligence (AI) for healthcare data analytics, the Internet of Things (IoT), blockchain, and machine learning, which provide highly personalized medical assistance and real-time solutions. The electronic health repositories are maintained and are shared globally by connecting patients, doctors, healthcare professionals, and medicine suppliers. But it also gives rise to challenges such as information security, data authenticity, and secure transmission of data worldwide. It also provides real-time health diagnostics using AI tools as well as buying prescribed medicines online.

1.2   Challenges in healthcare systems

The new Industrial Revolution has led to the growth of the healthcare sector along with the increase in challenges to retain its growth. Some of the crucial issues faced are:

- Rise in resources such as massive healthcare data generated day-by-day demands storage requirements. This in turn increases the cost of maintaining a stable and reliable e-healthcare storage system.
- Recent developments in the technical sector often require upgrading facilities as well as combining and processing health data for research.
- Advanced applications such as telesurgery and remote patient monitoring require uninterrupted and consistent availability of data for successful implementation.
- Security is a main concern when it comes to healthcare. Patient privacy is to be preserved and patient consent is required for use of healthcare data in academic research.
- Exchange of information and health data among hospitals, institutions, and mediclaim agencies is a vital part nowadays that requires a high level of confidentiality and integrity.
- Fake mediclaim are posing a threat to the e-healthcare sector because the whole process depends on the fidelity of the health record being communicated.

1.3   Motivation

A massive outbreak in digitization leads to the enormous growth of wireless communication technology, linking the world together. Distributing, archiving, updating, deleting, and maintaining digital data with proper infrastructure, authenticity, and security are worldwide concerns that induce various new ideas and studies in these areas constantly [3]. Many in the private sector are using cybersecurity frameworks such as NIST, HITRUST, CIS, and COBIT with their own policies and standards for regular maintenance of health records. Recently, blockchain-based healthcare applications have been framed by authors to protect privacy as well as to ensure the availability of healthcare data. Several models such as HaBiTs [4], AaYusH [5], and BinDaaS [6] are proposed to aid with patient monitoring and telesurgery applications. When it comes to such privacy protection, reversible data hiding plays a predominant role in handling sensitive patient data by hiding it inside the medical cover image such that the presence of patient data is undetectable. Thus, RDH helps in wrapping the sensitive details such as patient's name, ID, mediclaim details, diagnosis data, treatment, and prescriptions securely with the ability to unwrap them without any errors whenever necessary. Inspired by the privileges offered by blockchain technology and the RDH field, this chapter proposes an advanced secure framework for healthcare by combing interpolation-based reversible data hiding with blockchain.

1.4   Contributions

The main contributions of this chapter are listed below.

- An improved interpolation technique, altered neighbor mean interpolation (ANMI), is proposed along with the interpolated pixel adjustment with reduced mapping code (IPA_RMC) strategy for increasing the embedding capacity.
- The performance of the proposed IRDH method is validated using various performance metrics and compared with existing state-of-the art techniques.
- The crypto hashes of stego output as well as EPR are saved into blockchain such that the authenticity of both the medical image and patient's private information is explicitly verified and any tampering with medical data is also traceable with blockchain properties.

Thus, the proposed framework creates a secure platform for sharing medical health records among the members of the blockchain.

1.5 Organization

The rest of the paper is organized as follows. Section 2 gives brief notes on the backgrounds of blockchain and IRDH. Section 3 reviews various literature contributions in blockchain-based healthcare applications and the security of RDH systems. The proposed BAHDM framework integrated with the IRDH secured system is explained in Section 4. Experimental results are discussed in Section 5. Finally, Section 6 concludes the chapter.

2 Background

At present, the cloud is in use as a storage platform, which is a centralized network with a cloud manager. There is a risk of data leakage in the cloud as it is maintained by a cloud manager. Fear of data tampering, illegal replacement, or distribution of data in the cloud forced searches toward an alternate way of storing data securely. Blockchain is a solution to such a threat with blockchain nodes serving as a decentralized platform with trusted entities [7]. Every node in the blockchain is aware of every transaction inside it, making every transaction verifiable. With the help of the reversible data hiding technique combined with blockchain, healthcare management can be leveled up in confidentiality and integrity.

2.1 Blockchain technology

2.1.1 Structure of a blockchain

A system with a proposed protocol allowing anyone to join by sharing their physical device or virtual device forming a trusted network is the concept of blockchain. Transactions on every node are kept track of by all other nodes, making them transparent and so verifiable without any third-party agent [8]. The storage is immutable to avoid fraudulent activities. The structure of a blockchain is shown in Fig. 1.

The data are shared as chunks of blocks. Each block has three important sections: the user's data, the hash value of the current block, and the hash value of the previously linked block. The hash is the unique identifier for each block. Every transaction is

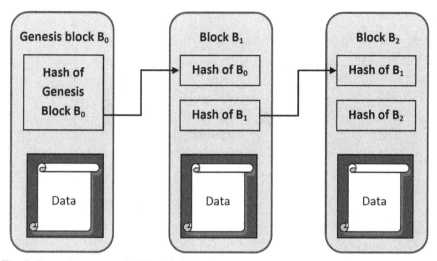

Fig. 1 General structure of a blockchain.

recorded in a ledger so that the chains of all blocks related to that transaction can be traced and audited. The beginning of a transaction is known as the genesis block, which contains the data and its hash value [9].

2.1.2 Working principle of blockchain

When a node is to be added or anyone wishes to add themselves to a blockchain, some rules are to be strictly followed to make all nodes in the network trustees. The rule framing process is called consensus [10]. Those nodes with the power of verifying the addition of another node are called miners. There are basically five common types of consensus, as shown in Fig. 2.

(i) *Proof of work (PoW)*: When a new node joins a blockchain, the active miner who recognizes the hash value first is given rights to acknowledge the new node's entry. But doing so is not an easy job. It needs higher computational power to maintain a higher hash rate and so they are rewarded with bitcoins in the case of Satoshi Nakamoto's first blockchain.

(ii) *Proof of stake (PoS)*: In PoW, high-end systems are required to do complex computations. To make it simple, the PoS approach is introduced where the miner with more coins has more probability for allowing a new block to be added.

(iii) *Delegated proof of stake (DPoS)*: In DPoS, a voting mechanism is followed where maximum coin holders can vote to change network requirements and are allowed to nominate a list of nodes for new additions to the blockchain.

(iv) *Proof of elapsed time (PoET)*: Unlike PoW, a time limit is set for validating the addition of a new node/transaction in the PoET consensus. Within this time limit, any trusted blockchain node gets a chance to validate.

(v) *Proof of authority (PoA)*: In PoA, some randomly chosen and high-staked nodes are appointed as trusted parties to do validation. These block validators are fixed in a blockchain.

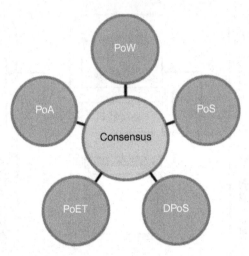

Fig. 2 Types of consensus.

2.1.3 Blockchain for healthcare

A simple blockchain scenario for healthcare is shown in Fig. 3. To avoid fake medical insurance claims, decentralized blockchain is of great advantage. All transactions are visible and verifiable in a blockchain network. Thus, blockchain contributes a big part in the management of the e-healthcare system.

2.2 Reversible data hiding technique

2.2.1 Traditional security systems

Security is one of the most sensitive needs of the telecommunication sector. Security, in a general sense, denotes the protection of data from unauthorized hands, uninterrupted resource access, and incorporating user privacy. Several technologies dedicated to data security cover cryptography, steganography, and watermarking [11]. The traditional method of protecting data from unidentified parties is the cryptography technique, where the readable information is changed into an unreadable format using encryption standards such as AES, RSA, etc. In case of authorship/ownership conflicts, watermarking proves the originality of data and the identity of a user with partial or invisible watermarks [12]. The usage of steganography prevents attacks from intruders because the existence of secret data inside the image is not visible to human eyes and hence it does not cause any suspicion while looking at it. Steganography scores higher in these techniques in sensitive areas, such as military applications, e-governance, e-commerce, intelligent services, remote sensing, and medical applications where covert communication and privacy are necessary. In the medical field, the use of steganography is investigated by hiding sensitive patient details, technically called EPRs or electronic health records (EHRs), inside the

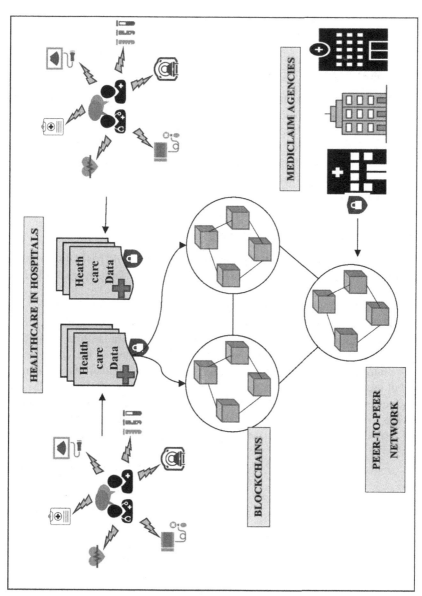

Fig. 3 A simple healthcare blockchain.

patient's medical image so that private information is not leaked or altered during transmission among hospitals, doctors, etc. [13,14]. However, the medical image that carries the EPR gets degraded in its quality due to the embedding process. But all these technologies lack important security concerns such as reversibility, invisibility, and perfect recovery. These characteristics altogether are had by reversible data hiding (RDH).

2.2.2 Advantages of RDH

RDH has become an isolated and curious study of interest because of its capability to perform all operations in a lossless manner throughout the hiding process. This is more suitable for medical data hiding where the cover medical image needs to be distortion-free for proper diagnosis, after recovering the secret data from it [15]. Also, the stego image, which is the resultant medical image after embedding, should not create suspicions for hackers. Hence, the tradeoff between embedding capacity and stego image quality remains a challenging task.

2.2.3 Classification of RDH approaches

The classification of reversible schemes mentioned here is purely based on the nature of the embedding process. The major classifications of five different types of RDH are explained in Fig. 4.

The first category is the difference expansion-based technique (DE), which is the traditional way of reversible embedding method where hiding is done between difference values of adjacent pixels in an image. Second, histogram shifting (HS)-based approaches are used where embedding is done at peak bins of the cover image [16]. The third category is the prediction error expansion technique, which is similar to DE but uses the errors between the predicted pixels of the cover image. This category gives promising results when compared with previous methods. Evolution in PEE leads to an embedding strategy called pixel value ordering (PVO), in which sorting is done on pixels before the prediction process [17,18]. Apart from these

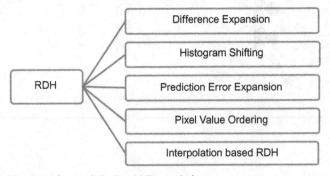

Fig. 4 Classification of reversible data hiding techniques.

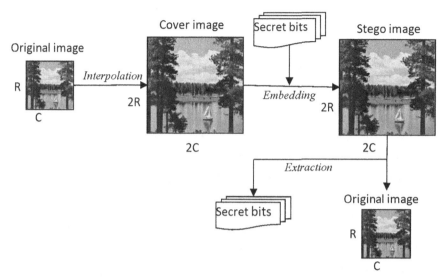

Fig. 5 General framework of IRDH technique.

techniques, a special methodology that enlarges a cover image to create space for embedding reaches a higher embedding rate. This technique is called the interpolation-based RDH technique (IRDH) [19].

2.2.4 Interpolation-based reversible data hiding

Limited capacity and high complexity are observed in older RDH methodologies. Interpolation is becoming a keyword for RDH, especially in medical data hiding. The general workflow of IRDH is shown in Fig. 5. The image taken as input is named the original image. This is scaled up by increasing the size by a factor of two, producing the so-called cover image [20]. The secret data hiding is done in this image on its interpolated pixels. The cover image carrying the secret data is now called a stego image. With this step, the embedding process is completed. At the extraction side, the original image and secret data are recovered [21].

3 Related works

3.1.1 Survey on blockchain-based healthcare systems

This section presents a survey on various models proposed by authors for interfacing blockchain with healthcare systems. Yue et al. [22] proposed a privacy-concerned blockchain model in healthcare. They developed a data access control mechanism for implementing the privacy of health records. Zhang et al. [23] designed two protocols for sharing and authenticating health records based on PSN. Table 1 lists recent applications of blockchain in telemedicine.

Table 1 Survey on existing works on a blockchain-based healthcare system.

Author	Year	Objective	Applications	Blockchain
Jigna J Hathaliya et al. [24]	2019	To provide secure access to patient EHRs	Biometric authentication	–
Sudeep Tanwar et al. [3]	2019	To improve data accessibility among healthcare providers	EHR sharing system	Hyperledger fabric blockchain
Rajesh Gupta et al., [3]	2020	Provides secure, tracking of UAV delivery	Healthcare medical supplies through UAV	Ethereum blockchain
Rajesh Gupta et al. [25]	2019	Highly reliable with quick response time for the communication channel.	Telesurgery	–
Pronaya Bhattacharya et al. [6]	2019	To ensure privacy and authentication of EHR.	Patient care services of Healthcare 4.0	Consortium blockchain
Rajesh Gupta et al. [4]	2019	To ensure interoperability among connected parties through a smart contract.	Telesurgery	Hyperledger fabric blockchain
Rajesh Gupta et al. [26]	2020	To expose the flaws of smart contracts and find solutions for security using AI tools.	Blockchain and cyberphysical system	–
Rajesh Gupta et al. [27]	2020	To develop an intelligent scheme incorporating AI, machine learning, and blockchain.	Telesurgery	Ethereum blockchain
Rajesh Gupta et al. [5]	2020	To develop secure and trustless smart contract	Telesurgery	–

3.1.2 Survey on interpolation-based reversible data hiding techniques

Jung and Yoo introduced the application of interpolation in reversible data hiding. The authors presented a new interpolation method, the neighbor mean interpolation (NMI), and embedded secret data into newly interpolated pixels [28]. The authors of [29] proposed an interpolation called interpolation by neighboring pixels (INP), which improved the visual quality of the stego image. In [30], the authors developed a better interpolation to increase the hiding capacity. The work in [31] extended the INP method using interpolation by maximizing the difference values between neighboring pixels (IMNP). It achieved a higher embedding rate than other techniques. Lu proposed utilized INP interpolation and the message recoding step to improve IRDH performance. This method uses small numbers to embed secret messages based on the message bit frequency [32]. In [33], the author presented a simple IRDH; the secret data quantity and stego quality are achieved by maintaining an appropriate threshold. The authors in [34] used reversible image watermarking using the interpolation technique. The interpolation error is used for embedding the watermarking, which is capable of high-quality visual clarity with low computational cost. With the exploitation of the direction order mechanism, errors are predicted for wall pixels while differences are calculated for nonwall pixels in [35]. Histogram shifting is the preferred choice for embedding. In [36], a weighted matrix and modulus function were proposed to embed secret data. The authors of [37] developed a directional interpolation method but used only difference expansion controlled by a threshold value.

In [38], a new reversible data hiding scheme was used that embeds data with high capacity and maintains the visual clarity of the embedded image. An improvised NMI method was used that doubles the efficiency of the original NMI. The authors of [39] proposed a data hiding technique that is semireversible. It uses an interpolation technique for enlarging the original image followed by LSB substitution of secret data. The authors of [40] also used an interpolation-based reversible data hiding technique called optimal pixel adjustment procedure and message adaptive error. The error between the interpolated pixel and the original pixel is calculated and used to hide the secret bits. The literature uses a chi-square test finally to check the secrecy of the embedded data. In [41], the authors proposed a method that depends on the IRDH scheme in which the original cover image pixels are left without embedding. Only the interpolated pixels are embedded in an ad hoc manner, which leads to high embedding capacity. Because the original pixels are left unchanged, this can be used in military applications. The authors of [42] propose the Lagrange interpolation-based reversible data hiding method, which finds the prediction image for odd pixels and even pixels separately. The secret information is embedded in the difference between the original and the prediction image by using the histogram shifting method. Because the embedding occurs at two stages of odd/even pixels, it assures a high embedding capacity. The work of [43] involves hiding confidential information in the encrypted image in a reversible manner. The interpolation error estimate method is applied to increase the embedding capacity. The use of a partitioned local histogram shift improves the image quality of the stego images. The authors of [44] embed secret data in a binary image using a technique called image magnification. Initially, they looked for any cross-shape patterns among the two types are selected. Based on the type of pattern selected, the original image is magnified. A technique called the inner-block flippable pixel selection strategy embeds the secret data in the scaled-up image, which ensures the stego image quality. The work of [45] aims to reduce the distortion of the stego image by proposing a reduction strategy. Basically, the secret data are handled in a manner such that its range is reduced to cause a minimal distortion effect in the interpolated pixels. It shows promising results when compared to other RDH.

In [46], the local characteristics of the image such as the complex region and smooth region are identified. Based on the classified region, the distribution of payload is performed, which helps in reducing the image distortion. In [47], the cover image is copied twice and both images are used for embedding, thereby increasing the embedding capacity of the cover image. They use the frequency count of the secret bit to reduce the value of the secret data so that the image quality remains unaffected, despite the maximum embedding capacity. The authors of [48] proposed an interpolation-based hiding scheme in which a mapping code reencodes the secret bit such that it lessens the degradation of image quality while concealing the data. Embedding blocks of various sizes are used to control the embedding rate.

4 Proposed work

This section presents the proposed blockchain-based authenticity of healthcare data for the mediclaim (BAHDM) model with interpolation-based RDH in two subsections. Fig. 6 shows the overall block diagram of the proposed method.

4.1 Interpolation-based reversible data hiding

In this section, we present our novel reversible data hiding using ANMI and interpolated pixel adjustment with reduced mapping code (IPA_RMC). The proposed RDH applies the ANMI method. Then, the interpolated pixels are processed in 3×3 blocks. Based on the difference value between the interpolated pixels and the neighbor pixels, the payload capacity of each interpolated pixel is calculated using the proposed strategy. Then the bits are embedded into the interpolated pixels with reduced codes without degrading the overall visual quality of the stego image. This stego is inserted into the blockchain. Next, the extraction algorithm is explained where both the cover and secret data are separated from the stego image reversibly after requesting the homogenous data hiding key by any node in the blockchain.

4.1.1 Altered neighbor mean interpolation

Image interpolation is a technique by which a low-resolution image can be scaled up to a high-resolution image without degrading the visual quality. The quality of such interpolated images can be calculated using the PSNR value. But the enlarged images

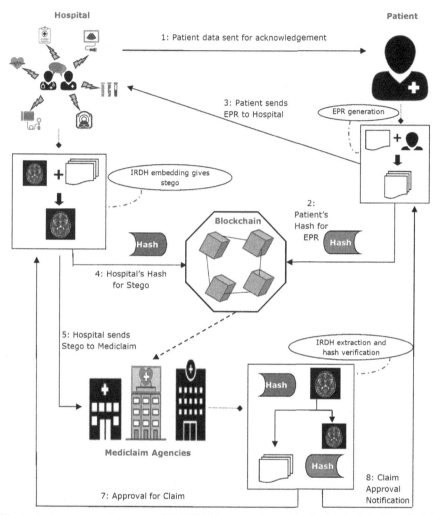

Fig. 6 Architecture of the proposed BAHDM framework combined with the IRDH method.

are larger in size than the given original images. To solve this problem, we consider the standard ground truth images of size 512×512 and reduce them to 256×256. This reduced image serves as the original image and is further upscaled using the interpolation technique to generate the cover image of a size equal to the ground truth image. The middle pixels are calculated as follows:

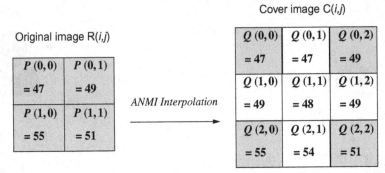

Fig. 7 Cover image built from an original image using the proposed ANMI.

$$C(0,1) = \left\lfloor \frac{C(0,0) + \dfrac{C(0,0) + C(0,2)}{2}}{2} \right\rfloor \quad C(0,2) = \left\lfloor \frac{C(0,2) + \dfrac{C(0,2) + C(2,2)}{2}}{2} \right\rfloor$$

$$C(1,0) = \left\lfloor \frac{C(0,0) + \dfrac{C(0,0) + C(2,0)}{2}}{2} \right\rfloor \quad C(2,0) = \left\lfloor \frac{C(2,0) + \dfrac{C(2,0) + C(2,2)}{2}}{2} \right\rfloor$$

$$C(1,1) = \left\lfloor \frac{C(0,0) + \dfrac{C(0,0) + C(0,1) + C(1,0) + C(2,2)}{4}}{2} \right\rfloor \tag{1}$$

Let $P(m,n)$ be the original image with dimensions 256×256 and $Q(m,n)$ be the resultant cover image with dimensions 512×512 from the proposed ANMI interpolation. The scaling procedure is described as follows. As pointed out in Fig. 6, for each 2×2 block of the original image, new pixels are inserted to form a 3×3 block. The blue pixels of cover image $Q(0,0), Q(0,2), Q(2,0)$, and $Q(2,2)$ are the reference pixels that are unchanged from original image $P(0,0)$, $P(0,1)$, $P(1,0)$, and $P(1,1)$, respectively, as shown in Fig. 7.

To share the influence of our proposed ANMI technique, the PSNR metric is used to show a comparison with other existing interpolation methods.

Table 2 compares the performance of the NMI, INP, CRS, IMNP, and proposed ANMI methods. From the table, it is evident that ANMI interpolation gives better results than other interpolation methods. Though a smaller increase is noticed, it will affect the stego quality to a certain extent, which will later be discussed.

4.1.2 Embedding using interpolated pixel adjustment and reduced mapping code

After interpolation, the next step is embedding. The proposed IPA_RMC exploits the relationship among the predicted pixels and original pixels of the cover image. The steps for embedding are given below in detail.

Table 2 PSNR comparisons of NMI, INP, CRS, IMNP, and proposed ANMI methods for interpolated image and ground truth image.

Images	NMI	INP	CRS	IMNP	Proposed ANMI
Airplane	33.93	34.29	33.15	34.09	35.27
Baboon	29.92	30.02	29.72	29.55	30.08
Barbara	30.87	31.10	30.49	31.34	32.14
Goldhill	31.78	32.15	31.25	31.96	33.13
Lena	33.63	34.13	32.94	33.53	35.11
Peppers	32.69	33.01	32.20	32.94	34.03

Input: Cover image C sized $2r \times 2c$ and secret bit stream denoted with symbol s.
Output: Stego image S sized $2r \times 2c$
Step 1: Divide cover into 2×2 sized nonoverlapping blocks.
Step 2: Find the difference values $d_k(k = 1, 2, 3)$ between the reference pixel $Q\ (m, n)$ and the interpolated pixels $Q(m, n+1)$, $Q(m+1, n)$ and $Q(m+1, n+1)$ as given in Eq. (2). The remaining pixels $Q(m, n+1)$, $Q(m+1, n)$,and $Q(m+1, n+1)$ are used for embedding.

$$d_1 = |Q(m, n) - Q(m, n+1)|$$

$$d_2 = |Q(m, n) - Q(m+1, n)|$$

$$d_3 = |Q(m, n) - Q(m+1, n+1)| \tag{2}$$

Step 3: Obtain the lower and upper bounds to determine the total bits to be embedded. The log base 2 values of d_k are denoted as l_k. The equations are as follows:

$$l_1 = \lfloor \log_2(d_1) \rfloor$$

$$l_2 = \lfloor \log_2(d_2) \rfloor$$

$$l_3 = \lfloor \log_2(d_3) \rfloor \tag{3}$$

Step 4: Allot the maximum capacity bits to be carried in an interpolated pixel using threshold value th. This threshold value is the user-defined value to balance the trade-off between stego quality and capacity

$$cl_k = \begin{cases} th & \text{if } l_k = \infty \\ th+1 & \text{if } l_k = 0 \\ th+2 & \text{if } l_k \in \{1, 2, 3\} \\ th+3 & \text{if } l_k \in \{4, 5, 6, 7\} \end{cases} \tag{4}$$

where $k = 1,2,3$ denotes the interpolated pixels $Q(m, n+1), Q(m+1, n)$, and $Q(m+1, n+1)$, respectively. The value c_k is the original length of the secret bits.
Step 5: Convert cl_k into the decimal equivalent c_k. Three cases are considered for embedding.
Step 5.1 *Case* (i). Those interpolated pixels whose intensity range falls less than 2^5 are embedded with the original length c_k by performing addition operations. In this case, overflow may occur and so subtraction is performed for overflow conditions. The

limitation variable $L1_{overflow}$ is used to check pixels for overflow cases. The corresponding equations are as follows:

$$L1_{overflow} = 255 - \left(2^{(th+3)} - 1\right) \tag{5}$$

$$S_{ref} = Q_{ref}$$

$$S_{intp} = \begin{cases} Q_{intp} + c_k, & \text{if } Q_{intp} \leq L1_{overflow} \\ Q_{intp} - c_k, & \text{otherwise} \end{cases} \tag{6}$$

Step 5.2 *Case* (ii). Those interpolated pixels whose intensity range falls greater than $(2^8\text{--}2^5)$ are embedded with the original length c_k by performing subtraction operations. In this case, underflow may occur and so the addition is performed for underflow conditions. The limitation variable $L2_{underflow}$ is used to check pixels for underflow cases. The corresponding equations are as follows:

$$L2_{underflow} = 2^{(th+3)} \tag{7}$$

$$S_{ref} = Q_{ref}$$

$$S_{intp} = \begin{cases} Q_{intp} + c_k & \text{if } Q_{intp} > L2_{underflow} \\ Q_{intp} - c_k & \text{otherwise} \end{cases} \tag{8}$$

Step 5.3 *Case* (iii). Those interpolated pixels whose intensity value lies in the middle range between greater than 2^5 and less than $(2^8\text{--}2^5)$ are embedded with reduced codes to improve stego quality. In this case, both overflow and underflow may occur. The limitation variables $L3_{overflow}$ and $L3_{underflow}$ are used to check pixels for overflow and underflow cases using the following equations:

$$L3_{overflow} = 255 - 2^{(c_k-1)} \tag{9}$$

$$L3_{underflow} = 2^{(c_k-1)} \tag{10}$$

Step 6: The third case relates to the code reduction step as shown in Table 3. For this case, the reduced mapping code (RMC) is generated by:

$$\bar{c}_k = \begin{cases} +\left\lceil \dfrac{c_k}{2} \right\rceil, & \text{if } c_k \text{ is odd} \\ -\left\lceil \dfrac{c_k}{2} \right\rceil, & \text{if } c_k \text{ is even} \end{cases} \tag{11}$$

Step 7: Embedding for the third case with their corresponding conditions are as given, $S_{ref} = Q_{ref}$

Table 3 Reduced mapping code.

Original decimal code of c_k	0	1	2	3	......	2k
Reduced decimal code of $\bar{c}_k$	0	+1	−1	+2	......	+k

$$S_{intp} = \begin{cases} Q_{intp} + \bar{c}_k, & \text{if } c_k \text{ is even and } Q_{intp} > L3_{underflow} \\ Q_{intp} + 2^{c_k} + \bar{c}_k, & \text{if } c_k \text{ is even and } Q_{intp} \leq L3_{underflow} \end{cases}$$

$$S_{intp} = \begin{cases} Q_{intp} + \bar{c}_k, & \text{if } c_k \text{ is odd and } Q_{intp} \leq L3_{overflow} \\ Q_{intp} - 2^{c_k} + \bar{c}_k, & \text{if } c_k \text{ is odd and } Q_{intp} > L3_{overflow} \end{cases} \quad (12)$$

Step 8: Go back to step 2 and repeat the same process until all the nonoverlapping blocks are processed. Finally, we get the stego image S.

4.1.3 Illustration of embedding algorithm

Consider the interpolated 2×2 block as shown in Fig. 8. The cover pixels belong to the third case $C(0,0) = 47$, $C(0,1) = 47$, $C(1,0) = 49$, $C(1,1) = 48$. Find the reference pixel, which is 47. The next step is to find the difference values, $d_1 = |47 - 47| = 0$, $d_2 = |47 - 49| = 2$, $d_3 = |47 - 48| = 1$. The difference values are in a varied range from 0 to 255. So, to group the interpolated pixels and allocate the capacity, log values are calculated for these difference values. $l_1 = \lfloor log_2(0) \rfloor = \infty$, $l_2 = \lfloor log_2(2) \rfloor = 1$, $l_3 = \lfloor log_2(1) \rfloor = 0$. Based on our proposed threshold allotment, th values are selected, $c_1 = th$, $c_2 = th + 2$, and $c_3 = th + 1$. The th is user-defined. Let us assume $th = 1$, then, $\bar{c}_1 = +1$, $\bar{c}_2 = +2$, and $\bar{c}_3 = -1$. The limitation variables $L3_{underflow}$ and $L3_{overflow}$ are checked. No overflow or underflow occurs. Let us consider secret message bits $s = 101110$. All three interpolated pixels are within range and hence stego pixels are formed by adding reduced integer values to interpolated pixels, $S(0,0) = 47$, $S(0,1) = 47 + 1 = 48$, $S(1,0) = 49 + 2 = 51$, $S(1,1) = 48 - 1 = 47$ as shown in Fig. 8.

4.1.4 Auxiliary information

The auxiliary data for extraction are the length of the total secret bits taken and the threshold. To represent the secret data length, a maximum of 20 bits is required. The maximum value of the possible threshold value is 5 and hence it requires three

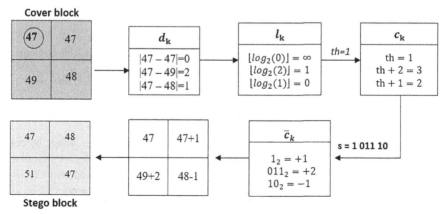

Fig. 8 Illustration of proposed IPA_RMC method with example.

$C(i,j)$	$C(i,j+1)$ l_{th} – 3bits	$C(i,j+2)$	$C(i,j+3)$ l_{s3} – 4bits
$C(i+1,j)$ l_{s1} – 4bits	$C(i+1,j+1)$ l_{s2} – 4bits	$C(i+1,j+2)$ l_{s4} – 4bits	$C(i+1,j+3)$ l_{s5} – 4bits

Fig. 9 Embedding of auxiliary information using LSB substitution in the first two 2×2 blocks.

bits. So, the additional data of $l_{th}+l_s$ are embedded into the first two blocks of the cover image using LSB substitution, as shown in Fig. 9. Then, the proposed embedding starts with the third block and proceeds until all required bits are hidden successfully.

4.1.5 Extraction algorithm

At the receiver side, to extract the secret data from the stego image and recover the original image, the proposed extraction algorithm is applied. The details of the extraction algorithm are given below.

Input: Stego image S sized $2r \times 2c$
Output: Original image R sized $r \times c$ and secret bit stream s
Step 1: Divide stego into 2×2 nonoverlapping blocks. Collect all the first pixels $S(i,j)$ from each block to get the original image R.

$$O(i,j) = S(2i, 2j) \, for \, all \, i, j \in \{0, 255\}$$

Step 2: Use the ANMI interpolation to get the interpolated image from the recovered original image (Eq. 1)
Step 3: Find the absolute difference between the interpolated image and the stego image. The difference value is the value of the integer hidden in the stego image.

$$Diff[n] = abs(S(x,y) - C(x,y))$$

Step 4: Follow the steps of embedding (Eqs. 4–6) to find the c_k value for each block. Convert the integer into binary bits of length $2c_k$ using Eq. (7)
Step 5: Extract all the secret bits and collect them to regain the secret data losslessly.

4.1.6 Illustration of extraction algorithm

At the extraction side, the original image is separated from the cover image by collecting the unchanged pixel $S(i,j)$ in every 2×2 block. In our example, the first pixel 47 is the original pixel. Now, the same ANMI interpolation is performed on the recovered original image. By finding the difference matrix between the interpolated image and the stego image, the secret bitstream is recovered losslessly, as shown in Fig. 10.

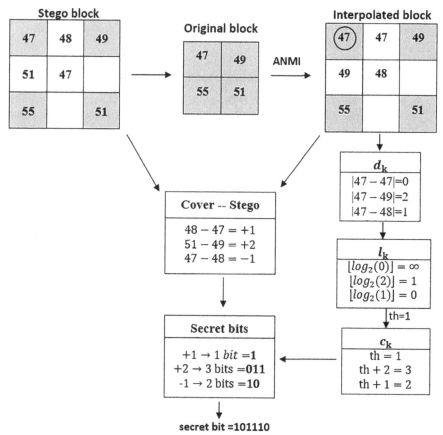

Fig. 10 Illustration of proposed extraction method with example.

4.2 Proposed BAHDM system

This section presents the proposed BAHDM system, which is combined with the proposed IRDH to achieve authenticity and integrity in mediclaim approvals. To build a blockchain for healthcare use, a simple consortium-based private blockchain system is considered that consists of three trusted parties: the hospital, patient, and mediclaim agency. A doctor from hospital X initially sends patient data to a particular patient Y who is a part of blockchain. = Patient Y approves the data by concatenating his picture with the data forming the EPR. Patient Y now generates cryptographic hash values for EPR and uploads into the blockchain. He also sends the EPR to X for mediclaim processing. By using the RDH technique, hospital X by embeds the EPR into his medical image, adds the generated hash of the stego medical image to the blockchain, and sends the stego medical image to mediclaim agency Z. Upon receiving the stego, Z verifies the genuineness of both the stego medical image and the EPR data using crypto hashes taken from the blockchain. Upon successful verification, the mediclaim is approved and payment is sent to hospital X while patient Y is also notified.

4.2.1 Procedural steps for blockchain creation and verification

Step 1: From hospital X, patient data (PD_X) are sent to patient Y as a request to verify the patient's identity and to generate the EPR. Y adds his signature by concatenating his picture (Y_{pic}) with patient data generating EPR.

$Request.1 : PD_X \rightarrow Y$

$Y : \Rightarrow EPR = PD_X \parallel Y_{pic}$

Step 2: The hash is generated using the previous block's hash value (H_{pre}) for EPR by Y and added to the blockchain. EPR in the original form is sent to hospital X.

$Y : \Rightarrow H_{cur} = H_{pre} \parallel Hash(EPR)$

$Upload.2 : Y : \Rightarrow H_{cur} \rightarrow Blockchain$

$Permission.3 : Y : \Rightarrow EPR \rightarrow X$

Step 3: Upon receiving the EPR, X performs interpolation-based reversible data hiding and embeds it into the medical image of Y (img). The hash for the embedded stego medical image is generated from previous hashes and added to blockchain. The original stego medical images (stego) are sent to Z.

$X :\Rightarrow stego = IRDH(img, EPR)$

$X :\Rightarrow H_{stego} = H_{cur} \parallel Hash(stego)$

$Upload.4 : X :\Rightarrow H_{stego} \rightarrow Blockchain$

$Request.5 : X :\Rightarrow stego \rightarrow Z$

Step 4: A request for mediclaim approval is sent to mediclaim agency Z along with the stego medical image. Z accesses the hashes from blockchain for verifying stego and EPR and grants the request. A notification is sent to patient Y.

$Access.6 : Z :\Rightarrow Authenticity(stego, H_{stego})$

$Z :\Rightarrow (img, EPR) = Extraction(stego)$

$Access.7 : Z :\Rightarrow Authenticity(EPR, H_{cur})$

$Approval.8 : Z :\Rightarrow Mediclaim \rightarrow X$

$Notify.9 : Z :\Rightarrow Notification \rightarrow Y$

5 Experimental results

This section presents the experimental results and a comparison of the proposed method with other state-of-the-art methods. Experiments were done on eight-bit grayscale medical images of size 512×512, as shown in Fig. 11. These images serve as ground truth. The interpolated cover image is compared with the ground truth (input image) image to show the performance of the interpolation scheme. So, the original image (carrier of secret data) is formed by reducing the input image to one-fourth of its size. For all the existing methods taken for comparison and the proposed method, we used bicubic interpolation for this reduction step. The secret data are formed by a concatenation Lena image of size 128×128 (considering the Lena image as the patient's picture) with the patient's electronic report. The secret data are then converted into binary bits for further processing.

The image quality of the embedded image can be evaluated using peak signal-to-noise ratio (PSNR) as follows:

$$\text{PSNR} = 10 * \log \left(\frac{255^2}{MSE} \right) \tag{13}$$

$$\text{MSE} = \frac{1}{MN} \sum_{i=0}^{M} \sum_{j=0}^{N} (S(i,j) - I(i,j))^2 \tag{14}$$

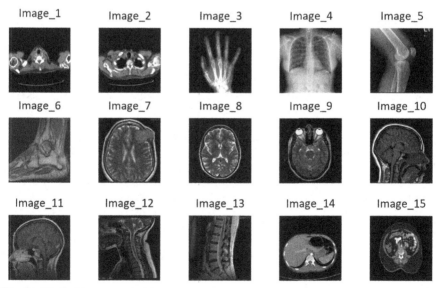

Fig. 11 Medical images as test images.

where PSNR and the mean square error (MSE) between the stego image $S(i, j)$ and input image $I(i, j)$ with dimension $M \times N$. The structural similarity index measure is given by

$$SSIM(x, y) = \frac{\left(2\mu_x\mu_y + c_1\right)\left(2\sigma_{xy} + c_2\right)}{\left(\mu_x^2 + \mu_y^2 + c_1\right)\left(\sigma_x^2 + \sigma_y^2 + c_2\right)}$$

$$c_1 = (k_1 L)^2, c_2 = (k_2 L)^2 \tag{15}$$

where μ_x and μ_y are average values; σ_x^2 and σ_y^2 denote variance; σ_{xy} is the covariance of x and y; c_1 and c_2 are variables for stabilization; $L = 255$ denotes pixel range; $k_1 = 0.01$ and $k_2 = 0.03$ are default constants; and x and y are stego and input images, respectively. The embedding capacity denotes the total number of bits that can be embedded into the cover image, called bits per pixel (BPP). The secret data are the randomly generated binary bits.

Table 4 shows the performance of different threshold values for the proposed IPA_RMC method for standard images as cover. Table 5 shows how the proposed system is efficient when compared to existing methods [7]. It is evident that the higher capacity is due to the increase in the number of pixels with n_k values 0 and infinity. Minimum bits are selected for those pixels with higher occurrences of n_k to maintain the stego image visibility. Table 6 shows the performance of different threshold values for the proposed IPA_RMC method for medical images as cover. The value of th is restricted between 1 and 3 to balance the tradeoff between capacity and PSNR. Thus, the user can define the th value according to their need.

Table 4 Performance of the proposed method with different thresholds for grayscale images.

Cover images	Proposed $th = 1$			Proposed $th = 2$			Proposed $th = 3$		
	PSNR	BPP	SSIM	PSNR	BPP	SSIM	PSNR	BPP	SSIM
Lena	44.48	1.58	0.9902	38.67	2.33	0.9631	33.98	3.08	0.8710
Baboon	41.10	2.11	0.9914	35.20	2.86	0.9674	31.63	3.61	0.8834
Jet	44.39	1.53	0.9912	38.63	2.28	0.9668	34.37	3.03	0.8827
Peppers	44.17	1.60	0.9886	38.41	2.35	0.9563	33.66	3.10	0.8491
Couple	42.89	1.77	0.9901	37.14	2.52	0.9623	32.90	3.27	0.8675
Boat	43.67	1.61	0.9912	37.87	2.36	0.9658	33.62	2.36	0.9658
Goldhill	43.76	1.74	0.9894	37.81	2.49	0.9593	32.89	3.24	0.8587
Man	41.57	1.80	0.9845	35.89	2.55	0.9385	32.18	3.30	0.8022
Lake	43.19	1.73	0.9907	37.32	2.48	0.9647	33.14	3.23	0.8757
Crowd	43.08	1.71	0.9919	37.26	2.46	0.9693	33.20	3.21	0.8903
Barbara	42.36	1.83	0.9906	36.42	2.58	0.9639	32.64	3.33	0.8719
Car	43.18	1.70	0.9915	37.32	2.45	0.9675	33.21	3.20	0.8847
Bee	45.59	1.42	0.9910	39.78	2.17	0.9658	34.85	2.92	0.8792
Traffic	43.00	1.71	0.9908	37.57	2.46	0.9652	33.31	3.21	0.8744
Elaine	44.68	1.65	0.9880	38.78	2.40	0.9544	33.41	3.15	0.8426

Table 5 Comparison of the proposed method with existing IRDH [7] for Image_3.

Range of c_k	Lee and Huang [7]				Proposed IPA_RMC (th = 1)			
	Number of pixels with c_k	Number of bits to be embedded per pixel	Total bits embedded for a given c_k	Total capacity (in bits)	Number of pixels with c_k	Number of bits to be embedded per pixel	Total bits embedded for a given c_k	Total capacity (in bits)
∞	120,495	0	0	0	141,345	th	141,345	141,345
0	12,684	0	0		25,651	$th+1$	51,302	51,302
1	17,058	1	17,058	155,139	16,704	$th+2$	50,112	87,099
2	18,711	2	37,422		8912	$th+2$	26,736	
3	14,671	3	44,013		3417	$th+2$	10,251	
4	8945	4	35,780		578	$th+3$	2312	2316
5	3400	5	17,000		1	$th+3$	4	
6	642	6	3852		0	$th+3$	0	
7	2	7	14	155,139	0	$th+3$	0	282,062

Table 6 Performance of the proposed method with different thresholds for medical images.

Cover images	Proposed th = 1			Proposed th = 2			Proposed th = 3		
	PSNR	BPP	SSIM	PSNR	BPP	SSIM	PSNR	BPP	SSIM
Image_1	45.14	1.12	0.9819	39.64	1.87	0.8834	34.99	2.62	0.6164
Image_2	44.30	1.20	0.9829	38.97	1.95	0.8943	34.57	2.70	0.6477
Image_3	46.55	1.08	0.9816	40.13	1.83	0.8859	35.27	2.58	0.6313
Image_4	46.08	1.40	0.9881	40.18	2.15	0.9470	34.67	2.90	0.8221
Image_5	46.75	1.15	0.9828	40.76	1.90	0.9006	35.48	2.65	0.6758
Image_6	45.67	1.46	0.990	40.04	2.21	0.9651	34.52	2.96	0.8763
Image_7	42.98	1.58	0.9882	37.40	2.33	0.9455	33.31	3.08	0.8193
Image_8	43.35	1.38	0.9907	37.71	2.13	0.9603	33.50	2.88	0.8544
Image_9	43.74	1.35	0.9789	37.80	2.10	0.8897	33.67	2.85	0.6685
Image_10	43.18	1.47	0.9881	37.43	2.21	0.9398	33.35	2.96	0.7971
Image_11	44.47	1.47	0.9881	38.32	2.22	0.9522	33.39	2.97	0.8328
Image_12	42.34	1.57	0.9853	36.44	2.32	0.9375	32.43	3.07	0.7862
Image_13	42.58	1.58	0.9836	36.70	2.33	0.9325	32.50	3.08	0.7765
Image_14	43.99	1.26	0.9826	38.80	2.01	0.8959	34.34	2.76	0.6523
Image_15	44.49	1.26	0.9813	38.51	2.01	0.8898	34.12	2.76	0.6306

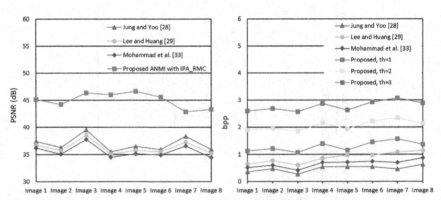

Fig. 12 Comparison of proposed ANMI with IPA_RMC and other existing methods.

Fig. 12 shows the PSNR and capacity comparison of the proposed scheme with other existing techniques. The capacity of the proposed technique is higher than all other methods. Despite this increment, our PSNR values are better than other existing techniques with lower capacity.

Fig. 13 shows the generated hash values for the stego medical image and the secret data. These hash values are used for verifying the originality of the contents by the mediclaim agencies for insurance approval. The hashes are stored in continuous links of blocks in a blockchain network.

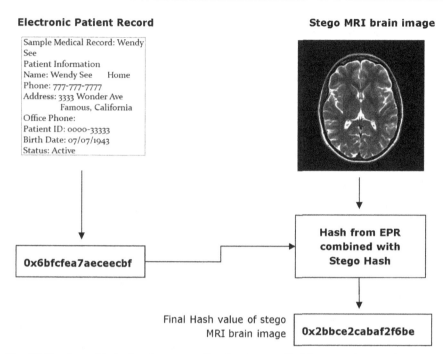

Electronic Patient Record

Sample Medical Record: Wendy
See
Patient Information
Name: Wendy See   Home
Phone: 777-777-7777
Address: 3333 Wonder Ave
         Famous, California
Office Phone:
Patient ID: 0000-33333
Birth Date: 07/07/1943
Status: Active

Stego MRI brain image

0x6bfcfea7aeceecbf

Hash from EPR combined with Stego Hash

Final Hash value of stego
MRI brain image   0x2bbce2cabaf2f6be

Fig. 13 Cryptographic hash values generation for stego medical image and secret data.

6 Conclusion

In this chapter, a novel ANMI and IPA_RMC proved to be efficient for interpolation interpolation-based information hiding. The proposed IRDH is combined with blockchain for developing the BAHDM framework. With BAHDM, the mediclaim agencies successfully verify the authenticity of medical images as well as the EPR using two cryptographic hashes generated by both the hospital and the patient. This prevents any disputes between alleged parties and provides security against false mediclaims. Experimental results showed the efficiency of the proposed IRDH technique and proved that it is suitable for medical applications where patient records must be securely saved into their medical images along with the benefits of blockchain technology.

References

[1] A.K. Sarangi, A.G. Mohapatra, T.C. Mishra, B. Keswani, in: S. Tanwar (Ed.), Healthcare 4.0: A Voyage of Fog Computing with IOT, Cloud Computing, Big Data, and Machine Learning. Fog Computing for Healthcare 4.0 Environments Technical, Societal, and Future Implications, Springer, 2021, pp. 177–210.
[2] R. Jain, M. Gupta, A. Nayyar, N. Sharma, in: S. Tanwar (Ed.), Adoption of Fog Computing in Healthcare 4.0. Fog Computing for Healthcare 4.0 Environments Technical, Societal, and Future Implications, Springer, 2021, pp. 3–36.

[3] S. Tanwar, K. Parekh, R. Evans, Blockchain-based electronic healthcare record system for healthcare 4.0 applications, J. Inform. Sec. Appl. 50 (2020) 102407.

[4] G. Gupta, S. Tanwar, S. Tyagi, N. Kumar, M.S. Obaidat, B. Sadoun, HaBiTs: blockchain-based telesurgery framework for healthcare 4.0, in: International Conference on Computer, Information and Telecommunication Systems (IEEE CITS-2019), Beijing, China, August 28–31, 2019, pp. 6–10.

[5] R. Gupta, A. Shukla, S. Tanwar, AaYusH: a smart contract-based telesurgery system for healthcare 4.0, in: IEEE Conference on Communications (IEEE ICC-2020), Dublin, Ireland, 07-11th June, 2020, pp. 1–6.

[6] P. Bhattacharya, S. Tanwar, S. Tyagi, N. Kumar, BINDaaS: blockchain integrated deep-learning as a service in healthcare 4.0 applications, in: IEEE Transactions on Network Science and Engineering, 2019, pp. 1–14.

[7] F. Frattolillo, A watermarking protocol based on Blockchain, Appl. Sci. 10 (21) (2020) 7746.

[8] P. Sarkar, S.K. Ghosal, M. Sarkar, Stego-chain: a framework to mine encoded stego-block in a decentralized network, J. King Saud Univ.-Comput. Inform. Sci. (2020). In press.

[9] A.H. Mohsin, A.A. Zaidan, B.B. Zaidan, K.I. Mohammed, O.S. Albahri, A.S. Albahri, M. A. Alsalem, PSO–Blockchain-based image steganography: towards a new method to secure updating and sharing COVID-19 data in decentralised hospitals intelligence architecture, Multimed. Tools Appl. (2021) 1–25.

[10] S. Shi, D. He, L. Li, N. Kumar, M.K. Khan, K.K. Choo, Applications of blockchain in ensuring the security and privacy of electronic health record systems: a survey, Comput. Secur. (2020) 101966.

[11] J. Shukla, M. Shandilya, A recent survey on information-hiding techniques, in: Data, Engineering and Applications, Springer, Singapore, 2019, pp. 57–70.

[12] A. Cheddad, J. Condell, K. Curran, P. Mc Kevitt, Digital image steganography: survey and analysis of current methods, Signal Process. 90 (3) (2010) 727–752.

[13] H. Sajedi, Applications of data hiding techniques in medical and healthcare systems: a survey, Network Model. Analysis Health Inform. Bioinform. 7 (1) (2018) 1–28.

[14] T. Yuvaraja, R.S. Sabeenian, Performance analysis of medical image security using steganography based on fuzzy logic, Clust. Comput. 22 (2) (2019) 3285–3291.

[15] G. Gao, X. Wan, S. Yao, Z. Cui, C. Zhou, X. Sun, Reversible data hiding with contrast enhancement and tamper localization for medical images, Inform. Sci. 385 (2017) 250–265.

[16] R. Abbasi, B. Luo, G. Rehman, H. Hassan, M.S. Iqbal, L. Xu, A new multilevel reversible bit-planes data hiding technique based on histogram shifting of efficient compressed domain, Vietnam J. Comput. Sci. 5 (2) (2018) 185–196.

[17] T.C. Lu, C.Y. Tseng, S.W. Huang, Pixel-value-ordering based reversible information hiding scheme with self-adaptive threshold strategy, Symmetry 10 (12) (2018) 764.

[18] M. Mahasree, N. Puviarasan, P. Aruna, An improved reversible data hiding using pixel value ordering and context pixel-based block selection, in: Proceedings of First International Conference on Computing, Communications, and Cyber-Security (IC4S 2019), 2020, pp. 873–887.

[19] M. Mahasree, N. Puviarasan, P. Aruna, High capacity reversible data hiding scheme with interpolation and threshold-based bit allocation technique, J. Mech. Continua Math. Sci. 15 (7) (2020) 704–717.

[20] M. Mahasree, N. Puviarasan, P. Aruna, Improved reversible data hiding in medical images using interpolation and threshold based embedding strategy, Int. J. Emerg. Trends Eng. Res. 8 (7) (2020) 3495–3501.

[21] S.Y. Shen, L.H. Huang, S.S. Yu, A novel adaptive data hiding based on improved EMD and interpolation, Multimed. Tools Appl. 77 (10) (2018) 12563–12579.
[22] X. Yue, H. Wang, D. Jin, M. Li, W. Jiang, Healthcare data gateways: found health-care intelligence on blockchain with novel privacy risk control, J. Med. Syst. 40 (10) (2016) 218.
[23] J. Zhang, N. Xue, X. Huang, A secure system for pervasive social network-based healthcare, IEEE Access 4 (2016) 9239–9250.
[24] J. Hathaliya, S. Tanwar, An exhaustive survey on security and privacy issues in healthcare 4.0, Comput. Commun. 153 (2020), https://doi.org/10.1016/j.comcom.2020.02.018.
[25] R. Gupta, A. Shukla, P. Mehta, P. Bhattacharya, S. Tanwar, S. Tyagi, N. Kumar, VAHAK: a blockchain-based outdoor delivery scheme using UAV for healthcare 4.0 services, in: IEEE International Conference on Computer Communications (IEEE INFOCOM 2020), Beijing, China, 27-30th April, 2020, pp. 1–8.
[26] R. Gupta, S. Tanwar, S. Tyagi, N. Kumar, Tactile-internet-based Telesurgery system for healthcare 4.0: an architecture, research challenges, and future directions, IEEE Network 33 (6) (2019) 22–29, https://doi.org/10.1109/MNET.001.1900063.
[27] R. Gupta, U. Thakker, S. Tanwar, M.S. Obaidat, K.F. Hsiao, BITS: a blockchain-driven intelligent scheme for telesurgery system, in: International Conference on Computer, Information and Telecommunication Systems (IEEE CITS-2020), Beijing, China, October 05-07, 2020, pp. 1–5.
[28] K. Jung, K. Yoo, Data hiding method using image interpolation, Comput. Stand. Interfaces 31 (2) (2009) 465–470. Elsevier.
[29] C. Lee, Y. Huang, An efficient image interpolation increasing payload in reversible data hiding, Expert Syst. Appl. 39 (8) (2012) 6712–6719. Elsevier.
[30] M. Tang, J. Hu, W. Song, A high capacity image steganography using multi-layer embedding, Optik 125 (15) (2014) 3972–3976. Elsevier.
[31] J. Hu, T. Li, Reversible steganography using extended image interpolation technique, Comput. Electr. Eng. 46 (2015) 447–455. Elsevier.
[32] T. Lu, An interpolation-based lossless hiding scheme based on message recoding mechanism, Optik 130 (2017) 1377–1396. Elsevier.
[33] A.A. Mohammad, A. Al-Haj, M. Farfoura, An improved capacity data hiding technique based on image interpolation, Multimed. Tools Appl. 78 (6) (2019) 7181–7205. Springer.
[34] L. Luo, Z. Chen, M. Chen, X. Zeng, Z. Xiong, Reversible image watermarking using interpolation technique, IEEE Trans. Inform. Forensics Sec. 5 (1) (2010) 187–193.
[35] X. Wang, C. Chang, T. Nguyen, M. Li, Reversible data hiding for high quality images exploiting interpolation and direction order mechanism, Digital Signal Process. 23 (2013) 569–577. Elsevier.
[36] J. Biswapati, G. Debasis, M.S. Kumar, Weighted matrix based reversible data hiding scheme using image interpolation, in: International Conference on Computational Intelligence in Data Mining (CIDM), vol. 2, 2015, pp. 239–248.
[37] P.V.S. Govind, M. Wilsey, A new reversible data hiding scheme with improved capacity based on directional interpolation and difference expansion, in: International Conference on Information and Communication Technologies (ICICT 2014), 2015, pp. 491–498.
[38] A. Rudder, W. Goodridge, S. Mohammed, Using Bias Optimization for Reversible Data Hiding Using Image Interpolation, arXiv preprint arXiv:1305.4102, 2013.
[39] K.H. Jung, K.Y. Yoo, Steganographic method based on interpolation and LSB substitution of digital images, Multimed. Tools Appl. 74 (6) (2015) 2143–2155.

[40] A. Benhfid, Y. Taouil, Reversible steganographic method based on interpolation by bivariate linear box-spline on the three directional mesh, J. King Saud Univ.-Comput. Inform. Sci. (2018) 1–10.

[41] M.A. Wahed, H. Nyeem, Reversible data hiding with interpolation and adaptive embedding, Multimed. Tools Appl. 78 (8) (2019) 10795–10819.

[42] C.F. Lee, C.Y. Weng, C.Y. Kao, Reversible data hiding using Lagrange interpolation for prediction-error expansion embedding, Soft. Comput. 23 (19) (2019) 9719–9731.

[43] X. Wang, X. Han, J. Xi, S. Wang, Reversible data hiding in encrypted image with separable data extraction from image decryption, Multimed. Tools Appl. 76 (5) (2017) 6127–6142.

[44] F. Zhang, W. Lu, H. Liu, Y. Yeung, Y. Xue, Reversible data hiding in binary images based on image magnification, Multimed. Tools Appl. 78 (15) (2019) 21891–21915.

[45] T.C. Lu, M.C. Lin, C.C. Huang, K.M. Deng, Reversible data hiding based on image interpolation with a secret message reduction strategy, Int. J. Comput. Softw. Eng. 1 (2016) 102–112.

[46] W. Hong, T.S. Chen, Reversible data embedding for high quality images using interpolation and reference pixel distribution mechanism, J. Vis. Commun. Image Represent. 22 (2) (2011) 131–140.

[47] T.C. Lu, L.P. Chi, C.H. Wu, H.P. Chang, Reversible data hiding in dual stego-images using frequency-based encoding strategy, Multimed. Tools Appl. 76 (22) (2017) 23903–23929.

[48] T.C. Lu, Interpolation-based hiding scheme using the modulus function and re-encoding strategy, Signal Process. 142 (2018) 244–259.

5G-enabled deep learning-based framework for healthcare mining: State of the art and challenges

18

Rahil Parmar, Dhruval Patel, Naitik Panchal, Uttam Chauhan, and Jitendra Bhatia
Computer Engineering Department, Vishwakarma Government Engineering College, Gujarat Technological University, Ahmedabad, India

1 Introduction

Technology has become an inextricable part of human life as a part of the modern workforce. Informatics advances the field of public health by combining techniques, skills, and ideas from both computer science and information science [1]. Healthcare informatics mainly focuses on the collection, storage, management, retrieval, and use of information obtained from data among medical professionals, organizations, and service providers. Medical data created in the form of electronic health record (EHR), biomedical data, and public health data have enhanced data access, traceability, and liquidity [2].

There has been a great evolution in the healthcare industry, which started with Healthcare 1.0 and is now at a much more evolved stage with Healthcare 4.0. In Healthcare 1.0, the doctor used to store and retrieve patient data manually [3, 4]. In Healthcare 2.0, data maintained manually by doctors were replaced with electronic records. Healthcare 3.0 introduced the real-time tracking of a patient's history through wearable devices. The electronic data, also known as EHR, were stored in a database that could be accessed through the Internet. Healthcare 4.0 implemented a centralized EHR system to keep track of a patient's health records and provide them with instantaneous services in real time [5].

A significant share of time of modern healthcare workers, professionals, and patients is spent in collecting, analyzing, and using gathered information for improvement, research, and quality measurement [1]. Biomedical and healthcare informatics (BHMI) is a discipline dedicated to the effective storage, acquisition, and use of information in healthcare [1].

There are various subbranches of BHMI including (Fig. 1):

- *Bioinformatics*: The cellular and molecular biology applications of informatics.
- *Imaging informatics*: Informatics involving images, which include the use of systems that store and retrieve images across all types of biomedicine and health applications.
- *Clinical informatics*: Applications of informatics in healthcare settings.
- *Public health informatics*: The use of informatics in public health applications such as monitoring, surveillance, and health promotion.

Blockchain Applications for Healthcare Informatics. https://doi.org/10.1016/B978-0-323-90615-9.00016-5
Copyright © 2022 Elsevier Inc. All rights reserved.

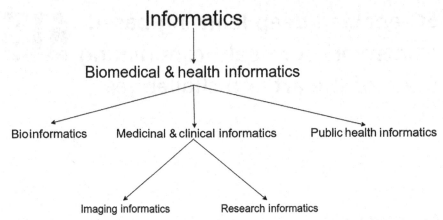

Fig. 1 Types of healthcare informatics.

- *Clinical research informatics*: The implementation of informatics to make clinical study easier.

There have been advances in artificial intelligence (AI) techniques applied to various domains in the previous decade. With the high volume and veracity of data produced, healthcare is one of the central focuses of researchers and industry experts.

Furthermore, wireless devices such as hand-held PCs, PDAs, messaging devices, electronic organizers, and smart phones have become more commonplace and widespread in recent years [6]. The mobile Internet and wireless technologies have expanded their services to a vast landscape. The addition of mobile technology to healthcare has improved healthcare service providers' responsiveness and healthcare customer satisfaction.

By 2024, millions of dollars are projected to be spent on 5G mobile edge computing (MEC), with industry deployments topping $73 million [7]. The sophistication of data grows each year. The growth in on-demand and customizable services has led to a rise in network complexity systems. For web access, linked automobiles, video downloads, online gaming, voice-over IP, and always-on Internet of things (IoT) device communications, Internet service providers must properly manage traffic. On-demand technologies impose these additional restrictions, which requires a fundamental overhaul of fixed and mobile access networks. To meet the growing volumes of traffic demand and variety, fifth-generation (5G) telecommunications networks are being constructed. To best serve core functions and complex network services, designers have had to reconsider the backbone and access of network architectures due to the rigorous technical specifications for 5G networks. Network providers are using cloud computing methods to deal with the dynamic traffic and demands of modern users. Software-defined networks and network feature virtualization can be used in 5G networks to save operating costs and allow on-demand services.

In the current pandemic, research related to health and healthcare has become a top priority. Researchers are continuously trying to find new ways to improve healthcare. Blockchain and deep learning are among the top developing research areas in healthcare. It has become possible to automate healthcare owing to these technologies [8, 9].

This chapter provides a background on topics such as blockchain and deep learning, and how they are used to improve healthcare with the advent of 5G networks. This chapter introduces some of the state-of-the-art technological advancements in healthcare. It also gives an overview of how 5G technologies can be used to improve healthcare services and handle big data generated from various technological devices.

The entire chapter is organized as follows: Section 2 covers inconsistency in the data produced from various healthcare technological devices. Section 3 includes technological advancements in healthcare technologies. Section 4 discusses the roles of 5G technologies in facilitating healthcare technologies. Section 5 provides the background high-performance computing (HPC) for healthcare mining enabled through 5G technologies. Section 6 describes types of big data and how they are managed using different technologies. Sections 7–9 explain the basics of deep learning and blockchain in healthcare, and disease prediction models in deep learning. Section 10 discusses issues and challenges, while Section 11 shows the future direction for further research. Section 12 provides a case study of maintaining security and privacy in healthcare informatics with deep learning and blockchain.

2 Lack of consistency in healthcare data

Due to the development in technologies and resources available in information and communication technologies (ICT), the amount of data generated from different sources has increased drastically in recent times. These data are generated from various sources such as sensors, medical instruments, reports, therapies, treatment, surveys, bills, etc. Such data are also known as EHRs. The healthcare industry is complicated because it includes a wide range of stakeholders, including surgeons, physicians, radiologists, nurses, pharmacists, and laboratory technicians, many of whom work together to treat patients. As the information generated in this domain covers a variety of data such as patient administration, organizational information, clinical data, and laboratory/pathology data, it is enormously complex.

Usually, the patients receive services from numerous doctors, pharmacies, laboratories, physicians, and school clinics based on the availability and required services. This has resulted in the fragmentation of medical data across organizations in proprietary heterogeneous networks. As a result, essential patient information cannot be retrieved to acquire a comprehensive and accurate picture of the patient's medical history. In one outpatient clinic, for example, an analysis revealed that the patient's data were unavailable in 81% of cases, with an average of four missing objects per case [10]. In addition, the healthcare delivered to the patient from different caretakers and organizations also results in errors due to various factors (such as environment, medical equipment used, etc.). In such a scenario, it becomes essential to maintain data quality. The data should be such that they could be used to improve the lives of people (Fig. 2).

Legacy systems (most frequently electronic medical records [EMRs]) store healthcare data and have limited interoperability capabilities. Because there are various schemas, fonts, metadata, and standard underlying data, integrating data are difficult [11]. Data privacy, confidentiality, control of information access, ownership,

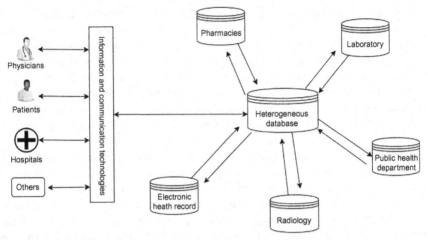

Fig. 2 Data from different sources.

and governance of the patients' information also plays an important role in data availability. They impede meaningful information exchange between patients and healthcare providers. The researchers have discovered that human contact with user interfaces has a significant impact on the pace, completeness, and quality of incident reporting in the system [12]. This reporting system that involves human interaction tends to generate better quality reports. Security and privacy issues are also prevalent, which results in challenges in the exchange of information. Unauthorized use of patients' information, unethical disclosure of patients' information, and unauthorized tampering of information are some of the reasons that discourage healthcare providers from sharing information using healthcare systems [11].

3 Technological advancements in healthcare: Current state of the art

Healthcare technology is a collection of information and techniques aimed at enhancing, maintaining, and sustaining humanity's health. Breakthroughs in the engineering development of healthcare technologies have increased people's quality of life and have significant technological, science, and cultural implications. IoT, mobile Internet, cloud computing, microelectronics, AI, big data, and 5G have enabled advancements in disease prediction and control, diagnosis and treatment, hospital administration, medical decision making, and medical science [13]. Healthcare data are becoming readily available to doctors, insurance companies, pharmaceutical industries, and patients due to the rapid growth of computer software and hardware technology. These facilitate the development of computational techniques that leads to data-driven insights for improving the quality of healthcare services delivered.

Some of the technological advancement in today's era include:

- *Virtual assistant*: Virtual assistants are the algorithms used for communication with users. They use various techniques such as speech recognition, machine learning, natural language processing (NLP), and neural networks. These techniques are trained on the patterns, insights, and information obtained from big data, and output is produced accordingly. Virtual assistant in healthcare makes it more convenient to deliver medical services. Virtual assistants in healthcare bridge the communication gaps among doctors, patients, and medical institutions. Google Assistant, Microsoft Cortana, and Apple Siri are some of the well-known general virtual assistants that help the user in accomplishing various tasks from creating reminders to automating the home. They can help the patient in recognizing symptoms and suggest a corresponding specialist consult. Virtual assistants can pass the relevant information to doctors, which ultimately helps doctors in managing patients and carrying out medical procedures and surgeries more conveniently. It helps a medical organization to collect insurance details, finance and procurement details, demographic details, patient history, data mining, and analysis of the available records.
- *Sensors, IoT, and wearable devices*: IoT has found its way with successful implementation in the healthcare service domain. Recently, the continuous collection of data is possible because of the advancements in sensing technologies. The patient's specific data can be accessed right away or saved in the archive for further retrieval and review [14]. The sensors are used in remote monitoring, management, and prevention of chronic disease. IoT-enabled devices have opened up the possibilities of remote monitoring of the patient, allowing greater flexibilities in providing treatment and medical services. When used with sensors, IoT provides the advantage of the broad spectrum of medical parameters in real time. It plays an important role in delivering quality of services with cost-effectiveness. The medical IoT system is a sophisticated set-up that consists of a wide range of mechanisms and systems, including medical equipment, smart sensors, network gateways, cloud computing, big data, and much more that contribute in controlling the healthcare environment [14]. Wearable devices such as smart watches, wearable electrocardiogram (ECG) monitors, blood pressure monitors, biosensors, etc., help in monitoring health issues in real time.
- *AI and big data*: AI is a technology that allows machines to imitate the cognitive functions of humans. It is achieved by using two tools: machine learning and deep learning. These tools use computer algorithms to predict certain outputs or make decisions. With the specific question pertinent to medical services, relevant information or patterns can be determined from the massive health-related data. With the current advancements in technology, the ability of AI to perform as humans has improved drastically. Robot-assisted surgery, virtual nursing assistance, and management in health information system workflow are some of the latest applications of AI in healthcare [14]. The ability to learn and self-correct based on responses aids in improving the performance accuracy of techniques in AI. The term "big data" in healthcare refers to the massive amount of data generated from various sources such as sensors, computers, or healthcare wearable devices. With the advent of big data, a considerable amount of useful information can be extracted for real-time reasoning in healthcare.

4 Role of 5G in healthcare

The term "5G" stands for the fifth generation of wireless transmission technology. It is expected to have a notable influence in various outlooks of contemporary society, which incorporates healthcare. The key features of 5G include data transfer rate, low latency, better coverage, network energy usage, low power consumption, high bandwidth, connectivity, and capacity. The theoretical expected speed of 5G is 10–30 Gbps while 4G is 300 Mbps. 5G has much lower latency compared to 4G, reaching as low as 1 ms. It also operates on microwave frequencies that have broad bandwidth. As a result, it will support a huge number of simultaneous users, approximately 100 times that of 4G.

5G will bind a greater number of IoT devices and share vast amounts of data over long distances. This IoT sensor(s) can monitor ECG signs, blood pressure, glucose levels, and body temperature, among other things. Wearable technologies equipped with different types of sensors can aid in the tracking of physical activities as well as patients suffering from chronic illnesses such as spinal cord trauma, stroke, cancer, and chronic respiratory diseases.

The treatment can be provided on the go to patients in the ambulance under the guidance of doctors. Doctors could get real-time vitals from patients using 5G-driven sensors in the ambulance and a mobile health tracking device [15]. This could help in saving lives in critical cases, where time is of prime importance. Doctors can attend to several patients without actually meeting them through video conferencing. Doctors can extract real-time vitals from the remote monitoring system and prescribe accordingly. In a time like this, when COVID-19 is prevalent, this becomes extremely useful. The doctors can avoid overcrowding and can prioritize patients who need immediate medical attention.

The medical equipment can be monitored in real time using sensors that are installed in the equipment. This can help in predicting hardware failures, which in turn minimizes the repair or replacement cost and time. Surgeons nowadays use augmented reality (AR) glasses to assist them during various surgeries and procedures about the vital information of patients and their conditions. Recently, virtual reality (VR) has gained lots of popularity for training the healthcare profession in simulating surgeries. With the low latency and high bandwidth of the 5G network, it can be achieved effortlessly. AI-powered robots with a minimal latency of 1 ms can be used to perform surgery by surgeons (Fig. 3).

An assistive-connected robotics could be used in hospitals to assist patients in need of critical care. The precision of such medical robot-assisted surgery can be increased. This can assist surgeons in improving postoperative outcomes [15]. These technologies will not only help in mutual training but also enhance the medical expertise. With excellent network efficiency and low-energy consumption in 5G, the energy used for data computation in IoT devices and robots can be reduced. It also aids researchers in accessing and analyzing data in real time by allowing them to send vast files across the globe in a limited period.

5   HPC 5G-enabled framework for healthcare mining

HPC stands for high-performance computing, which refers to the use of many interconnected computing devices to perform computations in parallel. The problem with big data is that there is a lot of data out there, but there is a lack of mechanisms or infrastructures in place to process, store, and transfer it between devices efficiently.

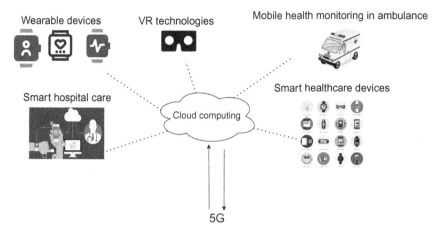

Fig. 3 Role of 5G in healthcare.

HPC attempts to solve the problem by computing with distributed machine resources. HPC refers to the ability to process data and computation at a high rate; it can solve complex problems and process massive datasets that local computing systems cannot manage. The scale of these datasets can range from terabytes to zettabytes. HPC attempts to process and calculate this data in real time, which ensures that results can be obtained in minutes or hours while some local computing systems would take days or weeks for the result. HPC is being used in many areas, including AI, genomics or bioinformatics, weather and environment, IoT, geographical data, big data analytics (BDA), and many more.

There are many HPC frameworks available, including open source, such as OpenHPC and Apache Hadoop, which are common HPC frameworks that support big data processing.

HPC working: HPC systems have many distributed computing systems, which are called clusters. The HPC cluster is composed of many compute servers that are connected through a network. Each of these computers is referred to as a node. These nodes operate in parallel to improve the performance and speed of processing.

Healthcare mining: There are several ways in which data mining can benefit the healthcare industry. In the healthcare industry, it is primarily used in medical research, genetics, hospital management, and disease prediction as well as to determine how successful a drug is against specific diseases. To maximize the efficiency of the HPC system, all clusters in the system must be able to keep up with each other. For example, the data are fed into an HPC system but if some of the nodes in the clusters are underperforming, then the overall performance of the system decreases. Likewise, if the data transmission speed between two nodes is slow, the HPC system cannot operate at full capacity.

Use of 5G: Higher data rates would be possible with 5G technology, in addition to linking millions of devices with quite specific requirements that will also be possible [16]. The above-mentioned HPC problems can be solved by using a network that provides higher bandwidth and lower latency for data transfer, allowing real-time data to be computed. These requirements can be fulfilled with 5G technology. In comparison to previous generations of cellular networks such as 4G technology, a vast number of nodes can be connected to the base stations at low power and latency by using the 5G network technology [17].

HPC systems can also be used in combination with cloud computing. Cloud computing can take advantage of the potential of large-scale distributed systems to increase the system's scalability. As HPC and cloud computing are combined, high-performance cloud computing (HPC2) is possible. HPC2 enables the provision of a cloud-based environment to the HPC cluster. This allows for faster access to computing resources, while simultaneously lowering costs and energy usage. There are several HPC frameworks available today, but there is still a lack of implemented 5G-enabled HPC infrastructures. If 5G technology can be used in addition to the previously mentioned HPC frameworks, it can increase the overall efficiency of the HPC system and make computing tasks even faster.

6 Handling healthcare big data

With the recent advancements in the Internet, IoT, and cloud computing, the amount of data collected in any organization has increased exponentially. As the size of data is rapidly growing, it is an essential step to process this data and produce patterns or information from it. BDA is a concept that refers to a collection of tools and techniques for transforming a large amount of data into useful information. BDA allows any enterprise to store, process, and generate useful information from a large amount of data at a high rate [18, 19].

The generated data can be of different types depending on the structure.

1. *Structured data*: The structured data follow a predefined format or structure and data types. For instance, these structured data may include information about various types of diseases, their symptoms, and the method for diagnosis in a hierarchical order.
2. *Semistructured data*: The semistructured data do not follow a proper format but the data may still be organized. It may include the output of sensors that monitors the patient's condition.
3. *Unstructured data*: This type of data does not follow any proper format and may include handwritten prescriptions or discharge summaries of patients.

There have been many advancements in molecular biology over the last decade, including genomics, proteomics, and other innovations. As a result, a massive amount of data has been collected. Also, the previous data in paper form are being converted into digital systems.

Healthcare data have its own set of characteristics, as it may include information from biomarkers, administrative health data, biometrics, and clinical imaging. Also, these data come from many different types of sources, including hospital registries, EHR, the Internet, and sometimes even the patient reports this data [20]. Medical data may include EHR, EMRs, public health records (PHR), medical practice management software (MPM), and several other healthcare data components [21]. In a healthcare system, an EMR is a digital form of a patient's medical history for a particular healthcare facility. This type of knowledge is only useful inside the hospital and is mostly used by pharmacists and healthcare professionals [9].

EHR is a more comprehensive version of EMR. An EHR contains a patient's entire medical history and is connected to the patient ID. Because EHR is valid in different organizations, it can be shared with other facilities [22]. The key concern now is figuring out how to handle this big data. The Hadoop ecosystem is a collection of applications and tools that can be used to manage massive amounts of data (Fig. 4).

Hadoop is an open-source big data framework used to process and analyze a massive amount of unstructured data. In Hadoop, the MapReduce algorithm is employed, with the map function producing intermediate key/value pairs of input records and the reduce function combining all values with the same key. The Hadoop distributed file system (HDFS) can provide scalable, reliable, replica-based storage of data [21]. 5G wireless networks can efficiently link data sources and data centers of big data. The design and operation of the 5G wireless network will be dependent on different big data features, and network capacity can be expanded to accommodate the large data volume. There are many methods for increasing 5G network capacity, including spectrum expansion, creating a dense network, and improving spectrum efficiency [24]. The Hadoop ecosystem includes a NoSQL database used to collect and process a huge amount of real-time data from various sources, including patient care units, hospital budgets, and payrolls [25].

Chen et al. proposed a 5G smart diabetes system used for monitoring, providing personalized diagnosis for diabetes, and effectively suggesting treatment. It monitors glucose levels using wearable 2.0 devices and analyzes the data using machine learning and big data. 5G technology is used to share data between social and personal data spaces [26]. Sivaparthipan et al. presented a system for the statistical assessment of diabetics analysis using big data. They used a statistical assessment method in this scheme, and the massive amounts of data were generated from medical devices and EHR. The Hadoop MapReduce method is used for statistical assessment [27]. Compared to other existing methods, their proposed system has increased performance, better precision, and higher accuracy for a diabetic cure. Sujitha and Seenivasagam introduced a classification system for lung cancer stages using machine learning and big data. They used the Apache Spark module for big data handling and Pyspark for multiclass classification in their proposed system. While both binary and multiclass classifiers satisfy accuracy and generate appropriate results, their proposed method allows the early detection of lung cancer with greater accuracy and improves the efficiency of other classifiers [28].

7 Deep learning and blockchain in healthcare

Machine learning is a field in which a variety of algorithms are used to process data and extract necessary information. Another technology that is quite useful in the healthcare field is blockchain. Blockchain is largely used for data security, privacy, and data protection. Moreover, it can help in maintaining data integrity. In the medical

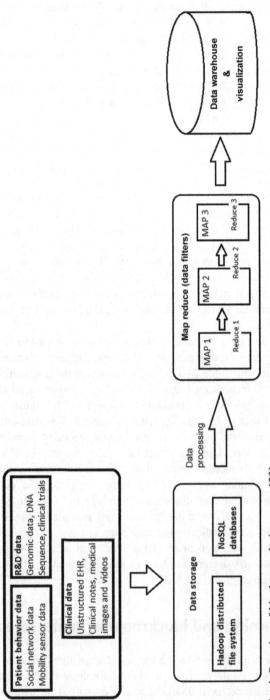

Fig. 4 Overview of big data analysis process.[23]

industry, these data primarily consist of EHRs. The use of blockchain in EHR improves access to a patient's medical history. It also allows hospitals to share and alter EHR data with one another through interoperability [29]. When data are appended to EHR on the blockchain, other machines vote on its eligibility and if these data are authenticated, then they will be appended. It means that any unacknowledged modifications to information are extremely difficult to apply, and as blockchain networks grow in size, it will take an exponential amount of processing power to alter the data. Aside from EHRs, blockchain can also be utilized to reduce fake medicines by tracking transactions and the locations of drugs as they are transported from one storage site to another [30].

There are potential applications for blockchain and deep learning in the current COVID-19 issue. The blockchain network can be useful in tracking the transmission of the Coronavirus by implementing it in people's mobile devices. Blockchain is useful in transactions such as medical billing, donations, insurance claims, and so on. Deep learning methods can be applied to predict the spread of viruses [31]. Both these technologies can be integrated, as proposed in the BinDaaS framework [32]. In this framework, the authors proposed a system that uses blockchain for the privacy and security of EHR data, and deep learning models for disease prediction based on the patient's EHR.

There are several deep learning techniques such as convolutional neural networks (CNN), recurrent neural networks (RNN), deep belief networks (DBN), backpropagation, and many more.

CNN: CNNs are used to process grid-structured data. A two-dimensional (2D) picture is a simple example of grid-structured data. In certain grid areas, CNNs have spatial dependencies [33].

RNN: RNNs are used for predicting sequences. Sequential data, such as sentences, time-series data, and genetics data such as DNA, can be processed with RNNs. This type of data has variable-length sequences. There are two types of RNNs, long-short term memory (LSTM) and gated RNNs [34].

Backpropagation: In multilayer networks, the backpropagation technique allows the deep learning model to learn about the loss function. It has two phases: a forward phase in which the inputs are given to the neural network and computations are performed, and a backward phase in which if any errors are found, the gradient of that error or loss function is measured and used to update the weight of the node. This procedure is carried out in a backward direction [33].

Many advancements have been made in the ability of computers to understand and process data using methods of deep learning. These methods are used on a variety of data forms, including languages, images, and audio. There are large quantities of data generated in healthcare, and deep learning can be very helpful in analyzing the data, which will support healthcare and medicine [35].

EHRs may hold a variety of details about a patient, including doctor's notes, test results, medical images, and genomics data. This EHR can be input into a deep learning model, which can then analyze and produce desired results such as disease prediction, drug prediction, diagnosis method recommendations, and several other things. For instance, RNN is useful for modeling sequential data such as languages, and EHRs are a decent input dataset for it. An RNN-based model was developed by Pham et al. [36]. It is used to predict patient medical outcomes by analyzing their previous health situations [37].

Another benefit of deep learning is that it helps in the detection of disease. The CNN model is used to process image data; it can take an input image and produce a labeled image as an output. As a result, images can be used to diagnose a disease. CNN, for example, can be used to enhance the detection of Glaucoma, which is an incurable eye disease [38]. Aside from that, CNNs have been used to interpret medical data such as magnetic resonance imaging (MRI), mammographies, X-rays, ultrasound, and radiographic imaging for classification, segmentation, and anomaly detection from these data [39].

8 Deep learning models for disease prediction

Deep learning is a subpart of machine learning techniques that mimics the structure and functions of a human brain. Similar to our brain, deep learning methods make use of neural network architectures. There are three layers in these networks: an input layer, a hidden layer, and an output layer. The input layer, as the first layer, is in charge of getting the initial data/values to the subsequent layers for processing. One or more hidden layers may be present in a neural network, and these are where the actual data processing computation takes place. These layers sit between the input and output layers and aid in the extraction of important data characteristics. The final layer, known as the output layer, is in charge of delivering the processed data results.

Deep learning applications in industries include image recognition, recommendation systems, NLP, self-driving vehicles, fraud detection, and many others. Another major application of deep learning is in the healthcare industry for medical image analysis. In the healthcare industry, deep learning collects a vast amount of data, which includes patient records, medical reports, and insurance records, and applies its neural networks to provide the best results. Doctors and researchers are using deep learning to uncover hidden patterns in data. Furthermore, it reliably analyzes any disease and assists doctors in properly treating it, resulting in better medical decisions. CNNs, for example, are often used to examine medical images such as X-rays, MRI, computed tomography (CT), and positron emission tomography (PET) [40].

Bifurcation of deep learning uses in healthcare:

- *Identifying diseases and diagnosis*: Predictive analysis using effective multiple machine learning algorithms aids in more accurate disease prediction and treatment of patients [41]. The concealed knowledge in healthcare data can be used to make effective decisions about a patient's health in the future.
- *Drug discovery and manufacturing*: Deep learning is used in the early stages of drug development to analyze and interpret biomedical data from clinical trials to predict the efficacy and side effects of a drug. As a result, better medical trials can be designed to find the most powerful treatments with the fewest side effects.
- *Outbreak prediction*: Deep learning is now being used to monitor and forecast epidemics all over the world. Scientists now have access to a vast amount of data gathered from a variety of

sources. Neural networks aid in the aggregation of this data and the prediction of a wide range of pandemics, from malaria outbreaks to extreme chronic infectious diseases.

Deep learning produces satisfactory results when it is used to perform tasks that are difficult for a conventional analysis method. Using genomic data to predict disease status for complex human diseases is a significant, but difficult, phase in personalized medicine. Many state-of-the-art machine learning algorithms underperform due to the so-called curse of dimensionality problem, which is one of many challenges [42]. On the other hand, deep learning's ability to predict disease status using genomic datasets is currently gaining traction.

Many studies have used ANN models to determine the difference between glaucoma and nonglaucoma [43, 44]. Sarki et al. [45] used the transfer learning concept to distinguish between mild diabetic eye disease (DED) and multiclass DED in their study. Two pretrained CNN models, VGG16 and InceptionV3, were compared for detecting DEDs in that study. Hon and Khan [46] used a transfer learning-based approach to diagnosing Alzheimer's disease from structural MRI images. They used two common CNN architectures in this study: InceptionV4 and VGG16. Sarraf et al. [47] used the LeNet and GoogleNet deep learning models to distinguish Alzheimer's disease-affected brains from healthy older adult brains. This was also the first time the functional MRI data were used in deep learning applications to predict Alzheimer's disease. These studies show that, even with limited training datasets, we can achieve an excellent disease prediction efficiency by integrating transfer learning and pretrained deep learning models. Mohanty et al. [48] used deep learning to identify plant disease by using a public dataset of healthy and diseased plant leaves. The trained model identified 14 crop species with 26 diseases. In their 60 experimental configurations, AlexNet and GoogleNet were used as pretrained models. Khamparia et al. [49] used a deep-stacked autoencoder to present a novel deep learning system for chronic kidney disease classification. In this classification problem, their model was able to achieve 100% accuracy. For lung disease classification, Tariq et al. [50] built a deep learning network. Using advanced data preprocessing techniques such as augmentation and normalization, they were able to achieve state-of-the-art classification accuracy. Table 1 highlights the above-referenced works, where different pretrained models were employed for disease classification.

Most of the above-referenced studies have employed a common workflow for implementing a disease prediction task by training a deep learning model on their respective datasets. First of all, the image dataset consisting of images of healthy and unhealthy body parts/organs is the input source for the disease prediction pipeline. Next comes the preprocessing step, where various techniques such as dimensionality reduction, data augmentation, etc., are applied to the input dataset. The output of this step serves as an input to deep learning-based neural network architecture. This step deals with the feature extraction process, which helps in training a good classification/prediction model for bifurcating different diseases based on features extracted. The trained deep learning model gives the classification/prediction results as output (i.e., whether an input image belongs to a healthy or an unhealthy class). Fig. 5 illustrates the general implementation of an image classification task using a deep learning model.

Table 1 Pretrained models used for disease prediction.

Author	Diseases classified	Pretrained models used
Chen et al. [43]	Glaucoma and nonglaucoma	–
Sarki et al. [45]	DED and multiclass DED	VGG16 and InceptionV3
Hon and Khan [46]	Alzheimer's	InceptionV4 and VGG16
Sarraf et al. [47]	Alzheimer's	LeNet and GoogleNet
Mohanty et al. [48]	26 Types of crop diseases	AlexNet and GoogleNet
Khamparia et al. [49]	Kidney	–
Tariq et al. [50]	Lung	–

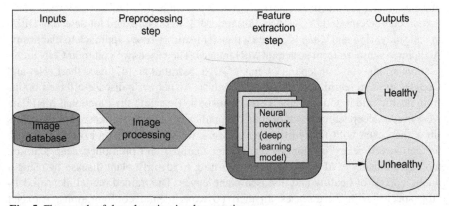

Fig. 5 Flowgraph of deep learning implementation.

9 Tools and libraries for deep learning applications

- *Caffe*: It is a deep learning framework developed at the University of California at Berkeley that provides C++ and Python interfaces. It is modular, expressive, fast, and multi-GPU compatible.
- *Keras*: Released in 2015, Keras is a library written in Python that utilizes as a backend either Theano or TensorFlow [51]. Keras contains numerous implementations of commonly used neural network building blocks.
- *MXNet*: Apache MXNet is another open-source deep learning framework to build, train, and deploy deep neural networks. It provides eight language bindings (Python, Scala, Julia, Clojure, Java, C++, R, and Perl), and supports distributed computing, including multi-GPU.
- *TensorFlow*: TensorFlow is an end-to-end open-source platform for machine learning. It was developed by Google and is used for various deep learning applications. It helps developers to build, train, and deploy machine learning applications.
- *PyTorch*: It is a machine learning library developed by Facebook's AI research lab based on the Torch library. Similar to Caffe, it also provides both Python and C++ interfaces. Various deep learning software are built on top of PyTorch for applications such as computer vision and NLP.
- *Theano*: It is a Python library and a compiler for manipulating and evaluating mathematical expressions, involving multidimensional arrays. It takes advantage of NumPy's efficient codebase. It was developed by the MILA group at the University of Montreal.

10 Issues and challenges

To improve the accuracy of the classification-based deep learning model, a large amount of data is required for training. One of the issues is that these types of datasets for medical imaging are not easily available. Furthermore, creating a dataset with correct annotations is a complicated and time-consuming process [52]. There is still the issue of data quality. Even if the data are usable for training, it is better to use high-quality data to train the deep learning model. The datasets available may contain noisy data with some missing values, which can reduce the accuracy of the model [53]. When working with EHR in deep learning, some issues arise, such as deciding which parameters to include and how to preprocess EHR data. The criteria may depend on the nature of the desired output. Data should be correctly preprocessed and segmented for deep learning model training, validation, and testing, which helps in a thorough evaluation of the deep learning model [37].

11 Future research direction

The current healthcare sector includes a variety of initiatives that are of national significance due to their scope of impact on individuals or society. Some of these initiatives are:

- As we have seen previously, machine learning and AI developments have become advanced in different fields. Due to the variety of data availability, the healthcare industry has attracted deep learning and machine learning researchers and experts. Wide databases from clinical management systems and medical research centers are marked by this shift in emphasis in the healthcare industry. This opens up the possibility of using deep learning techniques on sparse healthcare datasets.
- Gaining knowledge from diverse, heterogeneous, and high-dimensional biomedical data continues to be an important research path in the transformation of the healthcare industry. In the modern world of medical sciences, new forms of data are evolving. Deep learning has the potential to successfully reflect unstructured and complex instances.
- In recent years, data from EHRs have become increasingly relevant. Physical examinations, clinical laboratory reports, and operational papers are among the vast quantities of unstructured text contained in these records, many of which are difficult to approach [54, 55].
- The healthcare industry is currently faced with the challenge of interoperability, which refers to the ability of healthcare systems from multiple agencies, organizations, health centers, and regions to interact with one another [56]. Bottom-to-top approaches to interoperability based on clinical experience will tend to be highly important in the near future [57], as they should arise from a consensus among healthcare stakeholders about their needs and the availability and suitability of existing technologies to provide society with a response to those needs [58].
- Deep learning has been proposed to perhaps obtain a more accurate analysis of ECG signals due to its impressive increases in robustness to noise and uncertainty in many pattern recognition applications [57]. The use of ECG as a biometric trait for identification or authentication has gained traction, in addition to health monitoring and medical diagnosis [59, 60]. In comparison to other biometric traits, the ECG has proven to be one of the most promising, and researchers have recently begun to use deep learning methodologies in this field, which is still a pioneering endeavor [61].

- The establishment and adoption of a common language for describing medical terminology is an essential task that is required for the successful implementation of big data in healthcare [11]. This is to ensure the consistency, reusability, and shareability of healthcare information.
- We must promote policies to protect user privacy and information stored in blockchain-based systems because privacy and information protection are important in healthcare [62]. Future research may concentrate on developing protocols for managing private cryptographic keys for network nodes in particular. This will ensure the secure use of private keys and prevent data breaches caused by key mismanagement. There is also a need to improve blockchain technology conceptual expertise for specific issues such as diagnostics, biometric verification, and ongoing monitoring of senior patients.

12   Maintaining security and privacy in healthcare informatics

When blockchain and deep learning come together, patients will benefit from the deep learning model's ability to quickly analyze massive amounts of data and blockchain's power to secure health data. There is also a possibility of dramatically improving security by utilizing deep learning to manage the chain [32]. Blockchain technology has the potential to tackle the problems of data sharing and data reliability in healthcare data management. It increases the privacy and interoperability of a patient's health data by ensuring that health data are legitimate and transactions are safe. There have been very few studies carried out in this area. Kumar et al. [63, 64] used a combination of deep learning and blockchain to detect COVID-19 and lung cancer, respectively, in patients [65]. Both these studies employed datasets of different sizes but contained CT scan images of patients. The former study trained a deep learning model using blockchain technology. Besides training the model, the issue of privacy is solved using a special type of learning known as "federated learning." This learning process enables hospitals to keep their data private and only share the key parameters of the training process. The latter study is a similar one wherein the weights of the trained deep learning model are distributed to a blockchain decentralized network to train the global model. The blockchain network helps to exchange and distribute health data between hospitals, while ensuring the security of the data shared. Despite these advances in data sharing and model training with the use of blockchain and deep learning, some key challenges need to be addressed such as (1) securing health data from malicious attacks and (2) handling data inconsistencies such as different data formats used by various organizations, which makes it difficult to train a deep learning model.

13   Conclusions

Healthcare has advanced a lot due to technological advancements in the medical field and information technology. A huge amount of data is generated every day from various medical and IoT devices. These data can be used to improve the veracity of the services provided. A lot more has been made possible due to advancements in mobile technologies such as 5G technology. It is now possible to transfer data and carry out a task, which was not possible before due to technological limitations. Also, the data generated in various forms such as EHR, EMR, PHR, and many more can be handled with ease due to the development of big data technologies. Recently, there has been development and improvement in deep learning and machine learning. Various models have been proposed for disease prediction. They have been proved effective in the early diagnosis and prevention of various fatal diseases.

References

[1] J.A. Magnuson, B.E. Dixon, Public Health Informatics and Information Systems, Springer, 2020.

[2] X. Ma, Z. Wang, S. Zhou, H. Wen, Y. Zhang, Intelligent healthcare systems assisted by data analytics and mobile computing, in: 2018 14th International Wireless Communications & Mobile Computing Conference (IWCMC), IEEE, 2018, pp. 1317–1322.

[3] J. Vora, S. Tanwar, S. Tyagi, N. Kumar, J.J. Rodrigues, Home-based exercise system for patients using IoT enabled smart speaker, in: 2017 IEEE 19th International Conference on e-Health Networking, Applications and Services (Healthcom), IEEE, 2017, pp. 1–6.

[4] K. Shah, M.S. Obaidat, P. Modi, J. Bhatia, S. Tanwar, B. Sadoun, Amalgamation of Fog Computing and Software defined networking in Healthcare 4.0: the challenges, and a way forward, in: ICETE, 2020, pp. 25–32.

[5] A. Modi, S. Jani, K. Chauhan, J. Bhatia, Process model for fog data analytics for IoT applications, in: Fog Data Analytics for IoT Applications, Springer, 2020, pp. 175–198.

[6] K. Siau, Z. Shen, Mobile healthcare informatics, Med. Inf. Internet Med. 31 (2) (2006) 89–99.

[7] M. McClellan, C. Cervelló-Pastor, S. Sallent, Deep learning at the mobile edge: opportunities for 5G networks, Appl. Sci. 10 (14) (2020) 4735.

[8] J. Hathaliya, P. Sharma, S. Tanwar, R. Gupta, Blockchain-based remote patient monitoring in Healthcare 4.0, in: 2019 IEEE 9th International Conference on Advanced Computing (IACC), IEEE, 2019, pp. 87–91.

[9] S. Tanwar, K. Parekh, R. Evans, Blockchain-based electronic healthcare record system for Healthcare 4.0 applications, J. Inf. Secur. Appl. 50 (2020) 102407.

[10] O. Iroju, A. Soriyan, I. Gambo, J. Olaleke, Interoperability in healthcare: benefits, challenges and resolutions, Int. J. Innov. Appl. Stud. 3 (1) (2013) 262–270.

[11] I. Olaronke, O. Oluwaseun, Big data in healthcare: prospects, challenges and resolutions, in: 2016 Future Technologies Conference (FTC), IEEE, 2016, pp. 1152–1157.

[12] Y. Gong, Data consistency in a voluntary medical incident reporting system, J. Med. Syst. 35 (4) (2011) 609–615.

[13] S. Tian, W. Yang, J.M. Le Grange, P. Wang, W. Huang, Z. Ye, Smart healthcare: making medical care more intelligent, Glob. Health J. 3 (3) (2019) 62–65.

[14] S. Sikdar, S. Guha, Advancements of healthcare technologies: paradigm towards smart healthcare systems, in: Recent Trends in Image and Signal Processing in Computer Vision, Springer, 2020, pp. 113–132.

[15] S. Dananjayan, G.M. Raj, 5G in healthcare: how fast will be the transformation? Irish J. Med. Sci. (1971-) (2020) 1–5.

[16] R.A. Addad, D.L.C. Dutra, M. Bagaa, T. Taleb, H. Flinck, Fast service migration in 5G trends and scenarios, IEEE Netw. 34 (2) (2020) 92–98.

[17] I. Satoh, 5G-enabled edge computing for MapReduce-based data pre-processing, in: 2020 Fifth International Conference on Fog and Mobile Edge Computing (FMEC), IEEE, 2020, pp. 210–217.

[18] P. Kaur, M. Sharma, M. Mittal, Big data and machine learning based secure healthcare framework, Procedia Comput. Sci. 132 (2018) 1049–1059.

[19] K. Shah, P. Modi, J. Bhatia, Data processing and analytics in FC for Healthcare 4.0, in: Fog Computing for Healthcare 4.0 Environments, Springer, 2021, pp. 131–154.

[20] S. Shilo, H. Rossman, E. Segal, Axes of a revolution: challenges and promises of big data in healthcare, Nat. Med. 26 (1) (2020) 29–38.

[21] S. Dash, S.K. Shakyawar, M. Sharma, S. Kaushik, Big data in healthcare: management, analysis and future prospects, J. Big Data 6 (1) (2019) 1–25.

[22] S. Shafqat, S. Kishwer, R.U. Rasool, J. Qadir, T. Amjad, H.F. Ahmad, Big data analytics enhanced healthcare systems: a review, J. Supercomput. 76 (3) (2020) 1754–1799.

[23] Y. Wang, L. Kung, T.A. Byrd, Big data analytics: understanding its capabilities and potential benefits for healthcare organizations, Technol. Forecast. Social Change 126 (2018) 3–13.

[24] N. Zhang, P. Yang, J. Ren, D. Chen, L. Yu, X. Shen, Synergy of big data and 5G wireless networks: opportunities, approaches, and challenges, IEEE Wireless Commun. 25 (1) (2018) 12–18.

[25] S. Kumar, M. Singh, Big data analytics for healthcare industry: impact, applications, and tools, Big Data Mining Anal. 2 (1) (2018) 48–57.

[26] M. Chen, J. Yang, J. Zhou, Y. Hao, J. Zhang, C.-H. Youn, 5G-smart diabetes: toward personalized diabetes diagnosis with healthcare big data clouds, IEEE Commun. Mag. 56 (4) (2018) 16–23.

[27] C. Sivaparthipan, N. Karthikeyan, S. Karthik, Designing statistical assessment healthcare information system for diabetics analysis using big data, Multimedia Tools Appl. 79 (13) (2020) 8431–8444.

[28] R. Sujitha, V. Seenivasagam, Classification of lung cancer stages with machine learning over big data healthcare framework, J. Ambient Intell. Humanized Comput. 12 (5) (2020) 1–11.

[29] F.A. Reegu, M.O. Al-Khateeb, W.A. Zogaan, M.R. Al-Mousa, S. Alam, I. Al-Shourbaji, Blockchain-based framework for interoperable electronic health record, Ann. Romanian Soc. Cell Biol. 25 (3) (2021) 6486–6495.

[30] I. Yaqoob, K. Salah, R. Jayaraman, Y. Al-Hammadi, Blockchain for healthcare data management: opportunities, challenges, and future recommendations, Neural Comput. Appl. January (2021) 1–16.

[31] D. Nguyen, M. Ding, P.N. Pathirana, A. Seneviratne, Blockchain and AI-based solutions to combat coronavirus (COVID-19)-like epidemics: a survey, 9, IEEE, 2020, pp. 95730–95753.

[32] P. Bhattacharya, S. Tanwar, U. Bodke, S. Tyagi, N. Kumar, Bindaas: blockchain-based deep-learning as-a-service in Healthcare 4.0 applications, IEEE Trans. Netw. Sci. Eng. 8 (2) (2019) 1242–1255.

[33] C.C. Aggarwal, Neural Networks and Deep Learning, Springer, vol. 10, 2018, p. 978.

[34] P. Vadapalli, Top 10 deep learning techniques you should know about, upGrad Blog (2020). https://www.upgrad.com/blog/top-deep-learning-techniques-you-should-know-about.

[35] A. Esteva, A. Robicquet, B. Ramsundar, V. Kuleshov, M. DePristo, K. Chou, C. Cui, G. Corrado, S. Thrun, J. Dean, A guide to deep learning in healthcare, Nat. Med. 25 (1) (2019) 24–29.

[36] T. Pham, T. Tran, D. Phung, S. Venkatesh, Predicting healthcare trajectories from medical records: a deep learning approach, J. Biomed. Inf. 69 (2017) 218–229.

[37] J.R.A. Solares, F.E.D. Raimondi, Y. Zhu, F. Rahimian, D. Canoy, J. Tran, A.C.P. Gomes, A.H. Payberah, M. Zottoli, M. Nazarzadeh, Deep learning for electronic health records: a comparative review of multiple deep neural architectures, J. Biomed. Inf. 101 (2020) 103337.

[38] S. Borwankar, R. Sen, B. Kakani, Improved glaucoma diagnosis using deep learning, in: 2020 IEEE International Conference on Electronics, Computing and Communication Technologies (CONECCT), IEEE, 2020, pp. 1–4.

[39] A. Lavecchia, Deep learning in drug discovery: opportunities, challenges and future prospects, Drug Discov. Today 24 (10) (2019) 2017–2032.

[40] S.M. Anwar, M. Majid, A. Qayyum, M. Awais, M. Alnowami, M.K. Khan, Medical image analysis using convolutional neural networks: a review, J. Med. Syst. 42 (11) (2018) 1–13.

[41] A.C. Jamgade, S.D. Zade, Disease prediction using machine learning, Int. Res. J. Eng. Technol. 6 (5) (2019) 6937–6938.

[42] Q. Wu, A. Boueiz, A. Bozkurt, A. Masoomi, A. Wang, D.L. DeMeo, S.T. Weiss, W. Qiu, Deep learning methods for predicting disease status using genomic data, J. Biometrics Biostat. 9 (5) (2018) 417.

[43] X. Chen, Y. Xu, D.W.K. Wong, T.Y. Wong, J. Liu, Glaucoma detection based on deep convolutional neural network, in: 2015 37th Annual International Conference of the IEEE Engineering in Medicine and Biology Society (EMBC), IEEE, 2015, pp. 715–718.

[44] T.K. Yoo, S. Hong, Artificial neural network approach for differentiating open-angle glaucoma from glaucoma suspect without a visual field test, Invest. Ophthalmol. Vis. Sci. 56 (6) (2015) 3957–3966.

[45] R. Sarki, K. Ahmed, H. Wang, Y. Zhang, Automated detection of mild and multi-class diabetic eye diseases using deep learning, Health Inf. Sci. Syst. 8 (1) (2020) 1–9.

[46] M. Hon, N.M. Khan, Towards Alzheimer's disease classification through transfer learning, in: 2017 IEEE International Conference on Bioinformatics and Biomedicine (BIBM), IEEE, 2017, pp. 1166–1169.

[47] S. Sarraf, G. Tofighi, Alzheimer's Disease Neuroimaging Initiative, DeepAD: Alzheimer's disease classification via deep convolutional neural networks using MRI and fMRI, BioRxiv 1 (2016) 1–32.

[48] S.P. Mohanty, D.P. Hughes, M. Salathé, Using deep learning for image-based plant disease detection, Front. Plant Sci. 7 (2016) 1419.

[49] A. Khamparia, G. Saini, B. Pandey, S. Tiwari, D. Gupta, A. Khanna, KDSAE: chronic kidney disease classification with multimedia data learning using deep stacked autoencoder network, Multimedia Tools Appl. 79 (47) (2019) 1–16.

[50] Z. Tariq, S.K. Shah, Y. Lee, Lung disease classification using deep convolutional neural network, in: 2019 IEEE International Conference on Bioinformatics and Biomedicine (BIBM), IEEE, 2019, pp. 732–735.

[51] B.J. Erickson, P. Korfiatis, Z. Akkus, T. Kline, K. Philbrick, Toolkits and libraries for deep learning, J. Digital Imaging 30 (4) (2017) 400–405.

[52] M.I. Razzak, S. Naz, A. Zaib, Deep learning for medical image processing: overview, challenges and the future, Classif. BioApps 26 (2018) 323–350.

[53] A. Rajkomar, J. Dean, I. Kohane, Machine learning in medicine, New Engl. J. Med. 380 (14) (2019) 1347–1358.

[54] T. Ching, D.S. Himmelstein, B.K. Beaulieu-Jones, A.A. Kalinin, B.T. Do, G.P. Way, E. Ferrero, P.-M. Agapow, M. Zietz, M.M. Hoffman, Opportunities and obstacles for deep learning in biology and medicine, J. R. Soc. Interface 15 (141) (2018) 20170387.

[55] R. Miotto, F. Wang, S. Wang, X. Jiang, J.T. Dudley, Deep learning for healthcare: review, opportunities and challenges, Briefings Bioinf. 19 (6) (2018) 1236–1246.

[56] C. Soguero-Ruiz, I. Mora-Jiménez, J. Ramos-López, T. Quintanilla Fernandez, A. García-García, D. Díez-Mazuela, A. García-Alberola, J.L. Rojo-Álvarez, An interoperable system toward cardiac risk stratification from ECG monitoring, Int. J. Environ. Res. Pub. Health 15 (3) (2018) 428.

[57] L. Bote-Curiel, S. Munoz-Romero, A. Gerrero-Curieses, J.L. Rojo-Álvarez, Deep learning and big data in healthcare: a double review for critical beginners, Appl. Sci. 9 (11) (2019) 2331.

[58] B.E. Dixon, D.J. Vreeman, S.J. Grannis, The long road to semantic interoperability in support of public health: experiences from two states, J. Biomed. Inf. 49 (2014) 3–8.

[59] D. Wang, Y. Si, W. Yang, G. Zhang, T. Liu, A novel heart rate robust method for short-term electrocardiogram biometric identification, Appl. Sci. 9 (1) (2019) 201.

[60] J.J. Hathaliya, S. Tanwar, S. Tyagi, N. Kumar, Securing electronics healthcare records in Healthcare 4.0: a biometric-based approach, Comput. Electrical Eng. 76 (2019) 398–410.

[61] J.R. Pinto, J.S. Cardoso, A. Lourenço, Evolution, current challenges, and future possibilities in ECG biometrics, IEEE Access 6 (2018) 34746–34776.

[62] A. Tandon, A. Dhir, N. Islam, M. Mäntymäki, Blockchain in healthcare: a systematic literature review, synthesizing framework and future research agenda, Comput. Indus. 122 (2020) 103290.

[63] R. Kumar, A.A. Khan, J. Kumar, A. Zakria, N.A. Golilarz, S. Zhang, Y. Ting, C. Zheng, W. Wang, Blockchain-federated-learning and deep learning models for COVID-19 detection using CT imaging, IEEE Sensors J. 21 (14) (2021) 16301–16314.

[64] R. Kumar, W. Wang, J. Kumar, T. Yang, A. Khan, W. Ali, I. Ali, An integration of blockchain and AI for secure data sharing and detection of CT images for the hospitals, Comput. Med. Imaging Graph. 87 (2021) 101812.

[65] H. Ghayvat, M. Awais, P. Gope, S. Pandya, S. Majumdar, Recognizing suspect and predicting the spread of contagion based on mobile phone location data (COUNTER-ACT): a system of identifying COVID-19 infectious and hazardous sites, detecting disease outbreaks based on the Internet of things, edge computing, and artificial intelligence, Sustain. Cities Soc. 69 (2021) 102798, https://doi.org/10.1016/j.scs.2021.102798.

Criminal identification system using face detection with artificial intelligence

19

Neetu Mittal and Robin Singh
Amity Institute of Information Technology, Amity University, Noida, Uttar Pradesh, India

1 Introduction

In our daily lives, we usually remember people by their faces primarily, not their voice, fingerprints, or eyes. This is mainly because it is quickest to recognize someone by their face. This is because it is the most easily distinguishable feature on a human. Hence, face detection if done correctly is the best way to identify a person as anyone can quickly identify faces from far away. It is really simple for humans to do as they are born with this ability; however, it is exponentially more difficult for a computer to do the same. Humans have special nerve cells to identify specific features of any scene such as lines, edges, angles, etc., which is difficult for a computer to do [1]. However, there have been significant developments in facial detection and recognition technologies. This has once again opened doors for newer and better implementation of face recognition. Apart from the enhanced optical capabilities of newer security cameras, the processing power of computers has also increased considerably [2]. Now, these difficult and complicated calculations can be done on a single personal computer. This previously required specialized hardware only found with big organizations or a huge network of computers that split the work and were combined to give the results.

Much research has been done in the field and a lot of new models and algorithms have been developed by many renowned researchers [3–5]. All the newer algorithms solve some problems associated with face detection and recognition. The available datasets have also matured over time. Now, you can find an extensive dataset with just the click of a button on the Internet, which is enabling researchers with small budgets to also be able to perform their research and develop solutions for the existing and future problems [6]. Making sure that the model that is developed is future-ready is an important aspect of research. As it stands, technology is developing at an exponential rate and what is relevant today may be completely outdated in a few months. This has created a need for systems that can be upgraded and adapted easily to emerging trends and technologies. The same applies to face detection and recognition [7]. If a model works on the assumption that the image obtained will only be a certain way, it may fail to work in the near future as better optical hardware is developed or for example,

Blockchain Applications for Healthcare Informatics. https://doi.org/10.1016/B978-0-323-90615-9.00001-3
Copyright © 2022 Elsevier Inc. All rights reserved.

the image is being obtained using infrared light in the dark. Hence, flexibility is very essential when choosing the right model for your project. Another issue is performance improvement [8]. If the improvement gives a percent or two compared to a model being used widely, it makes switching to the new model not feasible as the gains obtained are diminished by the fact that it will take so much effort and expense to replace the existing systems with the new model. But the most significant developments have been on the software side, especially in artificial intelligence (AI). AI is now being used in various applications to automate things smartly and eliminate the need for human intervention to get work done faster and more accurately than ever before. However, AI is not a complete human replacement (at least for now) [9]. If there is noise or the image is not very clear due to some other reason, the accuracy decreases dramatically. Furthermore, hairstyles, make-up, and unnatural expressions are some factors that affect the accuracy of the results [10]. To minimize the effect of these factors, AI has been implemented to create artificial faces with different expressions from the image of faces obtained from digital cameras. Nowadays, AI can be used to augment the image obtained, which makes a significant difference in the accuracy of the results [11–15]. This is done with the help of new developments in graphic processing technology and intelligent three-dimensional (3D) mapping of the face, which can then be used to predict the missing parts. Blockchain with AI (Fig. 1) technology always provide a solution to integrity and security problems related to surveillance camera data with personal privacy.

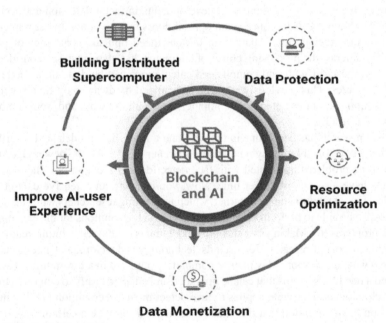

Fig. 1 Blockchain with AI.

2 Literature review

In the past, there has been a lot of research done on new methods for face recognition as well as criminal identification systems. To date, there have primarily been two major methods that have been used: a simple classifier and a modern approach with a neural network of learning features [16]. The domain where facial recognition is being applied the most is probably police work and surveillance. Videos have been chosen for surveillance, as they provide the most essential information for the desired application. They can be used for identification, video data, and face recognition for best biometrics [17,18]. The challenges with the face detection technique are the accuracy and detection price analysis. More challenges include a complicated background, too many faces in photographs, unusual expressions, illumination, pores, face occlusion, skin color, distance, orientation, and too many faces within the image. If the image incorporates too many human faces, that is tough for face detection. Furthermore, the resolution of the image may be very poor, which is likewise difficult for face detection. Skin-coloration pores and skin-coloration adjustments with geographical locations are factors. An excessive amount of distance between the camera and the human face may also lessen the detection of human faces in the photograph. Face orientation means a face with different angles [19–21]. Face aging can also be a challenge. How a person looked at the time their photo was taken for the database might not be how they look today. For this reason, a level of tolerance must be provided in the system to overcome these hurdles. Most systems available today provide age tolerance for as much as 20 years after training the model. However, in the case of minors, their faces change a lot in their teenage years and they may look very different in the future. There are no available systems that can predict the changes in the face with certain accuracy, which makes it exceptionally difficult to use the system in such scenarios. The only possible work-around to this without current technology is to keep updating the database pictures every few years [22]. Currently, most feature extraction [23] processes in face detection are done using Haar classifiers. Some common Haar features are edge features [24,25], line features, and center-surround features. They can also be called two-rectangle features, three-rectangle features, and four-rectangle features, respectively. The weights and sizes of these features are generated by applying machine learning algorithms [26]. For this purpose, having an extensive training dataset is essential to obtain the right values for the Haar classifiers [27]. There are, however, downsides to applying AI to these systems. AI operations [28] are very resource-consuming and usually take some time to complete the processing. This can sometimes result in a lot of time taken for processing a simple image, which can be done in much less time if using a traditional face recognition model. Furthermore, AI might sometimes give a completely different result than desired by altering the original image so much that it becomes completely unrecognizable, defeating the whole purpose of using AI. Hence, AI needs to be extensively trained [29] and should be smart enough to know when it is not required to perform any operations on the original image.

3 Proposed methodology

In this work, a software and hardware system has been proposed that will work in a systematic manner to identify and recognize criminals through surveillance cameras installed throughout the city. This can be done by deploying one mid-level hardware personal computer for 5–6 video sources each. There should be Internet connectivity throughout the day. Our system focuses on increasing the accuracy of the results. It tries to work even with little parts of the face showing by creating a three-dimensional (3D) map of the face and filling in the missing space using the power of AI.

The obtained images are of the highest quality possible in those situations by upscaling the resolution of the pictures with AI. Furthermore, this system helps narrow down the possible suspects to a small number from the database. The authorities can further filter these suspects using details such as height, history, etc.

The system will contain the following components:

- Input from surveillance cameras.
- Upscaling.
- Cropping the face.
- Creating a map of the face using AI.
- Feature extraction.
- Finding a match in the database.

3.1 Input from surveillance cameras

Video obtained from surveillance cameras is immediately pushed for preprocessing once the camera detects movement in the visible space. This saves memory and only the relevant frames are provided for further processing, as this is an expensive operation in terms of processing power. This video is then broken down into individual frames, which are then filtered on the basis of the visibility of the subject.

3.2 Upscaling

The obtained frames after preprocessing have their resolution upscaled using AI, for which GPU has been used. Upscaling the resolution provides better chances of getting distinguishable facial features in the later processes. This dramatically increases the reliability and accuracy of the system.

3.3 Cropping the face

The search for the visible parts of the face has been started now, no matter from which angle. All of these pieces are identified and cropped, and the system tries to identify which section of the face is for the next step of the process. The system tries to get as many pieces as possible of the fact that it can even if there are no clear views of the face from the front.

3.4   Creating a map of the face using AI

The collected pieces are then used to create a 3D map of the face. The AI tries to arrange the collected pieces like a puzzle until it fits together in a generic face template. The skin color is kept as a separate entity in this face and all the processing is done in greyscale. Now, the AI fills in the missing parts of the face by creating a gradient of the pixel values in the nearest pieces of the face that have been placed. This is generally very helpful in filling in small gaps in the face. Filling big gaps if done using the generic face template. The skin tone of the generic face is matched with the visible parts of the face obtained. A gradient is applied on the generic face being used to fill the gaps to blend it with the obtained image of the face.

3.5   Feature extraction

Feature extraction is the most important technique used for the identification and detection of function and extracting a special shape of dimensionality reduction. If the input statistics for an algorithm are very large and difficult to process with notoriously redundant data, then the input statistics will be converted into a decreased illustration set of features. Afterward, the human-face patches are extracted from photographs. It usually carries over 1000 pixels, which are too massive to build a robust popularity system. Two-dimensional (2D) face patches may additionally be taken from exceptional digital camera alignments, with exceptional face expressions and illuminations, and might also go through occlusion and litter. To conquer these drawbacks, feature extractions are done for information packing, size reduction, salience extraction, and noise cleansing. After this step, a face patch is typically transformed into a vector with a fixed dimension or a set of fiducial factors and their corresponding locations. Remodeling the input into a set of functions is called feature extraction [23].

3.6   Find a match in the database

After all the processing, the features are used to compare the data with the database to find possible matches, as shown in Fig. 2. The results obtained can then be manually filtered based on other information about the suspects in the database.

The proposed methodology is simple and helps to clearly distinguish the different methods' performances. The flowchart is described in Fig. 3. A comparison is done with the proposed system and a popular criminal identification system used actively in real-world applications on the basis of seven scenarios:

1. Subject is clearly visible from the front with bright lighting.
2. Subject is clearly visible with a slightly tilted face with bright lighting.

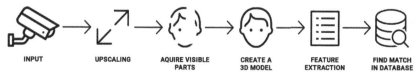

INPUT   UPSCALING   AQUIRE VISIBLE   CREATE A   FEATURE   FIND MATCH
                                      PARTS   3D MODEL   EXTRACTION   IN DATABASE

Fig. 2 Proposed methodology.

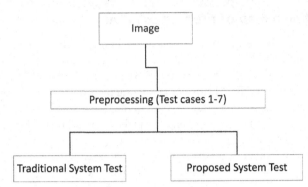

Fig. 3 Flowchart of proposed model.

3. Subject is clearly visible from the front with moderate lighting.
4. Subject is visible with a slightly tilted face with moderate lighting.
5. Subject is clearly visible from the front with low lighting.
6. Subject is visible with a slightly tilted face with low lighting.
7. Subject is not clearly visible with low lighting and slight blur.

The same videos have been provided to both systems and the results have been observed.

3.6.1 Advantages and disadvantages

Advantages:
The proposed system has the following advantages:

- Relatively cost-effective.
- Quick to process.
- Improved accuracy.
- Uses existing and widely available technology.
- Flexible and future upgradability.

Disadvantages:
The proposed system has the following disadvantages:

- Requires a very specific category of GPU.
- Requires PC to be locally connected with surveillance cameras.
- Requires an elaborate database of faces for comparison.

4 Results and discussion

The proposed system has been compared on the different parameters with the existing system. The results have been observed on the basis of the same frames and datasets provided to the system. In this analysis, seven different test cases have been identified and results have been recorded.

Table 1 Results of seven different test cases.

Test no.	Training period (without AI)	Training period (with AI)	Processing time (normal method)	Processing time (our method)	Accuracy (normal method)	Accuracy (our method)
1	10h	6h	5min	7min	80%	83%
2	10h	5h	8min	7min	73%	80%
3	11h	7h	10min	9min	78%	75%
4	10h	6h	10min	7min	70%	74%
5	10h	6h	10min	7min	64%	71%
6	10h	6h	10min	7min	62%	67%
7	10h	6h	10min	7min	58%	65%

In Table 1, not only does the proposed system work better, but also the training time and the processing time are lower due to the use of better parallel processing with the newer hardware. The GPU plays a big role in such scenarios and a powerful GPU that has been proven fit for such tasks should be used. Fig. 4 shows how stable the proposed system is while the results are much improved and more accurate compared to the traditional system, with a few exceptions. But it is much more reliable as depicted in Fig. 3. The proposed system performs much better than the traditional system, especially in conditions where the image obtained is not up to standards.

Less visibility of the subject is where the major difference has been observed in the accuracy of the results. In case number 3, the traditional system gets a slightly better result compared with the proposed system. It overcomes the lack of stable line across the graph with minimum deviation. With multiple cameras at different locations, the software can be programmed with their orientation and location to use images from all cameras together to better form the 3D map of the face.

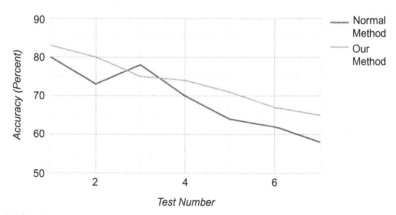

Fig. 4 Line plot comparison of accuracy.

5 Conclusion

The proposed system performs identical to the system that is the industry standard, with only the first few cases showing a slight advantage. Blockchains are used for storing crucial, sensitive personal data in a disk-free environment with the help of digital signatures and private keys in a secured way. However, the proposed system shows a distinct advantage due to better hardware and 3D mapping of the face, which are huge leaps compared to the current methods and systems. This is a clear indication of how AI is a much-needed feature in the criminal identification system. The proposed system is not only cheaper to implement, but also provides a localized approach to the problem, decreasing the load on database servers. The proposed system can also be implemented on a much larger scale due to the availability of the hardware and software required. This shows how there is still a lot to be done in the field of criminal detection and new developments in technologies such as AI, GPUs, and cameras can further improve this field.

6 Future work

- In the future, the proposed system can be incorporated with cameras that follow the subject to keep the subject in frame for longer as well as improvements in the algorithm to make the 3D mapping faster and more accurate.
- This process can also be improved in the future to search through the database faster. In future upgrades to the system, we can use Nvidia GPU ray-tracing capabilities to project artificial light on the subject in the captured video to artificially light up the scene further and have more options to search through the database.
- However, this will need to be very carefully calibrated for the system to understand exactly where in the space the subject is, as we are not using technologies like Lidar to find the exact distance of the subject from the camera.
- Further, the system may be used with proper calibration and multiple cameras that can determine the position of the subject in the 3D space by comparing the sizes of the images from two cameras at different positions facing the subject, which will eliminate the need for expensive tech like Lidar.

References

[1] P.N. Belhumeur, J.P. Hespanha, D.J. Kriegman, Eigenfaces vs. FISHERFACES: recognition using class specific linear projection, IEEE Trans. Pattern Anal. Mach. Intell. 19 (1997) 711–720.

[2] O. Bornet, Learning Based Computer Vision with Intel's Open Source Computer Vision Library, April 2007, Intel.com, 2005, May 19.

[3] R. Brunelli, T. Poggio, Face recognition: features versus templates, IEEE Trans. Pattern Anal. Mach. Intell. 15 (10) (1993) 1042–1052.

[4] S.T. Ratnaparkhi, A. Tandasi, S. Saraswat, Face detection and recognition for criminal identification system, in: 2021 11th International Conference on Cloud Computing, Data Science & Engineering (Confluence), 2021, pp. 773–777, https://doi.org/10.1109/Confluence51648.2021.9377205.

[5] S. Rath, S. Rautaray, A survey on face detection and recognition techniques in different application domain, Int. J. Mod. Educ. Comput. Sci. 6 (2014) 34–44, https://doi.org/ 10.5815/ijmecs.2014.08.05.

[6] A. Kumar, A. Kaur, M. Kumar, Face detection techniques: a review, Artif. Intell. Rev. 52 (2019) 927–948.

[7] E. Jose, M. Greeshma, M.T.P. Haridas, M.H. Supriya, Face recognition based surveillance system using FaceNet and MTCNN on Jetson TX2, in: 2019 5th International Conference on Advanced Computing & Communication Systems (ICACCS), 2019, pp. 608–613, https:// doi.org/10.1109/ICACCS.2019.8728466.

[8] U. Mande, Criminal identification system based on facial recognition using generalized Gaussian mixture model, Asian J. Comput. Sci. Inf. Technol. 2 (2012) 176–179.

[9] A. Karve, M. Balasubramanian, K. Chaudhari, S.B. Mane, Automated criminal identification system using face generation, in: A. Pandian, K. Ntalianis, R. Palanisamy (Eds.), Intelligent Computing, Information and Control Systems. ICICCS 2019. Advances in Intelligent Systems and Computing, vol. 1039, Springer, Cham, 2020, https://doi.org/ 10.1007/978-3-030-30465-2_63.

[10] P. Viola, M. Jones, Rapid object detection using boosted cascade of simple features, in: IEEE Conference on Computer Vision and Pattern Recognition, 2001.

[11] P. Viola, M. Jones, Robust real-time object detection, Int. J. Comput. Vis. 57 (2) (2002) 137–154.

[12] N. Mittal, H.P. Singh, R. Gupta, Decomposition & reconstruction of medical images in MATLAB using different wavelet parameters, in: IEEE International Conference on Futuristic Trends on Computational Analysis and Knowledge Management, 2015, pp. 647–653.

[13] A. Singh, M. Singh, B. Singh, Face detection and eyes extraction using sobel edge detection and morphological operations, in: 2016 Conference on Advances in Signal Processing (CASP), 2016, pp. 295–300, https://doi.org/10.1109/CASP.2016.7746183.

[14] N. Mittal, S. Tanwar, S.K. Khatri, Identification & enhancement of different skin lesion images by segmentation techniques, in: IEEE International Conference on Reliability, Infocom Technologies and Optimization, 2017, pp. 609–614.

[15] https://en.wikipedia.org/wiki/Cascading_classifiers.

[16] Open Computer Vision Library Reference Manual, Intel Corporation, USA, 2001.

[17] L. Sharma, An improved local binary patterns histograms technique for face recognition for real time applications, Int. J. Recent Technol. Eng. 8 (2019) 524–529, https://doi.org/ 10.35940/ijrte.B1098.0782S719.

[18] H.-X. Jia, Y.-J. Zhang, Fast Adaboost training algorithm by dynamic weight trimming, Chin. J. Comput. (2009) 32, https://doi.org/10.3724/SP.J.1016.2009.00336.

[19] Bureau of Justice Statistics, U.S. Department of Justice, in: SEARCH Group (Ed.), Legal and Policy Issues Relating to Biometric Identification Technologies, 1990, April, pp. 43–66.

[20] J. Cox, J. Ghosn, P.N. Yianilos, Feature-based face recognition using mixture distance, in: IEEE Computer Society Conference on Computer Vision and Pattern Recognition, 1996, pp. 209–216.

[21] G. Wang, H. Chen, H. Atabakhsh, Automatically detecting deceptive criminal identities, Commun. ACM 47 (2004) 70–76.

[22] D. Cristinacce, T. Cootes, Facial feature detection using adaboost with shape constraints, in: British Machine Vision Conference, 2003.

[23] N. Mittal, Automatic contrast enhancement of low contrast images using MATLAB, Int. J. Adv. Res. Comput. Sci. 3 (1) (2012) 333–338.

[24] B. Dhruv, N. Mittal, M. Modi, Study of Haralick's and GLCM texture analysis on 3D medical images, Int. J. Neurosci. 129 (4) (2018) 350–362.

[25] D. Zeng, R. Veldhuis, L. Spreeuwers, A Survey of Face Recognition Techniques under Occlusion, arXivarXiv:2006.11366v1, 2020.

[26] B. Dhruv, N. Mittal, M. Modi, Comparative analysis of edge detection techniques for medical images of different body parts, in: Data Science and Analytics. Communications in Computer and Information Science, 799, Springer, 2017.

[27] S. Dadkhah, M. Koeppen, S. Sadeghi, K. Yoshida, Bad Ai: investigating the effect of half-toning techniques on unwanted face detection systems, in: 9th IFIP International Conference on New Technologies, Mobility and Security (NTMS), 2018, 2018, pp. 1–5, https://doi.org/10.1109/NTMS.2018.8328726.

[28] S.S. Gupta, N. Mittal, M. Modi, Skin lesion detection in dermatological images using improved color space based thresholding, Skin Res. Technol. 25 (6) (2019) 846–856.

[29] https://en.wikipedia.org/wiki/Feature_extraction.

Analysis of supervised feature selection in bioinformatics

Neetu Mittal and Ashwani Kumar
Amity Institute of Information Technology, Amity University, Noida, Uttar Pradesh, India

1 Introduction

The advancements of different modern techniques such as blockchain, artificial intelligence (AI), and machine learning (ML) provide the easy utilization of services and a secured framework for the healthcare industry. Blockchain technology [1] provides a secured framework (Fig. 1) for the use of personal healthcare records of patients and helps to categorize the right therapeutic treatments while envisioning disease advancement [2].

The epidemiological study of data is for studying the disease as per the age group and how it affects health. The data collected are used for disease prevention and building strategies, measures, and antitoxins. Bioinformatics techniques are used for the better computational processing of the data collected as well as the factors causing disease spread and effect [3,4]. Data are used for building ML models for disease prediction and detection. But these data have a large number of attributes and variables, which may cause the generated model to overfit while it may also have too much noise. To avoid such limitations, they are trained on the features that are most responsible for the disease and cause the most variation in the results [5]. The selection of the key features is done by the feature selection, which is used to improve the prediction and detection of the generated models by using filter and wrapper methods [6]. The filter method works by a selection of features based on their uniqueness and based on its information and dependency [7,8]. Wrapper methods use an ML algorithm such as rigid regression or recursive feature elimination to evaluate the model on the basis of different selected feature. At the end, they provide an efficient model with a selected feature subset and feature ranking [9].

This chapter presents feature selection techniques and methods with their uses and significance with respect to ML. This study mainly focuses on experimental applications and explanations to better understand the methods and their implementation. To reduce the noise, the dimension of data and the selection of the best features are two techniques that are frequently used and applicable on the high-dimensional data of bioinformatics. Reducing the dimension of the dataset is the first step in any model training process. Quadratic discriminant analysis is a technique used for dimensional reduction by reducing the size of the dataset while also retaining the data without any major loss. This can also be seen in file compression techniques as the sizes of files such as datasets, images, and media are reduced and the data are not lost. But for this

Blockchain Applications for Healthcare Informatics. https://doi.org/10.1016/B978-0-323-90615-9.00008-6
Copyright © 2022 Elsevier Inc. All rights reserved.

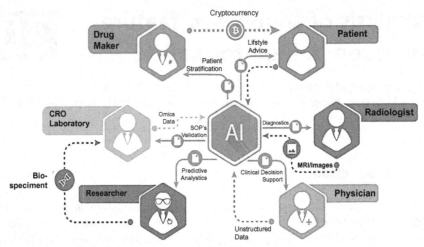

Fig. 1 Integration of blockchain and artificial intelligence.

test, linear discriminant analysis is used to preprocess data as well as reduce dimensions. It analyzes the set of good quality techniques and helps to transforming the huge amount of data into healthcare using advanced computational tools.

2   Literature review

The different applications of blockchain in the smart healthcare industry are mostly supported by many different smart techniques and technologies, as shown in Fig. 2. Datasets generated from epidemiological and bioinformatic analysis have a large number of features. These types of datasets are called high-dimensional datasets. They show high variability not only in the attribute range but also in their values. The high variability not only makes generating a prediction model an expensive task, but also makes it less efficient [10,11].

In ML, if you provide inferior data for model training, then the outcome of that processed model will be overfitting and will have noise. This is because the model

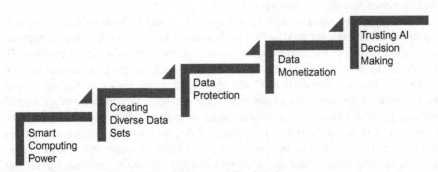

Fig. 2 Applications of artificial intelligence and blockchain.

Feature Selection Flow Diagram

Fig. 3 Flow diagram of feature selection.

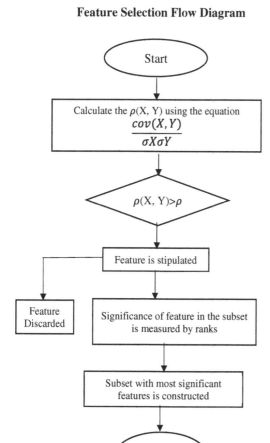

predicts and produces results based on its training on the data provided to it [12]. In datasets, there are two ways to select qualitative attributes; dimension reduction and feature selection are shown in Fig. 3. Dimension reduction is reducing the attributes by the generation of new attributes that are a combination of other attributes; this sometimes makes the model more complex. In feature selection [13,14], the original attributes are either included or excluded. It helps in building prediction model algorithms and results in less training time. The resulting models are less complex and have high accuracy. Sequence analysis has an established custom in bioinformatics. Sequence analysis has an established custom in bioinformatics with results and signal examining [15].

The substance examination revolves around the wide characteristics of a plan, for instance, a propensity to program for proteins or carrying through of a particular natural limit. Signal examination is also used to handle critical topics, for instance, quality essential segments [16] or managerial segments [17,18]. Besides the major features, an alternative has been used, i.e., amino acid at each position in a gathering, for instance, higher demand blends of these design squares can be surmised, their number growing drastically with the model length k [19,20]. For unimportant or overabundance, incorporate assurance procedures are then applied to anchor on the subset of significant parts [21,22]. Feature selection has various methodologies [23] that use the ranking of attributes for the qualitative selection of features [24]. Ranks are based on the statistical results of each feature. Methodologies are the filter method and the wrapper method [25,26].

Dimensional reduce is used to resize without alternation of the dataset [27]. This can also be seen in file compression techniques as the size of files, such as datasets, images, and media are reduced and the data are not lost. But for this test Linear Discriminant Analysis is used for preprocessing the data as well as reducing the dimensions [28].

2.1 Filter method

Filter methods perform best for data preprocessing and ranking of the attributes. They are not dependent on any external factors such as previous algorithms or any preprocessed results. They totally depend on statistical results and how much variability is seen in the result based on the exclusion or inclusion of a feature. Based on the ranks of the attributes, the features are included or excluded [29,30].

Set of Features > Selecting the Best Subset > Learning Ago > Performance

These methods are used for considering the covariance as well as a correlation of the datasets as well as analyzing them for better classification and representation; this is shown in Table 1.

Pearson's correlation is a measuring value for linear correlation between datasets or variables from datasets in a continuous form. The resulting value of a person's correlation lies between -1 to $+1$.

$$\rho x, y = \frac{\text{cov}(X, Y)}{\sigma X \sigma Y}$$

Linear discriminant analysis (LDA) is a classifier used for the dimension reduction of datasets. It preprocess the dataset so that it can be easily operated by ML

Table 1 Filter method correlation coefficient.

Feature/response	Continuous	Categorical
Continuous	Pearson's correlation	Linear discriminant analysis
Categorical	ANOVA	Chi squared

algorithms. It helps in extracting features from the data. LDA is used when the covariance of the matrices is the same, so plotting the two-dimensional (2D) graph of data is possible [31]. Discriminant analysis is based on the covariance of the data matrices. The discriminant is the coefficient function of a polynomial equation providing information about its root. The covariance is the joint variability of variables [32]. The LDA is composed of the same covariance. Dimension reduction is the key property of LDA that enables to work with more than two or three categories of data. It can reduce the dimensions of data sets given as plotting a 10-D or 50-D graph on a flat computer screen. Further, it can be reduced by dimension reduction techniques. The sets can be represented in most 2-D or 3-D model for easy representation and just with the increase in value in mathematical representation. This gives LDA an upper hand over QDA, PCA, or other DA methods [33,34].

$$\Sigma_1 = \Sigma_2$$

Analysis of variance (ANOVA) is used to analyze the difference in the mathematically instituted means of the samples. It is similar to LDA but is worked utilizing at least one clear-cut free highlight and one constant. It gives a factual trial or whether the methods for a few gatherings are equivalent.

Chi squared is a measurable test performed for the gatherings of rigid highlights to assess the probability of a connection or relationship among them utilizing their recurrence circulation.

2.2 Wrapper method

In the wrapper method, the aim is to find the best fitting subset of attributes of the dataset to get efficient results from the trained model [35]. The subset of attributes/ features (Fig. 4) is selected and then computed for the results. It is an expensive method. The results are stored then compared with the results of other subsets by clustering.

2.3 Forward selection

It starts with a regression model without features, and features are added one after one by the training model. The results are noted after each addition to keep track of efficient features to move forward [36,37]. The forward selection of attributes from

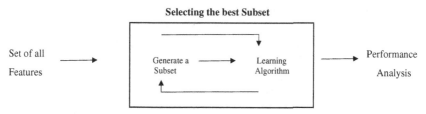

Fig. 4 Subset validation by performance analysis.

datasets is a very helpful process while adding the new attributes into the dataset. There is no need to start the process over again as the model can identify the significance of the attribute based on the previous attributes.

2.4 Backward elimination

The backward attribute elimination model is filled with all the attributes. Results are observed after those features are removed to check its variability in getting accurate results [38–40]. It is a multistep process. In backward elimination, there is a need to have the whole dataset at once and set one value as the bar for the attribute. If attributes do not score over the bar, they are removed. Otherwise, the model is trained on them and ranks the selected ones.

2.5 Recursive feature elimination

This method is based on a greedy search it goes through the array of attributes back and forth to create assemble models. Then eliminate the least costing attribute in the results. While eliminating the attributes, it also ranks the attributes to define the cost of the attribute in a particular test based on the results required [41,42]. It works on the pool of attributes and eliminates the features with the least absolute coefficient value, then rebuilds the model until the desired number of attributes and ranks are considered accordingly.

3 Methodology

The objective of the proposed work is to start with a high-dimensional dataset and reduce its dimensions by performing feature selection and ranking the attributes. According to the significance of the attributes in Phase I and use the ranks for selecting the attributes for constructing the subset of the dataset for Phase II.

In the second phase, the datasets are divided on the basis of significant attribute target with 1 and 0 values for comparing the results of both subsets.

To better understand the feature selection techniques and its methods, there is a need to work on high-dimensional medical data of the patients and their test reports. Instead of training models on whole datasets that could be expensive and even produce overfitted results, feature selection could make the task easier while the model will be more efficient. Sample medical data were taken from Kaggle, which is a UCI repository for datasets, for experimental predictions based on the significance of the attributes. Techniques from the filter and wrapper methods were used to preprocess the data and rank the attributes from the dataset based on their significance in the results. Ranks can be considered to select the attributes that could be used for training the model in less time and decreasing the noise and overfitting results of the model.

A quantitative unlabeled dataset was used in the conducted experiment using Jupyter Notebook and the virtual environment of Python. The dataset needs to be labeled first and then the operations in series—Chi squared has to be done. Further, preprocessing has been done and then selection of attributes, SelectkBest—to get the desired number of ranked attributes as preprocessed data. Logistic Regression has been done to get factual model and Recursive Feature Elimination are used. Finally, a deep study of the scientific uses of methods are discussed. While the examination test cannot be viewed as illustrative of the inhabitants of interest but generalizability is not the objective of the significant stimulus behind this research. Feature selection could work in an open setting. Feature selection methods give us techniques to shorten computation time, improve prediction, and better understand knowledge in model training, model testing, and sample acceptance application. Ridge regression is used to mark the coefficient terms, keep track of attribute rank, and improve the prediction model.

3.1 Phase-I

Data from heart disease patients from the UCI repository were used for experimental use. Various methodologies from filter and wrapper methods were applied to extract the asset attributes among all such as age, blood group, sex, chest pain type, bone density, resting blood pressure, RBC count, serum, cholesterol, WBC count, fasting blood sugar, and more, for a total of 14.

Various libraries and methods such as chi squared, SelectKBest, recursive elimination, and rigid regression are used for data preprocessing and ranking of features, which can be used in the further analysis for precise results and training.

Extracting best features by using filter and wrapper methods is the main motive of technique. Feature selection and achieve the model with the highest efficiency and with the least amount of noise and anomalies also taken care in this model.

The selected dataset is checked to ensure that there are an adequate number of attributes so the best could be selected and ranked accordingly.

Loading the data into the data frame (dataset taken from Kaggle) using Pandas and NumPy libraries to read and load dependencies is shown in Fig. 5. NumPy was used to work with multidimensional datasets and Pandas was used for analysis and manipulation.

Converting the objects of a data frame into NumPy Array for in time enumeration and segregate the data with different variables to separate values and their labels shown in Fig. 6. The values can be used for analysis and the labels can be ranked according to the order the values preserve in the early trained model.

Using filter methods for a statistical test of the attributes of the dataset:

1. Chi squared—Used for preprocessing of the attribute values for analyzing the independence of the attributes.
2. SelectkBest—Used to rank the attributes in the preprocessing and select the requested number of costly attributes from the set.

Results with the score of each attribute mentioned in Figs. 7 and 8 are the four attributes, best fit for the model to get result with least overfitting. This can be used further for accurate analysis models with high accuracy and speed. It will decrease the training time and cost of the model.

```
In [94]:  import pandas as pd
          import numpy as np
          data = pd.read_csv("heart1.csv")

In [95]:  data
```

(a)

```
Out[95]:
```

	age	sex	trestbps	chol	thalach	exang	oldpeak	slope	thal	target	bp	pulser	temp
0	63	1	145	233	150	0	2.3	0	1	1	138	76	38.2
1	37	1	130	250	187	0	3.5	0	2	1	140	75	39.2
2	41	0	130	204	172	0	1.4	2	2	1	145	88	38.6
3	56	1	120	236	178	0	0.8	2	2	1	136	89	39.8
4	57	0	120	354	163	1	0.6	2	2	1	129	95	37.9
5	57	1	140	192	148	0	0.4	1	1	1	133	82	38.3
6	56	0	140	294	153	0	1.3	1	2	1	138	73	38.4
7	67	1	160	286	108	1	1.5	1	2	0	110	62	37.1
8	67	1	120	229	129	1	2.6	1	3	0	115	63	37.2
9	62	0	140	268	160	0	3.6	0	2	0	98	62	36.8
10	63	1	130	254	147	0	1.4	1	3	0	120	65	37.2

(b)

```
In [96]:  data.head()

Out[96]:
```

	age	sex	trestbps	chol	thalach	exang	oldpeak	slope	thal	target	bp	pulser	temp
0	63	1	145	233	150	0	2.3	0	1	1	138	76	38.2
1	37	1	130	250	187	0	3.5	0	2	1	140	75	39.2
2	41	0	130	204	172	0	1.4	2	2	1	145	88	38.6
3	56	1	120	236	178	0	0.8	2	2	1	136	89	39.8
4	57	0	120	354	163	1	0.6	2	2	1	129	95	37.9

```
In [97]:  url = 'C:/Users/asus/Untitled Folder/heart1.csv'
          dataframe = pd.read_csv(url)
```

(c)

Fig. 5 (A–C) Loading the data into the model and data frame from the csv file.

```
In [98]:  array = dataframe.values
          X = array[:,0:13]
          Y = array[:,11]
          print(Y)

          [76. 75. 88. 89. 95. 82. 73. 62. 63. 62. 65. 68. 58. 65. 57.]
```

Fig. 6 Labeled attributes for statistical tests.

(A)

```
In [99]:  from sklearn.feature_selection import SelectKBest

In [100]: from sklearn.feature_selection import chi2
```

(B)

```
In [102]: test = SelectKBest(score_func=chi2, k=5)
          fit = test.fit(X, Y)

          np.set_printoptions(precision=5)
          print(fit.scores_)

          features = fit.transform(X)

          print(features[0:6,:])
```

(C)

```
[16.3365    3.31818 14.3038   95.954    24.22522  8.5      7.80946 7.76923
  3.35484  8.       25.46166 28.04824  0.30167]
[[ 63. 233. 150. 138.  76.]
 [ 37. 250. 187. 140.  75.]
 [ 41. 204. 172. 145.  88.]
 [ 56. 236. 178. 136.  89.]
 [ 57. 354. 163. 129.  95.]
 [ 57. 192. 148. 133.  82.]]
```

Fig. 7 (A–C) Importing libraries. Scores of the attribute in the significance test and selected attributes.

(A)

```
In [103]: from sklearn.feature_selection import RFE

In [104]: from sklearn.linear_model import LogisticRegression

In [105]: model = LogisticRegression()
          rfe = RFE(model, 5)
          fit = rfe.fit(X, Y)
          print("Num Features: %s" % (fit.n_features_))
          print("Selected Features: %s" % (fit.support_))
          print("Feature Ranking: %s" % (fit.ranking_))
```

(B)

```
Num Features: 5
Selected Features: [ True False  True  True  True False False False False F
alse  True False
 False]
Feature Ranking: [1 8 1 1 1 6 4 7 5 9 1 2 3]
```

Fig. 8 (A, B) Selecting top three attributes based on ranks.

Implementing recursive feature elimination–wrapper method to predict the target attribute.

Features selected by RFE are marked true and the rest are marked false on the basis of their significance in the trained model on the number of requested features.

Along with the 0–1 value, they also have a rank that can help in selecting more features for the model based on their rank. For the model building with the least noise

(A)

```
In [106]: from sklearn.linear_model import Ridge

In [107]: ridge = Ridge(alpha=1.0)
          ridge.fit(X,Y)

Out[107]: Ridge()
```

(B)

```
In [108]: def pretty_print_coefs(coefs, names = None, sort = False):
              if names == None:
                  names = ["X%s" % x for x in range(len(coefs))]
              lst = zip(coefs, names)
              if sort:
                  lst = sorted(lst,  key = lambda x:-np.abs(x[0]))
              return " + ".join("%s * %s" % (round(coef, 3), name)
                                            for coef, name in lst)
```

(C)

```
Ridge model: 0.001 * X0 + -0.009 * X1 + 0.001 * X2 + -0.0 * X3 + 0.001 * X4
+ 0.02 * X5 + -0.009 * X6 + 0.008 * X7 + 0.004 * X8 + 0.015 * X9 + 0.001 *
X10 + 0.997 * X11 + -0.002 * X12
```

Fig. 9 (A–C) Results with coefficient of each attribute.

and increased efficiency, and logistic regression with fundamental structure utilizes a calculated capacity to demonstrate a double reliant variable.

Rigid regression gives coefficient terms with the feature variable. It helps in selecting the essential features. It is also called L2-regularization and will, in general, get the comparable coefficient. These results can be used, as shown in Fig. 9, to improve the training time and result prediction of the model.

3.2 Phase-II

After ranking the attributes, they can be used for model training. The ranked features can also be used to make predictive decisions based on methods such as LDA as the result of the above experiment is linear data. The attributes have been selected on the basis of their ranks and those are used for model training. In the above dataset, the attribute has been targeted, which acted as a predefined significant feature, and the attributes at 11, 12, and 13. In this, the data set ranked 1, 2, 3 represents the top-ranked attribute for the prediction with the dependent attribute as a target.

$$\Sigma_1 = \Sigma_2$$

Steps for the experiment:

- Determine the global mean (M) of patients and nonpatients.
- Determine mean vector (M1) and covariance matrix (C1) with the use of M.
- Determine mean vector (M2) and covariance matrix (C2) with the use of M.
- Calculate within-class scatter matrix C.
- Compute the D functions

$$F_i = M_i * C^{-1} * X^T - 0.5 * M_i * C^{-1} * M_i^T + In(P_i)$$

Target 1—Attributes 13, 12, and 11.

Table 2 contains the attribute list of rank 1, 2, and 3, and their value of all targets 1 for separating according to the significant value as a subset of the dataset used in Phase I. It determines the mean vector M1 and

Constructing the covariance matrix C1.
Target 0—Attribute 13, 12, and 11.

Table 3 contains the attribute list of ranks 1, 2, and 3, and their value of all targets 0 for separating according to the significant value as a subset of the dataset used in Phase-I for determining the mean vector M2 and

Constructing the covariance matrix C2.

Global mean for all combined M

Table 2 Tuples with target value 1.

Blood pressure	Pulse rate	Temperature
138	76	38.2
140	75	39.2
145	88	38.6
136	89	39.8
129	95	37.9
133	82	38.3
138	73	38.4
Mean (M1)		
137	82.57	38.63

Table 3 Tuples with target value 0.

Blood pressure	Pulse rate	Temperature
110	62	37.1
115	63	37.2
98	62	36.8
120	65	37.0
118	68	37.1
102	58	37.3
106	65	36.9
111	57	37.0
Mean (M2)		
110	62.5	37.05

$$BP = (138 + 140 + 145 + 136 + 129 + 133 + 138 + 110 + 115 + 98 + 120$$
$$+ 118 + 102 + 106 + 111)/(7 + 8) = 122.6$$

$$PR = (76 + 75 + 88 + 89 + 95 + 82 + 95 + 82 + 73 + 62 + 63 + 62 + 65 + 68$$
$$+ 58 + 65 + 57)/(7 + 8) = 71.87$$

$$Temp = (38.2 + 39.2 + 38.6 + 39.8 + 37.9 + 38.3 + 38.4 + 37.1 + 37.2 + 36.8$$
$$+ 37 + 37.1 + 37.3 + 36.9 + 36.9 + 37)/(7 + 8) = 37.37.79$$

$$M = [122.6\,71.87\,37.79]$$

$$C1 = \begin{matrix} 229.65 & 140.0.1 & 13.09 \\ 140.0.1 & 174.27 & 8.90 \\ 13.09 & 8.90 & 1.08 \end{matrix} \quad C2 = \begin{matrix} 210.51 & 130.27 & 9.557 \\ 130.27 & 99.48 & 6.788 \\ 9.557 & 6.788 & 0.565 \end{matrix}$$

$$C = \frac{7}{7+8} * C1 + \frac{8}{7+8} * C2 = \begin{matrix} 219.44 & 134.82 & 11.208 \\ 134.82 & 134.38 & 7.772 \\ 11.208 & 7.772 & 0.804 \end{matrix}$$

Data of new person Z to be checked

$$X = [110\,62\,37]$$

Computing the F1

$$M1 * C^{-1} * X^T = 137\,82.57\,38.63 * \begin{matrix} 219.44 & 134.82 & 11.208 \\ 134.82 & 134.38 & 7.772 \\ 11.208 & 7.772 & 0.804 \end{matrix}^{-1} * 110\,62\,37^T$$
$$= 4679.31$$

$$M1 * C^{-1} * M1^T = 137\,82.57\,38.63 * \begin{matrix} 219.44 & 134.82 & 11.208 \\ 134.82 & 134.38 & 7.772 \\ 11.208 & 7.772 & 0.804 \end{matrix}^{-1} * \begin{matrix} 137 \\ 82.57 \\ 38.63 \end{matrix}$$
$$= 4722.57$$

$$F1 = M_1 * C^{-1} * X^T - 0.5 * M_1 * C^{-1} * M_1^T + In(P_1)$$
$$= 4679.31 - 0.5 * 4722.57 + In = 2317.26$$

Computing the F2

$$M2 * C^{-1} * X^T = 110\,62.5\,37.05 * \begin{matrix} 219.44 & 134.82 & 11.208 \\ 134.82 & 138.38 & 7.772 \\ 11.208 & 7.772 & 0.804 \end{matrix}^{-1} * 110\,62\,37^T$$
$$= 4645.81$$

$$M2 * C^{-1} * M2^T = 110\begin{matrix} 219.44 & 134.82 & 11.208^{-1} & 110 \\ 62.5 & 37.05 \end{matrix} * \begin{matrix} 134.82 & 138.38 & 7.772 \\ 11.208 & 7.772 & 0.804 \end{matrix} \begin{matrix} * & 62.5 \\ 37.05 \end{matrix}$$

$$= 4651.8$$

$$F2 = M_2 * C^{-1} * X^T - 0.5 * M_2 * C^{-1} * M_2^T + In(P_1)$$

$$= 4679.31 - 0.5 * 4722.57 + In\frac{8}{7+8} = 2317.26$$

$$F1 = 2317.26$$

$$F2 = 2319.28$$

F1 is smaller than F2 so that the data of Z show that the target 1 s are the patients ailing with the problem and target 0 s have a low probability of disease. In the above experiment, the linear discriminant from the filter method is used. It is efficient for preprocessing and reducing the dimension of the linear datasets. The research done in the medical field with LDA is phenomenal. Thyroid tests that used to take five tests in the diagnosis process can be done in two tests with the LDA process. Optimal linear combination is used in diagnosis based on features extracted from research and model training. The efficiency of the diagnosis model is higher than the previous one.

4 Conclusion

In the healthcare industry, the health service system with modern technology such as wearable devices, the Internet of Things, mobile Internet, blockchain, machine learning, and artificial intelligence provides the dynamic accessibility of information, the availability of materials, and the security of personal records. In the proposed work, the nature of feature selection's filter and wrapper methods along with some applications and ideas from implementation have been examined when applied suitably according to the need and inventions.

In machine learning, the performance of the model is dependent on the type of data provided to the system for training and testing purposes. The better the quality of data, the better the results of the training and analysis. Preprocessing the data with filter methods improves the quality of the data. Further analysis can be performed by using the wrapper method to select the best attributes of the dataset. This may also help to manage and update the medical framework in a smart means.

5 Key findings

- Feature Selection is vital when any data is collected or gathered by various means and especially bioinformatics.
- This can be used for designing and training the models for analysis-based results, diagnosis of the disease, patterns recognition, and various applications.

- Analyzing the cost of the attribute in data sets can help to rank and classify the data attributes for a clear outcome after the inclusion or exclusion of the attribute.
- This result in the final model based on the rank assigned during the whole process which can be used for models that can utilize the results for recognition or analyzing purpose.

References

[1] M.H. Miraz, D.C. Donald, Application of blockchain in booking and registration systems of securities exchanges, in: International Conference on Computing, Electronics & Communications Engineering (iCCECE), 2018, pp. 35–40.

[2] Z. Zheng, S. Xie, H.N. Dai, X. Chen, H. Wang, Blockchain challenges and opportunities: a survey, Int. J. Web Grid Serv. 14 (4) (2018) 352–375.

[3] Q. Abbas, I. Fondón, Unsupervised skin lesions border detection via two dimensional image analysis, Comput. Methods Programs Biomed. 104 (2011) 1–15.

[4] S. Piramuthu, Feed-forward neural networks and feature construction with correlation information: an integrated framework, Eur. J. Oper. Res. 93 (2) (1996) 418–427.

[5] Y. Saeys, I. Inza, P. Larrañaga, A review of feature selection techniques in bioinformatics, Bioinformatics 23 (19) (2007) 2507–2517.

[6] S. Ma, J. Huang, Penalized feature selection and classification in bioinformatics, Brief. Bioinform. 9 (5) (2008) 392–403.

[7] H. Wei, S.A. Billings, Feature subset selection and ranking for data dimensionality reduction, IEEE Trans. Pattern Anal. Mach. Intell. 29 (1) (2007) 162–166.

[8] B. Moska, D. Kostrzewa, R. Brzeski, Advances in Intelligent Systems and Computing, 1061, Springer, 2020, p. 77.

[9] T. Nguyen, B. Lechner, Y.D. Wong, Response-based methods to measure road surface irregularity: a state-of-the-art review, Eur. Transp. Res. Rev. 11 (1) (2019) 43.

[10] J. Cai, J. Luo, S. Wang, S. Yang, Feature selection in machine learning: a new perspective, Neurocomputing 300 (2018) 70–79.

[11] M. Fauvel, C. Dechesne, A. Zullo, F. Ferraty, Fast forward feature selection of hyperspectral images for classification with Gaussian mixture models, IEEE J. Sel. Top. Appl. Earth Obs. Remote Sens. 8 (6) (2015) 2824–2831.

[12] Dimension Reduction Techniques-Pulkit Sharma. https://www.analyticsvidhya.com/blog/2018/08/dimensionality-reduction-techniques-python/.

[13] Selecting Right Variables Saurav Kaushik. https://www.analyticsvidhya.com/blog/2016/12/introduction-to-feature-selection-methods-with-an-example-or-how-to-select-the-right-variables/.

[14] R.J. Urbanowicz, M. Meeker, W. La Cava, R.S. Olson, J.H. Moore, Relief based feature selection: introduction and review, J. Biomed. Inform. 85 (2018) 189–203.

[15] Y. Li, T. Li, H. Liu, Recent advances in feature selection and its applications, Knowl. Inf. Syst. 53 (2017) 551–577.

[16] B. Dhruv, N. Mittal, M. Modi, Comparative analysis of edge detection techniques for medical images of different body parts, in: Data Science and Analytics. Communications in Computer and Information Science, 799, Springer, 2017.

[17] B. Remeseiro, V. Bolon-Canedo, A review of feature selection methods in medical applications, Comput. Biol. Med. 112 (2019) 103375.

[18] M. Mafarja, S. Mirjalili, Whale optimization approaches for wrapper feature selection, Appl. Soft Comput. 62 (2018) 441–453.

[19] Y.U. Xue, B. Xue, Self-adaptive particle swarm optimization for large-scale feature selection in classification, ACM Trans. Knowl. Discov. Data 13 (2019) 1–27, https://doi.org/10.1145/3340848.

[20] R. Sheikhpour, M. Agha Sarram, S. Gharaghani, M.A.Z. Chahooki, A survey on semi-supervised feature selection methods, Pattern Recogn. 64 (2017) 141–158.

[21] L.M. Abualigah, A.T. Khader, E.S. Hanandeh, A new feature selection method to improve the document clustering using particle swarm optimization algorithm, J. Comput. Sci. 25 (2018) 456–466.

[22] J. Song, H. Wang, J. Wang, et al., Phospho predict: a bioinformatics tool for prediction of human kinase-specific phosphorylation substrates and sites by integrating heterogeneous feature selection, Sci. Rep. 7 (2017) 6862.

[23] N. Mittal, Automatic contrast enhancement of low contrast images using MATLAB, Int. J. Adv. Res. Comput. Sci. 3 (1) (2012) 333–338.

[24] B. Dhruv, N. Mittal, M. Modi, Study of Haralick's and GLCM texture analysis on 3D medical images, Int. J. Neurosci. 129 (4) (2018) 350–362.

[25] Y. Perez-Riverol, M. Kuhn, J.A. Vizcaíno, M.-P. Hitz, E. Audain, Accurate and fast feature selection workflow for high-dimensional omics data, PLoS One 12 (12) (2017) e0189875, https://doi.org/10.1371/journal.pone.0189875.

[26] A. Abu Shanab, T. Khoshgoftaar, Filter-based subset selection for easy, moderate, and hard bioinformatics data, in: IEEE International Conference on Information Reuse and Integration (IRI), 2018, pp. 372–377.

[27] Y.-H. Taguchi, Unsupervised Feature Extraction Applied to Bioinformatics: A PCA Based and TD Based Approach, Unsupervised and Semi-Supervised Learning, Springer Nature, 2019.

[28] B.F. Darst, K.C. Malecki, C.D. Engelman, Using recursive feature elimination in random forest to account for correlated variables in high dimensional data, BMC Genet. 19 (2018) 65.

[29] X. Huang, L. Zhang, B. Wang, et al., Feature clustering-based support vector machine recursive, feature elimination for gene selection, Appl. Intell. 48 (2018) 594–607.

[30] X. Lin, C. Li, Selecting feature subsets based on SVM-RFE and the overlapping ratio with applications in bioinformatics, Molecules (2018) 1420–3049.

[31] N. Mittal, H.P. Singh, R. Gupta, Decomposition and reconstruction of medical images in MATLAB using different wavelet parameters, in: IEEE International Conference on Futuristic Trends on Computational Analysis and Knowledge Management, 2015, pp. 647–653.

[32] N. Lazzarini, J. Bacardit, RGIFE: a ranked guided iterative feature elimination heuristic for the identification of biomarkers, BMC Bioinform. 18 (2017) 322.

[33] Y. Guo, F.-L. Chung, G. Li, L. Zhang, Multi-label bioinformatics data classification with ensemble embedded feature selection, IEEE Access 7 (2019) 103863–103875.

[34] R.J. Urbanowicz, R.S. Olson, P. Schmitt, M. Meeker, J.H. Moore, Benchmarking relief-based feature selection methods for bioinformatics data mining, J. Biomed. Inform. 85 (2018) 168–188.

[35] C. Croux, et al., Classification efficiencies for robust linear discriminant analysis, Stat. Sin. 18 (2) (2008) 581–599.

[36] P. Xu, G.N. Brock, R.S. Parrish, Modified linear discriminant analysis approaches for classification of high-dimensional microarray data, Comput. Stat. Data Anal. 53 (5) (2009) 1674–1687.

[37] S. Balakrishnama, A. Ganapathiraju, Institute for Signal and Information Processing Department of electrical and computer engineering Mississippi State University, Linear Discriminant Analysis—A Brief Tutorial.

[38] S. Wang, Z. Huang, Y. Qian, K. Yu, IEEE Trans. Audio Speech Lang. Process. 27 (11) (2019) 1686.

[39] S.J.D. Prince, J.H. Elder, Probabilistic linear discriminant analysis for inferences about identity, in: 2007 IEEE 11th International Conference on Computer Vision, 2007, pp. 1–8.

[40] N. Mittal, S. Tanwar, S.K. Khatri, Identification & enhancement of different skin lesion images by segmentation techniques, in: IEEE International Conference on Reliability, Infocom Technologies and Optimization, 2017, pp. 609–614.

[41] Y. Wang, An optimal linear discriminant analysis for pattern recognition, in: International Conference on Cyberworlds, Hangzhou, 2008, pp. 705–709.

[42] S. Zheng, C. Ding, F. Nie, H. Huang, Harmonic mean linear discriminant analysis, IEEE Trans. Knowl. Data Eng. 31 (8) (2019) 1520–1531.

COVID-19 identification and analysis using CT scan images: Deep transfer learning-based approach

21

Krishna Kumar Mohbey, Savita Sharma, Sunil Kumar, and Meenu Sharma
Department of Computer Science, Central University of Rajasthan, Ajmer, India

1 Introduction

COVID-19 is regarded as one of the most dangerous viruses on the planet. It has the ability to spread swiftly among individuals. People lose their lives because of COVID-19. COVID-19 affects the whole world. Scientists, epidemiologists, and virologists are continuously working to get different solutions for society. The number of COVID-19 patients began to increase unexpectedly, leaving authorities and health professionals unable to deal with the problem. Hospital rooms and ICU beds are limited number in the majority of developing nations. The health services in India are a particularly complicated situation because the country has the world's most diversified population (approx. 1.3 billion people). During the pandemic, hospitals struggled to provide adequate care to both COVID-19-infected and noninfected patients. Consequently, critically ill individuals are being refused entry to intensive care units. As a result, testing kit supplies are in short supply, and many hospitals worldwide are having difficulty detecting COVID-19 positive patients. In terms of medical professionals, it is projected that India has only one doctor for every 1666 people [1].

Healthcare services were not accessible for all COVID-19 patients in some of the worst-affected cities. As a result of a large number of verified cases, patients were returned home for quarantine and monitoring, possibly risking their loved ones to the virus. Outside of health facilities, high-risk patients must be observed regularly by examining symptoms such as fever, heart rate, oxygen saturation, and so on. Real-time monitoring technologies have a big influence on how health surveillance and treatment solutions are developed. The adoption of Healthcare 4.0 technology is one solution for this problem. Healthcare 4.0 [2–10] is driven by Industry 4.0 technology, such as wearable devices, artificial intelligence (AI), blockchain, cloud computing, IoT, robotics, 3D bioprinting, and so on. Various innovations in the e-healthcare industry, such as blockchain, AI, cloud computing, and IoT, have been combined to give dynamic medical treatments in real time. The IoT-WBAN [11] is comprised of the wireless communications of wearable devices. The information

Blockchain Applications for Healthcare Informatics. https://doi.org/10.1016/B978-0-323-90615-9.00011-6
Copyright © 2022 Elsevier Inc. All rights reserved.
447

gathered is subsequently utilized for various reasons, including in-hospital observation, remote diagnostics, outpatient monitoring, and emergency response. A wireless body area network (WBAN) has the potential to have a substantial influence on the control of COVID-19 transmission.

Inspired by that, many predictions such as plasma therapy, X-ray imaging [12, 13], and so on have come into existence. A lot of people died due to COVID-19 [14], and the disease's origin has yet to be discovered [15]. A primary strategy for better managing this pandemic is finding, isolating, and caring for patients as soon as possible. Our research aims to develop a computational transfer learning model for COVID-19 image classification. Due to online repository availability, we get images from CT scans of COVID-19-infected people and healthy people [16]. The indication of COVID-19 is a throat infection that leads to breathing problems. The COVID-19 patient should stay in isolation to protect healthy people because COVID is a highly contagious disease that transfers from one individual to another and forms a chain. Instead, many methods are used to reduce the impact of COVID-19. One of them is medical imaging [17], which is also helpful for analysis and predicting the effect of the virus on the human body. With CT scans, images of non-COVID-19 individuals and infected persons can be analyzed [18, 19]. Fig. 1 shows sample images of CT scans for COVID positive and negative patients.

For the proper treatment of COVID-19 patients, healthcare facilities can exchange data. Sharing data securely [20, 21] and training a global model to discover affected patients is a difficult challenge. Data collection from a variety of origins is a significant problem and a barrier in the development of intelligent [22] approaches. By adopting blockchain-based [23–25] federated learning, organizations can store their data privately and spread the data among institutions. An electronic medical record (EMR) based on a blockchain system has vast potential to provide safe, dependable, and resilient EMR storage. It will also enhance access to research data for study by scientists, healthcare professionals, and government agencies who can analyze it and make better choices. The decentralized system [26, 27] for information exchange among several facilities securely exchanges data without compromising the institutions' confidentiality. This distributed information can be analyzed to improve the global deep learning (DL) model to detect infected patients. Privacy, confidentiality, and data consistency are fundamental problems for storing and managing any patient data. As a result, blockchain-based [5] healthcare solutions are preferred for fostering user confidence, security, and privacy. Blockchain-based solutions can be used to improve the healthcare system. Healthcare systems can be enhanced with blockchain architecture and DL methods. A framework using blockchain and DL can also be used to anticipate future diseases and provide assistance to individuals.

For severe health issues such as COVID-19, the time and resources required to collect and marked images are difficult to acquire considerably large and openly accessible medical photographic data to train DL models. A different way of training DL models is transfer learning, which involves assigning precalculated weights to a DL network. The weights are acquired from previous experiments in various applications. This approach is commonly used for initializing DL techniques; other parameters are

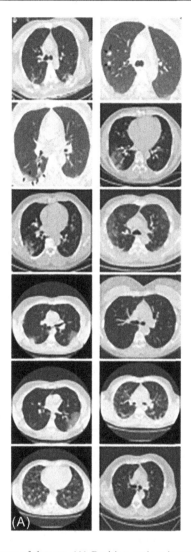

Fig. 1 Sample patient images of dataset. (A) Positive patient images;

(continued)

finalized using corpus available for clinical samples [28]. This analysis would look at how transfer learning can be incorporated to classify COVID-19 in CT scans. This could help physicians and academics provide a method to help highly constrained health providers decide about the next course of action. We have used the VGG-19 pretrained model to identify and classify the COVID positive and negative CT scan samples. The paper's key contributions include:

- We suggest a novel DL technique and evaluate it on a dataset with 5000 images to identify COVID-19 quicker.

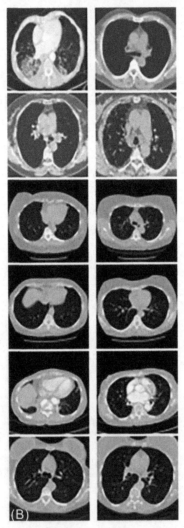

Fig. 1, cont'd (B) negative patient images.

- The proposed model is a transfer learning model based on VGG-19 architecture that can obtain an accuracy of 95%.
- We also discover in the experimental findings that our proposed model performs better in comparison to CNN and Xception Net.

We begin with a summary of the study relevant to this research in Section 2. After that, we discuss the suggested transfer DL model and compare the results with another model in Section 4. In Section 5, we present the output results along with discussions. Finally, we conclude the work and explain some future directions.

2 Related works

Afshar et al. [29] introduced a model using a capsule network to classify COVID-19 by analyzing CT scans. In this model, capsules and various convolution layers were used, which eliminates the class imbalance problem. In the experimental result, the authors showed the model's performance. They used the trained model that is publicly accessed on GitHub [30]. They showed that this model's accuracy is 95.7% sensitivity as 90%, the specificity of the model is 95.80%. In Ref. [31], the author proposed an AI model, in which machine learning (ML) and DL algorithms are utilized to identify the COVID-19-patient's X-ray. In Refs. [32, 33], the authors provide an analysis of MERS' radiologic features for treating sick individuals using X-rays. Still, they considered only a 30-year-old individual as having fever, stomach pain, and diarrhea. Further, this model applied on the X-ray and CT scans proved helpful. Also, in Ref. [34], the authors explain some protocols that should be implemented in hospitals to reduce the risks of spreading COVID-19 from infected persons to healthy persons.

In Ref. [35], the authors discussed the breakout cause of COVID-19. They raised the question of the cause of COVID-19. In their study, they assessed the impact of COVID-19 spread. In Ref. [36], the author proposed a model using the support vector machine (SVM) technique to classify the pneumothorax characteristics of a lung image mine using a local binary pattern. In the proposed model, they segmented the region of abnormal lungs using multiscale texture segmentation, which removes the chest image's impurities and gives us the area of interest. Later on, this transformation is used for a shift in texture to find multiple overlapping frames. Sobel edge detection identifies rib boundaries. Finally, the rib border is filled in between the aberrant patches to get a full disease region. In Ref. [37], the author uses CT scans of 21 COVID-19-infected individuals to demonstrate their work. In Ref. [38], the author extracted the features by using convolutional neural network (CNN) and SVM algorithms for classification by using COVID-19 corpus. This proposed model can be utilized to cure COVID-19 positive individuals. In Ref. [13], the author identified the impact of this viral disease from person-acquired lung diseases and pneumonia using deep algorithms applied on a chest CT scan. In Ref. [39], the author demonstrated the impact of COVID-19 on acute renal failures. In Ref. [40], the authors classified the collection of 50 COVID-19 patients within two classes as good and poor. Further, the potential risk for pulmonary infections and low recovery was found by the authors. Table 1 depicts a summary of works done for COVID-19 identification using various approaches.

In Ref. [48], the author analyzed COVID-19-infected persons and death due to the virus worldwide. In Ref. [41], the author introduced a DL model to diagnose a COVID-19-infected person with help from images. This method is very effective in the rapid identification of an infected person. This method gives 97.48% accuracy for lung classification by using different matrix parameters. In Ref. [49], the author demonstrated how the COVID-19 virus is revealed as a pneumonia infection. The authors' main aim is to propose a DL algorithm that is Covidx-net to cure COVID-19 automatically with the help of images. In Ref. [50], the authors proposed

Table 1 Comparative review of the existing work.

S. no.	Authors	Year	Approach	Accuracy (%)
1.	Hassanien et al. [41]	2020	Deep-based methodology with vector gadget classifier	98.48
2.	Afshar et al. [29]	2020	Capsule network	95.7
3.	Maghdid et al. [42]	2020	AlexNet pretrained	98
4.	Maghdid et al. [42]	2020	Modified CNN	94
5.	Thejeshwar et al. [43]	2020	KE Sieve Neural Network	98
6.	Jain et al. [44]	2021	Inception Net V3	93
7.	Jain et al. [44]	2021	Xception	97
8.	Aras et al. [45]	2021	ResNet50	94.7
9.	Ying et al. [46]	2021	DRE-Net	86
10.	Wang et al. [47]	2021	CNN	93

a distinct approach to identify COVID-19 positive individuals. It was concluded that COVID-19 automatically prevents the spread of coronaviruses through touch. Besides, the study of the COVID-19 correlation to pneumonia was performed and it was found that it is challenging to predict pneumonia caused by the coronavirus or any other symptoms. In Ref. [51], the author tried to find the lung abnormality by using chest radiography and concluded that the medical community depends on chest radiography due to the convenience and less spread control. In Ref. [30], the author used the front view of 123 X-ray samples to treat COVID-19 patients. In Ref. [42], the author presented the different AI techniques in medicine and the challenges faced using corpus-less image samples. They incorporate the pretrained AlexNet model and CNN to train on the dataset. As a result, the method has 98%, and modified CNN has 94.1% accuracy. In [52], the author extracted two subsets (16 × 16 and 32 × 32) generated from 530 X-rays and 150 CT scan samples labeled for COVID or non-COVID.

Hathaliya et al. [2] introduced a permissioned blockchain-based medical care ecosystem to improve the safety and confidentiality of client records. Remote health surveillance becomes increasingly sophisticated and versatile in Healthcare 4.0, allowing patients to be seen at any time and from any location via wearable sensors. The current telesurgery technology has security, privacy, and interoperability concerns, limiting its potential use in healthcare institutions throughout the world. To address these concerns, the authors [3] offered HaBiTs (blockchain-based telesurgery), a system in which security is accomplished by integrity and extensibility via smart contracts. To appropriately administer medicine, access to the health history of patients is vital, and blockchain may substantially strengthen the healthcare system. Various approaches are evaluated in this chapter [4], comprising tools and techniques to assess the performance of such systems for addressing existing limits of healthcare systems leveraging blockchain technologies, such as Hyperledger Fabric and Composer.

3 Proposed model

3.1 Convolutional neural networks

This is DL model, that is mostly used for image analysis and classifications [53–55]. A CNN model comprises one or more convolution layers, pooling layers, and fully connected layers. It has various applications such as handwriting recognition, medical image processing, sentiment analysis, and so on [56]. CNN can handle noisy images in image classification as well as overfitting problems in datasets [57, 58]. Nahid et al. proposed an image processing model to identify pneumonia [59]. In this model, they used X-ray images in the CNN framework and got 97.2% accuracy. In this work, they used feature learning and classification strategy together. Feature engineering comprises different convolutional and pooling layers. COVID-19 has been identified for 2020. After that various research works are carried out to identify COVID-19 using DL methods. We have also employed the CNN model for COVID-19 image identification with the following parameters (Table 2).

3.2 Transfer learning

It is a way of using one task's experience to increase the widespread use of another. The understanding of a previously qualified DL model is used to migrate the parameters learned by a network on any "task A" to a new "task B" [60].

It is often used in the processing of computer vision. The natural language where the labeled data are too small for a model to be trained from scratch and a network with a lot of information are preentrained on an identical problem (Fig. 2).

Following strategies can be used for transfer learning:

- *Use as a feature extractor*: DL networks are a layered architecture where multiple layers learn distinct features. All layers are connected to the last layer or the fully connected layer for final results. For other models, it can use DL models without their final layer as a fixed feature extractor (Fig. 3).
- *Use to fine-tuning*: In this method of transfer learning, we replace the final layer of the network and also selectively retrain some of the previous layers, which is shown in Fig. 4.

Table 2 CNN model parameter details.

Parameter	Value
Learning rate	0.001
Hidden layers	32
Batch size	32
Pooling	Maxpooling 2D
Activation function	Softmax
Number of classes	2
Optimizer	Adam

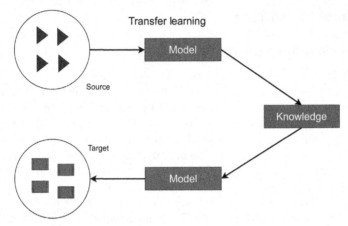

Fig. 2 Transfer learning concept.

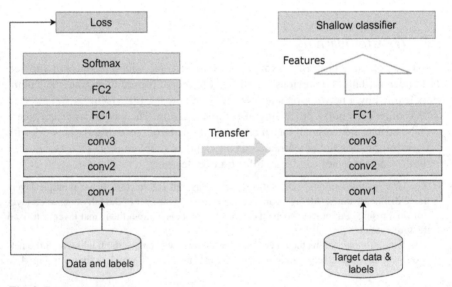

Fig. 3 Feature extractor.

3.3   Xception Net

At Google, Xception CNN has been created by Francois Chollet. It is an advancement
to the inception net; the changes are made in the structure by replacing the regular
inception module of the inception net by depth-wise separable convolutions [62]. It
has a parameter size close to that of the inception net, but it performs somewhat better
[63]. It consists of a combined layer containing 1×1, 3×3, and 5×5 convolution,
and it has 48 levels and hires an inception component. It is even known by the name
GoogLeNet [64]. It is shown in Fig. 5.

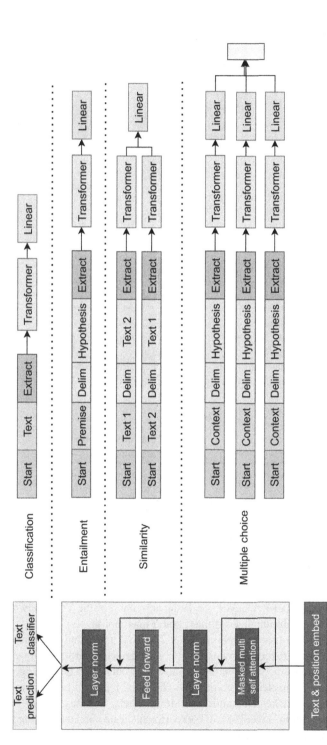

Fig. 4 Transfer learning using fine-tuning [61].

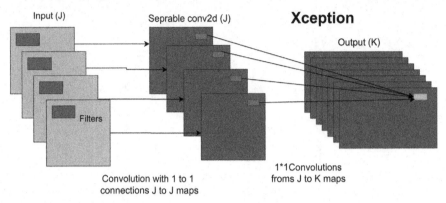

Fig. 5 Concept of Xception Net.

Table 3 CNN model parameter details.

Parameter	Value
Input shape	(224, 224, 3)
Weights	ImageNet
Optimizer	Adam
Loss function	Categorical_crossentropy
Activation function	Softmax
Epochs	60
Batch size	32
Dropout rate	0.5
Regularization	Batch_normalization
Pooling	Maxpooling2D

The experiments were conducted using the following parameters for Xception Net classification (Table 3).

3.4   VGG19 model

VGG is a deep CNN used for image classification. The Visual Geometry Group created it at Oxford in 2014. VGG19 is a 19-layer version of the VGG network (3 fully connected, 16 convolutional, 1 softmax, and 5 maxpool layers) [65].

The input to VGG-based CNN is a 224×224 RGB image that is preprocessed by a preprocessing layer. After preprocessing, they are passed to through the weight layers of the VGG19 model to 19 weight layers and 3 fully connected layers (Fig. 6). It comprises two fully connected layers of 4096 channels, followed by a completely connected 1000 channel layer to anticipate 1000 labels. Softmax feature is used for grouping by the last FC layer [65]. The experiments were conducted using the following parameters and architecture for VGG19 classification (Table 4 and Fig. 7).

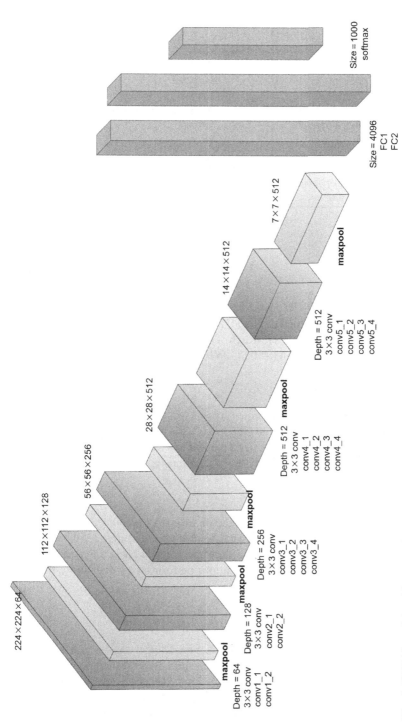

Fig. 6 VGG19 model architecture [65, 66].

Table 4 CNN model parameter details.

Parameter	Value
Input shape	(224, 224, 3)
Weights	ImageNet
Optimizer	Adam
Loss function	Categorical_crossentropy
Activation function	Softmax
Epochs	60
Batch size	32
Dropout rate	0.5
Regularization	Nil
Pooling	Maxpooling2D

4 Experiments

4.1 Dataset detail

The non-COVID and COVID instances of CT scan samples are included in this COVID-19 dataset [67]. A total of 5000 CT scan samples are utilized from the associated dataset for conducting this research. The dataset is divided into two subfolders of 2500 non-COVID images and 2500 COVID images.

4.2 Experimental setting

We use Python for the proposed model to analyze COVID-19 on a Windows 10 machine with an Intel Core i7-8700 CPU of a 3.20 GHz processor and RAM of 32 GB. First, we trained the models to extract the features. After that image classification was performed using different parameters in the transfer learning model.

4.3 Performance evaluation

Classifiers evaluate their performance based on precision, accuracy, recall, F1 score, accuracy, and area under the receiver operating characteristic curve (AUC). The measure shown by the confusion matrix is as shown in Table 5. These are used to retrieve the performance. The definitions of the various performance variables are shown in Table 6.

4.4 Experimental outcomes

We contrasted the experimental outcomes with other DL and transfer techniques, such as CNN, VGG19, and Xception Net, to assess the proposed DL model's efficiency. A comparison has been made based on accuracy, loss, AUC, F1 score, precision, recall, and confusion matrix. The proposed model VGG19 uses two classes, COVID and non-COVID. Figs. 8–10 show the accuracy and loss history of our model's test set

Layer (type)	Output Shape	Param #
input_1 (InputLayer)	[(None, 224, 224, 3)]	0
block1_conv1 (Conv2D)	(None, 224, 224, 64)	1792
block1_conv2 (Conv2D)	(None, 224, 224, 64)	36,928
block1_pool (MaxPooling2D)	(None, 112, 112, 64)	0
block2_conv1 (Conv2D)	(None, 112, 112, 128)	73,856
block2_conv2 (Conv2D)	(None, 112, 112, 128)	147,584
block2_pool (MaxPooling2D)	(None, 56, 56, 128)	0
block3_conv1 (Conv2D)	(None, 56, 56, 256)	295,168
block3_conv2 (Conv2D)	(None, 56, 56, 256)	590,080
block3_conv3 (Conv2D)	(None, 56, 56, 256)	590,080
block3_conv4 (Conv2D)	(None, 56, 56, 256)	590,080
block3_pool (MaxPooling2D)	(None, 28, 28, 256)	0
block4_conv1 (Conv2D)	(None, 28, 28, 512)	1,180,160
block4_conv2 (Conv2D)	(None, 28, 28, 512)	2,359,808
block4_conv3 (Conv2D)	(None, 28, 28, 512)	2,359,808
block4_conv4 (Conv2D)	(None, 28, 28, 512)	2,359,808
block4_pool (MaxPooling2D)	(None, 14, 14, 512)	0
block5_conv1 (Conv2D)	(None, 14, 14, 512)	2,359,808
block5_conv2 (Conv2D)	(None, 14, 14, 512)	2,359,808
block5_conv3 (Conv2D)	(None, 14, 14, 512)	2,359,808
block5_conv4 (Conv2D)	(None, 14, 14, 512)	2,359,808
block5_pool (MaxPooling2D)	(None, 7, 7, 512)	0
flatten (Flatten)	(None, 25088)	0
dropout (Dropout)	(None, 25088)	0
dense (Dense)	(None, 2)	50,178

Total params: 20,074,562
Trainable params: 50,178
Nontrainable params: 20,024,384

Fig. 7 Model architecture and configuration parameters.

Table 5 Confusion matrix.

		Actual value	
		Positive	Negative
Predicted value	Positive	True_Positive	False_Positive
	Negative	False_Negative	True_Negative

Table 6 Performance evaluation measures.

Matric name	Definition
Accuracy	$Accuracy = \dfrac{True\_Pos + True\_Neg}{True\_Pos + True\_Neg + False\_Pos + False\_Neg}$
Precision (P)	$Precision = \dfrac{True\_Pos}{True\_Pos + False\_Pos}$
Recall (R)	$Recall = \dfrac{True\_Pos}{True\_Pos + False\_Neg}$
F1 measure	$F1 - Measure = \dfrac{2*P*R}{P + R}$
AUC	$AUC = \left(R - \dfrac{False\_Pos}{False\_Pos + True\_Neg} + 1 \right) \Big/ 2$

after each training epoch. The flow of the plot that represents accuracy is saturated very soon when the loss function comes to a minimum local level and is steadily increasing as the learning rate decreases.

Our model's confusion matrix is seen in Tables 7–9. The model's classification labels are represented on the x-axis while the input image labels are represented on the y-axis.

The proposed model using VGG19 architecture is compared with the recent state of the art in terms of efficiency shown in Fig. 11. Table 10 displays the outcomes of three models in the COVID-19 CT scan image dataset. Overall, the quantitative findings among all six assessment metrics, including accuracy, precision, recall, F1 score, AUC, and loss, strongly showed that the suggested method outperforms existing approaches of COVID analysis. In particular, VGG19 can achieve an accuracy of 95% with a loss of 17%. Tables 7 and 8 show that our proposed model has marginally higher accuracy and lower loss, which means that the introduced model can accurately classify the images.

Overall, the quantitative findings show that VGG19 outperforms CNN and Xception Net in all six measurement criteria. Fig. 11 compares our approach to existing methods in terms of efficiency. CNN obtained a loss of 72% and an accuracy of 93%. Xception Net obtained a loss of 85% and an accuracy of 93%. Our proposed model has 17% loss and 95% accuracy and performs better than other models.

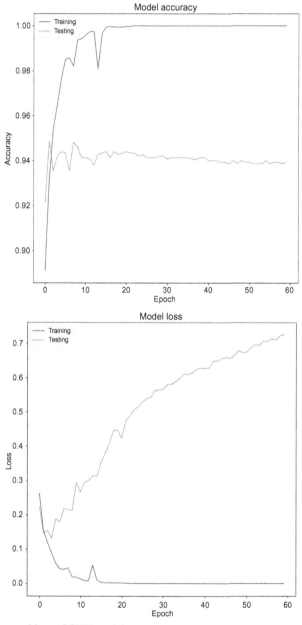

Fig. 8 Accuracy and loss of CNN model.

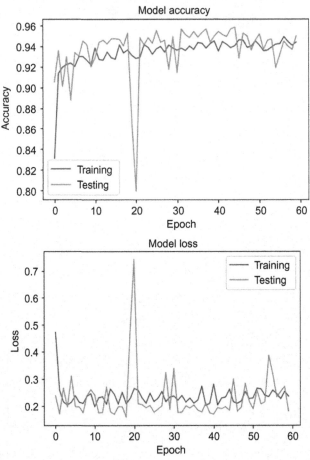

Fig. 9 Accuracy and loss of VGG19 model.

5   Conclusions

In our healthcare system, AI, DL, and blockchain approaches are all vital. They give a user-friendly and efficient automated system for maintaining health. COVID-19 identification and analysis using cutting-edge computational tools are the focuses of this chapter. We also employed the transfer learning concept to improve the predicted outcomes in this chapter. For COVID-19 detection and analysis, a transfer learning-based VGG19 pretrained model was used. A CT scan image dataset was used to assess the efficacy of the VGG19 model. Following a series of tests, it was discovered that the more convolution layers, a strong dropout, a high batch size, and a large number of epochs, the better the accuracy. The VGG19 model's findings were compared to the CNN and Xception Net models, and it was discovered that the VGG19 model outperforms the other two. The VGG19 model is based on a transfer learning technique

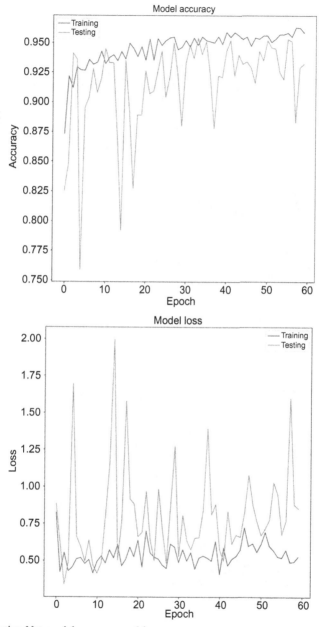

Fig. 10 Xception Net model accuracy and loss.

Table 7 The confusion matrix of the CNN model.

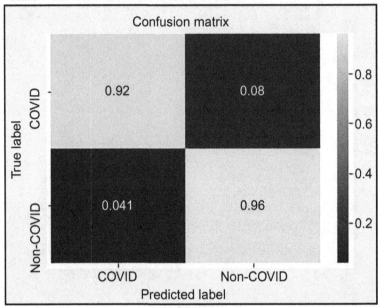

Table 8 The confusion matrix of the VGG19 model.

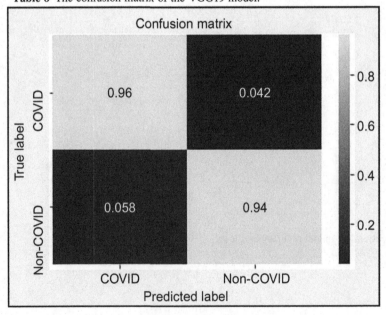

Table 9 The confusion matrix of the Xception Net model.

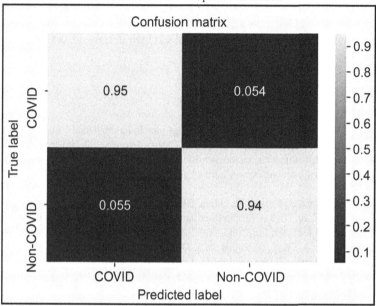

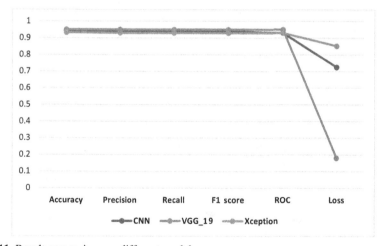

Fig. 11 Result comparison on different models.

Table 10 The performance comparison.

	Accuracy	Precision	Recall	F1 score	AUC	Loss
CNN	0.9393	0.94	0.94	0.94	0.93	0.7247
VGG19	0.9500	0.95	0.95	0.95	0.95	0.1797
Xception	0.9319	0.93	0.93	0.93	0.93	0.8525

that may be used in various domains. Blockchain architectures have several advantages over traditional systems, including seamless connectivity, faster data transfer, incident management, tracking, cost effectiveness, quick data access, and data security. We may combine DL-based models with blockchain designs in the future to increase the efficiency of healthcare systems.

References

[1] T. Sunder, Point of care healthcare technology in India-challenges and journey ahead: a clinician's perspective, IEEE Life Sci. (2013). (Accessed 2 November 2020. Available online: https://lifesciences.ieee.org/lifesciences-newsletter/2013/january-2013/point-of-care-healthcare-technology-in-india-challenges-and-journey-ahead-a-clinician-sperspective/.

[2] J. Hathaliya, P. Sharma, S. Tanwar, R. Gupta, Blockchain-based remote patient monitoring in Healthcare 4.0, in: 2019 IEEE 9th International Conference on Advanced Computing (IACC), 2019, pp. 87–91, https://doi.org/10.1109/IACC48062.2019.8971593.

[3] R. Gupta, S. Tanwar, S. Tyagi, N. Kumar, M.S. Obaidat, B. Sadoun, HaBiTs: blockchain-based telesurgery framework for Healthcare 4.0, in: 2019 International Conference on Computer, Information and Telecommunication Systems (CITS), 2019, pp. 1–5, https://doi.org/10.1109/CITS.2019.8862127.

[4] S. Tanwar, K. Parekh, R. Evans, Blockchain-based electronic healthcare record system for Healthcare 4.0 applications, J. Inf. Secur. Appl. 50 (2020) 102407, https://doi.org/10.1016/j.jisa.2019.102407.

[5] P. Bhattacharya, S. Tanwar, U. Bodke, S. Tyagi, N. Kumar, BinDaaS: blockchain-based deep-learning as-a-service in Healthcare 4.0 applications, IEEE Trans. Netw. Sci. Eng. (2019), https://doi.org/10.1109/TNSE.2019.2961932.

[6] R. Gupta, A. Shukla, S. Tanwar, AaYusH: a smart contract-based telesurgery system for Healthcare 4.0, in: 2020 IEEE International Conference on Communications Workshops (ICC Workshops), 2020, pp. 1–6, https://doi.org/10.1109/ICCWorkshops49005.2020.9145044.

[7] R. Gupta, A. Kumari, S. Tanwar, Fusion of blockchain and artificial intelligence for secure drone networking underlying 5G communications, Trans. Emerg. Telecommun. Technol. 32 (1) (2021) e4176.

[8] R. Gupta, A. Shukla, P. Mehta, P. Bhattacharya, S. Tanwar, S. Tyagi, N. Kumar, VAHAK: a blockchain-based outdoor delivery scheme using UAV for Healthcare 4.0 services, in: IEEE INFOCOM 2020—IEEE Conference on Computer Communications Workshops (INFOCOM WKSHPS), 2020, pp. 255–260, https://doi.org/10.1109/INFOCOMWKSHPS 50562.2020.9162738.

[9] J.J. Hathaliya, S. Tanwar, S. Tyagi, N. Kumar, Securing electronics healthcare records in Healthcare 4.0: a biometric-based approach, Comput. Electr. Eng. 76 (2019) 398–410, https://doi.org/10.1016/j.compeleceng.2019.04.017.

[10] D. Mehta, S. Tanwar, U. Bodkhe, A. Shukla, N. Kumar, Blockchain-based royalty contract transactions scheme for Industry 4.0 supply-chain management, Inf. Process. Manag. 58 (4) (2021) 102586, https://doi.org/10.1016/j.ipm.2021.102586.

[11] A. Manirabona, L.C. Fourati, A 4-tiers architecture for mobile WBAN based health remote monitoring system, Wirel. Netw. 24 (6) (2018) 2179–2190.

[12] H.J. Koo, S. Lim, J. Choe, S.-H. Choi, H. Sung, K.-H. Do, Radiographic and CT features of viral pneumonia, Radiographics 38 (3) (2018) 719–739.

[13] L. Li, L. Qin, Z. Xu, Y. Yin, X. Wang, B. Kong, J. Bai, Y. Lu, Z. Fang, Q. Song, Artificial intelligence distinguishes COVID-19 from community acquired pneumonia on chest CT, Radiology 296 (2) (2020) E65–E71.

[14] D.M. Hansell, A.A. Bankier, H. MacMahon, T.C. McLoud, N.L. Muller, J. Remy, Fleischner society: glossary of terms for thoracic imaging, Radiology 246 (3) (2008) 697–722.

[15] A. Narin, C. Kaya, Z. Pamuk, Automatic detection of coronavirus disease (COVID-19) using X-ray images and deep convolutional neural networks, Pattern Anal. Appl. 24 (3) (2021) 1207–1220.

[16] I.D. Apostolopoulos, T.A. Mpesiana, COVID-19: automatic detection from X-ray images utilizing transfer learning with convolutional neural networks, Phys. Eng. Sci. Med. 43 (2) (2020) 635–640.

[17] S. Wang, B. Kang, J. Ma, X. Zeng, M. Xiao, J. Guo, M. Cai, J. Yang, Y. Li, X. Meng, A deep learning algorithm using CT images to screen for corona virus disease (COVID-19), Eur. Radiol. 31 (8) (2021) 6096–6104.

[18] A.M. Ajlan, R.A. Ahyad, L.G. Jamjoom, A. Alharthy, T.A. Madani, Middle East respiratory syndrome coronavirus (MERS-CoV) infection: chest CT findings, Am. J. Roentgenol. 203 (4) (2014) 782–787.

[19] J.P. Kanne, Chest CT Findings in 2019 Novel Coronavirus (2019-nCoV) Infections From Wuhan, China: Key Points for the Radiologist, Radiological Society of North America, 2020.

[20] R. Gupta, S. Tanwar, F. Al-Turjman, P. Italiya, A. Nauman, S.W. Kim, Smart contract privacy protection using AI in cyber-physical systems: tools, techniques and challenges, IEEE Access 8 (2020) 24746–24772, https://doi.org/10.1109/ACCESS.2020.2970576.

[21] J.J. Hathaliya, S. Tanwar, An exhaustive survey on security and privacy issues in Healthcare 4.0, Comput. Commun. 153 (2020) 311–335, https://doi.org/10.1016/j.comcom.2020.02.018.

[22] D. Vekaria, A. Kumari, S. Tanwar, N. Kumar, ξboost: an AI-based data analytics scheme for COVID-19 prediction and economy boosting, IEEE Internet Things J. (2020), https://doi.org/10.1109/JIOT.2020.3047539.

[23] A. Shukla, N. Patel, S. Tanwar, B. Sadoun, M.S. Obaidat, BDoTs: blockchain-based evaluation scheme for online teaching under COVID-19 environment, in: 2020 International Conference on Computer, Information and Telecommunication Systems (CITS), 2020, pp. 1–5, https://doi.org/10.1109/CITS49457.2020.9232480.

[24] R. Gupta, A. Kumari, S. Tanwar, N. Kumar, Blockchain-envisioned softwarized multi-swarming UAVs to tackle COVID-I9 situations, IEEE Netw. 35 (2) (2021) 160–167, https://doi.org/10.1109/MNET.011.2000439.

[25] R. Gupta, U. Thakker, S. Tanwar, M.S. Obaidat, K.-F. Hsiao, BITS: a blockchain-driven intelligent scheme for telesurgery system, in: 2020 International Conference on Computer, Information and Telecommunication Systems (CITS), 2020, pp. 1–5, https://doi.org/10.1109/CITS49457.2020.9232662.

[26] U. Bodkhe, D. Mehta, S. Tanwar, P. Bhattacharya, P.K. Singh, W.-C. Hong, A survey on decentralized consensus mechanisms for cyber physical systems, IEEE Access 8 (2020) 54371–54401, https://doi.org/10.1109/ACCESS.2020.2981415.

[27] A. Kumari, S. Tanwar, A secure data analytics scheme for multimedia communication in a decentralized smart grid, Multimed. Tools Appl. (2021), https://doi.org/10.1007/s11042-021-10512-z.

[28] M.J. Horry, S. Chakraborty, M. Paul, A. Ulhaq, B. Pradhan, M. Saha, N. Shukla, COVID-19 detection through transfer learning using multimodal imaging data, IEEE Access 8 (2020) 149808–149824.

[29] P. Afshar, S. Heidarian, F. Naderkhani, A. Oikonomou, K.N. Plataniotis, A. Mohammadi, COVID-caps: a capsule network-based framework for identification of COVID-19 cases from X-ray images, Pattern Recogn. Lett. 138 (2020) 638–643.

[30] M.E.H. Chowdhury, T. Rahman, A. Khandakar, R. Mazhar, M.A. Kadir, Z.B. Mahbub, K. R. Islam, M.S. Khan, A. Iqbal, N. Al Emadi, Can AI help in screening viral and COVID-19 pneumonia? IEEE Access 8 (2020) 132665–132676.

[31] A.M. Alqudah, S. Qazan, A. Alqudah, Automated systems for detection of COVID-19 using chest X-ray images and lightweight convolutional neural networks, 2020, https://doi.org/10.21203/rs.3.rs-24305/v1.

[32] W.J. Choi, K.-N. Lee, E.-J. Kang, H. Lee, Middle East respiratory syndrome-coronavirus infection: a case report of serial computed tomographic findings in a young male patient, Korean J. Radiol. 17 (1) (2016) 166.

[33] E. Ayan, H.M. Ünver, Diagnosis of pneumonia from chest X-ray images using deep learning, in: 2019 Scientific Meeting on Electrical-Electronics Biomedical Engineering and Computer Science (EBBT), 2019, pp. 1–5, https://doi.org/10.1109/EBBT.2019.8741582.

[34] C. Basile, C. Combe, F. Pizzarelli, A. Covic, A. Davenport, M. Kanbay, D. Kirmizis, D. Schneditz, F. Van Der Sande, S. Mitra, Recommendations for the prevention, mitigation and containment of the emerging SARS-CoV-2 (COVID-19) pandemic in haemodialysis centres, Nephrol. Dial. Transplant. 35 (5) (2020) 737–741.

[35] I.I. Bogoch, A. Watts, A. Thomas-Bachli, C. Huber, M.U.G. Kraemer, K. Khan, Pneumonia of unknown aetiology in Wuhan, China: potential for international spread via commercial air travel, J. Travel Med. 27 (2) (2020), https://doi.org/10.1093/jtm/taaa008.

[36] Y.-H. Chan, Y.-Z. Zeng, H.-C. Wu, M.-C. Wu, H.-M. Sun, Effective pneumothorax detection for chest X-ray images using local binary pattern and support vector machine, J. Healthc. Eng. 2018 (2018) 2908517, https://doi.org/10.1155/2018/2908517.

[37] M. Chung, A. Bernheim, X. Mei, N. Zhang, M. Huang, X. Zeng, J. Cui, W. Xu, Y. Yang, Z. A. Fayad, CT imaging features of 2019 novel coronavirus (2019-nCoV), Radiology 295 (1) (2020) 202–207.

[38] J.P. Cohen, P. Morrison, L. Dao, K. Roth, T.Q. Duong, M. Ghassemi, COVID-19 image data collection: prospective predictions are the future, arXiv:2006.11988, 2020.

[39] B. Diao, Z. Feng, C. Wang, H. Wang, L. Liu, C. Wang, R. Wang, Y. Liu, Y. Liu, G. Wang, Human kidney is a target for novel severe acute respiratory syndrome coronavirus 2 (SARS-CoV-2) infection, MedRxiv 12 (1) (2020) 1–9.

[40] S. Fu, X. Fu, Y. Song, M. Li, P.-H. Pan, T. Tang, C. Zhang, T. Jiang, D. Tan, X. Fan, Virologic and clinical characteristics for prognosis of severe COVID-19: a retrospective observational study in Wuhan, China, medRxiv (2020), https://doi.org/10.1101/2020.04.03.20051763.

[41] A.E. Hassanien, L.N. Mahdy, K.A. Ezzat, H.H. Elmousalami, H.A. Ella, Automatic X-ray COVID-19 lung image classification system based on multi-level thresholding and support vector machine, medRxiv (2020), https://doi.org/10.1101/2020.03.30.20047787.

[42] H.S. Maghdid, A.T. Asaad, K.Z. Ghafoor, A.S. Sadiq, M.K. Khan, Diagnosing COVID-19 pneumonia from X-ray and CT images using deep learning and transfer learning algorithms, arXiv Preprint arXiv:2004.00038 11734 (2020) 99–110.

[43] S.S. Thejeshwar, C. Chokkareddy, K. Eswaran, Precise prediction of COVID-19 in chest X-ray images using KE Sieve algorithm, medRxiv (2020), https://doi.org/10.1101/2020.08.13.20174144.

[44] R. Jain, M. Gupta, S. Taneja, D.J. Hemanth, Deep learning based detection and analysis of COVID-19 on chest X-ray images, Appl. Intell. 51 (3) (2021) 1690–1700, https://doi.org/10.1007/s10489-020-01902-1.

[45] A.M. Ismael, A. Şengür, Deep learning approaches for COVID-19 detection based on chest X-ray images, Expert Syst. Appl. 164 (2021) 114054, https://doi.org/10.1016/j. eswa.2020.114054.

[46] Y. Song, S. Zheng, L. Li, X. Zhang, X. Zhang, Z. Huang, J. Chen, R. Wang, H. Zhao, Y. Zha, J. Shen, Y. Chong, Y. Yang, Deep learning enables accurate diagnosis of novel coronavirus (COVID-19) with CT images, IEEE/ACM Trans. Comput. Biol. Bioinf. (2021), https://doi.org/10.1109/TCBB.2021.3065361.

[47] S. Wang, B. Kang, J. Ma, X. Zeng, M. Xiao, J. Guo, M. Cai, J. Yang, Y. Li, X. Meng, B. Xu, A deep learning algorithm using CT images to screen for Corona virus disease (COVID-19), Eur. Radiol. (2021), https://doi.org/10.1007/s00330-021-07715-1.

[48] R.T.J. Hassani, O. Sandali, The novel coronavirus COVID-19: what are the ophthalmic risks? J. Fr. D'ophtalmol. 43 (4) (2020) 291–293, https://doi.org/10.1016/j. jfo.2020.02.001.

[49] E.E.-D. Hemdan, M.A. Shouman, M.E. Karar, Covidx-net: a framework of deep learning classifiers to diagnose COVID-19 in X-ray images, arXiv Preprint arXiv:2003.11055 (2020).

[50] M. Ilyas, H. Rehman, A. Nait-ali, Detection of COVID-19 from chest X-ray images using artificial intelligence: an early review, arXiv Preprint arXiv:2004.05436, 2020.

[51] A. Jacobi, M. Chung, A. Bernheim, C. Eber, Portable chest X-ray in coronavirus disease-19 (COVID-19): a pictorial review, Clin. Imaging 64 (2020) 35–42.

[52] U. Özkaya, Ş. Öztürk, M. Barstugan, Coronavirus (COVID-19) classification using deep features fusion and ranking technique, in: Big Data Analytics and Artificial Intelligence Against COVID-19: Innovation Vision and Approach, Springer, 2020, pp. 281–295.

[53] A. Krizhevsky, I. Sutskever, G.E. Hinton, Imagenet classification with deep convolutional neural networks, Adv. Neural Inf. Process. Syst. 25 (2012) 1097–1105.

[54] F. Chollet, Deep Learning With Python, Simon and Schuster, 2017.

[55] J. Wu, Introduction to convolutional neural networks, 5, National Key Lab for Novel Software Technology. Nanjing University, China, 2017, p. 23.

[56] D. Suryani, P. Doetsch, H. Ney, On the benefits of convolutional neural network combinations in offline handwriting recognition, in: 2016 15th International Conference on Frontiers in Handwriting Recognition (ICFHR), IEEE, 2016, pp. 193–198.

[57] R. Yamashita, M. Nishio, R.K.G. Do, K. Togashi, Convolutional neural networks: an overview and application in radiology, Insights Imaging 9 (4) (2018) 611–629.

[58] M. Koziarski, B. Cyganek, Image recognition with deep neural networks in presence of noise-dealing with and taking advantage of distortions, Integr. Comput. Aided Eng. 24 (4) (2017) 337–349.

[59] A.-A. Nahid, N. Sikder, A.K. Bairagi, M. Razzaque, M. Masud, A.Z. Kouzani, M. Mahmud, A novel method to identify pneumonia through analyzing chest radiographs employing a multichannel convolutional neural network, Sensors 20 (12) (2020) 3482.

[60] M.J. Horry, S. Chakraborty, M. Paul, A. Ulhaq, B. Pradhan, M. Saha, N. Shukla, COVID-19 detection through transfer learning using multimodal imaging data, IEEE Access 8 (2020) 149808–149824.

[61] A. Radford, K. Narasimhan, T. Salimans, I. Sutskever, Improving language understanding by generative pre-training, 2018.

[62] F. Chollet, Xception: deep learning with depthwise separable convolutions, in: Proceedings of the IEEE Conference on Computer Vision and Pattern Recognition, 2017, pp. 1251–1258.

[63] J. Ker, L. Wang, J. Rao, T. Lim, Deep learning applications in medical image analysis, IEEE Access 6 (2017) 9375–9389.

[64] M.A. Elaziz, K.M. Hosny, A. Salah, M.M. Darwish, S. Lu, A.T. Sahlol, New machine learning method for image-based diagnosis of COVID-19, PLoS One 15 (6) (2020) e0235187.

[65] K. Simonyan, A. Zisserman, Very deep convolutional networks for large-scale image recognition, arXiv Preprint arXiv:1409.1556 (2014).

[66] M. Ferguson, R. Ak, Y.-T.T. Lee, K.H. Law, Automatic localization of casting defects with convolutional neural networks, in: 2017 IEEE International Conference on Big Data (Big Data), 2017, pp. 1726–1735, https://doi.org/10.1109/BigData.2017.8258115.

[67] W. El-Shafai, F. Abd El-Samie, Extensive COVID-19 X-ray and CT chest images dataset, Mendeley Data v3 10 (2020), https://doi.org/10.17632/8h65ywd2jr.3.

Blockchain for 5G-enabled networks in healthcare service based on several aspects

Garima Jain[a] and Ankush Jain[b]
[a]Department of Computer Science and Engineering, Noida Institute of Engineering and Technology, Greater Noida, India, [b]School of Computer Science Engineering and Technology, Bennett University, Greater Noida, India

1 Introduction

The advancement in healthcare diagnosis and healthcare practitioners' uses cutting-edge technologies. Fig. 1 explains the characteristics of 5G. The healthcare industry has undergone several transitions from Healthcare 1.0 to Healthcare 4.0. Healthcare 1.0 is more physician-centric with structural flexibility to keep manual records of their patient's medical histories. However, in Healthcare 2.0, these manual records were gradually supplanted by digital records. Wearable devices were used for the real-time monitoring of patient healthcare history in Healthcare 3.0 [1]. With resources lacking, the healthcare systems were constrained and not integrated with computer data throughout this time. On the other hand, biomedical machines had not yet been invented so were not integrated with networked electronic equipment. Paper-based medications and reporting were commonly employed in healthcare organizations during this time, resulting in higher costs and time [2, 3].

Electronic health records (EHRs) must frequently be exchanged across healthcare organizations, medical and pharmaceutical companies, pharmacies, health coverage organizations, researchers, and patients to deliver appropriate healthcare. This creates a significant problem in maintaining the security and accuracy of the patients' sensitive data. During treatment, a patient may be transported to/from other hospitals. According to the US Department of Health and Human Services [4], a patient in such a case owns the right to their medical information and may need to set access control limits. Blockchain technology is a distributed database that is replicated across multiple servers in the network. We cannot modify it because the data are kept in independent blocks. As a result, the blockchain can boost privacy, visibility, and confidence.

The authors of Ref. [5] believe that the blockchain applications in healthcare have full potential for manage the process, facilitating research, and installing EHRs after analyzing the economic effect of technology by examining the scalability and impact of use cases in various industries. Due to its decentralized nature and supposed immutability, blockchain can tackle data management concerns in the healthcare business.

Blockchain Applications for Healthcare Informatics. https://doi.org/10.1016/B978-0-323-90615-9.00018-9
Copyright © 2022 Elsevier Inc. All rights reserved.

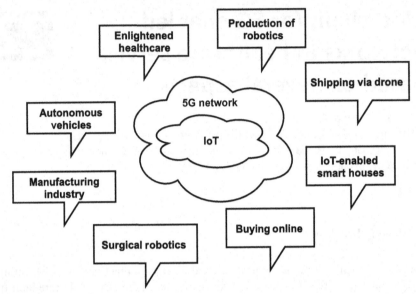

Fig. 1 Characteristics of 5G.

The system could simplify data sharing among numerous actors, improve effectiveness and efficiency, and provide anonymized academic file sharing [6].

With multiple taxonomies, this chapter will describe the leading technology and products for 5G security. It will detail a variety of attacks that have been detected in the 5G network as well as provide solutions. It examines whether we can use blockchain technology to transform our present healthcare system. Diverse healthcare participants (providers, users, patients, suppliers, producers, and academic institutions) play varied roles and have different requirements in the industry. This chapter aims to provide a deeper understanding by identifying the limitations of blockchain technology in the health field and determining the potential scope for blockchain for all health participants in a scientific test [7].

As far as healthcare is concerned, the urgency of development increases to more incredible speeds. The absence of systematic research on the topic and the separation of practice and academia make a detailed analysis of the new technologies' consequences for the healthcare sector difficult. By bringing study and practice together, both viewpoints may gain a better knowledge of critical issues. Reduced energy usage, lower latency, artificial intelligence (AI)-assisted programs, multimedia capability with AR/VR, increased security, and high data transmission rates are just a few of the benefits of 5G technology [7].

1.1 Motivation

As a result of the first stage of a comprehensive literature review, the following research objectives were generated to fill in the gaps, as shown in Table 1.

Table 1 Motivation and corresponding research objectives.

S. no.	Research question	Motivation
1	One of the most immediate issues among health professionals?	The goal is to bring attention to important challenges that are impeding the economic progress of the health sector.
2	How many blockchain features are being used to address the concerns that have been recognized?	The goal is to look into developing technology that helps to address problems and advance the area.
3	What are all the hurdles and difficulties with implementing blockchain?	The goal is to identify any concerns with blockchain deployment that have yet to be resolved.

1.2 Contribution

The following are the chapter's significant contributions:

- While the qualities of blockchain are appropriate for building a health service, these techniques are nonetheless costly in terms of runtime and data sent for record updates.
- Despite these costly methods, the blockchain paradigm can yield remarkable results, particularly in a measured approach. In this technique, patients and clinicians visit health records regularly to create a unified view from several hospitals for proper treatment or prediction of disorders using AI.

1.3 Structure of chapter

The rest of the chapter is organized as follows. The first section introduces technology and its role in the healthcare industry with contributions and research motivation. Section 2 delves into the characteristics of blockchain, including its features, architecture, and operation. The research approach in the healthcare system is described in Section 3. The implementation of 5G technology in the healthcare sector is summarized in Section 4. Section 5 discusses the likelihood of 5G in the blockchain. Section 6 explains how to use blockchain in healthcare records. Section 7 combines blockchain technology with the healthcare system. Section 8 ensures that blockchain technology in EHR is kept private and secure. Finally, Section 9 concludes the chapter.

2 Blockchain

The name "blockchain" was derived from the terms "chain" of "blocks" containing information, where the transactions made on a network are represented by a "block" and a string of blocks by a "chain" [8]. A blockchain is a decentralized, distributed, and public digital ledger. It is jointly maintained by multiple parties, using cryptography to ensure the security of transmission and access, achieve data storage consistency, make data tamper-proof, and prevent repudiation. It is also known as distributed ledger technology (DLT).

2.1   Characteristics of blockchain

The blockchain has the following properties compared to regular data duplication: First, there is the transition from double entry to distributed accounting [9]. Each accountant records independently in a typical information system, and each reconciling involves numerous different ledgers. Second, "insertion, deletion, selection, and update" has been replaced with "insertion and selection." Third, the management shifts from unilateral to multilateral. Fig. 2 classifies the architecture of blockchain.

In a blockchain, every block comprises data, a hash of the current block, and a hash of the preceding block.

- *Data*: The type of blockchain determines the data stored. For example, the data maintained on a Bitcoin blockchain include information about the transaction, such as "sender," "receiver," and "amount."
- *Hash*: Each block in a blockchain includes a hash, which is similar to a finger print. It uniquely recognizes the block with all its data. When a block is formed, a hash is generated, and changes to the league will cause the hash value to change.
- *Preceding block's hash*: Every transaction also comprises the preceding block hash, producing a blockchain network with every block pointing to the previous block [10]. Finally, a plug-in contract transforms into a built-in contract. Historically, the financial capital flow and administrative flow of information were two distinct aspects of a commercial organization. Bitcoin is a new sort of peer-to-peer digital currency first proposed in a paper published in 2008 by the enigmatic and anonymous inventor Satoshi Nakamoto, whose true name is unknown, with speculation that the moniker refers to a group of developers rather than a single individual. With crypto algorithms, a digital currency was created that could be

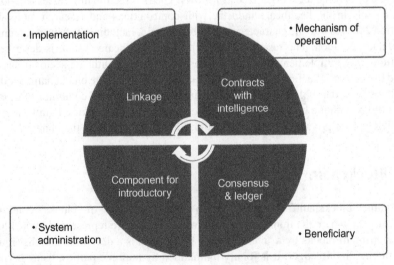

Fig. 2 Blockchain architecture.

utilized without any intermediaries or regulating authorities, allowing money to travel from one person to another without the need for a bank or other third-party middleman. Fig. 3 depicts the scenario of blockchain technology.

2.2 Working of blockchain technology

2.2.1 Technologies involved in blockchain cryptography

The workings of blockchain are complicated by several technologies, one of the most essential of which is cryptography, which uses public and private keys. The word "cryptography" comes from the Greek words "kryptos" (hidden) and "graphein" (writing). Cryptography is the art of writing in secret. It is a method of conveying a message from one person to another without allowing unwanted individuals access.

The public-key cryptography is one of the most popular technique among the various types of cryptography techniques. It consists of two keys: a "public key" and a "private key." Everyone can see the public key, but only the user who owns it can view the private key, which must be kept hidden [11, 12].

Fig. 4 depicts the working of a digital signature. In cryptography, the first stage is developing a private key, which is essentially a unique combination of letters (A through F) and integers. When a private key is generated, a sophisticated computational method is used to create its pair, known as the public key. The technological equivalent of the wax seal and stamp is a digital signature. The digital signatures are created using public and private key pairs [13]. The sender's private key is used to sign electronic communication before it is sent. Because the receiver knows the sender's public key, the recipient certifies that the sender's private key pair created the signature.

Nonce: A number that is used only once with a particular purpose and then is never used again is known as a once. One of its main applications is digital communication, which helps to avoid repeated operation that can be quite harmful and have bad repercussions.

Ledger: The ledger layer is in charge of the cryptocurrency system's storing information, which involves collecting user information, producing data blocks for local storage validity, and forwarding the patterned block to the blockchain. The ledger layer creates a blockchain data structure by embedding the preceding block's hashing into another block, ensuring the integrity of data and validity.

Consensus: The consensus layer is responsible for managing and ensuring the 10 Blockchain White Paper (2018) consistency of all end points in the data records of the channel. In blockchain technology, each node stores data independently. With the use of the consensus technique, the consensus layer synchronizes the books of each network, allowing it to execute functions such as node election, data integrity validation, and modern networking control.

Smart contract: The smart contract system is also responsible for constructing, installing, and executing the business processes of the blockchain network utilizing code as well as conditional triggers and automatic implementation of the established rules to reduce physical contribution.

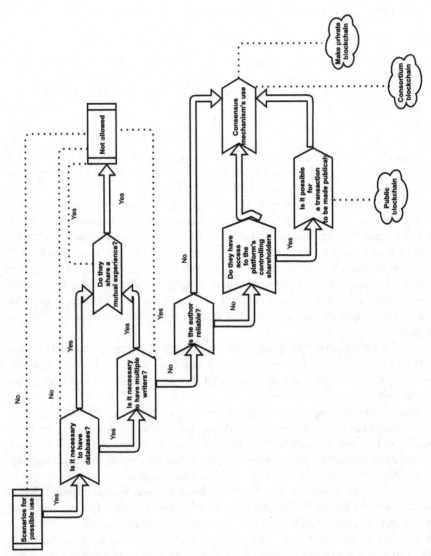

Fig. 3 Blockchain scenarios.

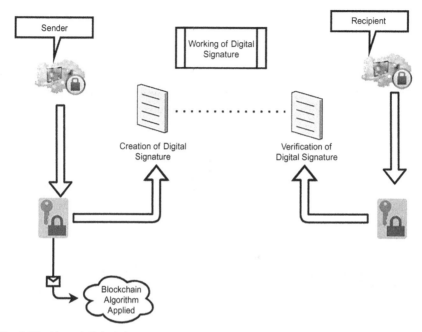

Fig. 4 Working of digital signature.

Interface layer: The major goal of the interface layer is to complete the encapsulating of opportunities for integration and provide a simple call to the application level. The remote procedure call (RPC) protocol is used to communicate with external networks at the application level, while the software development kit (SDK) toolbox is used to access and alter the private ledger data.

Application layer: The application layer is the part that the user sees in the end. The smart contract layer is called the primary purpose. The interface adjusts to numerous blockchain application scenarios to give consumers a variety of services and applications.

3 Healthcare system

Healthcare information needs to be more safe and private. Modification and destruction of stored data must be prohibited for this data. If an unauthorized individual has access to the data, it will be sold or misused. Because the amount of health records will grow due to 5G networks, security mechanisms to protect the data must also increase [14–16]. The field of healthcare encompasses a diversified set of tasks and procedures, and as a consequence, it confronts a wide range of issues. This review examines the difficulties that can be addressed by the literature through information technology, particularly blockchain. A healthcare scheme is a method of arranging healthcare in terms of finances, security, accessibility, data management, and retrieving.

Healthcare is the most critical factor in a country's overall development as it provides medical care to people worldwide to live healthy and prosperous lives.

As a result, as technology has advanced, the healthcare business has altered drastically. A healthcare system is based on accessible properties and public demands. Every patient's EHR could include critical information such as the patient's overall health, administrative data, and official papers. There has been significant progress in several fields of health, including telehealth, telesurgery, data collection, and diagnosis of illnesses.

3.1 Definition of healthcare

It is crucial to define the scope of the term "healthcare" to comprehend the context in which private blockchains can be applied. As stated earlier, several journals and definitions distinguish between the terms "health care" and "healthcare" as well as other terms such as "health system" and "healthcare business." Healthcare is a critical aspect in determining a region's or country's standard of living. The health sector is a collection of industries within the economy that provides services and products for the medicinal, preventative, curative, rehabilitative, and palliative care of patients [17].

4 5G in healthcare

This section highlights the clinical potential of 5G technology by presenting several clinically relevant use cases for 5G applications [18]. We will divide them into user groups and applications to standardize use cases and then identify the related goals and objectives, requirements, and timelines. Patients and caregivers, such as doctors, nurses, psychologists, companies, legislators, and legal organizations, are among the various users. The COVID-19 crisis exposed a vulnerability in many healthcare providers' processes, including hospitals and local/regional health authorities, which found themselves in the middle of the flood [19–21].

4.1 Need of 5G for future healthcare

Traditional healthcare systems are undergoing vast and ever-accelerating transformations. Enhanced or potentially developing information and communications technology (ICT) are driving these shifts.

More importantly, this technology suggests how 5G networks can evolve and enhance all the essential aspects of health insurance, a topic that is particularly relevant today given the propagation of the coronavirus, which has put immense strain on healthcare systems all over the world.

On multiple levels, the evolution of healthcare will occur in lockstep. In the start phase, the patient-care perspective evolves from the patient and illness to a decentralized physician healthcare setting, which is also overcoming healthcare providers' sector-specific barriers. Second, wellness data analysis results and treatment shift from inter-institutional to regional availability. In addition, health management is evolving from a broad and basic approach to one that introduces to individual patient. Furthermore, the emphasis of healthcare systems is shifting away from cancer therapy and toward preventive care. 5G can achieve speeds that are 100 times faster than 4G, while also handling many more users [22]. These benefits are shown by ultralow delays, the time it takes for a request to be processed by the network. This novel strategy, known as "4P" medicine (personalized, preventative, predictive, and participatory), necessitates the development of breakthrough technology to provide additional value to patients. Advanced digitalization concepts and virtualization methods will be among these technologies based on principles adopted from Industry 4.0 standards. In turn, to support new health, both will heavily rely on sophisticated data transmission abilities, including those provided by 5G technology.

4.2 Cutting costs for the provision of health services

By delivering dispersed physician care, decentralized healthcare services remote from facilities yet individualized and instantaneously available everywhere, information technology can continue to lower costs in the health domain. Another goal is to improve consistency and reliability by increasing the complexity of patient data and enhancing the products and service levels. 5G also enables a shift toward digitalization of treatments, allowing for individualized and designed treatments in hospitals to be delivered in nursing homes or elsewhere. This finding increases the chances of extra payments, while also improving the lives of patients and families.

5 5G security with blockchain

Blockchain is a term used in 5G security to describe novel and transformational technologies that verify and authenticate transactions, preserve information, and manage identities across multiple entities in a decentralized and secure manner [23, 24]. From existing literature, it seems that there is a breakthrough for future communication technologies in 5G. To ensure security in a 5G network, blockchain, a peer-to-peer decentralized database technology for storing distributed ledgers connected in chains, has many qualities: decentralizing, distributing, and others. Because it is a decentralized and spreading technology, it needs numerous applications such as smart health, innovative finances, supply chain management, and driverless cars [25]. Combining 5G with a blockchain system can significantly increase the economic value of data sharing. Because of the strength of 5G coverage enabled by blockchains, delay, fast throughput, and bandwidth have decreased, allowing IoT devices to be widely used. At the same time, these devices can use blockchain technology as a foundation layer to benefit from its security, decentralization, integrity, and agreement mediation. While most IoT transactions and contracts occur on the network layer, blockchain can provide consensus and protection, with the ability to settle account management and transactional issues on a chain. 5G will immediately benefit blockchain technology by expanding node involvement and decentralization and lowering block times, on-chain scaling, and IoT economy support. Blockchain technology allows many parties to share, transmit, and access data safely. The essential information is transferred to all parties via a distributed ledger in the blockchain. As a result, in the 5G network, blockchain technology delivers more security characteristics. In a transportation application, blockchain provides a secure data access system that allows relevant external bus transportation participants in the system to access a passenger's payment collection data.

In the 5G network, centralized and scalable IoT systems are also a big issue. Blockchain-based techniques, in this scenario, provide decentralized security and privacy mechanisms for various IoT applications in 5G. The taxonomies for several applications of 5G networks are shown in Fig. 5. Blockchain can efficiently access numerous users in the ultra-dense network (UDN) ecosystem for 5G, and it also provides a simple, secure authentication mechanism to solve the access-point group (APG) trusted generation and security problems. They DLT [26] states that multiple UDN systems generate a consortium blockchain and sensor node accessibility to the APG, which comprises various access points (APs). The UE (local support) service center manages the AP clusters (LSC). In the 5G environment, UE, on the other hand, employs blockchain technology to give secure and dependable access.

5G security applications and services for healthcare: The most significant claim in the 5G network is healthcare. Blockchain technology has a significant effect on decentralized systems that depends on several factors. The secure transmission of a patient's medical information is the most important criterion for providing advanced analysis in the healthcare domain because information leakage is a concern [27].

Big data analytics: In big data applications, the 5G network is critical for network data centers. Big data can successfully transfer massive volumes of complex information to data centers by utilizing the core features of 5G networks, cognitive radio

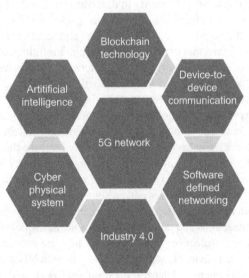

Fig. 5 Applications associated with a 5G network.

systems, and network infrastructure sections. One advantage of large datasets in 5G is the ability to detect anomalies quicker and in real time using a vast amount of data gathered from linked devices.

Internet of things: Every day, IoT devices generate massive volumes of data, necessitating efficient data transfer and huge quantities of throughput, something 4G-based networks have struggled to provide. Sensor nodes need more capacity, reduced latency, and faster data rates, which 5G networks can supply [21].

Automotive driving: Automotive driving is being examined in the context of the 5G network, such as completely autonomous car steering and mapping, as modern logistics milestones. Others may provide economic rewards or disincentives for adopting forms of conduct that reduce congestion.

Smart grid: It is part of Industry 4.0, which employs 5G technology to enable tailored solutions, flexibility, and cost savings in the manufacturing process.

Smart drones: With large number of links, 5G can significantly speed up the implementation of unmanned aerial vehicles (UAV) area networks, also known as drone access points.

5.1   Current technical and societal challenges

5G also brings with its several new issues. The use of this modern innovation establishes new benchmarks for infrastructure components. Even though 5G is commonly referred as a new technology, several features have been in use for years. For example, the radio-access technology (RAT) is quite similar to the widely used 3G and 4G technologies. The frequencies used by 5G devices, ranging from 450 MHz to 3.8 GHz, have been used since the early 1990s. It was first introduced when smartphone technologies incepted.

A mix of existing technologies and development areas of the network is used to provide novelty and additional value. For example, one of the most creative characteristics of the network infrastructure is "network slicing," which exploits the current frequency to develop new commercial services through virtualized channels of communication. Even though much of this technology was in use in recent decades, the demands on infrastructure have increased [28]. Many of the newest features have an increasing demand for processing power that older architectures cannot meet. As a result, additional expenditures in 5G infrastructure are required.

We must, however, invest in cutting-edge transmitter technology. On the other hand, many present communications are unsuitable for 5G applications. We feel that high investment costs and complex conversion stages are inhibiting the advancement of 5G technology. Governments will have to license all medical equipment, particularly software connected via 5G, and transferring patient data. Organizations will have to obey the relevant legislation for medical sensors and data protection. As a result, patients can rest assured that their information is secure. The hospital sector, in particular, has a high requirement for data security and safety. Indoor transmission within hospitals, for example, is tightly controlled and supervised in important application settings. In medical equipment factory, the functional interconnection is now getting difficult. New use cases and application possibilities are enabled by 5G as a high-performance communication link between medical equipment. Until they can benefit patients, these innovative applications must be researched and verified on a medical and technological level.

6 Blockchain for healthcare records

A total of 135 of the 150 publications (90%) emphasize the necessity for a blockchain-based implementation aimed at a specific type of EHR. A blockchain design can be considered a virtually incorruptible cryptographic database for storing crucial medical information.

Information technology has long been a part of a wide range of businesses, including healthcare. Technology has advanced by leaps and bounds in comparison to a few millennia ago. Fig. 6 depicts the architecture of medical record storage.

Patients, allied health professionals (e.g., doctors, nurses, and pharmacies), and executives are among the participants inside the bitcoin healthcare system model. To complete a healthcare transaction on the developed platform, the transaction is transferred to the public blockchain by the patient and allied health providers.

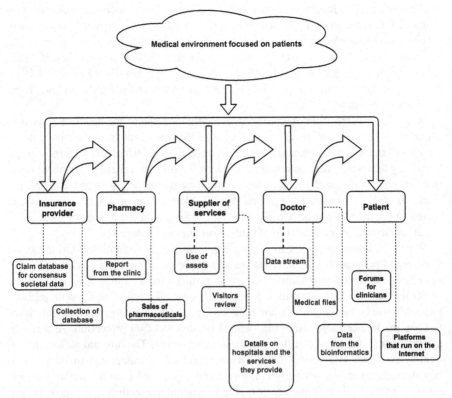

Fig. 6 Architecture of medical record storage.

Physicians and researchers authenticate the transaction, then transmit it to the administration, which acts as a miner. The transaction's block will be generated by the administrator and sent to all other institution administrators for repetition.

Several studies have used blockchain in therapeutic diagnostics to enable reliable health information preservation, processing, and exchange due to the decentralization and flexibility of the blockchain. Simonov et al. [29] examine the difficulties and possibilities for integrating blockchain into e-healthcare systems in depth. Liu and colleagues developed a blockchain-based data-sharing system to address the privacy issues of electronic medical records (EMR) sharing [30]. Fig. 7 defines the health data transfers using blockchain.

In the proposed system, the content extract signature approach and ciphertext-policy attribute-based encryption (CP-ABE)-based accessibility are introduced. To achieve human rights and verifiable health information storage, Li et al. [10] designed cryptocurrency medical data together. Ginn et al. [31] presented a confidentiality picture retrieval method for medical IoT devices that stored the feature representation for every image using modified digital ledger structures. Privacy-preserving image retrieval is based on feature vector extracts via smart contracts. The nature of the data contained in the EHRs is the fundamental cause of the concerns raised in the healthcare sector. Hussein et al. [32] said, "Data related to the diagnosis and treatment of a patient is considered extremely sensitive and private." Therefore, safeguarding and updating such information is a serious challenge and leads to barriers in adopting healthcare-related data systems [33]. Even if a sufficient amount of data is gathered in the system, the variety of sources and formats in which it is available extend the problem. While patient privacy must be assured, data should also be easily manageable and transferable [34]. Newly arising areas such as remote patient monitoring, telemedicine, and mHealth pose new challenges due to the need for speedy data manipulation and gathering based on the requirement of short reaction times.

Moreover, data can be exposed in an adequately safe facility to nasty user attacks [35]. Although storage modes may differ, cloud service providers, according to Kullo et al. [36], have difficulty persuading hospitals to employ their solutions due to concerns about third-party exploitation.

Interoperability is a critical factor that influences the development of new EHR management paradigms. While EHR and connectivity might be separate use cases in some ways, all focus on connection in the current level of blockchain development in healthcare. Hence, they will be examined together in the framework of this chapter. The definition of interoperability is, "The ability of healthcare systems to work together inside and across company boundaries in order to promote the successful delivery of healthcare for persons and communities." While some previously stated EHR-focused solutions address consistency, Pirtle and Ehrenfeld [37] raise an essential point. It introduces many new, blockchain-based solutions that address the EHR and integration use instances without issuing a concomitant standard. Agreeing on a unified system can result in a new interoperability issue. A new shift toward "patient-centered interoperability" is visible, in addition to interoperability among commercial entities such as hospitals, research institutes, and so on. The aim of giving clients

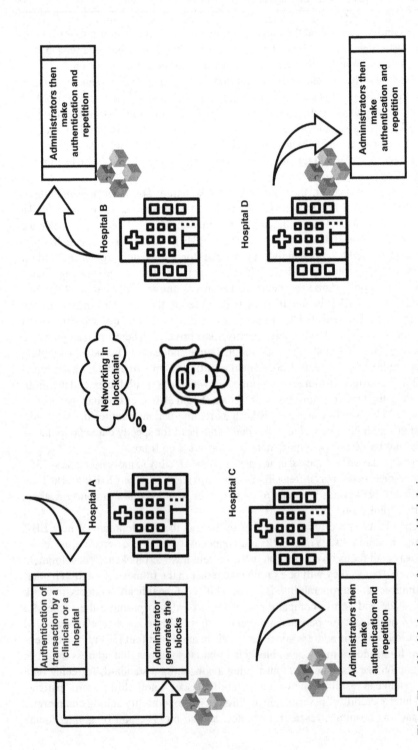

Fig. 7 Flow of health data transfers using blockchain.

information with their medical information, which goes hand in hand with EHR, brings significant privacy and security problems.

7 Healthcare system and blockchain technology

The blockchain is the Internet of the future. We believe that innovation will revolutionize the way that technology facilitates confidence in any system. In any transaction, we believe blockchain would be the most significant single "chain of trust." By eliminating intermediaries from the process, blockchain has the potential to increase the quality of our digital transactions. According to Forrester's "Top 10 Technology Trends to Watch: 2018 to 2021" research, "a viable distributed ledger business will be established" by 2020.

In the healthcare business, a blockchain is a collection of records known as blocks used to keep track of a growing number of online transactions, such as electronic health data (EHR) or EMR. A time stamp and a digital signature are included in each block and link to prior blocks. Several beginning businesses have been researching and developing blockchains for use in the healthcare sector. This shows that people are becoming more aware of the new technology's potential. It is critical to ensure that it is implemented on a large scale rather than simply in one system. However, cloud technology has vastly improved over time, which is excellent news for blockchain enthusiasts because a blockchain needs a lot of electricity to run. A high-end public cloud can assist in overcoming this constraint in the future. In the last few decades, the health sector has remained one of the most popular research areas. Researchers are constantly looking for new and more dependable ways to assist society and the health insurance industry.

The following are some of the blockchain systems that are already in use in various medical systems:

- Medical data are already kept on a blockchain, which makes them safer.
- The healthcare industry has been impacted by several software companies.
- Blockchain technology is already being used in several medication production processes and controls, including recording and storing parameters and providing services and shipments with automated judgments.
- Smart contracts have already been used to establish the stability of medical supplies by storing their temperature histories and monitoring them along the supply chain, including storage, shipping, and administration.
- Doctors might study the drug or treatment in different doses, or with other drugs or treatments.
- Using a blockchain to store and maintain medical data.

Distributed ledgers are all blockchains, but not all blockchain technology is a blockchain. Unlike conventional ledger systems, blockchain does not include a node with special permissions to amend or delete transactions. Blockchain technology is not new; it is a hybrid of numerous existing technologies combined in a novel way. The majority of blockchains rely on six primary technologies:

- Asymmetric encryption, which uses a two-way method of secret keys to secure data.
- Hash functions, which use an integer to validate the integrity of data.
- Merkle trees, which efficiently check data.

The following are some of the ways that blockchain can help healthcare:

Management of complaints and billing: All stakeholders will be aware of their portion of the predicted cost for services if blockchain is used in the claims adjudication and billing management processes. It can cut operating expenses even more by automatic invoicing and health coverage tasks.

Management of medical data: The use of blockchain technology can aid in promoting connectivity and securing healthcare data sharing. The ability to track patients instantaneously improves patient care, which is an important part of providing value-based and profitable care.

Fraud reduction: Fraud costs the healthcare industry more than $95 billion each year. Blockchain can help validate whether a contribution is real by securely collecting data from numerous sources at each step in the transaction, preventing fraudulent behavior. Clinical studies and medical research are two types of things while considering clinical trials. Clinical trials are predicted to go unreported in 70% of cases.

Blockchain improvements can address selective reporting and result manipulations using time-stamped data and results, reducing fraud and inaccuracies in clinical trial records; it is also known as counterfeit medication detection. Counterfeit pharmaceuticals cost medical businesses an estimated $500 billion each year. By documenting each step of the pharmaceutical supply chain at the particular medication level, blockchain might create a "single source of truth" around the flow of commodities and assist in maintaining integrity. They were securing confidential health data Protected Health Information. Between 2015 and 2021, 210 million patient records were compromised, impacting around 38 million patients.

Apart from hackers and malware, internal errors or misconduct accounted for 45% of breaches (220 occurrences). It is possible that the current healthcare IT architecture would not be enough to manage and safeguard linked devices (Internet of medical things [IoMT]). Concerns about privacy and reliability can be alleviated by using cryptocurrency.

7.1   How the blockchain's smart contract can change healthcare

The most powerful feature of blockchain implementation is smart contracts in a blockchain network. Smart contracts, which are part of a blockchain's consensus system, act as a portal for storing essential data on the network. Because most corporate blockchain implementations will be permitted, companies with sufficient permissions will access the data on the blockchain using an application interface (API) without difficulty. While using the API, businesses can request a specific block from the blockchain at any moment. Smart contracts can be thought of as the blockchain's business logic. They are specialized to a business or industry and are unique to each blockchain. Smart contracts, when properly configured, will be able to validate or reject a transaction on the blockchain system. Blockchains are being used in various settings and can address some of the healthcare industry's most pressing concerns. However, further research is required before real-time implementations of this technology can be deployed. There are four stages to the base classifier into the healthcare sector. The healthcare providers get direct access to the blockchain in the initial stage, and all clinical data are tracked and maintained in existing health IT systems. Patient IDs are used to provide various data connected to patients to the blockchain network via API. Inner transactions are then executed using a consensus protocol on blockchain technology.

All transactions are recorded in the public blockchain using patient public IDs that do not contain any personally identifiable information. The immutable ledger is used to build and chain the blocks. After that, all operations are completed and assigned a unique identifier. As a result, query processing or reverse mining begins with the health provider via APIs. Only semipatient data, such as ethnicity, age, and ailments, are stored in the block database. To gain in-depth knowledge, clinical data are evaluated. Finally, the patient can disclose their private key with the healthcare professional if they desire to share their identity. It is how the provider may have access to the patient's information and offer remedies or treatment for the complaints that have been recognized. To people who do not have the patient's private key, the information is private.

8 Blockchain applications to ensure the privacy and security of EHR

Blockchain technology is an innovation used to address privacy and security issues with EHR data in the cloud in a secured environment. Governments and relevant industrial sectors are becoming increasingly interested in digitalizing health systems, as indicated by various efforts taking place in many nations and industries. The possible advantages of EHR systems (e.g., public healthcare administration, online patient access, and patient medical data exchange) have attracted academic organizations' interest.

Blockchain is a peer-to-peer network-based distributed database that are organized in a chronological sequence. They can mitigate for a single point of failure with blockchain-based technologies. Furthermore, data stored in the distributed ledger and all nodes in the blockchain network have ledger backups that can retrieve this information. From any location, such a system promotes information sharing and aids in developing distributed node trust. It also makes data auditing and transparency easier by allowing users to track tamper-proof historical records in the ledger.

Data in the ledger can be stored in encrypted form using various cryptographic approaches, depending on the actual implementation, ensuring data privacy. Users can also use pseudoanonymity to conceal their true identities. To improve resilience, we can use smart contracts to enable various tasks for various application situations. Users can specify the criteria of the smart contract and will only perform the smart contract if the terms are met or fulfilled.

8.1 Blockchain

The success of Bitcoin helped popularize blockchain, enabling reliable and verified communications through an untrustworthy system without relying on a centralized third party.

In a chronological succession of blocks, a blockchain is a collection of detailed and legal transaction data. Each block is linked to the one before it by a reference (hash value), producing a lengthy chain. The genesis block is the parent block of a given block. The block body is derived from authenticated transactions from a specific time frame. The Merkle tree, in which every leaf node is a transaction, and every nonleaf node is indeed the hash of its two convolutional current nodes, is used to store all transaction details. Because any node could confirm the validity of any payment by the cipher value of the current branches instead of the whole Merkle tree, such a decision tree seems to be efficient for verifying transaction existence and integrity. Meanwhile, any changes to the contract will cause a new hash value to generate in the upper layer, resulting in a fraudulent root hash. Furthermore, the maximum number of users in a block is determined by the size of each money transfer and the block size.

These blocks are then tethered together in an encrypted configuration using a cryptographic hash function. Because it is impossible to change or delete recently identified data, new data are added in increased blocks chained with the preceding block. Any change to one of the blocks, as previously stated, will result in a different hash value and a different link similarity. As a result, integrity and protection are achieved.

8.2 Digital signature

In an unreliable environment, for transaction validation, asymmetric cryptography has well defined the use of storing data. Blockchain uses an asymmetric cryptographic mechanism to send transactions and validate transaction authenticity. It will verify the transfer and the sender's encryption key before being sent via the P2P network. In most extant blockchains, the symmetric encryption electronic signature technique (ECDSA) is used.

8.3 Consensus algorithms

The blockchain network has no central authority. As a result, attaining consensus for these operations among untrustworthy nodes in a distributed system is a major task, as highlighted by the Byzantine generals (BG) challenge. The Byzantine army is circling the area under the direction of a group of generals. According to the BG, they have no chance of success in the battle until they all assault at the exact moment. They are unsure, however, whether there would be traitors in a dispersed context. As a result, they must decide whether to assault or retreat. The blockchain network has the same problem.

8.4 Hashing

When evaluating the authenticity and appropriateness of blocks in consideration, the blockchain uses a consensus algorithm. Blocks are approved or rejected accordingly when a consensus is reached. There are several consensus techniques to choose from, including proof of work, proof of stake [38], proof of elapsed time, and Kafka [39]. A description of each is beyond the scope of this paper, and we direct the reader to the evidence given for more information.

8.5 Smart contracts

Smart contracts are conscience programs implemented on the blockchain and used in various industries, including service industries, health, and administration. By delivering a contract-invoking transaction to the contractual address, such a system can achieve complicated programmable operations. The consensus mechanism will then automatically execute the specified parameters in a safe environment.

8.6 Motivations for blockchain-based EHR systems

Generally, EHRs often include patient history, personal information (such as age and weight), lab results, and other information. As a result, ensuring the privacy and security of sensitive data is critical. Furthermore, hospitals in countries are subject to stringent regulatory oversight. Implementing and deploying health services in practice also presents several problems. As previously mentioned, centralized server models are prone to single-point attack constraints and malevolent insider assaults. Fig. 8 determines the standard design for database storage in an EHR system.

Users (e.g., patients) who have their information exported or maintained in these EHR systems lose ownership of their data and have no means of understanding who is viewing the data and for what purposes (i.e., violation of personal privacy). Such data may also be in danger of being leaked to some other organization by malicious users; for example, an insurance provider may reject coverage to a patient based on informed medical history. We will now define the essential aims in developing secure blockchain-based EHR systems depending on the specification of the latest iteration of certain EHRs and the character traits of blockchain:

- *Confidentiality*: Personal information will be utilized in a private manner, and only authorized persons will have access to the required information.
- *Security in terms of privacy, authenticity, and accessibility*:
  - *Privacy*: data can be accessed by authorized users.
  - *Authenticity*: data in transit would have to be authentic and not tampered with by an unauthorized entity.
  - *Accessibility*: access to data and knowledge for lawful users is not unfairly withheld.
- Transparency is a crucial aspect of security. Audit records, for example, primarily collect details on who has access to which EHR, for what purpose, and the time stamps of any activity throughout the life cycle [40].
- *Responsibility*: a person or an organization will be audited and held accountable for their actions.
- *Legitimacy*: the capacity to verify requester identities before granting access to sensitive data.
- *Secrecy*: Ensure security; it means that the things have no apparent identity. Absolute anonymity is difficult to achieve, hence pseudoanonymity is more widespread.

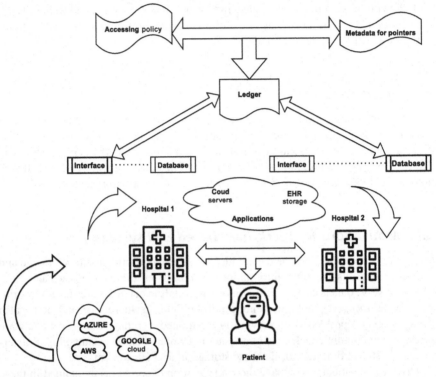

Fig. 8 Standard design for database storage in an EHR system.

9 Conclusion

Blockchain will have its own set of problems and difficulties. It is, nevertheless, a viable idea for allowing public and secured access to medical care data. In general public science and training, blockchain is still not developed enough, even for large-scale commercial adoption. This study discussed many technology products and benefits for 5G safety, such as availability, identification, authenticity, authentication, nonrepudiation, and secrecy, in light of recent developments and appropriate samples for 5G wireless networks.

Current trends such as globalization and digitalization, as stated in the chapter, necessitate change. The move from physical to untrusted virtual parties is one of the most significant adjustments brought about by these trends. The shift away from the old idea of trust necessitates a system that supports the new perspective. A distributed ledger device is expected to provide an additional degree of trust due to its architectural design. This layer establishes a standardized platform to make procedures more accessible around the globe. Healthcare data have value, especially given the vast amount of data available. It can reward data donors with a blockchain token.

It is critical to have an incentive program incorporated into the solution to keep the chain running smoothly. Create an interface that helps patients to contribute their information anonymously. It must determine the valuation method for various types of data. Another fascinating topic is connectivity between different public blockchains. It is likely that numerous blockchain systems, including those for medicine, would interact with one another. We can agree that all parties benefit from information processing and research and that confidentiality should be preserved and improved as technology advances. This concept proposes using a distributed ledger in 5G networks to encrypt data in cognitive health services and avoid potential fraud. When it comes to application, blockchain technology has various issues that need to be addressed with more research. Challenges to the study's validity, as described earlier, could lead to improved future research work.

References

[1] E. Gökalp, M.O. Gökalp, S. Çoban, P.E. Eren, Analysing opportunities and challenges of integrated blockchain technologies in healthcare, in: Eurosymposium on Systems Analysis and Design, Springer, 2018, pp. 174–183.

[2] R. Gupta, U. Thakker, S. Tanwar, M.S. Obaidat, K.-F. Hsiao, Bits: a blockchain-driven intelligent scheme for telesurgery system, in: 2020 International Conference on Computer, Information and Telecommunication Systems (CITS), IEEE, 2020, pp. 1–5.

[3] R. Gupta, S. Tanwar, S. Tyagi, N. Kumar, M.S. Obaidat, B. Sadoun, HaBiTs: blockchain-based telesurgery framework for Healthcare 4.0, in: 2019 International Conference on Computer, Information and Telecommunication Systems (CITS), IEEE, 2019, pp. 1–5.

[4] R. Gupta, A. Shukla, S. Tanwar, Aayush: a smart contract-based telesurgery system for Healthcare 4.0, in: 2020 IEEE International Conference on Communications Workshops (ICC Workshops), IEEE, 2020, pp. 1–6.

[5] J. Hathaliya, P. Sharma, S. Tanwar, R. Gupta, Blockchain-based remote patient monitoring in Healthcare 4.0, in: 2019 IEEE ninth International Conference on Advanced Computing (IACC), IEEE, 2019, pp. 87–91.

[6] I. Mistry, S. Tanwar, S. Tyagi, N. Kumar, Blockchain for 5G-enabled IoT for industrial automation: a systematic review, solutions, and challenges, Mech. Syst. Signal Process. 135 (2020) 106382.

[7] A. Ismail, S. Abdelrazek, I. Elhenawy, IoT wearable devices for health issue monitoring using 5G networks' opportunities and challenges, in: Blockchain for 5G-Enabled IoT, Springer, 2021, pp. 521–530.

[8] R. Gupta, S. Tanwar, S. Tyagi, N. Kumar, Tactile-internet-based telesurgery system for Healthcare 4.0: an architecture, research challenges, and future directions, IEEE Netw. 33 (6) (2019) 22–29.

[9] L. Ismail, H. Materwala, Blockchain paradigm for healthcare: performance evaluation, Symmetry 12 (8) (2020) 1200.

[10] H. Li, H. Huang, S. Tan, N. Zhang, X. Fu, X. Tao, A new revocable reputation evaluation system based on blockchain, Int. J. High Perform. Comput. Netw. 14 (3) (2019) 385–396.

[11] C. Stergiou, K.E. Psannis, B.B. Gupta, Y. Ishibashi, Security, privacy & efficiency of sustainable cloud computing for big data & IoT, Sustain. Comput. Inf. Syst. 19 (2018) 174–184.

[12] A. Tewari, B.B. Gupta, Security, privacy and trust of different layers in Internet-of-Things (IoTs) framework, Future Gener. Comput. Syst. 108 (2020) 909–920.

[13] S. Berenjian, S. Hajizadeh, R.E. Atani, An incentive security model to provide fairness for peer-to-peer networks, in: 2019 IEEE Conference on Application, Information and Network Security (AINS), IEEE, 2019, pp. 71–76.

[14] A. Naghizadeh, S. Berenjian, E. Meamari, R.E. Atani, Structural-based tunneling: preserving mutual anonymity for circular P2P networks, Int. J. Commun. Syst. 29 (3) (2016) 602–619.

[15] A. Naghizadeh, S. Berenjian, B. Razeghi, S. Shahanggar, N.R. Pour, Preserving receiver's anonymity for circular structured P2P networks, in: 2015 12th Annual IEEE Consumer Communications and Networking Conference (CCNC), IEEE, 2015, pp. 71–76.

[16] J.D. Halamka, A. Lippman, A. Ekblaw, The potential for blockchain to transform electronic health records, Harv. Bus. Rev. 3 (3) (2017) 2–5.

[17] J. Benet, IPFS-content addressed, versioned, P2P file system, arXiv preprint arXiv:1407.3561 (2014).

[18] V. Patel, A framework for secure and decentralized sharing of medical imaging data via blockchain consensus, Health Inf. J. 25 (4) (2019) 1398–1411.

[19] S. Kokolakis, Privacy attitudes and privacy behaviour: a review of current research on the privacy paradox phenomenon, Comput. Secur. 64 (2017) 122–134.

[20] N. Kshetri, Blockchain's roles in strengthening cybersecurity and protecting privacy, Telecommun. Policy 41 (10) (2017) 1027–1038.

[21] I. Lapowsky, How Cambridge analytica sparked the great privacy awakening, Wired (2019).

[22] R. Maull, P. Godsiff, C. Mulligan, A. Brown, B. Kewell, Distributed ledger technology: applications and implications, Strateg. Change 26 (5) (2017) 481–489.

[23] Q. Zhang, J. Liu, G. Zhao, Towards 5G enabled tactile robotic telesurgery, arXiv preprint arXiv:1803.03586 (2018).

[24] A. VishwaVidyapeetham, A blockchain and IPFS based framework for secure research record keeping, Int. J. Pure Appl. Math. 119 (15) (2018) 1437–1442.

[25] L. Lévêque, W. Zhang, C. Cavaro-Ménard, P. Le Callet, H. Liu, Study of video quality assessment for telesurgery, IEEE Access 5 (2017) 9990–9999.

[26] Y. Miao, Y. Jiang, L. Peng, M.S. Hossain, G. Muhammad, Telesurgery robot based on 5G tactile internet, Mobile Netw. Appl. 23 (6) (2018) 1645–1654.

[27] G.E. Simon, S.M. Shortreed, R.Y. Coley, R.B. Penfold, R.C. Rossom, B.E. Waitzfelder, K. Sanchez, F.L. Lynch, Assessing and minimizing re-identification risk in research data derived from health care records, eGEMs 7 (1) (2019), https://doi.org/10.5334/egems.270.

[28] M. Atzori, Blockchain technology and decentralized governance: is the state still necessary? Available at SSRN 2709713 (2015).

[29] M. Simonov, U. Ugwuowo, E. Moreira, Y. Yamamoto, A. Biswas, M. Martin, J. Testani, F.P. Wilson, A simple real-time model for predicting acute kidney injury in hospitalized patients in the US: a descriptive modeling study, PLoS Med. 16 (7) (2019) e1002861.

[30] J. Zhang, Y. Chen, S. Ashfaq, K. Bell, A. Calvitti, N.J. Farber, M.T. Gabuzda, B. Gray, L. Liu, S. Rick, Strategizing EHR use to achieve patient-centered care in exam rooms: a qualitative study on primary care providers, J. Am. Med. Inf. Assoc. 23 (1) (2016) 137–143.

[31] G.O. Ginn, J.J. Shen, C.B. Moseley, Hospital financial position and the adoption of electronic health records, J. Healthc. Manag. 56 (5) (2011) 337–352.

[32] S.A. Hussein, A.A. Al-Saboonchi, S.A. Al-Haji, Monthly variation in density of attached algae on solid plates in two lentic lotic localities from Basrah Province, Basrah J. Agric. Sci. 26 (1) (2013) 15–26.

[33] T.K. Mackey, T.-T. Kuo, B. Gummadi, K.A. Clauson, G. Church, D. Grishin, K. Obbad, R. Barkovich, M. Palombini, "Fit-for-purpose?"-challenges and opportunities for applications of blockchain technology in the future of healthcare, BMC Med. 17 (1) (2019) 1–17.

[34] A. Ozanne, D. Johansson, U. Hällgren Graneheim, K. Malmgren, F. Bergquist, M. Alt Murphy, Wearables in epilepsy and Parkinson's disease—a focus group study, Acta Neurol. Scand. 137 (2) (2018) 188–194.

[35] A. Ayadi, O. Ghorbel, A.M. Obeid, M. Abid, Outlier detection approaches for wireless sensor networks: a survey, Comput. Netw. 129 (2017) 319–333.

[36] I.J. Kullo, J. Olson, X. Fan, M. Jose, M. Safarova, C.R. Breitkopf, E. Winkler, D.C. Kochan, S. Snipes, J.E. Pacyna, The return of actionable variants empirical (RAVE) study, a Mayo clinic genomic medicine implementation study: design and initial results, in: Mayo Clinic Proc., vol. 93, Elsevier, 2018, pp. 1600–1610.

[37] C.J. Pirtle, J.M. Ehrenfeld, Information technology and patient protection, in: Precision Medicine for Investigators, Practitioners and Providers, Elsevier, 2020, pp. 511–517.

[38] F. Saleh, Blockchain without waste: proof-of-stake, Rev. Financ. Stud. 34 (3) (2021) 1156–1190.

[39] G. Wang, L. Chen, A. Dikshit, J. Gustafson, B. Chen, M.J. Sax, J. Roesler, S. Blee-Goldman, B. Cadonna, A. Mehta, Consistency and completeness: rethinking distributed stream processing in apache Kafka, in: Proceedings of the 2021 International Conference on Management of Data, 2021, pp. 2602–2613.

[40] M. Mashuri, M. Ahsan, M.H. Lee, D.D. Prastyo, PCA-based Hotelling's T2 chart with fast minimum covariance determinant (FMCD) estimator and Kernel density estimation (KDE) for network intrusion detection, Comput. Indus. Eng. 158 (2021) 107447.

Index

Note: Page numbers followed by *f* indicate figures and *t* indicate tables.

Printed in the United States
by Baker & Taylor Publisher Services